The Routledge Handbook of Translation and Philosophy

The Routledge Handbook of Translation and Philosophy presents the first comprehensive, state-of-the-art overview of the complex relationship between the field of translation studies and the study of philosophy. The book is divided into four sections covering discussions of canonical philosophers, central themes in translation studies from a philosophical perspective, case studies of how philosophy has been translated and illustrations of new developments. With twenty-nine chapters written by international specialists in translation studies and philosophy, it represents a major survey of two fields that have only recently begun to enter into dialogue. *The Routledge Handbook of Translation and Philosophy* is a pioneering resource for students and scholars in translation studies and philosophy alike.

Piers Rawling is Professor and Chair of Philosophy at Florida State University. He has wide-ranging interests and has published papers on a variety of topics, including decision theory, ethics (with David McNaughton), philosophy of language and applications of quantum theory (with Stephen Selesnick). He is co-editor (with Alfred Mele) of *The Oxford Handbook of Rationality* (2004).

Philip Wilson is Honorary Research Fellow in Philosophy at the University of East Anglia, where he teaches literature and philosophy. Publications include: *The Luther Breviary* (translated with John Gledhill, Wartburg 2007); *Literary Translation: Re-drawing the Boundaries* (edited with Jean Boase-Beier and Antoinette Fawcett, Palgrave Macmillan 2014); *The Bright Rose: German Verse 800–1280* (translated and edited, Arc 2015); *Translation after Wittgenstein* (Routledge 2015); and *The Histories of Alexander Neville* (with Ingrid Walton and Clive Wilkins-Jones, Boydell forthcoming). His research interests include the philosophy of history and translation.

Routledge Handbooks in Translation and Interpreting Studies

Routledge Handbooks in Translation and Interpreting Studies provide comprehensive overviews of the key topics in translation and interpreting studies. All entries for the handbooks are specially commissioned and written by leading scholars in the field. Clear, accessible and carefully edited, *Routledge Handbooks in Translation and Interpreting Studies* are the ideal resource for both advanced undergraduates and postgraduate students.

For a full list of titles in this series, please visit www.routledge.com/Routledge-Handbooks-in-Translation-and-Interpreting-Studies/book-series/RHTI.

The Routledge Handbook of Translation Studies and Linguistics
Edited by Kirsten Malmkjaer

The Routledge Handbook of Translation and Culture
Edited by Sue-Ann Harding and Ovidi Carbonell Cortés

The Routledge Handbook of Translation and Politics
Edited by Fruela Fernández and Jonathan Evans

The Routledge Handbook of Audiovisual Translation
Edited by Luis Pérez-González

The Routledge Handbook of Literary Translation
Edited by Kelly Washbourne and Ben Van Wyke

The Routledge Handbook of Translation and Philosophy
Edited by Piers Rawling and Philip Wilson

The Routledge Handbook of Translation and Philosophy

Edited by Piers Rawling and Philip Wilson

LONDON AND NEW YORK

First published 2019 by Routledge
2 Park Square, Milton Park, Abingdon, Oxon OX14 4RN

and by Routledge
605 Third Avenue, New York, NY 10017

First issued in paperback 2021

Routledge is an imprint of the Taylor & Francis Group, an informa business

© 2019 selection and editorial matter, Piers Rawling and Philip Wilson; individual chapters, the contributors

The right of the editors to be identified as the authors of the editorial material, and of the authors for their individual chapters, has been asserted in accordance with sections 77 and 78 of the Copyright, Designs and Patents Act 1988.

All rights reserved. No part of this book may be reprinted or reproduced or utilised in any form or by any electronic, mechanical, or other means, now known or hereafter invented, including photocopying and recording, or in any information storage or retrieval system, without permission in writing from the publishers.

Trademark notice: Product or corporate names may be trademarks or registered trademarks, and are used only for identification and explanation without intent to infringe.

Publisher's Note
The publisher has gone to great lengths to ensure the quality of this reprint but points out that some imperfections in the original copies may be apparent.

British Library Cataloguing-in-Publication Data
A catalogue record for this book is available from the British Library

Library of Congress Cataloging-in-Publication Data
A catalog record for this book has been requested

ISBN 13: 978-1-03-209477-9 (pbk)
ISBN 13: 978-1-138-93355-2 (hbk)

Typeset in Times New Roman
by Sunrise Setting Ltd, Brixham, UK

This *Handbook* is for Summer, Osea, and Mary Jane;
and for Kristin.

Contents

List of contributors	*x*
Acknowledgements	*xv*
Introduction Piers Rawling and Philip Wilson	1

PART I
Philosophers on translation   **15**

1 Schleiermacher   17
   Theo Hermans

2 Nietzsche   34
   Rosemary Arrojo

3 Heidegger   49
   Tom Greaves

4 Wittgenstein   63
   Silvia Panizza

5 Benjamin   76
   Jean Boase-Beier

6 Gadamer and Ricoeur   90
   Lisa Foran

7 Quine   104
   Paul A. Roth

8 Davidson   122
   Piers Rawling

Contents

9	Derrida *Deborah Goldgaber*	141
10	Current trends in philosophy and translation *Roland Végső*	157

PART II
Translation studies and philosophy — **171**

11	Translation theory and philosophy *Maria Tymoczko*	173
12	Context and pragmatics *Shyam Ranganathan*	195
13	Culture *Sergey Tyulenev*	209
14	Equivalence *Alice Leal*	224
15	Ethics *Joanna Drugan*	243
16	Feminism *Valerie Henitiuk*	256
17	Linguistics *Kirsten Malmkjær*	271
18	Meaning *Rachel Weissbrod*	289

PART III
The translation of philosophy — **305**

19	The translation of philosophical texts *Duncan Large*	307
20	Translating feminist philosophers *Carolyn Shread*	324
21	Shelley's Plato *Ross Wilson*	345

22	Translating Kant and Hegel *Nicholas Walker*	358
23	Translating Derrida *Oisín Keohane*	375
24	Levinas: his philosophy and its translation *Bettina Bergo*	391

PART IV
Emerging trends — **409**

25	Cognitive approaches to translation *Maria Şerban*	411
26	Machine translation *Dorothy Kenny*	428
27	Literary translation *Leena Laiho*	446
28	Mysticism, esotericism and translation *Philip Wilson*	461
29	Toward a philosophy of translation *Salah Basalamah*	476

Index — *490*

Contributors

Rosemary Arrojo is Professor of Comparative Literature at Binghamton University, US. She has published three books in Portuguese and several book chapters and articles in English, mostly on the interface between translation and contemporary thought. Her most recent book, *Fictional Translators – Rethinking Translation through Literature*, was published by Routledge (2018).

Salah Basalamah is Associate Professor at the School of Translation and Interpretation at the University of Ottawa, Canada. His fields of research include the philosophy of translation, translation rights, social and political philosophy, postcolonial, cultural and religious studies, as well as Western Islam and Muslims. He is the author of *Le droit de traduire. Une politique culturelle pour la mondialisation* [The Right to Translate. A Cultural Policy for Globalisation] for the University of Ottawa Press (2009). He is currently working on a book about the philosophy of translation and its implications beyond translation studies, the humanities and social science.

Bettina Bergo, Professor of Philosophy, Université de Montréal, Canada, is the author of *Levinas between Ethics and Politics* and co-editor of several collections: *'I Don't See Color': Personal and Critical Perspectives on White Privilege* (Penn State Press 2015), *Trauma: Reflections on Experience and Its Other* (SUNY 2009), and *Levinas and Nietzsche: After the Death of a Certain God* (Columbia 2008). She has translated three works of Emmanuel Levinas; Marlène Zarader's *The Unthought Debt: Heidegger and the Hebraic Heritage* (Stanford University Press 2005); Jean-Luc Nancy's *Disenclosure: The Deconstruction of Christianity* (Fordham 2008); and Didier Franck's *Nietzsche and the Shadow of God* (Northwestern University Press 2012). She is the author of numerous articles on phenomenology, psychoanalysis, and the history of psychology.

Jean Boase-Beier, Emeritus Professor of Literature and Translation at the University of East Anglia, UK, works on translation and style, and the translation of Holocaust poetry. Her publications include *A Critical Introduction to Translation Studies* (2011) and *Translating the Poetry of the Holocaust* (2015). She is also a poetry translator and editor.

Joanna Drugan is Professor of Translation at the University of East Anglia, UK. Her recent publications include the monograph *Quality in Professional Translation* (Bloomsbury 2013) and, with Rebecca Tipton, a co-edited special issue of *The Translator* on translation, ethics and social responsibility (2017). She is Principal Investigator of the AHRC/ESRC joint-funded Transnational Organised Crime and Translation project. Her main areas of research are translation quality, ethics and technologies.

Contributors

Lisa Foran lectures in European Philosophy at Newcastle University, UK. Her recent publications include *Derrida, the Subject and the Other. Surviving, Translating and the Impossible* (Palgrave Macmillan 2016) and the co-edited collection *Heidegger, Levinas, Derrida: The Question of Difference* (Springer 2016). Her research draws on phenomenology and hermeneutics to investigate the role of translation in ethical and political relations.

Deborah Goldgaber is an Assistant Professor of Philosophy at Louisiana State University, US. She is currently completing a book manuscript arguing that Derridean deconstruction offers a novel form of philosophical materialism. The project, entitled *Speculative Grammatology: Derrida and the New Materialism*, will appear in Edinburgh University Press's Speculative Realism series (2018). Her current research programme lies at the intersection of contemporary French philosophy, deconstruction and feminist theory. Her research has appeared in *Journal of Speculative Philosophy*, the *Notre Dame Philosophical Reviews* and *Postmodern Culture*.

Tom Greaves is Senior Lecturer in Philosophy at the University of East Anglia, UK. His publications include *Starting with Heidegger* (2010) and 'The Mine and the Mountain Range: Responding to Heidegger's Translation of the Sense of the Earth' in *In Other Words: The Journal for Literary Translators* (2011). His research interests focus on Heidegger, phenomenology and environmental philosophy, and he is Associate Editor of *Environmental Values*.

Valerie Henitiuk is Provost and Professor of Comparative Literature at Concordia University of Edmonton, Canada. Her recent books include the co-edited *Spark of Light: Short Stories by Women Writers from Odisha* (Athabasca University Press 2016) and *A Literature of Restitution: Critical Essays on W.G. Sebald* (University of Manchester Press 2013). She has served as Editor of the Routledge journal *Translation Studies* (2012–17) and, following a decade researching European translations of Classical Japanese women's writing, is now working on the translation of Inuit literature, supported by a research grant from the Social Sciences and Humanities Research Council of Canada.

Theo Hermans is Professor of Dutch and Comparative Literature at UCL and Director of the UCL Centre for Translation Studies, UK. Among his books are *Translation in Systems* (1999) and *The Conference of the Tongues* (2007). His main research interests are the theory and history of translation.

Dorothy Kenny is Professor at Dublin City University, Ireland. Her recent publications include the edited volume *Human Issues in Translation Technology* (Routledge 2017) and contributions to the journals *The Linguist* (2016) and *The Interpreter and Translator Trainer* (2014). She is co-editor of the journal *Translation Spaces*. Her main areas of interest are translation technology, translation pedagogy and corpus-based translation studies.

Oisín Keohane is a Lecturer in Philosophy at the University of Dundee, UK. Previously, he was a Mellon Postdoctoral Fellow at the University of Toronto, Canada. His monograph *Cosmo-nationalism: American, French and German Philosophy* will appear with Edinburgh University Press in 2018. He has published several book chapters, as well as articles in journals such as *Derrida Today*, *Paragraph* and *Nations and Nationalism*.

Contributors

Leena Laiho is Lecturer in German at the School of Languages and Translation Studies at the University of Turku, Finland. Her main areas of research are literary translation and the philosophy of art. Within this specific research context her publications on the translatability of literary works of art include contributions to *The Metalanguage of Translation*: 'A Literary Work – Translation and Original: A Conceptual Analysis within the Philosophy of Art and Translation Studies' (John Benjamins 2009) and to *The Handbook of Translation Studies*, Vol 4: 'Original and Translation' (John Benjamins 2013), both edited by Yves Gambier and Luc van Doorslaer.

Duncan Large is Professor of European Literature and Translation at the University of East Anglia, UK, and Academic Director of the British Centre for Literary Translation, UK. He has authored and edited five books about Nietzsche and German philosophy; he has also published two Nietzsche translations with Oxford World's Classics and one translation from the French with Continuum (Sarah Kofman's *Nietzsche and Metaphor*). He is co-editor of *Untranslatability: Interdisciplinary Perspectives* (Routledge 2018); with Alan D. Schrift he is also General Editor of *The Complete Works of Friedrich Nietzsche* (Stanford University Press).

Alice Leal is Senior Lecturer in Translation Studies at the University of Vienna, Austria. Her recent publications include a monograph on translation studies in Brazil (Frank & Timme 2014), a book chapter in *Transfiction* and in the *Handbook of Translation Studies* (both John Benjamins 2014), as well as contributions in *Versalete* (2017), *New Voices in Translation Studies* (2016), *trans-kom* (2014), *Target* (2013), *Translation Spaces* (2013) and *Across Languages and Cultures* (2013). Her main areas of research are translation theory, philosophy of language, multilingualism and poststructuralist discourse.

Kirsten Malmkjær is Professor of Translation Studies at the University of Leicester, UK, having previously taught at the universities of Birmingham, Cambridge and Middlesex, all in the UK. She is the editor of the *Routledge Linguistics Encyclopedia* (1991, third edition 2010) and (with Kevin Windle) of *The Oxford Handbook of Translation Studies* (2011). She is the author of *Linguistics and the Language of Translation* (Edinburgh 2005). Forthcoming publications include the *Routledge Handbook of Translation Studies and Linguistics* (ed.) and the collection of articles, *Key Cultural Texts in Translation* (John Benjamins), co-edited with Adriana Serban and Fransiska Louwagie.

Silvia Panizza is Lecturer in Ethics at the Norwich Medical School, University of East Anglia, UK. Previously, she taught English Literature and Translation at the University of Genoa. She is currently co-authoring a translation and edition of Simone Weil's *Venice Saved* (Bloomsbury) and is working on a joint project on mental capacity and non-human animals in scientific experiments. Her main areas of research are meta-ethics and moral psychology, animal ethics and Iris Murdoch's philosophy.

Shyam Ranganathan is a member of the Department of Philosophy, and York Center for Asian Research, York University, Toronto, Canada. His dissertation in philosophy (*Translating Evaluative Discourse,* York 2007), was on translation in general and translating philosophy in particular. He is translator of *Patañjali's Yoga Sūtra* (Penguin 2008) from the Sanskrit, editor and contributor to the *Bloomsbury Research Handbook of Indian Ethics* (Bloomsbury 2017), and the author of *Ethics and the History of Indian Philosophy* (MLBD

2007, second edition 2017) and *Hinduism: A Contemporary Philosophical Investigation* (Routledge 2018). His recent publications address the challenge of translation in light of colonialism and imperialism.

Paul A. Roth is Distinguished Professor in the Department of Philosophy, University of California-Santa Cruz, US. His most recent publications include *Refounding Analytical Philosophy of History: Steps Towards a Naturalist and Irrealist Account of Narrative Explanation* (forthcoming Northwestern University Press) and 'What Would It Be to Be a Norm?' in *Normativity and Naturalism in the Philosophy of the Social Sciences*, ed. Mark Risjord (Routledge 2016). Roth's work is examined in *Towards a Revival of Analytical Philosophy of History: Around Paul A. Roth's Vision of Historical Science*, ed. K. Brzechczyn (Brill 2018).

Maria Şerban is a philosopher of science currently working as a postdoctoral fellow of the 'Living Machines' Research Group at the University of Copenhagen, Denmark. Her recent publications include journal articles on the epistemology of neuroscience:'Learning from Large-scale Neural Simulations' and 'Constitution in Interlevel Experiments'. She is co-editor of a volume of essays on the philosophy of biology, to be published by Routledge in 2018: *Living Machines: Philosophical Interfaces between Biology and Engineering*.

Carolyn Shread is Lecturer in French at Mount Holyoke College, US. She has translated four books by French philosopher Catherine Malabou and is working on a fifth, *The Metamorphoses of Intelligence*. She has published articles in both translation and Haitian studies, including 'On Becoming in Translation: Articulating Feminisms in the Translation of Marie Vieux-Chauvet's *Les Rapaces*', which received the Florence Howe Award for Outstanding Feminist Scholarship in 2012. She works closely with Haitian publishing house LEGS ÉDITION, as managing editor of the *Voix féminines* series and the journal *Legs et littérature*, and is assistant editor to *Translation: A Transdisciplinary Journal*.

Maria Tymoczko is Professor of Comparative Literature at the University of Massachusetts Amherst, US. With an international reputation, she is a leading theorist and scholar in the field of translation studies. Educated as a literary scholar, a medievalist, and a specialist in Irish studies, she holds three degrees from Harvard University. Recent publications include articles on 'Internationalism and Knowledge about Translation', 'Translation and the Ethos of a Postcolony', 'Trajectories of Research in Translation Studies: An Update', and 'Victory by Verse'. Forthcoming are *Translation and Neuroscience* (Tartu Semiotics Library) and 'Translation as Organized Complexity: On the Agency of Translators'.

Sergey Tyulenev is Associate Professor in Translation Studies and the Director of the MA in Translation Studies at the University of Durham, UK. His recent publications include the monographs *Applying Luhmann to Translation Studies* (Routledge 2011), *Translation and the Westernization of Eighteenth-Century Russia* (Frank & Timme 2012) and *Translation and Society* (Routledge 2014). His main areas of research are the sociology, historiography and epistemology of translation.

Roland Végső is Susan J. Rosowski Associate Professor of English at the University of Nebraska-Lincoln, US. His primary research interests are contemporary continental philosophy, modernism, and translation theory. He is the author of *The Naked Communist: Cold*

Contributors

War Modernism and the Politics of Popular Culture (Fordham University Press 2013). He is also the translator of numerous philosophical essays as well as two books: Rodolphe Gasché's *Georges Bataille: Phenomenology and Phantasmatology* (Stanford University Press 2012) and Peter Szendy's *All Ears: The Aesthetics of Espionage* (Fordham University Press 2016). He is the co-editor of the book series *Provocations*, published by University of Nebraska Press.

Nicholas Walker has translated philosophical writings from German, Italian, Spanish, and French. He has translated texts by Kant, Heidegger, Gadamer, Benjamin, and Adorno. He has also published articles on Hegel, Hölderlin, Adorno, Habermas, and Wagner.

Rachel Weissbrod is an Associate Professor and Chair of the Department of Translation and Interpreting Studies at Bar-Ilan University, Israel. Her areas of research include theory of translation, literary translation into Hebrew, film and TV translation and the interrelation between translation and other forms of transfer. Her book *Not by Word Alone, Fundamental Issues in Translation* (in Hebrew) was published by The Open University of Israel in 2007. She has published in *Target*, *The Translator*, *Meta*, *Babel*, *Journal of Adaptation in Film and Performance*, *Translation Studies* and more.

Ross Wilson is Lecturer in Criticism in the Faculty of English, University of Cambridge, UK, and a Fellow of Trinity College. He is the author most recently of *Shelley and the Apprehension of Life* (2013) and of essays on the history and theory of literary criticism and English poetry from the eighteenth century. He is currently writing a book on the generic forms in which literary criticism has been written since around 1750.

Acknowledgements

The editors would like to express their gratitude to all at Routledge for their support, especially to Louisa Semlyen for suggesting and encouraging the project. The assistance of Hannah Rowe and Laura Sandford has been invaluable. Many thanks also to Jean Boase-Beier, for constant advice and support with translation studies, and to Gareth Jones, for constant advice and support with philosophy.

Introduction

Piers Rawling and Philip Wilson

This *Handbook* examines the relationships between translation studies and philosophy. Philosophy is one of the oldest intellectual practices known to humanity. Translation studies, by contrast, is a young discipline – a 1972 paper by James Holmes ([1972] 2004) is often viewed as its starting point – although translation as a practice predates even philosophy. The two disciplines are contingently linked because, as Jonathan Rée notes: 'no bookshelves are more heavily stocked with foreign books and translations than those of the philosopher' (2001: 231). However, Rée argues that the connection goes deeper: 'European philosophy has always been written with several languages in mind; and it has to be read, and translated, with multilingual eyes as well' (2001: 235). For Lawrence Venuti, translation is philosophy's 'dark secret' (1998: 115). The present volume shows how contemporary scholars are responding to the growing realisation that those working in translation studies and those working in philosophy have much to say to each other (see the study by Andrew Benjamin ([1989] 2015)). It will therefore help to establish dialogue between the fields as a norm, as well as being an important work of reference.

Willis Barnstone (writing in 1993) speaks of the 'mutual self-isolation of linguistic and philosophical studies on translation and the theory and practice of literary translators' (1993: 223), while Rosemary Arrojo (writing in 2010) argues that in the history of Western philosophy 'hardly any attention has been paid either to the practice of translation or to the philosophical questions it raises' (2010: 247). Arrojo, however, concludes that the situation is changing, a change evidenced by her own work. We note a growing number of conferences that bring together scholars in the two fields, as well as an increasing number of relevant publications, such as the essays in the volume edited by Lisa Foran (2012), which 'all point to the same claim: that translation is inherently philosophical and that philosophy not only demands, but also itself engages in, a type of translation' (Foran 2012: 11). Barbara Cassin's *Dictionary of Untranslatables* (2014) is a further instance of how translation and philosophy can be placed in the same field of enquiry. In a review of what he calls this 'extraordinary book', itself a translation from the French of 2004, Tim Crane argues that translation is 'almost never a straightforward conversion', which is what makes it a 'fertile subject for philosophy' (2015). The impact of Cassin's work is likely to take some time to be assimilated and sets the standard for a certain sort of enquiry, even though critical voices have been raised. Crane notes among other things the assumption in the *Dictionary* that French is the natural language of philosophy (ibid.), while Venuti (2016) argues that it operates with an underlying instrumental model of translation that makes many of its assumptions about untranslatability questionable, given that other models of translation are available. (See Akashi, Józwikowska, Large and Rose (forthcoming) for an overview of the emerging debate on untranslatability.)

Two important qualifications about the *Handbook* must now be made, two problems that are signalled as a call for action, for new overviews, which is something that is to be expected, because handbooks do not only map a field but also show where new explorations must be carried out.

First, the canonical philosophers discussed in Chapters 1–9 are all male. Such imbalance is symptomatic of a wider problem in philosophy, as Katrina Hutchison and Fiona Jenkins have shown (2013). Chapters 16 and 20 in the *Handbook* address this issue in the context of translation studies and philosophy. How can an unjust situation be improved?

Second, the *Handbook* is oriented to Western philosophy. In Part I, again, the male philosophers addressed have written in English, French and German only. Where are philosophers from non-Western traditions? Similarly, many of the debates described in Parts II–IV use Western discourse. However, even the very use of the term 'Western' is suspect. As Şebnem Susam-Saraeva points out, it renders the West more homogenous than it is and implies that not being Western is the 'only common denominator behind otherwise vastly different languages and cultures' (2002: 193). Such issues are further explored in Chapter 11, which addresses 'Eurocentrism', and in Chapter 12, where Western views are contrasted with a South Asian translation tradition.

A view from translation studies

Translation studies is what Mona Baker calls an 'interdiscipline' (2008), which of necessity looks outside for support. Jean Boase-Beier's work on creativity in translation, for example, draws on relevance theory (2006). If we accept Venuti's definition of translation studies as 'the formulation of concepts designed to illuminate and to improve the practice of translation' (2012: 13), then philosophy is an obvious area to which to turn for support, because it is a rigorous intellectual enquiry into the nature of reality. Thus translation studies anthologies typically include work by philosophers (Venuti reproduces statements by Walter Benjamin, Jacques Derrida, Friedrich Nietzsche, Friedrich Schleiermacher and George Steiner in an influential reader (2012)). Philosophy has given rise to a number of sub-disciplines, such as the philosophies of history, law and science, and there is no reason why it should not give rise to the philosophy of translation (see Large 2014: 182). The term 'philosophy of translation' can be understood in two ways: first, as an analytic activity in which philosophical tools are used to discuss translation issues – the ideas of moral philosophers can illuminate the debates of translation ethics, for example (see Chapter 15) – and, second, as a substantive activity that aims to formulate an overview (see Chapter 29). Not only translation scholars but also practising translators can use philosophy to examine and even to drive the way that they translate.

Such enquiry by translation scholars and by translators will enable boundaries to be redrawn between disciplines (see Boase-Beier, Fawcett and Wilson 2014: 8). Boundaries are never stable. Maria Tymoczko has used the work of Wittgenstein on family resemblance in order to view translation itself as a cluster concept with no fixed definition, for example (2007: 83–90). Figures such as Benjamin and Derrida draw attention from both university departments of philosophy and university departments of literature, while the work of many non-philosophers shows philosophical aspects – the sociologist Pierre Bourdieu is a case in point. One effect of this *Handbook* will be to destabilise boundaries further.

A view from philosophy

Ludwig Wittgenstein, in a letter to C.K. Ogden about Ogden's rendering of the 1921 *Tractatus Logico-Philosophicus*, remarked of translation in general: 'It *is* a difficult business!' (1973: 19). Wittgenstein's realisation is typical of what makes a philosopher reflect on translation: it is a phenomenon in need of explanation.

Most of the canonical thinkers who have written on translation come from the continental tradition (which privileges existential enquiry). In this volume, there are chapters in Part I on Friedrich Schleiermacher, Friedrich Nietzsche, Walter Benjamin, Martin Heidegger, Hans-Georg Gadamer, Paul Ricoeur and Jacques Derrida. But there have also been important contributions from the Anglo-American, or analytic, tradition (which privileges conceptual clarification), notably from Willard Van Orman Quine and Donald Davidson, who are addressed in Chapters 7 and 8 respectively. (Wittgenstein, the subject of Chapter 4, escapes the continental/analytic distinction.) One lesson of this *Handbook* is that valuable insights about translation can be gained from both traditions. We can move on from what Anthony Pym describes as 'not just a lack of dialogue but serious misunderstandings' (2007: 42) to more fruitful collaboration.

Investigating translation can not only tell us things that are of interest about what happens when we replace a word or a sentence in language A by a word or a sentence in language B, but can help us to theorise how people think. If I hold that meaning lies *behind* something, for example, then this may not only make me translate in a certain way but also show that I see essences underlying the use of language, which may carry over into how I view the things around me. If, on the other hand, I see meaning as publicly available – as determined by, and manifest in, the use of language – then I will translate differently and may have a different view of reality. Heidegger (see Chapter 3) goes as far as to assert (1996: 63):

> Tell me what you think of translation, and I will tell you who you are.

The stakes cannot get any higher.

An overview of the *Handbook*

Pym asserts that there are three ways in which philosophy and translation are linked (2007: 4):

1. Philosophers of various kinds have used translation as a case study or metaphor for issues of more general application.
2. Translation theorists and practitioners have referred to philosophical discourses for support and authority for their ideas.
3. Philosophers, scholars and translators have commented on the translation of philosophical discourses.

The *Handbook* has been divided into four parts. Parts I–III follow Pym's categorisation. Part I investigates how certain canonical philosophers have addressed translation, both as metaphor (as Pym describes) but also in its own right. In Part II, some key themes in translation studies are given philosophical clarification. Part III offers two overviews of translating philosophy, followed by four case studies. Finally, Part IV suggests five emerging research trends. The volume thus gives an overview of the state of research into translation studies and philosophy and also indicates ways in which students and researchers can continue to bring the two disciplines together. Each chapter indicates which other chapters in the *Handbook* can provide further illumination and includes a list of commented further reading.

Part I: Philosophers on translation

The first nine chapters, ordered chronologically, take the form of academic studies of the writings of the philosopher in question with respect to translation. The final chapter examines some contemporary trends in how the two fields of philosophy and translation studies speak to each other.

Theo Hermans discusses the views on translation of the German philosopher and theologian Friedrich Schleiermacher (1768–1834), whose famous 1813 lecture 'On the Different Methods of Translating' applies the principles of hermeneutics to interlingual translation. Hermans argues that Schleiermacher's views on translation are an integral part of his thinking on communication, language and understanding, and examines these views in their immediate context, in relation to Schleiermacher's other work and in relation to the translation of Plato that marks the beginning of Schleiermacher's hermeneutic thought. Schleiermacher's lecture, which is frequently anthologised by translation scholars and read by translation students, has at its core not the choice between the translator either bringing the author to the reader or taking the reader to the author, as is often stated, but the formidable difficulty faced by the hermeneutic translator who, having glimpsed the otherness of the foreign writer, has only the translating language to articulate the understanding gained. Translation cannot overcome difference, but as a project it can take us closer to the metaphysical ideal of absolute shared knowledge.

Even though Friedrich Nietzsche (1844–1900) left only fragments about translation, the impact of his thought on the development of some of the most important and productive trends that have emerged within the discipline of translation studies in the last few decades has been enormous, although, unfortunately, hardly acknowledged. **Rosemary Arrojo** shows how some of the main topics currently explored in translation studies – such as the recognition of the translator's inescapable visibility and agency, the transformational character of translation, the role of translation in processes of colonisation and evangelisation and the relationship between translation and gender issues – are deeply indebted to the work of Nietzsche, particularly as conveyed by his interpreters. If we consider, for example, that mainstream conceptions of the 'original' and its idealised relationship with translation are still very much reminiscent of Plato's theory of Forms and its devaluation of representations, it becomes evident how fundamental Nietzsche's conceptions of language, interpretation and the will to power have been for the ways in which we now think of the task of translators and the ethics that should guide their work.

Martin Heidegger (1889–1976) is an example of a canonical philosopher who addressed translation in detail. **Tom Greaves** describes how early discussions tended to focus on the difficulty, even the purported impossibility, of translating Heidegger's philosophical idiom and shows that recent discussion has focused increasingly on Heidegger's own translation practice – that is, the integral part that translation played in his understanding of philosophy and thought itself, together with the thematic discussions of translation in his writings. Greaves discusses three aspects of Heidegger and translation, the first of which is the radical rethinking of hermeneutics that the young Heidegger developed as the central feature of his development of phenomenology into a hermeneutic ontology. The second is the role that 'fundamental words' play in Heidegger's thinking and translation; Greaves explores possible justifications and potential limitations of this focus on fundamental words in Heidegger's developing thinking about language. Third, Greaves provides a brief overview of the history of English-language discussions of Heidegger's views on translation and how they have developed as more of his work has been published and understanding of his philosophy has changed.

Ludwig Wittgenstein (1889–1951) is widely regarded as one of the most important philosophers of language. He did not write extensively on translation, but **Silvia Panizza** shows how his insights and methods, which take pragmatic aspects of language to be of paramount importance, can be applied to both theory and practice. Four key concepts from Wittgenstein's 1953 *Philosophical Investigations* are discussed: language-games, forms of life, aspect-seeing and the surveyable representation. Language-games, for example, are the different contexts in which we use language, with particular aims and rules which give words their specific meaning. Instead of postulating a corresponding entity for each word, which the translator needs to find, a Wittgensteinian approach to translation suggests that we first need to understand which language-games texts are playing and within what kinds of forms of life they fit. The task of translation is to recreate similar contexts and effects rather than identifying an absolute referent. The chapter concludes with suggestions about how to evaluate different translations by appealing to Wittgenstein's conception of language.

'The Task of the Translator', by Walter Benjamin (1892–1940), is another text that is frequently anthologised and on many university reading lists. **Jean Boase-Beier** argues that though it does contain Benjamin's most complete statement of his views on translation, it is hard to understand in isolation. While certain pronouncements – that texts possess a quality of 'translatability', for example – are well known and relatively straightforward, others can appear merely idiosyncratic. The danger of taking from the essay only those ideas that are easy to understand is that the essay's extraordinary density is lost, and it can seem to be saying little of importance. If, however, we see this essay as a statement made at a particular point in Benjamin's intellectual development and read it in relation to his other works, especially those on language, philosophy and history, we not only see that there is no redundancy in the essay but also find it illuminated by his thoughts on those other topics. Boase-Beier's contextualisation of Benjamin enables us better to assess the relevance of his thought for both translation theory and practice.

Lisa Foran discusses the work of Hans-Georg Gadamer (1900–2002) and of Paul Ricoeur (1913–2005). For both thinkers, understanding is a condition of human existence, and they describe it as a form of translation involving a transformative relation between people, which produces meaning and which is never finished. Foran considers Gadamer's philosophical heritage, paying particular attention to the influence of Heidegger and the latter's accounts of thrownness and situated understanding, going on to describe how for Gadamer these and other concepts impact both on the aim of translation and how a practising translator can proceed. She then turns to Ricoeur and his shared phenomenological heritage with Gadamer. For Ricoeur, translation is a much broader concept that concerns not only an operation between languages but also offers itself as a paradigm for intersubjective relations. Translation necessarily gives rise to a number of ethical and political questions which are difficult to address. While both thinkers share a number of positions and concepts, the chapter's central claim is that Ricoeur's expanded account of translation is more attuned to those difficulties than Gadamer's.

Paul A. Roth considers the work of Willard Van Orman Quine (1908–2000), one of the twentieth century's most important philosophers in the Anglo-American tradition. On Roth's account, Quine shows earlier subscribers to this tradition to be committed to a problematic notion of meaning – problematic because it presupposes a notion of propositional content that is independent of contingent linguistic form. On this 'traditional' view, the translation of an utterance succeeds when it re-expresses (or 'recaptures') the pre-existing meaning of that utterance. Roth examines Quine's reasons for rejecting this view, with a focus on Quine's thesis of the 'indeterminacy of translation' and the philosophical assumptions that Quine sees this as calling into question. In the process, Roth closely examines just how Quine's thought experiment of *radical* translation – the case where one confronts a language previously unknown or untranslated – engenders compelling arguments for the indeterminacy of translation. Roth concludes with a comparison of Quine to Donald Davidson and sees both as rejecting the 'recapture' view of translation, with its assumption that a fixed and determinate meaning exists prior to translation, in favour of the view, forced upon us by the indeterminacy of translation, that meaning, in important respects, results from translation and cannot be independent of it.

Donald Davidson (1917–2003) made important contributions in several major areas of philosophy and is notable for his systematic approach. **Piers Rawling** begins by placing Davidson in the context of Quine and Wittgenstein and sees them all as united in rejecting the 'conventional' account of language. In addition, a key principle emerges: the manifestation principle. This states that there can be nothing more to the meaning of a speaker's words than can be gleaned from observation, where this observation is necessarily guided by certain maxims of interpretation, collectively known as the 'principle of charity'. But the principle of charity does not force unique interpretations. Indeed, interpretation, on Davidson's view, is inevitably indeterminate: there are myriad interpretations of a given speaker that all account for the data equally well, and no one of them is uniquely 'correct'. Other topics covered include 'radical interpretation', Davidson's application of Tarski's definition of truth, his argument to the effect that thought requires 'triangulation', his denial that there is any such thing as a 'conceptual scheme', his 'anomalous monism', holism about meaning and thought, and his claim that there is no thought without talk.

Deborah Goldgaber considers the work of Jacques Derrida (1930–2004), who is frequently studied by those outside philosophy departments, as noted above, and whose work powerfully critiques a certain philosophical view of language – logocentrism – and the ideal of translation it implies. According to this ideal, the function of language is to *express* meaning, while translation should find equivalents. Derrida's critique consists in showing that meaning is necessarily language-like; therefore it cannot anchor language, nor assure the possibility of successful linguistic equivalence between languages. According to Derrida, logocentric accounts of language assume what they ought to contest: the absolute difference between signifier and the signified. In fact, the signified element is not 'outside' the text, depending on language users to give and restore extra-textual meaning – it is inscribed on the 'inside'. Deconstructively speaking, translation is not a derivative linguistic practice with respect to establishing meaning but essential and primary. Texts are defined by their capacity to 'translate' heterogeneous texts. Derrida thus helps us to see the productive role of translation and the power of translational practices to enrich and shape language.

In the final chapter of Part I, **Roland Végső** examines what first might appear to be a central contradiction: while contemporary philosophy has turned against the heritage of the so-called 'linguistic turn' of the twentieth century and thus questions the absolute centrality of language, the category of translation has nevertheless remained a central concern for it as an ontological problem. He goes on to examine work by Alain Badiou, Michel Callon, Bruno Latour, Levi Bryant and Barbara Cassin, and he argues that today translation occupies in philosophical discourse the position of a limit in relation to ontology. In the case of Badiou, for example, ontology limits the function of translation, since mathematics as ontology tends towards the elimination of translation; for Cassin, translation limits the scope of classic ontology, as it is responsible for introducing a new kind of multiplicity to ontology; for Latour and Bryant, ontology is translation, and thus translation ceases to be an essentially linguistic problem, as it is tied to the more general problem of relationality.

Part II: Translation studies and philosophy

Philosophy can offer support to theorising about translation, and theorising about translation can contribute to philosophy. The approach in Part II is topic-based, addressing some of the major themes that have arisen in translation studies and offering a philosophical perspective.

Maria Tymoczko addresses the relationship between translation theory and philosophy, in a chapter that offers an overview of what is at stake in the whole project of this *Handbook*, by tracing the relationship between translation theory and the developments in Anglo-American philosophy which contributed to the shaping of the discipline of translation studies as it emerged in the twentieth century, issuing in the current state of the field. In certain respects, it can be argued that the two disciplines co-evolved, with philosophers of language frequently invoking translation in their arguments on the one hand and translation studies scholars and theorists using insights from philosophical arguments on the other. Because both disciplines focus on language (the defining trait of human cognition) in its pragmatic cultural contexts, there is significant convergence in the arguments of both fields. Topics explored include Quine's theory of the indeterminacy of translation/language (see also Chapter 7), Wittgenstein's work on meaning (see also Chapter 4), speech act theory and Rawls's theory of justice. Tymoczko also discusses aspects of translation theory that would enhance contemporary philosophical discourses and methods. Overall, the chapter forms a compelling argument for translation scholars to engage with philosophy and for philosophers to become familiar with work done in translation studies.

In his chapter on context and pragmatics, **Shyam Ranganathan** argues that the semantics or meaning of a text or utterance is its context-transcendent importance. Philosophers such as J.L. Austin and Paul Grice show us that pragmatics, in contrast, has to do with what we can accomplish within a context. Adopting the principle that it is the pragmatics of a text that is to be preserved in translation leads to indeterminacy: translations that contradict each other. Yet ignoring pragmatics while producing translations that aim at preserving linguistic meaning only results in translations that are failures. In contrast to a language-focused approach to meaning and translatable content characteristic of the Western tradition, Ranganathan closes by observing a promising line of thought in translation theory that identifies translation with genres. Drawing from the South Asian philosophy of Yoga, Ranganathan identifies a genre with a disciplinary practice. This allows for the identification of a nonlinguistic textual-meaning: the genre-relative pragmatics of a text. Translations that preserve textual meaning will not only have the same meaning as each other but will be pragmatically felicitous.

Sergey Tyulenev examines culture, one of the most problematic and yet central notions in the humanities in general and in translation studies. Why is culture so important? Why, despite all the problems of defining and describing it, can it be considered a success story in the crossdisciplinary terminological apparatus of the social sciences? Tyulenev draws on classical publications in anthropology and sociology and addresses questions of definition, including how to demarcate cultural and social aspects of translation and culturally and sociologically informed approaches in translation research. The history of the term and concept is presented by analysing *skopos* and polysystem theories. Translation is shown as both an intracultural mechanism and an indispensable factor in intercultural communication: it helps societies mediate between individuals and culture; it is a powerful mechanism of cultural evolution and a way for different societies to communicate and learn from each other. The chapter offers a discussion of methods of research into the relationship of culture and translation and recommendations for the practice of such research.

Alice Leal considers equivalence among languages as investigated by various philosophers, discussing approaches from the philosophy of language and asking whether we can draw insight from these reflections to enrich translation studies. Many key Western thinkers on language have not directly addressed the subject of equivalence, but it is still possible to discuss the implications of their work. Leal, following George Steiner, considers two main trends – the universalist and the relativist matrices – in a historical survey from Aristotle to Ricoeur. The traditional notion of equivalence in translation studies is deeply rooted in the universalist matrix, looking back to the Aristotelian notion of sign. Leal asks how far the matrix can be traced in subsequent philosophical movements and also examines the relativist matrix, ending by interrogating various philosophical attitudes to meaning and suggesting a working definition of equivalence within translation. The chapter shows how new light can be shed upon the questions that cluster around an ancient problem when philosophy is applied to translation.

Translation inevitably raises ethical questions, both in practice and theory. **Joanna Drugan** argues that from the earliest days of translation studies, scholars emphasised ethical aspects of linguistic equivalence or fidelity. Later, one of the pivotal 'turns' in the development of the discipline centred on calls for a 'return to ethics'. Researchers' focus simultaneously widened to embrace a broader range of issues and challenges and narrowed in on specific cultures, language pairs or domains in relation to ethics. These theoretical developments were accompanied by increasing deontic attention to ethics in relation to the practice of translation, particularly with the growth of professional associations and transformations in the technological and geopolitical context. In this, ethics remains relatively unusual in translation studies and in philosophy, since research has embraced both theoretical and practical camps, with each one studied, questioned and arguably enriched by the other. Drugan first traces significant developments in relation to ethics in translation studies chronologically, then considers some important ethical themes and questions for translation theory and practice in more detail.

Given how profoundly interconnected gender is to both identity and power, it inevitably informs and is informed by acts of translation, whether textual or cultural. **Valerie Henitiuk** describes the case of a young Inuit woman in the early 1950s, asked by a newly arrived missionary to provide a word list to help him learn her language. Mitiarjuk instead takes up the valuable tool of writing that she has only just acquired and begins writing stories. Feminists have addressed what it means to be a woman translator, particularly in cases where the source author is male and his text explicitly or even implicitly misogynous, and have highlighted the often parlous fate of women writers in translation. Further, they have helpfully criticised translation studies along with other disciplines for gendered language and constructions, uncovering engrained biases and proposing new paradigms and approaches. The journey of *Sanaaq*, originally composed in Inuktitut, through translations into French and then indirectly into English (both of which were produced by male anthropologists), functions in this chapter to help tease out the complex intersection of feminism and translation.

Kirsten Malmkjær discusses the sub-disciplines of linguistics and how they relate to aspects of translation in the context of philosophy. Phonetics, phonology, morphology and descriptive and theoretical grammar are linked to the uses of language in society and to the mental representation of language, as well as semantics, pragmatics, genre, text and discourse analysis and historical linguistics. Semantics is arguably closest to philosophy, which shares its interest in meaning. Of more interest in linguistics than in philosophical semantics has been the related sub-discipline of pragmatics, which deals with the study of language in use. Malmkjær introduces speech act theory in the context of the challenges posed for translators and interpreters, along with sociolinguistics and psycholinguistics. One relationship between socio- and psycholinguistics and philosophy lies in the notion of personality: speakers of one language may find speakers of another overly direct or impolite; and impositions on a people of a language can cause affront, alienation and anomie. The concerns of genre, text and discourse and conversational analysis are introduced, and the chapter ends with a discussion of the relevance-theory controversy.

Any attempt to address translation philosophically must at some point come to terms with what is meant by meaning, a notion that has been central to philosophy since Classical Greece and that is unavoidable in any discussion of how we can replace a word or a text in one language with a word or a text in another language. **Rachel Weissbrod** maps the different and often clashing approaches to the relationship between translation and meaning and introduces some of their main representatives. Her chapter surveys and critiques five approaches: first, translation is capable of transferring meaning – in fact, following Roman Jakobson, this is what translation is about; second, translation cannot transfer meaning but consists of textual equivalence, as asserted by Ian John Catford; third, meaning is not what translators are supposed to transfer, an idea associated with Benjamin; fourth, translators are authorised to create meaning rather than transferring it, as advocated – based on Derrida and other post-structuralist thinkers – by some feminist translators; fifth, translation studies is not about meaning. The concept of meaning can thus be a way to map translation studies, while highlighting its tight connections with philosophy.

Part III: The translation of philosophy

Rée asserts that 'of all the kinds of translation, none is trickier than the translation of philosophy', because philosophy is obscure, has a dialogical and literary nature and contains terms that often develop a life of their own (2001: 226–30). Because of this trickiness, most philosophy is translated by professional philosophers (Large 2014: 183). Chapter 19 sets the scene with a general discussion of the translation of philosophical texts, followed, in Chapter 20, by an investigation into the issues that arise when translating feminist philosophers in a male-dominated field. Part III ends with four case studies, each of which raises important questions for both translation theorists and philosophers.

Duncan Large notes how in most cases the reception of foreign-language philosophy has depended on translation. He traces a history of key translations since antiquity which have changed the course of the development of philosophy, both within the West and between Western philosophy and Chinese and Indian thought. It has been widely recognised that philosophical texts pose a particular challenge to the translator, comparable to translating scripture or poetry, and philosophy's conceptual language has regularly been considered 'untranslatable', but equally regularly philosophical texts have been translated (and retranslated). Five different purposes for philosophy translation are set out: cultural exchange, textual interpretation, linguistic enrichment, founding or furthering an indigenous philosophical tradition and the philosophical development of the individual translator. Although many of the most significant philosophy translations in history have been carried out by gifted amateurs, nowadays the task is increasingly falling to professional academic philosophers, of whom a steadily increasing number are women. The difficulties posed for the translator by conceptual and figurative language are considered, as is the relative creativity of some of the responses.

Carolyn Shread addresses the translation of feminist philosophers by presenting an inclusive sample of these thinkers and explaining how translation elucidates their philosophical views. Shread argues that, due to the historical oppression of women, feminist philosophy is often marginalised within the discipline and seen as a relatively new phenomenon. She notes that it was only in the 1970s that feminist voices in philosophy achieved institutional recognition, despite the fact that feminist philosophy – that is, philosophy informed by women's knowledge and experiences – has been a universal presence throughout history. In response to this longstanding exclusion, Shread argues, feminist philosophers have challenged the mainstream power structure within philosophy by offering perspectives, and proposing methodologies, that have fundamentally changed the discipline. Translation aids this feminist challenge by providing an escape route, a way to reach receptive audiences, and a method of canonisation. As Shread puts it, her chapter 'not only attests to a re-forming of philosophy, but also lies like a bomb within a handbook whose fourteen named philosophers are all, exclusively, men'.

It was noted above how Hermans identifies Schleiermacher's hermeneutic view of translation as originating in his translation of Plato. **Ross Wilson** gives a case study of a poet translating Plato and describes the issues that arise for translation studies. Percy Bysshe Shelley (1792–1822) famously wrote that translating poetry from one language to another was like casting a violet into a crucible in order to discover the formal principles of colour and odour. Wilson discusses how Shelley's stated views on translation can be reconciled with his own attempts at translating Plato, emphasising Shelley's description of Plato as, indeed, a poet, and thus the necessity of confronting Shelley's negative estimation of the translation of poetry in the case of his own translations. Wilson highlights how philosophy has literary aspects, and how translation can respond to literariness, despite the frequent assertions throughout time that poetry cannot be translated. Wilson's investigation of this encounter between a philosopher and a poet sheds light on both philosophy and translation. Of particular interest are the close readings of Shelley's translations that are undertaken.

Nicholas Walker examines the reception of German Idealist thought, principally of Immanuel Kant (1724–1804) and Georg Friedrich Wilhelm Hegel (1770–1831), in the English-speaking world in the second half of the nineteenth century and the first few decades of the twentieth, and the role and character of the translations which facilitated this process. Walker investigates how early translators conceived of their task and how they executed it, which involved in the first place choosing which texts to translate. Modern translations have often sought to demystify these authorships and free them from the weight of inherited interpretations, claiming to provide closer textual fidelity and greater terminological precision and consistency in relation to the freer and more tendentious approaches of earlier translators. Walker compares and contrasts specific translation choices in order to appreciate the potential losses as well as gains that may arise in some contemporary translation practice (such as the relative neglect of the literary quality and rhetorical features of the source texts in a desire to accommodate them to more standard forms of writing).

Oisín Keohane examines the consequences of translating Jacques Derrida into English over the last fifty years, arguing that the stakes have been dramatically increased in recent decades due to 'Anglobalisation', to use Keohane's term. To highlight these stakes, translations of Derrida from 1967 to 2017 are divided into four separate historical periods, from the first to the latest, produced by the Derrida Seminars Translations Project (DSTP), with each period individuated by means of its own specific set of translation strategies. Following this, critical issues and topics in translations of Derrida are further explored by examining how several translators of Derrida have rendered his phrase '*tout autre est tout autre*', which he used in numerous writings from the 1990s until his death in 2004. Gayatri Chakravorty Spivak's translation of Derrida is also a major focus, from the original 1976 translation of Derrida's *Of Grammatology* to the recent 2016 fortieth-anniversary retranslation. Finally, Geoffrey Bennington's critique of this retranslation and Spivak's response at the launch of the book in the UK are examined and critiqued.

In the final chapter of this section, **Bettina Bergo** offers a different way of approaching the translation of philosophy. What happens when the work of a thinker is juxtaposed with its translation? Examining the philosophy of Emmanuel Levinas (1906–95), Bergo discusses two translational desiderata: faithfulness to the letter of the source text and to its style and tone (which includes rhythm). And she does so in light of Levinas's own account of the 'ethical' suffering at the root of communication, responsibility and self-sacrifice [*la substitution*]. Beyond the difficulties of translating culturally hybrid texts while respecting these desiderata, Bergo demonstrates how the latter can enter into mutual tension and what this implies for the translator. She also shows how an investigation into the issues that arise when translating Levinas sets his later work between poetry, philosophy and what he called 'spirituality'. Above all, Levinas's writing poses the problem of how best to translate rhythms, affects and, ultimately, the silences that punctuate philosophical witnessing.

Part IV: Emerging trends

The contributors in Part IV map five possible directions for future enquiry. Prediction is a risky business, of course. Other directions are not only possible but inevitable.

Translators and translation scholars have for some time been interested in developments in cognitive science, both as a way of understanding translation and also of influencing practice. **Maria Șerban** shows how cognitive approaches to translation studies are driven by three interrelated aims: to understand the structure and organisation of the capacities of cognitive agents involved in processes of translation; to build better theories and models of translation; and to develop more efficient methods and programmes for translator training. Her chapter showcases some current research programmes that reflect the fruitfulness of the interdisciplinary structure of translation studies. Instead of thinking about cognitive research on translation as driven by a master cognitive theory, Șerban argues that it is more descriptively adequate and more fruitful to understand it as a family of projects based on multiple theories that are relevant for studying different aspects of the translation process. This perspective allows us to extract the *erotetic* structure of programmes organised around specific problems or questions shaped by previous research, well-established cognitive hypotheses and the current interests of the discipline of translation studies.

Dorothy Kenny discusses machine translation (MT), tracing its history from rocky beginnings in the aftermath of the Second World War and pointing up the technological and geopolitical factors that reinvigorated MT research on more than one occasion. Of particular significance was the shift in the late twentieth century from rule-based systems to data-driven systems, in which machines 'learned' probabilistic models of translation from an ever growing supply of human translations available in digital form. Kenny shows how the conceptualisation of meaning and translation changes with shifts in research paradigms: from the symbolism of rule-based systems, through the statistical approach that sees translation as a form of Bayesian optimisation and says little about meaning, to the connectionism of neural MT. The chapter also considers some of the more troublesome aspects of contemporary MT, including its complicated relationship with human translation. Despite occasional tensions, Kenny argues that MT provides the ideal locus for translation studies to engage with some of the most pressing questions of our time, questions linked to the resurgence of interest in artificial intelligence and to the future of human labour.

Leena Laiho examines theoretical approaches to literary translation, which involves exploring the very nature of the literary work of art. Her approach shows the heuristic value of labelling something as literary and discerns the literary work as aesthetic object in current theories of literary translation. Notions such as 'author', 'translator', 'original', 'translation', 'reader', 'text', 'meaning', 'similarity' and 'difference', all in general use when addressing literary translation, are ultimately related to 'literary work'. If literary translation is examined within frameworks such as phenomenology, hermeneutics, deconstruction or the philosophy of art, an explicit encounter with 'work identity' can be expected. However, when literary translation is considered more as an object of cultural relations and exchange (as in the context of the post-colonial approach), the aspect of work identity loses some relevance, and literary translation, embedded in cultural and political systems, can be understood as an issue of power relationships. Scholars from both translation and literary studies are considered in what is in effect a chapter on aesthetics.

Philip Wilson discusses the ways that translation has interacted with writings from mystical and esoteric traditions. Translation itself has been viewed as something supernatural, for example, by commentators on the third-century BCE Septuagint rendering of the Jewish scriptures, while writers on translation have also drawn on the vocabulary of mysticism and esotericism. Benjamin's 1923 essay 'The Translator's Task', for example, uses concepts from the Kabbalah, while tropes such as the Tower of Babel reoccur in translation literature. The chapter asks whether philosophy can help us theorise the phenomena under discussion and ends by discussing how translation theorists and philosophers can proceed. Are we dealing with a mystery or a problem? The answer to that question will vary according to one's philosophical views, so that the chapter as a whole establishes another link between philosophy and translation. It may be that the whole relationship has been a distraction from serious scholarship. On the other hand, it may be that the mystical and the esoteric tell us something very important about the mind and therefore about one of the mind's products, translation.

In the final chapter, **Salah Basalamah** argues for embedding a philosophy of translation within translation studies. He notes that, historically, translation studies has not been guided by the quest for a general theory but has, rather, evolved in a series of 'turns' – the linguistic, the cultural and the sociological. In parallel with this evolution, 'translation' has increasingly been used metaphorically in various disciplines (e.g. in molecular biology to portray genetic decoding) as well as in everyday language. Basalamah argues that a philosophy of translation should incorporate not only the various perspectives on translation as an object of study but also these metaphorical uses. Indeed, translation can be seen as a philosophical paradigm in itself, which can be studied and applied outside the bounds of language, culture and metaphor. Hermeneutics serves as a starting point, but any philosophy of translation needs to be conceptualised within translation studies, which may require a new epistemological sub-discipline. Once we have a suitably conceptualised philosophy within translation studies, further issues can then be explored at the inter- and transdisciplinary levels. Basalamah's chapter illustrates the substantive possibilities for the interaction between philosophy and translation.

Concluding remarks

It has been a privilege and a pleasure to edit this *Handbook*, the first major reference work to bring together these two fascinating fields. We are grateful to our contributors, who include philosophers, translation theorists and translators. Our own overview of the many issues involved has developed with the editing process, and we hope that readers find much here that is informative and much that will stimulate further debate.

References

Akashi, M., W. Józwikowska, D. Large and E. Rose (eds) (forthcoming) *Untranslatablity: Interdisciplinary Perspectives*, London: Routledge.
Arrojo, R. (2010) 'Philosophy and Translation', in Y. Gambier and L. van Doorslaer (eds) *Handbook of Translation Studies*, Amsterdam: John Benjamins, 247–51.
Baker, M. (2008) 'Foreword', in P. Nikolaou and M. Kyritsi (eds) *Translating Selves*, London: Continuum, xiii–xiv.
Barnstone, W. (1993) *The Poetics of Translation*, New Haven and London: Yale.
Benjamin, A. [1989] (2015) *Translation and the Nature of Philosophy*, London and New York: Routledge.
Boase-Beier, J. (2006) 'Loosening the Grip of the Text: Theory as an Aid to Creativity', in E. Loffredo and M. Perteghella (eds) *Translation and Creativity*, London and New York: Routledge, 47–56.
Boase-Beier, J., A. Fawcett and P. Wilson (eds) (2014) *Literary Translation: Redrawing the Boundaries*, Basingstoke: Palgrave Macmillan.
Cassin, B. (ed) (2014) *Dictionary of Untranslatables*, tr. by S. Rendall, C. Hubert, J. Mehlman, N. Stein and Michael Syrotinski, ed. by E. Apter, J. Lezra and M. Wood, Princeton: Princeton University Press.
Crane, T. (2015) 'Consciousness and Castles', *Times Literary Supplement*, January 30.
Foran, L. (ed) (2012) *Translation and Philosophy*, Oxford: Peter Lang.
Heidegger, M. (1996) *Hölderlin's Hymn 'The Ister'*, tr. by W. McNeill and J. Davis, Bloomington: Indiana University Press.
Holmes, J. [1972] (2004) 'The Name and Nature of Translation Studies', in L. Venuti (ed) *The Translation Studies Reader* [second edition], London and New York: Routledge, 180–92.
Hutchison, K. and F. Jenkins (eds) (2013) *Women in Philosophy*, Oxford: Oxford University Press.
Large, D. (2014) 'On the Work of Philosopher-Translators', in J. Boase-Beier, A. Fawcett and P. Wilson (eds) *Literary Translation: Redrawing the Boundaries*, Basingstoke: Palgrave Macmillan, 182–203.
Pym, A. (2007) 'Philosophy and Translation', in P. Kuhiwczak and K. Littau (eds) *A Companion to Translation Studies*, Clevedon, Buffalo and Toronto: Multilingual Matters, 24–44.
Rée, J. (2001) 'The Translation of Philosophy', *New Literary History*, 32, 2: 223–57.
Susam-Saraeva, Ş. (2002) 'A "Multilingual" and "International" Translation Studies?', in T. Hermans (ed) *Cross-Cultural Transgressions: Research Models in Translation Studies II, Historical and Ideological Issues*, Manchester: St. Jerome, 193–207.
Tymoczko, M. (2007) *Enlarging Translation, Empowering Translators*, Manchester: St. Jerome.
Venuti, L. (1998) *The Scandals of Translation*, London and New York: Routledge.
Venuti, L. (ed) (2012) *The Translation Studies Reader* [third edition], London and New York: Routledge.
Venuti, L. (2016) 'Hijacking Translation: How Comp Lit Continues to Suppress Translated Texts', *boundary 2*, 43, 2: 179–204.
Wittgenstein, L. (1973) *Letters to C.K. Ogden*, Oxford: Blackwell.

Part I
Philosophers on translation

1
Schleiermacher

Theo Hermans

The lecture 'On the Different Methods of Translating' ('Über die verschiedenen Methoden des Übersetzens'), which Friedrich Schleiermacher delivered at the Berlin Academy of Sciences in June 1813, is widely regarded as the beginning of modern translation theory. It also represents Schleiermacher's most extensive statement on the subject of translation. To understand its core ideas we need to know something of Schleiermacher's views on language and languages, and on the nature of communication and understanding. We need to be aware of his work as a translator as well. This chapter therefore, after a brief introduction, sketches Schleiermacher's writings on ethics and dialectics, and then addresses his translation of Plato. These different strands come together in his work on hermeneutics, which provides the key to the 1813 lecture. The final paragraph adds a note drawn from Schleiermacher's talks on psychology. Contextualising the 1813 lecture in this way will show that the traditional, decontextualised reading of it as presenting a choice between two opposing ways of translating (either the translator brings the foreign author to the reader or he/she takes the reader to the foreign author) is misguided. Even the apparent parallelism in the choice does not in fact exist. [Note: in the following pages, citations not preceded by a name are of Schleiermacher's work.]

Introduction

Today Friedrich Daniel Ernst Schleiermacher (1768–1834) is known principally as a liberal theologian who spoke in favour of the emancipation of women and of Jews. He became a public intellectual during the turbulent years of the Napoleonic wars and contributed substantially to what we now know as German Romanticism. In recent years he has been increasingly appreciated as a philosopher. Early in his career he read the Ancient Greek and Roman thinkers as well as Leibniz and Spinoza; he was heir to some of Herder's ideas, a contemporary of Kant and Hegel and familiar with the work of lesser figures such as Fichte and Schelling.

Schleiermacher studied at the University of Halle in 1787–90 and worked for a while as a private tutor and pastor. In the years around 1800, in the Berlin salon of the multilingual Henriette Herz, he became involved with the leading Romantic writers and intellectuals of the time, among them the brothers Friedrich and August Wilhelm Schlegel. He contributed to their short-lived but influential flagship journal *Athenaeum* and, at their instigation, published his first books (*On Religion*, 1799, and the effusive *Monologues*, 1800). He also undertook, initially with Friedrich Schlegel but then on his own, the translation into German of virtually the complete works of Plato; the first five volumes appeared as *Platons Werke* between 1804 and 1809, with a final sixth volume in 1828. He taught briefly at the University of Halle, but when in 1806 the town was overrun by Napoleon's troops and the university closed, he returned to Berlin, where he spent the rest of his life. While the French army occupied Prussia, Schleiermacher used his pulpit to preach resistance (Raack 1959; Vial 2005). In 1809 he played a role, alongside Wilhelm von Humboldt, in founding the University of Berlin. He served as its professor of theology and occasional dean for the next twenty-five years. He also became an active member of the Berlin Academy of Sciences, delivering some fifty lectures and speeches there between 1811 and 1834. The 1813 lecture 'On the Different Methods of Translating' was just one of these (1858; Nowak 2002).

Schleiermacher wrote prolifically, but a large part of his output remained in manuscript until after his death. His collected writings were first published between 1834 and 1864. The authoritative critical edition of the complete work (*Kritische Gesamtausgabe* (KGA)), currently in progress, is scheduled to comprise sixty-five volumes.

Most of what Schleiermacher issued in print during his lifetime is concerned with theology, although in terms of volume the Plato translation looms large. For his thinking about translation, his writings on ethics, dialectics, hermeneutics and psychology are all relevant. Yet he himself did not publish anything at all, or very little, in these fields. He did however lecture on them at the University of Halle and then in Berlin. What we have on these subjects, therefore, are lecture notes, by himself or sometimes by students, as well as various outlines and drafts from different periods in his life. He lectured on ethics at Halle in 1804–5 and in Berlin in 1808 (before the university was formally opened), 1812–13, 1816, 1824, 1827 and 1832 (1981: xiv). The lectures on dialectics took place in Berlin in 1811, 1814–15, 1818–19, 1822, 1828 and 1831 (2002a, 1: xxv–vi). He gave lectures on hermeneutics first at Halle in 1805 and then in Berlin in 1809–10, 1810–11, 1814 and 1819, and several more times in the 1820s and early 30s (2012: xix–xxix). The lectures on psychology began in 1818 and were then held in 1822, 1830 and 1833–4 (1862: viii). The manuscripts that are unrelated to his lecturing are often difficult to date, and some contain later additions and comments. He appears to have drafted a book on hermeneutics around 1810 but lost the manuscript and started anew in 1819. He was working on a book on dialectics when he died in 1834. The writings on ethics and dialectics in particular are often forbiddingly abstract.

Ethics

Chronologically, Schleiermacher's interest in ethics came first. He planned to translate Aristotle's *Nicomachean Ethics* as early as the late 1780s, when he was only around twenty years of age. In the next decade he published reflections on freedom, on sociability and on religious feeling, before composing a 'Draft towards an Ethics' ('Brouillon zur Ethik') in 1805–6, as his lecturing on the subject got underway.

His ideas, in this as in other domains, take shape around binary oppositions, such as real versus ideal, individual versus community, or particularity versus what he refers to as the shared 'identity' of human nature in all. The oppositions are not exclusive but mutually dependent and in constant interaction (which he calls 'oscillation'), so that one concept cannot be thought without the other and neither is ever present in an absolute form. Consciousness of one's own self presupposes a contradistinction with those who are not part of this self. Human nature is the same in all but manifests itself differently in every individual. We are open to the world around us but also project our own cognitive schemata onto it. Recognising the specific thoughts that each of us entertains permits the positing of a level of ideal or pure reason.

Human beings, for all their individuality, have a natural tendency to communicate and thus to form communities. Communication, for Schleiermacher, means that something that was internal to one person – for instance, a thought – is exteriorised and subsequently interiorised as the same thought by someone else. The means to achieve this is language: what is expression for the speaker functions for the interlocutor as a sign. Successful transfer depends on a shared schematism, a common way of thinking (1981: 65; 2002b: 49).

Communication enables sociability. It requires not only expression of one's own personality but also a receptive openness to others, a willingness to contemplate difference. The task is paradoxical because, on one hand, it will never be possible to really grasp another person's individual nature, while, on the other, a common humanity must be assumed (Berner 1995: 189–90). Sociability and individuality, although opposed, go together. The essence of sociability consists in respecting the other's closed world while inviting it to open itself up and, simultaneously, making ourselves available to others keen to get to know us ('das Wesen der Geselligkeit, welches besteht in der Anerkennung fremden Eigenthums, um es sich aufschließen zu lassen, und in der Aufschließung des eigenen, um es anerkennen zu lassen'; 1981: 265).

The uniqueness of each person's individuality, however, remains inaccessible to others and thus untranslatable; already the 'Brouillon zur Ethik' equates 'Eigentümlichkeit' ('individuality') with 'Unübertragbarkeit' ('non-transferability') (1977: 361). The adjective 'eigentümlich' and its associated noun 'Eigentümlichkeit' ('individual, individuality') will be key words in the 1813 lecture on translation. Nevertheless, since self-expression draws on language, and language is a means of communication, self-expression already contains within it a desire to be understood. In one sense, language also acts as a brake on idiosyncrasy. In a lecture on aesthetics Schleiermacher notes that, as a shared property and a relatively fixed system, language is not well equipped to express either strict singularity or fluidity ('die Bestimmtheit des Einzelnen'; 'das in sich Wechselnde'); it takes a creative artist to force it to do that (1977: 403).

Forms of sociability are determined primarily by language. Following Herder, Schleiermacher conceives of language as creating a bond, initially within the family, but then extending to the clan and from there to the nation. Nations and languages, like persons, have their own individuality (1981: 47; 2002b: 25). And since thinking and speaking are interdependent, communities speaking different languages also think differently. These differences constitute what Schleiermacher calls the 'irrationality' of language and of languages. The term, which is of prime importance and also appears in the 1813 lecture on translation (2002: 70; 2012a: 46), denotes the non-isomorphism and incommensurability between different ways of thinking and speaking (1830: 57). The 'Brouillon zur Ethik' already referred to ideas in a work of art as being 'irrational' in that they resist understanding ('daß die darin enthaltene Idee irrational ist gegen das Verstehen': 1977: 362), in a passage explaining the impossibility of ever reaching full understanding of another's discourse. In his outline of dialectics of 1814–15 Schleiermacher speaks of the 'irrationality' of the individual person as being counteracted by the use of language as such (1988: 109), because, as we just saw, language is always shared with others and, as he puts it in a draft on ethics in 1812–13, it imposes a degree of commonality on even the most individual thought (1981: 68–9; 1977: 410). Irrationality, then, is not absolute but increases the further languages and cultural traditions are removed from each other.

If irrationality troubles the relatively leisurely type of communication at the heart of sociability, it also haunts the more purposeful form of dialogue that drives dialectics.

Dialectics

Dialectics is concerned with the search for knowledge that would be both absolute and certain. The reasoning, in true German Idealist fashion, is that if individuals can gain a certain degree and kind of knowledge about a portion of the world, then the idea of complete knowledge that would be true to the whole world and shared by all can be posited. Knowledge as it resides in individual languages, Schleiermacher says in an Academy lecture in 1830, stands to absolute knowledge like refracted rays of light to light as such (2002: 675). Reason points the way towards such knowledge. Reason is universal, and all humans possess a fraction of it, each in their own way. While universal knowledge will remain an unattainable ideal, it acts as a regulatory principle in that it must be aspired to. Indeed, in practice, 'the whole history of our knowledge is an approximation to it' (2002a, 1: 149).

This approximation has to start from concrete reality and real people, and therefore from the recognition of difference, with the aim of reaching consensus. Taking his cue from Plato, Schleiermacher conceives of dialectics as dialogue, an exchange of ideas (2002a, 1: 81). The ideas themselves as well as their exchange require language. For the individual, knowledge that is more than vague intuition or a jumble of impressions can become cogent knowledge only when it is articulated in language. Thinking is silent speaking, as Schleiermacher never tires of repeating.

Knowledge becomes socially productive when it is shared with others. But communication, as we saw, is an uncertain undertaking. The search for perfect knowledge and consensus should therefore begin where the risk is lowest – that is, within one language. This is already difficult enough, due to the inaccessibility of the thoughts of individuals. The difficulties increase exponentially when knowledge is negotiated across languages, as in every field of knowledge different languages embody an ineradicable difference ('eine unaustilgbare Differenz') in ways of thinking (2002a, 1: 403). Schleiermacher refers to Cicero to drive the point home. Compare, he says, the self-assurance with which Cicero writes philosophy in his native Latin with the apprehension he betrays when he is translating from Greek; in the latter case he is like any other Roman, 'for whom the value of the translated Greek remained foreign' ('ein Römer, dem der Werth des wiedergegebenen griechischen fremd war': 2002a, 1: 402).

Like ethics, then, dialectics comes up against the irrationality of languages, and Schleiermacher supplies illustrations that are devastating for any concept of translation as the integral transfer of meaning or ideas. 'No knowledge in two languages can be regarded as completely the same, not even [the concept of] thing and A=A')' ('Kein Wissen in zwei Sprachen kann als ganz dasselbe angesehen werden; auch Ding und A=A nicht'), he notes in the 1814–15 draft on dialectics (2002a, 1: 98). He argues in the same passage that even mathematics, despite its language-independent notation, is thought differently in different cultural traditions. In one of his lectures on psychology he adds similar examples, from the top and the bottom end of the linguistic spectrum. Different words for 'and', he explains with reference to German 'und', Latin 'et' and Greek καὶ (kai), are not equivalent because they have different usages; and the German word for God ('Gott') differs from its Latin or Greek counterparts in that it is rarely used in the plural and then only to reflect foreign conceptions (1862: 173). The 1813 lecture on translation remarks in the same vein that not even the words 'God' and 'to be' are the same across languages (2002: 89; 2012a: 60).

The incompatibility between languages grows the more distant they are. In the 1832–3 manuscript of his dialectics Schleiermacher, clearly reflecting contemporary developments in comparative Indo-European linguistics (one of its pioneers, Franz Bopp, had been his colleague in Berlin since 1821), observes that, despite linguistic affinities stretching from Europe to India, the various local traditions are so different it is hard to find common philosophical ground. If this is true within the Indo-European sphere, what about cultures beyond it (2002a, 1: 405–6)?

Yet a universal language would not be the solution. Schleiermacher rejects the idea on several grounds. Its construction would be a logical impossibility since agreement would have to be reached in existing languages, making the universal tongue redundant. In any case, linguistic differences are valuable in themselves because their sum total reflects the richness of the human mind (2002a, 1: 404). Where a dead language like Latin has been employed as a transnational vehicle, its use has remained restricted to a social elite and, lacking the vibrancy of a living tongue, it would struggle to accommodate unfamiliar modes of thought (1862: 179).

In his 1811 lecture notes on dialectics Schleiermacher mentions another alternative to deal with the irrationality of languages. It consists in focusing on broader discursive and conceptual issues rather than on the non-synonymy of individual items: 'I cannot appropriate an alien singularity, I have to reconstruct it through the way the foreign concept is formed' ('Das Einzelne fremde kann ich mir nicht aneignen; aber ich soll es in der fremden Begriffsbildung nachconstruiren': 2002a, 1: 59). It may not be immediately clear what this means, but his own translation of Plato provides a clue.

Plato

When he tackled Plato around 1800, Schleiermacher was already an experienced translator. Apart from the *Nicomachean Ethics* mentioned above, he had rendered Aristotle's *Politics* into German, but the translation remained in manuscript. Also in the 1790s he took to translating from English: a travelogue by Mungo Park and sermons by Hugh Blair and Joseph Fawcett, the latter comprising two volumes. But the translation of Plato was of a different order and occupied him for several years (Lamm 2000, 2005). Covering the virtually complete works of Plato (minus *Laws* and *Timaeus*), it became an epoch-making version, not only for the quality of the rendering itself but also for the various introductions in which Schleiermacher offered comprehensive interpretations of the entire Platonic corpus (Schleiermacher 2000). These introductions were soon valued in their own right and appeared in English as early as 1836.

His preparation for the task was meticulous. He established a chronology for the separate dialogues and sought to understand each dialogue in its relation with all the others, and the work as a whole with reference to the individual dialogues. He also tried to grasp Plato's relation to the Greek language of the time, arguing that we need to know where Plato was constrained by the language at his disposal and where, being an artist as well as a philosopher, he was creatively shaping it in unusual ways. Plato, Schleiermacher argued, was crafting a philosophical Greek discourse even though the language was not quite ready for it. At the same time, as a Greek thinker, he thought in Greek.

Schleiermacher's German translation sought to give the German reader an inkling of this linguistic complexity and of the coherence of the entire oeuvre (Jantzen 1996). To achieve this, he followed two distinct routes. The first was captured by one of his friends, who read the translation in manuscript and praised it for 'nestling up to the original, without overdoing it' ('Anschmiegung ans Original, mit Vermeidung des Punkthaften': 2005: 166). Indeed, the translation often makes German follow the word order or even particular word formations of the Greek. These syntactic and morphological calques remind the reader, in German, that Plato is not a German but a Greek writer, and that his way of thinking and expression differs from standard German ways.

But Schleiermacher took another route, too. In some dialogues Plato ironically plays with the language, showing his mastery of it. In the *Cratylus*, for instance, a dialogue largely devoted to discussions about language, he lets his alter ego, Socrates, invent all manner of spoof etymologies for particular Greek words. In his introduction to this dialogue Schleiermacher admitted that this presented a challenge: 'This etymological part became the translator's cross, and it took him a long time to find a way out' ('Dieser etymologische Theil ist nun das Kreuz des Uebersezers geworden, und es hat ihm lange zu schaffen gemacht, einen Ausweg zu finden': 1807: 20). He adopted a bold solution: the German translation fields a German-speaking Socrates who therefore offers 'German German' linguistic derivations ('den einmal deutsch redenden Sokrates deutsches deutsch ableiten zu lassen': 1807: 21). In the case of proper names, however, this solution was not possible, and here the German version had to insert the Greek words between brackets. The coexistence of both types of solution within the same translation, Schleiermacher adds, should make the reader aware of the problematical nature of the whole exercise.

The annotations following each of the translated dialogues dramatise these dilemmas. The annotations to the spoof etymologies in *Cratylus*, for instance, frequently provide literal renderings from the Greek and then go on to explain that the translator has construed something equally fanciful using exclusively German words and derivations (e.g. 1807: 460, 461, 466, 468, 472). In *Phaedrus*, the opening dialogue in *Platons Werke*, he operates along similar lines, on one occasion basing another mocking etymology on a poem by August Wilhelm Schlegel published in 1800, just a few years before Schleiermacher's translation appeared in print and at the furthest possible remove from the world of Ancient Greek (1804: 101, 374; Hermans 2015: 87–8). The conspicuous anachronisms show, in German, Schleiermacher's understanding of Plato and of Plato's relation to Greek, while also counteracting the Greek-leaning flavour of Schleiermacher's German in other parts of the translation.

Hermeneutics

Shortly before the first volume of his Plato translation appeared in print Schleiermacher remarked in a letter to his publisher that not only was there much to be elucidated as regards Plato, but Plato was the right author to demonstrate understanding as such ('Es ist nicht nur am Plato selbst gar Vieles aufzuklären, sondern der Plato ist auch der rechte Schriftsteller um überhaupt das Verstehen anschaulich zu machen': 2005: 3). If understanding Plato was a precondition for translating him, translating Plato afforded insight into the art of understanding. In 1805, within a year of the publication of the first Plato volume, Schleiermacher began to outline a general theory of hermeneutics (2003: l–li). Hermeneutics, in turn, supplies the most direct key to Schleiermacher's pronouncements on translation, including the 1813 lecture.

Hermeneutics, ethics and dialectics are closely interlinked. As social beings, humans seek communication and community; they desire to be understood even as they project their inalienable individuality. Dialectics sets absolute and certain knowledge as its aim but has to proceed from concrete, individualised knowledge and to build dialogue on difference. Difference is also where hermeneutics begins. Understanding must be actively sought so as to overcome misunderstanding or uncertainty (1977: 92; 1998: 227–8; 2012: 127). The danger of misunderstanding is smallest within close-knit units like families, it is more or less manageable within one and the same language, and it is greatest across languages, because 'every language becomes the repository of a particular system of concepts and ways of combining', as he puts it in the ethics lectures of 1812–13 (2002b: 82; 'in jeder Sprache ein eigenthümliches System von Begriffen und von Combinationsweisen niedergelegt ist': 1981: 109). Negotiating these problems takes both discipline and imagination: hermeneutics is an art in that it is bound by rules, but there are no rules governing the application of the rules (1811: 38).

Not every text presents a hermeneutic challenge. When language merely repeats what is already known, or when it is transparent, as in 'common discourse in business matters and in habitual conversation in everyday life' (1998: 7; 1977: 76), hermeneutic effort is not required. The more language and thought are individual and original, however, the more hermeneutic effort and study are needed. Even then complete understanding will not be attained: hermeneutics remains an unending task, its outcomes forever conjectural (1977a: 41; 2012: 219). Full understanding, or what Schleiermacher in a lecture of 1829 calls 'a heightened understanding' ('ein erhöhtes Verständnis': 1977: 324), means understanding a discourse better than the speaker understood it himself, because it brings to consciousness what remained unconscious to the speaker and makes explicit the speaker's relation to the language (2012: 39, 75, 114, 128; 1998: 228, 266).

Hermeneutic study is demanding because it has to take in the relevant context, genre and period (1977a: 46; 1998: 231, 257). The level of difficulty increases the further we move away from our immediate surroundings. Only our native language is available to us in its naturally grown fullness; our access to utterances in foreign languages is inevitably fragmentary because, not having grown up in the foreign world, we can never acquire more than partial knowledge of their context (1977: 84). In a hermeneutics lecture of 1819 Schleiermacher remarks that 'man grows into his own language to such an extent that it is almost as hard to step out of one's language as it is to step out of one's skin' ('Der Mensch ist so hineingewachsen in seine Sprache, daß es nicht viel leichter ist, aus seiner Sprache, als aus seiner Haut herauszugehen': 2012: 244).

The actual process of gaining understanding follows two paths simultaneously, which Schleiermacher calls grammatical and technical interpretation (2012: 75, 121; 1977a: 42); in later writings technical interpretation is also called psychological or divinatory. The distinction reflects, on one hand, the interdependence of language and thought and, on the other, the dual notion of language as both a supra-personal system and a malleable instrument that creative individuals can bend to their will.

The two approaches are complementary, but, methodologically, grammatical interpretation comes first (2012: 101; 1977: 69–70; 1998: 232). Whereas grammatical interpretation concerns the utterance as a specimen of language, technical interpretation eyes the person who speaks and their thinking (2012: 75–6; 1977: 68; 1998: 229). In grammatical interpretation 'a speaker is regarded entirely as the organ of language', more particularly of the state of the language at the time the utterance was produced (1977: 85, 94; 1998: 230). Each language sets a limit to what can be said or thought in it. Technical interpretation proceeds as if one was trying to get to know the language from the speaker's discourse (1998: 230); it seeks insight into the speaker's individuality, and the linguistic expression of this individuality is what Schleiermacher calls style (2012: 102; 1998: 254–5; Pfau 1990). If grammatical interpretation investigates the state of the language at a given moment in its development and yields relatively certain knowledge, technical interpretation is both more dynamic and more speculative: it requires imaginative leaps on the part of the exegete who is now dealing with the innovations and transgressions of particular speakers imposing their will on the language and, through their interventions, forcing change on it. The complementarity between grammatical and technical interpretation appears also in what later became known as the hermeneutic circle: 'One must already know a man in order to understand what he says, and yet one first becomes acquainted with him by what he says' (1977a: 56; 2012: 25).

What is probably the first printed statement of Schleiermacher's hermeneutic principles appeared in his *Kurze Darstellung des theologischen Studiums* (*Brief Outline of the Study of Theology*) of 1811, a book concerned with the interpretation of canonical Christian works, especially the New Testament. The edition of 1811 was followed by a second, enlarged version in 1830.

The New Testament was written in Greek, even though most Christians in later ages read it in translation. Jesus of Nazareth and his disciples, however, spoke Aramaic, and the Greek of the New Testament still shows the Aramaic palimpsest underneath it. Schleiermacher's comments on these issues, in three short paragraphs, are telling:

> §16. No discourse can be fully understood except in the original language. Not even the most perfect translation overcomes the irrationality of language.
>
> §17. Even translations can be fully understood only by someone who is conversant with the original language.
>
> §18. Although the original language of the canon is Greek, much of it is translated directly from the Aramaic, and even more should be regarded as indirectly translated.
>
> (1850: 139–40)
>
> §16. Keine Rede kann vollständig verstanden werden als in der Ursprache. Auch die vollkommenste Uebersezung hebt die Irrationalität der Sprache nicht auf.
>
> §17. Auch Uebersezungen versteht nur derjenige vollkommen, der zugleich mit der Ursprache bekannt ist.
>
> §18. Die Ursprache des Kanons ist zwar griechisch, vieles aber ist unmittelbar Uebersezung aus dem Aramäischen, und noch mehreres ist mittelbar so anzusehen.
>
> (1811: 37)

'Irrationality', as the mark of difference, may not be absolute, but it cannot be wholly eradicated within a language, much less across languages, where equivalence does not exist. Translation cannot undo the irrationality of language. Strictly speaking, Schleiermacher notes in his draft General Hermeneutics of 1809–10, there are no synonyms even within the same language (2012: 94). Learning a foreign language, he notes in 1819, makes us 'reduce' foreign words to presumed mother-tongue equivalents, but this often ensnares us in errors (2012: 137–8; 1977: 112). The exegete seeking to understand a translation is therefore charged with interpreting the original as well as the translation and to appreciate the translation as an interpretation of the original.

The reference to New Testament Greek being a translation of sorts shows that Schleiermacher is perfectly aware of hybrid language. The New Testament writers, he suggests, were relatively simple people. Except for Paul, they were not quite capable of fully exploiting the resources of Greek. Apart from spoken Aramaic, they also drew on the Hebrew of the Old Testament and infused old Jewish terms with new Christian meanings. In addition, the Greek they wrote often harked back to the Septuagint translation of the Old Testament (2012: 130; 1977: 158; 1998: 82). The exegete needs to weigh these dependencies and remain alive to what Schleiermacher calls 'the language-forming power of Christianity' in the New Testament (1998: 86; 2012: 124, 205; 1977: 162), because the novel ideas of a new religion demanded innovative speech (1977: 382). Historical hindsight often dulls the freshness of what was once new but has become assimilated; in a later addition to his hermeneutic manuscripts Schleiermacher mentions Plato as just such a linguistic innovator, forging a written philosophical discourse out of everyday conversations in a manner that is hard for us moderns to appreciate (1977: 103). In a lecture of 1832 he broadened this out to the general statement that intellectual developments trigger linguistic change ('wenn in einem Volke eine geistige Entwicklung vorgeht, so entsteht auch eine Sprachentwicklung': 1977: 90).

The combination of, on one hand, the 'irrationality' of language and, on the other, the various factors which converge in singular ways in particular texts makes both hermeneutic understanding and translation challenging. This does not mean they are impossible. No-one can step outside their own skin, but in interpreting someone else's thought one must set one's own thoughts aside in favour of the other person's, as Schleiermacher stressed in his earliest notes on hermeneutics (2012: 7; 1977a: 42); to do otherwise is to sacrifice the understanding of otherness to the pursuit of one's own ends (1977: 213). In his very first lecture to the Academy, in 1811, he charged modern scholars of ancient thought with merely projecting their own ideas on the thinking of the ancients (2002: 33–4). But, as he recognised in a hermeneutics lecture of 1819, a special talent is needed to 'think oneself into' foreign languages ('Es ist ein Talent, sich in fremde Sprachen hineinzudenken': 2012: 244). It is a talent translators cannot do without.

'On the Different Methods of Translating'

Schleiermacher delivered his lecture 'On the Different Methods of Translating' ('Über die verschiedenen Methoden des Übersetzens') on two occasions at the Berlin Academy of Sciences, first to its philological section on 24 June 1813, then to the Academy's full session on 3 July. The time was one of heightened national sentiment in the wake of Napoleon's ignominious retreat from Russia six months earlier, and indeed Schleiermacher's journalism in the spring and summer of 1813 was concerned almost exclusively with the political and military situation (Meding 1992: 38–45). There is no evidence he attached much importance to the lecture on translation or that it made any impact. He dashed it off in less than four days (2002: xxxii). On the evening of its first presentation he spoke of it as 'a rather trivial piece' ('ein ziemlich triviales Zeug': 2002: xxxiii). He does not appear to refer back to it in any of his later writings. The text was printed in the Academy's Transactions (which were not sent out for review) in 1816 and then in Schleiermacher's posthumous collected works, but it remained forgotten until its reprint in Hans-Joachim Störig's anthology *Das Problem des Übersetzens* (*The Problem of Translation*) of 1963. The current high regard for it among scholars of translation is due to the work of Antoine Berman (1992) and Lawrence Venuti (2008: 83–98).

The lecture amounts to neither more nor less than the application of hermeneutics to translation. From a hermeneutic point of view, translation is nothing special: it simply means the extension of hermeneutic principles from the intralingual to the interlingual. At the same time, it is very special, due the irrationality of language being at its most acute here, and to the fact that, in order to articulate their understanding of the foreign text, translators have at their disposal only their own tongue as they address readers unfamiliar with the foreign tongue.

Schleiermacher opens his lecture by pointing out that the term 'translation', broadly conceived, can cover both intralingual and interlingual renderings, but he restricts it to the latter nevertheless. He also disposes of the oral interpreter ('Dolmetscher') in favour of the 'translator proper' (2012a: 44; 'der eigentliche Uebersezer': 2002: 68), who is concerned with written discourse. For the hermeneuticist, written discourse presents more of a challenge because, as Plato said in the *Phaedrus*, written discourse can dispense with the presence of a speaker and does not permit the kind of conversational exchanges during which interlocutors can clear up misunderstandings. Written discourse, Schleiermacher notes, is also the proper medium of the arts and sciences – where science ('Wissenschaft') appears to mean primarily philosophy; later in the lecture he cites Plato as a typical exponent of science (2012a: 60; 2002: 90).

Schleiermacher associates the world of commerce with oral interpreting because, he says, there the spoken word is the common currency (2012a: 44; 2002: 68). But translating journalism and travel literature is also more like oral interpreting than like translation proper because in these genres the subject-matter is the sole concern, everyone is familiar with the things being referred to, the phrases used are no more than counters determined by law or convention and so speakers are readily understood ('schlechthin verständlich': 2002: 70). Clearly, Schleiermacher is talking about texts which hold no hermeneutic challenge and so have 'zero' or minimum value in hermeneutic terms. Translating these texts is a mechanical exercise (2012a: 45; 2002: 70).

Translation proper, then, is concerned with hermeneutically challenging language and thought. In these texts the author's individual way of seeing and of making connections ('des Verfassers eigenthümliche Art zu sehen und zu verbinden': 2002: 69) prevails, and 'the author's free individual combinatory faculties' (2012a: 45; 'das freie eigenthümliche combinatorische Vermögen des Verfassers': 2002: 69) work on the language in such a way that substance and expression become inseparable. Schleiermacher's use of 'eigenthümlich', a term familiar from his other work, is key here: between them 'eigenthümlich' and the corresponding noun 'Eigenthümlichkeit' (he spells both with an 'h' in the middle) occur no fewer than eighteen times in the lecture, an insistence obscured in the English translations (1977b; 2002c; 2012a), which distribute the terms over different words ('particular', 'individual', 'peculiar', 'special' and corresponding nouns). The subject-matter in texts of this kind 'comes into existence only through being uttered and exists only in this utterance' (2012a: 45; 'erst durch die Rede geworden und nur zugleich mit ihr da ist': 2002: 69), and we encounter 'thought that is one with speech' (2012a: 46; 'der Gedanke [...] der mit der Rede eins ist': 2002: 71).

Transplanting these texts – the shift from a mechanical to an organic metaphor is deliberate, and Schleiermacher consistently invokes organic metaphors when speaking of 'proper' translation (2002: 67, 70, 79, 80, 83, 92, 93) – poses formidable problems, for two reasons. One is the irrationality of languages (2002: 70): the non-existence of cross-lingual equivalence. The other recalls the dual orientation towards language that is present in every utterance worth hermeneutic attention. On one hand, all speakers are in the power of language, which has 'preordained' (2012a: 46; 'vorgezeichnet': 2002: 71) what can be thought and said in it. On the other, creative minds shape the 'tractable' (2012a: 46; 'bildsam': 2002: 70) material of language to their own designs. This dual orientation of utterances reflects the distinction between grammatical and technical interpretation in Schleiermacher's hermeneutics. It is subsequently elaborated in exactly these terms in the first key passage in the lecture:

> Now if understanding works of this sort is already difficult even in the same language and involves immersing oneself in both the spirit of the language and the writer's characteristic nature, how much yet nobler an art must it be when we are speaking of the products of a foreign and distant tongue! To be sure, whoever has mastered this art of understanding by studying the language with diligence, acquiring precise knowledge of the entire historical life of a people and picturing keenly before him the individual works and their authors – *he*, to be sure, and he alone is justified in desiring to bring to his countrymen and contemporaries just this same understanding of these masterworks of art and science.
>
> (2012a: 47)

Wenn nun das Verstehen auf diesem Gebiet selbst in der gleichen Sprache schon schwierig ist, und ein genaues und tiefes Eindringen in den Geist der Sprache und in die Eigenthümlichkeiten des Schriftstellers in sich schließt: wie vielmehr nicht wird es eine hohe Kunst sein, wenn von den Erzeugnissen einer fremden und fernen Sprache die Rede ist! Wer denn freilich diese Kunst des Verstehens sich angeeignet hat, durch die eifrigsten Bemühungen um die Sprache, und durch genaue Kenntniß von dem ganzen geschichtlichen Leben des Volks, und durch die lebendigste Vergegenwärtigung einzelner Werke und ihrer Urheber, den freilich, aber auch nur *den*, kann es gelüsten von den Meisterwerken der Kunst und Wissenschaft das gleiche Verständniß auch seinen Volks- und Zeitgenossen zu eröffnen.

(2002: 72)

In this remarkable passage the hermeneutic project becomes the precondition for translating. Understanding in one's own language is already hard if the dual orientation of a discourse to the language as such and to the peculiarities ('Eigenthümlichkeiten') of the individual author are to be taken into account. Understanding works in a distant tongue deserves even more to be called a high art ('eine hohe Kunst'). This is so because a foreign language will always be available in fragmentary form only: the exegete has not grown up in and with that idiom and can therefore only ever grasp it partially and imperfectly, as an outsider. Becoming proficient in this most exacting division of the hermeneutic endeavour demands practice and dedication. Schleiermacher is emphatic on this point, rather more so than Susan Bernofsky's English rendering suggests: this proficiency is acquired through studying the language not just 'with diligence' but with *the greatest* diligence ('die eifrigsten Bemühungen'), *and through* detailed historical study, *and through* – the repetition of 'durch..., und durch..., und durch' is insistent – imaginative engagement with individual works and their authors. Only someone thoroughly versed in the art and travail of hermeneutics can dream of translating. And translating, in turn, consists in putting before the audience exactly that understanding of the foreign work which the translator has been able to achieve: the prolonged labour of 'Verstehen' ('understanding') results in an end product, 'Verständniß' ('understanding'), which now has to be articulated in the translator's language. Schleiermacher devotes most of the rest of the lecture to explicating what this means.

The task seems impossible, 'an utterly foolish undertaking' (2012a: 47). The translator has to make the reader understand ('verstehen': 2002: 72) not only the spirit of the foreign language ('den Geist der Sprache') in which the author felt at home ('einheimisch') and the latter's particular ('eigenthümlich') way of thinking and feeling as it is articulated in that language: he also needs to intimate to his readers the understanding ('Verständniß') he himself has reached, the effort ('Mühe') it took to get there, the pleasure ('Genuß') it yielded and the feeling of the foreign ('das Gefühl des fremden') that continues to inhere in the insight gained. The difficulty, specific to translation and consequent upon the hermeneutic engagement with the original, consists in the fact that, to give voice to all this and provide the reader with a vicarious experience similar to his own, the translator has only his own language.

It is at this point, and after he has cleared away two alternatives, paraphrase and imitation, which he says both sidestep the challenge, that Schleiermacher posits the two well-known options open to the translator: 'Either the translator leaves the writer in peace as much as possible and moves the reader towards him; or he leaves the reader in peace as much as possible and moves the writer towards him' (2012a: 49). The dichotomy, however, is not real. The second option is mentioned only to be dismissed. The first option is not what it seems either, as we shall see. Let us deal with the second option first.

This method, bringing the author to the reader, would have the translator write what the foreign author would have written had he not been foreign. But, Schleiermacher argues, if the author had grown up in our tongue, he would have been a different person entertaining different thoughts. This option assumes that the same thoughts can be thought in two different languages and that consequently thinking and language can exist separately. Schleiermacher rejects this belief as an untenable 'fiction' (2012a: 61; 'Fiction': 2002: 91) and in so doing declares the very foundation of this method invalid. He contrasts it with his own conviction, which affirms the principle of the identity of language and thought as underpinning all understanding, all hermeneutics and therefore all translating ('the inner, essential identity between thought and expression – and this conviction forms the basis for the entire art of understanding speech and thus of all translation as well': 2012a: 56; 'daβ wesentlich und innerlich Gedanke und Ausdrukk ganz dasselbe sind, und auf dieser Ueberzeugung beruht doch die ganze Kunst alles Verstehens der Rede, und also auch alles Uebersezens': 2002: 85). It follows that the aim of the method of bringing the author to the reader is 'null and void' (2012a: 56; 'nichtig und leer': 2002: 85), its applicability stands at 'well-nigh zero' (2012a: 59; 'fast gleich null': 2002: 89), its practice mostly resembles either paraphrase or imitation, and so it does not even qualify as proper translation at all ('dies würde streng genommen gar kein Uebersetzen sein': 2002: 91). At best, renderings made in this vein can prepare the ground: a nation not yet ready for proper translation may use imitation and paraphrase to feed an appetite for the foreign ('Lust am Fremden') and thus pave the way towards a more general understanding ('ein allgemeineres Verstehen': 2002: 76).

In fact, moving the reader to the author, the apparent opposite of the previous option, is equally impossible but for a different reason. The translator can gain at best a partial, fragmentary understanding of the foreign author. With even the translator denied full access, there can be no question of the reader being transported to the author. The point at which author and reader meet can only be the translator:

> The two separate parties must be united either at some point between the two – and that will always be the position of the translator – or else the one must betake himself to the other, and only one of these two possibilities lies within the realm of translation.
>
> (2012a: 49)

> Die beiden getrennten Partheien müssen entweder an einem mittleren Punkt zusamentreffen, und das wird immer der des Uebersezers sein, oder die eine muβ sich ganz zur andern verfügen, und hiervon fällt nur die eine Art in das Gebiet der Uebersezung.
>
> (2002: 75)

The alternative, which for Schleiermacher falls outside the realm of translation, would entail a reader becoming totally at home in the foreign language, or that language enveloping the reader to such an extent that he became a different person (2012a). It is therefore the translator who moves, taking the reader with him, and both firmly stay within the confines of their own tongue. The translator acts as the hermeneuticist does: he works to attain the best possible understanding of the foreign text, which nevertheless remains foreign, and then has to find a way to communicate to the reader unfamiliar with the foreign language exactly that understanding. In the process of seeking understanding the translator has moved some way towards the author, closer to the edge of his own tongue, so to speak. It is to this position, one foreign to the readers of the translation, that the translator moves his readers. This is the second key passage of the lecture:

> the translator endeavours through his labour to supply for the reader the understanding of the original language which the reader lacks. He seeks to communicate to the readers the exact same image, the exact same impression which he himself gained through his knowledge of the original language of the work as it is, and thus to move them to his own position, one in fact foreign to *them*.
>
> (2012a: 49; the italicised word represents my correction of Susan Bernofsky's translation, which, erroneously, has 'foreign to him')
>
> ist der Uebersezer bemüht, durch seine Arbeit dem Leser das Verstehen der Ursprache, das ihm fehlt, zu ersezen. Das nämliche Bild, den nämlichen Eindrukk, welchen er selbst durch die Kenntniβ der Ursprache von dem Werke, wie es ist, gewonnen, sucht er den Lesern mitzutheilen, und sie also an seine ihnen eigentlich fremde Stelle hinzubewegen.
>
> (2002: 74–5)

The hard-won familiarity with foreign works and authors sets translators apart from their compatriots. But the impression of the foreign work to be conveyed remains that gained by one who has diligently studied a foreign tongue while remaining aware of its foreignness. True, there are those rare prodigies to whom no language feels foreign, but Schleiermacher views them as exceptions for whom the value of translation is nil (2002: 77–8). At the other end of the spectrum stands a plodding schoolboy understanding ('schülerhaftes Verstehen': 2002: 76), which lacks a sense of the whole and its coherence – the kind of broader vision Schleiermacher had articulated in his Plato translation ten years earlier. Proper translation occupies the space between these extremes. It calls for an educated and dedicated translator proficient in the foreign language but for whom the foreignness of the foreign always remains ('dem die fremde Sprache geläufig ist, aber doch immer fremde bleibt': 2002: 78). The challenge for the translator is to deploy the translating language in such a way that it conveys to readers unfamiliar with the foreign language that particular sense of the foreign as it inhabits this specific work by this individual writer and as the translator, having looked over the fence, as it were, has apprehended it. Foreignness thus enters the translating language. This leads to Schleiermacher's observations on the translator creatively bending his language to the foreign tongue.

The form which that bending takes recalls Schleiermacher's Plato, which 'nestled up' to the original but left room for creative variation. Schleiermacher certainly does not mean strictly literal or metrical translation, which he dismisses as 'one-sided' (2012a: 52; 2002: 80). Rather, the translator must be granted a degree of linguistic flexibility. His discourse will in any case look less coherent than that of an original author who can build up a network of cognate keywords echoing one another across successive or related works (2012a: 52; 2002: 79). The remark echoes comments in the hermeneutic writings to the effect that we can gain only fragmentary knowledge of foreign cultures. Still, if the translating language is to accommodate the foreign ways of thinking embodied in the original, then the translator's usage will have to be innovative.

There is a wider, historical context as well. Schleiermacher projects the immature schoolboy grasp of the foreign on a national and temporal scale. In times when the educated part of a nation lacks a tradition of familiarity with foreign cultures, those who are ahead of their compatriots in dealing with the foreign cannot display their own more advanced understanding in their translations because they would not be understood (2012a: 50; 2002: 76). The comment recalls Schleiermacher's own anxiety, in a letter of 7 January 1804, that the German public might not have been ready for his Plato translation (2005: 186).

The conditions that enable proper translation to flourish, then, are twofold. It takes a language supple enough to be bent as required (French, caught in its neo-classical vice, will not do: 2002: 82, 92; 2012a: 54, 62) and a community of readers willing to accept unfamiliar linguistic usage. When these two conditions are met, a national translation culture can develop. The rhetorical finale of the 1813 lecture envisages a German nation obeying an 'inner necessity' to transplant foreign works, cultivating its national language 'through extensive contact with the foreign' and serving as a repository of the global treasure trove of culture (2012a: 62; 2002: 92). Schleiermacher concedes that this vision has yet to materialise, but '[a] good beginning has been made' (2012a: 62; 2002: 92). In a footnote to the printed version of the lecture he mentions Johann Heinrich Voss's four-volume translation of Homer (1793) and A.W. Schlegel's nine-volume Shakespeare (1797–1810) as shining examples of that beginning. No doubt he saw his own Plato translation as deserving a place in this list as well.

Approximation

The historical projection in the concluding paragraphs of Schleiermacher's 1813 lecture may look like a mere nationalistically inflected rhetorical flourish. It is more than that. In his 1812–13 manuscripts on ethics – contemporaneous with the lecture on translation – Schleiermacher notes how cross-cultural 'community' may arise from border traffic and is epitomised by language mixture ('Sprachmengerei': 2002b: 87; 1981: 115), something the cultural centre will normally disavow and oppose. Nations being unequal, one will usually exert and the other undergo influence. However, if national feeling in the receiving nation is sufficiently strong, it will assert its individuality, and 'this tendency to bring national particularity comparatively to consciousness gives rise to a community of translations' ('Aus dieser Tendenz aber die Nationaleigenthümlichkeit comparativ zum Bewußtsein zu bringen, entsteht die Gemeinschaft der Uebersezungen': 2002b: 87; 1981: 115). Because it engages with the foreign as foreign and puts the receiving language to work to create room for it, translation enables comparison, highlights cultural difference and serves as an index of national identity.

The somewhat later lectures on psychology add a twist to these ideas, complementing the notion of translation as marking difference with that of convergence and of approaching an ultimate goal. Discussing issues of linguistic diversity and cultural intertraffic, and using terminology reminiscent of his work on dialectics, Schleiermacher observes that 'as soon as several languages are in contact with one another, they also grow closer' ('Sobald dagegen mehrere Sprachen in Verkehr mit einander sind, so sind sie auch in einer beständigen Approximation begriffen': 1862: 179). As each develops, the exchange of knowledge among them intensifies and becomes easier, and the project of total and shared knowledge begins to look a little less utopian. And this, he claims, is already happening. 'The idea of knowledge that would not be enclosed within the borders of one language but would be the same for everyone, arises from the simple fact that this approximation is steadily being realised' ('Die Idee von einem Wissen, welches nicht in den Grenzen einer bestimmten Sprache eingeschlossen sondern ein gleiches für alle sein soll, beruht lediglich darauf, daß diese Approximation immer mehr realisirt wird': 1862: 180). But the road will be long, and just as the 1813 lecture on translation ended with a reminder of how much still needed to be done, so the lectures on psychology too stress the role of translation as marking at once the huge distance still to be travelled, the enormity of the task and the way in which it might nevertheless be accomplished:

> If we remind ourselves how far we are still from this goal, and how little we have achieved in resolving the modes of thinking of other peoples into our own, then we are a long way from claiming that the representational capacity of any language has evolved to the point where it could absorb other modes of thought. In translating from one language into another the differences in the respective elements become particularly clear, giving rise to the obvious task of balancing them out through a special art of combination and thus to make the content similar, which can be done to a certain degree. But this latter operation only then becomes truly approximative, when one simultaneously thinks in the other language, so that one would have to set as one's task the totality of thought in one language in order to translate from one language into another.
>
> Bedenken wir nun, wie weit wir noch von diesem Ziel entfernt sind und wie wenig wir darin geleistet haben, die Denkungsweise verschiedener Völker in die unsrige aufzulösen, so sind wird auch noch sehr weit entfernt zu behaupten, daß die Darstellung in irgend einer Sprache so weit gediehen sei, daß andre Denkweisen darin aufgingen. Bei der Uebertragung einer Sprache in die andre treten nun die Differenzen in den Elementen am meisten hervor, so daß die natürliche Aufgabe entsteht, diese durch eine besondere Art der Combination ausgleichen und so den Gehalt ähnlich zu machen, was bis auf einen gewissen Grad sich lösen läßt. Aber die lezte Operation wird dann erst recht approximativ, wenn man in der andern Sprache zugleich denkt, so daß man also die Totalität des Denkens in einer Sprache sich zur Aufgabe machen müßte, um aus einer Sprache in die andre zu übersezen.
>
> (1862: 180–1)

Translation brings difference to the fore because it cannot help proceeding from one word to another and inevitably runs into non-synonymy, the irrationality of language. The solution is to shift attention from the individual 'elements' to broader discursive and conceptual issues, as Schleiermacher had indeed recommended in his 1811 notes on dialectics, quoted above: 'I cannot appropriate an alien singularity, I have to reconstruct it through the way the foreign concept is formed' ('Das Einzelne fremde kann ich mir nicht aneignen; aber ich soll es in der fremden Begriffsbildung nachconstruiren': 2002a, 1: 59). This is a hermeneutic task, which only then truly contributes to the convergence of disparate knowledges when it aspires – a forlorn aspiration – to think the totality of thought in the foreign tongue. While the task cannot be accomplished, it can be done to a degree, and, as he states in an 1830 Academy lecture on ethics, cross-border intellectual traffic resembles both the multilingualism of individuals and 'the resulting if never more than approximative appropriation of what has been thought in other languages' ('die daraus entstehende immer nur approximative Aneignung des in fremden Sprachen gedachten': 2002: 675).

In his dialectics Schleiermacher envisaged a metaphysical ideal of absolute and true knowledge shared by all, and he sketched a dialogical path within and across languages leading, in the fullness of time, to that ultimate consensus. Here translation takes the role of that dialogue. Translation remains mired in difference, but it can be lifted to a higher plane. The utopia that translation entertains is that of a final convergence of modes of thinking that would abolish the irrationality of language. It is an almost Benjaminian vision.

Related topics

Benjamin; equivalence; ethics; meaning; Shelley's Plato.

Further reading

The *Kritische Gesamtausgabe* (KGA), currently in progress, is the authoritative edition of Schleiermacher's works in the original German. Each volume comes with a full critical apparatus, but it will be years before all sixty-five volumes are available. The best English-language general overview is the *Cambridge Companion to Schleiermacher* (Mariña 2005). It features a chapter on Schleiermacher as a translator of Plato but makes no mention of the 1813 lecture on translation. Andreas Arndt (2013, in German) and Christian Berner (1995, in French) offer comprehensive accounts of Schleiermacher's philosophical thought; a summary of Arndt's book is available in English (Arndt 2015), while Berner (2015) has a useful chapter, in German, on Schleiermacher's philosophy and the 1813 lecture on translation, in *Friedrich Schleiermacher and the Question of Translation*, ed. Larisa Cercel and Adriana Şerban.

References

Arndt, Andreas (2013) *Friedrich Schleiermacher als Philosoph*. Berlin and New York: Walter de Gruyter.
Arndt, Andreas (2015) 'Schleiermacher (1768–1834)'. Trans. Anita Mage. In *The Oxford Handbook of German Philosophy in the Nineteenth Century*. Ed. Michael Forster and Kristin Gjesdal. Oxford: Oxford University Press. 27–45.
Berman, Antoine (1992) *The Experience of the Foreign. Culture and Translation in Romantic Germany*. Trans. S. Heyvaert. New York: State University of New York Press.
Berner, Christian (1995) *La philosophie de Schleiermacher. Herméneutique, dialectique, éthique*. Paris: CERF.
Berner, Christian (2015) 'Das Übersetzen verstehen. Zu den philosophischen Grundlagen von Schleiermachers Vorlesung "Über die verschiedenen Methoden des Übersetzens"'. In Cercel and Şerban. 43–58.
Cercel, Larisa and Şerban, Adriana (2015) Eds. *Friedrich Schleiermacher and the Question of Translation*. Berlin and Boston: Walter de Gruyter.
Hermans, Theo (2015) 'Schleiermacher and Plato, Hermeneutics and Translation'. In Cercel and Şerban. 77–106.
Jantzen, Jörg (1996) 'Zu Schleiermachers Platon-Übersetzung und seinen Anmerkungen dazu'. In Schleiermacher. xlv–lvi.
Lamm, Julia (2000) 'Schleiermacher as Plato Scholar'. *Journal of Religion* 80, 2. 206–39.
Lamm, Julia (2005) 'The Art of Interpreting Plato'. In Mariña. 91–108.
Mariña, Jacqueline (2005) Ed. *The Cambridge Companion to Friedrich Schleiermacher*. Cambridge: Cambridge University Press.
Meding, Wichmann von (1992) *Bibliographie der Schriften Schleiermachers*. Berlin and New York: Walter de Gruyter.
Nowak, Kurt (2002) *Schleiermacher: Leben, Werk und Wirkung*. Göttingen: Vandenhoeck & Ruprecht.
Pfau, Thomas (1990) 'Immediacy and the Text: Friedrich Schleiermacher's Theory of Style and Interpretation'. *Journal of the History of Ideas* 51, 1. 51–73.
Raack, R.C. (1959) 'Schleiermacher's Political Thought and Activity, 1806–1813'. *Church History* 28, 4. 374–90.
Schleiermacher, Friedrich (1804) *Platons Werke. Vol. 1, 1*. Berlin: Realschulbuchhandlung.
Schleiermacher, Friedrich (1807) *Platons Werke. Vol. 2, 2*. Berlin: Realschulbuchhandlung.
Schleiermacher, Friedrich (1811) *Kurze Darstellung des theologischen Studiums*. Berlin: Realschulbuchhandlung.

Schleiermacher, Friedrich (1830) *Kurze Darstellung des theologischen Studiums*. 2nd revised ed. Berlin: G. Reimer.
Schleiermacher, Friedrich (1836) *Introductions to the Dialogues of Plato*. Trans. William Dobson. Cambridge and London: J. and J.J. Deighton & J.W. Parker.
Schleiermacher, Friedrich (1850) *Brief Outline of the Study of Theology*. Trans. William Farrer. Edinburgh: T. & T. Clark.
Schleiermacher, Friedrich (1858) *Aus Schleiermacher's Leben. In Briefen*. Ed. Wilhelm Dilthey. 2 vols. Berlin: G. Reimer.
Schleiermacher, Friedrich (1862) *Psychologie. Aus Schleiermacher's handschriftlichem Nachlasse und nachgeschriebenen Vorlesungen. Sämmtliche Werke 3, 6. Literarischer Nachlaß*, 4. Ed. L. George. Berlin: G. Reimer.
Schleiermacher, Friedrich (1977) *Hermeneutik und Kritik. Mit einem Anhang sprachphilosophischer Texte Schleiermachers*. Ed. Manfred Frank. Frankfurt: Suhrkamp.
Schleiermacher, Friedrich (1977a) *Hermeneutics: The Handwritten Manuscripts*. Ed. Hanz Kimmerle. Trans. James Duke and Jack Forstman. Missoula: Scholars Press.
Schleiermacher, Friedrich (1977b) 'On the Different Methods of Translating'. Trans. André Lefevere. In *Translating Literature: The German Tradition from Luther to Rosenzweig*. Ed. André Lefevere. Assen and Amsterdam: van Gorcum. 67–82.
Schleiermacher, Friedrich (1981) *Ethik (1812/13) mit späteren Fassungen der Einleitung, Güterlehre und Pflichtenlehre*. Ed. Hans-Joachim Birkner. Hamburg: Felix Meiner.
Schleiermacher, Friedrich (1988) *Dialektik (1814/15). Einleitung zur Dialektik (1833)*. Ed. Andreas Arndt. Hamburg: Felix Meiner.
Schleiermacher, Friedrich (1998) *Hermeneutics and Criticism and Other Writings*. Ed. and trans. Andrew Bowie. Cambridge: Cambridge University Press.
Schleiermacher, Friedrich (2000) *Über die Philosophie Platons. Die Einleitungen zur Übersetzung des Platon (1804–1828)*. Ed. Peter Steiner. Hamburg: Felix Meiner.
Schleiermacher, Friedrich (2002) *Akademievorträge. Kritische Gesamtausgabe* 1, 11. Ed. Martin Rössler. Berlin and New York: Walter de Gruyter.
Schleiermacher, Friedrich (2002a) *Vorlesungen über die Dialektik*. 2 vols. *Kritische Gesamtausgabe* 10, 1–2. Ed. Andreas Arndt. Berlin and New York: Walter de Gruyter.
Schleiermacher, Friedrich (2002b) *Lectures on Philosophical Ethics*. Trans. Louise Adey Huish. Ed. Robert Louden. Cambridge: Cambridge University Press.
Schleiermacher, Friedrich (2002c) 'On the Different Methods of Translating'. Trans. Douglas Robinson. In *Western Translation Theory from Herodotus to Nietzsche*. Ed. Douglas Robinson. 2nd ed. Manchester: St. Jerome. 225–38.
Schleiermacher, Friedrich (2003) *Kleine Schriften 1786–1833. Kritische Gesamtausgabe* 1, 14. Eds. Matthias Wolfer and Michael Pietsch. Berlin and New York: Walter de Gruyter.
Schleiermacher, Friedrich (2005) *Briefwechsel 1803–1804. Kritische Gesamtausgabe* 5, 7. Eds. Andreas Arndt and Wolfgang Virmond. Berlin and New York: Walter de Gruyter.
Schleiermacher, Friedrich (2012) *Vorlesungen zur Hermeneutik und Kritik. Kritische Gesamtausgabe* 2, 4. Ed. Wolfgang Virmond. Berlin and New York: Walter de Gruyter.
Schleiermacher, Friedrich (2012a) 'On the Different Methods of Translating'. Trans. Susan Bernofsky. In *The Translation Studies Reader*. Ed. Lawrence Venuti. 3rd ed. London and New York: Routledge. 43–63.
Störig, Hans-Joachim (1963) Ed. *Das Problem des Übersetzens*. Darmstadt: Wissenschaftliche Buchgesellschaft.
Venuti, Lawrence (2008) *The Translator's Invisibility. A History of Translation*. 2nd ed. London and New York: Routledge.
Vial, Theodore (2005) 'Schleiermacher and the State'. In Mariña. 269–85.

2
Nietzsche

Rosemary Arrojo

Introduction

Even though Friedrich Nietzsche (1844–1900) has left us only a couple of fragments that explicitly deal with translation, the impact of his thought on the development of some of the most productive trends that have emerged within the discipline of translation studies in the last few decades has been enormous, albeit hardly acknowledged. Even a cursory look at the main notions that have shaped such trends – the recognition of the translator's inescapable visibility and agency, the transformational character of translation, the role of translation in processes of colonization and evangelization, the relationship between translation and gender issues, just to name a few – will show that they are deeply indebted to key concepts directly associated with Nietzsche's philosophy, particularly as it has been re-examined by twentieth-century thinkers associated with poststructuralism. In fact, if we consider, for example, that mainstream conceptions of the so-called 'original' and the idealized relationship they propose between the original and its translations are still very much reminiscent of Plato's theory of forms and its devaluation of representations, it becomes evident why Nietzsche's conceptions of language, interpretation, and the will to power have been fundamental for the ways in which we are now able to think of the task of translators and the ethics that should guide their work. In order to address these issues I will start with a brief overview of the philosophical basis grounding recurrent conceptions of text and translation that have dominated the scholarship in the area for more than two millennia. After covering Nietzsche's own comments on translation, I will introduce the main theoretical questions that are relevant for an evaluation of the philosopher's seminal role in the shaping of contemporary translation studies and will cover key statements that have been associated with his thought.

More than two millennia of scholarship on translation: a brief historical overview

The long-standing, predominantly essentialist tradition

In his 1975 *After Babel – Aspects of Language and Translation*, arguably one of the first comprehensive treatises ever written on the topic, George Steiner divides the 'literature on the theory, practice, and history of translation' into four periods (Steiner 1975: 236). The first period starts with Cicero's recommendation not to translate word for word proposed in 'The Best Kind of Orators', written in 46 BC as an introduction to his translation of a speech by Demosthenes (Cicero 2002), as well as Horace's reiteration of this formula in the *Ars Poetica*, which appeared about twenty years later (Horace 2002). This initial phase covers major statements about translation in the Western tradition up to Friedrich Hölderlin's commentary on his translations of Sophocles's plays *Oedipus* and *Antigone*, published in 1804 (Hölderlin 1988). It includes Alexander Fraser Tytler's 1791 *Essay on the Principles of Translation* (Tytler 1978) as well as Friedrich Schleiermacher's 'On the Different Methods of Translating', published in 1813 (Schleiermacher 2002). According to Steiner, the common thread that brings together almost two-thousand years of scholarship on translation covered in this first period is the fact that the reflections proposed stem directly from the actual practice of translation. Some of the notable examples he mentions include Saint Jerome's and Luther's passionate defences of their Bible translations, recorded respectively in the 'Letter to Pammachius', from 395 CE (Jerome 2002: 23–30), and in the 'Circular Letter on Translation', which appeared in 1530 (Luther 2002: 84–9), as well as often quoted pronouncements by Joachim du Bellay, Michel de Montaigne, George Chapman, John Dryden, and Alexander Pope.

After this long initial period, the main focus of the scholarship in the area moves towards theory and hermeneutic inquiry, in which 'the nature of translation is posed within the more general framework of theories of language and mind' (Steiner 1975: 237), a trend that finds in Schleiermacher a precursor and in A. W. von Schlegel and W. von Humboldt central figures who have given the topic of translation 'a frankly philosophic aspect' (ibid.). Nonetheless, the tradition of commentary on the practice of translation obviously continued and, indeed, it is in this second phase that we find 'many of the most telling reports on the activity of the translator and on relations between languages' (ibid.). Among such reports, Steiner identifies statements by Goethe, Schopenhauer, Matthew Arnold, Paul Valéry, Ezra Pound, I. A. Richards, Benedetto Croce, Walter Benjamin, and Ortega y Gasset, statements that characterize the period as an age of 'philosophic-poetic theory and definition' extending to Valery Larbaud's *An Homage to Saint Jerome*, originally published in French in 1946 (Larbaud 1984) (Steiner 1975: 237). The third period, which is fully inscribed within modernity, is represented by the first papers on machine translation that begin to be divulged in the late 1940s alongside a keen interest in the possible implications for translation of statistics, information, and linguistics-inspired theories. Steiner also relates this period to the organization of professional translators' associations and the proliferation of international journals devoted to the topic. Besides this trend, which, for Steiner, is still unfolding as he is writing *After Babel* in the early 1970s, a fourth phase, which began emerging in the 1960s, can be identified in conjunction with a renewed interest in hermeneutics and the scholarship on translation developed in the wake of the 'discovery' of Walter Benjamin's piece on 'The Task of the Translator' (Benjamin 2000), first published in 1923, as well as the influence of Martin Heidegger and Hans-Georg Gadamer (Steiner 1975: 238).

However, as Steiner aptly argues, in spite of this long, rich history, 'the number of original, significant ideas on the subject remains very meagre' (ibid.: 239), a fact that contributes to his conclusion, later on, that 'all theories of translation – formal, pragmatic, chronological – are only variants of a single, inescapable question. In what ways can or ought fidelity to be achieved?' (ibid.: 261). Hence, even though the issue has been debated for more than two millennia, not much has been added, for example, to Saint Jerome's recommendation that, while a 'word for word' translation is adequate for the Scriptures, 'sense for sense' is the approach to be adopted for all the other genres (ibid.: 262). For Steiner, the indisputable fact that the spectrum of theoretical insights on such issues remains so limited, in spite of 'the wealth of pragmatic notation', can be attributed to the minor role played by translation in the history and theory of literature, in which it has 'figured marginally, if at all', with the exception of studies on 'the transmission and interpretation of the Biblical canon' (ibid.: 269). Although Steiner's point is well taken, we should also entertain the possibility of a highly plausible association between the chronic paucity of ideas on the matter and the general theoretical or ideological basis that has nurtured the great majority of narratives about translation surveyed in his book, at least up until what he considers to be the fourth period in the history of translation scholarship. To the extent that these narratives take for granted the possibility of a clear-cut dichotomy between 'letter' and 'spirit' or 'word' and sense', they share a conception of meaning and, consequently, also of text as a stable, potentially frozen entity that could remain mostly the same, preserved throughout time, and be transportable between different languages, a conception that is still behind the familiar views and clichés upheld both by translators and scholars alike. Therefore, it could be argued that it is precisely because the scholarship on translation developed in the West for more than twenty centuries has practically relied on the same conceptions of language and text that there has never been much left to add to what Cicero or Jerome had written about the subject, a conclusion that could also account, at least in part, for its marginality in the overall history of Western culture and philosophy. After all, if the translator's goal is generally viewed as the effort, often unsatisfactory, of impersonally repeating an unchangeable text in a different language and context, and if the result of such an effort is rarely viewed as having any major impact on the target language and culture, apart from representing (or misrepresenting) an idealized, untouchable original, translation can understandably be regarded as a minor, marginal activity.

This widespread, essentialist conception of translation 'is perfectly compatible with one of the foundational assumptions of Western metaphysics and the Judeo-Christian tradition, i.e., the belief that form and content (or language and thought, signifier and signified, word and meaning in similar oppositions) are not only separable but even independent from one another' (Arrojo 2010: 247). A classic illustration of the rationale that supports this kind of reasoning can be found in Plato's *Cratylus*, for example, in which Socrates argues that since 'things do not equally belong to all at the same moment and always', and are, thus, independent of us, they must 'have their own proper and permanent essence' (Plato 1961: 424–5, quoted in Arrojo 2010: 248). The belief in the possibility of these oppositions, as well as the possibility of clearly separating subject from object, is first and foremost what inaugurates the possibility of translatability, which is also the very possibility of philosophy. As Jacques Derrida has summarized this argument, 'the philosophical operation' defines itself 'as a project of translation': that is, 'as the fixation of a certain concept and project of translation' (Derrida 1985: 120). As he explains, 'what matters' for the philosopher, 'when he is being a philosopher', is 'truth or meaning, and since meaning is before or beyond language, it follows that it is translatable. Meaning has the commanding role, and consequently one must be able to fix its univocality or, in any case, to master its plurivocality' (ibid.). As a consequence, 'if this plurivocality can be mastered, then translation, understood as the transport of a semantic content into another signifying form, is possible' (ibid.). Following this line of thought, it can be argued that

> there is no philosophy unless translation in this latter sense is possible. Therefore, the thesis of philosophy is translatability in this common sense, that is, as the transfer of a meaning or a truth from one language to another without any essential harm being done.
> (ibid.)

In other words, 'the origin of philosophy is translation or the thesis of translatability, so that wherever translation in this sense has failed, it is nothing less than philosophy that finds itself defeated' (ibid.).

In the essentialist tradition, which treats language as a mere instrument for the carrying or the representation of meaning, translation is routinely considered as a basically mechanical activity that should (and could) be accomplished without the translator's unwelcome intervention in the 'content' of texts and words. Eugene Nida, for example, describes words as 'vehicles for carrying the components of meaning' that 'may be likened to suitcases used for carrying various articles of clothing' (Nida 1969: 492). As he resorts to this metaphor to describe the process of sense-for-sense translation, Nida points out that 'it really does not make much difference which articles are packed in which suitcase. What counts is that the clothes arrive at the destination in the best possible condition, i.e., with the least damage' (ibid.). As a consequence, the translator's role in the process of transferring meaning across languages is merely to make sure that the transportation of 'clothes' is adequately handled so that they do not get lost on the way nor are found to be irrevocably damaged as they reach their destination. Another recurrent major metaphor traditionally used to represent the split between word and meaning, signifier and signified, also resorts to clothes but this time as a representation of words as mere 'outward ornaments', intended to remind translators that while they must change the original's 'dress', they should not 'alter or destroy [their] substance', as John Dryden has prescribed in the preface to his translations of Ovid's *Epistles*, concluded in 1680 (Dryden 2002: 173). As Dryden explains,

> for thought, if it be translated truly, cannot be lost in another language; but the words that convey it to our apprehension (which are the image and ornament of that thought) may be so ill chosen as to make it appear in an unhandsome dress, and rob it of its native lustre.
> (ibid.; see also Van Wyke 2010: 23)

In his examination of the recurrent metaphor of bodies and clothes in connection with the basically essentialist notions of translation cultivated in the Western tradition, Ben Van Wyke calls attention to the implications for the translator's task of the conceptions of language and imitation exposed in Plato's Dialogues and, more specifically, in the example of beds and tables presented in Book X of *The Republic* (Plato 1991). In Plato's universe, the possibility of an absolute origin, or original, as an 'idea' or 'essence' whose 'natural author' is God, is not only taken for granted but constitutes the very foundation of his philosophical project (ibid.: 364). As the Platonic rationale goes, when a carpenter makes a particular bed, he is twice removed from the original, true bed because all he can do is imitate it and, therefore, produce only 'a semblance of existence' (ibid.: 363). At the same time, however, when a painter happens to paint the same bed constructed by the carpenter, he is nothing but 'the imitator of that which the others make' and, therefore, finds himself only 'in third in the descent from nature' (ibid.: 364). As Van Wyke argues, the traditional view of translation, which relies on the possibility of separating content from form, subject from object, 'follows a pattern that is similar to Socrates's notion of imitation' and Plato's theory of removes:

> [t]he original "essence" of a text is believed to stem from the author's thoughts, which are comparable to the first remove. These thoughts give rise to the original text (second remove), which is the basis for the translation (third remove imitation). [... Consequently, any] translation is but an image of the original because it is created without a direct link to truth.
> (Van Wyke 2010: 32–3)

As imitation is not only seen as an inferior form of representation but, also, because of its supposedly deceiving character, as potentially dangerous, '[m]any of the clichés related to translators and translation resonate with the comments Socrates makes about imitators' in the Dialogue mentioned above (ibid.: 33). On such grounds, the theoretical rationale that anchors this essentialist conception of translation, which is 'largely responsible for the age-old prejudices that have often considered translation a secondary, derivative form of writing', refuses to acknowledge 'the productive character of the translator's activity', and, hence, also 'the political role of translation and its impact on the construction of identities and cultural relations' (Arrojo 2010: 248).

The impact of Nietzsche's non-essentialist thought on translation

Nietzsche's aphorisms

After concluding, as commented above, that 'the range of theoretical ideas' on translation 'remains very small', Steiner predictably claims that the list of those who 'have said anything fundamental or new' about it is quite short: 'Saint Jerome, Luther, Dryden, Hölderlin, Novalis, Schleiermacher, Nietzsche, Ezra Pound, Valery, MacKenna, Franz Rosenzweig, Walter Benjamin, [and] Quine' (Steiner 1975: 269). Even though Steiner does not exactly elaborate on why Nietzsche has made the list, it seems that it was the philosopher's brief commentary on translation as a form of conquest – 'one conquered when one translated' – that qualified him to join those who have had anything notably significant to say in more than twenty centuries of discussion on the matter (Steiner 1975: 247). Steiner is alluding to an aphorism from *The Gay Science*, published in 1882, in which Nietzsche reflects on how Roman antiquity 'violently and yet naively [. . .] laid its hand on everything good and lofty in the older Greek antiquity' and unapologetically assimilated it 'into the Roman present' (Nietzsche 2001, 83: 82). Since the Romans 'did not know the pleasure of a sense for history, what was past and alien was embarrassing to them; and as Romans, they saw it as an incentive for a Roman conquest' (ibid.: 83). Indeed, translation was, for poets such as Horace and Propertius, an efficient strategy for their outright appropriation of the foreign:

> one conquered by translating – not merely by leaving out the historical, but also by adding allusions to the present and, above all, crossing out the name of the poet and replacing it with one's own – not with any sense of theft but with the very best conscience of the *imperium Romanum*.
>
> (ibid.)

Douglas Robinson ends his ambitious anthology *Western Translation Theory – from Herodotus to Nietzsche* (Robinson 2002) with the inclusion of the aphorism just mentioned together with another one from *Beyond Good and Evil*, published in 1887 (Nietzsche 2002). Even though Robinson recognizes that Nietzsche was 'one of the great modern philosophers', whose critique of 'civilized asceticism' laid 'the groundwork for psychoanalysis, deconstruction, and post-structuralist Marxism' (Robinson 2002: 261), he voices an opinion that clearly differs from Steiner's comment mentioned above. For Robinson, Nietzsche's 'passing remarks on translation from *The Gay Science* and *Beyond Good and Evil* are not particularly original' and only 'hold interest as late-nineteenth-century examples of romanticism' (ibid.: 262). Considering Steiner's and Robinson's conflicting takes on the 'originality' of Nietzsche's aphorisms, I will side with Steiner's, particularly after rereading them in conjunction with some pronouncements on translation made famous by the German Romantics, who were also quite aware of the translation practices adopted by the ancient Romans, while establishing, in their own context, an intimate association between translation, conquest, and nationalism.

In a letter written to A. W. Schlegel in 1797, Novalis, for instance, explicitly compared the Germans' interest in translation to the ancient Romans': '[w]e are the only nation (barring the Romans) who feel so irresistibly driven to translate and who have learned so immensely from it. Hence the many similarities between late-Roman literary culture and our own' (Novalis 2002: 212–13). As he expands, 'this drive is a sign of the German people's primordial nobility – a sign of that blend of the cosmopolitan and the forcefully individual that is true Germanness. Only for us have translations been expansions' (ibid.). Another relevant example can be found in Schlegel's proud acknowledgement of the Germans' interest in the foreign and their general approach to translation, also described as a form of (non-violent) conquest in his *History of Classical Literature*, which came out in 1802: 'today we make peaceful raids into foreign countries, especially the south of Europe, and return laden with our poetic spoils' (Schlegel 2002: 220). If we consider the comparison Schlegel establishes between the Germans' 'raids into foreign countries' and the ancient Romans' translation practices, it is remarkable that he sees violence in the Romans' initiatives but not in his fellow Germans':

> in antiquity the Romans – at least at first, while they were still, not without violence, modelling their language on Greek forms – seem to have made, as far as we can tell from a few fragments, reasonably faithful if also rather awkward and uneven translations of Greek poetry. In fact, translating started them off.
>
> (ibid.)

In 'On the Different Methods of Translating', Schleiermacher praises the role of translation in the construction of their national culture, a role that he compares to the enrichment of their soil and the improvement of their climate 'through the repeated introduction of foreign plants' (Schleiermacher 2002: 238). Allegedly, it is their 'vocation' to translate and to be open to the foreign that should ultimately 'destine the German people to incorporate linguistically, and to preserve in the geographical center and heart of Europe, all the treasures of both foreign and our own art and scholarship in a prodigious historical totality', and, as a result, their language would be the guardian of 'all the beauty that the ages have wrought' (ibid.). Even though Schleiermacher, Novalis, and Schlegel – as well as others associated with German Romanticism – clearly prescribe what they view as a foreignizing approach to translation while Nietzsche calls attention to the violence of the Romans' overtly domesticating translation practices, it is undeniable that both sides establish an obvious connection between translation and conquest. However, what distances Nietzsche from the German Romantics and, therefore, what makes his contribution germane and original, particularly in the context of Western nineteenth-century reflections on the topic, is that while the German Romantics unabashedly viewed the practice of translation as a form of appropriation of the foreign that should ultimately benefit the translator/conqueror's nation-building enterprise, the philosopher, in the aphorism mentioned, makes his non-prescriptive comments on the blatantly imperialistic strategies adopted by the Romans from a critical, almost proto-theoretical, perspective. Even though Nietzsche may seem to admire the Romans' boldness in appropriating Greek culture, as some have claimed (Schrift 1990: 178–9), he does note their disregard for the foreign or any sense of history in their translation practice. If we focus on this part of his commentary, it would not be far-fetched to argue that Nietzsche seems to anticipate the kind of scholarship on translation and processes of colonization that began to emerge at the end of the twentieth century under the sway of poststructuralist, postmodernist thought (see, for example, Rafael 1992), a thought that was largely nurtured in the philosopher's anti-essentialist conception of language and what it implies for a reflection on the relationship between translation and power, as will be discussed below.

In his aphorism on translation included in *Beyond Good and Evil*, Nietzsche focuses on the issue of 'tempo' as a reflection of the incommensurability of languages and cultures, an incommensurability that goes beyond mere semantics and syntax and raises doubts about the possibility of mere translatability, or any natural equivalence between languages. As he argues, 'the hardest thing to translate from one language into another is the tempo of its style, which is grounded in the character of the race, or – to be more physiological – in the average tempo of its "metabolism"'(Nietzsche 2002: 29). Since the Germans 'are almost incapable of a *presto* in their language' and, thus, also 'incapable of many of the most delightful and daring nuances of free, free-spirited thought', Aristophanes and Petronius, for example, are 'as good as untranslatable' (ibid.). Following this line of argument, how could 'the German language [...] imitate Machiavelli's tempo – Machiavelli who, in his *Principe*, lets us breathe the fine, dry air of Florence?' (ibid.). While the Italian 'cannot help presenting the most serious concerns in a boisterous *allegrissimo*', he is, 'perhaps, not without a malicious, artistic sense for the contrast he is risking: thoughts that are long, hard, tough, and dangerous, and a galloping tempo and the very best and most mischievous mood' (ibid.: 29–30). On that account, how could the Germans, who developed, in 'over-abundant diversity', everything 'ponderous, lumbering, solemnly awkward, every long-winded and boring type of style' (ibid.: 30), adequately translate the fundamentally different rhythms of Italian, Latin, or Greek into their language?

Even though Nietzsche's statements may be found to echo some of the German Romantics' general ideas, they also represent a significant departure from their core arguments and beliefs, and, in this sense, they could indeed 'point ahead to the hermeneutical translation theories of twentieth-century thinkers like Benjamin and Buber, Heidegger and Gadamer, Steiner and Derrida', as Robinson suggests in his brief statement about the philosopher's impact on the thought about translation developed in the West (Robinson 2002: 262). The notion of the incommensurability of languages, for example, is addressed by Humboldt in the introduction to his 1816 translation of *Agamemnon*, one of Aeschylus's best known tragedies: 'it has often been remarked, and both linguistic research and everyday experience bear this out, that with the exception of expressions denoting material objects, no word in one language is ever entirely like its counterpart in another' (Humboldt 2002: 239). Therefore, as he compares languages, Humboldt is motivated to encounter difference, rather than sameness or equivalence: 'each [language] puts a slightly different spin on a concept, charges it with this or that connotation, sets it one rung higher or lower on the ladder of affective response' (ibid.). Besides, 'difference' is certainly to be found even when translators do make an effort to express sameness:

> if one closely compares the best, most painstakingly faithful translations, one is astonished at the divergences that appear where the translator sought only sameness and similitude. One could even argue that the more a translation labours to be faithful, the more divergent it becomes.
>
> (ibid.)

Unlike Humboldt, however, and, more specifically, unlike Nietzsche, the German Romantics tended to believe in the possibility of fidelity to the foreign, even in the translation of poetry.

According to Schlegel, for instance, since fidelity 'entails making the same or a similar impression, [...] prose versions of poems are [...] reprehensible' (Schlegel 2002: 219). As a consequence, for him, one of the 'first principles of the art of translation must be to render a poem, so far as the target language allows, into the same metre as in the original', a principle that helps him advance the argument that 'the German language has the great merit of being till now the only one in which new metres introduced from classical languages have succeeded so far as to enter general circulation' (ibid.). Moreover, as he elaborates, the alleged 'superiority' of the German language properly reflects the 'willingness of the German national character to project itself into foreign mentalities, indeed to surrender utter to them', a trait that is 'so integral to our language as to make it the deftest translator for everyone else' (Schlegel 2002: 220) and which will turn German into 'the speaking voice of the civilized world' (ibid.: 221). Unlike Nietzsche, Schlegel explicitly prescribes a conception of translation whose interest in the foreign is clearly motivated by the effort to enrich his own language. As Schleiermacher has suggested, the true motivation behind the German Romantics' general interest in the foreign seems to be nothing less than the very end of translation:

> if ever the time should come when our public sphere gives birth on the one hand to a more profound and linguistically accurate conviviality, and on the other to increased space for the speaker's talents, then we may have less need for the translator in the advancement of our language.
>
> (Schleiermacher 2002: 238)

An outline of Nietzsche's notions of language and the subject and their import for questions of interpretation

The intimate association between philosophy and the possibility of translatability, highlighted by Derrida and briefly discussed above as the basis of essentialist thinking, has suffered a major blow with the critique of Western metaphysics undertaken by 'Nietzsche the philologist', who, according to Michel Foucault, was the first to connect 'the philosophical task with a radical reflection on language' (Foucault 1973: 305, quoted in Arrojo 2010: 248). This is a critique that 'has been pivotal in the development of anti-foundationalist trends in contemporary philosophy such as postmodern, poststructuralist thinking, deconstruction, and neopragmatism, opening up new paths of inquiry as the ones represented by gender and postcolonial studies' (Arrojo 2010: 248). In 'Nietzsche, Freud and Marx', first presented as a lecture in 1964 (Foucault 1998), Foucault identifies a common denominator in the work of the three thinkers that suggests a major change in the ways in which language is conceptualized, involving 'a transformation from an emphasis on the representative function of the sign', according to which it would merely represent a signified, or a 'thing', or its essence, towards 'a view of the sign as already a part of the activity of interpretation. This is to say, signs are no longer viewed as the reservoir of some deep, hidden meaning' that could be fully recovered or decoded, but, rather, as 'surface phenomena, linked in an inexhaustible network which condemns interpretation to an infinite task' (Schrift 1990: 78). As Nietzsche himself remarks, 'the essence of a thing' is only a few words said about it: that is, nothing more than an 'opinion about the "thing". Or rather: "it is considered" is the real "it is", the sole "this is"'(Nietzsche 1968, 556: 302).

Marx, Nietzsche, and Freud 'have put us back into the presence of a new possibility of interpretation; they have founded once again the possibility of a hermeneutic'

(Foucault 1998: 271–2) but a hermeneutic that implies a notion of interpretation 'as an infinite task' that can never be complete or exhausted (ibid.: 274). In the specific case of Nietzsche, Foucault ponders: 'What is philosophy for him if not a kind of philology continually in suspension, a philology without end, always farther unrolled, a philology that would never be absolutely fixed?' (ibid.: 275). As Foucault explains, Nietzsche teaches us that 'interpretation can never be completed' simply because 'each sign is in itself not the thing that offers itself to interpretation but an interpretation of other signs', and, as a consequence, 'everything is already interpretation' (ibid.: 275). Finally, since every signified is necessarily constructed with words, 'there is no original signified' that could be above or before language (ibid.: 276). These arguments were first developed in 'On Truth and Lies in a Nonmoral Sense', an unfinished essay from the early 1870s (Nietzsche 1999), in which Nietzsche outlines the foundation of a conception of language that 'is first and foremost anti-Platonic' (Arrojo 2010: 249). As he reasons, since languages are 'undoubtedly human creations', there is no absolute truth or immutable meaning or concept 'that could be clearly separated from its linguistic fabric and, therefore, be fully transportable elsewhere' (ibid.).

What language can offer us, rather than the representation of an extralinguistic core meaning, is nothing but 'relations of things to men' and, thus, 'metaphors' that are constituted in a process that Nietzsche describes in the following terms: in the very beginning,

> a nerve stimulus is transferred into an image: first metaphor. The image, in turn, is imitated in a sound: second metaphor. And each time there is a complete overleaping of one sphere, right into the middle of an entirely new and different one.
>
> (Nietzsche 1999: 82)

What makes language work is not its alleged capacity to convey ahistorical truths or meanings, but the fact that it is an arbitrary, conventional system, with which we create concepts – or 'fictions' – about everything that composes our human universe, including ourselves. Nietzsche illustrates this argument with a reflection on the concept of the 'leaf', which can be productively examined against the backdrop of Plato's example of the 'bed' commented on above. As Nietzsche ponders, just 'as it is certain that one leaf is never totally the same as another, so it is certain that the concept "leaf" is formed by arbitrarily discarding these individual differences and by forgetting the distinguishing aspects' (Nietzsche 1999: 83). Against Plato's belief in the possibility of ideal forms, Nietzsche's argument points to the conclusion that there is no such a thing as an original leaf, on the basis of which 'all the leaves were perhaps woven, sketched, measured, colored, curled, and painted – but by incompetent hands, so that no specimen has turned out to be a correct, trustworthy, and faithful likeness of the original model' (ibid.). However,

> even though we shall never find in nature, let's say, the ideal [or original] 'leaf' [. . .] we still manage to use it as a concept. In short, language works precisely because the conventions that make it possible teach us to forget certain differences so that we can sustain the illusion that the same could actually be repeated.
>
> (Arrojo 2010: 249; see also Van Wyke 2010: 35–6)

While it is 'originally *language* which works on the construction of concepts', the drive that leads humans towards such constructions is the 'fundamental human drive' (Nietzsche 1999: 88), later identified by the philosopher as the 'will to power'. On that account, the will to power, which is always channeled through some form of language, is not only that which creates all we know, but, also, that which interprets it: the 'will to power interprets [...] it defines limits, determines degrees, variations of power [...] In fact, interpretation is itself a means of becoming master of something' (Nietzsche 1968, 643: 342), a mastery, however, that can only be provisional and always circumscribed to a certain time and context. Since the object of all interpretation is always already a human creation, 'interpretation will henceforth always be interpretation by "whom"? One does not interpret what is in the signified, but one interprets after all: *who* posed the interpretation. The basis of interpretation is nothing but the interpreter' (Foucault 1998: 277–8). Consequently, for Nietzsche, interpretation 'exists [...] as an affect', 'not as a "being" but as a process, a becoming' (Nietzsche 1968, 556: 302). Furthermore, because the 'origin of "things" is wholly the work of that which imagines, thinks, wills, feels', even the subject, whether in a position of creator or interpreter, is also 'a created entity, a "thing" like all others: a simplification with the object of defining the force which posits, invents, thinks, as distinct from all individual positing, inventing, thinking as such' (ibid.).

As the philosopher who established inextricable associations between language, truth, and power, Nietzsche was not only the first to connect 'the philosophical task with a radical reflection on language', as commented above, but also the one

> who specified the power relation as the general focus [...] of philosophical discourse [...] Nietzsche is the philosopher of power, a philosopher who managed to think of power without having to confine himself within a political theory in order to do so.
> (Foucault 1980: 53)

Nietzsche is the one who transformed 'the question of truth' from, as it had been for millennia, 'What is the surest path to Truth?' into 'What is the hazardous career that Truth has followed?', a formulation that he has explored from the perspective of his 'genealogy of morals' (ibid.: 66). 'Truth' has then been redefined as 'a system of ordered procedures for the production, regulation, distribution, circulation, and operations of statements' and linked 'in a circular relation with systems of power which produce and sustain it, and to effects of power which it induces and which extend it' (ibid.: 133).

Key concepts associated with post-Nietzschean approaches to translation

As the arguments sketched above suggest, Nietzsche's thought radically undermines the theoretical ground that tends to support traditional conceptions of text and authorship as well as the relationships they are supposed to establish with translations and those in charge of producing them. These are the same conceptions that also shape the usual professional codes of ethics, for which the 'sanctity' of originals and the translator's invisibility are not simply indisputable possibilities but their most revered, non-negotiable principles. In the wake of Nietzsche's 'reversal of the Platonic conception of truth and representation', Van Wyke proposes to refashion the traditional body/clothes metaphor discussed above with a reference to a fragment from *The Gay Science*, which also alludes to bodies and clothes to explain the relationship between things and the meanings they acquire, but from a non-essentialist perspective. As Nietzsche's aphorism goes,

> the reputation, name, and appearance, the worth, the usual measure and weight of a thing, what it counts for – [...] thrown over things like a dress and quite foreign to their nature and even to their skin – has, through the belief in it and its growth from generation to

generation, slowly grown onto and into the thing and has become its very body: what started as appearance in the end nearly always becomes essence and *effectively acts* as its essence!

(Nietzsche 2001: 58, 69–70)

For Van Wyke, Nietzsche's conclusion that we 'cannot discover what things "are"'and can 'only inquire into what they are called, and by whom' is pertinent to translation because in its relationship with the original, 'not only will a translation act as another veil [or dress thrown over what we call the original], but it will be based, in part, on the many other veils [or dresses] that participate in naming the original' (Van Wyke 2010: 38). As an appropriate illustration, consider any text that we read and revere in translation and which becomes, for us, at least in practical terms, *the* actual original. When we take note that Plato's *Republic*, for example, was written around 380 BC, and that there have been innumerable versions not only in English, but in all the major known languages, all published both before and after the Jowett translation used in this chapter, it becomes evident that what we call Plato's text is ultimately a collection of countless, irrecoverable 'veils' that have shaped and transformed his original throughout more than two millennia, an original that can no longer be clearly distinguishable from all those translations and the many ways in which they have been read and disseminated.

A fundamental implication of these arguments points to the conclusion that no translation will ever manage to recover the alleged original as it can only reinterpret a certain given interpretation of it. In the wake of Nietzsche's philosophy, translation can no longer be conceived in terms of a transportation of stable meaning across languages and cultures. Rather, as Derrida has put it, for this notion of translation, 'we would have to substitute a notion of transformation: a regulated transformation of one language by another, of one text by another' (Derrida 1978: 20). In light of Foucault's interpretation of Nietzsche's views on language and power, we can add that what regulates the process of transformation taking place in every act of translation is never the translator's supposedly impersonal faithfulness to the original but the 'systems of power' that make it possible for any text to be translated and disseminated in a certain way, at a certain time, and within certain contexts and boundaries. Following this line of thought, we will also have to re-evaluate mainstream notions of authorship and the role usually played by the original's author in the scene of translation. Consider, for example, Foucault's well-known observations on the function of authors, according to which they can no longer be viewed as controlling masters or indisputable sources of their writing but, rather, as regulating factors, especially in association with texts that must be signed like those we call 'literary'. In post-Nietzschean terms, the author becomes 'a certain functional principle by which, in our culture, one limits, excludes, and chooses; in short, by which one impedes the free circulation, the free manipulation, the free composition, decomposition, and recomposition of fiction' (Foucault 1979: 159). Since the author's function is redefined as 'the principle of thrift' that helps interpreters tame the potentially infinite process of signification that can be triggered by any fragment of language (ibid.), the translator's agency must be obviously acknowledged as a decisive factor in the composition of the translated text. This conclusion also implies, however, that the visible translator, like the author, cannot be a fully present subject who can establish once and for all what readers may see in his or her text (for a discussion of 'the translator function', see Arrojo 1997).

Revealing elaborations of such conceptions and some of their practical consequences can be found in the work of Jorge Luis Borges, an early reader of Nietzsche, whose deep interest in matters of language and translation was documented in two often quoted insightful essays published in the 1930s – 'The Homeric Versions' (Borges 1999) and 'The Translators of *The Thousand and One Nights*' (Borges 1999a). Although some of his short stories have also been read as remarkable post-Nietzschean meditations on translation, I will briefly focus on the essays due to my limited space here (for a discussion of Borges's stories dealing with questions of translation and their connections with Nietzsche's thought, see Arrojo 2018, particularly chapters 4 and 5). It should also be made clear that even though one cannot objectively claim that Borges was directly influenced by Nietzsche, his comments on translation are clearly compatible with the philosopher's arguments outlined above and could be read as a fair representation of what a post-Nietzschean perspective on the translator's task might entail. I will begin with Borges's redefinition of the original as 'a mutable fact' and the consequent blurring of the usual hierarchical opposition meant to distinguish a text from its translations, an opposition that, as he argues in 'The Homeric Versions', is based on nothing but a 'superstition': '[t]o assume that every recombination of elements is necessarily inferior to its original form is to assume that draft nine is necessarily inferior to draft H – for there can only be drafts' (Borges 1999: 69). If interpretations, like the writing of texts, are never complete, or 'definitive', what different translations are able to offer readers is not in any sense the recovered original but, rather, 'a partial and precious documentation of the changes the text suffers' (ibid.). As they represent 'different perspectives' on the ever changing original, translations give us glimpses into the interpretations and the aesthetic values that may have motivated their translators' choices as well as the historical and cultural circumstances that made it possible for them to emerge and circulate (ibid.).

Borges's brief comments on different versions of the *Iliad* and *The Thousand and One Nights* suggest that the more visible the translators and their contexts are to him, as a reader, the more significant and 'precious' he will find their translations. For example, while William Cowper's 1791 *Iliad* is the 'most innocuous' for its literality, Alexander Pope's, whose six volumes were published between 1715 and 1720, is 'extraordinary' for its 'luxuriant language', which, among other things, 'multiplied' the hero's 'single black ship [...] into a fleet' (Borges 1999: 74). For Borges, since translations are not expected to be impersonal, ahistorical repetitions of an unchanging original at different times and in different languages and contexts, they should be evaluated for the kind of difference they actually make both for the original and for the cultural environment of the receiving language. In another example, Borges claims that Enno Littmann's 1920 German version of the *Nights* is 'mediocre', even though it was hailed by the *Encyclopedia Britannica* as 'the best one in circulation', because it offers readers 'nothing but the probity of Germany', which 'is so little, so very little' (Borges 1999a: 108). Along the same lines, what Borges admires in Dr Mardrus's French translation, published between 1898 and 1904, is the translator's 'happy and creative infidelity' (ibid.: 106). In fact, it is precisely Mardrus's infidelity, which brings to the *Nights* 'Art Nouveau passages, fine obscenities, brief comical interludes, circumstantial details, symmetries, [and] vast quantities of visual Orientalism', 'that must matter to us', since to celebrate his fidelity 'is to leave out the soul of Mardrus, to ignore Mardrus entirely' (ibid.).

Borges's appreciation of translations as historical documents seems to anticipate by more than six decades what Lawrence Venuti describes as the 'genealogical method' he adopted in *The Translator's Invisibility – A History of Translation*, one of the most important books to be published in the area in the 1990s (Venuti 2008: 32). As Venuti argues, such a method, 'developed by Nietzsche and Foucault', 'abandons the two principles that govern much conventional historiography: teleology and objectivity' (ibid.). Consequently, it allows us to witness that 'what is found at the historical beginning of things is not the inviolable identity of their origin; it is the dissension of other things. It is disparity' (Foucault 1977: 142, quoted in Venuti 2008: 32). This mode of analysis is fundamental for the achievement of his book's ultimate goal: that is, the elaboration of 'the theoretical, critical, and textual means by which translation can be studied and practiced as a locus of difference, instead of the homogeneity that widely characterizes it today' (Venuti 2008: 34). The main consequence of such a paradigm shift is that instead of ignoring or rejecting the translator's agency and all that it implies, we now focus on actively understanding its manifestations and consequences. As Borges has shown, perhaps better than anybody else, what motivates translators in the composition of their translations is not very different from what drives authors in the production of their originals. Indeed, his general characterization of the translators of *The Thousand and One Nights* as 'a hostile dynasty', according to which each translator 'secretly' translated *against* his main precursor (Borges 1999a: 92), could very well be viewed as an enlightening representation of translation as a manifestation of the will to power.

Final remarks

As this chapter has attempted to show, Nietzsche's redefinition of language as an instrument that inevitably produces meaning and is intimately associated with issues of power has turned upside down the usual relationships defining the translator's activity and seriously destabilized all the simplistic notions of fidelity and neutrality that have underestimated the practice of translation and its impact for more than twenty centuries. As claimed above, an acquaintance with Nietzsche's views on language will help translation scholars deepen their understanding of the important trends in contemporary theory that acknowledge and investigate the translator's visibility and its far-reaching implications as well as the asymmetrical relations of power that have defined intercultural relations. At the same time, this discussion is particularly relevant both for practising translators and for readers of translations. In the light of Nietzsche's insights, while readers are made aware of the fact that the translations they read can only be a product of their translators' interpretations, translators can no longer claim or aspire to be invisible in their work and, thus, will have to take responsibility for their interpretations of the so-called 'original' as well as their translation choices and strategies. As they can no longer imagine that it would be feasible to ignore differences and merely transport meaning across languages, and, therefore, as they necessarily transform originals – a 'transformation' that is regulated by their context and ideology – translators are urged to come to terms with their own agency (or their 'will to power') and, literally or metaphorically, to always sign their work and, thus, fully accept their role as legitimate authors of their translations.

Related topics

Schleiermacher; Heidegger; Wittgenstein; Derrida; current trends in philosophy and translation; translation theory and philosophy; culture; ethics.

Further reading

Those who are not familiar with Nietzsche's work should probably start with the philosopher's own aphorisms on translation (Nietzsche 2001, 2002), which have been discussed above. One of them can also be found in Venuti's *The Translation Studies Reader* (Venuti 2012: 67–8). Nietzsche's early essay 'On Truth and Lies in a Nonmoral Sense' (1999), also discussed above, is fundamental for an understanding of his conception of language.

As for studies devoted to the implications of Nietzsche's philosophy for translation, most of the material available in English has been mentioned above: Arrojo (2010, 2018), Borges (1999, 1999a), Van Wyke (2010), and Venuti (2008).

References

Arrojo, R. (1997) 'The "Death" of the Author and the Limits of the Translator's Visibility', in M. Snell-Hornby, Z. Jettmarova, and K. Kaindl (eds.) *Translation as Intercultural Communication*, Amsterdam and Philadelphia: John Benjamins, 21–32.

Arrojo, R. (2010) 'Philosophy and Translation', in Y. Gambier and L. V. Doorslaer (eds.) *Handbook of Translation Studies*, vol. 1, Amsterdam and Philadelphia: John Benjamins, 247–51.

Arrojo, R. (2018). *Fictional Translators – Rethinking Translation through Literature*, London and New York: Routledge.

Benjamin, W. (2000) 'The Task of the Translator', in H. Zohn (trans.), L. Venuti (ed.), *The Translation Studies Reader*, London and New York: Routledge, 15–23.

Borges, J. L. (1999) 'The Homeric Versions', in E. Weinberger (trans. and ed.), *Selected Non-Fictions*, New York: Penguin, 69–74.

Borges, J. L. (1999a) 'The Translators of *The Thousand and One Nights*', in E. Allen (trans.) and E. Weinberger (ed.), *Selected Non-Fictions*, New York: Penguin, 92–109.

Cicero, M. T. (2002) 'The Best Kind of Orators', H. M. Hubbell (trans.), in Robinson, 7–10.

Derrida, J. (1978) *Positions*, A. Bass (trans.), Chicago: University of Chicago Press.

Derrida, J. (1985) 'Roundtable on Translation', in P. Kamuf (trans.) and C. McDonald (ed.), *The Ear of The Other – Otobiography, Transference, Translation*, Lincoln and London: University of Nebraska Press, 93–161.

Dryden, J. (2002) 'The Three Types of Translation', in Robinson, 171–5.

Foucault, M. (1973) *The Order of Things – An Archaeology of the Human Sciences*. New York: Vintage Books.

Foucault, M. (1977) 'Nietzsche, Genealogy, History', in D. F. Bouchard (ed. and trans.) and S. Simon (trans.), *Language, Counter-Memory, Practice: Selected Essays and Interviews*, Ithaca: Cornell University Press, 139–64.

Foucault, M. (1979) 'What Is an Author?' in J. Harari (trans. and ed.), *Textual Strategies – Perspectives in Post-Structuralist Criticism*, Ithaca: Cornell University Press, 141–60.

Foucault, M. (1980) *Power/Knowledge. Selected Interviews and Other Writings, 1972–1977*, C. Gordon (ed. and trans.), New York: The Harvester Press.

Foucault, M. (1998) 'Nietzsche, Freud and Marx', J. Anderson and G. Hentzi (trans.), in J. D. Faubion (ed.), *Aesthetics, Method, and Epistemology*, New York: The New Press, 269–78.

Hölderlin, F. (1988) '"Remarks on Oedipus" and "Remarks on Antigone"', in T. Pfau (trans. and ed.), *Essays and Letters on Theory*, Albany: State University of New York Press, 101–18.

Horace, (2002) 'Imitating in Your Own Words', E. C. Wickham (trans.), in Robinson, 15.

Humboldt, W. von (2002) 'The More Faithful, The More Divergent', P. Carroll (trans.), in Robinson, 239–40.

Jerome, (2002) 'Letter to Pammachius', P. Carroll (trans.), in Robinson, 23–30.

Larbaud, V. (1984) *An Homage to Saint Jerome*, J.-P. De Chezet (trans.), Marlboro: Marlboro Press.

Luther, M. (2002) 'Circular Letter on Translation', D. Robinson (trans.), in Robinson, 84–9.

Nida, E. A. (1969) 'Science of Translation', *Language*, vol. 45, no. 3, 483–98.

Nietzsche, F. (1968) *The Will to Power*, W. Kaufmann (trans.), New York: Vintage Books.

Nietzsche, F. (1999) 'On Truth and Lies in a Nonmoral Sense', in D. Breazeale (ed. and trans.), *Philosophy and Truth – Selections from Nietzsche's Notebooks of the Early 1870s*, New York and Amherst: Humanity Books, 79–97.

Nietzsche, F. (2001) *The Gay Science*, J. Nauckhoff. (trans.) and B. Williams (ed.), Cambridge: Cambridge University Press.

Nietzsche, F. (2002) *Beyond Good and Evil*, J. Norman (trans.), R. P. Horstmann and J. Norman (eds.), Cambridge: Cambridge University Press.

Novalis, (2002) 'Translating Out of Poetic Morality', D. Robinson (trans.), in Robinson, 212–13.

Plato (1961) 'Cratylus', in B. Jowett (trans.), E. Hamilton and H. Cairns (eds.), *The Collected Dialogues of Plato*, Princeton: Princeton University Press, 424–5.

Plato (1991) 'Book X', in *The Republic*, B. Jowett (trans.), New York: Vintage, 360–97.
Rafael, V. (1992) *Contracting Colonialism – Translation and Christian Conversion in Tagalog's Society under Early Spanish Rule*, Durham: Duke University Press.
Robinson, D. (ed.) (2002) *Western Translation Theory from Herodotus to Nietzsche*, Manchester and Northampton: St. Jerome.
Schlegel, A. von W. (2002) 'Projecting Oneself into Foreign Mentalities', D. Robinson (trans.), in Robinson, 219–20.
Schleiermacher, F. (2002) 'On the Different Methods of Translating', D. Robinson (trans.), in Robinson, 225–38.
Schrift, A. D. (1990) *Nietzsche and the Question of Interpretation – Between Hermeneutics and Deconstruction*, New York and London: Routledge.
Steiner, G. (1975) *After Babel – Aspects of Language and Translation*, London and New York: Oxford University Press.
Tytler, A. F. (1978) *Essay on the Principles of Translation*. Amsterdam and Philadelphia: John Benjamins.
Van Wyke, B. (2010) 'Imitating Bodies, Clothes: Refashioning the Western Conception of Translation', in J. St. Andre (ed.), *Thinking through Translation with Metaphors*, Manchester and Northampton: St. Jerome, 17–46.
Venuti, L. (2008) *The Translator's Visibility: A History of Translation*, New York and London: Routledge, 2nd edition.
Venuti, L. (ed.) (2012) *The Translation Studies Reader*, New York and London: Routledge, 3rd edition.

3
Heidegger

Tom Greaves

Introduction

The thought of Martin Heidegger (1889–1976) was shaped to a quite unprecedented extent by the work of translation. Not only did he spend a great deal of time and effort translating and retranslating the words of early Greek thinkers, but those translations are interwoven with reflections on their own adequacy, on the (in)adequacy of other translations and on the difficulty and necessity of translation as a dimension of philosophical thought. For readers of Heidegger in English, or any language other than German, the necessity of reflecting on the translation adds further layers of complexity to this already complex hermeneutic situation. One consequence is that it is very difficult, sometimes even positively misleading, to try to separate out Heidegger's own translation practice from his reflections on translation, and those reflections in turn from the translations and reflections of his translators. Any such attempt, as Heidegger always insisted, already works with its own interpretive principles, which need to be opened up to dispute and modification.

Section 1 will set out Heidegger's views on the situation of the philosophical translator by outlining his radical rethinking of hermeneutics as involving the existential enactment of one's own hermeneutic situation. In Section 2 I explore a key instance of Heidegger's translation practice along with his reflections on translation. Section 3 gives a brief history of how thinking about Heidegger and translation has developed and of recent disputes that reflect back on attempts to translate some of his most difficult texts.

3.1 Heidegger's radical hermeneutics

Heidegger's early studies in theology made him familiar with German traditions in philology and hermeneutics. Having worked on both historical and contemporary problems in philosophy in his doctoral work and very first lecture courses, Heidegger delivered a series of lecture courses in the early 1920s, working intensively on the philosophy of Aristotle. He became convinced that what was really important for philosophical thought in these ancient texts had been covered over by centuries of interpretation and translation. A radical hermeneutic approach was thus needed that would *de-structure* the traditional interpretations and free up what was originally significant about the questions that Aristotle posed and the concepts that he developed, so that they could once more be appropriately understood by contemporary thinkers. Part and parcel of this attempt to radically retrieve Aristotle's philosophy for the 'the situation of a living present' (Heidegger 2009: 39) was the retranslation of his key concepts.

Certainly the dictum that every translation is an interpretation holds true for Heidegger. Yet to understand the full import of that dictum for him it is important to see that radical interpretation involves the enactment of the interpreter's own hermeneutical situation that is at one and the same time the retrieval or repetition of the hermeneutical situation of those thinkers that one is interpreting and translating.

Philosophy does not simply involve the production of a set of propositions that can be confirmed or disconfirmed through a process of thought that is neutrally available to anyone. The context in which such propositions appear and within which they need to be interpreted is not a ready-made or fixed conceptual scheme or framework. It is a lived situation that belongs to the thinker and is enacted in and through the thinking itself. In a report on the research that he was conducting into Aristotle's philosophy in 1922, Heidegger puts the point directly and clearly: '*To understand* does not simply mean to cognitively confirm, but rather to *repeat* primordially what is understood in terms of its ownmost situation and for that situation' (Heidegger 2009: 41). The enactment of our own hermeneutical situation, the point of view and way of understanding we adopt, is not anterior to or subsequent to the thinking enactment of the situation of those we are trying to understand, interpret and translate. The enactment of our own hermeneutical situation is at one and the same time the re-enactment of the situation to be understood.

The lectures from the summer semester of 1922, *Phenomenological Interpretations of Selected Treatises of Aristotle on Ontology and Logic*, that were distilled into the report just cited give a remarkable insight into Heidegger's developing translation practice and its centrality to his developing philosophical method. He translates long passages of Aristotle's texts for his students and comments on those translations, not as a preliminary to philosophical exposition and criticism but as itself a repetition of that hermeneutic situation that is to 'free up' the text for understanding. In the introduction to these translations as radical hermeneutic repetitions, Heidegger says the following about the practice of translation:

> The standard and character of a translation is always relative to the goal of interpretation. Here we are concerned not with exercises in style, but with a full appropriation of the interrelations of sense, i.e., of the meaningful matters, to re-enact the insights and interrelations of insights that originally brought forth those matters. The more precisely the translation is aimed at *that*, the stricter it is in each case. A so-called literal translation, that sticks to the words that are given and translates them as they are set down in the Lexicon, that in the translation takes them up and in doing so leaves them just as they are, is the most irrelevant imaginable. It works through single terms and meanings determined *by* '*words*'. This apparent definiteness brings to every word use, just as in philosophical expressions, leeway for the greatest ambiguity.
>
> (Heidegger 2005: 7)

It is only when we find expressions that re-enact the hermeneutic situation that there is a matter of concern for philosophy to think through at all. Philosophical translation does not aim at giving us access to an eternal conversation about matters of perennial and already determined significance. Nor does it aim to make a set of prior results available so that we can determine whether they are relevant to problems we have already set for ourselves. The sense of the words used is to be determined in the re-enactment of the situation in which something to be understood appears, and translation is an integral dimension of that re-enactment.

At first sight it can seem that Heidegger's translations are arbitrary and wilful, going not only against the grain of received renderings but twisting meanings, wrenching them out of context so as to suit his own philosophical purposes. Yet Heidegger insists that a proper context for philosophical translation and thought must be forged in the act of translation and thought itself. The hermeneutical situation is an inter-relation of meaning that we are thrown into, but it remains an arbitrary collection of accretions until a point of view is found that allows us to rethink the core matter of concern, which means opening up a 'range of view' within which 'the interpretation's claim to objectivity moves' (Heidegger 2009: 39). This range of view, the horizon of understanding, does not illicitly transpose the views and concerns of the translator-thinker onto a source text. Rather, it is what allows the translator to open up the matter of concern that the source text itself is concerned with. The most important feature of such a translation for Heidegger is therefore not that it presents us with a complete and ready-made doctrine, since thought itself is not a doctrine or set of doctrines, but that it allows an approach towards a matter of concern that opens and maintains a field of meaning. The translator needs to open that field of meaning once more so that readers can themselves rethink the matter of concern.

For Heidegger, then, philosophical translation must make use of what we might call an existential context principle. The context in which a translation takes place and makes sense is not simply a set of lexical items that can be arranged and rearranged. Translators find themselves in the midst of a tradition that both allows for a preliminary understanding and tends to fix that understanding into preconceived doctrines. The translation is the first and in many ways most significant moment in the process of 'destructuring' the traditional ways of thinking that we simply inherit, freeing them so that we can take them up and understand them for ourselves.

3.2 Thinking as translation of grounding words

In the light of the preceding summary of Heidegger's notion of the hermeneutical situation it is possible to begin to understand one of the most significant and peculiar features of his philosophical translation practice: the singling out of words. Despite his warning against 'literal' translations that exchange words for the supposed equivalents, some words, in Heidegger's view, form unique constellation points around which whole philosophical works, philosophical projects and even the spirit of a language and an historical people gather. As is made clear by the proper understanding of the hermeneutical situation, concentrating on single words in this way should not be seen as a violation of the context principle, that words only make sense in their context, but an existential radicalisation of that principle. These are what Heidegger calls fundamental, basic or grounding words.

Heidegger will frequently translate and retranslate such words from Greek philosophy, and the understanding of Heidegger's own thinking frequently turns on attempts to translate grounding words of his own. They should not be thought of as key words, as though we could find a corresponding key translation that would open up everything for us and make it instantly available. Grounding words do not give us access to a sense that is already locked away in them but are the constellation points of repeated attempts to make sense of what has been written and said. As such, they are themselves never completely unlocked or made wholly intelligible. As we translate and retranslate these words they are the source of any understanding of the text we achieve and, as such, should not simply be manipulated on each occasion to achieve one act of communication amongst others.

Following the course of Heidegger's repeated translations of a number of such grounding words can serve to exemplify both the practice of translation called for here and the various ways in which these words show us what he comes to understand by *being*: the coming about of a domain or dimension of intelligibility. Of the grounding words of Greek philosophy, Heidegger works his way back through the Aristotelian *ousia* and the Platonic *idea* as concepts that have been fixed in the Western philosophical tradition as ways to name being as *constant presence*. He then tries to shift this tradition back to question how it is that anything can come to be present, and so the question of being for him becomes the question of how *presencing* comes about.

Perhaps the best known of the grounding words that Heidegger returns to repeatedly and translates variously in his philosophical career is *alētheia*. Section 44 of *Being and Time* contains a justly famous analysis, rethinking and translation of this word, which is traditionally translated as 'truth' [*Wahrheit*]. Truth is traditionally conceived according to a series of Latin translations of Aristotle's phrase: *pathēmata tēs psychēs tōn pragmaton homoiōmata* [experiences of the soul that correspond to things] translated as *adaequatio intellectus et rei* by Thomas Aquinas. Heidegger traces this translation back to Avicenna and this to Isaak Israeli's *Book of Definitions*, which also uses the terms *correspondentia* [correspondence] and *convenentia* [coming together] for *adequatio* [agreement]. There is already a move, in tracing this series of borrowings and providing these translations, towards the thought that truth as correspondence is not simply what is the case in a relation between intellect and thing. There must be a 'coming together' of the two. What allows for any such coming together is what Heidegger calls the 'primordial' phenomenon of truth. This conception is what he finds hinted at in early Greek thought, but also the beginnings of its covering over (Heidegger 1962: 198; Heidegger 2010: 206; Heidegger 1993: 214).

There follows a threefold translation of *alētheia* that shows the increasingly primordial phenomena of truth. The truth that grounds a judgement is what has been discovered [*entdeckt*]. The discovery itself depends on being-discovering [*entdeckend-sein*] (Heidegger 1962: 261; Heidegger 2010: 209; Heidegger 1993: 218). Finally discovery itself of beings in the world depends on a sense of *alētheia* that Heidegger translates as the 'disclosure' [*Unverborgenheit*] of the world, the very domain of intelligibility in which anything can be discovered.

These translations are meant to return us to what the Greeks would have found 'self-evident' in the very word *alētheia*, rather than to present to us a new theory of truth:

> To translate this word as 'truth' and especially to define this word conceptually in theoretical ways, is to cover over the meaning of what the Greeks posited at the basis – as 'self-evident' and as pre-philosophical – of the terminological use of *alētheia*.
> (Heidegger 1962: 202; Heidegger 1993: 219)

The translation movement from 'discoveries' to 'discovering' and then to the 'disclosure' of the world allows us to re-enact the hermeneutical situation in which what was pre-philosophical and self-evident in the Greek understanding becomes explicit in a way that allows Heidegger himself to think through the matter in a way that was not immediately available to the Greeks. A further significant feature of *alētheia* that is covered over by its translation as 'truth' and revealed in Heidegger's translations is the *privative* character (signified in the

Greek by the prefix *a-*) that is restored in the words *dis*covery [*Ent*decktheit] and *dis*closure [*Un*verborgenheit]:

> Truth (discoveredness) must always first be wrested from beings. Beings are torn from concealment. The actual factical discoveredness is, so to speak, always a kind of *robbery*. Is it a matter of chance that the Greeks express themselves about the essence of truth with a *privative* expression (*a-lētheia*)? Does not a primordial understanding of its own being make itself known in such an expression – the understanding (even if it is only pre-ontological) that being-in-untruth constitutes an essential determination of being-in-the-world?
> (Heidegger 1962: 204; Heidegger 1993: 222)

Once more Heidegger's translations attempt to make explicit what is 'self-evident' in the Greek, a feature of *alētheia* that is not given explicit philosophical consideration and yet can be uncovered and freed up for such consideration through the right translation.

Heidegger will return to *alētheia* many times, highlighting and exposing the significance of its character as the revealing and unveiling that is the primordial phenomenon of truth (Wrathall 2011). In the 1930s in lecture courses on the Pre-Socratics and in an important series of 'being-historical' texts he comes to translate *alētheia* as 'sheltering en-closure' [*Entbergung*] (Heidegger 1992: 114; 2013: 4), which is a coinage of his own to rethink *alētheia* as the making of a space for sheltering. The 'robbery' of ripping beings out of concealment was implicitly at work in the Western tradition, shaping our ways of world disclosure. But 'concealing' need not be thought of as what needs to be eradicated in the coming about of disclosure and hence discovery. What is concealed can be sheltered from attempts to bring it into complete and exhaustive exposure and at the same time given space to reveal itself. At this point Heidegger's translation goes beyond what he thinks the Greeks implicitly or explicitly thought in the expression *alētheia* to what remained unthought in their expression.

It would be possible to trace Heidegger's translations of a number of other Greek 'grounding words' through his writings, showing the complex interactions of his philosophical rethinking and the reworkings of his translations in each case. Having sketched one prominent example of how Heidegger's way of thinking unfolds hand in hand with his translation of fundamental terms in Greek philosophy, I will now turn to what is perhaps the most important set of meditations explicitly concerned with translation in Heidegger's work, those elucidating his engagement with the famous choral ode in Sophocles' *Antigone*, in lecture courses from the mid 1930s. Heidegger first translates and interprets this ode from Sophocles in the lectures *Introduction to Metaphysics* from 1935, which were subsequently published in 1953 in German and translated into English by Ralph Manheim in 1959. It was thus one of the first of his extended writings to appear in English. The book was retranslated by Richard Polt and Gregory Fried in 2000, with a revised and expanded edition appearing in 2014 (Heidegger 2014: vii–xxvi). It has thus been and continues to be central to the English-speaking reception of Heidegger's work. In one of the most significant passages in this book, Heidegger provides his own complete translation of the famous choral ode together with two extended commentaries on its philosophical significance. It is the first two lines of the ode, however, that provide the impetus and the guiding thread:

> Polla ta deina kouden an-
> thrōpou deinoteron pelei
> [many the wonders nothing
> than-human-beings more-wonderful is]

Tom Greaves

Heidegger translates:

> Vielfältig das Unheimliche, nichts doch
> über den Menschen hinaus Unheimlicheres ragend sich regt.
> (Heidegger 1953: 112)

> Manifold is the uncanny, yet nothing
> Uncannier than man bestirs itself, rising up beyond him.
> (Heidegger 2014: 163 [trans Fried and Polt])

This translation and the commentaries that follow appear in a section of *Introduction to Metaphysics* entitled 'Being and Thinking', in which Heidegger sets out to explore various ways in which being, understood as presencing, underwent various 'restrictions' in the course of the 'history of being' that followed upon the early Greek thinkers. He is concerned here to understand the relationship of human beings to being. He emphasises the 'violence' [*Gewalt*] of human beings and their incursions into the realm of beings, which is generally taken to be the central message of the ode: that human beings essentially strive to tame violently the beings around them. However, Heidegger's translation suggests something beyond this thought:

> But why do we translate *deinon* as 'un-canny'? Not in order to cover up or weaken the sense of the violent, the overwhelming or the violence-doing: quite the contrary. *Deinon* applies most intensely and intimately to human Being [...]

> We understand by un-canny that which throws us out of the 'canny,' that is the homely, the accustomed, the current, the unendangered. The unhomely does not allow us to be at home.
> (Heidegger 2014: 167–8)

Heidegger makes *deinon* the focal point of his translation and understanding, not only of this ode but of Greek thinking about what is essential to human life. Human beings can exercise the particular kinds of controlling violence that they do because they themselves are subject to being thrown out of what is canny and thus becoming unhomely. This movement is what Heidegger performatively illustrates in this translation, moving the reader out of familiar translations of *deina* and into the unfamiliar.

That first move into the uncanny is revisited and recontextualised in an extensive treatment of the ode and its translation in the 1942 lectures *Hölderlin's Hymn 'The Ister'*. There Heidegger highlights the fact that his own translation is undertaken in dialogue with Friedrich Hölderlin's translations of Sophocles. He cites Hölderlin's two draft translations of these lines:

> Vieles Gewaltige giebts. Doch nichts
> Ist gewaltiger, als der Mensch.

> There is much that is powerful [or 'violent']. Yet nothing
> Is more violent than the human being.
> (Hölderlin 1801)

> Ungeheuer ist viel. Doch nichts
> Ungeheuerer, als der Mensch.

> There is much that is extraordinary [or 'monstrous']. Yet nothing
> More extraordinary than the human being.
>
> (Hölderlin 1804)
> (cited in Heidegger 1996: 69–70)

Heidegger's commentary on these translations suggests that he discerns in the retranslation of *deinon* from *Gewaltige* to *Ungeheuer* the possible thought that at the core of the violence that human beings perpetrate against the beings that surround them is the very movement of being thrown open to those beings in the first place. *Ungeheuer* would usually be translated by 'monstrous' or some variant, and Heidegger claims that the modern sense will be primarily of what is 'immense'. McNeill and Davis translate it as 'extraordinary' to follow Heidegger's claim that the word can suggest the 'not ordinary' [*das Nicht-Geheuer*] and so become a precursor to his own translation of *deinon* as the un-canny. Yet significantly Heidegger also claims that this is presumably not what Hölderlin had in mind, evidenced by his return to rendering *deinon* as the *gewaltig* at other points in the text (1996: 71).

This is precisely what thoughtful and poetic translation at its best can achieve, according to the extended 'Remark Concerning Translation' that Heidegger interjects into this lecture immediately preceding his commentary on the translation of these words:

> There is no such thing as translation if we mean that a word from one language could, or even should, be made to substitute as the equivalent of a word from another language. This impossibility, should not, however, mislead one into devaluing translation as though it were a mere failure. On the contrary: translation can even bring to light connections that indeed lie in the translated language but are not explicitly set forth in it. From this we can recognize that all translating must be an interpreting. Yet at the same time, the reverse is also true: every interpretation, and everything that stands in its service, is a translating. In that case, translating does not only move between two different languages, but there is a translating within one and the same language.
>
> (Heidegger 1996: 62)

The point here is not that we should avoid focusing on single words instead of on the sense of the text as whole. The open sense of the whole can only be established in confronting the translation of grounding words, and it is to this that Heidegger directs his efforts. The point is rather that those words carry with them traces of connections of sense that are not only implicit for the writer and his or her contemporaries but, even beyond that, are unavailable until the translation draws them out. The poetically and thoughtfully translated word can release possibilities of sense that were not explicit in the source text or in the translation itself. That is why Heidegger goes on to make the bold claim that translation is not only required in translating Sophocles' Greek into German, as he has been doing in confrontation with Hölderlin, but that proper engagement with Hölderlin's own poetical works or philosophical works, like those of Kant and Hegel, require for German speakers 'translation within our own German language' (1996: 62). This is a point that has recently been taken up and elaborated upon in some detail by commentators, especially Parvis Emad. Emad considers the distinction between inter- and intra-lingual translation as crucial and yet ultimately derived from an originary sense of translation into the realm of *alētheia*, like the translation of the human into 'becoming unhomely' that these passages undertake (Emad 2010).

What we find in these later lectures is an elaboration and working out of the radical hermeneutics of Heidegger's early work. The enactment of the hermeneutic situation is renewed in confrontation with these grounding words, each of which carries with it the potential to confront us with the singular source of sense from which our ways of understanding the world are unfolded. The ultimate aim of this kind of thoughtful and poetical translation is therefore, according to Heidegger, not so much to enable the understanding of what is expressed in a foreign language but to confront oneself with the source of the sense that one makes of the world in one's own language:

> 'Translation' [*Übersetzen*] is not so much a '*trans*-lating' [Über-*setzen*] and passing over into a foreign language with the help of one's own. Rather, translation is more an awakening, clarification, and unfolding of one's own language with the help of an encounter with the foreign language.
>
> (Heidegger 1996: 66)

Understanding the specific philosophical and poetic aims of such a translation helps us to see how and why Heidegger thinks it appropriate to take what many have regarded as extreme liberties in translation. In the translation of the *Antigone* ode, for example, Heidegger makes the plural *ta deina* into the singular *das Unheimliche*, and makes the 'many' things that are designated by this term into a 'manifold' of the uncanny. In the 1942 lectures he elaborates on what he considers to be a 'threefold' set of meanings that can be found in the grounding word *to deinon*: the fearful, the powerful and the inhabitual. Each of these senses incorporates a contrary: the fearful as that which frightens and as that which is worthy of honour; the powerful as that which looms over us and that which is merely violent; and the inhabitual as that which is extraordinary and that which is skilled in everything. The translation itself does not try to amalgamate all these senses with their various contraries but to find a way back to the singular essence which allows for this manifold of sense to unfold: 'What is essential in the essence of the *deinon* conceals itself in the originary unity of the fearful, the powerful and inhabitual. What is essential in all essence is always singular' (1996: 64). So Heidegger's translation as *das Unheimliche* is aimed at finding a way to return us to the 'singular' essence of sense-making.

As translators we can take inspiration from this practice even if it is not always our sole and only task to transport ourselves and others back to this origin of sense-making. A glance at the history of English translations of the Sophocles ode shows us that 'Many are the wonders . . .' or some variation of that rendering has been standard for many years and still features in many contemporary efforts. At the very least an engagement with Heidegger's confrontation with Sophocles and Hölderlin's translations of Sophocles should cause a translator to consider whether this standard formulation does justice to the singular multiplicity that Heidegger points us towards. Some renderings simply add 'fearful' or 'terrible' to 'wonder' as predicates to describe the many things that surround us. Others, more promisingly, search for formulations such as 'formidable', which may move us in what Heidegger considers to be the right direction: that is, not just to an understanding of how Sophocles understood the human place in nature and how we make sense of the world we find ourselves in, but to a situation in which each one of us is confronted with that task as poet, thinker, translator and reader (for further discussion see, for example. de Beistegui 2003: 169–84; Greaves 2011).

3.3 Heidegger in translation

In the preceding two sections I gave an outline of Heidegger's thinking about translation and pointed to some prominent examples of how his translation practice informs and is informed by that thinking. In Section 1 we saw that the young Heidegger developed a radical hermeneutics, thinking of context as the projective enactment of a situation whereby translation plays an essential role in the task he sets himself of retrieving and destructuring the tradition of Western thought. In Section 2 we looked at some prominent elaborations of this thought and translation practice in his translations of *alētheia* and then in the 1930s in an ongoing dialogue with Hölderlin as translator-mediator of Greek poetic thinking.

I turn now to the recent reception history of Heidegger's thinking about translation. Fittingly, given his understanding of the open projection of a situation, this is still very much an ongoing project, with various scholars contributing to both the translation and retranslation of Heidegger's texts and to the interpretation of his philosophy of translation. These projects often go hand in hand, and in recent years they have become so intertwined this it is no longer especially helpful to try to separate them from one another.

George Steiner might be said to have opened the phase of interpreting Heidegger's understanding of translation as an ineluctable element of hermeneutics as such. His pioneering work *After Babel* first appeared in 1975, three years before he published a short book on Heidegger's thought, *Martin Heidegger*, in 1978. In *After Babel* Steiner invokes Heidegger as the thinker whose greatest contribution to the study of translation was to point towards a necessary violence, a point of breaking open a text, that forms the second in a series of four moments in the 'hermeneutic movement of translation', comprising trust, aggression, incorporation and retribution. Drawing heavily on the discussions of 'violence' [*Gewalt*] in *Introduction to Metaphysics*,[1] Steiner suggests the following image:

> The translator invades, extracts, and brings home. The simile is that of the open-cast mine left an empty scar on the landscape. As we shall see, this despoliation is illusory or is a mark of false translation. But again, as in the case of the translator's trust, there are genuine borderline cases. Certain texts or genres have been exhausted by translation. Far more interestingly, others have been negated by transfiguration, by an act of appropriative penetration and transfer in excess of the original, more ordered, more aesthetically pleasing.
>
> (Steiner 1992: 314)

It remains unclear whether Steiner thought that Heidegger himself ultimately fell prey to this image of false translation. Heidegger was certainly acutely aware of the dangers of texts being 'exhausted' by translation. He understood that unthinking and automatic reliance on received translations derives from and perpetuates the danger of extractive and exploitative attitudes towards language. However, Heidegger conceived of the necessary moment of violence as a disruption of precisely that flattening of meaning, not through an act of 'appropriative penetration' that is willed by the translator but by allowing one's own understanding to be appropriated by the singularities of sense in the language that one inhabits. For Heidegger, the contrast with exploitative exhaustion is not the creating of a more ordered and aesthetically pleasing text, which would be another result of the same kind of attitude towards language; instead, in the 1942 lectures discussed above, which were not initially available to Steiner, Heidegger offers his own image of how the translator should seek to inhabit the landscape of language, which resonates and contrasts with that offered by Steiner:

> The peak of a poetic or thoughtful work of language must not be worn down through translation, nor the entire mountain range levelled to the flatlands of superficiality. The converse is true: Translation must set us upon the path of ascent towards the peak.
>
> (Heidegger 1996: 62)

The contrast between these images of mine and mountain takes us towards one of the central concerns of Heidegger's thinking and a core debate in translation studies in the 1990s: the 'domestication' versus 'foreignisation' debate. In the course of a powerful argument for translation that does not elide the 'foreignness' of its source texts Lawrence Venuti points out in *The Scandals of Translation* that Heidegger responded to Friedrich Schleiermacher's concern that translation bring the domestic reader to the foreign text (Venuti 1998: 120). Of course, much depends on what one understands by the 'domestic' and 'foreign' and the ways that they are built and come to be. The appropriation of linguistic resources for one's own purposes offers a very different image of 'domestication' to that of becoming familiar with a landscape through ascents that radically alter one's own perspective. Venuti praises both Heidegger's own translations of Greek philosophers and those of his translators, such as David Farrell Krell, for finding ways of drawing out the foreign in both source and target languages (Venuti 1998: 120). The danger in this debate is not only the temptation to laud 'foreignisation' for its own sake but the setting up of the 'domestic' and the 'foreign' as pre-established categories into which our experiences of translation can be divided. Heidegger thinks of the two quite differently, as essential elements of the ultimate possibility of the human: 'becoming homely in being unhomely' (Heidegger 1996: 115) – that is, a never complete becoming familiar with the sense of beings through the disruption of established sense.

In 2004 Miles Groth's *Translating Heidegger* set a new benchmark for studies of all aspects of Heidegger's relation to translation. Groth traces the history of the early critical reception of Heidegger's works and what he judges to be significant mistranslations of fundamental words, which he argues have formed a significant barrier to understanding. He then sets out a powerful reading of Heidegger's own views of translation that draws upon a number of important sources, including the crucial remarks from the 1942 Hölderlin lectures. Groth focuses on the significance of single words in Heidegger's thought and translation. He describes Heidegger's own translation practice as following a paratactic method – as opposed to the syntactic method of translations, which insist that the proposition is the locus of thought – and he illustrates this method in action by following very closely the translation of Parmenides, Fragment VI in the 1951–2 lecture course *What Evokes Thinking?* Groth's central point is well taken, that 'Heidegger's translations are based on the elucidation of single words. He does not see the proposition as the bearer of thought' (Groth 2004: 141). This has formed a point of convergence for many scholars and translators of Heidegger's own works. However, Groth also makes some problematic claims, especially in his attempts to demarcate Heidegger's thought from Schleiermacher and the rest of the hermeneutic tradition. Most problematic, I would suggest, is the claim that for Heidegger, 'because thinking does not occur in words, the words that comprise a text are only a representations of an author's thought, which is the actual focus of hermeneutic activity' (2004: 116). Whilst we may be able to agree that Heidegger would not describe thinking as a 'linguistic process', his criticism of the tradition of 'representational thinking' is prominent and pervasive. From early on Heidegger continually emphasised the rootedness of thought in speech and utterance, and that is one reason that the translation of a work of thought cannot be thought as the simple replacement of one representation with another.

In recent years there has been a burgeoning of interest amongst Heidegger scholars in questions concerning translation, both in terms of the interpretation of his remarks on the topic and how best to bring that understanding to bear on the translation of his works. The majority of the projected 102 volumes of the *Gesamtausgabe* [*Collected Edition*] have been published in German, so there is now a great deal more material available which directly or indirectly bears upon the issue. At the same time those volumes are steadily becoming available in translation and, in many cases, retranslation. *Being and Time* is available in two English translations, with a revised edition of the second (Heidegger 1962 and Heidegger 2010), as is *Introduction to Metaphysics*, both texts that Heidegger published during his lifetime and that have always been central to any engagement with his work. Lecture courses from various stages of Heidegger's career that formed the basis for published lectures and books have also been translated and have enriched our understanding of his philosophical development. A good bibliography of the German texts and their English translations can be found in Sheehan (2015: 307–30).

Inevitably this burgeoning of translations has brought with it complexities in the reception history of these works. For example, John Macquarrie and Edward Robinson took the extremely significant decision to leave the term *Dasein* untranslated in their 1962 translation of *Being and Time*. *Dasein* names for Heidegger that kind of being which has its own being as an issue for it and is able to open itself to the question of being. The German word has now been absorbed as a term of art in the vast majority of commentary and interpretation. In everyday usage and in the philosophical tradition the term signifies the general existence of anything at all, but Heidegger clearly wants to signal the specific structure of the word as appropriately designating an open questioning being. The *Da* is now meant to say something about the kind of being we are considering. Rather than meaning 'here' or 'there', and thus signifying a being situated in a preformed and designated place, as it might well in other contexts, a strong case has been made that *Da* should be translated as 'open' and thus *Dasein* as 'open-being' (Sheehan 2015: 136–7). The situation is made more complex by the fact that Heidegger himself asked Joan Stambaugh, the second translator of *Being and Time*, to hyphenate *Da-sein* in her translation, when it is not hyphenated in the German text. This highlights the structure of the word just discussed, but it also creates confusion, in that this hyphenated word was already used to designate not those beings that are open but the kind of being that they have as open: that is, their openness (2015: 135). Furthermore, Heidegger hyphenates *Da-sein* in later texts where it is unclear to what extent he is expanding upon or shifting the sense that the term was given in *Being and Time*. The revised edition based on the Stambaugh translation returns to the unhyphenated but still untranslated use of *Dasein* (Heidegger 2010).

Just as Heidegger's engagement with the philosophical tradition took the form of an open-ended rethinking and retranslation of its grounding words, we should neither expect nor hope for definitive renderings of such words in his own works. One such word from the later Heidegger is *Das Ge-stell*, the word that Heidegger uses to indicate the essence of technology. The word is used in this way in the well known 1953 lecture *Die Frage nach der Technik*. William Lovitt's widely read and very influential 1977 translation 'The Question Concerning Technology' renders this term as 'enframing', making an active notion from the usual sense of *Gestell* as a frame such as a bedframe or bookcase (Lovitt 1977). This coinage was accepted by most commentators until the recent translation of the 1949 lectures held at Bremen, 'Insight into That Which Is', by Mitchell (2012). Parts of these lectures formed the basis for the later technology lecture and essay. Mitchell renders *Das Ge-stell* as 'positionality', pointing to a number of passages in which Heidegger explicitly distinguishes the sense he intends from a frame to be filled with a content or even an internal structure like a skeleton (Mitchell 2012: xi). What Heidegger has in mind is the positioning, placing or setting [*stellen*] that can be found in a range of German words including *Vor-stellen*, representation, *Her-stellen*, production and *Be-stellen*, ordering. As Eric Meyer points out, however, 'positionality' requires as much commentary as 'enframing' to make this clear, and it loses a sense of something potentially menacing taking place (Meyer 2013: 235). Furthermore, whilst what is taking place is not simply the setting up of one frame or another, it is not at all clear that this 'coarse sense of structure or framing' is not to be heard here at all in the word, as Mitchell claims it is not to be heard in 'positionality' (Mitchell 2012: xi). The great difficulty for the translator here is that we are supposed to hear *both* the everyday sense of the term *and* find ourselves opened up to unfamiliar possibilities for making sense of things, each carried in the idioms that challenge translation. To this end Theodore Kiesel's suggestion that we render *Das Ge-stell* as 'syn-thetic com-posi[tion]ing' seems felicitous. Even whilst it is inevitably unable to indicate everything that Heidegger's term does, it makes its own important connections that Heidegger himself must explain, such as those terms connected to the Latin *thesis* (Kisiel 2014).

This same core difficulty in opening unfamiliar senses of familiar and idiomatic words runs through the heart of Heidegger's thinking about language and translation to the core of sometimes acrimonious disputes that mark attempts to translate Heidegger's texts. These disputes have recently been focused on a set of texts from the late 1930s and early 1940s, including 'being-historical' works and numerous notebooks, including the already infamous 'Black Notebooks', the first of which was recently translated into English by Richard Rojcewicz as *Ponderings* (Heidegger 2016). The ongoing question of the nature and extent of Heidegger's commitment to National Socialism obviously accounts for some of the intensity of these disputes. Debates about whether Heidegger's philosophy was in some sense allied to Nazism even before the 1930s often revolve around questions of translation. That the question will to one extent or another never be closed is related to the core problem of Heidegger's understanding of translation. He takes up contemporary, often politically charged, terminology and tries to open up its significance, sometimes leaving it ambiguous as to whether or in what way he is endorsing that unfamiliar sense and what it means in each case for his commitment to the familiar sense. Much of the recent debate, for example, has centred on the translation of *Bodenlosigkeit* (usually rendered 'groundlessness' of thought in this context) in the much disputed §77 of *Being and Time*. Some commentators have tried to defend Emmanuel Faye's translation of the term as 'absence of soil', with the suggestion of Nazi 'Blut und Boden' [blood and soil] ideology, whilst others see this as a groundless projection that does nothing to help in the actual uncovering of Heidegger's Nazi affiliation (Fritsche 2016; Sheehan 2016).

For those attempting to translate Heidegger's texts or read them in translation, the difficulty is often stark. *Beiträge zur Philosophie (vom Ereignis)*, first published in German in 1989, has already been translated into English as *Contributions to Philosophy (from Enowning)* by Parvis Emad and Kenneth Maly in 1999 and *Contributions to Philosophy (of the Event)* by Richard Rojcewicz and Daniella Vallega-Neu in 2012. The difference between the translations is already suggested by the two renderings of the title words in parentheses. With the word *Ereignis* [event] Heidegger again takes an everyday word and suggests that its structure could indicate a new post-metaphysical thinking of what takes place to bring beings into their own. The first translation created a substantial controversy, largely because even with a lengthy translators' foreword explaining many of the translation decisions, it is very difficult to make sense of the English without extensive reference to the German source text. Emad and Maly argue for the inadequacy of earlier translations of the grounding word of this text, *Ereignis* (the list of attempts now includes: 'Event of Appropriation', 'Eventuation', 'Befitting', 'Ap-propria-tion' and 'Event'), on the basis of their misleading connotations from the history of philosophy (Emad and Maly 1999: xix–xxii). Yet these arguments are rarely as decisive as the translators suggest and in the end start to lead us towards the conclusion, quite at odds with Heidegger's views, that there could be an intelligible rendering that escaped all such potentially misleading connotations. Whilst one might begin to move in the reverse direction to Heidegger's, drawing out the unfamiliar in the familiar, eventually becoming familiar with 'enowning', as many readers have become familiar with 'enframing', there are limits to what can be made intelligible in any hermeneutic situation (see de Beistegui 2007). On the other hand, the Rojcewicz and Vallega-Neu translation is clearly intended as a corrective to what many have taken as the excesses of the Emad and Maly version. They write in a very concise translators' foreword of the unfamiliar senses of words that Heidegger opens up, that:

> [O]ur translation aims to invite the reader into the task of disclosing the new sense and does not presumptuously impose that sense from the start through idiosyncratic terminological choices. For example, what 'essence' and 'event' come to mean in the course of these ponderings is up to the reader to decide.
>
> (Rojcewicz and Vallega-Neu 2012: xvi)

The problem here is the danger of falling into 'literal' translation of the kind that we saw Heidegger frequently criticise: that is, translation that assumes that 'essence' and 'event' were in some sense appropriate translations and that the reader could be invited into the disclosure of new senses of these terms without any indication, beyond the statement that the old senses have become problematic. There are dangers on both sides and they will never all be avoided. What Heidegger's own remarks suggest is that what is problematic in this situation is what needs to be cultivated rather than annulled. The movement through and between familiar and unfamiliar senses may not be possible in a single translation, and to follow the movement of thought that Heidegger initiates may require us to work between translations. This will become especially true as more and more translations and retranslations of Heidegger's work are undertaken and become available in future years.

Note

1 See Chapter 16, this volume, for a discussion of the feminist critique of Steiner's imagery.

Related topics

Schleiermacher; Derrida; equivalence; meaning; the translation of philosophical texts.

Further reading

Groth, Miles . (2004) *Translating Heidegger.* New York: Humanity Books. (A very significant study divided into two parts. The first part is a history of early translations of Heidegger, focusing on English-language translations. The author argues that mistranslations have contributed significantly to misunderstandings of Heidegger's thought. The second part is a reading of Heidegger's philosophy of translation together with an extended case study of his translation practice.)

Schalow, Frank. (2011) *Heidegger, Translation and the Task of Thinking: Essays in Honor of Pavis Emad*. Dordrecht: Springer. (This volume includes a wide range of essays on Heidegger's philosophy of translation, many of which connect his translation practice to specific topics and themes from his whole range of writings.)

References

de Beistegui, Miguel. (2003) *Thinking with Heidegger: Displacements*. Bloomington: Indiana University Press.

de Beistegui, Miguel. (2007) Mindfulness (Besinnung), review Martin Heidegger, *Mindfulness (Besinnung)*, trans. Parvis Emad and Thomas Kalary, Continuum, 2006. *Notre Dame Philosophical*

Reviews. Available at: http://ndpr.nd.edu/news/25281-mindfulness-besinnung/ [Accessed 22 July 2016].

Emad, Parvis. (2010) Heidegger and the Question of Translation: A Closer Look. *Studia Phaenomenologica*, X, 293–312.

Emad, Parvis and Kenneth Maly. (tr.) (1999) *Martin Heidegger: Contributions to Philosophy (From Enowning)*. Bloomington: Indiana University Press.

Fritsche, Johannes. (2016) Absence of Soil, Historicity, and the Goethe of Heidegger's *Being and Time*: Sheehan on Faye. *Philosophy Today*, 60(2), 429–45.

Greaves, Tom. (2011). The Mine and the Mountain Range: Responding to Heidegger's Translation of the Sense of the Earth. *In Other Words: The Journal for Literary Translators*, 37, 3–16.

Groth, Miles. (2004) *Translating Heidegger*. New York: Humanity Books.

Heidegger, Martin. (1953) *Einführung in die Metaphysik*. Tübingen: Max Niemeyer Verlag.

Heidegger, Martin. (1962) *Being and Time*. John Macquarrie and Edward Robinson (tr.). Oxford: Blackwell.

Heidegger, Martin. (1992) *Parmenides*. André Schuwer and Richard Rojcewicz (tr.). Bloomington: Indiana University Press.

Heidegger, Martin. (1993) *Sein und Zeit*. 17th ed. Tübingen: Max Niemeyer Verlag.

Heidegger, Martin. (1996) *Hölderlin's Hymn 'The Ister'*. William McNeill and Julia Davis (tr.). Bloomington: Indiana University Press.

Heidegger, Martin. (2005) *Phänomenologische Interpretationen ausgewählter Abhandlungen des Aristoteles zur Ontologie und Logik (Gesamtausgabe 62)*. Frankfurt am Main: Vittorio Klostermann.

Heidegger, Martin. (2009) *The Heidegger Reader*. Günter Figal (ed.). Jerome Veith (tr.). Bloomington: Indiana University Press.

Heidegger, Martin. (2010) *Being and Time*. Dennis J. Schmidt (ed.). Joan Stambaugh (tr.). Albany: State University of New York Press.

Heidegger, Martin. (2013) *The Event*. Richard Rojcewicz (tr.). Bloomington: Indiana University Press.

Heidegger, Martin. (2014) *Introduction to Metaphysics*. Revised and expanded tr. by Gregory Polt and Richard Polt. New Haven and London: Yale University Press.

Heidegger, Martin. (2016) *Ponderings II–VI: Black Notebooks 1931–1938*. Richard Rojcewicz (tr.). Bloomington: Indiana University Press.

Kisiel, Theodore. (2014) Heidegger and Our Twenty-first Century Experience of Ge-Stell. *Research Resources*, 35. http://fordham.bepress.com/phil_research/35 [Accesssed 29 May 2018].

Lovitt, William. (tr.) (1977) *Martin Heidegger: The Question Concerning Technology and Other Essays*. New York: Harper and Row.

Meyer, E. D. (2013) The Task of the Translator, Or, How to Speak to Martin Heidegger's Texts. *Philosophy Today*, 57(3), 323–32.

Mitchell, Andrew J. (tr.) (2012) *Martin Heidegger: Bremen and Freiburg Lectures: Insight into That Which Is and Basic Principles of Thinking*. Bloomington: Indiana University Press.

Rojcewicz, Richard and Daniella Vallega-Neu. (tr.) (2012) *Martin Heidegger: Contributions to Philosophy (Of the Event)*. Bloomington: Indiana University Press.

Sheehan, Thomas. (2015) *Making Sense of Heidegger: A Paradigm Shift*. London: Rowman and Littlefield International.

Sheehan, Thomas. (2016) L'affaire Faye: Faut-il brûler Heidegger? A Reply to Fritsche, Pégny, and Rastier. *Philosophy Today*, 60(2), 481–535.

Steiner, George. (1992) *After Babel: Aspects of Language and Translation*. 2nd ed. Oxford: Oxford University Press.

Venuti, Lawrence. (1998) *The Scandals of Translation: Towards an Ethics of Difference*. London and New York: Routledge.

Wrathall, Mark A. (2011) *Heidegger and Unconcealment: Truth, Language, History*. Cambridge: Cambridge University Press.

4
Wittgenstein

Silvia Panizza

Introduction

The work of Ludwig Wittgenstein (1889–1951) is best known for offering an account of language which pointed the philosophy of language away from a view of words conceived as referring to abstract and universal ideas, towards a conception of language and meaning as grounded within specific practices. His work constitutes a significant part of the 'linguistic turn' of the twentieth century, which saw an increasing preoccupation with language in various disciplines, including philosophy. It is not surprising, therefore, that Wittgenstein has a lot to offer to translation theory and to translators. However, perhaps because Wittgenstein himself did not write explicitly about translation issues, his work is still not widely used in translation, although some recent studies, on which I will draw in this chapter, are starting to fill the gap and to show fruitful possibilities for thinking about translation (Glock 2008; Gorlée 2012; Kusch 2012; Oliveira 2012; Tymoczko 2014; Wilson 2016).

This chapter begins by outlining Wittgenstein's thought on language and his methods, after clarifying two common points of contention among Wittgenstein scholars – that is, the difference and continuity between the 'early' and 'later' Wittgenstein, and the debate on whether Wittgenstein can be said to offer a 'theory' of language. Wittgenstein's thought will then be presented by focusing on some key ideas that are particularly helpful for translation, specifically the notions of 'language-games', 'forms of life', 'aspect-seeing' and 'surveyable representation'. The emphasis is not on how Wittgenstein has been translated but on how his ideas can help in the theory and practice of translation by offering a distinctive view of language.

Controversies in Wittgensteinian scholarship

It is common practice to divide Wittgenstein's philosophical output into two phases, separated by a long break from philosophy, during which Wittgenstein thought he had solved all the problems of philosophy (see the 'Preface' of the *Tractatus Logico-Philosophicus* (Wittgenstein [1921] 1990, hereafter *Tractatus*) and spent time working as a gardener, architect and schoolteacher. The first phase, known as 'early Wittgenstein', is represented by the work published in German in 1921 as *Logisch-Philosophische Abhandlung* and in English in 1922 as *Tractatus Logico-Philosophicus*. There, in a series of numbered propositions from 1 to 7 with many sub-numerals, Wittgenstein is usually understood as setting limits to language through an analysis of how language represents states of affairs in the world, using logic and formal methods. Language is said to 'mirror' the world: there is a direct relationship between language conceived as formally analysable propositions and the structure of facts in the world. 'A proposition is a picture of reality... a model of reality as we imagine it' (*Tractatus* 4.01).

The second phase, represented by the *Philosophical Investigations* (Wittgenstein [1953] 2009, hereafter *PI*), takes a different approach and suggests a different analysis of language. Here a greater number of remarks, stories, vignettes, dialogues and exhortations encourages the reader to think of the actual use of certain words and concepts and how some conceptual schemes are more or less useful in understanding the object of philosophical investigations, among which is language. Unlike the logical and semantic approach of the earlier text, we have here a pragmatic perspective which revolves around the observation of ordinary language and its role in actual, particular contexts. 'Just as', Wittgenstein writes, 'a move in chess doesn't consist simply in moving a piece in such-and-such a way on the board – nor yet in one's thoughts and feelings as one makes the move: but in the circumstances that we call "playing a game of chess", "solving a chess problem", and so on' (*PI* 33). Similarly, his approach to the question of whether other human beings are conscious is to ask in what contexts the worry would make sense: 'Suppose I say of a friend: "He isn't an automaton". – What information is conveyed by this, and to whom would it be information? To a human being who meets him in ordinary circumstances? What information could it give him?'(*PI II* 20).

Interpretative controversies populate the reading of both early and later work. The above presentation summarises the reading that has been orthodox since the beginning of Wittgensteinian scholarship and, to some extent, still is. Recently, however, a different way of understanding Wittgenstein has emerged and is growing in popularity, partly but not wholly encapsulated by the label 'New Wittgenstein'. The founding articles of this approach are to be found in Crary and Read (2000), including papers by Cora Diamond, James Conant, Stanley Cavell, Hilary Putnam and John McDowell. This line of thought includes: a) the idea that the early and late Wittgenstein do not in fact propose two different philosophies but that there is a strong continuity between the two; b) the impossibility of spelling out the message of the *Tractatus*, as I have done above, because the book is 'framed' by a discourse that rejects the formulation of totalising theses, such as what the limits of language are; and c) the suggestion that the same rejection of theories is to be applied to the *Investigations* as well, so that a line of continuity is formed which takes Wittgenstein in all his work to be proposing a philosophical method based on observation as opposed to theory. This alternative interpretation suggests that Wittgenstein's work contains not theories but a form of 'therapy', which engages with mistaken or, rather, content-less philosophical ideas in order to dispel them and thus aims to 'cure' the thinker/reader by exposing the emptiness of those theories.

The problems relating to theory, whether it applies to the early Wittgenstein, the later or both, are particularly difficult for the reader who wishes to apply Wittgenstein's insights to another area, such as, in our case, translation. If Wittgenstein does not offer any positive statement about language, what is the use of reading him for translation? To answer this question we need to clarify the 'no-theory' line of interpretation, establish its plausibility and so discuss to what the rejection of theory actually amounts.

Reading Wittgenstein as rejecting theories or as a therapeutic philosopher does not amount to being unable to derive anything intellectually and practically helpful from his work. Dispelling misguided philosophical frameworks, or, in Wittgenstein's language, 'pictures', is indeed negative work and an ineliminable aspect of Wittgenstein's contribution. But in doing so, Wittgenstein is, on the one hand, claiming to remove something that was never truthful or helpful anyway and, on the other, he is *pointing at* what is truthful and helpful, not in the form of other theories, but in the form of everyday practices which deserve to be observed more carefully. In this sense, philosophy is not about building up abstractions but returning to what one already, in some sense, knew, but which was too obvious to be seen (*PI* 129).

The fundamental insight of Wittgenstein's work, according to the therapeutic or no-theory reading, is that language cannot be surveyed from a perspective external to it – as Alice Crary explains (Crary and Read 2000: 1). Philosophical theories of language (and, if we take some of its statements seriously, and not just as 'therapy', the *Tractatus*) purport to do just that: to offer an exhaustive representation and analysis of language which, by necessity, places itself outside the bounds of language, as it were, looking in. Only in that way can language be exhaustively theorised. Wittgenstein rejects that possibility, claiming instead that language needs to be observed from within, which includes our perspectives as users of language and as agents engaged in the practices within which language arises and is used. That is, after all, the only perspective we *can* occupy.

As far as the later Wittgenstein, the author of the *Investigations*, is concerned, this view is less controversial, and both orthodox and therapeutic readers come to some agreement about the more pragmatic perspective to be found there. They differ, still, on how radically Wittgenstein's contention is to be taken and on whether what Wittgenstein is offering in the *Investigations* can, in turn, be understood as another theory of language. The difference can be seen to hinge on the distinction between 'saying' and 'showing': is Wittgenstein offering a positive view of language as a context-dependent activity, to be judged on the basis of what we can *do* with it, or is he simply pointing out examples of language use and urging us to come to our own conclusions about them? Even if we follow the latter approach, and take Wittgenstein to be merely 'pointing', he is still pointing at examples of language use and of ways in which language does or does not make sense depending on the context; in sum, he seems to be both indicating and performing – though not theorising or asserting – a view of language as necessarily embedded in human contexts and practices, rather than being independently linked to the world through a logical connection.

Whichever reading of the *Investigations* one favours, therefore, a specific view of, and approach to, language (but not only language) can be discerned in the later Wittgenstein. This view and approach is what can offer a fundamental starting point for the translator and the translation theorist: as Bertrand Russell wrote of philosophy in the Introduction to the *Tractatus*, that it is 'not a theory but an activity' (see also *Tractatus* 4.112), so speaking, writing, understanding each other – and indeed translating – are, Wittgenstein shows us, to be understood as activities, which can only be observed in their midst and in the process of engaging in them, rather than from a theoretical, abstract 'outside' – which is not a wrong position but, rather, an impossible one. The problem, to quote William James (an author dear to Wittgenstein), is that 'the theorising mind always tends to the oversimplification of its material' (James 1902: 31). Language is complex and the life in which language is used even more so. The first suggestion from Wittgenstein that translation can take on board is, therefore, to try and stay with the complexity and pay close attention to language in its natural context before taking any further step.

Whether we side with the 'New Wittgensteinians', who identify deep continuity between early and late Wittgenstein, or with the orthodox interpretation, the *Investigations* offers a more useful perspective for translation and a more explicitly original view of language as praxis. Moreover, Wittgenstein himself wanted this to be the work that would be published after his death to represent his thought. For these reasons, this chapter focuses on the Wittgenstein of the *Investigations* and the contribution that his later work can make to translation.

Applying Wittgenstein to translation

Because Wittgenstein's contribution is at least as significant in terms of its methodology as in terms of its content, his philosophy can be helpful to other fields in two interconnected ways: as showing a method for understanding various phenomena and as offering a specific view of language and meaning. Both aspects make Wittgenstein applicable to the field of translation, where he can illuminate thought about language as such as well as in specific instances. As Read (2007) argues, part of the value of Wittgenstein's philosophy lies in what it allows us to do, or in how we can *apply* Wittgenstein to life, including other disciplines. It is not surprising, therefore, that some degree of attention has already been paid to Wittgenstein in the field of translation studies (Toury 1980; Chesterman 1997; Steiner 1998; Robinson 2003; Tymoczko 2007; Kross and Ramharter 2012; Gorlée 2012; Wilson 2016). What is more surprising is that such attention has been relatively scant. This chapter draws significantly on Philip Wilson's work in applying Wittgenstein to translation.

As Wilson suggests, the reason for the relative lack of Wittgensteinian approaches to translation may be twofold. First and most significantly, Wittgenstein, while clearly concerned with language, said very little about translation, as opposed to other philosophers such as Martin Heidegger. The second reason may be that Wittgenstein studies have been for a long time the almost esoteric preoccupation of scholars, more concerned with clarifying what Wittgenstein meant than with using his insights to solve other problems; this may have made Wittgenstein's work appear less approachable from the perspective of disciplines more focused on application than on exegesis (Wilson 2016: 5). Neither reason, however, signifies that applying Wittgenstein is either fruitless or overly difficult. In fact, his method and approach to language can reveal important aspects of the presuppositions and activity of translation, as the rest of this chapter shows.

The contribution of Wittgenstein's thought to translation can be articulated along a number of key concepts, which are central to Wittgenstein's philosophy as a whole but which can also be applied to translation in its various aspects. These are: language-games, forms of life, aspect-seeing and the surveyable representation. I give more space to the exploration of the first two concepts, as they are more important for the present purposes. It will become clear, however, that these concepts are not to be taken separately, but they all emerge and interact when considering how language operates. Each of these Wittgensteinian concepts is considered below in relation to translation in its various aspects. Wilson (2016) divides his work into three parts, considering respectively 'reading the source text for translation', 'writing the target text' and 'theorising the target text'. All three aspects will be considered, with the aim of showing how Wittgensteinian ideas can illuminate translation as a whole; however, in line with Wittgenstein's stress on praxis, more emphasis will be given to the practice of translating, in the context of reading and writing texts for translation.

Using Wittgenstein's method in translation

Before we begin the exploration of the key Wittgensteinian concepts, the central methodological principle – although here the word 'principle' should be taken with some caution – needs to be spelled out. Wittgenstein's rejection of dogmatism (and perhaps of theories) has important consequences for his way of doing philosophy and, in turn, for how we think and practise translation after Wittgenstein. This guiding idea can be found in *PI* 66: 'Don't think, but look!' Looking – observing attentively the phenomena under consideration – is contrasted with thinking, theorising, abstracting, simplifying. Looking is a way of taking seriously the object of investigation, without trying to fit it into a preconceived shape or pattern or trying to extract an 'essence' from it. Looking is paying attention to the object, something that does not only require a good pair of eyes but also, as we shall see, serious training, sensibility, knowledge and even some degree of virtue and self-awareness.

We have already briefly observed what philosophical dangers may arise from a tendency to 'think' before, or instead of, 'looking'. The same holds true for the translator and the translation theorist: inspired by Wittgenstein, the translator needs to be able to look at the source text carefully and then to write a target text that displays the same observational capacity in relation to the context of that text. Similarly, the translation theorist needs to be able to survey the activity and texts of translation without attempting to unify them under a single feature, but with the awareness that translation itself is a discipline that can only be understood through sensibility to differences. It is telling that Wittgenstein considered using 'I'll teach you differences' from William Shakespeare's *King Lear* as a motto for his book.

Looking is, for Wittgenstein, an antidote to a very common and natural, yet equally pernicious, way of approaching phenomena that is frequently referred to in the scholarship as 'being in the grip of a picture': 'A picture held us captive. And we could not get outside it, for it lay in our language and language seemed to repeat it to us inexorably' (*PI* 115). Pictures are ways of framing the world, or some aspects of it, so that everything is seen through their structures. Thinking that language essentially operates through correspondence, for instance, with one word being directly linked to an object in the world, is a picture which, Wittgenstein warns, can lead us deeply astray. In translation, this is manifest in one 'supermeme' (or extremely pervasive idea, as described by Chesterman 1997) – that is, equivalence: according to the meme of equivalence, a translation is a way of 'carrying-across' meaning from one language to another, true to its etymology (Lat. *trans-latus*). Translation thus supposedly identifies the meaning 'behind' the words and reproduces the same (equivalent) meaning in the target language. This depends on the possibility of identifying an 'essence' to words and sentences, which is in principle separable from the contingencies of their use. Being in the grip of this picture could entail, for instance, not being sensitive to how sentences operate differently depending on context and thus missing relevant aspects of the source text.

While Wittgenstein is not asking us to eliminate pictures, his suggestion is that, first, pictures should be held undogmatically – that is, without presuming that they are more than helpful tools for understanding and describing particular situations, and, second, that even some non-dogmatic pictures are not helpful or not fitting for the phenomena in question and are better abandoned for more useful and appropriate ones. Wittgensteinian anti-dogmatism is also an appeal to plurality. Another danger in translation, identified in various contexts by Wilson (2016), is that of thinking in dualities. Dualism can take the shape of a dichotomy between form and content. This kind of dualism is closely linked to the essentialist view of language and the equivalence ideal in translation. If form is seen as something separable from meaning or content, a mere ornament, then it is possible to translate while ignoring how something is said and looking for the pure meaning behind the form. But what is that pure meaning supposed to be? It may be possible to translate a CD-player instruction manual by disregarding the stylistic choices of the source text (we could safely replace alliteration, for instance, with non-alliterative sentences), but in the translation of other texts – say, a literary text – formal decisions are an integral aspect that cannot be ignored. There, formal elements are as much part of the meaning of the text as any other aspect, so that form *is*, in fact, content (Madden 2006). We do not need to appeal to literary cases to make this point, however. The role of form in creating meaning goes way beyond texts with artistic intent. Think, for example, of the various implicit ways of foregrounding an element in conversation, as in the example below:

1. Jean kissed Sophia
2. It was Jean who kissed Sophia
3. Sophia was kissed by Jean

All three sentences refer to the same state of affairs in the world, but do they convey the same meaning? In sentence (2), the phrasing signals that there may have been some doubt as to the identity of the person who had kissed Sophia, doubt that has just been cleared; sentence (3) foregrounds Jean, whose name is now at the beginning of the sentence, her role in the situation acquiring more salience (see Douthwaite 2000). A translator who ignores these aspects of the source text may miss a significant amount of what the source text is trying to convey.

This brief discussion of the form–content dichotomy exemplifies two Wittgensteinian insights, both related to the importance of being aware of multiplicity in and among phenomena. First, simplifying phenomena by dividing them into a limited number of cases ignores the wide range of possibilities available, so form does not need to stand in opposition to content, but form and content interact in different ways in different texts. Second, translation itself can operate very differently with different texts which have different purposes and different world views. Thus Tymoczko (2007) defines translation as a 'cluster concept', to describe the great variety of phenomena that translation both includes and engages with in texts. Widely different translations of the same text can serve different ends and hence be adequate on their own terms. Wittgenstein's appeal to the multiplicity of phenomena and his stress on context enables us to appreciate this possibility.

Language-games

The importance of context for language and the multiplicity that goes with it introduce the first key concept of Wittgenstein's under examination, that of language-games. In *PI* 23, Wittgenstein states that it is impossible to enumerate and classify sentences: there are countless sentences, because they come into existence and disappear according to the particular communicative need in particular situations. He goes on to say that 'the word "language-*game*" is used here to emphasize the fact that the *speaking* of language is part of an activity, or a form of life'. He then lists examples of language-games:

> Giving orders, and acting on them –
> Describing an object by its appearance, or by its measurements –
> Constructing an object from a description (a drawing) –
> Reporting an event –
> Speculating about the event –
> Forming and testing a hypothesis –
> Presenting the results of an experiment in tables and diagrams –
> Making up a story; and reading one –
> Acting in a play –
> Singing rounds –

Guessing riddles –
Cracking a joke; telling one –
Solving a problem in applied arithmetic –
Translating from one language into another –
Requesting, thinking, cursing, greeting, praying.

These are examples of different games, or activities, that we perform with language, or activities *within* which words and sentences acquire the particular meaning they have. The image of the 'game' is significant for several reasons: like games, language has rules, which are established intersubjectively; these rules are not fixed once and for all, nor independently of the aim of the game, but their purpose is making the game *work*; individual moves in a game, like words in a language, acquire their meaning in relation to the game they are part of: a piece of chess, outside the game of chess, could be used for other purposes (a child may use the knight to represent a horse in a farm) or have no use at all – so words acquire their meaning within the language-game they are part of, and the same word may mean something very different in a different game (where 'cool' may signify an attractive and fashionable person in a conversation among teenagers, or the right temperature to drink wine at a wine tasting) or have an indeterminate meaning if no game is specified (this is particularly clear with indexicals, like 'here').

Bearing in mind the variety of language-games should help the reader – and the translator when reading and writing a text – to avoid meaningless queries, such as 'What is a question?' (*PI* 24). Language-games are part of the anti-essentialist view introduced above: just as it makes no sense to look for the essence of the word 'dog', so it is impossible to look for the essence of a question, statement or remark: they are what they do, and they do something different in different language-games. The essentialist *picture* is dispelled by Wittgenstein's reminder that language operates in contexts, and through games with many aspects and different rules.

The other familiar picture that language-games dispel is the denotative view of language. Wittgenstein introduces it with a passage from Augustine (*PI* 1), who describes his own language acquisition as proceeding through a series of ostensive definitions, so that a word was uttered and an object pointed at. Ostensive definitions are presented by Augustine as the model for learning a language, which depends on a correspondence view of language: words correspond directly to objects in the world (which is the view found in the *Tractatus*, whether we believe it is meant to be rejected or not). If correspondence is accepted, translation is a matter of identifying in the source text the states of affair denoted by the sentences, and the objects denoted by the words, and identifying which sentences and words denote the same states of affair and objects in the target language. But Wittgenstein objects: while this may sometimes be the case, what Augustine describes is only a fraction of what we call 'language' (*PI* 3). Pointing and denoting are one way in which we use language, but this system only applies to names, and not even to names in every case. It does not, however, apply at all to a vast number of linguistic items, such as verbs, adverbs, etc. Furthermore, the very practice of pointing, on its own, does not guarantee the successful learning of the word in relation to the object: even in this case, we need to be aware of what pointing itself means; we need to know that we need to follow the finger and not look at the other arm, etc. Pointing is, we can say, a language-game in itself, and only within that game does the apparent 'pure' denotation make sense. Or, as Wittgenstein puts it in *PI* 9, 'the pointing occurs in the *use* of the words too and not merely in learning the use'.

Denotation is here contrasted with use. Language-games are instances of language *in use*, where meaning is dependent on what we do with words, who does it, where, when, how and why. The emphasis on use, to determine the meaning of a text, runs through the *Investigations*, and the remark extrapolated from *PI* 43, 'meaning is use', is frequently taken as the later Wittgenstein's motto:

> For a *large* class of cases of the employment of the word 'meaning' – though not for *all* – this word can be explained in this way: the meaning of a word is its use in the language.
>
> And the *meaning* of a name is sometimes explained by pointing to its *bearer*.
>
> (*PI* 43)

Let us note, again, the anti-dogmatic stance that Wittgenstein takes, and that he invites his readers to take with him: 'sometimes' the meaning of a name is explained by pointing, but more often it is not. At the very heart of Wittgenstein's philosophy is the impossibility of successfully making generalising statements ('for a *large* class of cases ... though not for *all* – note his italics), because that would introduce an element of necessity that is incompatible with taking seriously the individual concrete case. Multiplicity and openness characterise language-games.

It is significant that translating is here considered as a language-game in its own right. This is one of the few remarks Wittgenstein explicitly makes about translation, but it is telling: translation is not seen as an activity that abstracts itself from language, surveying it from above and transferring an independent meaning from one language into another; rather, it is a linguistic activity like many others, with its own rules, contexts and variety of applications. In translating, we are doing something with language and are as embedded in the practices and conventions of this particular activity as we would be in any other. Translation is a language-game that interacts with other language-games, taking them as its object in reading the source text and attempting to play them in writing the target text. The language-games that translation can deal with are countless. Let us take, drawing from Wittgenstein's examples in *PI* 23, the language-games of giving orders and of praying. The translator needs to be aware which language-game the words she is translating are part of. The same words – for example, 'please make sure that the dog stays safe' – can be an order given by a domineering person entrusting the care of their dog to a dog-sitter or the words of a child praying to God that his little spaniel stays free from harm. Identifying the language-game will enable the translator to select the appropriate translation.

> 1 Please make sure that the dog stays safe
> 1a Assicurati che il cane non si faccia male
> *Ensure that the dog does not get hurt*
> 1b Per favore, proteggi il cane
> *Please protect the dog*

(1a) and (1b) are appropriate translations into Italian of (1), although both depart significantly from a word-by-word translation, especially (1b). The two translations are possible because each identifies a different language-game: in (1a), the order omits the politeness word 'please', which in English can have a perfunctory use; politeness forms like 'prego' or 'per favore' [please] are used far less frequently in Italian than in English. The emphasis is also on the health and physical wellbeing of the dog, so that the dog not 'getting hurt' is the person's main concern. In the prayer in (1b), the intention of politeness and indeed reverence is emphasised, by contrast, by the use of 'per favore', which is more salient in Italian because it is more rarely used, and the sense of safety is generalised in a request to protect the animal from any form of harm, appropriate in a prayer to an omnipotent being. These contextual observations can justify the differences in the two translations.

Forms of life

The elements that allow us to identify the appropriate translation in the example above derive from the correct identification of the language-games. However, language-games alone could not quite take us to the conclusions that we were able to reach, particularly to a full explanation of the use of 'please'. The 'surroundings' of the text, to use a Wittgensteinian expression (*PI* 250, 583–4), participate in giving it its meaning, and they can be broader than the particular language-games. Discussing the feelings of love and hope, Wittgenstein remarks:

> What is happening now has significance – in these surroundings. The surroundings give it its importance. And the word 'hope' refers to a phenomenon of human life. (A smiling mouth smiles only in a human face.)
>
> (*PI* 583)

The surroundings in which a word is used are fundamental to the word's meaning, not only, and more familiarly, because a word needs to be understood in context, but more deeply, because words, like anything else we do as human beings, only make sense as part of the kind of life we live, which has particular concerns, needs, perspectives, constraints, ways of organising and perceiving the world. These are all aspects of what Wittgenstein calls 'a form of life'. If we return to the quote above, we can see that Wittgenstein introduces the notion of language-game by pairing it with that of forms of life: 'the word "language-*game*" is used here to emphasize the fact that the *speaking* of language is part of an activity, or a form of life' (*PI* 23).

Forms of life have been interpreted as ranging from very broad (humanity as a whole) to very narrow (e.g. the translator's form of life), and language often acquires meaning according to its role in more than one form of life. When reading for translation and when writing a text in translation, the difficulty is to remain aware of the various language-games and how they are embedded in different forms of life at the same time. Wilson (2016: 31–2) shows how the word 'dog' can have very different meanings and, therefore, should be translated differently, depending on the local form of life that it is part of. For instance, we understand 'There is a dog in the kitchen. He is called Ben' in the context of a form of life where dogs are kept as pets and are treated as part of the family, given names and referred to by gendered pronouns. Conversely, 'He was as sick as a dog' can be understood through our awareness of the form of life where dogs are regarded as inferior to humans (Wilson 2016: 32). This awareness is necessary to reading the source text for translation competently. Then, when translating these texts, we will need to ask ourselves whether the language we are translating into belongs to a culture in which practices involving dogs are the same or different. If the latter, that would mean, potentially, changing the reference to 'dog' to some other animal, which plays a similar role in the target text's form of life. This recommendation itself, however, also depends on the context and aim of the translation: if the translation was intended to stress the foreign nature of the source text (a novel about explorers, a travel guidebook, etc.), it would be appropriate to refer to the same animal *precisely because* dogs play a different role in that form of life.

Awareness of forms of life helps the translator to deal with difficult cases, like words which seem to exist in one language but not another. The Italian 'tamponare', for instance, refers to the act of lightly bumping into another car – say, at a traffic light perhaps out of distraction or impatience. This phenomenon is to be understood in the context of a culture where drivers are known for being slightly more aggressive than elsewhere, and where bumping into another car is not considered to be a major source of worry, being so common, so that is can be taken with some lightness and even irony. ('Tamponare' also mean 'to dab', as when one dabs a part of the body with a cotton pad, hence it evokes a more gentle image than the context requires.) English does not have a word which describes exactly this phenomenon. The English word 'to bump' is broader, including somewhat more serious instances of collision, and lacks the ordinariness and light-heartedness that can be associated with 'tamponare'. Here, a Wittgensteinian approach would: a) start by identifying all of the above features of the word, only available through a sound grasp of the form of life in which it is used; b) identify the specific language-game that the source text engages in with the word. Is it someone reporting an accident to the police? Someone telling an anecdote to a friend in an amused manner? A driving manual? c) look for what word, phrase or sentence could do the *same work* in the target language, here English. Many options, depending on the language-game and purpose of the translation, are available: 'bump', 'hit', 'touch', 'collide', etc. Wittgenstein's lesson, applied to this example, is that it would not be helpful merely to recur to a bilingual dictionary, looking for the answer to the question: 'What does "tamporare" mean?'

The example of forms of life in translation may lead the reader to believe that forms of life generally coincide with a culture or a country. That does not need to be the case: forms of life can be both broader and narrower than cultures, nor are they fixed; they are constantly evolving and changing in the same way that human lives do, and language with them (see *PI* 23). An example of a more local form of life, with its impact on language, can be found in the gender attributed to the sea in Spanish. Unlike other languages in which the sea is gendered as either masculine (Portuguese 'o mar') or feminine (French 'la mer'), in Spanish 'mar' is both feminine and masculine. In *The Old Man and the Sea*, Ernest Hemingway's main character tells us that the difference lies, primarily, in the geographical and emotional closeness of people to the sea: people who live by the sea and love it give her a feminine gender, calling it 'la mar', comparing the sea to a woman who may be moody but is always to be respected and appreciated; younger people, who take a more detached and instrumental approach to the sea, use the traditionally more antagonistic gender and call it 'él mar' (Hemingway 1995: 29–30).

This description reminds the translator that she needs to pay attention to the narrower or more local forms of life as well, here, for example, that of the young fishermen, whose use of the masculine noun signifies a different way of thinking about the sea: this difference is significant, and the translation should find ways to preserve the world view that goes with the choice of gender. We could use Hemingway's observations about forms of life, for example, to understand these lines by Lope de Vega:

Pasé la mar cuando creyó mi engaño
que en él mi antiguo fuego se templara
('A Lupercio Leonardo', Vega 2012: 28)
[*I crossed the sea when I believed my fancy
That in it my ancient fire would be quenched*]

These lines are striking because the sea is feminine in the first lines ('la mar') and masculine in the second ('él'). A possible interpretation, following Hemingway, is that – according to traditional views on gender – the sea is feminine when seen as a welcoming mass of water, carrying the poet and promising peace, and masculine when it is placed alongside the poet's 'fire' ('fuego'), which it is meant to extinguish, where the sea works as a more active contrast to the individual.

How are we to translate these lines into a language where the sea is neuter or where it has a fixed gender? The aim is to find a translation that 'not only says what the original poem says, but does what the original poem does', as Phyllis Gaffney says about Pierre Leyris's translations of Gerald Manley Hopkins into French (1999: 57). If we agree with Wittgenstein, a translated poem cannot really say what the original says unless it also does what the original does. To that purpose, we could find ways to convey the sense of passage in the first line and of conflict in the second by, for instance, adding an adjective to the first occurrence of 'sea' which conveys ease, and by preserving the masculine pronoun in the second line. Many possibilities are open to the translator, as long as the forms of life and language-games of the original and of the target are recognised.

Seeing aspects

The richness that can be conveyed by a word, when understood in the context of its use in the particular language-game and form of life, leads us to consider another key Wittgensteinian concept that can illuminate crucial aspects of translation: seeing aspects. The multiplicity and complexity of phenomena and hence of language means that each phenomenon, and each word in context, will have a variety of aspects, which will be more or less apparent to the observer/translator. Wittgenstein introduces the idea of aspects with the well-known 'duck–rabbit' drawing in *PI* II 118, where one can see at first either a duck or a rabbit, and then, if the aspect 'dawns' on one, see the other animal *in* the picture. Yet unlike this simple image with only two visible aspects, most texts and their words in context present a potentially unlimited number of aspects, or ways of seeing them. Crucially, seeing aspects does not depend only on having a sharp sight. It requires, using Wittgenstein's example, conceptual mastery (having the concepts 'duck' and 'rabbit'), participation in a form of life (where ducks and rabbits exist) and the ability to recognise the 'surroundings' which make it more likely that a duck or a rabbit is the relevant aspect (e.g. whether the image is presented with a lake in the background). In the same way, the translator, in order to be aware of all the relevant aspects, needs to be familiar with the form of life of both source text and target text, to master the relevant concepts in the context of those forms of life, to be aware of the 'surroundings' or language-games the text is part of and generally be able to exercise her sensibility and imagination in bringing possibilities to light. All this requires not only linguistic training, but cultural awareness and training in observation, as well as the exercise of imaginative faculties (see Oliveira 2012 for a more thorough reflection on aspects in translation). The importance of immersing oneself in the forms of life of the source text in order to see the relevant aspects is highlighted by Wilson through his example of his own translation of *Das Hildebrandslied* [the song of Hildebrand], an Old High German poem, where he comments that, by seeking to understand the context, culture, and way of seeing the world that shaped the source text, in effect 'translation becomes anthropology' (Wilson 2016: 42). The richness of the Spanish 'mar' discussed in the section above is another example of the importance of seeing aspects when reading and writing a text in translation: lacking awareness of the multiplicity of aspects that the word can disclose could result in a misunderstanding of the meaning it has in its original context, and hence in a translation that is either limited to fewer aspects or misunderstands the original meaning altogether.

Evaluating translations

In the midst of such multiplicity and openness, how do we determine what a good translation looks like? The task is not impossible but requires some qualifications. First, while with the same text it is possible to have translations that are better and others that are worse, if we follow Wittgenstein, we cannot claim that there is a single best translation of a text. The merit of each translation will depend on various factors, which are also contingent on the aim and context of the translation. Thus Dinda Gorlée (2012) describes translation as an open-ended and future-oriented process, which can always be improved and changed in new contexts and with the rise of new language-games. In this way, the very idea of 'ideal' or 'standard' translation becomes, in Gorlée's words, 'an oxymoron' (2012: 19). Second, following the discussion on aspects, good translations will be sensitive to as many aspects of the source text as possible and will show sufficient knowledge of the forms of life and language-games of source and target text by maintaining as many observable relevant aspects as possible. However, it would be impossible to determine exactly how many aspects a text has, because new ones can always be discovered. For these reasons, as Gideon Toury (1995) suggests, it would be more appropriate to talk about an 'adequate' translation than a 'good' one. An adequate translation fulfils the particular need for which it is required, is able to recognise and recreate a sufficient number of aspects in the source and target texts and can have a role in the target language which is similar to the role the original has in the source language. In other words, it can be *used* similarly.

The aim to create a text that can do similar 'work' to the original in these ways can be described, to introduce one final Wittgensteinian concept, as the identification and creation of a 'surveyable representation' (*PI* 122), which, on the one hand, allows the translator to see the source text as a whole, and in the context to which it belongs, with its more and less salient aspects; on the other hand, a surveyable representation of the target text offers the possibility of evaluating it against the source text, by presenting an overview of its elements and the role it plays in its own context. Finally, the idea of surveyable representation can be applied to translation theory, where instead of analysing or prescribing (both of which go against Wittgenstein's method; see *PI* 66) the aim is to describe the multi-faceted activity of translation and to acknowledge that there may be no single, or even a set of, common denominators. Descriptive Translation Studies take this kind of approach (Toury 1980).

Looking at translation through a Wittgensteinian lens can allow us to find greater freedom in both the practice and theory of translation. By directing our attention to the actual phenomena and their complexity, Wittgenstein frees us from misleading pictures which include the temptation to believe that each word must refer directly to an object in the world, or that a single essence must be behind the phenomenon of translation. Wittgenstein's stress on multiplicity removes the habit of thinking in polarities and leads us away from unhelpful dualisms, such as form versus content, which disappear when thinking of language as fundamentally embedded in context. Finally, Wittgenstein draws attention to the difficulty of doing justice to the facts, in this case the texts, not only because of their complexity but also because of the different skills and abilities and virtues involved in doing so: from a Wittgensteinian perspective, a good translator is not only a linguistic expert but also someone with extensive knowledge of different fields and of different cultures, a well developed sensibility and imagination and the self-awareness and humility required to hold possibilities in mind, to not project a form of life onto the text and to remain aware of differences.

Related topics

Quine; context and pragmatics; equivalence; ethics; literary translation.

Further reading

Wilson, Philip. (2016) *Translation after Wittgenstein*. London: Routledge. (A book-length study of the application of Wittgenstein to translation. It examines the practices of reading for translation, writing a text in translation and theorising about translation from a Wittgensteinian perspective.)

Kross, Matthias and Esther Ramharter (eds). (2012) *Wittgenstein Übersetzen*. Berlin: Parega. (A collection of papers on Wittgenstein and translation.)

Gorlée, Dinda. (2012) *Wittgenstein in Translation: Exploring Semiotic Signatures*. Berlin and Boston: De Gruyter Mouton. (A study on translation from the perspectives of Wittgenstein and C.S. Peirce, exploring the possibility of 'semiotranslation'.)

References

Chesterman, Andrew. (1997) *Memes of Translation*. Amsterdam: John Betjeman.
Crary, Alice and Rupert Read (eds). (2000) *The New Wittgenstein*. London and New York: Routledge.
Douthwaite, John. (2000) *Towards a Linguistic Theory of Foregrounding*. Torino: Edizioni dell'Orso.
Gaffney, Phyllis. (1999) '"The achieve of, the mastery of the thing!" Pierre Leyris's Verse Translation of Gerald Manley Hopkins', in Jean Boase-Beier and Michael Holman (eds) *The Practices of Literary Translation*. Manchester: St. Jerome, 45–58.
Glock, Hans-Johann. (2008) 'Relativism, Commensurability and Translatability', in John Preston (ed) *Wittgenstein and Reason*. Oxford: Blackwell, 21–46.
Gorlée, Dinda. (2012) *Wittgenstein in Translation: Exploring Semiotic Signatures*. Berlin and Boston: De Gruyter Mouton.
Hemingway, Ernest. (1995) *The Old Man and The Sea*. New York: Simon & Schuster.
James, William. (1902) *The Varieties of Religious Experience*. London: Longmans, Green & Co.
Kross, Matthias and Esther Ramharter (eds). (2012) *Wittgenstein Übersetzen*. Berlin: Parega.
Kusch, Martin. (2012) 'Wittgenstein on Translation', in M. Kross and E. Ramharter (eds) *Wittgenstein Übersetzen*. Berlin: Parega, 57–75.
Madden, Matt. (2006) *99 Ways to Tell a Story*. London: Jonathan Cape.
Oliveira, Paulo. (2012) 'Übersetzung, Aspekt und Variation', in M. Kross and E. Ramharter (eds) *Wittgenstein Übersetzen*. Berlin: Parega, 123–72.
Read, Rupert. (2007) *Applying Wittgenstein*. London: Continuum.
Robinson, Douglas. (2003) *Becoming a Translator*. London and New York: Routledge.
Steiner, George. (1998) *After Babel*. Oxford: Oxford University Press.
Toury, Gideon. (1980) *In Search of a Theory of Translation*. Tel Aviv: Porter Institute for Poetics and Semiotics.
Toury, Gideon. (1995) *Descriptive Translation Studies and Beyond*. Amsterdam: John Betjeman.
Tymoczko, Maria. (2007) *Enlarging Translation, Empowering Translators*. Manchester: St. Jerome.
Tymoczko, Maria. (2014) 'Cultural Hegemonies and the Erosion of Translation Communities', in Sandra Bermann and Catherine Porter (eds) *A Companion to Translation Studies*. Chichester: Wiley-Blackwell, 165–78.
Vega, Lope de. (2012) *Poemas*. Barcelona: Linkgua Digital.
Wilson, Philip. (2016) *Translation after Wittgenstein*. London: Routledge.
Wittgenstein, Ludwig. [1921] (1990) *Tractatus Logico-Philosophicus*. Tr. by C.K. Ogden, London and New York: Routledge.
Wittgenstein, Ludwig. [1953] (2009) *Philosophical Investigations*. Tr. by G.E.M. Anscombe, P.M.S. Hacker and J. Schulte, Chichester: Wiley-Blackwell.

5
Benjamin

Jean Boase-Beier

5.1 Introduction

One of the difficulties involved in understanding Walter Benjamin's work on translation, and in assessing its importance for current discussions on translation and philosophy, is that he is generally known to Translation Studies students and scholars through only one piece of writing: 'Die Aufgabe des Übersetzers' [The Task of the Translator, Benjamin 1992a, cited here as T].[1] Another is the complexity of his writing style. These two difficulties are linked: because Benjamin's writing can seem complex and esoteric, there is a tendency for those who study translation not to read his other works, relying solely on this much anthologised essay, written in 1920–1 as Benjamin's introduction to his translations of the 'Tableaux parisiens' [Paris Tableaux] from Baudelaire's 1857 *Les fleurs du mal* [Flowers of Evil, Baudelaire 2015].

A third difficulty comes from what might appear to be conflicting strands of thought in 'The Task of the Translator'. It was only after its publication that he became seriously interested in Marxism and materialism, but we can already see the influence of Karl Marx's *Das Kapital* [Capital] (Marx 1961), which he read in 1921, in his concern with the influence of the foreign, the effects of history on the present, and the image of the *Wehen* (birth pangs) of language (T, p. 55; Marx 1961: 6–8).

His friend Gerhard (later Gershom) Scholem says Benjamin's philosophy of language at this time was 'openly theological' (Scholem 1981: 147, Harry Zohn's translation), and strands of his theological view are indeed apparent in references to scripture and the 'Messianic' (T, pp. 64, 56). But in fact there is no conflict: Benjamin always balanced his materialist thinking (the view that the material means of human existence determine the organisation of society, and more generally that the material and the practical are of primary importance as opposed to the view that the spiritual, the cognitive, or the idealistic is primary) with a more metaphysical view, which looks beyond what could be explained scientifically. He was clearly influenced by Ernst Bloch's *Geist der Utopie* [Spirit of Utopia, Bloch 1973], which he had read three years earlier, and which emphasises the religious aspects of Marxism and the link between Marxist and Messianic revolution. Benjamin's short piece 'Kapitalismus als Religion' [Capitalism as Religion], which he also wrote in 1921, brings together some of his thoughts on Marxism, capitalism, organised religion and theology (Benjamin 1996: 288–91).

Anthologies play an important role in re-contextualising the thoughts of scholars within a particular discourse, besides providing convenient teaching materials. But we can observe with other figures whose writing was not primarily on translation, for example Roman Jakobson (see e.g. Jakobson 2012), that the essay with 'Translation' in its title, though understandably the most anthologised within Translation Studies, is never the only source of the particular scholar's thinking on the topic of translation. Nor can it be properly understood out of context. The same is true of Benjamin.

Benjamin emphasises that in order to get to the truth of experience we must destroy the unity of accepted categorisations and conventional modes of thought (1992a: 5–6). While we might argue that this is exactly what anthologies do, by taking a piece of work out of the context of the thoughts of a particular thinker and juxtaposing it with the thoughts of others, it is important to apply this idea to the anthologies themselves and look at their parts separately and in their original contexts. When Benjamin wrote 'The Task of the Translator', he was as concerned with the sense of 'task' (*Aufgabe* – literally that which we have been given to do) as with the sense of what it was to be a translator. If we consider Benjamin's other works, we see that *Aufgabe* is a word he uses frequently, describing 'the task of the critic' (Benjamin 1985: 171–5), of the first human beings (1992a: 42), of the poet (1992a: 5), of philosophy (1965: 7) and of linguistic theory (1992a: 31), and it therefore needs to be understood against the background of all Benjamin's uses of the word.

*

Walter Benjamin, literary and cultural critic, philosopher, linguist, poet, translator, was born in Germany's capital city, Berlin, in 1892, into an assimilated, well-to-do middle-class Jewish family. He committed suicide in 1940, in the French-Spanish border town of Port Bou, while attempting to escape to the US (Birman 2006). The death notice the following month in the *New York Weekly* describes him as a 'scientist' (Birman 2006: 17). His editor, Rolf Tiedemann, follows Benjamin's colleague Theodor Adorno in maintaining that his work belonged 'emphatically to philosophy' (Tiedemann 1992: 173). Benjamin himself, in 1925 (1996: 422), had written that his main scholarly interest was in aesthetics and that this brought together his literary and philosophical interests. Common to all the areas he worked in was a concern with language.

Benjamin was, from early childhood, a keen observer of the world around him. In *Berliner Kindheit um 1900* (Berlin Childhood around 1900), written thirty years later (Benjamin 2010), he describes in precise and lyrical prose the many objects he observed – trees, toys, pictures, shops, animals, the telephone – that, viewed from the perspective (and especially the materialist perspective) of the adult, could be seen to have awakened his interest in the historical and cultural significance of everyday things. He became interested in the philosophy of youth culture under the teaching of educational reformer Gustav Wyneken in 1905 and 1906: Benjamin's first publications were in a journal for which Wyneken wrote, *Der Anfang* [The Beginning]. Having left school at the age of 20 with good grades, he went to university in Freiburg, Berlin and Munich, studying philosophy, publishing a number of journal articles and completing his PhD in 1919 with 'The Concept of Criticism in German Romanticism', where he examined the development of a modern understanding of art by engaging critically with Kant's thinking on knowledge and reflection (Eiland and Jennings 2014: 107–13). It was published in 1920. It had been Benjamin's intention to obtain his *Habilitation* so he could pursue an academic career, but he was finally forced to abandon the idea in 1925, having been told that his work was 'extremely difficult to read' (Eiland and Jennings 2014: 231). But this was almost certainly not the only reason: Benjamin's interdisciplinary and unconventional work was (and has remained) hard to locate within a particular area.

The work Benjamin had hoped would secure his *Habilitation*, *Ursprung des deutschen Trauerspiels* [Origin of the German Mourning Play], was published in 1928 (Benjamin 1993), and he continued to write prolifically on literature and culture, developing an approach to the philosophy of history which was increasingly influenced by the Marxism of Bertolt Brecht, with its concern for the economic and material (see e.g. Adorno et al. 2007). He intended much of his philosophy to be brought together in *Das Passagenwerk* [The Arcades Project], but it was unfinished at his death and was not published in its entirety until more than forty years later (Benjamin 1999).

Though we can indeed read very clearly what Benjamin thought in the early 1920s about translation in 'The Task of the Translator', it is hard to understand what we are reading unless we are prepared to see it in the context of the prehistory of these thoughts in his earlier work and their continuing development in his later work.

5.2 Historical perspectives

In 'Über den Begriff der Geschichte' [On the Concept of History, Benjamin 1992a: 141–54, cited here as H], Benjamin says that history is not chronology: the past is not merely what once happened; the present must be able to 'recognise itself' as an 'intended' part of the image we carry of the past (H, p. 143) (note that Zohn translates this statement the other way round: Benjamin 1992b: 247).

If we take Benjamin's view seriously, it suggests that, in order to understand 'The Task of the Translator', we need to relate what it says not only to his situation at the time, and to debates then current, but also to what its consequences were to be. Some of these consequences for current research are examined in Section 4, and for translation practice in Section 5. In this section, I consider the context in which he was writing and the essay's place within his development as a philosopher.

As we have seen, Benjamin began writing for publication before the outbreak of the First World War and continued up to his death in the second year of the Second World War. These wars necessarily had an influence on his life and work. He rarely commented on the first war (Scholem 1981: 31), but, though not a pacifist (Scholem 1981: 32), he broke with Wyneken in 1914 when the latter argued for the importance of the war in a way which Benjamin saw as narrowly nationalistic (Eiland and Jennings 2014: 75). The rise of Nazism and the outbreak of the second war led to his exile, flight and suicide.

While much of his early writing consisted of poems and literary prose, and he was involved in several literary groups, his concern for politics was already evident in leadership roles in the youth movement in Berlin and Freiburg and in work such as the 1915 essay 'Das Leben der Studenten' [The Life of Students, Benjamin 1996: 37–47].

Through his friendship from 1915 on with Scholem, originally a mathematician and later an expert on Jewish mysticism and the Kabbalah (see Scholem 1995, 1996), he became interested in Jewish theology. When he wrote 'The Task of the Translator' in 1920 and 1921, he had thus known Scholem for several years, and it is probably Scholem's influence that can be seen in the theological references.

His relationship with musician and philosopher Adorno, whom he first met in 1923 but did not get to know well until some years later, and with other critical theorists from the Frankfurt Institut für Sozialforschung [Institute for Social Research], as well as with Brecht, were to have profound influences on his work, especially from the late 1920s.

Benjamin got to know Brecht in 1924, the year after Scholem emigrated to Palestine, and around then Scholem felt he perceived a split in Benjamin's thinking (1981: 149–50), as his Marxism became more entrenched and was, Scholem felt, in conflict not only with his metaphysics but also with their earlier shared 'anarchistic convictions' (1981: 149). In the late 1920s, Benjamin's Marxism developed as a more explicitly anti-Fascist view (Benjamin 1992b: 248–51). Hitler became Chancellor in 1933, and Benjamin, who had been working on French literature, and especially on Baudelaire, since his student days, left to live in Paris.

Benjamin liked to keep his friendships separate, perhaps realising that not every strand of his thinking would appeal to every friend. He spoke of his 'Janus face', one side of which, Scholem remarks, was offered to him and one to Brecht (Scholem 1981: 249). It is true that his friends often disapproved of one another: both Adorno and Scholem felt that Brecht had a pernicious influence on him (Scholem 1981: 284–8; 293; Eiland and Jennings 2014: 607–8).

Yet it should not be thought that Benjamin merely absorbed the influence of others. His work pushed Adorno, already a materialist thinker, in a more 'revolutionary' direction (Adorno et al. 2007: 102; see also Eiland and Jennings 2014: 357). His thinking on translation greatly influenced Scholem's, and it almost certainly influenced Scholem's practice as a translator (Sauter 2015). And Scholem considers it likely that Benjamin's interest in sinology influenced Brecht's philosophy of the theatre (Scholem 1981: 59; Brecht 2015: 149–59).

Though Benjamin's interactions with Scholem, Brecht, Adorno and others were clearly important for his philosophical development, the greatest influence, it could be argued, remained that of his university studies in philosophy in Freiburg, Berlin and Munich between 1912 and 1917. Even before his studies he had read Fritz Mauthner's linguistic theory of philosophy, taking from Mauthner the view that all philosophical issues come down to questions of language. Mauthner had felt that Kant did not fully appreciate the centrality of language to reasoning (Weiler 1970: 3). In 1915, at university, Benjamin confessed to Scholem that he failed to understand Kant (Scholem 1981: 16), but he saw himself as a neo-Kantian throughout his life (Eiland and Jennings 2014: 33). He also read von Humboldt and the Christian philosopher Johann Georg Hamann, who had influenced Goethe and Hegel (Smith 1960: 17). Traces of Hamann's (and, to a lesser extent, von Humboldt's) views of the importance of language and the link between language and theology can be seen in many of Benjamin's works, such as 'Über Sprache überhaupt und über die Sprache des Menschen' [On Language per se and on the Language of Human Beings, here cited as L], originally written in 1914, and 'The Task of the Translator', as can Hamann's interest in fragments rather than systems (Smith 1960: 22). He also read (and disliked) work by Heidegger, to whom his use of the term *Dasein* can partly be traced, though it had been used by earlier philosophers, for example von Humboldt (Menninghaus 1980: 57) and also Hamann (Smith 1960: 19). Benjamin himself seems to suggest that Novalis is the source (1992a: 6) and that the word means 'a necessity of being there' (ibid.).

In spite of Benjamin's comment about his 'Janus face', we should not underestimate the degree to which he saw metaphysics and Marxist materialism as compatible, for Benjamin saw in Judaic and Christian theology, with their different views of the Messianic, just as in Marxism, a concern for the revolution that was to come. In his early 'Capitalism as Religion', this connection is as clear as it is in his last work, 'On the Concept of History', which Benjamin said was influenced by Scholem's *Trends in Jewish Mysticism* (Scholem 1995; Eiland and Jennings 2014: 659). In the latter essay, Benjamin also makes clear another link: 'The class struggle ... is a struggle for the raw and material things, without which there are no fine and spiritual ones' (H, p. 143). There are two important points here. One is a non-teleological view of history: we don't act in order to affect the future because history makes things happen and revolution (Messianic or Marxist) represents the end, not the aim, of history. The other is a concern with the effects of the practical and material on the way thought comes to be expressed. He was very interested in bookbindings and paper (see Scholem 1981: 87, who disapproved) just as he was in fragments of language that have the potential to be put together and bring about spiritual redemption (see Section 3). But Benjamin's metaphysics was never, in spite of what Scholem thought (1981: 147), essentially religious. There was indeed a spark of the spiritual in language, as in all 'material things', and it came from God, but it was not so much a way to know God as a way to grasp the essence of the thing itself.

5.3 Critical issues and topics

In the previous two sections, I have been suggesting that in order to understand Benjamin's ideas about translation we need to see them within the broader context of his philosophy of history and language. There are seven linked ideas in 'The Task of the Translator' that are particularly important for an understanding of his views on translation: (1) translation is at the heart of language; (2) language is not just a tool for talking about things; (3) there is a spiritual essence in language, the 'pure language', and translation helps reveal it; (4) translation arises from a quality of 'translatability' in the text; (5) translation is a stage in the development of a text that allows it to live on; (6) translation is not based on equivalence; and (7) there are good and bad ways of translating. It is worth considering each of these ideas, and their relation to what he says in other writing, in more detail.

1. Translation is at the heart of language

Translation helps us understand how language came into being, and how it thus retains a spiritual element, and it shows us the nature of the connection between languages: all languages 'want to say' the same thing (T, p. 53) even if they do not always refer to the same things (a distinction also being made in structuralist linguistics around that time; see Saussure 1916). In giving us these insights, translation allows us to get at the real essence (*Wesen*, L, p. 31) of language, and to move from seeing language as a set of instrumental signs to realising that language is a topic for consideration in its own right (T, p. 62).

The first human beings, by a process of naming, 'translated' the essence of what God had created into human language (L, pp. 41–2): a way of recognising the divine, retained in language as a divine spark, its 'magic' (L, p. 32). Recognising the true nature of what God created through language to be subsequently named in human language is the task (*die Aufgabe*) of humans, and it is repeated whenever we translate and only then (L, p. 43). Knowing about translation thus changes our understanding of the relation of language to the things it denotes, and of language itself; in translation, unlike in original writing, we can glimpse the 'true language' that it is the task of the translator to find (L, p. 45; T, pp. 55, 58–9, 62).

Not only is translation at the heart of language per se, but it is also at the heart of linguistic theory (L, p. 42). And, indeed, in a 1927 interview, Benjamin declared that translation was at the heart of his philosophy (Eiland and Jennings 2014: 284).

2. Language is not just a tool for talking about things

Because translation allows us to see language as the thing we talk about rather than just as the tool we use to talk about other things, it counteracts the 'bourgeois' view (L, p. 30) of language as merely instrumental. On the contrary, words aim towards silence (Benjamin

1996:6), a notion taken up later by poet Paul Celan (see Section 5). It seems likely that by silence Benjamin meant a lack of referential meaning, of instrumentality and of *Geschwätz* (chatter), a word that Benjamin appears to attribute directly to Kierkegaard (L, p. 44), though Kierkegaard, writing in Danish, used various different words to refer to what in English translation is often 'chatter' (see, for example, Kierkegaard 2010: 46). *Geschwätz* is a word also used by Celan (1982: 27), to describe the instrumental overlay on language. In 'On Language *per se*', Benjamin linked the capacity of language for revealing truth if viewed non-instrumentally to a similar capacity in both time and history, a point he also made in his work on the *Trauerspiel*, begun shortly before 'The Task of the Translator' (Eiland and Jennings 2014: 87).

Eiland and Jennings argue that the non-instrumental character of language allowed him, following Hamann, to transcend the Kantian dichotomy of subject and object (how can I subjectively grasp what objectively is?) (2014: 87). In fact Benjamin does not really try to transcend it: qualities inherent in things – translatability in a text (T, p. 52), communicability in language (L, p. 36), language in everything including those things that cannot speak (L, p. 30) – are inherent in them independently of there being any human being to take them up.

3. There is a spiritual essence in language, the 'pure language', and translation helps reveal it

Poetry is also non-instrumental and does not use language to convey messages (T, p. 50); the translation of poetry must take this into account. Indeed, the translator, more than the original writer, is concerned with the integration of all languages, which Benjamin saw as the re-integration, following the kabbalistic tradition of Judaism, where *tikkun*, or redemption, is the mending of the vessels which were unable to contain the divine essence and thus broke (Scholem 1995: 265–8). As Scholem points out (1995: 267), the initial breaking of the vessels was necessary and thus had a cathartic element, an idea that led Benjamin to equate it with revolution in the Marxist sense (1992b: 247). Different languages are like fragments of a whole and we see how they fit together when translating, allowing us to understand the 'true' or 'pure' language (T, p. 59) as a possible agent of redemption. The pure language has a less instrumental character than individual languages (T, p. 62); like pure art, it belongs to itself (1992a: 28).

The view that language is essentially non-instrumental foreshadows Chomsky's writing on linguistics. There is no evidence that Chomsky read Benjamin, and he would be unlikely to be sympathetic to the mystic element in Benjamin, just as Brecht was not referring to it as 'a load of mysticism' and 'abominable' (Brecht 1993: 10).

But the spiritual essence of language, the pure language, is not to be understood merely in linguistic terms; Benjamin does not mean something historically prior to contemporary languages, such as the Proto-Indo-European discussed by Franz Bopp (1816), nor does he mean the sort of Universal Grammar first mooted by the Port-Royal Grammarians in 1660 (Crystal 1998: 84) and taken up by linguists since, to be made precise by Chomsky as a set of innate linguistic principles (see e.g. 1986). Benjamin instead links the essence of pure language with language before the fall (L, pp. 44–5), as spoken by God as a means of creation. In human language, we have now lost the close connection of the name to the thing but sense it again in translation, because translation reveals not meaning but those original connections.

The pure language will emerge from individual languages as they grow towards 'the Messianic end of their history' (T, p. 56) – that is, towards *tikkun*. And, as later in *The Arcades Project* (Benjamin 1999), it is the pure language that counteracts the bourgeois view of language as instrument (L, p. 30).

Just as, in his dissertation on German Romanticism, written a few years before 'The Task of the Translator', Benjamin develops the idea that criticism helps us see individual works in relation to a whole (Eiland and Jennings 2014: 112), here he says that translation helps us see individual languages in relation to a whole, the pure language (T, p. 62). The task of the translator is no less than to assist in this process of eventual linguistic (and therefore spiritual, since the origin of language is divine) redemption (T, p. 59).

Assembling fragments that might be connected into a whole also characterises Benjamin's method of writing. This can be seen particularly in *The Arcades Project* (Benjamin 1999), where we also see a development of another idea from 'The Task of the Translator': the word is an 'arcade' (T, p. 61) that allows us passage, in translating, through the barrier of syntax to the pure language. In *The Arcades Project*, he describes the arcade as that in which the horizontal passage always draws the eye heavenwards (1999: 160).

4. Translation arises from a quality of 'translatability' in the text

Because translation, like language, and like poetry, is not instrumental, it is not simply aimed at new readers (T, p. 50), but instead it taps into a quality in the text itself, its 'translatability' (T, p. 51). Translation is inherent in a text, as is criticism; he had explained the latter point in his 1919 dissertation, and he did so again in 1930 in 'Die Aufgabe des Kritikers' [The Task of the Critic, Benjamin 1985: 171–85]. Translation is particularly inherent in texts that do not convey information in a straightforward way (T, p. 63). By translating we bring out the latent translatability of the text – its ability to transcend language boundaries and history, and to live on (T, p. 52). The distinction between translation and translatability is crucial for Benjamin, as is the distinction between communication and communicability. The first term in each case expresses a material and instrumental instantiation of a metaphysical essence, which the second expresses, but which is *not* derived from the first. Translatability is an essentially God-given quality of the text (L, p. 42). But the real essence (and translatability) of the text, Benjamin implies, resides in the part that cannot easily be translated, because it shows us the foreignness of texts to one another and thus points to the possibility of reconciliation of that foreignness (T, p. 57); this is most clearly illustrated in the sacred text, with a non-syntactic interlinear gloss.

5. Translation is a stage in the development of a text that allows it to live on

In Benjamin's non-instrumental view, history is not just a way of organising events chronologically for our own purposes. The present moment must be seen in relation to, not merely in chronological sequence with, its past and its future. And the present in which we live is, for the past, the future (1992a: 143).

However, the continuity is not linear: moments in cultural history can only be understood in relation to past moments, not because they developed out of them, but because related ideas, which may have been forgotten in the meantime, are present in both historical periods. Benjamin describes the German *Trauerspiel* in *Ursprung des deutschen Trauerspiels* [Origin of German Mourning Play, Benjamin 1993] in this way, and also the Parisian Arcades in *The Arcades Project* (Benjamin 1999).

Through translation, a literary work, like a language, grows and changes over time; thus there is little point in the translator trying to mimic the original work (T, p. 54). Benjamin praises Goethe and Hölderlin for allowing translation to be a means for effecting change in the target language (T, pp. 63–4). Etymological (i.e. linear) change alone, however, is not sufficient to express the relations of languages to one another (T, p. 55), because they are also related by what they mean, or aim to mean (T, p. 55).

6. Translation is not based on equivalence

Translation that strives for equivalence with the original text is not possible (T, p. 54). On the contrary, translation is a 'continuum of changes' by which a second language expresses what a first has said (L, p. 42). This idea appears to be linked, for Benjamin, to the reassembling of the fragments of the broken vessel (T, p. 60). Fragments need to fit together, something they could not do if they resembled one another; translation (like *tikkun*) only works if they are *not* similar.

7. There are good and bad ways of translating

Benjamin is more concerned with what translation *is* rather than with evaluating it. But a poor translation is a poor example of what it is. Two things characterise a poor translation: (i) it conveys the message of the original (T, p. 50); and (ii) it does this inexactly, because it does not convey what is essential – that is, the poetic (T, p. 50). We need to consider each point in turn.

i Texts, like language itself, like history and like translation, are not simply instrumental: they are not merely 'about' something. But a poor translation tries to be faithful to meaning (T, p. 60). Yet poetic meaning in particular is not *what* words mean, but how what they mean is tied to *how* they mean. That is, poetic meaning lies in the link between meaning and style (not, I think, as Harry Zohn translates it, that it 'derives from the connotations conveyed by the word chosen to express it', Benjamin 1992b: 78). There is thus little point in trying merely to achieve equivalence with the source text, since it is in the nature of texts to change (T, p. 54). We should instead look at the way words represent what they refer to and consider how that relationship differs in the original and the translation. The image of the dissimilar fragments of a vessel thus has a practical consequence: trying to achieve equivalence of meaning will result in poor translations.
ii To avoid conveying what is inessential, the translator must find the 'intention towards the language translated into that allows the echo of the original to be awakened in it' (T, p. 58). 'Intention' should here be understood as 'directedness of consciousness toward' (Szondi 1992: 167). The translator, therefore, *muß dichten* (must write poetry, T, p. 50). A good translation will find a style that allows the translated text to carry an echo of the original; it will be a foreignising translation in today's terms (see e.g. Venuti 2013: 2). Foreignising translation also makes sense because it allows the target language to change under the influence of the source language, and, as we have seen, it is in the nature of languages to change (T, p. 63). A good translation evokes a sense of *Sprachergänzung* (linguistic complementation); complementation was crucial for Benjamin, also in human relationships (Eiland and Jennings 2014: 357; Sauter 2015).

5.4 Current contributions and research

Though Benjamin's work was, in his lifetime, often rejected as incomprehensible (Scholem 1981: 157), he has come to be regarded since his death as one of the most important philosophical critics of modern times, and yet some do find his work difficult. David Bellos declares himself 'baffled' (Bellos 2010: 194) and is clearly unable to understand the essay at all. And Willis Barnstone, though very sympathetic to Benjamin, calls it 'puzzling' that he compares translation to fragments of a broken vessel, saying the fragments need not match yet gives 'the gloss that insists on the correspondence of even the smallest linguistic units' as the true model for 'salvational translation' (1993: 237).

However, Benjamin's pronouncements do not appear puzzling if we realise that he was not talking about translation per se. In 'Curriculum Vitae', written in 1925, he calls 'The Task of the Translator' a 'preface on the theory of language' (Benjamin 1996: 423): the task of the translator is not merely to translate but to show us how to understand language. And in fact Benjamin does not compare translation to fragments of a broken vessel, as Barnstone assumes (1993: 237), but to a process of putting those fragments back together. And he does not even compare it, for translation is not a metaphor for *tikkun*; it is a process that allows us to glimpse what *tikkun* might be. Of course the fragments must *not* match, or they could not fit together. An exact gloss of a phrase in language A, given in language B, points exactly to the *non*-equivalence of A and B.

Many other scholars, for example Eagleton (1981), Witte (1985), Steiner (1985: 344–5), and Niranjana (1992: 110–62), have written about Benjamin's work. He has influenced art critics (Berger 1972), Jewish scholars (Alter 1991) and Holocaust scholars (Glowacka 2012), and he has been interpreted and commented on from different perspectives, such as philosophy (Benjamin and Osborne 1994) or theology (Plate 2005).

I shall here limit my discussion of current work on or influenced by Benjamin to the area of Translation Studies. We can distinguish theoretical engagement with his work from possible consequences for the practice of translation. The latter aspect will be considered in Section 5. Relevant theoretical engagement with his work, which I shall consider in this section, is of two types: on the one hand, there is engagement with Benjamin's work within Literary Studies, which provides a context for work in Translation Studies, and, on the other, there are discussions within Translation Studies itself.

As an example of the first case consider Attridge (2004). Attridge speaks of translation as a response to a text, just like criticism (2004: 75), echoing Benjamin's 'The Task of the Critic' and 'The Task of the Translator'. Attridge, like Benjamin, sees both criticism and translation as part of a work's afterlife, thus suggesting the need to treat translations as part of the remit of Literary Studies rather than as a separate subject area.

The second type of critical engagement, that within Translation Studies itself, is concerned with what Benjamin's views suggest for translation theory. Besides pointing to the non-equivalence of languages, they might suggest that a translation, if done with due regard for the way language is used in the original, will be written in a new language: the language of a translated text is different from the language of non-translated texts.

Translation scholar Clive Scott subscribes to Benjamin's view of translation as a 'co-operative enterprise' between the source and target languages (2012: 179). However, he says that Benjamin's view of translation 'restores too great a prominence... to the metalinguistic' and involves the 'sacrifice of spontaneity' in measuring 'the appropriate equivalence' (Scott 2000: 79). While it is true that Benjamin sees translation as something that looks beyond the task at hand, it is not at all clear that this involves a loss of spontaneity, and we have seen already that Benjamin specifically stresses *non*-equivalence. His Baudelaire translations capture register, rhythm, rhyme but are in no sense slavishly close to the originals, nor can they be said to lack spontaneity (Benjamin 2013). Indeed Scholem, himself a translator, on hearing Benjamin read his translations aloud, took them for the work of poet Stefan George (Eiland and Jennings 2014: 194). Given that Benjamin was not primarily a poet, and George's versions of Baudelaire were hugely successful, this suggests the quality of Benjamin's work.

Another recent scholar, Dorota Glowacka, focuses on 'The Task of the Translator' in her work on Holocaust testimony, *Disappearing Traces* (2012). Emphasising the link between theology and linguistics in Benjamin's essay, she points out that translation brings out the 'higher kinship' (2012: 92) of languages and reinterprets this as responding to an inherent 'demand' in the text itself that it 'remain unforgotten' (2012: 93). Quoting Jacobs (1975: 756), she says that translation makes our own language foreign to us, by showing it in comparison to another (Glowacka 2012: 232, note 38). For Glowacka, this is 'an injunction to a national language to be deeply self-reflective about what it has excluded, and to confront its investments and assumptions' (2012: 93).

5.5 Consequences for practice

There are two types of consequence for translation practice that we might derive from reading Benjamin's works. The first is based on a recognition of his possible influence on the text to be translated, and the second on a recognition that his thinking might affect our view of the process of translation and thus lead us to translate differently.

In the first case, it is important to be aware that, though Benjamin's work was available in English translation only from the late 1960s, it influenced German writers much earlier. When translating from German we must consider that influence. Because Benjamin's influence on Brecht was significant, it is not possible to translate Brecht's plays or poems, or the work of later writers who were responding to Brecht (e.g. Volker von Törne; see also Leeder 2006), without considering Benjamin. Though von Törne specifically alludes to Brecht (e.g. 'Ballade für bb', von Törne 1981: 70), it is Benjamin's linking of the destructive breaking of the vessels and the redemptive reassembling of *tikkun* with political revolution that is echoed in much of von Törne's work, where Biblical imagery of flood and fire and destruction is juxtaposed with the need to overthrow bourgeois society, as in the poem 'Erinnerung an die Zukunft' [Memorial to the Future, von Törne 1981: 75–80].

Even more obvious is Benjamin's influence on Paul Celan. Much of Celan's imagery – of destruction, fragmentation, piles of rubble – shows the influence of Benjamin, whose work he read in 1959 (Felstiner 1995: 96) but had certainly come across earlier: 'Totenhemd' [Winding Sheet], published in 1952, echoes Benjamin's 'Metaphysics of Youth' (Benjamin 1991: 91–104) very closely. The poem 'Weggebeizt' [Cauterised] is almost impossible to understand without realising that many of its expressions, such as 'das bunte Gerede des An-/erlebten' (the colourful talk of secondary experience), are influenced by Benjamin's concern with the words themselves, their direct relation to things and the *Geschwätz* that overlays them (L, p. 44) and obscures both that relation and the essential nature of language (Felstiner 1995: 144–5). Celan's frequent multilingual wordplay recalls Benjamin's view that the essential nature of language is revealed particularly when languages come up against one another (T, p. 56). Consider Celan's use of '*Neige*' (decline), followed by '*Schnee*' (snow), which is *neige* in French, in 'Bei Wein und Verlorenheit' [With Wine and Lostness, Celan 1980: 15]. And, just as Benjamin said that etymology alone did not explain the connection between languages (T, p. 55), Celan's poetics uses not only real etymologies, such as that between German *Trümmer* (rubble) and English 'drum' in 'Totenhemd' [Celan 1952: 51], but also apparent but not actual etymologies and connections of sound, for example between *Trommel* (drum) and *Trümmer*. Poetic connections of sound similarity, or connections with absent but implied words, often take the place of actual etymological connections (Boase-Beier 2015: 109–12).

John Felstiner, Celan's translator, is aware of Benjamin's influence on Celan's work, and thus illustrates this first way of considering the implications of Benjamin's philosophy for practice. But Felstiner also shows what the second type of influence might mean: an influence on translation practice itself. George Steiner, writing in the *Times Literary Supplement*, and quoted on the front of Felstiner's 1995 book, calls it 'the first approach to the Celan-world so far available'. In this Felstiner is emulating Benjamin: he uses translation not merely as a means to make Celan's work available to English readers but to do something more profound: to enter Celan's world by considering the questions of language and its relation to thought in his poems. Though Felstiner shrugs off the 'grandiose expectations for a secondary act and art' with which he thinks Benjamin invested translation (Felstiner 1995: 91), nevertheless he is clear that, in approaching Celan's work in a Benjaminian spirit, 'the translator enters its evolution' (ibid.). And in an image taken from Benjamin's view of history (H, p. 146), he says that each line, 'reflecting backward to its origin', is moving into the future (ibid.). In practice, this way of translating allows Felstiner to use, for example, the actual words 'der Tod ist ein Meister aus Deutschland' [Death is a Master from Germany] in 'Todesfuge' [Deathfugue, Felstiner 2001: 30–3] in order to show, by questioning the German in its use of the word *Meister*, that we must question our own use of its cognate 'master'. That is, rather than give us an equivalent in English, Felstiner encourages us to question both the German word and its easy translatability into English.

Benjamin's emphasis on the non-instrumentality of language thus leads the translator away from its meaning-conveying function and towards the materiality of the stylistic detail of the text (Boase-Beier 2015: 125–6). His view that translation lies at the heart of language, that it shows us how language works, and indeed how thought works, is of course not new. Benjamin took it from earlier philosophers such as Hamann, and it has been taken up by later philosophers, such as Midgley (2014: 48). But its consequences for translation itself are different. Here this view suggests that translation is not what happens between a monolingual source text and a target but between one text in which translation already inheres and another. So the translator already looks for the relation between source-language and target-language words in the original poem. For example, when I read 'Totenhemd' prior to translating it, the relationships between *weben* (to weave), *wecken* (to wake) and *wehen* (to drift or blow) and words connected to them by etymology, sound or meaning in English (though of course not actually present in the text), such as 'weave', 'weft', 'wake' and 'waft', were striking. It was these relationships within the original poem that led to my decision to translate *wehen* as 'waft' rather than the more obvious equivalent 'blow' (used, for example, by Hamburger, 2007: 77). The decision was a direct result of considering the source text not simply as German but as in essence both multilingual and inherently embodying translation.

Benjamin's notion of the 'afterlife' of the text also has practical consequences. If translation is what allows a further, natural stage in the growth of a text, then translation is not an approximation or a loss, or second-best, but rather an essential stage of the text's development. As I argue elsewhere (Boase-Beier 2015), this suggests translation should be clearly marked as such and contextualised so that readers knowingly engage with the translation and what it means that the text has been translated.

5.6 Future directions

In considering how Benjamin's philosophy could influence our thinking on translation in the future, we need to consider it as part of a historical development. Because 'The Task of the Translator' is so often anthologised, it has become part of the current discourse on translation (see e.g. Venuti 2012: 71–2). But there is little understanding of Benjamin's work on translation in its philosophical, theological, linguistic, political and historical context. Such a study would allow a fuller discussion of Benjamin's ideas from the point of view of current debates in Translation Studies.

Using Benjamin as an example, we might also revisit those other much anthologised figures in Translation Studies, such as Schleiermacher, Nietzsche, Jakobson, Steiner and

Derrida. If each were seen in the context in which they were writing, against the background of thought to which they were responding, and through subsequent developments of their thought within their own and other fields, it would be possible to draw more interesting consequences for both translation theory and translation practice.

But possibly the most important work to be done in the future is a thorough study of Benjamin as translator. By considering his exceptional translations of Baudelaire (Benjamin 2013) in the light of his remarks written at the same time, and by comparing them with other translations (such as Roy Campbell's, published 1952, or Jan Owen's, published 2015), we will perhaps obtain greater insight into how he himself thought his philosophy related to the practice of translation.

Note

1 Abbreviations for works by Benjamin cited in this chapter are as follows: T: 'The Task of the Translator'; L: 'On Language *per se* and on the Language of Human Beings'; H: 'On the Concept of History'. Pages refer to the German originals in Benjamin (1992a), *Sprache und Geschichte: Philosophische Essays*, Stuttgart: Reclam. Translations are mine unless otherwise stated.

Related topics

Schleiermacher; Derrida; culture; meaning; mysticism, esotericism and translation.

Further reading

Eiland, H. and Jennings, M. (2014), *Walter Benjamin: A Critical Life*. Cambridge, MA: Harvard University Press. (An extremely detailed study of Benjamin's life, relationships, influences and the way his various works came into being.)

Scholem, G. (1981), *Walter Benjamin: The Story of a Friendship*, trans. H. Zohn. New York: New York Review Books. (An engaging account of the friendship between Scholem and Benjamin, which gives fascinating insight into Scholem's view of the development of Benjamin's ideas.)

Eagleton, T. (1981), *Walter Benjamin, or Towards a Revolutionary Criticism*. London: Verso. (A careful, detailed, and thorough study of Benjamin as a Marxist thinker.)

Benjamin, A. and Osborne, P. (1994), *Walter Benjamin's Philosophy: Destruction and Experience*. London and New York: Routledge. (A collection of critical engagements with Benjamin's philosophy.)

Wizisla, E. (2009), *Walter Benjamin and Bertolt Brecht: The Story of a Friendship*, trans. C. Shuttleworth. London: Libris. (A study that provides important background to the relationship between Brecht and Benjamin.)

References

Adorno, T., Benjamin, W., Bloch, E., Brecht, B., Lukács, G. (2007), *Aesthetics and Politics*. London: Verso.

Alter, R. (1991), *Defenses of the Imagination: Jewish Writers and Modern Historical Crisis*. Philadelphia: The Jewish Publication Society of America.

Attridge, D. (2004), *The Singularity of Literature*. London and New York: Routledge.

Barnstone, W. (1993), *The Poetics of Translation: History, Theory, Practice*. New Haven, CT and London: Yale University Press.

Baudelaire, C. (2015), *Les fleurs du mal*. Mont-Royal: Éditions Alliage.

Bellos, D. (2010), 'Halting Walter', *Cambridge Literary Review*, 3: 194–206.

Benjamin, A. and Osborne, P. (1994) *Walter Benjamin's Philosophy: Destruction and Experience*. London and New York: Routledge.
Benjamin, W. (1965), *Zur Kritik der Gewalt und andere Aufsätze*. Frankfurt am Main: Suhrkamp.
Benjamin, W. (1985), *Gesammelte Schriften, Vol. 6*, ed. R. Tiedemann and H. Schweppenhäuser. Frankfurt am Main: Suhrkamp.
Benjamin, W. (1991), *Gesammelte Schriften, Vol. 2*, ed. R. Tiedemann and H. Schweppenhäuser. Frankfurt am Main: Suhrkamp.
Benjamin, W. (1992a), *Sprache und Geschichte: Philosophische Essays*. Stuttgart: Reclam.
Benjamin, W. (1992b), *Illuminations*, ed. H. Arendt, trans. H. Zohn. London: Fontana Press.
Benjamin, W. (1993), *Ursprung des deutschen Trauerspiels*. Frankfurt am Main: Suhrkamp.
Benjamin, W. (1996), *Selected Writings. Vol. 1, 1913–1926*, ed. M. Jennings. Cambridge, MA: The Belknap Press.
Benjamin, W. (1999), *The Arcades Project*, trans. H. Eiland and K. McLaughlin. Cambridge, MA: The Belknap Press.
Benjamin, W. (2010), *Berliner Kindheit um 1900*. Frankfurt am Main: Suhrkamp.
Benjamin, W. (2013), *Baudelaire Übertragungen*. n.p.: Edition Mabila.
Berger, J. (1972), *Ways of Seeing*. London: BBC/Penguin.
Birman, C. (2006), *The Narrow Foothold*. London: Hearing Eye.
Bloch, E. (1973), *Geist der Utopie*. Frankfurt am Main: Suhrkamp.
Boase-Beier, J. (2015), *Translating the Poetry of the Holocaust: Translation, Style and the Reader*. London: Bloomsbury.
Bopp, F. (1816), *Über das Conjugationssystem der Sanskritsprache*. Frankfurt am Main: Andreäische Buchhandlung.
Brecht, B. (1993), *Journals*, ed. J. Willett, trans. H. Rorrison. London: Methuen.
Brecht, B. (2015), *Brecht on Theatre*, ed. M. Silberman, S. Giles and T. Kuhn. London: Bloomsbury.
Campbell, R. (trans.) (1952), *Poems of Baudelaire*. New York: Pantheon Books.
Celan, P. (1952), *Mohn und Gedächtnis*. Stuttgart: Deutsche Verlags-Anstalt.
Celan, P. (1980), *Die Niemandsrose; Sprachgitter: Gedichte*. Frankfurt am Main: Fischer.
Celan, P. (1982), *Atemwende*. Frankfurt am Main: Suhrkamp.
Chomsky, N. (1986), *Knowledge of Language*. New York: Greenwood Press.
Crystal, D. (1998), *The Cambridge Encyclopedia of Language* (2nd edn.). Cambridge: Cambridge University Press.
Eagleton, T. (1981), *Walter Benjamin, or Towards a Revolutionary Criticism*. London: Verso.
Eiland, H. and Jennings, M. (2014), *Walter Benjamin: A Critical Life*. Cambridge, MA: Harvard University Press.
Felstiner, J. (1995), *Paul Celan: Poet, Survivor, Jew*. New Haven, CT: Yale University Press.
Felstiner, J. (trans.) (2001), *Paul Celan: Selected Poems and Prose*. New York and London: W.W. Norton.
Glowacka, D. (2012), *Disappearing Traces: Holocaust Testimonials, Ethics, and Aesthetics*. Seattle, WA: University of Washington Press.
Hamburger, M. (trans.) (2007), *Poems of Paul Celan*. London: Anvil.
Jacobs, C. (1975), 'The Monstrosity of Translation', *MLN* 90: 755–66.
Jakobson, R. (2012), 'On Linguistic Aspects of Translation', in L. Venuti, ed. *The Translation Studies Reader* (3rd edn.). London and New York: Routledge, pp. 125–31.
Kierkegaard, S. (2010), *The Present Age/On the Death of Rebellion*, trans. A. Dru. New York, NY: HarperCollins.
Leeder, K. (trans. and ed.) (2006), *After Brecht: A Celebration*. Manchester: Carcanet.
Marx, K. (1961), *Das Kapital*. Berlin: Dietz.
Menninghaus, W. (1980), *Walter Benjamins Theorie der Sprachmagie*. Frankfurt am Main: Suhrkamp.
Midgley, M. (2014), 'I am More than the Sum of My Parts', *Times Higher Education*, 3 April: 47–9.
Niranjana, T. (1992), *Siting Translation: History, Post-Structuralism, and the Colonial Context*. Berkeley, CA: University of California Press.

Owen, J. (trans.) (2015), *Charles Baudelaire: Selected Poems from Les Fleurs du Mal*. Todmorden: Arc Publications.

Plate, S. (2005), *Walter Benjamin, Religion, and Aesthetics: Rethinking Religion Through the Arts*. London and New York: Routledge.

Saussure, F. de (1916), *Cours de linguistique générale*, ed. C. Bally and A. Sechehaye. Lausanne: Payot.

Sauter, C. (2015), 'Hebrew, Jewishness, and Love: Translation in Gershom Scholem's Early Work', *Naharaim* 9 (1–2): 151–78.

Scholem, G. (1981), *Walter Benjamin: The Story of a Friendship*, trans. H. Zohn. New York: New York Review Books.

Scholem, G. (1995), *Major Trends in Jewish Mysticism*. New York: Schocken Books.

Scholem, G. (1996), *On the Kabbalah and Its Symbolism*, trans. R. Manheim. New York: Schocken Books.

Scott, C. (2000), *Translating Baudelaire*. Exeter: University of Exeter Press.

Scott, C. (2012), *Translation and the Perception of Text: Literary Translation and Phenomenology*. London: MHRA/Maney.

Smith, R. (1960), *J.G. Hamann 1730–1788: A Study in Christian Existence*. London: Collins.

Steiner, G. (1985), *Language and Silence: Essays 1958–1966*. London: Faber and Faber.

Szondi, P. (1992), 'The Poetry of Constancy: Paul Celan's Translation of Shakespeare's Sonnet 105', trans. H. Mendelsohn, in R. Schulte and J. Biguenet, eds., *Theories of Translation: An Anthology of Essays from Dryden to Derrida*. Chicago: University of Chicago Press, pp. 163–85.

Tiedemann, R. (1992), 'Zur vorliegenden Auswahl', in W. Benjamin, ed., *Sprache und Geschichte: Philosophische Essays*. Stuttgart: Reclam, pp. 173–75.

von Törne, V. (1981), *Im Lande Vogelfrei: Gesammelte Gedichte*. Berlin: Wagenbach.

Venuti, L. (ed.) (2012), *The Translation Studies Reader* (3rd edn.). London and New York: Routledge.

Venuti, L. (2013), *Translation Changes Everything: Theory and Practice*. London and New York: Routledge.

Weiler, G. (1970), *Mauthner's Critique of Language*. Cambridge: Cambridge University Press.

Witte, B. (1985), *Walter Benjamin*. Reinbek: Rowohlt.

6
Gadamer and Ricoeur

Lisa Foran

Introduction

Hans-Georg Gadamer (1900–2002) and Paul Ricoeur (1913–2005) are in many senses the founders of what is known as philosophical hermeneutics. Both thinkers engage with a particularly pragmatic reading of the ancient philosophers Plato and Aristotle, notably the idea of philosophy as practice. Both also combine the work of phenomenologists such as Edmund Husserl and Martin Heidegger with a broader tradition of textual exegesis found in the work of Romantic philosophers such as Wilhelm Dilthey and Friedrich Schleiermacher. Of particular note is the account of human existence offered by Martin Heidegger in his seminal 1927 text *Being and Time*, itself indebted to a combination of hermeneutics and phenomenological method. For both Gadamer and Ricoeur, what distinguishes human existence is the manner in which it is always directed towards meaning. The task of philosophy is to uncover the structures or mechanisms by which meaning is established and created. Evidently, the question of translation holds particular importance in each of their works. Translation arises in Gadamer's works primarily as an example or illustration of a particular hermeneutic point; it is in some sense a specific or extreme case of interpretation in general. However, for Ricoeur, translation is a more explicit topic in and of itself and acts as a broader paradigm which offers insight into our social and political situation.

Gadamer: historical perspectives

Gadamer was born in Marburg, Germany in 1900. He initially read German literature at Breslau but returned to Marburg, where in 1922 he completed his doctoral dissertation on pleasure in Plato under the supervision of Paul Natorp. Natorp was part of a school of thought known as Neo-Kantianism, which saw philosophy primarily as an epistemological enterprise which should provide the conditions of the possibility of (scientific) knowledge. This transcendental focus was reflected in Natorp's readings of Plato and Aristotle, which, unlike traditional readings of these thinkers, emphasised their similarities rather than their differences. This approach was later mirrored in Gadamer's own reading of Platonic and Aristotelian thought (see in particular Gadamer [1978] 1986, [1931] 1991). Natorp was also influential in the emerging school of phenomenology founded by Edmund Husserl at the turn of the century (Luft 2009). In 1923 he sent Gadamer an unpublished manuscript on Aristotle by Martin Heidegger, a student of Husserl and soon to be appointed as a lecturer at Marburg University. The manuscript had a profound effect on Gadamer, who felt he had found in Heidegger what he had been looking for in philosophy all along. Gadamer attended Heidegger's lectures at Marburg and completed his *Habilitation* under the supervision of Heidegger and Paul Friedlander in 1927. This was subsequently published as *Plato's Dialectical Ethics* in 1931 (Gadamer [1931] 1991).

While certainly not an explicit supporter of Hitler, during the 1930s and throughout the war years Gadamer was somewhat apolitical and compliant with the Nazi regime. Jean Grondin sees Gadamer's compliance during this period as an imposed silence and credits Gadamer for maintaining what distance he could (Grondin [1999] 2003: 10; see also Grondin [1999] 2011). Certainly, Gadamer distanced himself from Heidegger during this period at least in part because of the latter's involvement with Nazism (Gadamer [1988] 1989). He also, however, admits that this period was not a 'noble' one for him but that his silence and even compliance with the regime was motivated by the desire to protect his family. Philosophically, his focus during this time was on Plato, and he delivered lectures such as 'Plato and the Poets' (1934) and 'Plato and State Education' (1942), the latter of which can be read as a subtle critique of the Third Reich. In 1939 he became professor of philosophy at Leipzig, where he was almost solely responsible for the philosophy curriculum. He was appointed as rector of Leipzig University after the war in 1945. He briefly moved to Frankfurt in 1947, where Theodore Adorno and Max Horkheimer were working after their return from the US. In 1949 Gadamer took over Karl Jaspers' chair at Heidelberg and remained there until his retirement.

It was not until 1960, however, that Gadamer published his first major work and one that propelled him into the international scene. *Wahrheit und Methode*, translated as *Truth and Method*, remains Gadamer's most important and systematic work. After his official retirement from Heidelberg in 1968, Gadamer became visiting professor at a number of universities in North America and Europe. Throughout his career he engaged in dialogue with many of his contemporary thinkers, most notably Jürgen Habermas and Jacques Derrida. Although these dialogues did not reach any real conclusions or agreement as such, they testify to Gadamer's hope that dialogue can produce new understanding. Gadamer died in Heidelberg in March 2002.

Gadamer: critical issues and topics

For Gadamer, human existence is one of understanding, and the medium of understanding is language (Gadamer [1960] 2004). While defining man in terms of linguistic capability has a long philosophical tradition, Gadamer's account of language is closer to Heidegger than Aristotle. For Gadamer, the crucial point about language is that it *precedes* us. We are born into a language that exists before us and that contains a certain understanding of the world – a history or a tradition. We understand the world around us through tradition and this is deposited in language. Language is not, as it was for Aristotle, the mere translation of internal thoughts into external expressions (Aristotle 1962: 115). Rather, all thought for Gadamer is made possible by the fact of language. This of course can, and indeed has, led to charges of linguistic relativism and linguistic idealism. But we should tread carefully here. Gadamer does not claim that there is only understanding *in* language but rather that understanding is what it is and the way it is *because of* language. That is, the *kind* of understanding we have, which is the only understanding there is, is always inflected by the fact of language.

Even when we look at an artwork, an experience we might think of as totally separate to language, Gadamer claims that because we *could* discuss this experience in language (even inadequately), we have the experience that we do (Gadamer [1960] 2004: 399). When discussing the artist as painter or composer who may well claim that their work cannot be adequately dressed in words, Gadamer claims that this failure of language itself reveals that another linguistic description is possible. As Jean Grondin sums it up: 'The failure of words can only be measured by what they fail to say. The limits of language thus confirm – and very eloquently – the universality of language' (Grondin 2002: 42). It is not that all experience must be reduced to a propositional statement but rather that the linguistic element (*Sprachlichkeit*) in which we live colours all of our experiences. We are linguistic beings because we are hermeneutic beings: that is, beings whose existence is defined by the search for meaning.

Language is never a neutral medium of understanding; because it is historical and cultural, it reflects historical and cultural prejudices. However, it is here in the account of prejudice that we find Gadamer's distinction from Romantic hermeneutics. For Dilthey, following Schleiermacher, hermeneutics was envisaged as a method, or *Kunstlehre*, for the Human Sciences (Dilthey 1989, in particular 53–79, 431–41). The aim of hermeneutics was to interpret a text without prejudice and to understand it better than the author herself. In *Truth and Method*, Gadamer's target is the very idea of method itself, which, from the hermeneutic method of Dilthey to the phenomenological method of Husserl, sees meaning as something which is there (in the text or in the world) to be discovered and which can be discovered as some neutral thing without context. In contrast, Gadamer claims meaning is something produced or created through play. If we take the fact of our situation seriously, we must acknowledge not only the positivity but the very necessity of prejudice. When I approach something which I want to understand, I do so from a particular context and with particular interests in mind. It is my interest in something that motivates my desire to understand it. This interest and the context from where I begin – linguistic, historical, cultural and so on – constitute my prejudices, which give me a path towards what is to be understood.

It may seem, then, that Gadamer advocates a subjectivism of sorts, but he protests strongly to the contrary. Prejudice or prejudgements (*Vorurteil*) are what open up the matter to be understood. This was something already apparent in Heidegger's account of understanding and what is known as the hermeneutic circle in *Being and Time*. For Heidegger, our understanding is made up of a tripartite structure of *Vorhabe*, *Vorsicht* and *Vorgriff*: fore-having, foreseeing and fore-conception. In other words, when we try to understand something we have already a vague or yet to be worked-out grasp of what the thing is and some idea of how our understanding will proceed and possibly terminate. For example, if I am a translator trying to understand a foreign text, I already understand – at the very least – that it is a text, probably what kind of text it is, and I have some vague impression regarding how my interpretation will finish. From this background fore-structure of understanding I proceed in interpretation, at the end of which I may find my preconceptions were misplaced or indeed entirely wrong. I can thus modify them accordingly, and perhaps these revised impressions will later form part of a set of preconceptions or fore-structure I have when approaching a similar text or a text by the same author. For Heidegger, then, background understanding (*Verstehen*) is our starting point, and this is worked out or developed in interpretation (*Auslegung*). Interpretation and understanding feed into each other, forming the hermeneutic circle. As we begin understanding (albeit vaguely) what we want to understand or interpret it may seem like this is a vicious circle, but for Heidegger the hermeneutic circle is positive; it is where we always already dwell and through which meaning, in its broadest sense, is refined

(Heidegger [1927] 2009: 190–2; Gadamer [1960] 2004: 267–73). The hermeneutic circle for Heidegger concerns the very nature of our existence; it describes our way of understanding everything we encounter and is not restricted to linguistic exegesis. In *Truth and Method* Gadamer takes up Heidegger's account of understanding but modifies it, returning it to something closer to the account found in Dilthey and Romantic hermeneutics more generally, specifically in terms of the hermeneutic circle (Grondin 2002).

For Gadamer, in contrast to Heidegger and in keeping with his Romantic predecessors, the hermeneutic circle is the play between whole and parts. This subtle distinction between the two thinkers is down to a difference in what they see as the *object* of hermeneutics. For Heidegger, the hermeneutic nature of existence has at its core the basic human understanding of being itself. Each time I understand something – a text, a room I walk into, a political situation – I fundamentally grasp that it *is*. Heidegger's concern, then, with hermeneutics is to work out what this 'that it is' or 'Being' is. Gadamer, when discussing the hermeneutic circle, is more concerned with understanding a text or a dialogue. Thus the circle for Gadamer is made up of understanding the parts in light of the whole and vice versa. For example, if as a translator I approach a textbook to be translated, I begin with a certain anticipation of what the textbook is; at the very least I know it is a textbook and most likely what kind of textbook. I will thus have an anticipation of how my translation will proceed. This anticipation – combined with various other factors – will constitute my prejudice (*Vorurteil*). In translating the text I work through parts (maybe chapters or paragraphs) and in so doing my prejudices or anticipated understandings become confirmed, rejected or simply modified. Thus translating parts of the text modify my anticipation of the whole text. Eventually, when the translation is complete, the parts are integrated into the whole. This to-ing and fro-ing between parts and whole in my understanding constitutes the hermeneutic circle for Gadamer ([1960] 2004: 267).

In discussing translation explicitly Gadamer refers to two different situations: the first is that of a dialogue with an interpreter as third party, and the second is that of a translator approaching a written text ([1960] 2004: 385–90). For Gadamer, in a conversation the aim is not to come to an understanding of the other person but rather to come to an understanding of the subject matter itself. When you are telling me about your bike breaking on the way to work, we are reaching an agreement (or understanding) about the broken bike and the circumstances of your journey, not what kind of person you are. Understanding is always a situated event; I understand things through the situation I am in, including the language I speak, the culture I inherit, the time period I live through and so on. These things make up my horizon of understanding. The ordinary meaning of horizon is the line that marks out the field of what we can see; it is where sky meets earth. We can see everything (with more or less clarity) up to that line but not beyond it. In phenomenology horizon denotes a similar field of possible experience but applies to all experiences not just visual ones. For Husserl, when we are thinking about something (or remembering, or talking about it) we are directed towards it as an object. This object of thought has 'predelineated potentialities': horizons that mean there is a field of possible ways of thinking about or experiencing it (Husserl [1931] 1995: 45). Taking up this idea of horizon in terms of understanding, Gadamer describes a 'fusion of horizons' as that which ideally happens in conversation with another person. My situation and perspective on the world that allow me to understand it confronts your situation and perspective. Through conversation our perspectives are opened up to each other, fusing together and enlarging both our horizons. When you are telling me about your broken bike, my horizon of understanding becomes fused with yours and we are together directed towards the thing itself (the broken bike). In this Gadamer comes close to Heidegger's account of assertion in *Being and Time*. When I tell you something – 'my bike is broken', for example – we are together towards the object I speak about (i.e. the bike). However, for Heidegger what is crucial in this is that we share a way of being (here, of being-towards the broken bike); what I am talking about or the subject matter is of secondary concern (Heidegger [1927] 2009: 197–9). In contrast, for Gadamer what we share is not the understanding of a particular way of being but rather the play of language through which meaning, as the understanding of the subject matter, emerges. In this ordinary conversational situation language is the medium through which understanding takes place. Such conversation is in fact only possible for Gadamer when 'the two speakers speak the same language' ([1960] 2004: 387). A conversation in two different languages disrupts understanding, and in this disruption we can see what normally has to be in place for understanding to happen. In other words, the disruption of understanding reveals the conditions of ordinary understanding. Taking a situation of breakdown to establish 'normal' conditions of a given experience is a particularly phenomenological move on Gadamer's part. A conversation in two different languages, understood by both speakers, results in one language establishing mastery. If I speak to you in French and you respond in English, at a certain point the conversation is given over to either French or English as the medium of understanding (Gadamer [1960] 2004: 386). However, ordinarily a conversation in two languages requires the mediation of an interpreter who translates between the speakers. In such a situation the two people do not really have a conversation, only the interpreters do. Translation here involves the two interlocutors giving up their authority in order to try to bridge a gap that can never be fully closed (Gadamer [1960] 2004: 386).

Every translation is the culmination of the translator's interpretation of either the speaker's words or the words of the text. The difference between the task of the translator and the task of the interpreter is one of degree rather than kind. Grondin describes Gadamer's notion of translation as the 'application' of understanding so that every case of understanding, insofar as it attempts to understand what is initially foreign, is a case of translation (Grondin 2002: 43). However, it seems to me that for Gadamer translation is a little narrower than this, in that it is always between two different languages, so that while every translation is an interpretation, not every interpretation is a translation. For Gadamer, translation is not necessary when we really master a language, and we do this – we understand a language – by living in it: 'Where there is understanding there is not translation but speech' ([1960] 2004: 386).

Nonetheless, it is not speech but the written text that constitutes the real hermeneutic task. This focus on the written text emerges from Gadamer's account of tradition and his prioritising of the past in any act of interpretation. For Gadamer, as for Heidegger, we find ourselves in a world that has already been interpreted in a certain way, and that interpretation of the world is left behind in tradition deposited in language. Gadamer introduces the idea of *Wirkungsgeschichte*, or 'effective history', which is the manner in which history produces our pre-understanding, or 'prejudice', of a matter to be understood. If I am trying to understand, interpret (and perhaps eventually translate) a text, it matters that I am doing so in the twenty-first century, that I was born in Europe, that my mother tongue is English, that I am a woman and so on and so forth. In other words, my context, which is always historical, affects my interpretation insofar as it circumscribes my horizon of understanding. Meaning for Gadamer is not a fixed thing 'in' the text which I as interpreter have to dig out. Ideas do not lie about in some sort of 'linguistic storeroom' to be discovered, claims Gadamer ([1960] 2004: 390). Rather, meaning emerges in the play between the interpreter and that which is being interpreted. The horizon of the text and the interpreter's horizon become fused to create a new horizon in which the subject matter is brought to light. Both interpreter and text 'have a share' in this coming to light. All understanding is interpretation, and all interpretation takes place in the medium of language. This linguistic nature of understanding is '*the concretion of historically effected consciousness*' ([1960] 2004: 391, italics in original). In other words, our understanding is made possible by our linguistic nature, and this linguistic nature bears the traces of our historicality. We understand because we have language, and language is where the understanding of prior generations or traditions is accumulated.

The role of the written text is particularly important here. While it may be the case that writing is secondary to speech, or 'comes after' speech, that language *can* be written is 'not incidental'. 'In writing language gains its true ideality, for in encountering a written tradition understanding consciousness acquires its full sovereignty. Its being does not depend on anything' ([1960] 2004: 392). The written text surpasses both an oral tradition and the remnants of a tradition discovered in monuments or architecture. In the first instance of an oral tradition – of, for example, retelling of myth or narrative – the story never fully detaches from the speaker and therefore never fully detaches from the conditions of each retelling. In other words, if a myth is retold over and over again from one generation to the next, it becomes inflected by these various stages of its retelling. In this way, the myth does not allow a past humanity to become present to us again as the story has become mixed with various moments in the past. In contrast, a written text is an 'enduringly fixed expression of life' ([1960] 2004: 389) which has a certain autonomy to live on as itself. The reader of a written text becomes the authority on that text's meaning.

Crucially, for Gadamer the reader is not concerned here with the meaning intended by the author of the text. This is in contrast with the aim of hermeneutics as described by Schleiermacher, for whom the interpreter aims to first understand the text as well as the author and then even better than the author (Schleiermacher [1972] 1998: 33). Schleiermacher played down the role of writing in order to emphasise the manner in which interpretation is at play even in the understanding of an oral utterance. The aim of the interpreter for Schleiermacher (and for Dilthey) was to follow the 'outward' signs of speech towards their 'inner' origin in the speaker's mind. In other words, meaning was situated in the inner life of the author or their psyche. For Gadamer, when we interpret we are not aiming towards the psychological state of the author or speaker but rather towards the matter itself – what is being spoken or written about. Contra the nineteenth-century aim of reconstructing the author's intention, the benefit of the written text for Gadamer is that it allows greater detachment from such psychological approaches to a text. For an interpreter to attempt to understand what 'the author meant' is to miss the point; what counts is what is said, not who is saying it. Of course the author's intention is there, but for Gadamer this is simply not the goal of hermeneutics (Gadamer [1960] 2004: 393; Grondin 2002: 41).

Nor is the goal to attempt to understand a text as a so-called 'original reader' might have understood it. For where exactly is this original reader situated? At the time the author was writing or within fifty years of their death? Or one-hundred years? How do we draw the line between 'past' and 'present' reader? As Gadamer asserts: 'The idea of the original reader is full of unexamined idealization' ([1960] 2004: 396). A reader, who is always an interpreter, can only approach the text with the goal of understanding the subject matter itself. Recourse to a psychological or a historical approach is valid only when no agreement or understanding regarding the subject matter can be reached. Even in such extreme cases, where what is being said is too closely linked with who is saying it to be separable, there still must be a basic understanding of the subject matter before there is an understanding of the author's intention towards it.

To return to the issue of translation, this is for Gadamer an extreme case of interpretation. Like the interpreter (or reader in general), the translator in approaching the text is not attempting to 'reawaken' the author's intention but is rather *recreating* the text to be translated in another language ([1960] 2004: 387). Like all interpretation, translation 'highlights' aspects of the text; it emphasises certain features of the text at the expense of others. The translator must decide which parts of the text to emphasise and which to underplay, meaning that any translation could always unfold in a different way according to different decisions taken by the translator. While this is of course true of any interpretation, translation is a particularly difficult attempt at understanding, where the difference between the translator's view of the subject matter and the subject matter itself, as it is in the text, is ultimately unbridgeable. A translator can find a solution, but it will only ever be a 'compromise', since for Gadamer there is an 'insurmountable' gulf between different languages ([1960] 2004: 388).

The aim of a translation is to bring into one language the subject matter found in the text of another, and the subject matter can never be separated from the language in which it is expressed. This is why the translator cannot be reduced to one who performs the technical operation of removing one set of linguistic clothes to replace them with another; the translator rather *recreates* the meaning of the original in the language into which she translates. And it is for this reason that the translator's horizon fused with that of the original text opens up a new horizon on the subject matter. This is a rather positive view of translation that accords the translator a certain authority, which is of course in line with the authority accorded elsewhere by Gadamer to the reader. Nonetheless, Gadamer is ambiguous on the issue of translation. He claims that 'every translation is clearer and flatter' than the original in that it must make clear what was in the original dense or ambiguous. It must '"unfold" what was in the original "folded"'to use Antoine Berman's phrase (Berman [1985] 2000: 290). It seems that for Gadamer translation is an unfortunate event that occurs where optimal understanding between speakers or between reader and text cannot take place. Furthermore, Gadamer's account of translation is quite literal; he discusses it only as the transposition of meaning from one language to another. By contrast, Ricoeur views translation as a broader model that illustrates cultural and political understanding.

Ricoeur: historical perspectives

Paul Ricoeur was born in 1913 in Valence, France. He was orphaned at the age of two and raised with his sister in Rennes by his grandparents. He graduated from the University of Rennes with an Arts degree in 1933 and continued his studies at the Sorbonne where he achieved his *aggregation* in 1935. This competitive state exam entitled him to a teaching position at a *lycée* and he taught first at Colmar in Alsace and later in Lorient. During this period Ricoeur published short articles with a focus on Christian Socialism and an early article on phenomenology (Reagan 1996: 7). While these articles do not reveal Ricoeur's philosophical project, they do demonstrate his early and continued commitment to philosophy as socially and politically engaged – a commitment reflected in his approach to translation. Called up for military service in 1939, Ricoeur was captured by the German army in 1940 and remained a prisoner of war until the liberation in 1945. The camp where Ricoeur was held became something of university in itself, with lectures given by inmates to each other. It was during this time that Ricoeur began reading and translating Husserl, as well as studying the existentialist thinker Karl Jaspers. Ricoeur and Gadamer, then, lived substantially different 'wars', and while it is always dangerous to read biography too far into philosophical works, there can be no doubt that these different war experiences inflected the philosophical projects of each thinker.

After the war Ricoeur lectured at the University of Strasbourg, and in 1950 he published his first major work, *Freedom and Nature: The Voluntary and the Involuntary* ([1950] 2007). The relationship between human freedom and the various restrictions on that freedom – from our physical constitution to our moral responsibility – had long been a theme in philosophy, at least since Kant. However, Ricoeur's account in this 1950 work is particularly marked by its phenomenological and existential framing as found in the work of both Heidegger and Jean-Paul Sartre. For Heidegger, we choose our way of being from a situated context over which we have no control, what he terms 'thrownness' (*Geworfenheit*). Thrownness makes up things like our physical capabilities, the historical period in which we find ourselves, the language we are born to and so on. We are delivered into this context and from it alone can we freely create our own identity. This tension between context and freely choosing one's identity became a central theme in French appropriations of phenomenology, such as the work of Maurice Merleau-Ponty, Sartre and Simone de Beauvoir. For Sartre, the tension is between the in-itself – brute material existence – and the for-itself – man's freedom from this material existence through his imaginative capacity. In contrast to Sartre, Ricoeur's account in his 1950 work of the tension between what he terms the voluntary and involuntary aspects of existence sees both sides as necessary.

In 1956 Ricoeur was appointed Chair of Philosophy at the Sorbonne. He published two major works in 1960, *Fallible Man* and *The Symbolism of Evil*, both of which in some sense continue his previous work on the relationship between freedom and nature. In *Fallible Man* we find one of Ricoeur's central and perennial themes: that our identity is never unified but rather marked by a radical disjunction between our finite, subjective and physical existence – *bios* – and our capacity for objective and universal reason – *logos* ([1960] 1986). Because of this central dis-unity at the heart of our existence, we can go wrong and make mistakes; but we can also do good. In other words, the tension which makes us fallible also allows us to make amends. The play between these two modes of being gives us both our unique identity and our unity with others through communication founded on universal reason.

Later in the 1960s Ricoeur began a shift not so much away from phenomenology as towards a means of supplementing it with philosophical methodologies which might better explain the self's relation to itself and others. In 1965 he published *Freud and Philosophy: An Essay on Interpretation*, demonstrating engagement with psychoanalysis, and in 1969 a collection of essays, *The Conflict of Interpretations*, was published. This collection dealt more explicitly with hermeneutics as well as psychoanalysis and structuralism. Both works indicate Ricoeur's contention that understanding – of oneself or of the world – is always mediated. This inevitable mediation means interpretation is a necessary part of human existence and, simultaneously, that that interpretation, itself subject to mediation, will never be conclusive. In 1967 he took a position at the University of Paris at Nanterre (now Paris X) where he worked until his retirement in 1980. In the same year, 1967, he was appointed John Nuveen Professor of Philosophical Theology at the University of Chicago, where he worked until 1992.

He was the recipient of a number of honorary doctorates from universities, including Göttingen, Chicago and McGill, as well as numerous awards, including the Karl Jaspers Prize and the French Academy Grand Prize for Philosophy. Like Gadamer, Ricoeur saw philosophy as a dialogue between thinkers, and, also like Gadamer, Ricoeur was immensely influenced by phenomenology, Romantic hermeneutics and Ancient Greek thought, in particular Aristotle. However, Ricoeur's engagement with French structuralism, Freudian psychoanalysis and Anglo-American philosophy provides his work with a larger palette of concepts, producing perhaps a more original and idiosyncratic approach to the various philosophical themes he tackled. He died in 2005 at the age of ninety-two.

Lisa Foran

Ricoeur: critical issues and topics

For Ricoeur, I understand my existence through signs found in the world, and language is a system of signs that mediates my understanding. However, *pace* structuralist thinkers such as Ferdinand de Saussure and Roman Jakobson, Ricoeur argues that language must always be taken as 'discourse' rather than simply a system of self-referential signs. Discourse is always realised temporally by a subject referring to a world in an address to an other (Ricoeur [1971] 1973). Interpretation, then, is always concerned with interpreting discourse: what someone said about something to someone else. This means that interpretation will always be temporal and therefore subject to change in the future. Interpretation will be subjective, bringing the interpreter's own situation into play. And interpretation will have broader ethical implications insofar as it concerns the relation between one and the other. For Ricoeur, translation is a very particular situation and one which can offer a paradigm for understanding all relations between self and other, whether at a socio-political or individual level. Translation occurs as an explicit theme in his writings from the early 1990s onwards. Here I will discuss translation in two different, although not unrelated, senses: first, translation as that which takes place between two different languages and, second, how this maps onto or acts as a model for translation as that which takes place between two different people and/or cultures.

Translation between languages, argues Ricoeur, is as old as humanity itself. There has always been translation simply because there have always been many languages. The myth of Babel (Genesis 11: 1–10) is the biblical narrative of the origin of this linguistic multiplicity, wherein the tribe of Shem sought to build a tower to the heavens. Their ambition was thwarted by God, who scattered the tribe across the world and imposed many languages upon them. While this narrative is often interpreted to read multilingualism as a kind of punishment, Ricoeur sees it as something far more benign. It is rather a myth describing something fundamental about the human condition: that we can speak one language and have the capacity to learn another (Ricoeur [2004] 2006: 12–14). Babel, argues Ricoeur, is simply one step in the broader Genesis narrative of separation: first, the chaotic universe is separated into its ordered parts, then Adam and Eve are separated from their naivety in the Garden of Eden and given responsibility in the world, then the fratricide of Abel separates fraternity as an ethical relation and, finally, man is scattered across the Earth in multiple languages. Read as such, Babel simply explains that humans speak many languages in the same way that the expulsion from Eden explains that we are conscious creatures capable of reflection upon our condition ([2004] 2006: 18).

Historically, translation has been characterised as a balancing between the translatable and the untranslatable. This framing of translation has produced what Ricoeur terms 'two ruinous alternatives'. Either: translation is impossible because different languages are radically heterogeneous; or translation only happens because all languages share a common fund which can either be found or created ([2004] 2006: 13). The first approach, that translation is in theory impossible, arises from the view that any given language reflects a particular world view – not only that there are different words for the same things but that these words and the manner in which they are conjoined into sentences produce such a unique way of understanding the world that it would be impossible to 'carry this across' into another linguistic environment. While it is true that 'languages are different not only owing to the way that they carve up reality but also owing to the way they put it together again at the level of discourse' ([2004] 2006: 30), this does not mean that no bridge between languages can be built. If it did, Ricoeur wryly argues, we would end with a situation where 'bilinguals have to be schizophrenics' ([2004] 2006: 14). In this Ricoeur follows Donald Davidson's dismissal of the idea of 'conceptual schemes' (Davidson 1974).

The second approach we usually find about translation under the translatable/untranslatable framing has two strands: either translation is possible because all languages derive from a lost original language, or all languages are based on a hidden structure, meaning that we can recreate a universal lexicon which would eliminate all the confusion of multilingualism. The idea of a lost prelapsarian language of Eden is found in strands of thinking as diverse as Gnosticism, Kabbalah and even anti-Semitic tales of the original 'Aryan' language (Ricoeur [2004] 2006: 16). Part of the Nazi narrative emerged from a desire to appropriate Sanskrit and Sanskrit manuscripts as a European cultural heritage. Linking Sanskrit to an 'original' or 'pure' Aryan race that had become 'contaminated' permitted a dangerous and wholly unfounded nostalgia both for a 'pure race' and 'pure language'. That language and political identity are tied together may seem somewhat obvious, but if we follow Ricoeur's point all the way through here, we can see how our view of translation reflects deeper cultural and ethical commitments. If we think we can 'go back' to a pure language, where translation becomes unnecessary, then we are committed to thinking our current state is a fallen one. We are committed to thinking our future lies in reproducing a mythical past where difference of any kind has been eliminated. The dangers of such thinking are illustrated not only in the horrors of World War Two but any time today that we see policies of exclusion implemented under the disguise of unity.

The other strand of this view of translation is based on the idea of *a priori* codes. Here the argument is that translation is possible because all languages share a certain hidden structure, which, once deciphered, will allow us to recreate a single universal language. Such views are found in Bacon's desire to eliminate language's imperfections and Leibniz's dream of a universal lexicon. Such dreams must be abandoned, argues Ricoeur, because they fail for two reasons. First, there is no consensus on what would be included in such a 'universal lexicon', nor could there ever be. Ideas of a universal lexicon are committed to a total equivalence between sign and thing ([2004] 2006: 17). They are akin to ideas of a 'third text': that to find the perfect translation between two texts we just need to create a sort 'neutral' third text between them. Of course the creation of this text requires at least a bilingual reader to proof it; that is, it requires a translator, and so we return the problem of translation again ([2004] 2006: 7). The second reason that the *a priori*-codes route fails for Ricoeur is that it is tied to an ahistorical and universal view of language. It must deny the various historical events that led to the various multiplicities of languages. As is so often the case, the gap between the universal and the empirical, between the *a priori* and the historical is insurmountable. This gap remains whether we are talking about the differences between languages or the differences between people ([2004] 2006: 8).

Ricoeur concludes that translation happens all the time – it is not impossible – yet it can never be finished – it is not conclusive. Translation between languages is thus imperfect and unfinished, but this should not surprise us, for even within a single language it is always possible to say the same thing in a different way. We can only criticise a translation through a retranslation, and these retranslations happen all the time. Think of how often so-called classic texts have been translated over long periods of time: the works of Aristotle or Virgil or Dante. New translations emerge over time because language is always changing; the English of the nineteenth century sounds archaic to a modern ear. 'Language is full of life': it changes and so it translates itself even within a so-called single language (Ricoeur [2004] 2006: 24). The 'problem' of translation between languages, notes Ricoeur, finds its 'origin in language's reflection on itself' ([2004] 2006: 28). Understanding always requires two interlocutors, two people in a conversation (even if that conversation is between self and self as other), and between these two people misunderstanding is always possible. Yet it is this very risk of misunderstanding – what Schleiermacher described as the source of hermeneutics – that makes understanding possible (Schleiermacher [1972] 1998: 21–2). Each time we engage with another we seek to 'open out the folds of an argument', to explain what it is we or they are talking about, and each time we do this we translate – we say in another way (Ricoeur [2004] 2006: 25).

Given the ubiquity of translation, either between languages or within a single language, it no longer makes sense to hold onto the traditional dichotomy of translatable/untranslatable. It is far more productive, claims Ricoeur, to take up instead the practical alternative of faithfulness and betrayal ([2004] 2006). The translator is situated between two partners: the foreign text (or author or culture) and the future reader of the translation. The translator strives to achieve a balance between bringing the author to the reader and the reader to the author, as Schleiermacher phrased it (Ricoeur [2004] 2006: 4, 23). Occupying this mediator's role, the translator vows to be faithful to both partners and yet inevitably must betray them both to some extent by balancing each of their concerns. Compromises must always be made, and the translator must sacrifice her faithfulness to one partner in order to fulfil her vow to the other. It is because translation entails this balancing of betrayal that we can have so many retranslations; the translator's choice of whom to be faithful to can always be remade.

Employing the Freudian term 'work' in the sense of 'working-through' (*durcharbeiten*) (Freud [1914] 2001: 145–56) to describe what the translator does between bringing the reader to the author and the author to the reader, Ricoeur supplements the traditional hermeneutic balancing act with two tasks undertaken by the translator: the work of remembering and the work of mourning. It is through these two tasks that we see the way translation for Ricoeur acts as a paradigm for ethical encounters between people and cultures.

A successful work of mourning in Freud entails accepting the loss of a loved one and finding a way to imagine a new future in a world without that person. Once this work is completed the ego becomes 'free and uninhibited again' (Freud [1917] 2001: 245). In terms of translation, Ricoeur argues that the translator must give up the ideal of the perfect translation ([2004] 2006: 8). Such an ideal can become oppressive, restricting or even preventing the translator from beginning her work for fear that translation by its very definition is only ever 'bad translation' ([2004] 2006: 5). In contrast, when the translator accepts her task as the creation of 'equivalence without adequacy' ([2004] 2006: 10) – when she gives up and mourns the 'perfect translation' – she is liberated to find happiness as a host welcoming the foreign at home.

Together with this work of mourning is the work of remembering which 'attacks the view that the mother tongue is sacred, the mother tongue's nervousness around its identity' (Ricoeur [2004] 2006: 4). Following Berman, Ricoeur notes that the mother tongue, or target language, often resists translation or 'the test of the foreign (*l'épreuve de l'étranger*)' because it fears that contact with what is other will put its own identity in danger (Ricoeur references Berman [1984] 1992 frequently in his discussion of translation). The relation between same and other is always inhabited by this fear of attack, a fear which can very quickly turn welcome into rejection (Ricoeur [2003] 2004: 81–2). This fear of the other is one of three causes of what Ricoeur calls the 'fragility of identity'.

One of the other causes of this fragility is the strange relation between identity and time; how is it that someone can stay the 'same' over time? This is the question addressed in Ricoeur's 1992 work *Oneself as Another*. Here Ricoeur argues that personal identity is made of two parts: *idem* identity and *ipse* identity. *Idem* identity responds to the question 'what are you?' It is that which remains the 'same' over time and has a certain 'immutability'. It is a sort of structural identity and is made up of all the things that would allow others and myself to identify me across the span of my life. Ricoeur also describes this as our 'character': 'the set of lasting dispositions by which a person is recognized' ([1990] 1994: 121). On the other hand, *ipse* identity responds to the question 'who are you?' and does not have an unchanging core but is rather the ability to begin a new action and to commit oneself to a promise ([1990] 1994: 167). Rather than being immutable it is described as constancy: an ongoing action of keeping one's word, of testifying to being the 'same' person. It is individual selfhood and agency that allows us to take responsibility for our actions. Personal identity emerges in the play between these two modalities of *idem* (same) and *ipse* (self) to reveal a narrative identity, an identity that is part of a broader fabric of intersubjectivity. The work of remembering in this context involves remembering that each of us is one among many and that the story of who we are is a narrative constructed by both ourselves and others. It also entails remembering our responsibility in constructing and preserving the narratives of others.

The third cause of the fragility of identity is related to the first and second and entails the heritage of founding violence. Ricoeur notes that 'there is no historical community that has not arisen out of what can be termed an original relation to war' ([2003] 2004: 82). There are two kinds of violence at play here: on the one hand is the manner in which nations emerge from a war in which they define, contest, and defend their identity; on the other is the manner in which these founding events are remembered or misremembered. A founding narrative invariably entails strengthening one identity over and against some other. Simply put, the story of a war told by one country will emphasise the heroism of its citizens and the brutality of its enemies; yet the same war narrated from the other side will reverse this structure: 'The same events are thus found to signify glory for some, humiliation for others' ([2003] 2004: 82).

The translator engaged in this work of remembering, then, not only reminds the mother tongue of its status as just one language among others, thus guarding against the aforementioned linguistic ethnocentrism; she also takes responsibility for welcoming the foreign language and preserving its identity as other. This work of linguistic remembering constitutes translation as an act of hospitality where 'the pleasure of dwelling in the other's language is balanced by the pleasure of receiving the foreign word at home' ([2004] 2006: 10).

Understood as such, it is no surprise that translation is one of three interrelated models of integration that Ricoeur proposes as a means for integrating Europe (1996). Translation as a model of integration would provide the European political landscape with two things. First, a pragmatic multilingualism whereby the learning of at least two living languages would be standard practice; learning at least two languages means learning at least two cultures and so, at what Ricoeur terms a 'spiritual level', the model of translation would, second, give rise to a 'translation ethos', leading to both cultural and spiritual hospitality as well as linguistic hospitality ([1992] 1996: 5). The second and third models of European integration are related to this first model of translation, especially when we remind ourselves that translation is a work of memory and mourning.

The second model is the exchange of memories. Since identity is a play of both *idem* (same) and *ipse* (self), identity is always mobile and active. However, narratives of founding events often 'freeze the history of each cultural group into an identity which is not only immutable but also deliberately and systematically incommunicable' (Ricoeur [1992] 1996: 7). To counteract this danger, the model of the exchange of memories would allow cultures to reread historical events from a plurality of perspectives. The third model is that of forgiveness. Through the hospitality afforded by the model of translation, and through the exchange of memories in the second model, this third model would require the remembrance of suffering. It would call on each cultural group in Europe to remember the suffering they have inflicted upon others. In doing so they would not only plead for forgiveness but perhaps also be more willing to offer forgiveness to those who have caused them suffering. This forgiveness would not be a forgetting but, on the contrary, a constant and vigilant remembering. In this way the burden of the past and its weight of guilt might be lightened. These three models together emphasise exchange and mediation in an effort to reconcile 'the right to universality and the right to historical difference' ([1992] 1996: 12). They allow us to reimagine the past in the present, which in turn permits a new imagining of the future.

Translation, then, for Ricoeur reveals something fundamental about the human condition; not just that we speak languages and learn others but, more fundamentally, that our experience unfolds between the universal and the particular. Balancing these two modalities requires an ethical engagement and openness to what is other. The fact of translation reveals that balancing the concerns of the one and the other is always possible, even if it remains an infinite task that can always take place in a different way.

Related topics

Schleiermacher; Nietzsche; Heidegger; Davidson; equivalence; Levinas: his philosophy and its translation; mysticism, esotericism and translation.

Further reading

Ricoeur, P. (2006) [2004] *On Translation*. Translated by Eileen Brennan. London and New York: Routledge. (This volume brings together three late essays on translation by Ricoeur dealing with themes such as equivalence, the untranslatable and the idea of translation as a paradigm for understanding intersubjective relations.)

Gadamer, H.G. (2004) [1960] 'Language as the Medium of Hermeneutic Experience'. Translated by Joel Weinsheimer and Donald G. Marshall. In *Truth and Method*. London and New York: Continuum. 401–23. (While translation arises frequently in Gadamer's *magnum opus*, this section gives his most explicit account of how translation fits within his broader hermeneutic theory.)

Mootz, F.J. and Taylor, G.H. (2011) *Gadamer and Ricoeur: Critical Horizons for Contemporary Hermeneutics*. New York: Continuum. (A collection of twelve essays comparing Gadamer and Ricoeur on various key themes, some of which are best suited to those with a strong background in philosophy. However, the editors' introduction provides readers with a clear and accessible general overview of the similarities and differences between both thinkers.)

Brennan, E. (ed.) (2015) *Ricoeur Studies* 6 (1), available from: https://ricoeur.pitt.edu/ojs/index.php/ricoeur/issue/view/12 [accessed 13 August 2017]. (This special issue of *Ricoeur Studies* is devoted to the topic of translation in his work. There are five essays (one of which is in French) covering comparisons with other thinkers such as Jacques Derrida and Emmanuel Mounier; the relation between history and translation; and an account of Ricoeur's 'translation theory' that draws on a broad range of his work (not just on those texts that explicitly deal with the theme).)

References

Aristotle (1962) 'On Interpretation'. Translated by Harold P. Cook. In *Aristotle: The Categories, On Interpretation, Prior Analytics*. London: Heinemann. 114–79.

Berman, A. [1984] (1992) *The Experience of the Foreign: Culture and Translation in Romantic Germany*. Translated by S. Heyvaert. New York: SUNY Press.

Berman, A. [1985] (2000) 'Translation and the Trials of the Foreign'. Translated by Lawrence Venuti. In Lawrence Venuti (ed.) *The Translation Studies Reader*. London and New York: Routledge. 284–97.

Davidson, D. (1974) 'On the Very Idea of a Conceptual Scheme'. *Proceedings and Addresses of the American Philosophical Association* 47, 5–20.

Dilthey, W. (1989) *Selected Works Vol. I: Introduction to the Human Sciences*. Edited by Rudolf A. Makkreel and Frithjof Rodi. Princeton, NJ: Princeton University Press.
Freud, S. [1917] (2001) 'Mourning and Melancholia'. Translated by James Strachey. In *The Standard Edition of the Complete Psychological Works of Sigmund Freud, Volume XIV*. London: The Hogarth Press. 243–58.
Freud, S. [1914] (2001) 'Remembering, Repeating and Working Through (Further Recommendations on the Technique of Psychoanalysis II)'. Translated by James Strachey. In *The Standard Edition of the Complete Psychological Works of Sigmund Freud, Volume XII*. London: Vintage. 145–56.
Gadamer, H.G. [1978] (1986) *The Idea of the Good in Platonic-Aristotelian Philosophy*. Translated by P. Christopher Smith. New Haven, CT and London: Yale University Press.
Gadamer, H.G. [1988] (1989) 'Back from Syracuse?' Translated by John McCumber. *Critical Inquiry* 15 (2), 427–30.
Gadamer, H.G. [1931] (1991) *Plato's Dialectical Ethics*. Translated by Robert M. Wallace. New Haven, CT and London: Yale University Press.
Gadamer, H.G. [1960] (2004) *Truth and Method*. Translated by Joel Weinsheimer and Donald G. Marshall. London and New York: Continuum.
Grondin, J. (2002) 'Gadamer's Basic Understanding of Understanding'. In Robert J. Dostal (ed.) *The Cambridge Companion to Gadamer*. Cambridge: Cambridge University Press. 36–51.
Grondin, J. [1999] (2003) *The Philosophy of Gadamer*. Translated by Kathryn Plant. Montreal: McGill-Queen's University Press.
Grondin, J. [1999] (2011) *Hans-Georg Gadamer: A Biography*. New Haven, CT and London: Yale University Press.
Heidegger, M. [1927] (2009) *Being and Time*. Translated by John Macquarrie and Edward Robinson. Oxford and Cambridge, MA: Blackwell.
Husserl, E. [1931] (1995) *The Cartesian Meditations*. Translated by Dorion Cairns. Dordrecht: Kluwer Academic.
Luft, S. (2009) 'Reconstruction and Reduction: Natorp and Husserl on Method and the Question of Subjectivity'. In Rudolf Mackreel and Sebastian Luft (eds.) *Neo-Kantianism in Contemporary Philosophy*. Bloomington, IN: Indiana University Press. 59–91.
Reagan, C.E. (1996) *Ricoeur: His Life and His Work*. Chicago: University of Chicago Press.
Ricoeur, P. [1971] (1973) 'The Model of the Text: Meaningful Action Considered as a Text'. *New Literary History* 5 (1), 91–117.
Ricoeur, P. [1960] (1986) *Fallible Man*. Translated by Charles A. Kelbley. New York: Fordham University Press.
Ricoeur, P. [1990] (1994) *Oneself as Another*. Translated by Kathleen Blamey. Chicago: University of Chicago Press.
Ricoeur, P. [1992] (1996) 'Reflections on a New Ethos for Europe'. Translated by Eileen Brennan. In Richard Kearney (ed.) *Paul Ricoeur: The Hermeneutics of Action*. London: Sage. 3–13.
Ricoeur, P. [2003] (2004) *Memory, History, Forgetting*. Translated by Kathleen Blamey and David Pellauer. Chicago: University of Chicago Press.
Ricoeur, P. [2004] (2006) *On Translation*. Translated by Eileen Brennan. London and New York: Routledge.
Ricoeur, P. [1950] (2007) *Freedom and Nature: The Voluntary and the Involuntary*. Translated by Erazim V. Kohak. Evanston, IL: Northwestern University Press.
Schleiermacher, F. [1972] (1998) *Hermeneutics and Criticism*. Translated by Andrew Bowie. Cambridge: Cambridge University Press.

7
Quine

Paul A. Roth

Introduction

This paper examines what philosophical assumptions Quine calls into question in maintaining indeterminacy of translation and his reasons for doing so.[1] For while many have noted that Quine rejects a certain notion of meaning, or 'mentalistic semantics', this has often been misread as question-begging, reflecting only a bias in favour of behaviourism in particular and physicalism in general (see chapter 8 of Hylton 2007 for a survey and critique of such charges). But this charge of question-begging only arises, or so I argue, because commentators ignore what characterizing translation as *indeterminate* implies for Quine. By putting together Quine's worries about meaning and unpacking the determinacy/indeterminacy distinction, the stage is set for a close examination of just how Quine's thought experiment of *radical* translation – the case where one confronts a language previous unknown or untranslated – makes both explicit and compelling arguments for indeterminacy of translation (this account draws upon but modifies Roth 1978 and Roth 2003a).

In a paper published as 'Meaning and Translation' in an anthology entitled *On Translation* (Quine 1959), Quine broaches one of his earliest formulations of a problem he labels a 'difficulty or indeterminacy of correlation' (Quine 1959: 172; see also Quine 1960: 78). Portions of that paper resurface a year later as part of chapter 2 of *Word and Object*, where he rebrands this 'difficulty' as 'a principle of indeterminacy of translation' (Quine 1960: 27). He there also expands his exposition and switches titles to 'Translation and Meaning' (Quine 1960). This switch signals, I suggest, an invitation to rethink how translation and meaning relate and connect.

A translation may plausibly be viewed as *underdetermined* by the available evidence – that is, the evidence itself perhaps cannot settle the question of which of competing translations to choose. But by placing the term 'translation' before 'meaning', Quine hints translation is *prior* to determination of meaning. Unpacking Quine's hint yields a defence of Quine's claim that accounts of meaning suffer from a problem additional to that of underdetermination, one that originates in an 'indeterminacy of correlation'. This clearly reverses any assumption that translation merely *recaptures* or *recapitulates* a prior meaning. A 'recapture' view of translation assumes a fixed or determinate meaning existing prior to translation. Indeterminacy of translation suggests that meaning in important respects *results* from a translation and cannot be independent of it.

Intuitions about meaning

Analytic philosophy has at its canonically identified points of origin commitments to a problematic notion of meaning, one found, I would maintain, both in G. Frege and in G. E. Moore. Moore proves to be a more convenient stalking horse for purposes of making explicit what Quine opposes. Consider the following claim by Moore in this regard:

> I shall, therefore, use the word in the sense in which I think it is ordinarily used; but at the same time I am not anxious to discuss whether I am right in thinking that it is so used. My business is solely with that object or idea, which I hold, rightly or wrongly, that the word is generally used to stand for. What I want to discover is the nature of that object or idea.
> (Moore 1968/1903: 6)

This conveys a certain notion of propositional content, of ideas or concepts that terms and statements express independently of their contingent linguistic forms. Determinacy connotes just this presumed independence of a notion of meaning irrespective of expressive form. In the course of the evolution and development of analytic philosophy, Quine, Wittgenstein, Sellars, and Davidson all come to criticize and reject this view of meaning.

Nonetheless, such a 'Platonist' view of meaning persists (I suspect still predominates) even among those who seemingly regard themselves as heirs to the analytic tradition.

> Understanding does not presuppose translation, but *the other way around*. One cannot translate something one does not understand. To translate e_1 from L_1 is to find an expression from L_2 that means the same, and this can be done only by someone who knows what e_1 means. ... It is equally absurd to maintain that *meaning* presupposes translation. Translating an expression e_1 from L_1 by an expression e_2 from L_2 is legitimate only if e_2 means roughly the same in L_2 as e_1 does in L_1. Consequently, the very notion of translation presupposes that the expression to be translated are meaningful independently of translation, namely by virtue of being used and explained in their home language.
> (Glock 2003: 204)

On this view, translation translates expressions '*independently*' of translation, namely by virtue of being used and explained in their home language'. Call translation of meaning so conceived the 'recapture view'. On this account, when translation succeeds it 'recaptures' or re-expresses whatever meaning the target statement had. (For further evidence of how pervasive this view remains in philosophy and linguistics, see the literature reviewed in Begby 2016.) The reference to a home language here proves critical, for the thought (not Quine's) is that one's 'home' (native, first) language determines (in a sense yet to be specified) a meaning to be so recaptured.

In order to make vivid what intuition fuels the *recapture view*, imagine a 'translation' version of Moore's 'open question' test. This develops from Moore's challenge to naturalism in ethics, and so lends itself, *mutatis mutandis*, to challenges to the sort of naturalistic semantics for which Quine advocates. In the ethical case, this test can be used to challenge any list of natural attributes that purports to define a normative term – for example, 'good' as pleasure.

The test asks of the proposed definiens, 'But is it/are they good?' Now if the item(s) defined 'good', this question should strike a competent speaker as uninformative or tautological, but the question is not obviously either. This Moore takes to show that it remains an 'open question' as to what to properly counts as the meaning of 'good', and so establishes that a list of non-normative properties cannot be taken as *prima facie* definitional.

In the case of meaning, an analogue would be the paradox of analysis (of which the 'open question' test is also a variant). That is, for any proposed translation, it likewise remains at least *prima facie* intelligible – an open question that any competent speaker could legitimately pose – to ask, 'But is that what the original statement *really* means?' This would seem sufficient to establish that translation links in some fashion to an intended or prior meaning, and that intended meaning must be what a correct translation recaptures. In this case, 'intended meaning' functions as the non-natural property that a purely naturalized semantics – for example, one that relied on behavioural criteria such as signs of agreement – might well miss. This translation 'test' thus links to that pervasive intuition that a statement has a determinate (one fixed by an intention or other non-natural factor) meaning that any proposed translation attempts to 'recapture'. So while competent speakers can disagree about meaning – for moral terms or other lexical items, this poses no threat or challenge to this belief in an underlying distinction between actual and attributed meaning.

Nonetheless, I maintain that Quine targets this intuitive distinction by asserting indeterminacy of translation.

> The metaphor of the black box, often so useful, can be misleading here. The problem is not one of hidden facts, such as might be uncovered by learning more about the brain physiology of thought processes. To expect a distinctive physical mechanism behind every genuinely distinct mental state is one thing; to expect a distinctive mechanism for every purported distinction that can be phrased in traditional mentalistic language is another. *The question whether, in the situation last described, the foreigner really believes A or believes rather B, is a question whose very significance I would put in doubt. This is what I am getting at in arguing the indeterminacy of translation.*
> (Quine 1970a: 180–1, emphasis mine; see also Davidson and Hintikka 1969: 303–4)

What makes for better or worse in translation, in other words, cannot be pegged to a metaphysical distinction between real and attributed meaning. In this regard, the tie between the 'open question' test and meaning resides not just in it paralleling Moore's anti-naturalism in ethics but in a much deeper intuition that ties together meaning and intentionality. 'To accept intentional usage at face value is, we saw, to postulate translation relations as somehow objectively valid though indeterminate in principle relative to the totality of speech dispositions' (Quine 1960: 221; see also 220). In sum, the notion of meaning at issue rests on very basic anti-naturalistic intuitions about language – a type of meaning realism, so to speak.

Determinacy and indeterminacy/truth and meaning

Quine's 1959 characterization of indeterminacy goes as follows:

> Containment in the Low German continuum facilitated translation of Frisian into English, and containment in a continuum of cultural evolution facilitated translation of Hungarian into English. These continuities, by facilitating translation, encourage an

illusion of subject matter: an illusion that our so readily intertranslatable sentences are diverse verbal embodiments of some intercultural proposition or meaning, when they are better seen as the merest variants of one and the same intracultural verbalism. Only the discontinuity of radical translation tries our meanings: really sets them over against their verbal embodiments, or more typically, finds nothing there.

(Quine 1959: 170–1; cf. Quine 1960: 76)

Notice that Quine's remarks here (as elsewhere) *never* allege difficulties or faults with *actual* translations. To the contrary, he speaks explicitly of 'our so readily intertranslatable sentences'. As Quine's long-time colleague and philosophical confidant Burton Dreben rightly insists, 'Quine never denies that translation, good translation, takes place. And he raises no genuine problem of radical translation that calls for a straight-forward answer, that must be solved in its own terms' (Dreben 1992: 304; see also Hylton 2007: 201). Quine does *not* conjure up some 'special' sceptical problem regarding the *practice* or the *product* of translation. In short, the indeterminacy of translation does *not* identify a philosophical problem that calls for a solution.

Rather, he takes aim at a core *philosophical* assumption regarding what translations translate. As the phrase 'indeterminacy of *correlation*' suggests, Quine questions those theories of meaning that hold that 'sentences are diverse verbal embodiments of some intercultural proposition or meaning'. Translation functions as his metaphor for rethinking what imputations of meaning impute. To term translation indeterminate represents a critique of a conception of meaning, not an alternative *theory* of meaning. Quine, then, rejects what we might think of as a 'traditional' understanding of meaning, since nothing meets the criteria that this understanding presupposes: we need a new understanding.

How could one establish an 'indeterminacy of correlation' in a way that unsettles such pervasive intuitions about meaning? Recall that Quine never maintains that indeterminacy equates to *meaninglessness*. Quine sometimes glosses 'indeterminacy' as a case where there exists 'no fact of the matter'. But note that for Quine notions such as factuality and determinacy have significance only when construed *intratheoretically* – that is, relative to a theory. 'Factuality, like gravitation and electric charge, is internal to our theory of nature' (Quine 1981: 23). Now Quine uses the term 'theory' in both a broad and narrow sense. Broadly used, he equates the terms 'theory' and 'language' at least to the following extent.

> In *Word and Object* and related writings my use of the term 'theory' is not technical. For these purposes a man's theory on a given subject may be conceived, nearly enough, as the class of all those sentences, within some limited vocabulary appropriate to the desired subject matter, that he believes true.
>
> (Davidson and Hintikka 1969: 309; see also 310)

More narrowly taken, 'theory' can be understood as scientific theory, ideally canonically formulated (i.e., in logical form).

These broader and narrower uses of theory connect in turn to the continuum that Quine understands between ordinary language and natural science. 'Science is not a substitute for common sense, but an extension of it. The question for knowledge is properly an effort simply to broaden and deepen the knowledge which the man in the street already enjoys, in moderation' (Quine 1966: 219). As humans refine whatever lore has been bequeathed them, common sense becomes science. On this view, notions such as truth and meaning can be made fully determinate only relative to an explicit theory, for only when logically regimented do the structurally determinate features become explicit.

I suggest putting together 'no fact of the matter' and determinacy so understood in the following way: specifically, a sentence can be deemed as determinate relative to a framework provided that the syntax settles whether it is valid or contravalid (Ricketts 2003: e.g., 266–7) – that is, determines whether or not a sentence can be logically derived given the rules (syntax) of a system. More generally, for a framework, L-rules (logical or syntactical rules) specify what sentences are valid or contra-valid (i.e., what follows by virtue of logical rules), and the P-rules (those that apply to sentences implying an empirical content) specify the descriptive (or physical) predicates, ones that include 'formalization of physical laws and even reports of individual observations' that may supplement the L-valid sentences of the language (Ricketts 1996: 238). Ricketts observes that for Carnap the 'union of these two classes comprises the determinate sentences of the language' (Ricketts 1996: 238–9). Ricketts later characterizes this move as one of 'transposing epistemology into *Wissenschaftslogik* [logic of science]' (Ricketts 2003: 267).[2] Fixing as this does what 'determinacy' means for Carnap provides, I maintain, a critical marker for appreciating how Quine comes to use the term 'indeterminacy'.

In this context, indeterminacy obtains when a sentence or its negation cannot be regarded as a logically or empirically determinable consequence of some specific *theory*.

> It is rather when we turn back into the midst of an actually present theory, at least hypothetically accepted, that we can and do speak sensibly of this and that sentence as true. Where it makes sense to apply 'true' is to a sentence couched in the terms of a given theory and seen from within the theory, complete with its posited reality.
> (Quine 1960: 24; see also Quine 1975: 316)

The case is likewise for translation, for Quine views even understanding ourselves as just a limiting case of translation – 'homophonic' translation as he terms it:

> Specifying the universe of a theory makes sense only relative to some background theory. ... Commonly of course the background theory will simply be a containing theory, and in this case no question of a manual of translation arises, but this is after all just a degenerate case of translation still – the case where the rule of translation is the homophonic one.
> (Quine 1969: 55)

Radical translation proves to be no different in kind than the problem inherent in acquiring and speaking one's native tongue. '[T]he resort to a remote language was not really essential. On deeper reflection, radical translation begins at home. ... Our usual domestic rule of translation is indeed the homophonic one' (Quine 1969: 46; cf. Quine 1969 5: 27–8; Quine 1960: 59). Analogous with Tarski-style theories of truth, a semantics for a language can only be given in a meta-language, one that must be utilized in order to provide an interpretation of an object language. This generates a potential infinite regress of interpretations. But Quine accepts this. That is, translation only becomes possible by taking some interpretation (meta-language) for granted. *But this 'taken for granted' should not and cannot be confused with having in hand a fixed interpretation for a meta-language.*

Radical translation proves to be only a metaphor for a general problem of explaining how people come to share a language. A final turn of the screw here involves Quine's discussion of where a parallel between attributions of truth and meaning as intratheoretically determined attributes fails to hold.

This indefinability of synonymy by reference to the methodology of analytical hypotheses is formally the same as the indefinability of truth by reference to scientific method. Also the consequences are parallel. Just as we may meaningfully speak of the truth of a sentence only within the terms of some theory or conceptual scheme, so on the whole we may meaningfully speak of interlinguistic synonymy only within the terms of some particular system of analytical hypotheses.

(Quine 1959: 170; cf. Quine 1960: 75)

But having acknowledged a parallel to this extent, Quine pointedly adds, 'May we conclude that translational synonymy at its worst is no worse off than truth in physics? To be thus reassured is to misjudge the parallel' (Quine 1960: 75; in Davidson and Hintikka 1969: 303, Quine also characterizes indeterminacy of meaning as 'parallel but additional' to the underdetermination of truth). But, countless commentators have complained, how could the parallel fail on Quine's own grounds? If the parallel fails to fail, then meaning, like truth, suffers from underdetermination by the evidence, but nothing more. No *special* lack of a fact of the matter would then obtain, and so no indeterminacy.

Evidence and explanation

To begin to understand why Quine does not beg any questions against mentalistic semantics, one must appreciate a distinction between *evidence for* meaning and a *theory of* meaning. Quine's behaviourism belongs to his notion of evidence for scientific explanation, an account which places a premium on observability. In contrast with classical empiricism, which takes what appears to individuals as explanatorily basic, empiricism *externalized* explains by taking the publicly available as where explanation must begin (Quine 1980a: 259). Consistent with his thoroughgoing naturalism and fallibilism, Quine positions even empiricism as an *intratheoretic* assumption of science as now understood, support for which rides on the explanatory success of the sciences (Quine 1990: 20–1; see also Roth 2006). Conversely, whatever plays no legitimate role in scientific explanation has no claim to being counted as a fact of the matter.

When it comes to meaningful communication, science self-applied takes as its explanandum science itself – that is, 'how surface irritations generate, through language, one's knowledge of the world' (Quine 1960: 26).[3] More colourfully put, science studies the 'relation between meager input and the torrential output ... for somewhat the same reasons that always prompted epistemology; namely, in order to see how evidence relates to theory, and in what ways one's theory of nature transcends any available evidence' (Quine 1969: 83). Quine's emphasis in short underscores the primacy of behaviourally available evidence in formulating explanations of language learning and translation.

In an exchange with Chomsky (Davidson and Hintikka 1969), Quine (no doubt to Chomsky's own surprise and frustration) readily takes on board Chomsky's well-known critique of behaviourism as an *explanation* of language acquisition. As Quine remarks,

Chomsky's remarks leave me with feelings at once of reassurance and frustration. What I find reassuring is that he nowhere clearly disagrees with my position. What I find frustrating is that he expresses much disagreement with what he thinks to be my position.

(Davidson and Hintikka 1969: 302)

And with regard to Chomsky's dismissal of indeterminacy as a special problem, Quine's response could hardly be blunter: 'Chomsky did not dismiss my point. He missed it' (Davidson and Hintikka 1969: 304).

Quine's evident frustration here concerns the fact that he never proposes a *theory* of meaning in terms of behaviour. Rather, he insists that behavioural *evidence* underwrite any entities imputed as explanantia.

> Meanings are, first and foremost, meanings of language. Language is a social art which we all acquire on the *evidence* solely of other people's overt behaviour under publicly recognizable circumstances. Meanings, therefore, those very models of mental entities, end up as grist for the behaviourist's mill.
>
> (Quine 1969: 26, emphasis mine)

Quine's own expositions of his behaviourism tend to be terse and, if anything, to distance himself from standard readings of the term. He does strongly endorse, however, a more developed account that Sellars provides (Sellars 1980; Quine 1980b). Most significantly for purposes of explicating indeterminacy, for both Sellars and Quine behaviourism exercises its firmest and most important philosophical grip precisely in cases of initial language acquisition – that is, infant language learning. Infants constitute a fundamental and pervasive natural experiment in radical translation, and so an ongoing site for philosophical lessons about meaning.

In particular, what distinguishes what can be learned from behavioural evidence and what not? Here Sellars explicitly warns against a temptation to posit preexisting mental capacities, for this may create more mysteries than insights. Invoking preexisting mental states can only be licensed by making them pay their way in terms of what evidence requires explanation.

> §25 ... But from the standpoint of methodology the binding principle was to be: Don't simply *borrow* concepts and principles from the framework of introspective knowledge. Use all the analogical and suggestive power of Mentalistic concepts and principles, but be sure that the concepts and principles you introduce have no more Mentalistic structure than can be justified in terms of their ability to explain observable behavior phenomena.
>
> §26 As I see it, this was – and remains – the methodological stance of a sophisticated behaviorism.
>
> (Sellars 1980: 6–7)

How much to attribute to innate capacities awaits on this view a more general theory of learning. But the unjustifiable methodological move here would be to posit innate structures in the absence of what can or cannot be otherwise learned. Quine concurs. 'His [Sellars] moderate behaviorism is exactly to my taste' (Quine 1980b: 26). Given how little behaviour can be made sense of by appeal to rules, this underscores the need for methodological caution (see Roth 2003b for additional arguments on this point).

What work must posits do to earn their theoretical keep? They must abet explanation but without adding 'unexplained explainers'. For example, attempting to explain a pattern of behavior by terming it a 'practice' introduces a term as explanatory that itself cries out for explanation A basic strategy for positing theoretical entities commensurate with Quine's behaviourist view of evidence can be found by considering Quine's argument for innate quality spaces. This provides a model for introducing a posit of this type. 'A standard of similarity is in some sense innate. ... Needed as they are for all learning, these distinctive spacings cannot themselves all be learned; some must be innate' (Quine 1969: 123). In this case, a theoretical posit – for example, of a genetic/innate disposition to notice colour difference – explains observed behaviours – a set of stable responses – that would be required for learning even to be possible. The fact that something like these must be present for learning to begin explains, so to speak, what makes them necessary. Conversely, positing a 'deep structure' as explanatory of linguistic competence when no one can produce such algorithms and no evidence can be adduced for the necessary existence of them represents a case of 'unexplained explainers'.

What makes a posit a posit concerns its *explanatory* role in accounting for causes of what we observe. Behaviour is to be explained; posits help pave the explanatory route. This illuminates why Quine complains that the 'problem of *evidence* for a linguistic universal is insufficiently appreciated' (Quine 1972: 390, emphasis mine). He complains, that is, that he finds it 'bewildering' to take behavioural evidence as evidence for 'the doctrine of unconscious preferences among extensionally equivalent grammars. I'd like to think that I am missing something' (Quine 1972: 389). Unlike the case for positing innate quality spaces, the posit of an 'unconscious preference' imputes, relative to the observed linguistic behaviour, that such a grammar would be not just rule-fitting but actually rule-guiding (Quine 1970b: 386ff.). Yet the rationale for positing innateness here fails to parallel the case of quality spaces where no alternative to some innate mechanism exists. As explained in more detail below, no explanatory mandate exists for assuming a rule guiding preference, let alone an innate one.[4]

This also illustrates the distinction between the factual and the theoretical on which both Quine and Sellars insist:

> What is utterly factual is just the fluency of conversation and the effectiveness of negotiation that one or another manual of translation serves to induce ... Such was my parable of the trimmed bushes, alike in outward form but wildly unlike in their inward twigs and branches.
>
> (Quine 1990: 43–4; cf. Quine 1960: 8)

Again, what makes for the 'utterly factual' ties to its being publicly observable. There exists 'no fact of the matter' when, for example, there are no determinate inferential relations among statements. Manuals of translation might generate these, but nothing underwrites any assumption that what translation translates represents the result of some framework a speaker possesses and a translation 'recaptures'. The point is *not* that a speaker might be using a different manual than a translator. *Quine challenges the assumption that a speaker has some prior framework in place.*

Note that the worry here should not be interpreted as a concern that a field linguist settles upon the 'wrong' translation. No, for this misses the point to which Quine alludes above regarding behavioural conformity masking a very different underlying structure (Quine 1960: 8). Yet what makes Quine's topiary imagery something other than a metaphor? Does Quine have an argument for the conclusion that the evidence favours his picture of 'difference all the way down' as opposed to a Chomskian-like hypothesis of shared grammatical structures? Note here the important philosophical point that the topiary metaphor suggests. Meaning, truth, and factuality can only be made *determinate* within some theoretical structure or another. But what if the evidence does not license an inference to the existence of a there being a *prior* theory? The consequence would *not* be that another's word and gestures are meaningless, but rather that they lack any *determinate* meaning – that is, a structure that logically fixes its implicative relationships. Structure/theory provides such determinacy; its absence makes for indeterminacy.[5]

Quine has, I suggest, at least two distinct arguments *against* the plausibility of inferring determinacy on the basis of behavioural evidence. One I will term the rule argument, and it emphasizes the point that behavioural evidence cannot distinguish between rule-guiding and rule-fitting. This has been clearly and forcefully developed by Thomas Ricketts in a series of papers, and I outline the argument below. The other argument I call the argument from language learning, and it emphasizes what I have elsewhere termed the 'paradox of language learning' (see especially Roth 1978) and Quine's holism. The paradox is this. Taking an infant as the paradigm case of a radical translator, and given Quine's assumption that statements have meaning not individually but only as part of a larger whole, this suggests that all infants learn meaningful language even though exposed only to parts that are, *ex hypothesi*, meaningless (e.g., individual terms or sentences). I speculate (Roth 1978) that Quine's account of observation represents an attempt to suggest how each person overcomes this paradoxical situation. Quine takes the paradox to count decisively against the assumption that each individual finds the same route from part to whole. This is the substantive philosophical point behind his topiary metaphor. Together, these two arguments – the rule argument and the argument from language learning – provide powerful reasons against presuming translation as a process between determinate languages (in the sense discussed earlier). The 'recapture' view fails for Quine because these arguments both underwrite the conclusion there was nothing (i.e., no determinate framework) there in the first place to recapture. *No initial or prior determinacy of meaning can be plausibly presumed.*

Quine, like the Wittgenstein of the *Philosophical Investigations*, uses the publicly available evidence for meaning – behavioural evidence – in an effort to undo the lure of mentalistic semantics. Indeterminacy of translation in this respect represents a *negative* result regarding what theories of meaning *cannot* plausibly take for granted but yet do. Both arguments for the indeterminacy of correlation or translation move from what everyone agrees to – the behaviourally/publicly available evidence – to an unwanted or unexpected conclusion – that that *evidence* provides no support for determinacy of meaning.

> For an uncritical mentalist, no such indeterminacy threatens. Every term and every sentence is a label attached to an idea, simple or complex, which is stored in the mind. When on the other hand we take a verification theory of meaning seriously, the indeterminacy would appear to be inescapable. *The Vienna Circle espoused a verification theory of meaning but did not take it seriously enough.*
>
> (Quine 1969: 80, emphasis mine)

> In mentalistic philosophy there is the familiar predicament of private worlds. In speculative neurology there is the circumstance that different hookups can account for identical verbal behavior. In language learning there is a multiplicity of individual histories capable of issuing in identical verbal behavior. Still one is ready to say of the domestic situation *in all positivistic reasonableness* that if two speakers match in all dispositions to verbal behavior there is no sense in imagining semantic differences between them. It is ironic that the interlinguistic case is less noticed, for it is just here that the semantic indeterminacy makes clear empirical sense.
>
> (Quine 1960: 79, emphasis mine)

It would be reasonable to impute semantic determinacy, provided that the behavioural evidence supported attributing to speakers of a language either logical principles immune to revision (and so determinate at least relative to a home language, thus fixing an inference structure) or clear empirical ties of sentences to experience and to other sentences (thus fixing empirical consequences or meaning). The rule argument sinks the former hope, and the language-learning argument squashes the latter.

In sum, what positivists failed to take 'seriously enough' turns on the question of whether or not one can verify on the basis of available evidence that speakers possess a determinate linguistic framework. If no such determinate framework can be argued for given the evidence, then there exists no basis for imputing determinacy of translation (in the sense specified earlier). If no determinacy, then as noted in the previous two quotes from Quine, indeterminacy 'would appear to be inescapable' because it 'makes clear empirical sense'.

Pressing from above:[6] fitting versus following rules

Carnap takes the notion of shared linguistic frameworks to have explanatory utility, specifically with regard to accounting for scientific rationality. For Carnap, sentences that are unrevisable because not subject to empirical test (L-rules) in a framework specify in what scientific rationality consists. Quine's challenge to Carnap asks what evidence justifies making a distinction between what cannot be revised and what can, and so what (apart from being listed under one heading rather than the other) makes a rule an L-rule and not a P-rule. Carnap, Ricketts suggests, attempts to meet this challenge by appeal to behavioural criteria.

> Carnap attempt to meet this challenge by presenting a 'behavioristic, operational procedure' for identifying the analytic sentences of a person's language by reference to the person's speech dispositions... [T]hese dispositions are those which mark a sentence a rationally unrevisable. Description of these dispositions is, however, couched in concrete, more or less behavioral terms. ... Thus it, unlike the previously described criterion, avoids illicitly presupposing the availability of a criterion of analyticity. Carnap hypothesizes that the procedure for attributing linguistic frameworks could be cast into the form of a handbook, a manual.
>
> (Ricketts 1982: 125)

Carnap's hypothesized behavioural criterion promises a basis in observable evidence for distinguishing the 'merely' empirical and the rationally unrevisable. But this view of the formal language piggybacking on speech dispositions engenders more general questions regarding what distinguishes a calculus and what makes it an instance of a language. Ricketts maintains that the enduring core of Carnap's view of this relation is that a proposed calculus represents an attempt to formally codify an '"agreement with the actual historical habits of speech" of a linguistic community' (Ricketts 2003: 261). The difference between L-rules and P-rules – what belongs to the logical and what to the empirical – will as a result reflect 'speakers' standing dispositions to accept some sentences and to reject others, together with their dispositions to infer certain kinds of sentences from certain other kinds' (Ricketts 2003: 261). However, Ricketts claims, this does *not* coincide with Carnapian pragmatics, by which Carnap means 'the interdisciplinary science of language as a behavioral and biological phenomenon' (Ricketts 2003: 264). For Carnap, pragmatics involves an interdisciplinary, historical study of actual language use. Pragmatics, in this sense, informs formalization insofar as it inclines (simply as a contingent fact of received and established usages) speakers to respond to or categorize statements in one way rather than another (see also Ricketts 2003: note 14). Yet no reason can be given for assuming that pragmatics in this sense must apply to those languages of interest for *Wissenschaftslogik*. On this view, there exists no prior (to framework formulation) sorting of the logical and the physical. Articulation of a framework occurs purely in an *ex post facto* fashion, for purposes of 'projecting' or stipulating a fixed inferential structure that provides for objective evaluation as a *Wissenschaftslogik* demands. Ricketts concludes:

> It will not include statements like 'Such and so utterance is an utterance of an L-valid formula of system S'. Carnap – behaviorist that he is – does not think of such statements as playing any role in the explanation of linguistic behavior. ... The projection of calculi onto actual or hypothetical used languages is a stipulation solely for the purpose of *Wissenschaftslogik*, of recasting epistemic evaluations as the syntactic (later semantic) descriptions of sentences – and so of investigators' linguistic behavior – that this projection makes available.
>
> ... The coordination of calculi and languages yields an understanding of the linguistic activity of scientists as the formulation and empirical testing of theories. ... Via the potential projection of calculi onto languages, old epistemological distinctions are explicated by syntactic surrogates. And for Carnap, in this setting, explication is replacement.
> (Ricketts 2003: 264)

On this account, any distinction between what counts as logical and what as empirical achieves its clarity only after a framework has been formulated (Ricketts 2003: 267). Frameworks create or impose determinacy; they have no claim to recapturing some prior notion. Rather, a virtue of a framework lies in the fashioning of these distinctions in a way that is clear and precise. As Ricketts puts it, 'The definition of L-validity stands on its own, making precise a way in which mathematical sentences of a language are formal auxiliaries to the substantive sentences' (Ricketts 2003: 267). Or, alternatively, 'Carnap is happy simply to stipulate the primitive logical vocabulary as a part of the description of a semantic system' (Ricketts 2003: 269). One may be judged by one's choices, but choice remains practical – one that is ours to make – precisely because even the notion of justification itself emerges as exact only from within a framework. Put another way, the notion of justification and so of normativity emerges only *intratheoretically*.

As Ricketts observes, 'the thesis of indeterminacy of translation is Quine's response to Carnap. Quine's examination of the role independently describable speech dispositions play in guiding and constraining translation show Carnap's criterion to be a counterfeit' (Ricketts 1982: 127) – counterfeit because it presupposes a framework and has no status apart from one. The problem importantly does not concern the worry that a translator imagines a speaker to be using one set of rules but in actuality a speaker uses another set. *What is lacking is an argument that the observed behaviour can only be a product of some determinate set of rules or another in the first place.* What translation requires does not entail that some prior determinate set of rules or another must be employed by a speaker. Nothing entitles translators to read back into the minds of speakers what they find explanatorily convenient.

Ricketts nicely captures this last point by his reading of Quine's dispute with Chomsky. Chomsky becomes just one more case of explanation by attribution of a shared framework, and so mistakes convenience for a necessity.

> Quine could take Chomsky to be arguing with him, one scientist to another. In particular, Quine could construe Chomsky as offering a rival approach to Quine's behaviorism. ... To dismiss Chomsky's challenge here, Quine need only, from the vantage point of the physical theory of which psychology is a component part, express

his justified confidence that every instance of speech behavior admits of a physical explanation. The failure of behaviorism shows only that we will not have very much to say by way of systematic explanation of verbal behavior until neurophysiology is far more advanced than it is today.

(Ricketts 1982: 135)

Quine can readily and without any harm to his philosophical point concede that behaviourism fails as an *explanation* of verbal behaviour. His behaviourism insists, rather, that whatever *evidence* speakers have for meaning ties back to what can be acquired publicly. The fundamental status of behavioural *evidence* remains unchallenged by failures of behavioural theory to be explanatorily determinative of linguistic behaviour.

In short, what marks out mental or logical kinds as members of those kinds cannot be given a *defining* behavioural correlate. Quine endorses Davidson's anomalous monism for this very reason.[7]

> The point of anomalous monism is just that our mentalistic predicates imposes on bodily states and events a grouping that cannot be defined in the special vocabulary of physiology. Each of those individual states and events is physiologically describable, we presume, given all the pertinent information.
>
> (Quine 1990: 71)

No behavioural fact distinguishes a wink from a blink, hence to infer determinacy of translation – to attribute a fixed or settled meaning – to distinguish between them outruns anything evidence supports. This does not imply, of course, that one makes a mistake to distinguish one from the other, but what meaning one draws from it will depend on what structure a translator imposes on it.

As Ricketts rightly insists,

> In Carnap's view, there is no clear conception of empirical statement, empirical fact, or empirical possibility, apart from the incorporation of observation predicates in to a language with its consequence relation. This is part of the force of the Principle of Tolerance.
>
> (Ricketts 1996: 237)

Carnap's principle counsels pluralism with respect to choice of a framework; such choices can be made freely and without being judged 'right' or 'wrong'. There is no 'right' answer to questions such as 'Do numbers exist?' One's choice of a logical framework determines how one answers such a question. Indeed, it would saddle Carnap with a commitment to the very sort of philosophical controversy – the 'real' nature of mathematical and logical truth – that he means to deflect.

Ricketts notes that Carnap's understanding of how to demarcate descriptive statements, and so factual content, shifts markedly with his move from syntax to semantics (see especially Ricketts 2003: 269). As he remarks,

> In *Introduction to Semantics*, Carnap presents the general semantic characterization of the logic-descriptive dichotomy as an open question – one that Carnap never answer. . . . In the meantime, Carnap is happy simply to stipulate primitive logical vocabulary as a part of the description of a semantic system.
>
> (ibid.)

This is why any talk of right or wrong, satisfactory or unsatisfactory, *presupposes* the adoption of a formal framework, for only in this context can such judgements be made.

Carnap's emphasis assumes that practical choices are there to be made, once metaphysical constraints have been lifted. But if one sees, as does Quine, choices guided from the outset by pragmatic (in the specified sense) notions about how at least some matters need to turn out, the insistence that logic should not be based on prior prohibitions proves idle. One has no free choice here. Pragmatics stands, contingently yet inescapably, as the 'metaphysics' initially influencing all speculation about methods of inquiry. From Quine's standpoint, to imagine that a choice of *Wissenschaftslogik* somehow escapes such prior constraints would appear hopelessly naive. This would include naivety, for the very reasons just rehearsed, regarding what counts as logic and what does not. Just as with metaphysical allegiances, so-called practical choices will be guided by some prior sense (itself a function of the contingencies of time, place, and language first learned) of the appropriate or the possible.

Thus, on the interpretation suggested, 'pressing from above' shows that choice of theory is never innocent; there is no truly external stance from which to judge choices of language in terms of theoretical preferences. As historically located individuals, one starts with a received science and a community that already accepts or rejects certain ways of expressing oneself. 'Pressing from below' reiterates the point about underdetermination – that is, that evidence alone can at best determine what translations appear to be rule-conforming. The inference from rule-conforming behaviour to a theory that captures supposed rule-following just represents a type of metaphysical inference that Quine argues against.

What remains of meaning?

In this regard, Charles Morris's discussion of the issues (Morris 1936), in a talk delivered around the time that Quine published 'Truth by Convention' (in 1935: Quine 1966), proved prescient. Morris notes, 'Pragmatism distinguishes itself from English empiricism by its emphasis upon biological and social categories (it is not falsely described as bio-social positivism' (Morris 1936: 130). Morris goes on to denigrate logical positivism's early commitment to traditional empiricism as an 'unexamined individualistic hangover' that compares unfavourably to 'the pragmatic emphasis upon the social aspects of meaning and knowledge' (Morris 1936: 132). But emphasis on the social dimension comes at a philosophic price, at least for those with a commitment to traditional empiricism. What, then, of objective knowledge? Imagine, Morris suggests, that each individual makes a list of sentences he or she verifies:

> In such a list of propositions it is clear that there is no absolute line of demarcation to determine when a proposition is to be given an honorific status in the domain of knowledge. ... And since the list is never completed, there can be no certainty that the rank of any specific propositions will henceforth undergo no change.
> (Morris 1936: 134).

This turn to the pragmatic/social and away from the individual/empirical has consequences as well for understanding efforts to formalize languages. In particular,

> when we choose the rules of operation for a constructed language we must understand in a non-formal sense what operations the rules permit. In both cases we can later formulate

the rules themselves in formal terms, but only by using language not itself at that moment in the purely formal mode.

(Morris 137)

Now Quine:

[I]t is not clear wherein an adoption of the conventions, antecedently to their formulation, consists; such behavior is difficult to distinguish from that in which conventions are disregarded. ... [B]ut when a convention is incapable of being communicated until after its adoption, its role is not so clear. In dropping the attributes of deliberateness and explicitness from the notion of linguistic convention we risk depriving the latter of any explanatory force and reducing it to an idle label. We may wonder what one adds to the bare statement that the truths of logic and mathematics are a priori, or to the still barer behavioristic statement that they are firmly accepted, when he characterizes them as true by convention in such a sense.

(Quine 1966: 99)

The belief that choice of conventions need not reflect any epistemic/philosophic prejudices proves illusory. Against Carnap, choice must be guided by historically and culturally contingent but ineliminable preconceptions. The flight from metaphysics proves to be the proverbial appointment in Samarra – no one can choose unconstrained by unscientific thoughts about how matters must be. Social/behavioural conformity cannot serve as a proxy for empiricism since it utterly fails to explain what acquires social endorsement in the first place. The social and behavioural, that is, cannot be a philosophic proxy for classical empiricism because the social is 'always already' theoretical.

Quine, I suggest, realizes all this. Thus when he writes at the end of the opening paragraph of *Two Dogmas* of 'blurring the lines between speculative metaphysics and natural science', he realizes full well that the blurring occurs because recognition of the line presupposes that one knows the realm in which practical reason (freedom) can be exercised. Carnap saw metaphysics as limiting that realm. Quine appreciates, however, that we never have more than pragmatics, a scientific/systematized attempt at understanding our own inherited language use. Any attempt to hive off a space of the practical apart from the pragmatic seeks what cannot be had, a 'point apart' from where history has destined us to begin. So, Quine goes on to famously state, once we acknowledge that any formalization of a language can be no more than the imposition of a structure on some of our preconceptions in favour of others, this marks a 'shift towards pragmatism' and away from a belief that such decisions represent a free choice. Our contingencies of birth function as our inevitable *de facto* metaphysics. These may be altered by inquiry, as history demonstrates, but they condition our starting points.

Quine's remarks on the indeterminacy of translation ought to inform how one reads certain important statements by Davidson on the topic of translation. Although this cannot be argued here, Davidson's views on translation evolved and (I would say) became radical over the course of his career. A clear signal of what I regard as Davidson's radicalization can be found in his justly famous presidential address to the APA. There Davidson too gave explicit voice to the thought of meaning/translation as a result of an *imposed* framework.

It would be wrong to summarize by saying we have shown how communication is possible between people who have different schemes ... For we have found no intelligible basis on which it can be said that schemes are different. It would be equally wrong to announce the glorious news that all mankind – all speakers of language, at least – share a common scheme and ontology. *For if we cannot intelligibly say that schemes are different, neither can we intelligibly say that they are one.*

(Davidson 1974: 20, emphasis mine)

That is, as I read Davidson, there exists no prior conceptual scheme to recapture. There only exist those that one implicitly or explicitly formulates for purposes of understanding others (or oneself). I take Davidson here to explicitly deny that truth, ontology, or meaning exist as an 'uninterpreted reality'. Like Quine, he insists that these notions make sense only intra-theoretically. He also explicitly acknowledges that interpreters impose a scheme; there does not exist a conceptual scheme awaiting discovery or recapture.

When Davidson returns to this theme a decade later, his thought takes an even more radical tack, for now he explicitly endorses, or so I suggest, Quine's scepticism about meaning that results from 'pressing from above' – that is, assuming that there exists a conceptual scheme that constitutes the one people actually follow, as opposed to one to which they merely conform.

> The problem we have been grappling with depends on the assumption that communication by speech requires that speaker and interpreter have learned or somehow acquired a common method or theory of interpretation – as being able to operate on the basis of shared conventions, rules, or regularities. The problem arose when we realized that no method or theory fills this bill. The solution to the problem is clear. In linguistic communication nothing corresponds to a linguistic competence as often described. ... I conclude that there is no such thing as a language, not if a language is anything like what many philosophers and linguists have supposed. There is therefore no such thing to be learned, mastered, or born with. We must give up the idea of a clearly defined shared structure which language-users acquire and then apply to cases.

(Davidson 2006: 265)

This does not mean to imply that Davidson merely parrots Quine or simply acquiesces to his conclusion. Important differences exist between the two regarding what bits of language can be analysed and how to do so. But these differences notwithstanding, they do converge clearly and forcefully on the conclusion that a belief in a shared structure as explanatory of meaning must be rejected. Whatever their paths to this conclusion, it remains a conclusion that they share.

This does not return us to some alternative theory of meaning; there exists nothing to be a theory of. Rather, it emphasizes the fundamental importance of what Morris terms the pragmatics of language. Note as well that whatever pragmatics reveals by way of its analysis of language, that account will be underdetermined. But, finally, pragmatics so conceived simply cannot assume a realm of meaning prior to (and apart from) whatever a 'manual of translation' provides, for to insist on this would be to place unwarranted metaphysical constraints on any manual of translation by making assumptions about what *must* be guiding a choice of logic (of translation in this case) *prior* to any scientific/systematic inquiry into the issue. Indeed, the constraints appear to involve just the same confusion of the philosophical and the pragmatic – that is, mistaking empirical results achieved by application of a specific theory for some general insight into how matters must necessarily be for any theory on the topic.[8] Thus does the dead hand of a 'metaphysics of meaning' continue to weigh like a nightmare on the brains of the living.

Notes

1. For biographical information on Quine, see his autobiography (Quine 1985). See also the web page devoted to writings by and about Quine's life and works, including the transcripts of numerous interviews: http://www.wvquine.org/. Regarding Quine on translation, this paper draws upon as well as amplifies my earlier efforts to reconstruct an argument for the indeterminacy of translation. Primary among these are (Roth 1978, 2003a). My exegetical emphasis remains focused on Quine's challenges to any notion of a *framework* for translation and how claims to indeterminacy tie to assumptions about a *prior* framework.
2. Although beyond the scope of this discussion, issues surrounding putative distinctions between the logical and the empirical (so-called L-rules and P-rules) and the project of developing a *Wissenschaftslogik* shadow this whole debate. Roughly speaking, the fundamental philosophical issue concerns the possibility of distinguishing between the psychological and the logical, and so what is empirical/contingent (and thus a matter for empirical science) and what is purely formal and not subject to empirical determination (and so a matter for philosophy). Because it was thought that the inference rules and consequence relations of formal logic could be fully *syntactically* specified, logic was held to be free of all metaphysical assumptions. A pure 'science of logic' – *Wissenschaftslogik* – would thus preserve what could be salvaged of Kant's distinction between the *a priori* and the *a posteriori* in light of advances in logic and science. Given some vestige of Kant's distinction, there then remains an area of 'reason' not subject to empirical determination. Surrendering Kant's distinction, however, would be to effectively give up philosophy as an autonomous branch of scientific knowledge. Quine's attack on the analytic/synthetic distinction, which includes the indeterminacy of translation, challenges this last remnant of Kant's bifurcation. Regarding the signification and status of *Wissenschaftslogik*, see, for example, Richardson (1996) and Ricketts (1994, 1996, 2007, 2009).
3. Talk of 'surface irritations' signals only that Quine takes it that contemporary science licenses empiricism – that is, the view that information reaches individuals *only* through the senses. As I argue in Roth (2003a), Quine is neither a reductionist nor a conventional behaviourist. In particular, his behaviourism ties to his account of *evidence*.
4. I owe this way of putting the point to Piers Rawling.
5. Space does not permit discussion of relationships and differences here between Quine's rejection of determinacy in the sense specified and Robert Brandom's inferentialism.
6. I adapt and deploy Quine's characterizations of arguing for indeterminacy by 'pressing from above' and 'pressing from below' (Quine 1970a: 183) to my own purposes.
7. See Chapter 8, this volume, for a discussion of anomalous monism.
8. Although this cannot be argued here, my position certainly implies that the principle of charity constitutes at most a *pragmatic* constraint on interpreters.

Related topics

Wittgenstein; Davidson; current trends in philosophy and translation; meaning.

Further reading

Hylton, P. (2007) *Quine*. New York: Routledge. (The most comprehensive, systematic, and scholarly study available of Quine's philosophy.)

Kripke, S. (1982) *Wittgenstein on Rules and Private Language*. Cambridge, MA: Harvard. (Although not primarily about Quine, this still represents one of the most interesting discussions of scepticism about the notion of meaning of the type that Quine inspires.)

Quine, W. V. (1960) *Word and Object*. Cambridge, MA: MIT Press. (One of the major twentieth-century works in Anglo-American philosophy of language and a good place to begin for those interested in Quine's account of translation. (Quine introduces his famous thought experiment regarding the referent of 'gavagai' in §12.))

References

Begby, E. (2016) Deranging the Mental Lexicon. *Inquiry*, 59, pp. 33–55.
Davidson, D. (1974) On the Very Idea of a Conceptual Scheme. *Proceedings and Addresses of the American Philosophical Association*, 47, pp. 5–20.
Davidson, D. (2006) A Nice Derangement of Epitaphs. In: E. Lepore and K. Ludwig, eds. *The Essential Davidson*. Oxford: Clarendon Press, pp. 251–65.
Davidson, D. and J. Hintikka, eds. (1969) *Words and Objections: Essays on the Work of W. V. Quine*. Dordrecht-Holland: Reidel.
Dreben, B. (1992) Putnam, Quine – and the Facts. *Philosophical Topics*, 20, pp. 293–315.
Glock, H-J. (2003) *Quine and Davidson on Language, Thought and Reality*. New York: Cambridge University Press.
Hylton, P. (2007) *Quine*. New York: Routledge.
Moore, G. E. (1968/1903) *Principia Ethica*. Cambridge: Cambridge University Press.
Morris, C. 1936. The Concept of Meaning in Pragmatism and Logical Positivism. *Actes du huitième congrès international de philosophie* (Prague 1936), pp. 130–8.
Quine, W. V. (1959). Meaning and Translation. In: R. Brower, ed. *On Translation*. Cambridge, MA: Harvard University Press, pp. 148–72.
Quine, W. V. (1960). *Word and Object*. Cambridge, MA: MIT Press.
Quine, W. V. (1966) *Ways of Paradox and Other Essays*. New York: Random House.
Quine, W. V. (1969) *Ontological Relativity and Other Essays*. New York: Columbia University Press.
Quine, W. V. (1970a) On the Reasons for the Indeterminacy of Translation. *Journal of Philosophy*, 67, pp. 178–83.
Quine, W. V. (1970b) Methodological Reflections on Current Linguistic Theory. *Synthese*, 21, pp. 386–98.
Quine, W. V. (1975) On Empirically Equivalent Systems of the World. *Erkenntnis*, 9, pp. 313–28.
Quine, W. V. (1980a) Linguistics and Philosophy. In: H. Morick, ed. *Challenges to Empiricism*. Indianapolis, IN: Hackett, pp. 257–9.
Quine, W. V. (1980b) Sellars on Behaviorism, Language and Meaning. *Pacific Philosophical Quarterly*, 61, pp. 26–30.
Quine, W. V. (1981) *Theories and Things*. Cambridge, MA: Harvard University Press.
Quine, W. V. (1985) *The Time of My Life*. Cambridge, MA: Harvard University Press.
Quine, W. V. (1990) *Pursuit of Truth*. Cambridge, MA: Harvard University Press.
Richardson, A. (1996) From Epistemology to the Logic of Science: Carnap's Philosophy of Empirical Knowledge in the 1930s. In: Ronald N. Giere and Alan W. Richardson, eds. *Origins of Logical Empiricism*. Minneapolis: University of Minnesota Press, pp. 309–32.
Ricketts, T. (1982) Rationality, Translation, and Epistemology Naturalized. *Journal of Philosophy*, 79, pp. 117–35.
Ricketts, T. (1994) Carnap's Principle of Tolerance, Empiricism, and Conventionalism. In: Peter Clark and Bob Hale, eds. *Reading Putnam*. Cambridge: Blackwell, pp. 176–200.
Ricketts, T. (1996) Carnap: From Logical Syntax to Semantics. In: Ronald N. Giere and Alan W. Richardson, eds. *Origins of Logical Empiricism*, Minneapolis: University of Minnesota Press, pp. 231–50.
Ricketts, T. (2003) Languages and Calculi. In: Gary L. Hardcastle and Alan W. Richardson, eds. *Logical Empiricism in North America*. Minneapolis: University of Minnesota Press, pp. 257–80.
Ricketts, T. (2007) Tolerance and Logicism: Logical Syntax and the Philosophy of Mathematics. In: Michael Friedman and Richard Creath, eds. *The Cambridge Companion to Carnap*. Cambridge: Cambridge University Press, pp. 200–25.
Ricketts, T. (2009) From Tolerance to Reciprocal Containment. In: Pierre Wagner, ed. *Carnap's Logical Syntax of Language*. New York: Palgrave Macmillan, pp. 217–35.
Roth, P. A. (1978) Paradox and Indeterminacy. *Journal of Philosophy*, 75, pp. 347–67.

Roth, P. A. (2003a) Why There Is Nothing Rather than Something: Quine on Behaviorism, Meaning, and Indeterminacy. In: D. Jacquette, ed. *Philosophy, Psychology, and Psychologism*. Boston, MA: Kluwer, pp. 263–87.

Roth, P. A. (2003b) Mistakes. *Synthese*, 136, pp. 389–408.

Roth, P. A. (2006) Naturalism without Fears. In: S. Turner and M. Risjord, eds. *Handbook of the Philosophy of Science, Volume 15: Philosophy of Anthropology and Sociology*. Boston, MA: Elsevier, pp. 683–708.

Sellars, W. (1980) Behaviorism, Language and Meaning. *Pacific Philosophical Quarterly*, 61, pp. 3–25.

8
Davidson

Piers Rawling

Introduction

Donald Herbert Davidson (1917–2003) was one of the foremost Anglo-American philosophers of the second half of the twentieth century. He made important contributions in several major areas of philosophy – including philosophy of language, philosophy of action, philosophy of mind, and metaphysics. He is notable for his systematic approach: his contributions are multiply interconnected. Davidson published much of his work in essays that appeared in a wide variety of venues over many years, but many of these have been usefully collected in Davidson (2001a, 2001b, 2001c, 2005a). References to essays that appear in these volumes will refer to the volume in question.

I cannot hope to do justice here to Davidson's innovative and impressive edifice, but I shall try to elucidate the parts that are relevant to translation theorists as well as raise some criticisms. I begin by placing Davidson in the context of Quine and Wittgenstein, and see them all as united in rejecting the 'conventional' account of language and meaning. In addition, a principle that is key to understanding many of Davidson's views emerges: the manifestation principle. This states that there can be nothing more to the meaning of a speaker's words than can be gleaned from observation, where this observation is necessarily guided by certain maxims of interpretation, collectively known as the 'principle of charity' (a principle of particular relevance to translators and translation theorists). But the principle of charity does not force unique interpretations. Indeed, interpretation, on Davidson's view, is inevitably indeterminate: there are myriad interpretations of a given speaker that all account for the data equally well, and no one of them is uniquely 'correct'.

Other topics covered include 'radical' interpretation, Davidson's application of Tarski's definition of truth, his argument to the effect that thought requires 'triangulation' (2001c: 128–30), his denial that there is any such thing as a 'conceptual scheme' (2001b: 183–98), his 'anomalous monism' (2001a: 207–27), holism about meaning and thought (2001c: 98–9), and his claim that there is no thought without talk (2001c: 95–105).

I shall paint with a broad brush, and no doubt some will disagree with my interpretation of Davidson's views. But I hope at least to present a comprehensible version of part of his overall picture of language and thought, and how its components fit together. (It may be helpful to bear in mind that much of Davidson's approach is 'transcendental' in the broad sense that he explores the conditions for the possibility of interpretation, of language, and of thought.)

Historical perspectives, the rejection of the conventional account of language, and the manifestation principle

Quine (see Chapter 7, this volume) was a major influence on Davidson, with both acknowledging similarities between parts of their views and those of Wittgenstein (who is discussed in Chapter 4, this volume) (see Quine 1960: 76–7; Davidson 2001c: 129). And both can be seen as adopting a view commonly associated with Wittgenstein – the claim that the meanings of expressions are determined by their observable use:

> For a *large* class of cases of the employment of the word 'meaning' – though not for all – this word can be explained in this way: the meaning of a word is its use in the language.
> (Wittgenstein *PI* 43)

This might be taken as advocating a focus on pragmatics (see Chapter 12, this volume). However, pragmatics might, in turn, be seen as presupposing what I'll call a 'conventional' account of meaning, and as simply supplementing that account – consider, for instance the following, from the entry on pragmatics in *The Stanford Encyclopedia of Philosophy*:

> Pragmatics is usually thought to involve a different sort of *reasoning* than semantics. Semantics consists of conventional rules of meaning for expressions and their modes of combination. ... In contrast, pragmatics involves ... reasoning that goes beyond the application of rules, and makes inferences beyond what is established by the basic facts about what expressions are used and their meanings.
> (Korta and Perry 2015)

However, Quine and Davidson have something far more radical in mind – something more akin to the views ascribed to Wittgenstein by Kripke (1982 – see pp. 55–8 for Kripke's explicit comparison of Quine and Wittgenstein). On the view of meaning that we find in, say, Frege (1892), an expression has a meaning ('sense') that is grasped by competent speakers – and it is this grasp that implies the existence of standards of application: mistakes are possible. The later Wittgenstein ([1953] 2009) can be interpreted as arguing that this is entirely the wrong picture – there is nothing about a speaker that could constitute her grasp of a meaning (where such a grasp would dictate how the expression so grasped should be applied), and hence there are no conventional meanings (if there were, they would be graspable). If this scepticism holds, there is simply no fact of the matter about how expressions should be applied – it is impossible to make mistakes, not because speakers are infallible, but, rather, because there are no meaning facts to be mistaken about. Kripke sees Wittgenstein arriving at this sceptical conclusion via the latter's 'rule-following considerations': no finite sequence of applications of any 'rule' can dictate how further applications should proceed. So Kripke sees Wittgenstein as worrying that language is impossible but then proposing a way out – namely, that language is essentially social (1982: 79, 88ff.). And it is here, according to Kripke, that Wittgenstein's discussion of the impossibility of a private language comes in: there is no room for such a language if language is essentially social.

On Kripke's account of Wittgenstein, then, the sceptical problem is that there are no meanings – no language of any sort: 'Wittgenstein's main problem is that it appears that he has shown *all* language, *all* concept formation, to be impossible, indeed unintelligible' (1982: 62). Wittgenstein's 'sceptical solution' (1982: 4), according to Kripke, involves 'widen[ing] our gaze . . . to the wider community' (1982: 89), and it is this appeal to the social nature of language that renders private languages impossible: 'It is [Wittgenstein's] solution that . . . contains the argument against "private language"; for allegedly, the solution will not admit such a language' (1982: 60).

Neither Quine nor Davidson appeals to Wittgenstein's arguments explicitly, but both agree with one of their upshots – namely, there are no such things as 'meanings' to be uncovered. This claim is perhaps of a piece with Derrida's rejection of 'logocentrism' (see Chapter 9, this volume), and Davidson can be interpreted as endorsing it when he writes:

> In linguistic communication nothing corresponds to a linguistic competence as often described . . . I conclude that there is no such thing as a language, not if a language is anything like what many philosophers and linguists have supposed. There is therefore no such thing to be learned, mastered, or born with. We must give up the idea of a clearly defined shared structure which language-users acquire and then apply to cases. And we should try again to say how convention in any important sense is involved in language; or, as I think, we should give up the attempt to illuminate how we communicate by appeal to conventions.
>
> (2005a: 107)

How do Quine and Davidson arrive at the rejection of conventional meaning? Let us return to Wittgenstein's directive to focus upon meaning as use. On Kripke's account, this directive emerges as part of Wittgenstein's sceptical solution, and the underlying idea is shared by Quine and Davidson. In the latter pair's hands, this idea finds expression as the thought that all an interpreter can do is focus upon the use of language by her interpretee and the claim that there can be no more to what someone means than what she can make manifest to an observer. There is thus a reversal of the conventional direction of dependence of use upon meaning – rather than meaning largely determining correct use, it's the other way around: use determines meaning. Let's call this claim that meaning must be manifest in, and is wholly determined by, use the 'manifestation principle'. But how do Quine and Davidson argue for it?

Quine opens the preface to *Word and Object* (1960: ix) thus:

> Language is a social art. In acquiring it we have to depend entirely on intersubjectively available cues as to what to say and when. Hence there is no justification for collating linguistic meanings, unless in terms of men's dispositions to respond overtly to socially observable stimulations. An effect of recognizing this limitation is that the enterprise of translation is found to be involved in a certain systematic indeterminacy . . .

This expresses not only a commitment to the manifestation principle but also the claims that this thesis follows from considerations of language acquisition, and that use does not yield unique translation.

Davidson's approach is more Wittgensteinian, at least in his argument to the effect that thought requires what he calls 'triangulation' with other thinkers (2001c: 128–30). The Wittgensteinian argument against conventional meaning appeals, as we have seen, to normative considerations – where 'normative' is used in its prescriptive sense. A norm in this sense is something that *should* be followed, not something that is followed. One mark of normativity in this prescriptive sense is that error is possible: you can do as you shouldn't. Prescriptive normativity (henceforth, 'normativity'), then, is essential to language on the conventional account rejected by Wittgenstein – linguistic mistakes are possible. Wittgenstein argues that nothing about a speaker considered in isolation, however, could constitute her being normatively bound in this way. It is only when we consider her as part of a community that normativity can enter. Davidson, roughly speaking, shares this conclusion, and, although he argues for it in a somewhat different way, his focus is, like Wittgenstein's, upon normativity.

Here's how Davidson sets things up:

> The basic situation is one that involves two or more creatures simultaneously in interaction with each other and with the world they share; it is what I call *triangulation*. ... [This triangle] is essential to the existence ... of thought. For without the triangle, there are two aspects of thought for which we cannot account. These two aspects are the objectivity of thought and the empirical content of thoughts about the external world.
>
> (2001c: 128–9)

By 'the objectivity of thought', Davidson means simply that thought 'has a content which is true or false independent (with rare exceptions) of the existence of the thought or the thinker' (2001c: 129). Thus thought is objective just in case we can be in error, so Davidson seeks to show that the possibility of error depends upon social interaction, as in the 'triangle':

> Where do we get the idea that we may be mistaken, that things may not be as we think they are? Wittgenstein has suggested, or at least I take him to have suggested, that we would not have the concept of getting things wrong or right if it were not for our interactions with other people. The triangle I have described stands for the simplest interpersonal situation. In it two (or more) creatures each correlate their own reactions to external phenomena with the reactions of the other. Once these correlations are set up, each creature is in a position to expect the external phenomenon when it perceives the associated reaction of the other. What introduces the possibility of error is the occasional failure of the expectation; the reactions do not correlate. Wittgenstein expresses this idea when he talks of the difference between following a rule and merely thinking one is following a rule; he says that following the rule (getting things right) is at bottom a matter of doing as others do. Of course, the others may sometimes be wrong. The point isn't that consensus defines the concept of truth but that it creates the space for its application. If this is right, then thought as well as language is necessarily social.
>
> (2001c: 129)

However, in this passage, Davidson seems to move from the thought that if we cannot help but believe we may be in error, then we may be in error – and hence beliefs are either false or true, so that thought is objective. This is reminiscent of Kant's transcendental idealism, roughly: if we cannot help but think things are thus and so, then things are thus and so. And this form of reasoning is subject to challenge. But let us set that aside and move on to the other component, 'the content of thoughts about the external world':

> Social interaction, triangulation, also gives us the only account of how experience gives a specific content to our thoughts. Without other people with whom to share responses to a mutual environment, there is no answer to the question what it is in the world to which we are responding. The reason has to do with the ambiguity of the concept of cause. It is essential to resolve these ambiguities, since it is, in the simplest cases, what causes a

belief that gives it its content. In the present case, the cause is doubly indeterminate: with respect to width, and with respect to distance. The first ambiguity concerns how much of the total cause of a belief is relevant to its content. The brief answer is that it is the part or aspect of the total cause that typically causes relevantly similar responses. What makes the responses relevantly similar in turn is the fact that others find those responses similar; once more it is the social sharing of reactions that makes the objectivity of content available. The second problem has to do with the ambiguity of the relevant stimulus, whether it is proximal (at the skin, say) or distal. What makes the distal stimulus the relevant determiner of content is again its social character; it is the cause that is shared. The stimulus is thus triangulated; it is where the causes converge in the world.

(2001c: 129–30)

One difficulty here is an apparent regress. If there were facts of the matter about brute similarity, then it would be possible for an isolated individual privately to go on in the 'same way' or respond similarly to similar stimuli. And there would be a fact of the matter as to whether or not she should do either, independently of what she or others happen to judge (we could not, in my view, analyse this 'should' in non-normative terms, but why expect that?). Davidson argues against this possibility by pointing to what he sees as the need to have someone else confirming, or not, an individual's response to some stimulus. What makes two stimuli similar, it seems, are similar responses, and what makes two responses 'relevantly similar in turn is the fact that others find those responses similar'. However, what constitutes others' finding these responses similar? Presumably, these others must have similar responses to them, which responses must in turn be found similar by other people. But where does this end (bearing in mind that it cannot end in individuals making solo judgements)?

Even ignoring these difficulties, however, the question arises as to whether these considerations justify the manifestation principle. Davidson does not claim that they do, but I am not aware of any other argument that he supplies in its favour, and exploring the claim that thought is necessarily 'social' looks promising. However, as Davidson notes (2001c: 130), while, on his account, triangulation is 'necessary to thought[, i]t is not sufficient'. He then asks, 'What more is needed for thought?' and answers, 'language'. Animals that 'we do not credit with judgement' can 'triangulate'; it is language that distinguishes those that judge from those that merely respond. (Davidson realizes, of course, that 'this is not much help, since it is obvious that a creature that has language can think'. However, there is still an issue of interest, which he then goes on to explore – namely, 'why language is essential to thought'.)

The upshot is that Davidson does not establish, via his triangulation argument, the social nature of language, in the sense expressed in the manifestation principle. Indeed, he seems simply to assume that language is 'social', as revealed in the concluding sentence to the second of the passages on triangulation cited above: 'If this is right, then thought as well as language is necessarily social'. Perhaps, then, Davidson does not see the need to justify the manifestation principle. Be that as it may, it plays, as we shall see, a central role in much of his thinking about language.

The principle of charity, radical interpretation, and indeterminacy

Suppose you find yourself stranded on a desert island with one fellow castaway. Unfortunately, you rapidly discover that you cannot communicate with her. In your attempt to determine whether she has a language, and, if so, what she means by her utterances, you must engage in what Davidson calls 'radical interpretation'. If you are to communicate, you must build your interpretation from the ground up. Davidson asks: how is this possible? He pursues the answer by laying down criteria that interpretation must meet. In order for interaction to be mutual interpretation, the parties must make assumptions about each other – assumptions that could not turn out to be false lest their enterprise fail to be interpretation. In this sense, then, no interpretation is built entirely from nothing, and it is this that helps make radical interpretation possible. The ineliminable assumptions we must make, in limiting what counts as interpretation, provide a structure without which radical interpretation would be impossible.

Why focus on radical interpretation rather than a situation in which we are interpreting someone who speaks a more familiar tongue? One reply is that our reliance upon the assumptions that are necessary for all interpretation might be at least partially obscured if we do not attend to the radical interpreter. In interpreting a language that is to some degree familiar at the start, our reliance upon these assumptions might remain merely implicit. The radical situation forces them out into the open.

What are these assumptions? Wilson (1959) coined the term 'principle of charity' to name the following principle: 'We select as designatum that individual which will make the largest possible number of... statements true'. Quine appeals to this idea in formulating a key 'maxim of translation':

> assertions startlingly false on the face of them are likely to turn on hidden differences of language. This maxim is strong enough in all of us to swerve us even from the homophonic method that is so fundamental to the very acquisition and use of the mother tongue.
>
> The common sense behind the maxim is that one's interlocutor's silliness, beyond a certain point, is less likely than bad translation – or, in the domestic case, linguistic divergence.
>
> (1960: 59)

A crucial form of silliness for Quine is the flouting of logic: 'fair translation preserves logical laws'. To call this 'charity' is, of course, an intentional misnomer: to be uncharitable is to disengage from the practice of translation. Davidson (2001b: xix) goes beyond Quine in 'apply[ing] the Principle of Charity across the board. So applied, it counsels us quite generally to prefer theories of interpretation that minimize disagreement' in such a way as to secure understanding. As Davidson puts it, he 'use[s] Quine's inspired method in ways that deviate, sometimes substantially, from his [Quine's]' (1990: 319).

What makes interpretation possible, according to Davidson, 'is the structure the normative character of thought, desire, speech, and action imposes on correct attributions of attitudes to others, and hence on interpretations of their speech and explanations of their actions' (1990: 325). In other words:

> The possibility of understanding the speech or actions of an agent depends on the existence of a fundamentally rational pattern, a pattern that must, in general outline, be shared by all rational creatures.
>
> (2005b: 63)

Davidson seeks to show how it is possible to attribute meanings and other propositional attitudes (beliefs and desires and their ilk) when observable behaviour is our only evidence. He gives us a sketch of how an idealized interpretation might proceed. However, the sketch is not to be taken literally: Davidson's exercise is 'conceptual' (1990: 325), and what emerges is certainly not intended as a manual for the field linguist. Rather, the function of the sketch is to illustrate the structural restrictions on interpretation. Interpretation is possible because the interpreter is forced to interpret the behaviour of interpretees as conforming to patterns dictated by a general form of the principle of charity: it is constitutive of the propositional attitudes that they be largely rational, where rationality encompasses, amongst others, norms of evidence, preference, desirability, and action. This is not to say that there is no room for irrationality; but it cannot be too pervasive. Just as there is no chaos unless against a background of order, so there is no irrationality unless against a background of rationality.

Here is a sketch of part of Davidson's interpretational procedure (see also Davidson 2005b: 61ff.; Rawling 2003). He envisages the interpreter as having worked out that her interpretee holds true a sentence S, hence S expresses one of the interpretee's beliefs – but which one? If the interpreter knew that S means that p, then she could conclude that S expresses the interpretee's belief that p. Alternatively, if S expresses the belief that p, then S means that p. But the interpreter's problem is that she seeks two outputs, belief and meaning, from one input: S is held true. How is she to proceed? This is where charity comes in. The charitable presumption here is that, if the interpreter is prompted to believe that p in the circumstances that prompt her interpretee to hold true S, then S expresses the interpretee's belief that p (and hence S, in the interpretee's idiolect, means that p). That is, the interpretee's basic beliefs must turn out to be true by the interpreter's lights: 'it makes for mutual understanding, and hence for better interpretation, to interpret what the speaker accepts as true as true when we can' (Davidson 2001c: 149). And this breaks the logjam to a degree – the remaining difficulty being that in many cases, perhaps all, there will be 'indeterminacy': the interpreter will not be able to determine which of several true beliefs the circumstances prompt. Thus more than one belief-meaning pair will account for the interpretee's holding true some sentence.

At this point, the relevance of this line of thinking may be questioned, since, in practical terms, working out first which sentences an interpretee holds true is unrealistic. But, as noted above, this is a conceptual exercise, so perhaps it's best to think of matters this way: suppose the interpreter could work out that her interpretee holds various sentences true, to what extent would that pin matters down? The point is that even if an interpreter could get this far, it's not far enough to preclude indeterminacy.

The strictures of charity notwithstanding, then, complete interpretations are far from unique: even if we were able to acquire all of the relevant evidence, the principle of charity would still leave many interpretations open: 'the evidence on which all these matters depend gives us no way of separating out the contributions of thought, action, desire, and meaning one by one. Total theories are what we must construct, and many theories will do equally well' (Davidson 2001b: 241; see also LePore and Ludwig 2005, chapter 15 and the Davidson references therein).

All interpretations that save the behavioural phenomena and satisfy charity are, then, on a par. And there will be many such adequate interpretations of any given interpretee. Here's how Davidson sums up the relationship between interpretations and the evidence for them:

> What we *should* demand, however, is that the evidence for the theory [of meaning for a speaker] be in principle publicly accessible ... The requirement that the evidence be publicly accessible is not due to an atavistic yearning for behavioristic or verificationist foundations, but to the fact that what is to be explained is a social phenomenon. Mental phenomena in general may or may not be private, but the correct interpretation of one person's speech by another must *in principle* be possible. A speaker's intention that her

words be understood in a certain way may of course remain opaque to even the most skilled and knowledgeable listener, but what has to do with correct interpretation, meaning and truth conditions is necessarily based on available evidence. As Wittgenstein has insisted, not to mention Dewey, G. H. Mead, Quine, and many others, language is intrinsically social. This does not entail that truth and meaning can be *defined* in terms of observable behavior, or that they are 'nothing but' observable behavior; but it does imply that meaning is entirely determined by observable behavior, even readily observable behavior. That meanings are decipherable is not a matter of luck; public availability is a constitutive aspect of language.

(2005b: 55–6)

It is crucial to note that there are two different notions of indeterminacy implicit here, both of which are familiar from the philosophy of science. Consider first the claim that the evidence for interpretation must be publicly available. This parallels science – an interpretation is a theory, and the evidence for scientific theories must also be publicly available. And in both cases evidence underdetermines theory – more than one theory is adequate in the sense of being consistent with all our observations (which is not to say that in science even one has been formulated). In the case of interpretation, then, we have what I shall refer to as 'epistemic indeterminacy': there are many distinct adequate interpretations of any given interpretee. And this epistemic indeterminacy is not contingent upon the fact that our evidence is limited to what we have so far observed: even if, *per impossibile*, we knew how our interpretee would behave under all possible circumstances, the claim is that our knowledge would still underdetermine interpretation – as Quine puts it: 'translation [is] indeterminate in principle relative to the totality of speech dispositions' (1960: 221). Thus, even in the observational limit, as it were, there will be many competing adequate interpretations of a given interpretee.

The second notion of indeterminacy tracks an instrumentalist response to underdetermination in science. Scientific realists maintain that, even though many incompatible theories are adequate in that they 'save the phenomena', there is exactly one true theory amongst them. Instrumentalists, by contrast, maintain that there is no fact of the matter here. Davidson's second notion of indeterminacy results from a combination of epistemic indeterminacy with the manifestation principle – the thesis 'that meaning is entirely determined by observable behavior'. This combination entails that there are many competing interpretations that save the behavioural phenomena, and that there is no fact of the matter concerning which of them is correct. To cite Quine again, the 'point is not that we cannot be sure whether [our translation] is right, but that there is not [in the case of translation that lacks the possibility of direct observational test] an objective matter to be right or wrong about' (1960: 73). I shall refer to this absence, which parallels the combination of underdetermination and instrumentalism in the discussion of scientific theories, as 'metaphysical indeterminacy'.

So far we have been appealing to a restricted form of the manifestation principle: meaning must be manifestable in, and is wholly determined by, use. But meaning and the propositional attitudes are interdependent: to attribute a meaning to an utterance is to attribute a propositional attitude that it expresses. Thus Davidson appeals to a general form of the manifestation principle: there can be nothing more to meaning *and the propositional attitudes* than the (potentially) observable phenomena provide. And hence, on his view, there appear to be facts of the matter neither concerning what we mean by (many of) our words, nor the contents of (many of) our propositional attitudes. (Note that this seems inconsistent with Davidson's idea from the previous section that 'triangulation... gives us the only account of how experience gives a specific content to our thoughts'; but I shall not delve further into that here.) And thus it seems that Davidson must renounce the attitudes, since they are individuated by their contents (what distinguishes the belief that grass is green from the belief that snow is white is that the first has the content *that grass is green,* whereas the second has the content *that snow is white*). But, amongst many other difficulties (such as the fact that we couldn't believe the theory he is propounding), Davidson's abandoning the propositional attitudes undercuts radical interpretation: radical interpretation requires charity, and charity requires the existence of beliefs (not only must the interpretee have beliefs, but they must rationally cohere, and many of them must be true).

Davidson, however, claims that the multiplicity of interpretations is no more problematic than, say, the multiplicity of scales of length measurement – interpretation is analogous to measurement. The basic idea of Davidson's analogical strategy is clear enough (Davidson 2001c: 53–67). We use sentences to track the propositional attitudes of an agent; we use the real numbers to track, say, the lengths of objects. The sentences in the former attribution play the role of the real numbers in the latter. We might maintain that there is an 'indeterminacy of length': there are infinitely many serviceable schemes for attributing lengths (feet, inches, metres, etc., and we could come up with infinitely many more). Similarly, there are many serviceable schemes for attributing meanings and the other attitudes to a given interpretee. And the latter indeterminacy, Davidson claims, is as benign as the former. But the details of the analogy need spelling out.

Davidson does not deny that there are many disanalogies between the two cases. There is, for example, an algorithm for moving from one scale of length measurement to another (multiply by the relevant positive constant – for example, multiply by three to move from feet to yards); there is no such algorithm in the case of interpretations. However, we do need at least something that is invariant across interpretations if there is to be any analogy at all. What does invariance amount to in the measurement theoretic case? First, there are invariant relata. In the case of length, for instance, we attach the numbers to physical objects (the relata), and these remain the objects to be measured as we move from one scale to the next. And each scale preserves the relation 'is at least as long as': the greater the number on any given scale, the longer the object; and if it's longer on one (say feet), it's longer on all the others (metres, inches, etc.).

What remains invariant across interpretations? We needn't insist on pushing the analogy all the way, but at least we should be able to find a class of relata whose membership is fixed across different interpretations. It might initially appear that these relata are the propositional attitudes of the interpretee. But these do not remain invariant across different interpretations – it is precisely they that vary. On Davidson's picture, indeterminacy is simply the fact that we can use different locutions to locate the same node in some pattern. But what are the invariant nodes? They cannot be propositional attitudes: the belief that p, say, under one scheme, will be the belief that q under another – two different propositional attitudes (both attributions are couched in the one idiolect of the interpreter). Since we identify propositional attitudes in part by their contents, the relata cannot comprise the propositional attitudes themselves, because their content is exactly what varies between schemes of interpretation. (I discuss these matters in detail in Rawling 2013.)

One might respond here by wondering whether there is not some 'neutral' way of identifying propositional attitudes – so that, despite appearances to the contrary, the belief that p and the belief that q are in fact the same belief. But the problem is worse than so far suggested. Propositional attitudes in one scheme need not even map one to one onto propositional attitudes in another. Consider the following possibility: on one interpretation, a piece of behaviour, B, is interpreted as a signal; on another interpretation (that also saves all the relevant phenomena), B is interpreted as a simple scratch.[1] Thus, on the first interpretation, B is explained by a complex of propositional attitude states that is simply larger than that invoked in the second. Or, indeed, the explanation of B on some scheme might invoke no propositional attitudes at all.

As I see matters, then, Davidson remains in the position of denying the existence of propositional attitudes and with them the attribution of meanings to utterances (spoken or written). To avoid this conclusion, Davidson must relinquish either the epistemic or the metaphysical indeterminacy of interpretation. That is, either he must argue that use makes manifest a unique interpretation, or he must abandon the manifestation principle.

Of course, we have to begin with use when interpreting someone, particularly in the case of radical interpretation. We observe how others use language and try and match usage to likely referents on the basis of salience and so forth – use alone, as it were, is insufficient: we need guidance in the form of the principle of charity. But with Davidson's high standards of verification (see e.g. 2001b: 227–41), we'll never pin down a unique interpretation. However, it doesn't follow from the fact that interpreters can never be sure they've got matters correct, that there's nothing to be correct (or incorrect) about, unless we accept the manifestation principle.

Further views

Considerations of space limit coverage of Davidson's other views, but I shall briefly discuss some of the more well-known ones.

(a) There is no such thing as a language

This claim was addressed above, and, in one sense, it is of piece with the manifestation principle, since meaning is (purportedly) dependent upon use, and use can, as it were, 'go off the rails' at any point (recall Wittgenstein's rule-following considerations). But the claim is reinforced by metaphysical indeterminacy: there is no fact of the matter concerning what anyone means by their utterances and hence no 'conventional' meaning to be had.

(b) Holism

Holism, as it applies here, is the claim that propositional attitudes can occur only in interdependent patterns. Charity dictates that an interpretee's attitudes must meet certain criteria of rationality: for instance, there are strong presumptions that if an agent believes that $P \& Q$, then she believes that P. And there are other forms of interdependence – for example:

> In order to believe the cat went up the oak tree I must have many true beliefs about cats and oak trees, this cat and this tree, the place, appearance and habits of cats and trees, and so on; but the same holds if I wonder whether the cat went up the oak tree, fear that it did, hope that it did, wish that it had, or intend to make it do so.
>
> (Davidson 2001c: 98–9)

Two questions immediately arise: how rigid is the interdependence, and how large must the pattern be?

Davidson rejects a sharp analytic–synthetic distinction, which, in this context, is tantamount to denying that conceptual grasp depends upon a fixed list of particular beliefs:

> can the dog believe of an object that it is a tree? This would seem impossible unless we suppose the dog has many general beliefs about trees: that they are growing things, that

> they need soil and water, that they have leaves or needles, that they burn. There is no fixed list of things someone with the concept of a tree must believe, but without many general beliefs, there would be no reason to identify a belief as a belief about a tree ...
>
> (2001c: 98)

This passage suggests both a flexible interdependence and a degree of flexibility concerning the size of the pattern of beliefs that is concomitant with any particular belief.

However, Davidson makes remarks that can be interpreted as denying such flexibilities. For instance:

> Since the identity of a thought cannot be divorced from its place in the logical network of other thoughts, it cannot be relocated in the network without becoming a different thought.
>
> (2001c: 99)

This remark can be interpreted as attributing such rigidity to the interdependence of the attitudes that, for example, I cannot move from believing that today is Tuesday to believing that today is Wednesday, because my concept of 'today' will not remain invariant across the two beliefs.

But this misstates Davidson's intent (at least as conveyed in verbal remarks) and misconstrues the nature of the interdependence.[2] There are dependences in which changes in one factor can leave other factors stable. Consider Ohm's law: voltage (in certain ideal circuits, at least) is the product of resistance and current (V=RI). Here we have three mutually interdependent quantities, and certainly a change in one of them must result in a change in *one* of the others; but the third can remain fixed (e.g. by increasing the voltage in a circuit of fixed resistance, we increase the current). In the case of the contents of propositional attitudes and utterances, of course, we have a vast number of variables, but the same point applies: changes cause disruptions, but their scope will typically affect only a very small portion of the network of propositional attitudes and meanings. And I can share part of your network without sharing all of it (two circuits can share a potential difference of three volts, while differing in current and resistance).

(c)   There is no thought without talk (Davidson 2001c: 95–105)

Dogs, for example, cannot manifest any propositional thoughts because they cannot provide sufficient 'use' for us to determine enough about their putative propositional mental states (see the examples in (b), above). Speech is required in order for propositional attitudes to be manifestable. Hence, by the generalized manifestation principle, dogs have none.

(d)   Anomalous monism (Davidson 2001a: 207–27)

This is the view that, although there are no psycho-physical laws, mental events are also physical events (see also Chapter 7, this volume). One of Davidson's arguments for the first claim (2001a: 222–3), roughly speaking, is that in attributing propositional attitudes, we appeal to the canons of rationality, whereas physics appeals to no such norms, and thus if we attempt to formulate psycho-physical laws at one point in time, they will inevitably be violated, as time unfolds, due to the disparate ways in which we identify mental states and physical brain states.

Monism follows from the facts that (a) the mental causally interacts with the physical; (b) if one event causes another, there must be descriptions of them under which they instantiate a causal law; and (c) there are physical events that have no mental descriptions. Let *P* be such a physical event that causes (or is caused by) a mental event *M*. So there must be descriptions of *P* and *M* under which this causal happening falls under a law. But, as just argued, there are no psychophysical laws, thus *M* must have a physical description and hence is a physical event.

One well-known complaint about this view is that it has 'epiphenomenalist tendencies' (Kim 1993). If a yellow ball breaks a window, it does not do so in virtue of its colour (under typical circumstances) – rather, other properties of the ball and window do, as it were, the causal work; and one mark of this is that these are the properties that fall under laws. The claim against Davidson's account is that mental properties are the analogue of the ball's colour, and thus Davidson saves the mental at the expense of its efficaciousness.

(e) There are no 'conceptual schemes' (Davidson 2001b: 183–98)

This is one of Davidson's most celebrated claims, and it can be seen as following from the generalized manifestation principle. To have a conceptual scheme is to think in a certain way, and hence, by the manifestation principle, conceptual schemes must be interpretable by us (this being implicit in the principle: it is we who are observing the use of language). Hence there can be no conceptual schemes radically incommensurable to ours, since these would be, by hypothesis, inaccessible to us. This brings out the parochial nature of the manifestation principle: by its lights, there can be, in fact, nothing more to any speaker's meanings or thinker's thoughts than can be made manifest to *me* (or *you*). Thus it is criterial of a conceptual scheme that it be interpretable by me, and so it cannot be incommensurable to mine in any fundamental way. Hence there is but one 'conceptual scheme' – but, says Davidson, 'if we cannot intelligibly say that schemes are different, neither can we intelligibly say that they are one' (2001b: 198).

Davidson himself, however, in arguing for this claim, does not appeal explicitly to the manifestation principle. He points out, for example, that authors who propose examples of incommensurable schemes inevitably end up giving comparisons between them that undermine the very thesis purportedly being exemplified. And he argues that all of the metaphors proposed to capture the idea of incommensurable conceptual schemes fail to do so. One of these metaphors is that of a scheme 'fitting some entity', and Davidson concludes:

> Our attempt to characterize languages or conceptual schemes in terms of the notion of fitting some entity has come down, then, to the simple thought that something is an acceptable conceptual scheme or theory if it is [largely] true. ... And the criterion of a conceptual scheme different from our own now becomes: largely true but not translatable. The question whether this is a useful criterion is just the question how well we understand the notion of truth, as applied to language, independent of the notion of translation. The answer is, I think, that we do not understand it independently at all.

> We recognize sentences like '"Snow is white" is true if and only if snow is white' to be trivially true. Yet the totality of such English sentences uniquely determines the extension of the concept of truth for English. Tarski generalized this observation and made it a test of theories of truth: according to Tarski's Convention T, a satisfactory theory of truth for a language L must entail, for every sentence *s* of L, a theorem of the form '*s* is true if and only if *p*' where '*s*' is replaced by a description of *s* and '*p*' by *s* itself if L is English, and by a translation of *s* into English if L is not English. This isn't, of course, a definition of truth, and it doesn't hint that there is a single definition or theory that applies to languages generally. Nevertheless, Convention T suggests, though it cannot state, an important

feature common to all the specialized concepts of truth. It succeeds in doing this by making essential use of the notion of translation into a language we know. Since Convention T embodies our best intuition as to how the concept of truth is used, there does not seem to be much hope for a test that a conceptual scheme is radically different from ours if that test depends on the assumption that we can divorce the notion of truth from that of translation.

(2001b: 194–5)

Davidson's application of Tarski's definition of truth is the topic of the next section. Here I want to note some features of this argument. The basic idea is that if conceptual schemes 'fit' something, then they must all be true of it. But, since 'Convention T embodies our best intuition as to how the concept of truth is used', we don't understand what it is for a scheme to be true of something unless we can translate the contents of the scheme into our own language. However, such translation would enable us to compare any purportedly incommensurable scheme to our own.

The first thing to note is the transcendental underpinning of this argument: the implicit move from our claimed inability to understand truth independently of translation into our own language to the claim that truth is dependent upon such translation. Or, to put it another way, if we lack a test for incommensurability, there is none. And this is the manifestation requirement in a different guise: if there were an incommensurable scheme, its content would have to be (as is impossible) available to us via interpretation.

The second feature to note, which is of relevance to the next section, is the relation between Tarski's convention T and the concept of truth. Tarski (1944) is dismissive of discussions of what we might call 'truth simpliciter' – that is, truth as a concept independent of its application to a language. As he puts it:

we must always relate the notion of truth, like that of a sentence, to a specific language; for it is obvious that the same expression which is a true sentence in one language can be false or meaningless in another.

(Tarski 1944: 342)

To borrow an example of Davidson's:

the sounds 'Empedokles liebt' do fairly well as a German or an English sentence, in one case saying that Empedokles loved and in the other telling us what he did from the top of Etna.

(2001b: 98)

Thus the sentence, 'Empedokles liebt', taken phonetically, might be true in English but not in German. Truth, then, is relative to a language in this sense. And it is truth relative to a specified language that Tarski defines, not truth simpliciter.

But can we not countenance discussion of truth simpliciter? Davidson, as cited above, may appear to be in sympathy with denying that we can, but in later work (2005b) he seems more open to such discussion. In my view, unless we can appeal to truth simpliciter, then Convention T is arbitrary: why would we be so keen to get the result that

'Snow is white' is true in English if and only if snow is white

if we had no prior grip on truth simpliciter? I appeal to this point in the next section.

Davidson's application of Tarski's definition of truth

Davidson (1994: 126) asks: 'What would it suffice an interpreter to know in order to understand the speaker of an alien language, and how could he come to know it?' He suggests that 'a theory of truth, constructed more or less along the lines of one of Tarski's truth definitions, would go a long way toward answering the first question' (his account of radical interpretation, as we have seen, is his answer to the second). To begin with, I'll set aside Davidson's claim that there is no such thing as a language.

Given that interpreters have finite minds, languages are learnable, and that, if the project is to be realized, interpretation manuals need to be finitely expressible, Davidson sought some finite way of expressing what it suffices for an interpreter to know (a theory of interpretation). (Note that Davidson makes no claim to the effect that the sort of theory he proposes is explicitly known by any interpreters.) In addition, such theories should reveal compositionality (how the meaning of a sentence depends on the meanings of its parts) and not quantify over meanings and their ilk (since, in Davidson's view, there are no such things). Finally, the outputs of such a theory should enable interpreters to conclude truths of the form:

(M) S means-in-L that p

where L is the language being interpreted (the object language), S is any sentence of L, and the metalanguage here is English.

One obvious problem is that, although L is assumed to have a finite vocabulary, it will have arbitrarily long sentences, provided, as in natural languages, and as I shall assume, some of its vocabulary items are iterable. Hence there is no upper bound to the number of L sentences. Of course, in practice, there is an upper limit to sentence length in natural languages, but iteration poses a difficulty nonetheless. The appeal of applying Tarski's definition of truth (Tarski 1944, 1956), then, is that the definition is finite, neatly accommodating iteration via recursion clauses (at least for classical logical constants), and it reveals compositionality. However, the obvious difficulty is that the outputs are not of form (M) but, rather, of form:

(T) S is true-in-L if and only if p

What, then, is Davidson's proposal? Space precludes full discussion, but here is a brief account (see LePore and Ludwig 2003, 2005 and Rawling 2003 for more details).

(For readers unfamiliar with recursive definitions, the following may help. Consider the 'shriek' (UK usage) or 'factorial' (US usage) function, where, for example, $5! = 5 \times 4 \times 3 \times 2 \times 1$. How are we to express the function for an arbitrary natural number, n? We could write:

$n! = n(n-1)(n-2)\ldots$ (1)

But this is unsatisfactory for programming a calculator – it can't 'understand' the ellipsis. So here's a better definition:

For any natural number n: $(n+1)! = (n+1)n!$ and $0! = 1$

This definition is 'odd', since the first clause, known as a 'recursion clause', has an occurrence of '!' on both sides of the equation. But the definition works (try it) – and does so for an infinity of inputs, despite itself being finite.)

Piers Rawling

In the enterprise of formal logic, the object language can be specified in purely syntactic terms. And the semantics are provided by interpretations. Consider a simple language, *SL*, in which the only sentences are:

A, *B*, *C*, and #*a*, *(a*b)*, where *a* and *b* are sentences

(thus '#' and '*' are iterable – e.g. '##(##(A*C)*#(#C*B))' is a sentence)

And for which an interpretation, **I**, assigns to each of *SL*'s sentences exactly one of T, F (designating true and false respectively). Suppose the recursion clauses for the interpretation of the iterable items are:

For any sentences *a*, *b*:

(*a*b*) is T on **I** if *a* is T on **I** and *b* is T on **I**; (*a*b*) is F on **I** otherwise

#*a* is T on **I** if *a* is F on **I**; #*a* is F on **I** otherwise

All interpretations agree on these recursion clauses (hence '*' and '#' are logical constants); interpretations are differentiated by their differing distributions of Ts and Fs over the sentential letters. The recursive 'trick', of course, enables a finite definition of sentencehood to classify infinitely many objects as sentences, and a finite specification of **I** to assign unique values from {T, F} to all of them.

There are three perspectives one can take on interpretations. Tarski supposes that we know in advance that '*' is to be translated as 'and', and '#' as 'it is not the case that'. Then, supposing a prior grip on the concept of truth simpliciter, we can see a specific interpretation, **I**, as giving truth-on-**I** values for every sentence in the language. And it is the definition of an interpretation that constitutes Tarski's definition of truth for *SL*.

For the purposes of Davidson's project, however, it is assumed that we do not know in advance the 'meanings' of '*' and '#', and we are not defining an interpretation but, rather, constructing it as an empirical theory. The interpreter is, as it were, collecting evidence to the effect that: *a* is true-on-**I** if and only if *a* is true-in-the-speaker's-language (these relativized truth predicates presuppose, as with Tarski's definition of truth, a prior notion of truth simpliciter). To say that '*' (in the speaker's language) means the same as 'and' (in English) is simply to say that **I** is correct. And note that **I** reveals the compositionality of the speaker's language with respect to truth – how the truth value of a complex sentence depends on the truth values of its parts. In the interpretation of a natural language along these lines, the idea is that compositionality with respect to 'meaning' will be revealed.

The third perspective is the one with which I began this exercise, on which the language is defined in purely syntactic terms. On the perspectives I have attributed to Tarski and Davidson, the language is specified partly in semantic terms. On the first, the intended interpretation of '*' is 'and'; on the second, this interpretation emerges as evidence is collected. On either of these first two perspectives, but not the third, change the 'meaning' of '*' and you change the language. Natural languages are, of course, partly specified in semantic terms: change the semantics and you change the language.

There are, however, many well-known difficulties with Davidson's application of Tarski. Consider, for example, that the following biconditional is true:

'Es regnet' [It's raining] is true-in-German if and only if: it is raining and 2+2 = 4

Yet 'Es regnet' does not mean in German that: it is raining and 2+2 = 4. From the perspective of a theory of meaning, we might say that the equivalence has arisen via a 'deviant' derivation within the truth theory. If a theory of truth is to serve as a theory of meaning – in other words, if it is to be 'interpretative' – we have to ensure that (T) (above) holds because, and only because, (M) does (Davidson 2001b: 137–9; LePore and Ludwig 2003). We can, perhaps, ensure this by placing restrictions on permissible derivations within the truth theory. But why not go for 'means that' directly?

One immediate problem is how to deal with, say, the recursion clause for 'und' [and] in our (English) theory of German. In the interpretative truth theory, we straightforwardly have:

S^'und'^T is true-in-German if and only if
S is true-in-German and T is true-in-German
(where '^' abbreviates 'concatenated with')

But it's unclear how to fill in the right-hand side of:

S^'und'^T means-in-German that . . .

However, Ray (2014) shows how to get to 'means that' via a theory that issues in theorems of the form:

'S means-in-L that p' is true-in-English.

And, as he shows, his account solves a variety of problems.

In addition, it does so utilizing only basic extensional quantificational logic in the meta-languages (there are two levels) and without quantifying over meanings and their ilk. Also, as Ray points out, his theory remains neutral about such matters as the analysis of intensional idioms involving that-clauses – we are not pushed, for example, into a paratactic analysis of indirect discourse (Davidson 2001b: 93–108). I side with Ray (2014: 92–3) in seeing this neutrality as an advantage of his approach – after all, this part of Davidson's project, in my view, was merely to give an account of how to write a finite interpretation manual that meets the criteria outlined in the second paragraph of this section, and this Ray accomplishes.

One thing to note is that the notion of a 'logical constant' is in the following way irrelevant in this enterprise – whether on Davidson's original approach or Ray's update. In the case of Tarski's definition of truth for first-order logic (setting aside functors and identity), iterability and logical constanthood coincide. However, it's not logical constants, per se, that necessitate recursion clauses to ensure the finitude of the theory – rather, it's iterability that does this. In Davidsonian manuals of interpretation, then, all and only iterable items of the object language require recursion clauses – in the case of English, these include not only the classical logical connectives like 'and' and 'or' but also intensional idioms involving that-clauses (this is tricky on Davidson's paratactic approach – see Sennet 2013: 197–8), adverbs such as 'very' ('it's not merely very good, it's very, very, very, good'), and so on.

How does this application of Tarski square with Davidson's rejection of the conventional account of language and meaning (which issue I set aside at the beginning of this section)? As a result of Davidson's truck with Tarski, Kripke (1982: 71–2, n.60) sees Davidson's views as closer to the *Tractatus* (Wittgenstein [1921] (1990)) than to the *Philosophical Investigations*. However, nothing said in this section is inconsistent with Davidson's unconventional view of language. First, he sees interpretations as fleeting – what he describes as 'passing' (2005a: 101ff.): there is no implication of a long-term commitment to linguistic 'conventions'. Second, logic (as per the principle of charity) and compositionality (as per Tarskian form) don't force unique interpretations of the interpretee but merely lay down some of the criteria of adequacy for all of the multiple interpretations that, according to Davidson, apply to her at a given point in time.

Recommendations for practice

Davidson's central concern, qua systematic philosopher of language, was to explore such issues as the conditions for the possibility of interpretation. He was not much concerned with the actual practice of translation. Furthermore, much of his discussion of interpretation applies most directly to the spoken word. So what does he have to say to translators of the written word?

Perhaps the most obvious point is that the principle of charity certainly applies, so that, to adapt one of Quine's remarks cited above to the translation of philosophy, a philosopher's 'silliness, beyond a certain point, is less likely than bad translation' – that is, if the translator cannot make sense of her own translation of some particular philosopher, perhaps the most likely possibility is that her translation is bad. And, of course, the point applies across the board – consider Davidson's (2005a: 103) own discussion of Mrs Malaprop and her use of 'epitaph' to mean 'epithet'.

Concluding remarks

Recall the following passage:

> What we *should* demand, however, is that the evidence for the theory [of meaning for a speaker] be in principle publicly accessible ... The requirement that the evidence be publicly accessible is not due to an atavistic yearning for behavioristic or verificationist foundations, but to the fact that what is to be explained is a social phenomenon. ... That meanings are decipherable is not a matter of luck; public availability is a constitutive aspect of language.
>
> (Davidson 2005b: 55–6)

In part, Davidson is here protesting, in effect, that the manifestation principle is not merely the result of 'an atavistic yearning for... verificationist foundations'. But an argument for the principle is required to avoid the charge of verificationism – merely asserting that language is 'a social phenomenon' does not suffice. Wittgensteinian and Quinean arguments notwithstanding, I, for one, remain to be convinced that such an argument is available.

But, even if the manifestation principle fails, Davidson's work in showing us where it leads is invaluable. We are left, perhaps, with a '*modus ponens – modus tollens* stand-off': both sides agree that the manifestation principle has various consequences. One side denies at least some of these consequences (such as metaphysical indeterminacy) and thus rejects the principle; the other accepts the principle and hence its consequences.[3]

Notes

1 This example is similar to one suggested to me by Kirk Ludwig.
2 I am not the first person to note this: Graham Priest, for example, makes the point (1981: 78).
3 I owe many thanks to all those over the years who have educated me about Davidson's views, by far the most helpful of whom was Donald Davidson himself. Errors are mine alone, of course.

Related topics

Wittgenstein; Quine; Derrida; meaning.

Further reading

Davidson, D. (2005) *Truth and Predication*. Cambridge, MA: Harvard University Press. (In this posthumously published book, Davidson addresses not only truth and predication but also, amongst other topics, interpretation.)

Kusch, M. (2012) 'Wittgenstein on Translation'. In M. Kross and E. Ramharter (eds) *Wittgenstein Übersetzen*. Berlin: Parega: 57–75. (A discussion of Wittgenstein on translation, responding to a paper by Hans-Joachim Glock, which brings in Davidson on conceptual schemes.)

Malmkjær, K. (2005) *Linguistics and the Language of Translation*. Edinburgh: Edinburgh University Press. (On pp. 52–8, Malmkjær discusses Quine and Davidson within the context of equivalence in translation, concluding that philosophy shows that equivalence is a problem not only on a practical but also on a theoretical level.)

LePore, E. and K. Ludwig (eds) (2013) *A Companion to Donald Davidson*. Chichester: Wiley-Blackwell. (This edited volume contains many useful essays on Davidson's views.)

Ludwig, K. (ed.) (2003) *Donald Davidson*. Cambridge: Cambridge University Press. (This shorter edited volume also contains useful essays on Davidson's views.)

References

Davidson, D. (1990) 'The Structure and Content of Truth'. *Journal of Philosophy* 87(6): 279–328.
Davidson, D. (1994) 'Radical Interpretation Interpreted'. In Tomberlin: 122–8.
Davidson, D. (2001a) *Essays on Actions and Events*, 2nd edition. Oxford: Clarendon Press.
Davidson, D. (2001b) *Inquiries into Truth and Interpretation*, 2nd edition. Oxford: Clarendon Press.
Davidson, D. (2001c) *Subjective, Intersubjective, Objective*. Oxford: Clarendon Press.
Davidson, D. (2005a) *Truth, Language, and History*. Oxford: Clarendon Press.
Davidson, D. (2005b) *Truth and Predication*. Cambridge, MA: Harvard University Press.
Frege, F.L.G. (1892) 'Über Sinn und Bedeutung'. In *Zeitschrift für Philosophie und philosophische Kritik* 100: 25–50. Translated as 'On Sense and Reference' by M. Black in *Translations from the Philosophical Writings of Gottlob Frege*, P. Geach and M. Black (eds). Oxford: Blackwell, 3rd edition, 1980.
Heil, J. and A. Mele (eds) (1993) *Mental Causation*. Oxford: Clarendon Press.
Kim, J. (1993) 'Can Supervenience and "Non-Strict Laws" Save Anomalous Monism?' In Heil and Mele: 19–26.
Korta, K. and J. Perry (2015) 'Pragmatics'. *The Stanford Encyclopedia of Philosophy* (Winter 2015 Edition), Edward N. Zalta (ed.), https://plato.stanford.edu/archives/win2015/entries/pragmatics/.
Kripke, S.A. (1982) *Wittgenstein on Rules and Private Language*. Cambridge, MA: Harvard University Press.
LePore, E. and K. Ludwig (2003) 'Truth and Meaning.' In Ludwig: 35–63.
LePore, E. and K. Ludwig (2005) *Donald Davidson: Meaning, Truth, Language, and Reality*. Oxford: Oxford University Press.
LePore, E. and K. Ludwig (eds) (2013) *A Companion to Donald Davidson*. Chichester: Wiley-Blackwell.
Ludwig, K. (ed.) (2003) *Donald Davidson*. Cambridge: Cambridge University Press.
Priest, G. (1981) 'Review of *Theory and Meaning* (by D. Papineau; Oxford: Clarendon Press, 1979)'. *Philosophical Quarterly* 31: 77–9.
Quine, W.V.O. (1960) *Word and Object*. Cambridge, MA: MIT Press.
Rawling, P. (2003) 'Radical Interpretation'. In Ludwig: 85–112.
Rawling, P. (2013) 'Davidson's Measurement-Theoretic Analogy'. In LePore and Ludwig: 247–63.
Ray, G. (2014) 'Meaning and Truth'. *Mind* 123: 79–100.

Sennet, A. (2013) 'Parataxis'. In LePore and Ludwig: 191–207.
Tarski, A. (1944) 'The Semantic Conception of Truth and the Foundations of Semantics'. *Philosophy and Phenomenological Research* 4(3): 341–75.
Tarski, A. (1956) 'The Concept of Truth in Formalized Languages'. In Woodger: 152–78.
Tomberlin, J. (ed.) (1994) *Philosophical Perspectives: Logic and Language* (Vol. 8). Atascadero, CA: Ridgeview.
Wilson, N.L. (1959) 'Substances without Substrata'. *Review of Metaphysics* 12: 521–39.
Wittgenstein, L. [1921] (1990) *Tractatus Logico-Philosophicus*, tr. C.K. Ogden. London and New York: Routledge.
Wittgenstein, L. [1953] (2009) *Philosophical Investigations*, tr. G.E.M. Anscombe, P.M.S. Hacker, and J. Schulte. Chichester: Wiley-Blackwell.
Woodger, J. H. (ed.) (1956) *Logic, Semantics, Metamathematics*. New York: Oxford University Press.

9
Derrida

Deborah Goldgaber

Introduction and definitions

Derrida's critique of logocentrism

The work of Jacques Derrida (1930–2004) presents a radical critique of traditional philosophical accounts of language and meaning. This critique bears directly on his account of translation. Like Wittgenstein, Derrida argues that philosophers have relied upon a certain picture or image of language and linguistic function. This picture is not distinctively philosophical or theoretical. It is the model of language implicit in our everyday ways of talking about language. On Derrida's view, *philosophical* accounts differ from folk-theories of language insofar as they attempt to formalize and vindicate this picture. Throughout his early work, Derrida refers to this shared image of language and linguistic function as 'logocentrism'.

What is the *logocentric* image of language and why is it problematic? A logocentric picture imagines language as involving the exchange of extra-linguistic meanings analogous to the way we might imagine paper money as the exchange of some intrinsic value to which it is pegged (e.g. gold). We can develop this analogy between money and meaning further. Just as the relation between currencies would be determined by an underlying fixed value, the relation between languages would be understood in terms of the underlying structure these languages express. For Derrida, when we say that words or texts *have* meaning, this is not merely a metaphorical way of talking about language that sophisticated philosophical accounts transcend or correct. We have something like the monetary model in mind – a belief that our words and texts can be redeemed, that their meaning can be cashed in and transferred.

Derrida argues that philosophical accounts of language tend to agree that language functions as the exchange of meanings and depends upon the fungibility of semantic content. Indeed, not only does philosophy share a basic thesis about translation – that it is 'the transport of semantic content into another signifying form' – but Derrida argues that the 'thesis of philosophy is translatability' (Derrida 1985: 120). What Derrida means here is that Western philosophy is oriented around explaining and vindicating the possibility of Meaning – purely self-present, self-transparent meanings – that would escape the opaqueness and equivocity of the linguistic signifier in any particular language and the Babel-ian diversity of empirical languages more generally. Even linguistic accounts that emphasize the 'free-play' of the signifier – here Derrida has in mind 'structuralist theories' – understand the latter to be 'constituted upon a fundamental immobility and a reassuring certitude, which is itself beyond the reach of the free-play' (Derrida 1978: 279). This reassuring certitude is provided by the theoretical posit of what Derrida calls the 'transcendental signified'.

Transcendental signifieds, translation and the 'reduction to meaning'

According to Derrida, theories of linguistic function have almost always involved the possibility of 'reducing' empirical language to meaning (Derrida 1972: 134). Philosophers and 'lay' speakers assume that words refer to and are underwritten by cognitive entities or items distinct from the language we use. To access these underlying meanings, it follows, we must, as it were, cash in the 'materiality of the signifier' – the material element of language exemplified by a written mark or spoken word – for the value it represents. Successful uses of language – reading, writing, translating – would each involve restoring to mind ('re-presenting') the underlying meanings that have been transferred through language. Philosophical accounts propose various theoretical entities that serve the required functional role of Meaning. Derrida refers to the theoretical entities philosophers introduce as 'transcendental signifieds' (Derrida 1978: 279–80). This term captures the necessary condition for anything to serve the functional role of Meaning: ultimately, meaning must be transcendent to or outside language.

According to Derrida, logocentric, or meaning-centric, accounts of linguistic function have determined how philosophers and theorists have thought about translation. But a certain understanding of translation may also have given rise to logocentrism. Derrida writes that the *theological* ideal of unequivocal translatability may be behind our logocentric beliefs. 'In effect, the theme of a transcendental signified took shape within the horizon of an absolutely pure, transparent, and unequivocal translatability' (Derrida 1981: 20). Today's debates about translation standards – for example, whether translators should seek fluency of translation versus fidelity to the syntactical structure of the original – have deep theological roots. This makes intuitive sense – in theological contexts where authority is grounded in sacred source texts, the stakes of translation are magnified. Questions related to the possibility of their faithful interpretation dominated centuries of debates. Derrida suggests that this theological context conditions apparently secular debates about the nature of translation.

Derrida is hardly alone in linking contemporary accounts of linguistic function and translation to long-standing theological debates. George Steiner, in *After Babel*, writes that theologians have long since sketched out the relevant alternatives for achieving 'fidelity' to the source text.

> All theories of translation . . . are only variants of a single inescapable question. In what ways can or ought fidelity to be achieved? What is the optimal correlation between the A text in the source language and the B text in the receptor language. But is there anything of substance to add to St. Jerome's statement of the alternatives, *verbum e verbo*, word by word in the case of the mysteries, but meaning by meaning, *sed sensum exprimere de sensu*, everywhere else?
>
> (Steiner 1975: 261–2).

There, where meaning is not assured, where some aspect of the text interrupts the reduction to meaning, the principle of translation is word for word; everywhere else, the translator should seek to convey the meaning. Steiner restates the metaphysical view of language that Derrida associates with logocentrism:

> The underlying structure of language is universal and common to all men. Dissimilarities between human tongues are essentially of the surface. Translation is realizable precisely because those deep-seated universals, genetic, historical, social, from which all grammars derive can be located and recognized as operative in every human idiom... to translate is to descend beneath the exterior disparities of two languages in order to bring into vital play their analogous and, at the final depths common principles.
> (Steiner 1975: 73)

Adopting this metaphysical view of language allows philosophers to effectively bracket off almost every question about translation and translingual practices. The nature of translation or the experiences of the translator pose no *new* philosophical problems or difficulties.

According to the logocentric model, both inter-lingual and intra-lingual translation, to refer to Jakobson's distinction (2012: 127), involve only an extra loop of the basic linguistic operation – the reduction (of the signifier) to its meaning. First, the signifier is reduced to the signified – to arrive at the meaning of the word or phrase – and then the signified is matched to the signifier in the target language or another equivalent signifier in the same language. The signified element always goes *untranslated*, remaining outside the economic 'play' of signifiers. In contrast to the sort of economic questions that Steiner suggests have dominated the practice of translation since St. Jerome – word for word or sense for sense – philosophers, Derrida argues, have most often been interested only in the question of establishing the *a priori* possibility of translation. Put in another way, we might say that philosophers have been concerned with language's *translatability* – establishing the conditions of translation's possibility through discourses on the nature of meaning – rather than with *translation* and its concrete practices.

Critical issues

Philosophical and deconstructive critiques of the transcendental signified

Derrida argues – controversially – that all (Western) philosophical theories of language have been captured by logocentrism. This claim will sound implausible if one takes it to mean that nobody before Derrida has ever been critical of the concept of transcendental signifieds. It will sound equally implausible if it leads one to expect that all (Western) accounts of language equally endorse the idea that there are pure, ideal (self-present or self-interpreting) semantic items without which language could not function. While there are philosophers who do seem to endorse this view – Edmund Husserl would perhaps be the most relevant example for Derrida – most contemporary philosophers would likely distance themselves from the pure logocentric ideal that Derrida argues philosophers attempt to vindicate.

Derrida does not deny a *certain* diversity among philosophical theories of language and meaning, nor that philosophers have been critical of this ideal. However, he would argue that the apparent diversity of philosophical opinion is a function of the various ways philosophers conceive of the transcendental signified, which does not always appear in the form or guise we might expect – it may appear here as speaker's intention, there as context, in the notion of a word's history of use or reception. As Derrida shows in his own critical readings, we are likely to find philosophers critiquing one version of the transcendental signified only to replace it with another version. Derrida is predominantly interested in thinkers like Charles Pierce, J.L. Austin, Ferdinand de Saussure and Walter Benjamin, who have in one way or another criticized the logocentric ideal but whose critiques, he insists, fall short of the sort of radical critique of logocentrism that deconstruction performs. With respect to these logocentric critiques, Derrida writes, 'the force and the efficiency of the [logocentric] system [of concepts] regularly change transgression into "false exits"' (Derrida 1972: 135). Philosophers attempt to 'exit' logocentrism only to reaffirm it again in another form.

For all their surface diversity – and genuine effort to break out of the logocentric logic – philosophical accounts fall back on the view that something *external* to language, texts or signs is necessary to explain how the latter have or come to have meaning. Logocentrically speaking, what is *essential* to language – the meaning it is said to convey – is missing, and language is defined by this essential lack. Meaning *qua* transcendental signified is, as Derrida writes, language's essential supplement. Setting himself up, then, against what he takes to be the entire philosophical tradition, Derrida famously argues in *Of Grammatology* that 'there is nothing outside the text' ['il n'y a pas de hors-texte'] (Derrida [1976] (1998): 158–9). Meaning is not and cannot be what is outside language. There is nothing like transcendental signifieds; there are no non-language-like elements that will allow us to explain how language or texts function. What is required is not an account that explains linguistic function by a reduction *to* meaning but rather a reduction *of* meaning, as Derrida writes at the conclusion of his essay 'Ends of Man' (1972). We have to learn to see meaning 'as the effect of structure or a formal organization that itself has no meaning'. Such a structure or formal organization, as we will see below, is what Derrida refers to with terms such as 'text' and 'iterability' (Derrida 1972: 134).

Derridean 'eliminativism', or texts without meanings

Derrida identifies logocentrism with the claim that, linguistically speaking, meaning is elsewhere, thus texts and all properly linguistic phenomena would be radically dependent on sources of meaning external to them. By contrast, the deconstructive position entails that meaning is 'inside' the text or that meaning is text-like. This would give texts a kind of independence and self-sufficiency that logocentrism, as we shall see, has no way of conceiving.

The claim that there is no meaning (viz., transcendental signified) outside the text, or that meaning is essentially textual, can only be registered as absurd from within the logocentric framework. From the logocentric point of view, if meaning were textual in the relevant sense, it would cease to be meaning and texts would cease to function. Logocentrism, as we saw above, assumes that while texts *have* meanings – where to have a meaning is to have an assignable transcendental signified to which the text refers – texts themselves are intrinsically *meaningless*, so many arbitrary sounds or marks. The only alternative to this claim seems to be its negation: namely that texts have *no* meaning (no assignable transcendental signified) and hence are empty, all arbitrary form and no content. As a result, Derrida's claim that meaning is textual has often been interpreted by his critics as a claim that texts have no meaning. For this reason, Derrida tends to eschew use of the term 'meaning' altogether. He takes it to be too invested with logocentric assumptions. Instead he uses the less 'loaded' term 'signified'. In this sense, we can think of Derrida as an eliminativist with respect to Meaning, in the same way that philosophers like Patricia and Paul Churchland are eliminativists with respect to terms like 'consciousness'.

According to John Searle, there are precisely two ways we can talk about how texts have meaning. Either we say that the text's meaning derives from the author's intention, or we say that its meaning is established at its reception. Derrida seems to reject both options with his claim that there is no exit from the text. Yet, Searle argues, Derrida seems to offer no alternative account of meaning to replace that which he rejects:

> For Jacques Derrida meaning is a matter of, well, what? Meanings are 'undecidable' and have 'relative indeterminacy', according to Derrida. Instead of fully determinate meaning, there is rather the free play of signifiers and the grafting of texts onto text is within the textuality and intertextuality of the text.
>
> (Searle 1994: 637)

Searle suggests that either Derrida must say there are only texts (that never amount to any meaning), in which case Derrida's account is nonsensical, or there are meanings after all, in which case Derrida will have to decide which account of the transcendental signified he prefers.

One of Derrida's philosophical strengths is to emphasize the philosophical disorder that the reduction of meaning – or the elimination of the transcendental signified – produces for logocentrism. Derrida recognizes that, from the logocentric point of view, to say that meaning is textual or sign-like ruins the very concept of the sign and meaning (Derrida [1976] (1998): 50). This disorder, however, should not cause us to reassert the priority of the transcendental signified but to accept the possibility that our conceptual armature needs to be radically revised. The significance of his claim cannot be heard until and or unless we have a radically revised account of the sign or text. Before we turn to the question of what revised account of the sign Derrida offers, if any, it is important to get a better sense of precisely why the claim that the signified element is structured like a language ruins the notion of a sign.

Derrida presents the problems that follow from asserting the text- or language-like character of signified elements in his reading of the semiology of Pierce in *Of Grammatology*. As Derrida reconstructs it, Peirce argues that the referent of a sign – any possible semantic item – is necessarily subject to the same conditions of interpretation that apply to linguistic signifiers. Signs produce signs as their interpretents that then require interpretents *ad infinitum*. 'From the moment that there is meaning there are nothing but signs. We *think only in signs*' (Derrida 1998: 50). When it comes to those items at which signifiers point – where we would expect to find the 'meaning' of signs – Peirce finds only more signs.

If Peirce's logic is right – and Derrida argues it is perfectly warranted – then the signified element is structured internally by the same difference that structures the external relation between signifier and signified, word and meaning, sentence and propositional content. Unless we want to claim that some signs turn out to be self-interpreting and self-transparent, we must admit, as Samuel Wheeler writes, that the semantic strata of language necessarily suffer from the same indeterminacy with respect to *their own meaning* as do the signifying strata (Wheeler 2000: 23–5). It follows that the meaning of anything that is sign-like cannot be determined, since the element that would determine its meaning is always subject to one more interpretation.

In his reading of Peirce, Derrida argues that an account of linguistic or cognitive function that requires us to think that there are signs 'all the way down' is ruinous of the very concept of the sign. Peirce's recognition that 'from the moment that there is meaning there is nothing but signs' amounts 'to ruining the notion of the sign at the very moment when ... its exigency is recognized in the absoluteness of its right' (Derrida 1998: 50). If everything is a sign – from the point of view of the logocentric assumptions that determine our understanding of the sign – nothing can be a sign, since signs only make sense with reference to a (transcendental) signified element.

An image might help to show the logic of Derrida's argument. Picture the spinning pinwheel that appears on a computer screen as the processor attempts to carry out a command. The pinwheel, we assume, represents that time it takes for the command to be executed. We hope, when such a pinwheel appears, that it will eventually disappear. The operation will come to a happy ending and we can continue with the task. Now imagine the process of thought as involving Peircean signs. In order to interpret a sign, we are directed by the sign to open another file (the 'interpretent'): this intrepretent redirects us to open another file, which, in turn, sends us to a third. If this process were literally, as Peirce suggests, without end, it seems that rather than an account of the possibility of thought we have an account of its radical impossibility. The picture of thinking/language that Peirce leads us to is, from a theoretical perspective, dysfunctional. Logocentric assumptions require a 'file' that will put an end to the referential play, to what Derrida calls the sign's difference and deferral – or, on his economic coinage, *différance*.

In a famous thought experiment, Searle argues that the very paradox that Derrida identifies in his reading of Peirce is grounds to insist on (rather than reject) the existence of transcendental signifieds (Searle 1982). He asks us to imagine an English monolinguist, alone in a room, charged with the task to respond to a text written in Chinese characters. The monolinguist does not speak or read Chinese but has all the resources necessary to produce a legible and apt response – for example, all the rules that govern permissible syntactical transformations along with the statistical knowledge of the appearance of certain syntactical strings. The monolinguist would thus be able to access a list of common responses to common phrases.

Assuming the monolinguist has sufficient time, we would have good reason to think that s/he could produce an adequate response to the message. However, Searle argues that from the possibility of this performance we would not be warranted in saying that our monolinguist understands Chinese. Understanding is something more than the successful outward, syntactical transformation of a phrase, if only because any adequate account of 'success' would seemingly need to make reference to a language-user capable of understanding the text produced. Searle's 'Chinese room' argument functions as a *reductio ad absurdum*. There must be something extra-textual about language, because if there were not, then we would all be, with respect to our own language and our own thoughts, like the monolinguist in the Chinese room. Since this would be an absurd conclusion, belief in transcendental signifieds is warranted.

As we have seen, Derrida comes to the opposite conclusion to Searle – insisting that there is no 'outside-the-text', that language necessarily functions through an ineliminable and interminable *différance*. He takes the absurdity that seems to result from thinking of all semantic content as sign-like not as evidence that, at some level, language necessarily involves a transcendental signified but as the effect of the logocentric assumption that there is an *absolute* difference between signifier and signified. Logocentric accounts cannot make sense of – indeed, they require us to deny – the *différance* that characterizes every level of linguistic function.

Though it challenges the view that the signifier and signifier are absolutely or radically distinct, deconstruction does not seek to collapse the difference between signifier and signified – indeed, Derrida's reading of Peirce points out the unacceptable effects of such a collapse. Rather, it aims to rethink the nature of this difference, to think the *différance* of language in a way that gives us a revised account of linguistic function. This deconstruction of the transcendental signified must be undertaken 'with prudence' to avoid losing the theoretical means to account for their difference. Without preserving the difference, we could not explain linguistic function – in particular, the possibility of translation that relies on this difference.

> [It is not a question] of confusing, at every level, and in all simplicity, the signifier and the signified. That this opposition or difference cannot be radical or absolute does not prevent it from functioning, and even from being indispensable within certain limits – very wide limits. For example, no translation would be possible without it ... In the limits to which it is possible, or at least appears possible, translation practices the difference between signified and signifier. But if this difference is never pure, no more so is translation.
> (Derrida 1982: 20)

If the possibility of translation – and language use more generally – depends upon a difference between signifier and signified that 'is never pure', then conceptions of translation that assume this purity must be revised. 'For [this] notion of translation we would have to substitute a notion of transformation: a regulated transformation of one language by another, of one text by another' (ibid.).

Translating the difference between signifier/signified

How, then, shall we understand the relation between signifier/signified differently? How can we think of both signifier and signified as language-like, without this entailing that linguistic texts are intrinsically meaning-less? Derrida suggests, as we saw in the quote above, that critical reflection on the field of translation is a privileged milieu for developing a non-logocentric account of linguistic function. Translation '*practices* the difference between signifier and signified'. Whereas for logocentrism translation is a peripheral concern, derivative with respect to establishing the possibility of a reduction to meaning, for a deconstructive account of language it is central and paradigmatic. If, deconstructively speaking, translation can no longer be imagined as the transfer of meaning or transcendental signifieds, how should it now be understood? How can the practice of translation guide our intuitions to a new understanding of linguistic function? Translation, Derrida writes, must be understood as the regulated 'transformation of one text by another' – as an inter-textual transformation. What does Derrida mean by this 'transformation'?

As we saw in the quote above, Derrida argues that linguistic function depends upon the possibility of distinguishing – in a non-absolute fashion – between a linguistic signifier and its signified. Language functions within what Derrida characterizes as the 'very wide limits' of this (non-absolute) difference. The puzzle we face as we attempt to free ourselves from the logocentric picture of language is how to conceive this difference – and linguistic function more generally – when all of the concepts that pertain to language, according to Derrida, have been determined logocentrically. To borrow Husserl's expression, the deconstructive thinker must go 'back to things themselves'; in this case, to the linguistic phenomena being described. If logocentric accounts get the relation of signifier and signified wrong, how have they misinterpreted the phenomena they have described? What alternatives exist? By dint of what features or properties does one item play the role of the signifier and the other signified?

In the formulation we used earlier, logocentrism defines language in terms of an essential lack. Searle's Chinese room aimed to vindicate our intuitions with respect to this logocentric claim. We receive a message in a foreign script and readily recognize it as a text, but we cannot read it. As a text, we assume it has a meaning – for the reader/speaker of this language – but that meaning is inaccessible to us because we cannot match the script to the (underlying)

Meanings. On this view of language, we will, in principle, have no way of deciphering the text. What is essential to the text is lost (at least for us). Its meaning can only be restored in the presence of a speaker/reader or the discovery of a bridging text – a Rosetta stone that provides sufficient context for translation.

If, from the logocentric point of view, meaning is radically absent from a text, where is it? As Searle schematizes, meaning, roughly speaking, is what is in the head of either speaker/author or receiver/reader; meaning is what is assigned to the text either at its production or at its arrival (or both). In between, during the time of its transmission, the meaning of a text is presumed absent. Derrida argues, most explicitly in 'Signature, Event, Context' (1998), that this assumption about meaning's radical (textual) absence does not hold up to a careful analysis of textual phenomena. The apparently absent, signified element that has hitherto defined linguistic phenomena is, in fact, not absent and elsewhere. It is not and never was in the head of its author or intended receiver, at least insofar as the latter are assumed as outside-the-text. As Derrida writes, in one of the most cited – though perhaps least well understood – passages in his oeuvre:

> In order for my 'written communication' to retain its function as writing, i.e., its readability, it must remain readable despite the *absolute* disappearance of any receiver, determined in general. My communication must be repeatable – iterable – in the *absolute* absence of the receiver or of any empirically determinable collectivity of receivers. Such iterability – (iter, again, probably comes from itara, other in Sanskrit, and everything that follows can be read as the working out of the logic that ties repetition to alterity) structures the mark of writing itself, no matter what particular type of writing is involved . . .
>
> (Derrida 1988: 7)

What has been poorly understood, I argue, is this notion of 'readability'.

Structural readability and iterability

Derrida asserts: 'a writing that is not structurally readable – iterable – beyond the death of the addressee would not be writing'. He is asking us to consider what remains of a text's meaning if we imagine the death not of this or that addressee but the death of any possible author and any possible receiver. For a logocentrist like Searle, the answer must be: 'nothing'. The signified, the 'text's' inner meaning or content is lost, as it is not with the text. Under these conditions, the text is no longer readable. Writers and readers are the condition of possibility of readability. By contrast, Derrida argues that in the absence of all possible readers the text remains 'structurally readable' or, what is for him synonymous, 'iterable'. In what sense does a text with no possible readers remain readable? To what sort of possibility does 'structural readability' refer?

The notion of 'structural readability' refers to the status of the text's heterogeneous, signified element, the absence of which defines the logocentric concept of a text or message. For the logocentric, the death of all possible (human) readers names the conditions under which the text becomes structurally *un*readable. Against these logocentric intuitions, Derrida insists that the text remains *readable*. Moreover, the 'structural readability' beyond the horizon of any human subject, Derrida argues, actually defines texts. Here Derrida's notion of 'iterability' moves us away from an anthropocentric notion of language, defining the latter by the possibility of its survival and function beyond the human.

Language, for Derrida, is defined by *iterability*, a form of repetition – distinct from its logocentric determination – necessarily linked to alterity. Texts as iterable – 'readable' outside the horizon of all readers – presuppose the survival of the heterogeneous element we refer to as meaning. But this semantic element is not elsewhere – it is intra-textual. Derrida's neologism 'iterability' specifies the sort of *differantial* structure linguistic function entails – a structure 'foreign to the order of presence', in which a repeatable mark (a signifier) *repeats* a heterogeneous difference (signified). But what is the manner or nature of this double repetition? How does it occur?

Derrida writes, 'iterability alters, contaminating parasitically what it identifies and enables to repeat "itself"' (Derrida 1988: 62). The relation between signifier and signified is something like the relation between a parasite and its host, where the parasite exists in and through the body of its host. If we follow this metaphor, the signifying strata composed of its pattern of differential elements would be the host or medium in and through which the 'parasitic' signified elements are expressed. This 'parasitic' structure is nested, with the 'parasitic' pattern encoding the host pattern. While this description of the sign may sound unfamiliar and even fantastical, Derrida suggests that such structures are, in fact, perfectly ordinary and common. The life of language and texts is a parasitic life. Meaning survives *parasitically* – beyond the horizon of all speakers and readers – insofar as it is encoded in another text.

A pattern of difference can only appear as such by altering, modifying, or in-forming – 'parasitically', as Derrida writes – another pattern of differences. Differences nest in heterogeneous differences. Differences live on, or survive, only in the 'flesh' of the heterogeneous differences they alter or transform. 'Language-like' structures refer to differences or systems of differences characterized by 'play' or modifiability. The repetition characteristic of language is not limited to, nor can it be exemplified by, the story of a conventionally adopted, arbitrary mark, which once adopted would be indefinitely repeatable. Such an account of linguistic repetition suffers from a one-sidedness that the account of language as iterability diagnoses and makes visible. Iterability, as opposed to the logocentric determination of linguistic repetition, draws our attention to the incalculable manifold of encoded differences repeated along with any repetition of the surface or 'host' text.

The structure of iterability helps us to understand in what sense we can account for the difference between the signifier and signified in non-absolute (or non-logocentric) terms. We can say that one experiences something as a signifier, or understands the meaning of a signifier, when one performs – however spontaneously or unconsciously – something like a reverse translation. Reading, in its everyday sense, amounts to retrieving or reconstructing the 'parasitic', or what we might equally call the hetero-modal text. However, as Derrida points out, a text remains structurally readable without anyone actually performing such an act of translation – or even recognizing it as a text. A celebrated example will help illustrate the point.

James Gleick in *The Information* (2012) retells the famous story of the drum language of the Etele in Africa (Gleick 2012: 19). In his account of the 'talking drums', Gleick describes Kele as a tonal language with two sharply distinct tones: each syllable is either low or high. The Kele language is 'spoken' – one may also say 'written' – by a pair of drums that, *isomorphically*, produce two distinct tones. Kele words are 'pronounced' on the drums in a sequence of high and low tones that mimic the tonal pattern in the spoken language. Kele, like any spoken language, is rich in contrastive oppositions; tonal differences would be just one of the contrastive magnitudes. But tonal differences are important enough contrasts to allow other marked differences to be dropped (n th wy w cn drp vwls frm phntc nglsh) in the drum speech or writing while still allowing the latter to represent speech. Gleick notes that the

Europeans who did not know how to 'read' the drum language could not hear the messages that were nonetheless 'readable' everywhere around them.

The story of the talking drums and the way that they 'speak' Kele is even more interesting if we consider that the distinctive sounds of the talking-drums account, according to some musicologists, form some of the distinctive structures of American popular music and dance, including jazz, rock 'n' roll and tap. One might hypothesize that the musical forms descended from Kele drumming are replete with messages and texts structurally readable to a Kele speaker, though such messages would be produced without any sort of intention on the part of the drummer or tap dancer. The readability of such messages is entirely unaffected by the presence or absence of Kele speakers. In the drum writing, Kele spoken language is found in and as the pattern of differences the drums repeat – in much the same way that spoken language is found in phonetic writing. It is true that the textual iterability exemplified by the talking drums – the same iterability we find in phonetic writing – may seem a poor model for understanding the difference between signifier and signified precisely because neither case seems to implicate the signified or 'conceptual' element in language. From this example, one might think that Derrida's notion of the iterable or parasitic text is apt for describing the morphogenetic relations between speech and phonetic writing (which stays at the level of the signifier) but does not help us to define the relationship between signifier and signified. If iterability names a generalized structure, as Derrida insists, it must apply to the link between signifier and signified. We must assume that the signified or semantic content can also be preserved in and as the differential patterns that define speech or the signifying strata of language.

Derrida notes that we are, without warrant, accustomed to thinking of speech as closer to the signified (Derrida 1998). Whether in speech or in writing, the signified elements must be structurally 'readable' or preserved. Just as the distinctive patterns of differences characteristic of graphic (phonetic) writing provide us with enough information – provided one knows *how* to read, decompress and extract them – to reconstitute the differences in speech, so do the differences in speech provide us with enough information to reconstitute the 'conceptual' information encoded in speech. This seems harder to credit than the Kele drum example. How can a heterogeneous text heard in speech provide us with the satisfying meaning-effect?

To get a sense for how this might work in language, we might consider a case of 'intermodal' (or inter-sensory) translation. Neurologist Amir Amedi's laboratory reports producing a sensory substitution device called EyeMusic. EyeMusic is 'a system [for the congenitally blind] that turns [visual] images into sequences of sound' (Arbel et al. 2014). Using Derrida's notion of iterability, we might produce an inter-lingual translation of Amedi's description. EyeMusic involves the 'regulated transformation' of one text by another. Visual texts are transformed into and made to appear in and through differences in sound. The differences characteristic of visual images (e.g. light/dark) are transformed into differences in sound (e.g. high/low frequency) in such a way that the user of EyeMusic can 'see' through sound. With the right user training, differences in sound come to 'mean' or signify differences in sight. In other words, Amedi's programme 'practises the difference between signifier and signified' in and through the regulated transformation of one sensory 'language' by another. The possibility of inter-modal translation, suggests that sensation, is also structured like a language, is iterable or textual, and as such is in the purview of translation studies. Indeed, *translatability* – or what Derrida refers to as 'the regulated transformation' of one text by another – refers to the survival of a text in and through its modification of and repetition in another text.

One of the insights that we can glean from these examples – those of the speaking drums and EyeMusic – is that the object, or 'signified', of any signifying modality cannot, in principle, be identified with respect to its origin or its essence. Texts are, originally, speaking, inter-modal. The original translatability (or iterability) of essentially inter-modal phenomena forecloses the possibility of identifying any signified with an original field of appearance. With these examples it should be clearer why thinking of language in terms of generalized iterability allows Derrida to re-describe meaning-effects (of all kinds) in terms of translation. 'Meaning', in its narrow linguistic sense and in its more general sense of signification, in Derrida's account, is the effect of generalized translation.

The theory of translation we can reconstruct on the basis of Derrida's work offers a distinctive account of the nature of translation that exceeds the ambit of both literary and linguistic phenomena. Nonetheless, this theory gives us insight into the specific nature of literary phenomena and the specific task of the translator, as defined by literary objects. Derrida figures the task of translation both in terms of preservation and transformation, of reproduction and creation. There is, of course, nothing particularly innovative about that description. What makes Derrida's view of translation distinctive is that it is not linguistic meaning that a translator reproduces or represents in a target language. As we have seen, Derrida understands language not as a vehicle for meanings but from the point of view of its structure. Structurally speaking, language involves inscribed or compressed patterns, patterns of difference that store or encode other, heterogeneous patterns. What a translator *re-stores* through regulated transformation is something closer to the resonance-patterns ('traces') possible in one language in the resonance-patterns of another. The task of translator involves waking up language – or unfolding or decompressing the patterns stored in language – and putting language to work, in order to make one language resonate in another.

Derrida's translational practices

Derrida and Benjamin: translation beyond the human

The notion of translatability that Derrida evokes with iterability recalls Walter Benjamin's notion of translatability in 'The Translator's Task', (1923 [2012]) a resonance Derrida explores at length in the indispensable 'Des Tours de Babel' (1985). Benjamin writes that

> translation is a form. In order to grasp it as such, we have to go back to the original. For in it lies the principle of translation, determined by the original's translatability ... Accordingly, the translatability of linguistic structures would have to be considered even if they were untranslatable for human beings'.

While Derrida will have little use for Benjamin's notion of an original work – for Derrida it is rather the relation of parasitism that would be original – he shares with Benjamin the sense of translation as having fundamentally to do with a text's form and how this form implies a function or mode of survival that escapes the horizon of the human.

In what sense is translation a form? In 'The Translator's Task', Benjamin notes, 'word-for-word translation completely thwarts the reproducing of sense and threatens to lead directly to incomprehensibility' (Benjamin 2012: 81). Translation, then, cannot be a matter of reproducing the outward form of a source text. Instead, Benjamin writes, translation consists in awakening the 'pure language spellbound in the foreign language', of 'liberating the language imprisoned in the work by rewriting it' (Benjamin 2012: 83). This notion of a pure language 'in' language, liberated by translation, sounds suspiciously logocentric, where 'pure language' would name one more version of a transcendental signified. Indeed, Derrida's reading of Benjamin suggests that the latter's conception of language is not entirely free of its logocentric assumptions. Nonetheless, Derrida finds in it much to support the deconstructive (post-logocentric) account of language. The notion of a 'pure language spellbound' in a text suggests that the form in question is that of a text in which a heterogeneous text is spellbound, an intra-textual relation entangling signifier and signified. For Benjamin, the necessity of translation is linked to the mode in which language and meaning live and survive.

As Derrida underlines in his reading, the 'original' text *requires* translation even if there is no translator 'fit to respond to this injunction, which is at the same time demand and desire in the very structure of the origin'.

> This structure is the relation of life to sur-vival. This requirement of the other as translator, Benjamin compares it to some unforgettable instant of life . . . it is unforgettable even if in fact forgetting finally wins out. It will have been unforgettable. . . . The requirement of the unforgettable – which is here constitutive – is not in the least impaired by the finitude of memory. Likewise the requirement of translation in no way suffers from not being satisfied, at least it does not suffer in so far as it is the very structure of the work.
>
> (Derrida 1985: 205)

Derrida suggests that where Benjamin's account of translation risks obscurity, his notion of iterability offers clarification. That which is 'remembered' or remains 'unforgettable' in the text is not conditioned by the finitude of human memory or human life. The necessity and the possibility of translation is part of the 'very structure of the work', a requirement, furthermore, that does not suffer from not being satisfied. The task of translation can wait, indefinitely. In the same way that the death of the author/reader functions to define the form of the text's survival in his account of iterability in 'Signature, Event, Context', Derrida suggests in 'The Translator's Task' that the death of all possible translators – that is, the finitude of human memory and the empirical impossibility in the case of humans of *not* forgetting – does not impugn a text's translatability. The structure of the work – that is to say, the structure of the iterable text – is constitutively linked to that which in it is 'unforgettable'. Hence, so long as there is a text, there is the requirement or demand for translation/remembering. This is the same as saying that the text is, primarily, and before it is anything else, structurally, a form of memory, an archival form, a form of preservation that cannot be defined in terms of that which it makes possible – namely the familiar uses humans may put this form to. The text provides all the necessary conditions for its own translation.

What lives in language – according to Derrida's gloss of Benjamin – is revitalized in and through translation. Successful translation 'liberates' the pure language imprisoned within the source language – that which we habitually refer to as the text's meaning. In contrast to the ideal of a translation governed by the reproduction of a source text's meaning, for Benjamin this liberation is not re-productive but productive (Derrida 1985: 182–3). The liberation of pure language/meaning produces (more) meaning.

> The original gives itself in modifying itself; this gift is not an object given; it lives and lives on in mutation: For in its survival, which would not merit the name if it were not mutation and renewal of something living, the original is modified. Even for words that are solidified there is a postmaturation.
>
> (Derrida 1985: 183)

The original language or text survives only in its translation – in its modification-transcription in another text. We will see below, more concretely, how we are to understand this enrichment or 'postmaturation' in terms of Derrida's own translation practice.

What is a 'relevant' translation?

Derrida is clear that what interests him in translation is less the problem of producing equivalences between languages than showing how translation involves the modification of one language by another language in a way that is productive and transformative. As Lydia Liu notes, the productivity implied is bi-directional.

> Benjamin's notion of complementarity acquires a fresh importance in Derrida's reconsideration of the concepts of origin, intention, and the relations between the languages involved in translation processes. That is to say, translation is no longer a matter of transferring meaning between languages 'within the horizon of an absolutely pure, transparent, and unequivocal translatability.' The original and translation complement each other to produce meanings larger than mere copies or reproduction.
>
> (Liu 1995: 15)

As we have already seen with the term 'iterability' (which, recall, etymologically conveyed the seemingly unrelated and even opposed senses of repetition and alterity), Derrida is particularly interested in words – conceptual words – that convey multiple, even opposing senses. Such words make visible the differences that swarm beneath the apparent unity of the signifier. In *Dissemination* (1972), Derrida famously reminds us that Plato describes writing as a *pharmakon*, emphasizing the strange way in which writing both supplements (aids, benefits) and supplants (undermines, usurps) memory. According to Derrida, the *pharmakon* of writing cannot be reduced to the series of oppositional concepts that it conditions or makes possible (Derrida 1981: 103). If the reader, philosopher or translator were to decide in favour of one of the semantic resonances of *pharmakon* [remedy /poison], then the whole problem that writing poses to philosophy – as presented in this text – would collapse.

That Plato had recourse to the Greek word *pharmakon* was fortuitous; had he no such recourse, one might speculate that he would have had to invent a word. In *Dissemination*, Derrida chose to keep *pharmakon* untranslated. This arguably makes for a better choice than introducing a clunky neologism – say, 'usurp-plant-ation' – which would preserve something of the difference signified by the original. Elsewhere, faced with a similar translational task, Derrida opted for an interlingual translation:

> In 1967, to translate a crucial German word with a double meaning (*aufheben, Aufhebung*), a word that signifies at once to suppress and to elevate, a word that Hegel says represent the speculative risk of the German language, and that the entire world had until then agreed was untranslatable – or if you prefer, a word for which no one had agreed with anyone on a stable, satisfying translation into any language – for this word, I had proposed the noun *relève* and the verb *relever*. This allowed me to retain, joining them in a single word, the double motif of the elevation and the replacement that preserves what it denies or destroys, preserving what it causes to disappear.
>
> (Derrida 2001: 196)

Looking back on the history of his own translation, Derrida recounts the fortuity of his selection of *relever* as a way of rendering Hegel's *Aufhebung*. Rehearsing the common wisdom that *Aufhebung* is untranslatable, because it is so linked to the particular semantic possibilities of the German language, Derrida nonetheless defends the relevance and productivity of the translation he proposed. This relevance is not based on equivalence but rather on the way that the term 'sounds' – the image proposed here is percussive – some of the most important semantic notes in the original, 'raising up' or 'bringing to the surface' that which has been submerged. This process involves a choice or selection that is never fully calculable. There is something, then, of the aleatory in all translation.

Derrida notes that despite the controversy surrounding his own work and name, the translation he proposed came to be widely accepted. However, the stabilization and validation of this particular Franco-German exchange covers over, he suggests, the contingency of his own initial proposal. Derrida insists that if *relever* is a good, apt, *relevant* translation, it is not for the reasons that are commonly adduced – that *relever* is somehow an equivalent for the German. Rather, if *relever* is relevant – good or apt – it is because it is itself – in a recursive movement – a *relève /Aufhebung* of *Aufhebung*. Indeed, Derrida suggests, that translation is always a kind of *Aufhebung*. The alteration-modification of the 'original' term is not something that can be avoided.

As we have seen in Derrida's reading of Benjamin, translation involves what Liu, as we saw above, called complementarity. Translations can have a strange backward effect, transforming or enhancing what we might be tempted to see as the linguistic past. Derrida demonstrates the effects of this complementarity in his reading and translation of Shakespeare's *The Merchant of Venice*. The latter will again offer an occasion to reflect on the productivity of *relever*. Derrida suggests that Portia's famous line 'when mercy seasons justice' might best (most relevantly) be rendered in a French translation by the term *relever*. The standard translation by François-Victor Hugo, which renders 'seasons' as *tempère*, Derrida finds formally unproblematic – but less relevant: 'It isn't an erroneous choice' (2001: 195). He will, however, suggest *relève*, which he justifies for three reasons: 1) it leaves the sense of 'season' idiomatically intact, as it is found in the context of cooking [*assaisonner*]; 2) it has the sense of elevation as the original suggests the elevation of divine justice (mercy) over earthly justice (retributivism); 3) as the history of its translation attests, *relever* suggests a way to understand Portia's claim about the relation between mercy and justice. In doing so, the translation of 'season' by *relève* 'threatens' to enrich the original text with the idea that (Christian – New Testament) mercy is the *Aufhebung* of (Jewish – Old Testament) justice – a movement away from the literality of retributivism to its suspension-overcoming in divine mercy.

Derrida is here advocating for a certain willingness to take risks that is indistinguishable from the willingness to wield the power inherent in the act of translation. In much of Derrida's work on translation, as we have seen, metaphysical concerns – ones that position translation in a way that de-centres the human – trump both political and ethical questions concerning the uses and abuses of translation in *human* contexts. This makes Derrida's wide-ranging thinking on translation particularly relevant for the contemporary context – where we see the rapid, inexorable development of machine translation in all its senses. However, this, no doubt, requires a deconstructive analysis of the ethics and politics of translation. I have suggested readings that make valuable strides in this direction below.

Related topics

Benjamin; translation theory and philosophy; equivalence; meaning; the translation of philosophical texts; translating Derrida; machine translation; toward a philosophy of translation.

Further reading

Liu, L. (1995) *Translingual Practice: Literature, National Culture, and Translated Modernity*, Stanford, CA: Stanford University Press. (Interrogating translational practices at the nexus of Western-Sino-Japanese national literatures, Liu's work dilates on many of the deconstructive insights we find in Derrida's texts and points to forms of power that translingual theorists are uniquely positioned to make visible.)

Cassin, B. (ed.) (2014) *Dictionary of Untranslatables: A Philosophical Lexicon*, translated by S. Rendall, C. Hubert, J. Mehlman, N. Stein and Michael Syrotinski, edited by E. Apter, J. Lezra and M. Wood, Princeton, NJ: Princeton University Press. (Following closely Derrida's own usage, an 'untranslatable', Barbara Cassin, project editor, specifies, is not what *cannot* be translated but the *'sign* of the way in which, from one language to another, neither the words nor the conceptual networks can simply be superimposed'. This book is important because of the way it takes up both Derrida's challenge to logocentrism, or what it calls 'linguistic universalism', and his injunction to philosophize in more than one tongue [*plus d'une langue*].

Ertel, E. (2011) 'Derrida on Translation and His (Mis)reception in America', *Trahir* (September 2011): 1–18. (This article provides an indispensable critical overview of Derrida's work on translation, including excellent reconstructions of his argument of 'Des Tours de Babel', 'What is a Relevant Translation' and 'Living On', another text in Derrida's oeuvre that takes up the notion of textual 'survival' introduced in Derrida's reading of Benjamin.)

Metzgler, E. (2002) 'Translation, Poststructuralism and Power', in M. Tymoczko and E. Gentzler (eds) *Translation and Power*, Amherst and Boston: University of Massachusetts Press. (This work provides an important overview of how deconstructive thought on translation practices has been taken up outside of the American academic context, particularly by scholars and translators in Brazil and francophone Canada. Focusing on the dimension of politics and power evidenced in translational practices, Metzgler explores some political implications of Derrida's work on translation.)

References

Arbel, R., Maidenbaum, S., Amedi A., *et al.* (2014) 'Vision through Other Senses: Practical Use of Sensory Substitution Devices as Assistive Technology for Visual Rehabilitation', *MED 2014*. doi: 10.1109/MED.2014.6961368.

Benjamin, W. [1923] (2012) 'The Translator's Task', trans. S. Rendall, in L. Venuti (ed.) *The Translation Studies Reader* [third edition], London and New York: Routledge, 75–83.

Derrida, J. (1972) 'The Ends of Man', trans. A. Bass, *Margins of Philosophy*, Chicago: University of Chicago Press, 109–36.

Derrida, J. [1976] (1998) *Of Grammatology*, trans. G. Spivak, Baltimore, MD: Johns Hopkins University Press.

Derrida, J. (1978) 'Structure, Sign, and Play in the Discourse of the Human Sciences', trans. A. Bass, *Writing and Difference*, Chicago: University of Chicago Press, 278–94.

Derrida, J. (1981) *Positions*, trans. A. Bass, Chicago and London: University of Chicago Press (1988, *Limited Inc.*, ed. G. Graff, Evanston, IL: Northwestern University Press).

Derrida, J. (1982) *Margins of Philosophy*, trans. A. Bass, Chicago: University of Chicago Press.

Derrida, J. (1985) 'Des Tours de Babel', trans. J. F. Graham, in J. F. Graham (ed.) *Difference in Translation*, Ithaca, NY: Cornell University Press, 165–207.

Derrida, J. (1988) 'Signature Event Context', in *Limited Inc.*, trans. S. Weber and J. Mehlman, Evanston, IL: Northwestern University Press, 9.

Derrida, J. (2001) 'What Is a "Relevant" Translation?' trans. L. Venuti, *Critical Inquiry* 27: 174–200.

Gleick, J. (2012) *The Information: A History, a Theory, a Flood*, New York: Vintage Books.

Jakobson, R. [1959] (2012) 'On Linguistic Aspects of Translation', in L. Venuti (ed.) *The Translation Studies Reader* [third edition], London and New York: Routledge, 126–31.

Liu, L. (1995) *Translingual Practice: Literature, National Culture, and Translated Modernity*, Stanford, CA: Stanford University Press.
Searle, J. (1982) 'The Chinese Room Revisited', *Behavioral and Brain Sciences* 5 (2): 345.
Searle, J. (1994) 'Literary Theory and Its Discontents', *New Literary History* 25th Anniversary Issue (Part 1) 25 (3): 637–67.
Steiner, G. (1975) *After Babel*, Oxford: Oxford University Press.
Wheeler, S. (2000) Deconstruction as Analytic Philosophy, Stanford, CA: Stanford University Press.

10
Current trends in philosophy and translation

Roland Végső

Introduction

To a large extent, the twentieth century turned out to be the century of language for Western philosophy in the sense that both the continental and analytic traditions witnessed a 'linguistic turn'. This state of affairs, needless to say, boded quite well for the fate of translation as a philosophical problem. Elevating language to the status of a central concept also implied that translation had to play an important role in our theoretical systems. Of course, this general tendency did not in the least imply any kind of uniformity, and individual philosophers granted different degrees of importance to translation. But even if translation never quite occupied the position of being one of the most important problems for philosophy, the concept of translation was nevertheless endowed with more and more heuristic power. It became at least a silent partner in some of the most spectacular enterprises of philosophy.

But the new century began on a quite different note. Already by the 1990s, it had become clear that the twentieth century will be over only when the hegemony of language is finally broken and becomes a thing of the past. Since a significant section of contemporary philosophy is motivated by a barely disguised fatigue with questions of language, signification, textuality, hermeneutics, and deconstruction, a rather dark eventuality began to rise on our horizon: the possibility that translation might not be such an interesting problem for philosophy after all. This turn away from language, which also implied a turn away from translation, was more often than not couched in the form of a rejection of 'post-structuralism'.

A clear example of this turn away from translation can be detected in the works of Alain Badiou. First and foremost, this shift is clearly legible on a stylistic level. Although Badiou's writing and argumentative style is not without its own poetic appeal, it is explicitly motivated by a rejection of the rhetorical excesses and stylistic bravado of some of his contemporaries. Apologizing for the 'abstruse' nature of what they are going to present in their introduction, the translators of Badiou's *Infinite Thought*, Oliver Feltham and Justin Clemens, offer the reader the freedom to skip over these difficult materials. As they point out, they feel justified in this move by Badiou himself:

> He effectively tries to speak to those who do not spend their lives in professional institutions, but act and think in ways that usually exceed or are beneath notice. As

> Badiou himself puts it: 'Philosophy privileges no language, not even the one it is written in'.
>
> (Badiou 2003: 2)

These words suggest that the egalitarian nature of Badiou's philosophy manifests itself on the level of style as well. In a more philosophical tone, Alberto Toscano introduced his translation of Badiou's *Logics of World* by referring to the ideal at work in Badiou's philosophy as 'the rationalist imperative of transmissibility which would tend towards the nullification of human speech' (Badiou 2009: xv). In the same spirit, then, Toscano adds: 'I have worked to make the act of translation as unobtrusive as possible'. The formula is clear: since the problem of translation tends towards nullification in Badiou's philosophy, the translation of Badiou's works itself should move in the direction of the elimination of the obtrusive signs of translation.

Thus, the ideal of mathematical formalization that motivates much of Badiou's thinking points in the direction of a universal language that renders translation a secondary concern. To be more precise, translation does not simply disappear from this system. The point is that everything can be translated into the language of set theory. But once this translation has taken place, there is no need for future retranslations. Translation is still necessary but only as an incidental concern that in itself does not have to become the object of detailed philosophical analysis. Quite paradoxically, it is the universal possibility of translation (everything can be translated into the language of mathematics/philosophy, and pure thought travels among languages universally) that renders translation unimportant.

We find one of the clearest formulations of this problem in Badiou's article on the French language in *The Dictionary of Untranslatables*. Badiou starts by identifying a conflict between the desire to write in the mother tongue and the official academic language of philosophy (Badiou 2014: 350). In the French context, this conflict first manifested itself in Descartes' works as the necessary choice between the French language and Latin. The seemingly counter-intuitive point, however, is that it is the choice of French that represents a genuine universalism here, not Latin. By choosing to write in French, the philosopher responds to the essentially democratic call of philosophy to speak to everyone. Thus, as Badiou puts it, the privilege given to the French language '*had nothing to do with the language as such*' (Badiou 2014: 350). In Badiou's account, Descartes' 'principled universalism' is based on a triple foundation: 1) reasoning (whose paradigm is geometrical writing) is axiomatic in nature and 'travels across languages universally'; 2) thinking in the form of the intuition of immanent ideas is essentially non-linguistic; 3) the transcription of these ideas may take place in any dialect (Badiou 2014: 350). All three of these criteria shift the focus away from the specificity of a language to the universality of reason.

And yet the specificity of French does not simply disappear in this argument. Badiou clearly delineates the subtle differences between French, German, English, and Italian. He calls French a 'thin' language because it prioritizes syntax over substance. His conclusion captures the duality of philosophical language and national dialect in the following terms:

> Axiomatizing, deriving, and thereby even emptying speech of any individuality that sparkles too much, of any predication that is too colorful; purifying this speech, these excessive turns of phrase like repentances and uncertainties – these are the very acts of philosophy itself, once it orders its Idea in this material *place* that grasps it, runs through it: a language, *this* language, French.
>
> (Badiou 2014: 354)

This point is fully in line with Badiou's general argument that a Truth is transworldly in nature but still needs a worldly body in order to assume appearance (Badiou 2011: 26). As a result, the possibility and necessity of translation is clearly designated a specific ontological location in Badiou's system. But translation is simply the worldly body in which the universality of the Idea appears: the Idea is not untranslatable; it simply does not need translation anymore.

Nevertheless, it would be a mistake to assume that the translator has nothing to learn from Badiou's philosophy. If we decide to concentrate on some of the more general questions raised by his writings (rather than exclusively on his philosophy of language), we might find that several of his central categories – like the event, truth, and the subject – are potentially useful tools for conceptualizing what takes place in acts of translation. For example, it is an interesting coincidence that one of the central concepts for Badiou that tie these three categories (event, truth, subject) together is that of 'fidelity' – a central problem for theories of translation as well. Therefore, if we conceive of Badiou's philosophy as a philosophy of praxis (Ashton, Bartlett and Clemens 2006), we might be able to use a number of his ideas to formulate a theory of translation as an ethical and political practice (Végső 2012).

Towards a sociology of translation

In addition to Badiou, one of the most important influences behind the current transformation of the philosophical interest in translation came from a field strictly speaking different from philosophy: science studies. Even at an early stage of its development, actor–network theory (ANT) defined its methodology as a 'sociology of translation'. Unlike Badiou (who removes translation from the centre of attention but retains the basic linguistic nature of translation), ANT promotes translation into a central concept but no longer treats it as an essentially linguistic phenomenon. In this context, 'translation' becomes the preferred term for what in a more general philosophical lexicon we often call 'mediation'. As such, linguistic mediation (that is, the common understanding of translation) is only one possible example of translation, which now becomes a praxis that has to be located at the level of the ontology of the social: translation constitutes networks.

The expression 'sociology of translation' is usually derived from Michel Callon's works of the 1980s. In his 1986 article 'Some Elements of a Sociology of Translation', Callon outlines his theory of the sociology of translation through a case study examining the production of scientific knowledge concerning scallop farming in 1970s France. It is in this context that Callon formulates his influential theory of translation as a process in which 'the identity of actors, the possibility of interaction, and the margins of manoeuvre are negotiated and delimited' (Callon 1999: 68). Callon follows the story of three researchers who return home to France from a trip to Japan and attempt to revitalize a local economy through the domestication of a specific species of scallop. In order to examine how the central actors of the story (scientists, fishermen, and scallops) interacted with each other, Callon formalizes the process of translation in the following formulas:

1. 'Translation is a displacement' (Callon 1999: 81): in the process of this production of new scientific knowledge a whole series of displacements had to occur that involve human and nonhuman actors alike.
2. 'It is to establish oneself as a spokesperson' (Callon 1999: 81): but translation also involves expressing in one's own language what other actors say and want, how they act and interact. At the end of the process, a unified discourse has to bring these actors into a more or less stable relationship with each other.

3. 'Translation is a process before it is a result' (Callon 1999: 81): after this unification, however, the work of translation is not over yet as the possibility of new displacements opens up immediately and new spokespersons emerge to unify these relations in new configurations.
4. 'Translation is the mechanism by means of which the social and natural worlds progressively take form' (Callon 1999: 82): what is ultimately at stake in the processes of translation is the very definition of the two grand domains of human existence. As Callon puts it, the 'result is a situation in which certain entities control others' (Callon 1999: 82). In other words, power relations are established.

As far as ANT is concerned, then, translation (understood as the process whereby actors are constituted through the establishment of specific relations) cannot be defined exclusively as a linguistic mediation of social relations. Callon's last point calls attention to a crucial dimension of translation: translation constitutes the very division between the social and the natural worlds. It is in this sense that the problem of translation must be located on the level of the ontology of the social.

This definition of translation is also the foundation of Bruno Latour's take on the social. In a sense, we could say that Latour argues for a pure mediation without a social totality. This argument involves a reversal of causality: in science studies, 'the social was to be explained instead of providing the explanation' (Latour 2005: 108). If the sociology of translation can identify and describe mediators as actors, it will not need the hypothesis of a 'society' that lies behind these mediations:

> As I have said in the introduction, to use the word social for such a process is legitimated by the oldest etymology of the word *socius*: 'someone following someone else', a 'follower', or 'associate'. To designate this thing which is neither one actor among many nor a force behind all the actors transported through some of them but a connection that transports, so to speak, transformations, we use the word *translation* – the tricky word 'network' being defined in the next chapter as what is *traced* by those translations in the scholars' accounts. So, the word 'translation' now takes on a somewhat specialized meaning: a relation that does not transport causality but induces two mediators into coexisting. [...] I can now state the aim of this sociology of associations more precisely: there is no society, no social realm, and no social ties, *but there exist translations between mediators that may generate traceable associations.*
>
> (Latour 2005: 108, emphasis in original)

This focus on mediation also explains Latour's well-known historical argument that modernity is constituted by the repression of the ontological function of translation. The exclusion that constituted modernity guaranteed that the act of mediation carried out by translation remained hidden. As Latour puts it, modernity was defined by two distinct practices:

> The first set of practices, by 'translation,' creates mixtures between entirely new types of beings, hybrids of nature and culture. The second, by 'purification,' creates two entirely distinct ontological zones: that of human beings on the one hand; that of nonhumans on the other.
>
> (Latour 1993: 10–11)

The paradox of modernity was that the more it denied the processes of translation in the name of purification, the more it promoted the proliferation of hybrids.

The ultimate goal of this critique of modernity is to outline a new 'relationalist' ontology (Latour 1993: 114). The first step in this project is the generalization of the logic of mediation:

> An intermediary – although recognized as necessary – simply transports, transfers, transmits energy from one of the poles of the Constitution. It is void in itself and can only be less faithful or more or less opaque. A mediator, however, is an original event and creates what it translates as well as the entities between which it plays the mediating role.
> (Latour 77–8)

Thus, a genuine act of mediation translates but in such a way that it itself creates both the mediated entities and the relations among them. Translation, in this sense, does not pre-exist the identities and relations that it puts into relation with each other. It is in the event of the mediation itself that the identities of all the agents are created.

Latour's term for this new ontology is 'relative relativism' (Latour 1993: 113). Translation cannot be inscribed in the logic of 'absolute relativism', since the latter is essentially based on the denial of the very possibility of establishing relations among ontologically distinct entities. To put it differently, absolute relativism is based on the ideal of untranslatability since it cannot establish a common measure among different entities. But Latour's famous principle of irreducibility clearly rejects this position: 'Nothing is, by itself, either reducible or irreducible to anything else. Never by itself, but always through the mediation of another. How can one claim that worlds are untranslatable, when translation is the very soul of the process of relating?' (Latour 1993: 113).

It is in this context that we can understand Latour's critique of the 'linguistic turn' in continental philosophy:

> Whether they are called 'semiotics', 'semiology' or 'linguistic turns', the object of all these philosophies is to make discourse not a transparent intermediary that would put the human subject in contact with the natural world, but a mediator independent of nature and society alike. This autonomization of the sphere of meaning has occupied the best minds of our time for the past half-century. If they too have led us into an impasse, it is not because they have 'forgotten man', or 'abandoned reference', as the modernist reaction is declaring today, but because they themselves have limited their enterprise to discourse alone.
> (Latour 1993: 63)

As Latour points out, the price to be paid for this autonomization of language was the rejection of the problem of reference and the identity of the speaking subject: 'Language has become a law unto itself, a law governing itself and its own world' (Latour 1993: 63). On the one hand, these philosophers discovered the crucial difference between genuine mediators and mere intermediaries. In other words, an intermediary occupies a place of transmission where no genuine act of translation takes place. It is a more or less transparent transportation of information and identity between two positions. A genuine act of mediation, however, is constitutive in the sense that it itself brings into being the very entities it translates as well as their relations. In the same way, Latour suggests, for the philosophers of the linguistic turn language effectively functioned as a means of constituting subjects, objects, and their relations. When the subject becomes a 'meaning effect' and the object a 'reality effect' of language, the latter takes on the role of a constitutive force that creates the very entities that it mediates.

On the other hand, however, Latour argues that this absolutization of language missed a crucial point. In its essence, it amounted to a confusion of the problem of mediation with the problem of language. To put it differently, it was a welcome development in the history of philosophy that these thinkers provided a more precise articulation of the problem of mediation by analysing the intricacies of language, signification, and textuality. But, in the same move, they misunderstood the nature of mediation by reducing it to nothing but linguistic mediation. They confused mediation with its one of its possible instantiations.

Thus, we could say that the primary accomplishment of the sociology of translation is that it elevates translation to an ontological concept in a way that is quite different from earlier paradigms. Yes, translation has been 'ontologized' before (by Heidegger, Derrida, etc.), but here it is ontologized in a way that goes well beyond the ontology of language (which holds that language is by definition translation) as well as linguistic ontologies (which argue that everything is constructed by language). Translation is no longer a regional ontology (restricted to our understanding of language as signification) but a general ontological principle of the very constitution of the social (and its opposite, 'nature'). Linguistic translation is merely one possible example of this universal principle.

In more practical terms, we could argue that this approach to translation promises to liberate translation from some of its inherited institutional constraints. Of course, the generalization of translation as the fundamental paradigm of social practice does incur the risk of turning it into an empty concept whose potential field of application is so broad that it loses any practical value whatsoever. But the mobilization of ANT for translation theory might help us develop broader frameworks of interpretation that take into consideration a surprising array of actors moving along a number of different networks as they bring into being various relations of translation. To say the least, such an expansion of our understanding of translation would imply that (even if we want to concentrate on traditional forms of linguistic translation) we have to break out of the restrictive basic model that conceives of translation exclusively in terms of an encounter between an original text and a (professional) translator. In other words, we would have to try to understand how linguistic translation functions within larger networks of social mediation. In place of the dual model, we would have to construct unpredictably polymorphous frameworks as we follow translation through a number of different institutions (presses, translation schools, universities, distribution centres, etc.) with the goal of discovering new actors (publishers, editors, professional teachers of translation studies, teachers of literature, etc., but also nonhuman actors such as Google Translate, new forms of digital publication, data-mining algorithms, etc.).

Towards a flat ontology of translation

New materialisms, speculative realism, object-oriented ontology: these are the names under which the rejection of a specific conception of language and translation proceeds today. What is common in these philosophical movements is a turn away from an exclusive focus on subjectivity towards a new concern with the object, reality, and materiality. While it was easy for us to accept the proposition that the ontology of the subject is defined in an essential manner by practices of translation, it is not entirely self-evident that objects are capable of acts of translation. But this is precisely the thesis that motives a whole nascent branch of philosophy today.

The clearest formulation of this thesis can be found in Levi Bryant's *The Democracy of Objects*: 'Above all, ontological realisms refuse to treat objects as constructions of humans. While it is true, I will argue, that all objects translate one another, the objects that are translated are irreducible to their translations' (Bryant 2011: 18). The ultimate goal of Bryant's project is to construct a 'flat ontology' – that is, an ontology without the traditional inherited metaphysical hierarchies. In a strictly ontological sense, all existing beings are equal even if they enter into unequal relations. Relying on Ian Bogost's pithy formula, Bryant puts this thesis in the following words: 'The democracy of objects is the ontological thesis that all objects [. . .] equally exist while they do not exist equally' (Bryant 2011: 19; Bogost 2012: 11). Bryant formulates what he considers to be the four fundamental theses of a flat ontology (or what he calls 'onticology'): 1) all objects are withdrawn (that is, no object possesses full presence and, therefore, no object is ever exhausted by the relations it might be able to enter); 2) the world does not exist (in other words, in an ontological sense, we cannot speak about a harmonious totality of objects); 3) the human being does not possess a privileged position in relation to being (as a result, the human/object relation is really only a subcategory of the more general problem of the object/object relation); 4) all objects are on 'an equal ontological footing' (if every existing object is equally real, we need to start thinking in terms of expanded collectives of objects that often exist on radically different scales) (Bryant 2011: 32).

As we can see, just as in Latour's work, the starting point of this philosophy is the attempt to rethink the human/nonhuman distinction itself. Quite surprisingly, however, it is translation (a seemingly purely anthropocentric concept) that carries the majority of this argumentative burden:

> In short, the difference between humans and other objects is not a difference in kind, but a difference in degree. Put differently, all objects translate one another. Translation is not unique to how the mind relates to the world. And as a consequence of this, no object has direct access to any other object.
>
> (Bryant 2011: 27)

Translation is no longer treated as a capability specific to the human being and becomes the generalized condition of objectivity as such. Translation names the way objects relate to each other. For example, when a book lies on a table, a certain type of information exchange takes place between the book and the table: the book receives information about its environment from the table; but this information is distorted in nature because its production is strictly internal to the book's intrinsic composition as a system (hence the term 'translation'). The book, therefore, interprets the table only in terms of the internal structures of the book itself.

In order to establish this last point, Bryant relies on Alfred North Whitehead's process philosophy and Niklas Luhmann's autopoietic systems theory. From Whitehead, Bryant borrows the idea that every existing entity grasps in specific ways the other entities that it comes into contact with. Whitehead calls this process 'prehension' in order to distinguish it from human 'comprehension'. What follows from this position is that human comprehension is only one specific manifestation of the larger problem of prehension that applies to all existing entities. The important point for Bryant is that this prehension always takes on subjective forms that are specific to the prehending entity (Bryant 2011: 135–6).

Thus, to account for the 'subjective' nature of prehension in more objective terms, Bryant relies on Luhmann's theory of autopoietic systems. The latter designate autonomous entities composed of a set of elements that are themselves constituted by the system itself (in other words, they do not pre-exist the system in which they will function as elements). As a result, the identity of an autopoietic system is determined by a network of dynamic processes whose effects remain internal to the system. Consequently, these systems are self-referential (their operations refer only to themselves and are products of the system itself) and closed in on themselves (they do not directly relate to their environment). They maintain only selective relations with their environments and systems in their environments that are always coded in terms of the internal structures of the given system (Bryant 2011: 140).

To simplify things, what counts for Bryant is that objects (modelled on autopoietic systems) interact with each other by producing 'information'. But what is the status of this information? Understood in this specific sense, information is not something simply given in the system's environment that could be exchanged between two entities. Rather, it names the way a concrete perturbation of the system is transformed into processes internal to the system. This transformation also implies that information is always constituted by the system experiencing the perturbation and always assumes system-specific forms (Bryant 2011: 156). Playing with the word itself, Bryant gives two new meanings to the term: 1) information means that something is 'in formation' – that is, it has no fixed identity and is capable of transformation; 2) but information is also 'in-form-ation' – that is, it designates the way objects take on new forms (Bryant 2011: 165).

When Bryant directly picks up the problem of translation in this context, he presents his discussions within the framework of the Lacanian theory of the 'cause'. As Bryant explains, Lacan distinguishes a genuine cause from the deterministic chain of the law (which defines our common understanding of causality). The point for Lacan is precisely that in the case of a cause we find an irreducible gap between cause and effect. In other words, a cause manifests itself precisely when something does not work according the law of causality. Thus, in the surprise of a cause, we encounter effects in excess of what we expected in relation to our traditional understanding of causality (Bryant 2011: 174–5):

> The gap functions in a very specific way in Lacan's conception of the mechanisms of the unconscious, but we can say that Lacan also makes a broader and more profound point about the gap and the relationship between cause and effect that holds for all inter-object relations. Here we can coin the aphorism, 'there is no transportation without translation', or, alternatively, 'there is no transportation without transformation'.
>
> (Bryant 2011: 178)

Two points should be emphasized here. First, we should note that Bryant provides yet another take on the old adage according to which translation is necessarily a form distortion (see the Italian *traduttore, traditore* [to translate, to betray]). At the same time, however, it is also clear that this distortion now receives a specific form: it is the production of something new. Bryant's comments on translation suggest something that goes against the usual definition of translation as a form of fidelity to the original. A genuine act of translation must be a surprising event that exceeds its actual causes. It is worthy of the name translation only if it breaks with the law and graces us with the advent of the new.

Ultimately, this argument leads to a new ontology of translation. We could break this argument down into three major moments. First, as Bryant insists, translation has to be generalized as an ontological relation: 'To be sure, every entity translates the other entities to which it relates, yet these translations must be rigorously distinguished from the entities that are translated' (Bryant 2011: 265). Second, the constitutive limitations of this generalized condition must be clearly articulated:

> Objects never directly encounter one another, but rather only relate to one another as translations or information. And information is never something transmitted or exchanged by objects, but rather is constituted by each object as a function of its own internal organization and distinctions.
>
> (Bryant 2011: 281)

Finally, what follows from the previous points is the hypothesis of the absolute de-essentialization of translation:

> There are as many forms of translation as there are types of objects. Indeed, there are as many forms of translation as there are objects. Moreover, new forms of translation come into being all the time with the emergence of new objects and with the development of objects.
>
> (Bryant 2011: 282)

This last point raises a crucial issue: translation strictly speaking does not have an ontology. It is reinvented every time an object enters into new relations with other objects. To put it differently, translation is an ontological category to the degree that it itself cannot be fully ontologized.

In a certain sense, then, this flat ontology radicalizes the conclusions of the sociology of translation. As we have seen, the conclusion is not simply that the society/nature distinction itself is a product of processes of translation and purification, but that every existing object translates the other objects that it encounters. The expansion of the notion of translation reaches here one of its logical limits: translation is no longer simply the general principle of human language; it is no longer merely the essence of all human or animal communication (be that linguistic or not); it is no longer the fundamental mechanism of the human mind; it is no longer the general logic of social action; it is the way every existing object persists in being. The good news here for practitioners of linguistic translation appears to be once again the liberation of the act of translation from inherited institutional limitations. For if every object reinvents translation when it enters into a relation with new objects, there must be an infinity of possible definitions of translation itself. This thesis could be taken as an ontological starting point for new forms of experimentation with the very definition of translation that exceed our received ideas about what a translator is supposed to do and accomplish at the end of the day when the work of translation is declared to be done.

Towards a new sophistics of translation

As far as the philosophy of translation is concerned, one of the most significant events of the new century turned out to be the grand project spearheaded by Barbara Cassin that was published in French in 2004 and translated into English under the title *Dictionary of Untranslatables: A Philosophical Lexicon* (Cassin 2014b). Cassin, while a frequent collaborator of Badiou, champions a philosophical tradition that was rejected by the proudly Platonist Badiou: the Sophists. This reinvention of sophistics amounts to a rearticulation of the role of language for a post-deconstructive era. Cassin's basic provocation is to offer an alternative history of philosophy. She uncovers a sophistic tradition that functions as an alternative to the dominant ontological and phenomenological traditions. In this sense, sophistics is the repressed 'other' (or even 'bad other') of ontology: 'Sophistic texts are the paradigm of what was not only left to one side but transformed and made unintelligible by their enemies' (Cassin 2014a: 2).

According to Cassin, while the fundamental model of philosophy remained Parmenides' *Poem* and Platonico-Aristotelian ontology, the sophistic countermodel constitutes a 'logology', an altogether different relation to *logos*. As Cassin explains, she borrows the term 'logology' from Novalis, who used it to refer to discourse that was primarily concerned with itself (Cassin 2014a: 2). For Cassin, however, the focus on the self-reflexive nature of discourse means that sophistics is a performative discourse. In other words, unlike ontology it is not trying to say what is but makes what it says *be*. In this sense, sophistic discourse 'creates as it speaks' (Cassin 2014a: 3). While ontology describes being as *phusis*, logology performs a *polis*: hence its political dimension. Yet Cassin is careful to emphasize that her ultimate goal is not the 'rehabilitation' of the Sophists. The point is not to turn the Sophists into rigorous philosophers but to understand why philosophy wanted to exclude them from its canon and to show why they disturb philosophy even today (Cassin 2014a: 14).

As Cassin explains, at the heart of this new (and simultaneously very old) sophistics, we find the idea of a 'consistent relativism'. In order to understand what Cassin means by this term, we must emphasize that she rejects the general understanding of the term that reduces it to a kind of moral nihilism:

> What is relativism? It is not the rejection of values, nor is it the idea that everything is of equal worth, but rather the rejection of values that will remain exactly and eternally the same, for all places and for all times.
>
> (Cassin 2014a: 326)

To put it differently, in spite of the fact that relativism is based on the critique of universal Truth, 'not everything goes, or, if you wish, relativism is not subjectivism' (Cassin 2014a: 268).

In place of Truth, then, Cassin offers up what she calls a 'dedicated comparative'. The basis for this redefinition of our relation to truth is Protagoras ('Man is the measure of all things'):

> Protagoras changes the parameters, quite radically: he switches from the binary opposition between true and false to the comparative 'better'. We learn that there is no such thing as Truth with a capital 'T', the Platonic idea that allows the philosopher-king to reign supreme over all men (and women, too, for sure), but rather that some things are 'truer' than others. There is no absolute, only a comparative; and, more specifically still, what I would call a 'dedicated comparative': the 'truer' is a 'better for'; as the better is defined as 'the more useful', the better adapted to (the person, the situation, all that makes up the moment in question, the moment the Greeks call *kairos*, 'the opportune moment').
>
> (Cassin 2014a: 237)

Eventually, Cassin finds the concrete political counterpart of this metaphysical pragmatism in one of Desmond Tutu's remarks in the South African Truth and Reconciliation Commission's report:

> 'Enough of the truth for': it is this expression that stops me in my tracks. It goes against the idea that there is one unique and absolute truth, *the* truth: rather, there is some truth, a bit, bits of truth. It is a partitive – some bread, some water, some truth. And there is enough of it for it to serve and be useful: it is instrumentalized truth.
>
> (Cassin 2014a: 262)

The philosophical foundation of the critique of Truth (in the name of this 'enough of the truth for') is Cassin's rejection of the Aristotelian principle of noncontradiction. Cassin presents Aristotle as the primary opponent of the Sophists. More than Plato, Aristotle was 'the philosopher who was mostly responsible for marginalizing them' (Cassin 2014a: 6). The important point is that Aristotle demonstrates 'the principle of all principles, the law of noncontradiction' (Cassin 2014a: 4) by a refutation of the sophistic position. Cassin argues that Aristotle can conceive of meaning only in terms of univocity and tries to excise ambiguity, homonymy, and polysemy from the domain of legitimate speech. Since the Sophists fell outside of the principle of noncontradiction, as far as Aristotle was concerned, they were like 'plants' (Cassin 2014a: 6).

In this historical struggle between the dominant onto-phenomenological logos and sophistic logology, the forces of translation clearly align themselves with the latter subterranean tradition. In this sense, for Cassin, translation constitutes a limit to ontology itself. As we have seen, the problem with classic ontology is that it presupposes the unity of *logos*. But, as Cassin puts it, 'a model other than the universality of the *logos* has to be found' (Cassin 2014a: 10). The foundation of this new model is the plurality of languages. This is where translation emerges as a central question of philosophy: 'languages perform different worlds' (Cassin 2014a: 11). As a result, the very nature of philosophy changes if we take the necessity of translation seriously: 'We philosophize in words and not in concepts: we have to complicate the universal with languages' (Cassin 2014a: 11).

We can find one of Cassin's most direct philosophical engagements of the problem of translation in her essay 'The Relativity of Translation and Relativism' (Cassin 2014a: 297–316). As the title suggests, translation becomes here the primary terrain for the articulation of the meaning of relativism since translation is the primary site for posing the question of the relation 'interpretive plurality and truth' (2014a: 298). As Cassin puts it: 'Translation [. . .] regularly violates the principle of noncontradiction because the principle of noncontradiction is based on the requirement of univocity: one word, one meaning – or, in any case, no two meanings at a time, no two meanings at the same time' (Cassin 2014a: 312). But the essence of translation is that it mobilizes the inherent ambiguities of two languages in such a way that the translator is always in the midst of a dynamic system of possibilities. Thus, the best model for the process of translation would be that of a 'calculus with its compossibilities': 'Accordingly, translation would be of the order of arborescence rather than that of the line' (Cassin 2014a: 303).

The essay is primarily concerned with the possible translations of Parmenides' poem often referred to under the title 'On Nature'. After tracing in detail the complications of textual transmission and surveying already existing translations, in the end Cassin reaches a surprising conclusion. At a crucial point of the essay, Cassin decides to hold on to two (rather than one) translations of a specific line of the poem (Cassin 2014a: 305) and adds: 'I do not want to choose between these two translations, nor can I choose' (Cassin 2014a: 309). Yet Cassin insists that this choice does not imply that all other options would have been equally valid: 'They make more sense to me than the others. They present a meaning to which it is necessary to be sensible' (Cassin 2014a: 309). In this sense, the process of translation meets one of its internal limits in the act of a choice: 'This choice, which presents itself as a choice [. . .] highlights the type of consistence that characterizes normal interpretive operations: cultural construction, textual fixion, trafficking in the letter, and translation as the terminal point of interpretation' (Cassin 2014a: 309).

Following Protagoras' lead, then, we should see translation as a manifestation of this consistent relativism that involves a shift from 'the binary opposition of true/false to the comparative "better" and, more precisely, to what I call "dedicated comparative": "better for"' (Cassin 2014a: 315). Immersed in the mire of possible options, the translator is urged to make a choice. But the choice should not be that of absolute Truth. As Cassin suggests, the translator must choose something that is 'better' and, more precisely, 'better for' the historical moment that constitutes the *kairos* of the act of translation. This is where the political dimension of translation also surfaces: 'Politics does not consist of the universal imposition of Truth (or the imposition of universal truth). It consists of the differential aid to choose the better' (Cassin 2014a: 316).

The end(s) of translation

How can we briefly formalize the relation among these definitions of translation? What is common to all of the authors examined here is the fundamentally ontological orientation of their definitions of translation. The ultimate horizon of contemporary philosophical engagements of translation appears to be what we call the ontology of translation. In the present context, we can use the expression 'the ontology of translation' in two senses. First, it can refer to the fact that the question of the ontological consistency of translation practices surfaces with a new intensity. At worst, philosophers slide over this question and take a specific definition of translation for granted; at best, translation gains a new kind of ontological openness. The second meaning of the expression refers to the tendency to elevate translation to the level of an ontological concept. In this sense, translation becomes the fundamental paradigm of human praxis, social mediation, or the very constitution of beings in general.

This development, which is hardly without historical precedents, does not necessarily mean that other questions (epistemological, ethical, political) completely disappear from the philosophy of translation. It means only that the decision concerning the very being of translation takes on a new urgency. In fact, one thing that also connects these theories of translation is that the ontological reflection is always framed in the context of a theory of politics. To put it differently, the contemporary ontology of translation is oriented by a principle of egalitarianism. Badiou's fundamentally rationalist egalitarianism is based on the transworldly nature of the event of truth, which, beyond a certain point, transcends translation. Radical equality becomes possible when we no longer need translation. In the case of Latour and Cassin, we find that a properly formulated relativism establishes simultaneously the necessity of translation and the conditions of political practice. For Bryant, a genuinely flat ontology is also an ontology of translation. The essential equality of all beings is predicated upon the hypothesis that being is in a perpetual state of translation.

Thus, we could argue that today translation occupies in philosophical discourse the position of a limit in relation to ontology. In the case of Badiou, ontology limits the function of translation (since mathematics as ontology tends towards the elimination of translation); for Cassin, translation limits the scope of classic ontology (as translation is responsible for introducing a new kind of multiplicity to ontology). For Latour and Bryant, ontology is translation, and the very problem of the limit is internalized; but for both of them, translation ceases to be an essentially linguistic problem as it is tied to the more general problem of relationality.

At the two extremes, the field of contemporary philosophical engagements of translation is defined by two ways of avoiding translation. On this level, the turn away from translation and the universalization of translation coincide. One position holds that translation is real but, in the end, a matter of philosophical indifference. The other, however, claims for it an excessive relevance. Everything is always already translation, so the specificity of translation disappears in this abstract universality. Both approaches, therefore, show us ways of suspending translation while retaining it at the same time. Between these two extremes, the question of the very possibility of translation (the debate concerning the untranslatable) emerges as the third dominant way of questioning translation today. The aporia of our times appears to be best captured in the maxim according to which the systematic demonstration of untranslatability is the ultimate and only possible affirmation of translation. This paradigm (which already has a long history) contains a risk that leads us down the road toward the fetishization of the untranslatable. Once again, translation is saved by the declaration of its very end.

Related topics

Translation theory and philosophy; the translation of philosophical texts; cognitive approaches to translation; toward a philosophy of translation.

Further reading

Apter, E. (2013) *Against World Literature: On the Politics of Untranslatability*, New York: Verso. (One of Cassin's collaborators on the English translation of the *Dictionary of Untranslatables,* Apter provides an influential contemporary example of how the problem of untranslatablity can be put to use in the study of literature.)
DeLanda, M. and G. Harman (2017) *The Rise of Realism*, Cambridge: Polity. (The conversations between these two thinkers provide a good context for understanding the role of translation in speculative realism and object-oriented ontology; part IV is especially relevant here.)
Law, J. (1997) *'Traduction/trahison:* Notes on ANT', Department of Sociology, Lancaster University, http://cseweb.ucsd.edu/~goguen/courses/175/stslaw.html [accessed 06/28/2017]. (An important overview of actor–network theory with a special emphasis on the problem of translation.)
Serres, M. (1982) *Hermes: Literature, Science, Philosophy*, ed. J. Harari and D. Bell, Baltimore, MD: Johns Hopkins University Press. (An influential precursor of the sociology of translation that formulates a philosophy of science based on the problem of communication and translation. In spite of the fact that his style was often compared to deconstruction, Serres was an important influence on Latour.)
Venuti, L. (2016) 'Hijacking Translation: How Comp Lit Continues to Suppress Translated Texts', *boundary 2* 43.2, 179–204. (A critique of Cassin's and Apter's treatment of the untranslatable by one of the leading theoreticians of translation today.)

References

Ashton, P., A. J. Bartlett, and J. Clemens (2006) 'Disciples: Institution, Philosophy, Praxis', in P. Ashton, A. J. Bartlett, and J. Clemens (eds.) *The Praxis of Alain Badiou*, Melbourne: re.press, 3–12.
Badiou, A. (2003) *Infinite Thought*, tr. O. Feltham and J. Clemens, London: Continuum.
Badiou, A. (2009) *Logics of Worlds: Being and Event*, 2, tr. A. Toscano, New York: Continuum.
Badiou, A. (2011) *Second Manifesto for Philosophy*, tr. L. Burchill, Cambridge: Polity.
Badiou, A. (2014) 'French', in B. Cassin (ed.) *Dictionary of Untranslatables: A Philosophical Lexicon*, tr. S. Rendall, C. Hubert, J. Mehlman, N. Stein, and M. Syrotinski, ed. E. Apter, J. Lezra, and M. Wood, Princeton: Princeton University Press, 349–54.
Bogost, I. (2012) *Alien Phenomenology, or, What It's Like to Be a Thing*, Minneapolis: University of Minnesota Press.
Bryant, L. (2011) *The Democracy of Objects*, Ann Arbor: Open Humanities Press.
Callon, M. (1999) 'Some Elements of a Sociology of Translation: Domestication of the Scallops and the Fishermen of St. Brieuc Bay', in M. Biagoli (ed.) *The Science Studies Reader*, London: Routledge, 67–83.
Cassin, B. (2014a) *Sophistical Practice: Toward a Consistent Relativism*, New York: Fordham University Press.

Cassin, B. (ed.) (2014b) *Dictionary of Untranslatables: A Philosophical Lexicon*, tr. S. Rendall, C. Hubert, J. Mehlman, N. Stein, and M. Syrotinski, ed. E. Apter, J. Lezra, and M. Wood, Princeton: Princeton University Press.

Latour, B. (1993) *We Have Never Been Modern*, tr. C. Porter, Cambridge: Harvard University Press.

Latour, B. (2005) *Reassembling the Social: An Introduction to Actor-Network-Theory*, Oxford: Oxford University Press.

Végső, R. (2012) 'The Parapraxis of Translation', *CR: The New Centennial Review* 12.1 (Spring 2012), 47–68.

Part II
Translation studies and philosophy

11
Translation theory and philosophy

Maria Tymoczko

Introduction

Philosophers writing in the Eurocentric tradition have often used translation as a vehicle or extended metaphor for discussing problems in philosophy because translation epitomizes and sets in high relief many aspects of language, cultural asymmetry, and problems related to communication among human beings.[1] Translation speaks to differences in language and culture both with respect to individuals and whole societies. Hence it goes to the heart of philosophical problems related to philosophy of mind, including the nature of knowledge, decision making, and perception of other minds, and to cognitive and social functions such as intention, action, communication, and ethics. Translation has also been used at times to frame discussions of specialized domains of knowledge including the philosophy of science or the understanding of history and the workings of ideology in societies.

Thus translation studies deals with many of the same concerns and problems that engage philosophers. Although discussions of these topics in translation studies at times lack the abstract sophistication and specialized vocabulary used in the long tradition of Eurocentric philosophy, philosophers should find explorations of these issues by translation studies scholars of interest. Their value for philosophy in part results from the fact that translation studies is grounded in the broad context of global linguistic and cultural variation that translators work with and that many of the findings about translation are concrete and demonstrable in case studies. By contrast, the examples deployed by philosophers in the Eurocentric tradition of philosophy are typically restricted to Indo-European languages and cultures, often closely related ones or, as in the case of W.V.O. Quine, invented examples that are not convincing when considered pragmatically (Tymoczko 1999: 146–62). Moreover, the arguments in philosophy are often about abstract or putative case studies. Thus awareness of theoretical discourses in translation studies can remediate some of the parochial approaches of philosophy. Conversely philosophers raise issues that translators and translation scholars must consider in relation to both the theory and practice of translation.

Translation studies is a discipline that consolidated after World War II. Although it is young and still building its theoretical foundation, much has been accomplished. In an entry in the *Encyclopedia of Applied Linguistics* (Tymoczko 2013) I identified and discussed at greater length the following principles of translation theory that have achieved general consensus among translation scholars internationally.[2]

1. Translation involves negotiating fundamental linguistic and cultural asymmetries and anisomorphisms.[3]
2. Translation involves decisions and choices about meanings in the source text (ST) and constructions of meaning in the target text (TT).[4]
3. Meaning in a ST or a TT extends far beyond semantic meaning. In translation a practitioner must pay particular attention to functional aspects of languages and texts.
4. Because translation involves decisions, choices, and constructions related to meaning, there is no single correct way to translate. Translation equivalence is *a posteriori* in nature. The particular configuration of equivalence in a translation can be defined only by descriptive studies of the actual translation in relation to context.[5]
5. An entailment of the decisions, choices, and constructions involved in translating is that translation is a metonymic process. Translations are partial representations of their STs. In addition translators introduce into their translations elements that have metonymic reference to the target language and context.[6]
6. Translation equivalence can be stipulated explicitly or implicitly, as can any linguistic behavior.
7. Translation is a form of rewriting and as such has many commonalities with other forms of rewriting, including adaptations to media other than language.
8. Because translation involves choices and because strategies of translation vary so widely, like other forms of cultural production, translations are best seen in the context of cultural systems.
9. Translations are an ideological and political form of cultural production.
10. Translation is a cluster concept. Ideas about translation have varied widely across time, place, culture, and language.

Although these theoretical statements seem simple, they are powerful. In my earlier article on translation theory cited above I elaborate on these principles and discuss the entailments of each. Because there is little point in reproducing those earlier elaborations, here I concentrate on discussing the relation between translation theory and the Eurocentric tradition of philosophy, specifically the Anglo-American tradition. I focus on some of the common theoretical issues shared by translation studies and philosophy, as well as issues that could be further explored to the mutual advantage of both fields.

We should begin by observing that the practice of translation is enormously difficult to theorize because of the complexity of translation and the sheer number of parameters involved, each of which potentially introduces significant variation. A partial list of these parameters includes the large number of human languages (currently more than 6,000), any two of which in translation present their own dilemmas related to linguistic asymmetries from sound system to registers and styles; the large number of distinct human cultures, each with its own subcultures associated with those languages; variations of each of these cultures in all cultural domains including law, customs, mores, ethics, social structures, religion, and textual and literary conventions; divergence in cultural contexts (both spatial, including geography, climate, and so forth affecting human lifeways, and temporal and political contexts, including history and relations to other cultures); and distinctive social systems related to such things as social structure, material culture, politics, and ideology. In addition to this enormous number of nested parameters pertaining to the source and target cultures there are specific parameters associated with each translation, including the patron, the translator, and the context and function of the translation.

Moreover, because generativity is a fundamental characteristic of human language and human culture, each of these parameters of translation is potentially in flux, such that new variations are continually emerging. In turn the generativity of human language and culture results in the development of new parameters, such as those being introduced to translation practice by digital culture at present. As a result of this multifaceted and unbounded complexity, translation theory is very difficult to formulate, and it must be flexible and open enough to account for new factors related to translation that are generated globally. Translation studies is not the only discipline that faces these challenges in formulating theory: they are common to theory in most disciplines related to human culture, including literary theory, sociology, and so forth. At present translation scholars are investigating the implications of complexity theory itself for translation as a practice and for formulating translation theory.

At times practitioners and teachers of translation approach language somewhat simplistically, ignoring the ways that philosophers have discussed and problematized language, regressing to a positivist framework for language, or inventing terminology rather than using the established vocabulary of linguistics in articulating problems related to asymmetries across languages. Sometimes statements about translation seem to ignore dominant theories of language or sociolinguistics that are current or taken for granted in the discourses of philosophy and linguistics. It is also evident that some translators and translation scholars lack a basic grounding in frameworks for ethics established in philosophical discourses and other domains, considering ethics to be located primarily at the level of word choice during the act of translating. Thus greater familiarity with philosophical discourses about all of these questions can add grounding and weight to discourses in translation studies about the ethics, ideology, and political dimensions of translation as well as about many facets of language.

This broad context frames the following discussion of some of the established discourses that should be considered and reconsidered in light of the intersection of the fields of philosophy and translation studies in any discussion of the general principles or theory of translation. Obviously it is impossible to give a comprehensive account of the intersection of the two fields in a chapter of this size, not least because philosophy is a very broad and open field, differing considerably across linguistic and cultural traditions, and thus defined and delineated in many different ways in cultures around the world. The concept indicated by the English word *philosophy* and its cognates in European languages, together with the many words in languages other than European ones that are used to translate this word, has a diverse and open field of reference.[7] Like translation, philosophy is an example of a cluster concept, concepts whose referents are held together by what Wittgenstein called 'family resemblances'.[8] Globally philosophy includes a broad range of discourses and discourse types, many texts and text types, and privileged areas of concern that go far beyond those discussed in Eurocentric philosophy or those considered below.

Here I focus on the relations between translation theory and Anglo-American philosophical traditions, which are the philosophical discourses that I am best qualified to discuss. Nonetheless, because some of the figures referenced below were formed in other cultural and philosophical traditions (for example, Ludwig Wittgenstein by German philosophy, and Roman Jakobson by Russian Formalism, the Prague School, Saussure, and other European movements and figures), the actual reach of the discussion here is broader than Anglo-American thinking on the topics in focus. Parallel succinct entries, however, could and ultimately should be written on the intersection of philosophy and translation theory in

European Continental philosophy, Chinese philosophy, the philosophical traditions of south Asia, and non-Eurocentric philosophies in general.

This survey begins with Quine, whose work is canonical in translation studies and speaks to the largest questions of whether translation is ever determinate, reliable, or definitive in its representations. I then turn to the work of Wittgenstein and the Anglo-American school of the philosophy of language. Wittgenstein's approach to language is important for understanding specific cruxes in translation related to translation theory and practice. Equally important, his resistance to constructing universalizing philosophical frameworks is consistent with the theoretical structures needed in translation studies because of its complexity, supporting the approach to translation theory summarized above.[9] Both Wittgenstein and the Anglo-American school of the philosophy of language offer many invaluable entry points for interrogating specific linguistic features of translations in their cultural contexts, and vice versa. The third section of this chapter focuses on John Rawls's approach to ethics and illustrates the mutual value of integrating approaches and discourses about ethics in philosophy and translation studies. Studies of ethical translation practices and ethics in translation theory can be deepened by Rawls's view of subject positions in determinations of justice; conversely translation data can broaden philosophical discourses and provide tangible examples with ethical implications illustrating Rawls's approach to ethics. The chapter concludes with a brief consideration of epistemology and the ways that findings and approaches in translation studies complicate philosophical discourses and theoretical investigations about how human beings 'know' things.

Despite and at times even because of disagreements in philosophical circles about all these questions, teachers of translation, translation studies scholars, and translators themselves have much to gain from consideration of the large questions raised by philosophers, critical responses to philosophical arguments, and the substantive value of philosophical writings when tested against the body of descriptive translation data and the theoretical frameworks that have grown up within translation studies. Philosophy problematizes many facets of translation that are often assumed or elided by translators and translation studies scholars. The converse is, of course, also true: philosophers often have a naive view of the processes and practices of translation across diverse cultures through time. Thus philosophers will benefit from familiarity with discourses developed in translation studies and the range of concrete cases discussed in descriptive studies of translation.[10] Along with the large body of empirical data gathered in translation studies and the analyses and theorizations of those data, some of the best means of assessing broad philosophical considerations about thought, language, communication, and other fundamental features of human activity are found in studies of translation. Empirical and theoretical studies of translation offer strong measures for testing the durability of many specific propositions in philosophy, particularly those related to language and culture. Thus both philosophy and translation studies can be deepened by intersecting at the levels of both data and theory.

Quine and the indeterminacy of translation

The essay by W.V.O. Quine (1908–2000) titled 'Meaning and Translation' (1959) contains his signature argument about the indeterminacy of translation. The article appeared in one of the first compendia of essays about translation, *On Translation* (1959), edited by Reuben Brower and published by Harvard University Press. The book showcases the views about translation of its contributors, many of whom were well-known translators and highly respected professors associated with Harvard University in a variety of disciplines ranging from classics to the emerging field of computer science.

The book is in part a response to World War II, which left none of the essayists untouched. That global conflagration brought people into contact who spoke hundreds of languages, making translation a pressing security and intelligence issue and contributing to the establishment of translation studies as a discipline. The collection of essays appeared in the heat of the Cold War, and it is possible that it was prompted and financed by intelligence interests in the US government either directly or indirectly. Harvard had served as a haven for many refugees during World War II and for those fleeing the Soviet Union at the end of the war and thereafter, many of whom would have supported this sort of endeavour.[11] The essays may also have been seen as an initial exploration of issues to be incorporated into programmes for computer translation, which could by then be seen as necessary in order to process the vast store of intelligence being collected by the US from many nations of the world and in many languages during the Cold War. It is significant that Anthony Oettinger (a linguist and an early computer scientist interested in machine translation before computer science was established as an independent discipline) contributed to the book.[12]

The volume constitutes a conversation about the nature of translation, the process of translating, and the reliability of translations. The essays range from descriptions and analyses of translation as texts to theoretical statements. Some of the essays are not fully consistent with each other as abstract arguments per se, but as pragmatic advisories to intelligence operations they would all have been useful. In this context Quine's argument about the indeterminacy of translation and Jakobson's response that reliable translation is always possible – epitomized by his statement 'all cognitive experience and its classification is conveyable in any existing language' (1959: 234) – constitute a key dialogue in the book about the nature of translation. In many ways these two essays are the most important and durable essays in the collection; both are foundational for the theory of translation and often anthologized in translation studies.

The book addresses the extent to which translation is 'possible', 'certain', or 'reliable', and the extent to which it is subject to indeterminacy; this is a central theoretical issue that translation scholars grapple with and that translators themselves must think about deeply. In his essay Quine uses the term *indeterminacy* only once, at the end of the essay, after he has discussed at length all the contingencies of understanding what an utterance might mean; the term appears in the phrase 'indeterminacy of correlation' (1959: 172). Quine's stance on translation is consonant with the most important shifts in scientific and mathematical thinking of the twentieth century, epitomized in Einstein's theory of relativity, Heisenberg's uncertainty principle, and Gödel's incompleteness theorem. These scientific theories and principles undermined the certainties that until then people had assumed about the world in the domains of physics and mathematics and by extension in social and cultural life generally. The principles articulated by Einstein, Heisenberg, and Gödel continue to serve as the foundation for the scientific and technical revolutions that frame our lives and for our broad outlook on the social world.

It is telling that in his essay Quine uses other terms to signal indeterminacy, including the term *relativity* (1959: 152), and that toward the conclusion of his argument he invokes science: 'The indefinability of synonymy by reference to the methodology of analytical hypotheses is formally the same as the indefinability of truth by reference to scientific method' (1959: 170). In choosing to focus on the indeterminacy of translation thus, Quine deliberately creates a discourse that evokes the great revolution away from positivism that occurred in mathematics and the natural sciences in the first half of the twentieth century. He signals his view that like the natural world, human life and the social world also have uncertainty and relativity at their core because language itself, the defining characteristic of human cognition, has its own forms of uncertainty, relativity, incompleteness, and indeterminacy in any act of communication. These uncertainties and relativities can be symbolized by the indeterminacy of translation.[13]

Quine's arguments about translation are metonymic for language as a whole: they stand for intralingual translation as well as interlingual translation and for communication internal to a language community as well as communication across languages. This relationship is underlined in Quine's book on the topic that appeared the following year, namely *Word and Object* (1960), in which he elaborates on the indeterminacy of translation directly. After a preliminary consideration of terminology, the first substantive chapter is titled 'Translation and Meaning' (pp. 26–79, sections 7–16). Quine turns immediately to translation as a way to make points about communication 'less abstractly and more realistically' (1960: 27). After considering fundamental aspects of language that pose problems related to communication, he sums up as follows.

> One has only to reflect on the nature of possible data and methods to appreciate the indeterminacy. Sentences translatable outright, translatable by independent evidence of stimulatory occasions, are sparse and must woefully under-determine the analytical hypotheses on which the translation of all further sentences depends.
> (1960: 72)

The chapter ends with a seven-page section titled 'On failure to perceive the indeterminacy', which presents arguments that help 'to make the principle of indeterminacy of translation less surprising' (1960: 78). Quine concludes with an irony that explicitly links the difficulties of intralingual communication and translation.

> The indeterminacy of translation has been less generally appreciated than its somewhat protean domestic analogue. In mentalistic philosophy there is the familiar predicament of private worlds. In speculative neurology there is the circumstance that different neural hookups can account for identical verbal behavior. In language learning there is the multiplicity of individual histories capable of issuing in identical verbal behavior. Still one is ready to say of the domestic situation in all positivistic reasonableness that if two speakers match in all dispositions to verbal behavior there is no sense in imagining semantic differences between them. It is ironic that the interlinguistic case is less noticed, for it is just here that the semantic indeterminacy makes clear empirical sense.
> (1960: 79)

Therefore Quine effectively refutes the naive view that the goal of translation is to preserve the 'meaning' of a source text, challenging assumptions that such a goal is even possible in either intralingual or interlingual communication.[14]

In his work on translation thus, Quine sets not only translation but language itself with its indeterminacies in the same framework as the relativities and uncertainties of postpositivist theories about the natural world. In the closing statement of the chapter that outlines arguments about the indeterminacy of translation Quine is also explicit that he repudiates positivism, thus locating his work in a postpositivist context. Language – as demonstrated concretely in translation – takes its place in the constellation of relativity, uncertainty, and incompleteness that twentieth-century sciences and mathematics had posited. These watershed realizations mark the break between a positivist world view and the postpositivism of the contemporary world. For Quine translation is a metaphor, analogue, and tool for establishing the larger uncertainties of all communication. Nonetheless Quine is also correct in perceiving that these indeterminacies are epitomized in translation and that they are both literally and theoretically true of translation.

The status of Quine's foundational work on translation indicates that translation studies grew up within the larger postpositivist revolution that shaped formulations in the natural sciences, the social sciences, and the humanities during the last century. Understanding this nested structure of thought within which translation theory and translation studies as a discipline are situated is foundational for philosophers and for translation scholars alike. Indeed the best philosophical discourses about language and translation speak eloquently to the necessity of modern postpositivist frameworks in inquiry related to translation and communication. Quine's view of language and of the uncertainties of language is also influenced both by Wittgenstein, as we will see, and by American pragmatism, a contribution to the Eurocentric philosophical tradition that is original to philosophy in the US. This pragmatic strain in Quine's position serves translation studies well.

Because translation studies is a much more pragmatic field than philosophy and because it includes both the theory and practice of translation, scholars and practitioners alike realize that at the end of the day (or year), a translation must be completed. In many cases the proverbial statement applies: a translation is never finished; it is just abandoned. Often questions about the indeterminacy of translation are the sticking points of the practice of translation. In the realm of translation theory, however, problematics related to uncertainty have resulted in a rich array of questions that themselves have opened out into a variety of domains and theoretical investigations in translation studies. For example, which of the indeterminacies are linguistic (e.g. dependent on semantic fields, grammatical constructions, linguistic asymmetries, and other features of language per se)? And which are cultural (e.g. related to cultural prescriptions and proscriptions, and to other cultural asymmetries of various types, from climate, social structure, material culture, customs, and religion, to literary and textual forms)? Indeterminacy can also be indexed with reference to the translator: the translator's skill, knowledge of the source and target languages and cultures, and knowledge of the subject matter of the source text, among other factors. Explorations of these and other domains of uncertainty have been of central importance in the development and articulation of modern translation theory, and they index the complexities underlying translation theory.

Following Quine, translation theory thus indicates that translators will benefit from having a somewhat sceptical view of their own certainties while translating. Translators are helped by recognizing the indeterminacies that they inevitably face not only in relation to the language and meaning of the source texts they work with but to the sufficiency of their own knowledge, experience, and skills for creating the translations they produce. At the same time, despite these insufficiencies and indeterminacies, translation entails decisions; paradoxically the indeterminacies are also the locus of the power inherent in a translator's choices and agency. These foundational principles of translation theory go back to Quine's philosophical discourses and to the revolutions in the sciences and mathematics that he invokes as a framework for his views of language and translation.

The potential benefits of understanding this relationship for the two fields of philosophy and translation studies are reciprocal. Philosophers are enriched by considering the frameworks of inquiry offered by translation studies, the insights built into contemporary translation theory, and the data these frameworks are founded on. Unlike philosophy, translation studies has the strength of being grounded in tangible practices issuing in tangible products and case studies. Although the theoretical dilemmas of indeterminacy in translation cannot be 'resolved', translation studies has constructed a broad base of empirical data documenting ways that specific translators at specific times in specific languages and cultures have responded to cultural and linguistic asymmetries and to the difficulties and indeterminacies of translation. Pragmatic examples and insights related to the theoretical problems of the indeterminacy of translation are found in descriptive studies of translated texts, studies of translators' activities, common-sense observations of translators, and the self-reflection of translators. Moreover, where a philosopher might be able to propose the consideration of a problem in the abstract, translation studies scholars normally contextualize problems by deploying specific examples of translations from multiple cultural contexts, thus assessing both dilemmas and answers to theoretical problems with respect to a variety of concrete frameworks.[15] Translators also frequently work across languages and cultures that are not related and that hence are highly divergent both linguistically and culturally, making their observations about language and culture less parochial than many philosophical arguments about the same domains of inquiry. Not least of the strengths of translation studies and its theoretical scaffolding for philosophy is that translators do in fact undertake what Quine (1959: 148) calls '*radical* translation, i.e. translation of the language of a hitherto untouched people', including peoples of the past. Thus translation theory diverges from and remediates some philosophical discourses because of its empirical grounding: as a field, translation studies tests its theory with reference to empirical evidence.

Wittgenstein, the philosophy of language, and translation

Ludwig Wittgenstein (1889–1951) prefigured many of Quine's positions on language discussed in the previous section, namely that language is often ambiguous or indeterminate in its meaning and that the indeterminacies are varied in type. In his later and most influential work, published posthumously in 1953 as *Philosophical Investigations* (hereafter *PI*) in a bilingual (German and English) edition, Wittgenstein's writing takes the form of a set of numbered fragments of varied lengths related to discourses that frequently focus on language and the difficulty of establishing meaning and achieving communication.

Typically Wittgenstein is both more metaphorical in his philosophical explorations than Quine and more detailed as well. Thus, for example, Quine (1959: 148 and *passim*) develops the hypothetical case of the 'jungle linguist', who is trying to understand and find a translation for a 'native' utterance about a rabbit seen in the visual field. By contrast, even in his early work, Wittgenstein starkly summarizes difficulties of communication and of comprehending language across cultural difference and life forms through hyperbolic and puzzling statements, such as 'If a lion could speak, we could not understand him' (*PI* II xi 223). Wittgenstein's arguments about incommensurability and the problems of communicability across languages are thus arresting but also challenging to parse. Nonetheless, for translation studies these cryptic statements are acute: translators who work with difficult texts such as complex arguments, dead languages, or poetry at times feel as if they are trying to understand and speak for the lion, but even translators working with relatively easy texts confront impasses pertaining to meaning. In contrast to this oblique way of making philosophical points, at times Wittgenstein expatiates and is highly detailed in his arguments about language, as we will see.

An Austrian, Wittgenstein went to Cambridge as a student in 1911 to work with philosophers there, particularly Bertrand Russell, and was recognized almost immediately as brilliant. He stopped his studies to enlist in the Austrian army when World War I began, drafting parts of his first book in a prison camp. After the war his *Tractatus Logico-Philosophicus* (1922) was published (originally, in 1921, in German), but the response was discouraging to him and accordingly he decided to try other professions, ultimately becoming a schoolteacher. His early philosophical work is sometimes seen as a form of – or at least compatible with – logical positivism, but after teaching school children for a number of years he returned to Cambridge in 1929 to resume philosophy on a very different basis, taking a postpositivist stance toward many problems he had earlier felt could be resolved with certainty. Teaching schoolchildren between his two periods at Cambridge, Wittgenstein had perhaps become more aware of the messiness of language and the difficulties of communication, despite its manifest possibility.

Lecturing in Cambridge after he returned, Wittgenstein effectively became the founder of a substantial movement in Anglo-American philosophy focused on new approaches to the philosophy of language; Quine's work falls in that school. In Wittgenstein's later writing he draws attention to the pragmatics of ordinary language, raising questions about the actual usage of language. Implicitly he discusses differences that exist across languages (or dialects and idiolects) by investigating the sorts of asymmetries that might be found across what he calls 'language games' [*Sprachspiele*] associated with different 'forms of life' [*Lebensformen*], namely patterns of language use and representations that are adopted individually or communally by members of a language community or by language communities as a whole. His emphasis on use and pragmatics as the touchstones for language is expressed clearly in his *Philosophical Investigations*, where he states that 'For a *large* class of cases – though not for all – in which we employ the word 'meaning' it can be defined thus: the meaning of a word is its use in the language' (*PI* 43, original emphasis). He also focuses on the often puzzling representations of ordinary language in relation to action and behaviour. All these approaches to the meaning, usage, asymmetries, and pragmatics of language entered into his subsequent philosophical discourses.

A substantial contribution by Wittgenstein to epistemology, the theory of language, and translation theory is found in his work on concepts. Prefiguring the work of Quine, Wittgenstein moved away from viewing language as a simple match between words and objects. Where Quine focuses on the problem of understanding words in the context of reference and linguistic information, however, Wittgenstein's discussions of concepts point to the difficulty of understanding the same word in a variety of utterances and multiple contexts in ordinary language. Among his signature examples, he discusses the German word *Spiel* (pl. *Spiele*) and the English word *game* (pl. *games*), demonstrating that in both languages the lexemes denote a wide range of activities that are not unified or defined by circumscribed properties (i.e. necessary and sufficient conditions of the category) but rather by pragmatics and observable forms that games take (*PI* 65–77). Thus Wittgenstein indicates that many concepts are not defined by logical positivist definitions but by a cluster of shifting and loose relationships, no one or small set of which is essential or sufficient for identifying members of the category. He argues that the conceptual field of such concepts is constituted by 'family resemblances' in which 'the various resemblances. . . overlap and criss-cross' and thus 'form a [conceptual] family' (*PI* 67). Note that Wittgenstein does not say that such concepts are characterized by 'prototypes'. Instead his conception of language and language usage avoids privileging some of the conceptions of a specific culture at a specific time, say by invoking a prototype of *game* which would mute the difficulty of understanding the meaning of an utterance both within a language community and in a global context. Accordingly his ideas about cluster concepts are more useful for translation studies than the investigations by later scholars such as Rosch (1977) and Lakoff (1987).[16]

Wittgenstein's *Philosophical Investigations* is of interest in translation studies partly because it was published originally in an authorized bilingual edition. Thus it straddles the boundary of two languages and ipso facto raises questions about language interface and translation.[17] Accordingly the edition (and Wittgenstein's teaching) presupposes success in finding 'equivalents', or at least satisfactory homologies, for coping with differences across two (albeit closely related) languages and cultures, a task he accomplished for 30 years while lecturing at Cambridge, despite the philosophical complexities that he writes about. Paradoxically, however, his philosophical arguments do not grapple with the most difficult aspects of the questions that he raises in his discussion of concepts that cluster around family resemblances, namely that those fields of resemblance can be very disparate across cultures that are significantly different in language family, history, and cultural traditions. In such cases the use (and thus the meaning in Wittgenstein's view) will be quite divergent and hence particularly difficult to translate. Notwithstanding the fact that Wittgenstein avoids the problems of translating concepts that map differently across radically divergent cultures and languages, his arguments clearly raise questions that translation studies must address in its theory and practice related to asymmetrical conceptual fields in languages as well as asymmetries in pragmatics related to the understanding or translation of ordinary language. This aspect of Wittgenstein's philosophy is thus key to important aspects of translation theory.

Wittgenstein's focus on the functionalism of language is significant for translation studies and is central to his concept of language games. He writes, 'the term "language-*game*" is meant to bring into prominence the fact that the *speaking* of language is part of an activity, or of a form of life' (*PI* 23, original emphasis). He then gives a list of language games that goes far beyond assertion, question, and command, and includes such things as giving and obeying orders, describing the appearance of an object, reporting and speculating about an event, forming and testing a hypothesis, making up a story, making a joke, and translating, in addition to 'asking, thanking, cursing, greeting, praying' (*PI* 23). He indicates that there are countless kinds of sentence:

> countless different kinds of use of what we call "symbols", "words", "sentences". And this multiplicity is not something fixed, given once for all; but new types of language, new language-games ... come into existence, and others become obsolete and get forgotten.
>
> (*PI* 23)

Wittgenstein emphasizes the open nature of language, the countless number of language games, and the ever changing nature of language, all of which are essential for understanding the practice of translation and formulating translation theory. It is essential in translation theory to make room for all these types of slippage and variation in communication across languages, cultures, and time. Moreover, in reminding us that translation itself is a language game and that there is a recursive aspect to developing translation norms and translation theory, Wittgenstein makes room in translation studies for many ways of playing that game across time and space and semiotic forms.

The term 'form of life' [*Lebensform*] deserves additional comment in the context of translation theory. Wittgenstein does not develop this concept at length, but his meaning is nonetheless reasonably clear in his arguments. The flexibility of the term makes it useful in theoretical discussions because it can be deployed to refer to any group that has cultural and linguistic coherence. Thus it allows for nested structures of speech communities, including dialect or regional groups or even groups linked by kin, religion, and so forth. It admits into theoretical paradigms a great deal of variety and flexibility about what counts as a cultural group whose patterns of usage must be accommodated in translation. Moreover, the term can be used to refer to cultures across time. All these types and levels of cultural and linguistic translation are part of the complexity of translation and are encountered by translators who act as mediators for the particularities of language usage and cultural forms. Such forms of language must also be accommodated in translation theory.

The timeline of Wittgenstein's work coincides with the beginning of modern linguistics, which superseded philology as a field. Both in its early and late stages, Wittgenstein's philosophy served 'first, as a critique of language' (Biletzki and Matar 2016: 3.7). His explorations of language led to the development of a broader field of interest in the philosophy of language that transcended linguistic issues narrowly conceived. Anglo-American philosophers of language, including Quine, continue Wittgenstein's work, focusing on the concrete use of language. Rarely discussing translation as such, philosophers in this school nonetheless often identify and explore issues that translators face in working across languages and cultures, dilemmas that are or should be included in translation pedagogy, and points that translation studies is often called upon to address in its theoretical formulations.

A central achievement in the philosophy of language is the development of speech act theory which illustrates the type of contribution that philosophy makes to translation theory and practice. Growing out of Wittgenstein's discussions of language games, many philosophers of language have worked on speech act theory, notably Austin (1962), Searle (1969), and Grice (1975). Discourses about speech act theory focus on the pragmatics of language rather than the semantics: in this framework language is a mode of action and of doing things, epitomized in the title of Austin's *How to Do Things with Words* (1962). Where semantics focuses on the linguistic information in a sentence, speech act theory takes up the functional effects and the value of linguistic acts as utterances in context. Philosophers argue that the meaning of a sentence or text is complex. It includes the linguistic meaning indicated by such things as its grammar and lexemes, but as an utterance the text must also be considered in terms of its contextual force or function. Thus, in addition to its locutionary (sentential) meaning, it will have illocutionary meaning which depends on identifying the function of the speech act involved. The locutionary meaning of an utterance might be interpreted in a variety of ways – for example, from assertion to irony depending on context, as in the phrase 'he's making the country great again'. The illocutionary force of the utterance disambiguates the locutionary meaning, which often occurs semiotically in speech (say, by tone or gesture). Moreover, an utterance has perlocutionary meaning associated with the speaker's goal for the recipient's response and the (desired) effects of the utterance – for example, persuasion, alarm, anger, and so forth.

In speech act theory, therefore, the meaning of an utterance has many layers. Ideally a translator would attend to all three aspects of an utterance to be represented in translation, namely the locutionary, illocutionary, and perlocutionary dimensions. Knowing the source and target languages well enough to be aware of the asymmetries of the two languages with respect to speech acts and being acquainted with a sufficiently wide range of means for achieving these aspects of communication in each language are both essential in order for a translator to decide how (or even whether) to represent these intertwined aspects of speech in the target language. Like Wittgenstein's arguments about the diverse fields of reference in concepts and variations in the meaning of words, speech act theory points to the difficulty of determining and communicating meaning in language and across languages. Thus Wittgenstein obliquely contributes to some of Quine's discourses about the indeterminacy of language and translation as well.

The complexity of unpacking the meaning of an utterance is indicated by examples showing that the locutionary form of a speech act can vary with respect to the same illocutionary force and conversely that the illocutionary force can vary with respect to the same locutionary form. Although philosophers have discussed the implications of speech act theory both abstractly and concretely in terms of specific examples (usually in English), they have not yet adequately explored the ways that these features of language intersect across languages and through translation, which would seem a minimal exercise for understanding and theorizing the phenomenon in a sufficiently broad context. Clearly issues pertaining to speech acts also can be and should be incorporated more usefully into the pedagogy and practice of translation, and a more adequate theorization of the translation of speech acts – which experienced translators accomplish all the time – remains to be undertaken in translation studies as well as philosophy.

Speech act theory intersects with the broadest functionalist approaches to language as action, namely language as a means of doing things in the world at the geopolitical level. Thus this aspect of the philosophy of language anticipated analyses of translations as examples of political and ideological action and as exercises in cultural power. Such questions about the politics and ideology of translation have motivated central discourses in translation studies for three decades; in part motivated by cultural studies, many case studies have been generated, resulting in significant theoretical formulations, as indicated at the beginning of this chapter. The development of these discourses also is indebted to sociolinguistics and sociological approaches to translation that both describe and theorize the pragmatics of translation. As a consequence translation theory has become increasingly intertwined with frameworks from the social sciences, a trend that is apparent throughout the field of translation studies internationally, but these aspects of inquiry also reflect the influence of the ideological tenor of European Continental philosophy. In work exploring the implications of speech act theory, translation studies is thus indebted not merely to the Anglo-American interest in the philosophy of language but also to the political formulations of Continental philosophy and to the social sciences as a whole.[18]

Speech act theory is but one example of the areas explored in Anglo-American philosophy of language that are of interest to translation studies scholars. Like the later Wittgenstein, philosophers of language focus on the functional and social aspects of communication and point the way toward deeper understanding of the cultural aspects of both language and translation. They move beyond denotation to connotation and beyond conventional linguistic implicatures to conversational implicatures. Translation studies enlarges these perspectives, going beyond the local contextual implicatures to those at the level of the interface of languages and cultures in geopolitical contexts. This pyramid of linguistic functions needs further exploration and theorization in both philosophy and translation studies.

This brief foray into contributions by Wittgenstein and the Anglo-American school of the philosophy of language illustrates that both before the publication of Quine's 1959 article and afterward philosophers had problematized communication in ways that support Quine's argument about the indeterminacy of translation, where translation can be seen both literally as text production and also metaphorically as a means of exploring the fundamental nature of language and the uncertainties in human communication as a whole. This trajectory is one reason that translation theory stresses the importance of decisions and choices in translation processes; in any act of translating, the various functions and implicatures of text in context must be considered at both the local and geopolitical levels. Although translation is a metonymic process and inevitably a representation of the source text will be partial (Tymoczko 1999: 41–61), nevertheless translators want to make informed decisions about their choices. Thus the intersections of the philosophy of language and the theory and practice of translation are of key importance to translation studies. In turn, because translation studies deals with communication across languages and cultures that are potentially highly asymmetrical, this survey indicates why knowledge of translation theory and practice can benefit philosophers.

In both fields, moreover, one can see a tendency to extrapolate from awareness of the general uncertainties in communication to a focus on the ideological entailments of language and translation where the social implicatures of translation choices and the power of translation become signifiers of power and resistance. Thus influences in translation theory from Anglo-American philosophy of language converge with theoretical trajectories related to ethics and ideology, questions taken up in the following section.

Rawls, justice, and the ethics of translation

Because questions related to political and ideological aspects of translation have become more central, ethics has constituted one of the most lively areas of discourse in translation studies since the 1990s. The interest in ethics has also been heightened by exploration of the engagement of translators in social issues, by interest in the intersection of language and ideology, and by the increasingly global reach of the field of translation studies. Influenced by cultural studies and literary investigations of postcolonial texts, as well as Continental philosophy, translation scholars have explored ethical issues related to the role of translation in decolonization and liberation movements; representations of other cultures in translation; the role of translators and translation in situations of conflict including war; the intersection between translation and power, resistance, and activism; the ethics of interpreting in courts, tribunals, and asylum hearings; gender and translation; and other relevant topics.[19]

The omission of focused attention to the sociocultural frameworks and ideological concerns in the arguments of both Quine and Wittgenstein has thus become a limiting factor in their ongoing usefulness for current theorization of translation. Although Wittgenstein and his followers in the philosophy of language moved toward the inclusion of contextual concerns in discussions of language, the contexts investigated were relatively small in scale. Sociolinguistic implications were largely discussed in terms of personal contexts or generalized aspects of language and culture rather than communication in the public sphere, the interrelation of language and political or ideological facets of culture, social engineering via language, and other large-scale social phenomena involving the ethics of language.

This blind spot about the ideology of language in relation to cultural power in much of the work in the philosophy of language is particularly ironic in the case of philosophy in the US during the second half of the twentieth century because the country was roiling with political activism for decades during that period as a result of such things as the Civil Rights Movement, the Vietnam War, the Second Wave of Feminism, and the so-called War on Poverty. Although many Anglo-American philosophers were writing some of their most significant works at the time and although many of them were activists, few engaged in sustained philosophical examinations of the core ethical, political, and ideological issues of the time. Later philosophers of language consider questions that relate to broad social contexts more extensively and more directly than do Wittgenstein and Quine, but issues about the ethics of language in relation to power and ideology are relatively muted in Anglo-American philosophy.

The political philosophy of John Rawls (1921–2002), however, indirectly addresses the ferment of his times and offers tools to address issues pertaining to ethics in relation to translation theory and practice. In *A Theory of Justice* (1971/1999) Rawls makes the argument that justice can be conceptualized via the concepts of fairness and equity, an approach relevant to issues that translators face particularly when translating texts across languages and cultures with significant differentials in power and prestige. Rawls's argument is to a large extent abstract and oriented toward the organization of political systems, but nonetheless he raises issues relevant to internal inequities debated in the US throughout the twentieth century as well as to long-standing inequities in international relations. Rawls proffers no detailed ethical principles or prescriptions, but his view of ethics turns on questions related to positionality as a basis of equity and justice.

Rawls argues that positionality based on fairness and reciprocity (Rawls 1999: 447) is a fundamental criterion for assessing the justice of social arrangements. He indicates that fairness, equity, and reciprocity can best be judged by the willingness of members of a group to establish social structures and practices without knowing what positions they will hold in the resulting society. We can extrapolate that the same would be true in the case of transnational or transcultural circumstances as well. Such arrangements are key because in a social context thus arranged a person should be satisfied that there is equity and fairness whatever subject position the individual might subsequently achieve, hold, or be assigned from the array of possible positions in the polity. Rawls posits therefore that liberal societies ideally would establish their principles and frameworks of justice behind what he calls a 'veil of ignorance' with respect to the positions that individuals would occupy (1999: 11, 118–23, section 24).

Clearly when Rawls began his work, equity and fairness of subject positions were not at all characteristic of the situations motivating social debates in the US or the world. Race, gender, wealth, education, equality before the law, and war were all motivating factors for demonstrations and protest turning on ethical issues resulting from unequal social conditions. The inequities of race, gender, and wealth were appallingly clear, as was inequality before the law. The US is of course not the only nation in the world for which this could have been said in the second half of the twentieth century, nor has it been the only one since the end of the Cold War. These questions were, however, burning issues in the US for decades as Rawls was formulating his theory of justice and when his book was first published. In his political philosophy, therefore, Rawls proposed an approach that attempts to achieve fairness and equity in social issues with immediate and general ethical relevance and with implications for issues debated in a lively manner in translation studies.

Although Rawls does not focus on translation in his discourses about ethics, his arguments suggest frameworks for evaluating the ethics of specific translation strategies, translators' choices, and the texts themselves that become part of global discourses through translation. Rawls's key principles of fairness and reciprocity in positionality can be used to reassess practices for translating texts as well as patterns of texts chosen for translation. By extension Rawls's work also provides an index for assessing theoretical assertions or discourses promoting specific translation practices that have emerged in translation studies either from descriptive studies or prescriptive argument. Earlier I indicated that translation studies scholars have explored the role of translations in the construction and exercise of power, the framing of resistance, the engagement of translators in activism, and so forth. To some extent these factors have been theorized as well (Tymoczko 2013), but there is a great deal of room for additional work on issues pertaining to these questions in both translation studies and the philosophy of language. Many of the case studies analysed by translation studies scholars provide excellent data for further work in both fields.

Rawls's view of positionality and 'the veil of ignorance', for example, can be used as a point of departure for assessing the ethics and reciprocity of specific translation strategies. One could ask how members of a specific culture – writers, citizens, or bilingual readers of a text and its translation – would want a text of importance to themselves and their culture to be translated into other languages. Would they prefer a strategy that is literal or free? Would it be preferable to adopt an approach to translation that involves formal equivalence focused on linguistic criteria or dynamic equivalence focused on functional impact, as proposed in the formulations of Nida (1964)? Similarly invoking the veil, one could ask whether key texts of a culture should be transmitted via a translation strategy involving domestication to the receiving culture's norms or foreignization involving strict adherence to the source text's norms, as suggested in the formulations of Venuti (1995, 1998). And so forth. Moving beyond binaries, one might ask what metonymies of the source texts of a culture would be imperative for translation in the view of members of a source culture in lieu of privileging the response of readers in the target culture (Tymoczko 1999: 41–61). In other words, how would members of the source culture prefer to be represented in translation to the receiving culture?

To think about these choices entailed in translation from behind a 'veil of ignorance' that prevents a translator from knowing whether the text to be translated is from the translator's home culture or elsewhere changes the stakes and the dynamic considerably. The resulting choice of translation strategy and choices for specific decisions would be much more likely to be equitable and just in the representation of the source text and its culture. When Rawls's 'veil of ignorance' is invoked, the ethics of specific translation strategies has a much more immediate relevance if the source text might be canonical in the translator's own culture. The question of representation associated with various translation strategies can thus be reformulated for translation studies using Rawls's terminology, resulting in more acute approaches for assessing the ethics or justice of translation modalities. Indeed Rawls's theory of justice can actually be generalized as a tool for assessing any particular translation strategy advocated by translation scholars or documented in the protocols identified in decades of descriptive studies of translation. Recasting translation shifts in style, modes of discourse, abridgement, omissions, and so forth in terms of justice and equity of representation and invoking a 'veil of ignorance' about which culture is the source or receiving culture might hence be productive for assessing the ethics of translation decisions, strategies, and working methods in general.

In my experience questions of this type generate lively discussion, particularly on the part of bilinguals. Usually people do not want the important texts of their own cultures to be represented in a defamiliarized way that would be jarring, awkward, or alienating for international readers; when asked, people usually express their preference for fluent but 'accurate' translations. Finding such a balance is obviously not easy, particularly when cultural or linguistic practices of one culture are ipso facto offensive or alienating to another. Nonetheless the questions lead outward to assessing the ethics of global cultural flows and to the examination of whether there is justice in the representation of both the central texts of powerful cultures (including former colonial powers) and less powerful cultures. Such investigations also lead directly to theoretical and practical questions about positionality and ethics: who is asked to accommodate to what? How does the issue of accommodation (say, to offensive material) relate to cultural power and inequities of subject positions geopolitically? How does the question of translation strategies relate to the number of works from a culture that enter general worldwide circulation in translation? These are all fundamental ethical questions about translation that address the largest political and social frameworks within which we currently find ourselves as a result of globalization. Some of these questions have in fact been discussed in translation studies, but the formulations here suggest that approaches to translation decisions mediated by the principles of justice elaborated in the work of Rawls would nuance established discourses in translation practice and scholarship considerably.[20] Consideration of translation in terms of the formulations about justice by Rawls could deepen and expand theoretical insights about ethics and ideology in translation studies. In turn considering justice in global contexts and global communication as mediated by translation would deepen philosophical discourses as well, not least because the concreteness and specificity of translations are useful as empirically grounded examples for philosophical constructions.

Rawls's perspective on justice thus streamlines the framework for discussion and adds clarity to the dilemmas presented by cultural and linguistic interface within structures of power and inequity. Rawls's approach to equity and justice is less overtly ideological than related discussions by Continental philosophers; in fact his approach fits with the 'ordinary language' orientation of Anglo-American philosophy, which makes it more transferable to other disciplines. Moreover, coming at questions of ethics (in this case pertaining to translation and translation theory) from such an angle mutes the necessity for allegiance to a particular 'committed' stance as a prerequisite for engaging with a set of philosophical arguments about ethics. By contrast commitment to a definitive ideological framework is often implicit in the work of Continental philosophers and assumed to be forthcoming from their readers. Thus the work of Rawls offers a solid basis for a wide readership to discuss principles of ethics pertaining to the philosophy of language; for selecting ethical strategies for translating and making specific translation choices; for assessing, evaluating, and describing existing translations; for moving toward greater justice in international discourse mediated by translation; and for building an ethical theory of translation with geopolitical applicability.

Rawls's test pertaining to positionality is simple, but applied to translation it entails consideration of many complex parameters, as we have seen, including issues such as choice of texts, choice of translation strategy, assessment of the publishing industry, the quality and quantity of translations from diverse cultures, analysis of norms implicit in translated texts, geopolitical power as reflected in translation practices, and reception of a translated text at every level from the individual to the global market and world systems. As the case of translation indicates, moreover, the approach to justice developed by Rawls can be used at many levels: for personal, social, national, and global discourses. The advocacy for and application of his principles of justice by translators and the field of translation studies would constitute a major ethical step forward, as it would in many other fields and situations. Rawls observes (1999: 447), 'By giving justice to those who can give justice in return, the principle of reciprocity is fulfilled at the highest level'. This might also be a way forward to justice with respect to complex global issues that can be understood by ordinary citizens of our multilingual multicultural world.

Epistemology, translation, and philosophy

Here we consider very briefly questions related to epistemology, indicating again that translation studies and philosophy will be mutually enriched by sharing inquiry into a subject with which both fields engage. In the case of epistemology, groundbreaking research on translation points to issues that remain to be adequately theorized in translation studies and that bear discussion in philosophy as well.

It is well known that branches of knowledge are often not fully homologous across cultures and languages. The discipline of history in China, for example, included the study of astrology. One of the best studies documenting patterns of conceptual and epistemological asymmetry that are revealed in translation is found in Scott L. Montgomery's *Science in Translation: Movements of Knowledge through Cultures and Time* (2000). Montgomery begins with a sustained study of the history of translating astronomy in the West, tracing the passage of Greek astronomy via Roman translations to medieval manuscripts in Latin.

He contrasts that trajectory with astronomy in the East, namely the Syriac and Persian-Indian translations and conversions of Greek knowledge, which later became the foundation for Arabic science and mathematics. In turn during the later Middle Ages, Arabic scientific and mathematical traditions transformed the medieval European Latin legacy that had come directly through Roman translations. Thus Montgomery demonstrates that 'the same' scientific materials were 'known' in many different ways in distinct linguistic and cultural traditions. In his second case study Montgomery examines the origins of modern Japanese science and the effects of language (Chinese, German, and English) on the developments of Japanese approaches to science, focusing on chemistry.

The translation of science is an interesting point of entry into epistemology, because science and mathematics are popularly viewed as the surest of the sure and hence would seem to rest on common epistemological bases. Montgomery painstakingly demonstrates, however, that in the passage across languages and cultures fundamental conceptualizations and practices of a scientific discipline often shift. This is, of course, a finding that Quine and Wittgenstein would probably both have anticipated. Moreover, Montgomery shows that at times asymmetries of language affect the content of scientific knowledge itself. Thus his investigations use translation to raise questions about epistemology itself through exploring the meaning of knowledge in terms of scientific materials that are generally held to be known with the greatest convergence.[21]

This is a concrete example of an epistemological crux at which concerted work in the two fields of translation studies and philosophy would be profitable and mutually beneficial. Most likely it would deepen theoretical understandings of epistemology in both domains. A close study of the metamorphosis of subject matter and the significance of the shifts when knowledge passes across languages and cultures through translation is a body of incisive evidence that translation studies can contribute to the investigation, while philosophers have their own contributions to make to theorizing the larger patterns relating translational transformations and philosophical discourses about epistemology in general. Again the global reach of translation studies in terms of the cultures and languages it investigates can make a substantial contribution to the discourses of philosophy, and vice versa where philosophy potentially contributes approaches to the vast field of data revealed by work in translation studies.

Montgomery's conclusions about the dispersion of epistemological perspectives on science are congenial in many respects to Pierre Bourdieu's views of epistemology. Bourdieu invokes the concept of the *habitus*, which he defines as 'a system of lasting, transposable dispositions which, integrating past experiences, functions at every moment as *a matrix of perceptions, appreciations, and actions* and makes possible the achievement of infinitely diversified tasks' (1977: 82–3, original emphasis). Involving both dispositions and practices, Bourdieu's work makes room for the cultural dispersion of systems of knowledge with resulting divergent epistemological stances even in the natural sciences, which are attributable to framing effects of the habitus. For his part Montgomery provides concrete data about the way that such cultural asymmetries can create longstanding divergence and disparities between the epistemologies of specific cultures. Understanding epistemological asymmetries and their relation to the habitus of both the source and receiving cultures is a central challenge in translation, often requiring considerable initiative and creativity on the part of translators to resolve. Findings from translation practice and the history of translation, such as those of Montgomery, should be part of the basic data used by philosophers to investigate the epistemology of individuals and societies. Because the subject matter of translation studies is concrete and its descriptive methods are empirical, translation data are a good foundation for studies of epistemology.

Conclusion

If we look back to the principles of translation theory listed at the beginning of this chapter that have achieved consensus since World War II, we can see that almost all of them intersect with the philosophical explorations discussed above. Both Wittgenstein and Quine discuss the difficulties, ambiguities, uncertainties, and indeterminacies of understanding language intralingually and interlingually. Thus their work is related to the first, second, and fourth points of translation theory in the list: the anisomorphisms of language and culture, the necessity for decisions and choices in translation, and the fact that equivalence in translation is *a posteriori*. The third principle – the importance of scrutinizing function in considering meaning – is a cardinal pillar of Wittgenstein's later work and central to Anglo-American philosophy of language, specifically speech act theory. The fifth point, that translation is a metonymic process, follows implicitly from the first four principles of translation theory, and thus all of the first half of the list is linked to philosophical discourses.

Although philosophical discussions pertaining to rules have not been explored here, they are addressed in the work of Wittgenstein and Quine, as well as the philosophy of language as a whole. In general philosophical discourses about language recognize the possibility that an individual or society can stipulate normative language. Normative language would hence encompass translation strategies as indicated above in the sixth point of translation theory, namely that a specific type of translation equivalence can be prescribed to a translator (both explicitly by an employer or a teacher or implicitly by cultural norms). Principle number 9, that translation is an ideological and political form of cultural production, is also related to many philosophical discourses, but they are primarily those elaborated in Continental European philosophy rather than the Anglo-American discipline. Clearly, however, Rawls's political philosophy is highly relevant to this principle of translation theory, as the earlier section on Rawls makes clear. The tenth point, that translation is a cluster concept, is actually a foundational starting point for understanding translation that could be positioned first on the list. This principle can be traced directly to the work of Wittgenstein. Although cluster concepts have been explored extensively by linguists, often the treatment of this issue in linguistics is much thinner than discourses in philosophy and translation studies. Ironically this is the case because many linguists are more interested in theories of language than on data pertaining to the diversity of languages per se.

Principles number 7 and 8, namely that translation is a form of rewriting and that translation is best seen within the context of systems theory, were initiated within translation studies by André Lefevere and Itamar Even-Zohar respectively, both translation scholars whose research is foundational for the field. Their hypotheses gained assent as theoretical principles about translation because they were validated by empirical research in translation studies (see Tymoczko 2013 for references). These two principles of translation theory have proven useful and durable and hence have become central to translation theory. Descriptive research on translation has verified their significance in case studies of widely disparate materials across time and culture. Principle 7 is indebted primarily to literary studies (though of course 'rewriting' is an extension of the capacity in ordinary language to express ideas in multiple ways, a topic discussed widely in philosophy). Principle 8, the integration of systems theory and translation theory, is part of a widespread trend in many disciplines, with systems analyses salient in cultural, social, and political theory, and in literary studies as well. Systems studies was originally initiated in engineering.

Thus almost all the elements of translation theory that are widely accepted in the field of translation studies intersect with philosophy, illustrated here with respect to Anglo-American philosophical traditions. Much of the same could be demonstrated with respect to other philosophical traditions, and those intersections remain to be explored.

Quine's focus on the indeterminacy of translation points to his perception of the commonalities of uncertainty, incompleteness, and relativity between communication and the large cosmic frameworks within which human life plays out. This is an important starting point for both translation theory and philosophy. It may be that human beings are able to perceive and plumb the uncertainties of the universe because for hundreds of thousands of years we have evolved the capacity to communicate with other groups of people despite indeterminacy. This capacity has grown as human beings dispersed from their common home in Africa and began to generate distinct languages. Our ability to accept the uncertainties of communication, the indeterminacies of language, the difficulties of 'accessing' other minds, and the incompleteness of linguistic utterances that bombard us daily has paved the way for our more recent realizations that we are creatures in a cosmic realm that itself has uncertainty at its heart. Our own abilities to communicate across language difference despite indeterminacies have primed us for millennia to perceive, tolerate, and function as communities despite the uncertainties of the social and material worlds. They have also allowed us to navigate the uncertainties and relativities of mathematics and physics.

Focusing on the indeterminacies of communication by exploring multilingual contexts of language – highlighted in the processes and products of translation – is central to recognizing the complexities of language as a form of action in the world. The depth of those complexities can only be fully realized by investigations of language that reach across all the language families used by the human community. The uncertainties of language are clear in considering the various cluster concepts that can be identified in broad cross-cultural contexts where the use of prototypes breaks down because of the variety and multiplicity of life forms and languages. The global reach and depth of international data about languages and cultures in translation studies has the potential to offer correctives to philosophical investigations and discourses limited by cultural or linguistic parochialism. In addition the findings of translation studies related to the ethics and ideology of language use and cross-cultural communication promise to add heft to philosophical discourses, particularly in the Anglo-American tradition. Conversely the precision of vocabulary, argument, and the long tradition of abstract discourse in philosophy can add rigour to discourses and theories about translation.

The challenges revealed by examining the intersection of philosophy and translation theory show that both fields have important investigations and parallel developments ahead and that each field will be enriched by the findings of the other. The extensive overlap of concerns in translation studies and philosophy indicates that mutual awareness of the discourses across the two fields will improve translation theory and deepen inquiry in philosophy. In turn appreciation of those intertwined explorations will be heightened by a mutual commitment to the ethical principles of equity, reciprocity, and justice that allows us to value the positionality of others across disciplines and across the world.

Notes

1 The term *Eurocentric* is used to refer to cultures around the world shaped primarily by European linguistic and cultural traditions, as well as to European cultures themselves.
2 In translation studies there is a very large literature on each of the following points. See Tymoczko (2013) for a more extended discussion of each theoretical issue enumerated below as well as extensive suggestions for further reading on each aspect of translation theory discussed.

3   An *an*isomorphism is a relationship in which there is no systematic (or isomorphic) one-to-one relationship between two items, whether they are lexical, grammatical, or cultural features of texts and cultural systems.
4   Where a 'text' is understood as being either oral or written, as well as creations in another medium. The latter is, however, beyond the scope of this article.
5   There has been considerable debate in translation studies about equivalence and meaning. For further reading on these issues see Tymoczko (2013, 2007: 265–309).
6   A lengthy treatment of this question is found in Tymoczko (1999: 41–61).
7   For example, in Hindu tradition it is impossible to separate the fields of philosophy and theology (Flood 1996: 224–49).
8   *Philosophical Investigations* (hereafter *PI*) 67. See the following section, on Wittgenstein. A more extensive discussion of cluster concepts in relation to translation is found in Tymoczko (2007: 54–106) and sources cited.
9   See Biletzki and Matar (2016) on Wittgenstein's 'anti-systematic' approach to philosophy.
10 Many useful references to the literature of translation studies related to the specifics of translation theory are found in the sources cited in Tymoczko (2013).
11 For example, the great linguist Roman Jakobson (1896–1982) and Anthony Oettinger (1929–) were both refugees who contributed foundational essays related to translation theory.
12 Oettinger, a pioneer in artificial intelligence and machine translation, later served as a consultant to the US National Security Council (1975–81) and the President's Foreign Intelligence Advisory Board, among other governmental positions associated with US intelligence and security.
13 The importance of Quine's arguments can be lost on readers because of the racism in his language and examples: a 'jungle linguist' is trying to understand 'a native' with 'an alien' culture, whose 'heathen tongue' and 'heathen term[s]' the linguist is trying to construe. The problem is exacerbated by Quine's alternation between this sort of language and the use of 'a Martian' as an alternate paradigm for difficulties of communication (e.g. 1960: 47). In a global field such as translation studies, Quine's work would be more appreciated if his language were not so objectionable.
14 I am indebted here and *passim* to the careful reading given this essay by John M. Connolly, Sophia Smith Professor of Philosophy Emeritus, of Smith College. Professor Connolly saved me from numerous errors and helped to sharpen my arguments at various points.
15 See, for example, the various English translations of a single early Irish text in relation to their diverse cultural and political contexts, discussed in Tymoczko (1999: 62–83).
16 A prototype approach to concepts is a modified form of the traditional philosophical approach to defining concepts in terms of necessary and sufficient conditions which Wittgenstein rejects. Because prototypes are culturally specific, this approach does not work well for translators in dealing with concepts where the prototypes can diverge significantly across cultures, even in the case of closely related cultures. For example, one might argue that in the US *football* American-style represents the prototype of a field game, whereas in most of the world (where the game is played) the prototype of a field game would be *football* in the sense of soccer. A more detailed discussion of cluster concepts in relation to translation is found in Tymoczko (2007: 54–106).
17 Although the German manuscript of section I was prepared for publication by Wittgenstein in 1945, at his instructions the book was published posthumously, appearing in 1953 with Wittgenstein's German text translated into English by G.E.M. Anscombe, his authorized literary executrix. Anscombe's translation reflects her deep familiarity with Wittgenstein's thought derived from both the German text and extensive exposure to his lectures and discussions that presented his arguments and examples in Wittgenstein's own English wordings.
18 On these issues see, for example, Tymoczko (2016), Graham (1985), and Inghilleri (2005).
19 See, for example, Baker (2006), Inghilleri (2012), Simon (1996), Tymoczko (1999, 2010), Tymoczko and Gentzler (2002), and Venuti (1995, 1998).
20 The work of Venuti (1995, 1998) addresses some of these questions but within a very different framework from that of Rawls. See as well the relevant works cited in Tymoczko (2013).
21 Montgomery's study indirectly indicates why a great deal of innovative scientific inquiry in the world is currently being conducted and published in English: a common link language facilitates convergence in the epistemology of the subject under investigation.

Related topics

Wittgenstein; Quine; context and pragmatics; culture; equivalence; ethics; meaning.

Further reading

Chan, Leo Tak-hung. 2004. *Twentieth-Century Chinese Translation Theory: Modes, Issues, and Debates*. Amsterdam: John Benjamins.
Cheung, Martha P. Y. ed. 2006a. *An Anthology of Chinese Discourse on Translation*. Vol. 1. Manchester: St. Jerome. Vol. 2, ed. Robert Neather. London: Routledge. (These two collections represent Chinese theoretical and philosophical discourses on translation that (from one long and prestigious tradition beyond Eurocentric cultures) counterbalance the Eurocentrism about translation theory and philosophy in translation studies as a discipline.)
Cheung, Martha P. Y. 2006b. 'From "Theory" to "Discourse": The Making of a Translation Anthology'. *Translating Others*, ed. Theo Hermans, 2 vols. Manchester: St. Jerome. 1.87–101. (Cheung argues that the very concept of 'theory' does not fully apply to Chinese texts discussing translation as a phenomenon from a meta-perspective; that is, she argues that the concept *theory* is itself a cultural construct.)
Tymoczko, Maria. 1999. 'On Translating a Dead Language'. *Translation in a Postcolonial Context: Early Irish Literature in English Translation*. Manchester: St. Jerome, 146–62. (This essay represents another theoretical approach and a more pragmatic one to Quine's argument about the indeterminacy of language and translation.)
Tymoczko, Maria. 2007. *Enlarging Translation, Empowering Translators*. Manchester: St. Jerome. (A general survey of translation studies, offering a postpositivist history of the field and discussing basic problems of defining translation, representing source texts in translation, and the use of such concepts as meaning, speech acts, and agency in translation. The work of many philosophers is discussed including Wittgenstein, Quine, Austin, Searle, Kripke, Sartre, Paul de Man, and Foucault.)
Tymoczko, Maria. 2013. 'Translation Theory'. *The Encyclopedia of Applied Linguistics*, ed. Carol A. Chapelle. 10 vols. Chichester: Wiley-Blackwell, 5928–37. (This is a very compact survey of elements of translation theory that have achieved general consensus in the field of translation studies, with extensive suggestions for reading on each point.)

References

Austin, John L. 1962. *How to Do Things with Words*. Oxford: Oxford University Press.
Baker, Mona. 2006. *Translation and Conflict: A Narrative Account*. London: Routledge.
Biletzki, Anat, and Anat Matar. 2016. *The Stanford Encyclopedia of Philosophy*, ed. Edward Z. Zalta. https://plato.stanford.edu/archives/fall2016/entries/wittgenstein/
Bourdieu, Pierre. 1977. *Outline of a Theory of Practice*. Trans. Richard Nice. Cambridge: Cambridge University Press.
Flood, Gavin. 1996. *An Introduction to Hinduism*. Cambridge: Cambridge University Press.
Graham, Joseph F. ed. 1985. *Difference in Translation*. Ithaca: Cornell University Press.
Grice, Paul. 1975. 'Logic and Conversation'. *Studies in the Way of Words*. Cambridge: Harvard University Press, 1989. 22–40.
Inghilleri, Moira. 2012. *Interpreting Justice: Ethics, Politics, and Language*. New York: Routledge.
Inghilleri, Moira. ed. 2005. *Bourdieu and the Sociology of Translation and Interpreting*. Special issue of *The Translator* 11:2.
Lakoff, George. 1987. *Women, Fire, and Dangerous Things: What Categories Reveal about the Mind*. Chicago: University of Chicago Press.
Montgomery, Scott L. 2000. *Science in Translation: Movements of Knowledge through Cultures and Time*. Chicago: University of Chicago Press.

Nida, Eugene A. 1964. *Toward a Science of Translating: With Special Reference to Principles and Procedures Involved in Bible Translating*. Leiden: E. J. Brill.
Quine, W.V.O. 1960. *Word and Object*. Cambridge: MIT Press.
Quine, W.V.O. 1959. 'Meaning and Translation'. *On Translation*, ed. Reuben A. Brower. Cambridge: Harvard University Press. 148–72.
Rawls, John. 1971/1999. *A Theory of Justice*. Cambridge: Harvard University Press.
Rosch, Eleanor. 1977. 'Human Categorization'. *Studies in Cross-Cultural Psychology*. Vol. 1, ed. N. Warren, London: Academic Press, 1–49.
Searle, John. 1969. *Speech Acts: An Essay in the Philosophy of Language*. Cambridge: Cambridge University Press.
Simon, Sherry. 1996. *Gender in Translation: Cultural Identity and the Politics of Transmission*. London: Routledge.
Tymoczko, Maria. 2016. 'Trajectories of Research in Translation Studies: An Update with a Case Study in the Neuroscience of Translation'. *Asia Pacific: Translation and Intercultural Studies* 3:2, 99–122.
Tymoczko, Maria. 2013. 'Translation Theory'. *The Encyclopedia of Applied Linguistics*, ed. Carol A. Chapelle. 10 vols. Chichester: Wiley-Blackwell, 5928–37.
Tymoczko, Maria. ed. 2010. *Translation, Resistance, Activism*. Amherst: University of Massachusetts Press.
Tymoczko, Maria. 2007. *Enlarging Translation, Empowering Translators*. Manchester: St. Jerome.
Tymoczko, Maria. 1999. *Translation in a Postcolonial Context: Early Irish Literature in English Translation*. Manchester: St. Jerome.
Tymoczko, Maria, and Edwin Gentzler, eds. 2002. *Translation and Power*. Amherst: University of Massachusetts Press.
Venuti, Lawrence. 1998. *The Scandals of Translation: Towards an Ethics of Difference*. London: Routledge.
Venuti, Lawrence. 1995. *The Translator's Invisibility: A History of Translation*. London: Routledge.
Wittgenstein, Ludwig. 1953. *Philosophische Untersuchungen, Philosophical Investigations*. Trans. G.E.M. Anscombe. New York: Macmillan.
Wittgenstein, Ludwig. 1922. *Tractatus Logico-Philosophicus*. Trans. D.F. Pears and B.F. McGuinness. London: Routledge and Kegan Paul.

12
Context and pragmatics

Shyam Ranganathan

Introduction

Pragmatics, semantics and syntax are basic distinctions in linguistics. Syntax has to do with rules that constrain how words can combine to make acceptable sentences. Semantics concerns the meaning of words and sentences, and pragmatics has to do with the practical aspects of communication – a matter so wide that pragmatics has been called the 'wastebasket of linguistics', encompassing everything that does not neatly fit into syntax or semantics. Yet the three are connected. Syntactic constraints in language can entail semantic constraints. A language with (obligatory) gendered nouns (such as Latin-derived languages) introduces semantic layers that are absent in a largely genderless language. In French, nouns are gendered, so objects are either 'masculine or feminine', while in English they are not usually either, and hence speaking about the same object in French or English is semantically different to this extent. Semantic constraints can also influence the practical use we make of language. The English third person singular pronoun 'it' is reserved for objects and not persons, and this makes it difficult to talk about a single third person in English without characterizing them as either 'he' or 'she' – pronouns that are inappropriate and misleading when referring to someone who is (biologically, psychologically or as a matter of choice) non-binary. We can, as some do, invoke 'they' (originally a third person plural pronoun) for such cases, but this is semantically at odds with the plurality of 'they' and may thus be pragmatically infelicitous: our interlocutors may believe we are speaking about a group when we use 'they' in this progressive way. So while we may wish to easily separate syntax and semantics from pragmatics, it is complicated.

The need for translation can arise for multiple reasons, even within a language. We might want to replace an acceptable original statement with an equally acceptable new statement, and the new statement (*prima facie*) will be a translation of the original statement. If we want to engage in such intralingual translation to get our point across, our motivation is pragmatic. But our interest in translation across languages is also *prima facie* a matter of pragmatics: we often want to understand what is said in a far removed context using symbols that we do not understand, and the correct translation will have the pragmatic effect of rendering something foreign, domestic (Neubert and Rothfuss-Bastian 2003).

To flush out the elements involved in working out the place of pragmatics in translation, I shall distinguish between three possible criteria of translation: *S*, *M* and *P*. Because our motivation for translation is often pragmatic, it is difficult to imagine the need for *S*: accuracy in translation is about preserving syntactical features of a source text (ST), such that if the syntax of a target text (TT) is not the same as the ST, then we have grounds for rejecting it as a good translation. The reason this is implausible is that we typically feel the need for translation in cases where an original communicative act occurs in a source syntactic system that is different from the target syntactic system, rendering the original syntax without some change inaccessible in the target system. For instance, Sanskrit words are heavily altered to show their syntactic properties to the point that word order does not matter. We cannot do this in English: *word order matters in English* for word order is part of how we understand the relationship of words within a sentence. We could not, for instance, write *English matters word order in* and expect anyone to take the two sentences to have the same meaning. You can do that in Sanskrit so long as all the sentential components are properly formatted as each word would have a tag built into it that allows us to understand its relationship to other words in the sentence. However, if we were to translate Sanskrit sentences word for word in the order they come into English, the resulting sentences will likely not respect the rules of English syntax though the individual translated words would be meaningful – and the result would certainly be *pragmatically* infelicitous (uncommunicative), not just syntactically incorrect. If we expect the syntax of a TT to be the same as the ST, then translation would apparently be impossible in many cases. Far more plausible is *M*: accuracy in translation is about preserving the meaning of an original, such that if the meaning of the TT is not the same as the ST, then we have grounds for rejecting the TT as a good translation of the ST. Even when the source language (SL) and target language (TL) are syntactically different, if we can produce a TT that has the same meaning as the ST (perhaps, sentence for sentence, section for section), then we may have good reason to believe that we can understand what is communicated in the ST, for, as noted, semantics seems to constrain the pragmatics of what is said.

If I start out with an unscientific ST of poetry about flowers, and I end up with a TT that is a botanical catalogue of flowers, then I will have reason to doubt the accuracy of the translation as these are *prima facie* semantically different: it is a failure by *M*. But the pragmatics of the ST and TT in this case are widely at odds, in no small part because of the divergence in meaning: poetry and botany occupy different communicative spheres of our lives. So on this score, too, we might have grounds to doubt that translation in this case has been a success on the grounds of *P*: accuracy in translation is about preserving the pragmatics of an original, such that if the contextual use of a TT is different from the ST, we have grounds for rejecting it as a good translation.

To fix such problems, we might desire to combine *M* and *P* so that an accurate translation will preserve both meaning and pragmatics. But what preserves semantics in translation may not preserve pragmatics in translation.

For instance, the Christian Bible in a devout Christian culture has a certain use, communicative and contextual cachet (as the culture's most basic sacred text) that it will not enjoy when *semantically* translated (by way of *M*) into the language of a devout Muslim culture, even if the resulting translation is semantically equivalent to the original. Muslims will be able to acknowledge such a translation as accurate by way of *M*, but they would reject it as their most basic religious text. Similarly, the translation of the Quran into the language of a devout Christian culture could be faithful according to *M*, but the Christians in such a culture would not thereby give up acknowledging their Bible as their most basic religious text. Yet conservative Christians and Muslims in the two cultures would agree that the Bible and the Quran play isomorphic social roles in the two cultures (as the most basic religious text) – indeed, if the Christians and the Muslims in these cultures want to disagree with each other about the text each other should adopt as the basic religious text, they would have to grant that much. But, surprisingly, if we were to adopt *P*, then we would thereby treat the Bible and the Quran as translations of each other because of their isomorphic contextual roles as the basic sacred book in the two cultures. This is *prima facie* absurd, but the absurdity requires an explanation. Otherwise, it is a mere prejudice.

Naïve views about translation are frustrated because neither *M* nor *P* seem to be without problems (not to mention that *S* is not an option), and merely combining them seems implausible as they seem to be in competition with each other. What complicates the matter is that meaning, context and pragmatics are (philosophically) controversial. What you take to be pragmatics depends in part on what you take to be semantics, as *pragmatics* is the use we can make of meaning in a context, while *semantics* – meaning – is context-transcendent (Szabó 2006). So we might agree to *M*, for instance, but arrive at very differing translations if our picture of meaning differs. But correlatively, what we take to be the pragmatics of a text or an utterance to be translated will not be absolutely divorced from its semantics, as the pragmatics is the use of such meaning. Hence we might agree to *P* and yet arrive at different translations of an ST due to their differing accounts of the ST's semantics. There is no way to consider the question of pragmatics in translation in isolation from questions of meaning.

In this chapter on pragmatics and context as it relates to translation, I will take a closer look at *M* and *P*, after reviewing historical perspectives on semantics and pragmatics. *M* and *P* are translation-theoretic counterparts of two divergent approaches to the relationship between semantics and pragmatics. *M* is associated with the prioritization of semantics in an account of pragmatics (semantics-first), while *P* is associated with a prioritization of pragmatics in an account of semantics (pragmatics-first). The trouble with *M* as we shall see is that it sacrifices *P*, and the problem with *P* is that it sacrifices *M* – and either way something about the contextual significance of an ST is lost in the process. We shall review recent research in translation theory that recommends a bridge principle in the assessment of translation to help us be selective about the semantic and pragmatic features of an ST that are to be preserved in translation. This strategy leads to acknowledging a distinct meaning to be preserved, defined in part by pragmatics. We arrive back at *M* but not without taking *P* seriously.

Historical perspectives

Gottlob Frege may be seen as an early proponent of a semantics-first approach. In his 'Über Sinn und Bedeutung' (Frege 1892: translated as 'On Sense and Reference', 1980), for example, he famously proposes that proper names have a sense and a reference. To take a standard example, 'Mark Twain' and 'Samuel Clemens' have the same reference – the man in question – but express different senses, where the sense of a proper name is, roughly, the way in which one represents its reference to oneself. It is this that explains the difference in 'cognitive significance' between 'Mark Twain is identical to Mark Twain' and 'Mark Twain is identical to Samuel Clemens' – both are true, but the latter is informative, in a way in which the former isn't, to someone who doesn't associate the same 'modes of presentation' with 'Mark Twain' and 'Samuel Clemens' and thus doesn't know that the two names denote one and the same man. (Frege's view is challenged by Kripke (1980).)

Frege's account leaves little room for pragmatics, it seems – sense and reference do all the communicative work. But Austin (1955) showed, with his theory of speech acts, that mere meaning does not tell the whole story. Consider the making of a promise. Arguably, the words

'I promise to take you to lunch' have the same meaning in the performance of a play as they do in a conversation with a colleague at work, but only in the latter context do they place the speaker under an obligation. Austin also noted that most meaningful claims, such as 'it is raining outside', are never true in isolation: rather they are true or false when they are statements (said at a particular time and place by some persons), and this shows us that the pragmatics of language use is important to questions of truth – but also more broadly to the question of what we are talking about. Similarly, Paul Grice later showed that there is a host of *pragmatic implicatures* in communication – implications that are understood by listeners, which go beyond the mere meaning of what is said (Grice 1961: §3; 1975: 24). An example of such implicature is my claim in English that 'I am full' when someone asks me whether I want a second serving of food. Those who understand English will typically infer, pragmatically, from this declaration that I do not want more food (true in this case) even though I did not say that I did not want more food. Here the implicature reveals a distinct meaning (I DO NOT WANT MORE FOOD) with its own truth.

Both Austin's and Grice's observations show how semantics alone is insufficient to account for communication, truth and even meaning: rather pragmatics fills the gap. Pragmatics is largely context-bound and hence the pragmatics of language cannot be abstracted from contexts of use: rather it has to do with the impact language has on language users' use in the context of utterance. The importance of pragmatics is *prima facie* evidence for *P*. In response to this kind of insight, philosophers in the early part of the twentieth century began moving away from a semantics-first theory to a radical pragmatics-first approach called *functionalism*, according to which the meaning of a word is its effect on a speaker. It was explored and defended in C.K. Ogden and I.A. Richards' *The Meaning of Meaning* (1923) and in Bertrand Russell's *Analysis of Mind* (1921). If *functionalism* were true, then we would have to collapse the meaning of a term with its influence on us. Ludwig Wittgenstein in his unpublished notes shows why this account is too crude. He writes: 'If I wanted to eat an apple, and someone punched me in the stomach, taking away my appetite, then it was this punch that I originally wanted' (quoted in Monk 1990: 291). In conflating the meaning of a word with its influence on us, an apple's ability to remove our appetite would be equivalent to an injury that does the same thing. Wittgenstein's (1958) own view in his *Philosophical Investigations,* with its focus on 'meaning as use' (*Investigations* 43), is in line with a stress on pragmatics.

Much of contemporary philosophy of language can be characterized as a debate between the proponents of a semantics-first position and those who are more open to the importance of pragmatics (see Salmon 2005). In the post-Wittgensteinian world, it is difficult to find proponents of functionalism. Yet it is popular outside of philosophy. The linguist J.R. Firth accounts for meaning thus: 'What do the words "mean"? They mean what they do' (1964: 110). This view has been taken up with vigour among translation theorists – for example, Susan Bassnett:

> In translating ... it is the function that will be taken up and not the words themselves, and the translation process involves a decision to replace and substitute the linguistic elements in the TL. And since [a] phrase [in English] is, as Firth points out, directly linked to English social behavioural patterns, the translator putting the phrase into French or German has to contend with the problem of the non-existence of a similar convention in either TL culture.
>
> (Bassnett 2002: 27)

Bassnett concludes: 'The emphasis always in translation is on the reader or listener' (2002: 30). But Bassnett is not alone. We find a similar position defended by Eugene Nida. Nida's

Toward a Science of Translating, with Special Reference to Principles and Procedures Involved in Bible Translating (1964) is one of the most cited works in Translation Studies over the last fifty years. Nida endorses a functionalist account of meaning (Nida 1964: 37), cites other theorists who agree and, more importantly, proposes a functionalist criterion for evaluating translations (Nida 1964: 162–4). This trend of adopting functionalism is mirrored in *skopos* theory, according to which what normatively guides translation is not fidelity to the ST but rather a goal (Greek *skopos*) that is a result of the negotiation between the translator – who is in all matters related to translation an expert – and the agent who *commissions* the translation. The commissioning of a translation, on this account, *assigns* a purpose both to the ST and the process of translation, and the norms that govern a translation are those set out by the commission of the translation (Vermeer 1989: 174–84). This approach to textual reconstruction might be called *localization* by others who endorse *M*. Companies and businesses have to engage in the process of localization to render their products user-friendly for a target market, and this process will arise out of a dialogue between the commissioning agents and the facilitators of localization, who should be knowledgeable about the pragmatics of the target culture. But for *skopos* theory, this is also the core of translation.

Critical issues and topics

In this section, we will investigate the challenges and conflicts that arise from semantics and pragmatics in translation. These are the critical issues of translation in relation to pragmatics, and the topics we shall address are the indeterminacy of translation and possible pragmatic solutions.

Consider the translation of South Indian kinship terms, from languages such as Tamil. In Tamil, one's parent's same-sex siblings are considered parents, not aunts and uncles. One's mother's older sister is one's 'Periyamma' ('periya' is BIG, 'amma' is MOTHER: BIG MOTHER) and her husband would be 'Periyappa' (BIG FATHER). One's mother's younger sister is 'Chiththi' (SMALL MOTHER) and her husband is your 'Chiththapa' (SMALL FATHER). Likewise one's father's brothers would be respectively 'Periyappa' or 'Chiththapa' (if they are older or younger than your father) and their wives would be your 'Periyamma' or 'Chiththi'. Your mother's brother is your 'Māmma' and his wife 'Māmy', which are also the terms of address that juniors would use for their unrelated seniors in informal settings. One's father's sister is one's 'Aththai' and her husband (in high-caste Tamil) is 'Athimbēr' (a term that also refers to one's older sister's husband) or more standardly 'Athai kozhunan'. What is the right translation of these terms? In English, we would collapse most of these into 'aunt' and 'uncle', but this would not translate the literal meaning of these expressions. The problem is that the pragmatics of 'big mother' in English is not at all what it is in Tamil. (Indeed in Tamil, unlike in English, with the rare exception of 'big brother or sister', the concepts of BIG and SMALL can also generally do for 'older' and 'younger'.) A literal translation will consist in loss of meaning and distortion; nevertheless, translating 'big mother' as 'aunt' is semantically inaccurate and would result in a pragmatic loss of implications of parental intimacy, care and responsibility involved in acknowledging one's big mother.

Quine (1960) had noticed a similar problem in his *Word and Object*: we can arrive at competing incompatible translations that are consistent with the totality of (empirical) evidence with no (possible) evidentiary way to decide the case. This is the empirical component of what Quine dubs the '*indeterminacy of translation*' (see Chapters 7 and 8, this volume, for further discussion). Translations of 'Periyamma' into English as either 'big mother' (literal translation) or 'aunt' (pragmatic, functional translation) are likely examples of this kind of indeterminacy, as these are not compatible in English and yet both are suggested by the evidence. The indeterminacy here arises because we are faced with equally bad or good literal and pragmatic translations that are not compatible. Given that the pragmatics of our expressions are context-bound and often particular to languages and cultures, we should not be surprised that translators will be faced with such dilemmas in translation as a matter of course and, moreover, that we are led to these dilemmas because both the literal and pragmatic translations of expressions are suggested by the evidence.

Problems like this are what motivate the adoption of *P* and the rejection of *M* by translation theorists: we get rid of the dilemma of indeterminacy by merely siding with the user-friendly pragmatic translations. If we reject *M*, we would reject trying to semantically translate 'Periyamma' as (the infelicitous) 'big mother' and settle for 'aunt' when we are moving from Tamil to English.

One might try to justify this kind of translation via *M* by identifying a sentence in Tamil and a sentence in English as semantically equivalent on the grounds that they have the same truth conditions. There may be a sentence in English about one's aunt that is true and false in exactly the same cases as a Tamil sentence about one's Periyamma, and while the words 'aunt' and 'Periyamma' are not semantically equivalent, the sentences they occur in may be taken as a single unit. Sentences such as 'My aunt is coming for dinner' and 'My Periyamma is coming for dinner' seem to share a truth condition (said by me, in a specific context – when my mother's older sister is coming for dinner) and hence are translations of each other.

A problem with this approach is that it sacrifices 'compositionality': the principle that the meaning of a sentence is a function of the meanings of its parts. Compositionality is a central tenet of a semantics-first approach, for it explains how the meaning of words, not their use, is central to the meaning of what is said. Disregarding compositionality in favour of treating sentences as units is to move into an Austinian frame where we take the context-relative utterance of a sentence as critical to understanding its significance. Then it is the pragmatics of these sentences that allows us to treat them as translationally equivalent, and so we are committed to *P*, not *M*. Récanati (2010) argues that, in general, the way we understand the significance of sentences is by grasping their contextual use, which overrides compositionality. This is a pragmatics-first approach to significance that would license *P*.

So *P* on balance looks like the more honest way to understand how a Tamil sentence about one's Periyamma is translatable into an English sentence about one's aunt as equivalent statements. *P* does not require us to pretend that such sentences share a meaning: it rather asks us to judge the accuracy of the translation purely on pragmatic grounds.

The problem with *P* is that on its own it is absurd. It is absurd because it does not guarantee that a TT has to be a derivation of an ST. If a conclusion is derivable from premises, logicians say that the premises and conclusion relate to each other as a *valid* argument. In this case, if the premises are true, the conclusion has to be true. (Validity is not about whether a premise is true or whether they can be true, and hence valid arguments can contain within them claims that are necessarily false, like contradictions, and even claims that cannot be true or false, such as commands: P1 *If you had better run, then take the umbrella*; P2 *You had better run; Therefore, take the umbrella*. They can contain interrogatives: P1 *To be or not to be, that is the question. Therefore, to be or not to be?*). So, for instance, the inference *q* therefore *q* is a valid inference for this reason, as are many rules of inference (such as *modus ponens*: if *p* then *q*, *p* therefore *q*). If translations conformed to *M*, then an accurate TT would be a mere semantic restatement of an ST and would hence have to meet the minimal requirement of being a deductive derivation from the ST. Hence if the Christian Bible ST is true, then the candidate Christian Bible TT would be true too. (This is a minimum standard, for TTs can meet it and fail to be accurate STs, when, for instance, they are partial translations of the ST. Yet it is rational to expect it as a minimum requirement of translation.) But if the Christian Bible ST is true, it does not follow that a TT Quran is true; and correspondingly if a Quran ST is true, it does not follow that a Bible TT is true. Yet this is exactly what we would have to contend with if we adopted *P*: we would have to put up with the notion that the Bible and the Quran are intertranslations in respective conservative Christian and Muslim societies irrespective of the fact that we cannot derive the one, logically, from the other. So *P* is objectionable because it is irrational: it violates a most basic standard of reason, namely validity. But defenders of *P* might note that the problem here is not *P* but *functionalism*. If we adopt Récanati's approach, then we only ever treat an SL and TL utterances as equivalent when they share a truth condition relative to a context of use. So it would seem in such cases, the TT could never be false if the corresponding ST is true. Yet it is not clear that this defence is successful.

When we evaluate validity, we are not typically evaluating statements but rather propositions in the abstract: it is the relationship of these propositions in the abstract that can entail each other. So, too, with translation. Translation does not obviously take statements as its objects. When we convert statements in one language into another, we are engaged in (what we could call) *interpretation*. An example of such activity is *simultaneous interpretation* (when, for instance, an interpreter converts what an SL speaker says into corresponding TL sign-language for a deaf audience, in real time). Is this not mere hair-splitting? Why is this pairing of SL and TL claims not also a form of translation? The difference between interpretation and translation is the preservation of truth (as we find in valid deductions). As Davidson notes in his 'A Nice Derangement of Epitaphs', when people err in speech, we interpret what is said much like Récanati later claims: we understand the content of what is said as what we take to be true in the context, and we ignore the error (Davidson 1996: 472–3). So, too, with interpretation: the goal is to follow the content of what is said in context, and so interpreters would be obliged to ignore errors of speech when producing interpretations (this is an aspect of the 'principle of charity': see Chapter 7, this volume, for further discussion). While to avoid absurdity translations need to be derivable from an ST, in the case of interpretation, the TT correction is not derivable from the ST but the ST usage. Interpretation is guided by pragmatic considerations that characterize *P*. Also in the case of translation, we are often interested in preserving errors for two reasons. First, in the translation of science or philosophy, we are often unsure what is true or relevant, so we are not in a position to match sentences on the basis of their truth or relevance – even when relativized to a context. Second, errors can be important for the translator to preserve. For example, the translation of the testimony of a witness in a court case that sanitized the witness's errors would be tantamount to tampering with evidence that bears on the credibility of the witness. Yet *P*, with no concern for meaning, takes us here.

Current contributions and research

P and *M* are the odd couple of translation. If we choose either, we land in trouble: preserving literal meaning and pragmatic features of the ST is a competitive endeavour. If we save literal meaning, we often sacrifice pragmatics, and if we save pragmatics, we often sacrifice meaning.

The plausible solution to this problem of needing both *M* and *P* is to propose a bridge principle that leads us to account for, and preserve, both the semantic and pragmatic features of the ST. So we assess the accuracy of the translation not in terms of *M* or *P* but in terms of the bridge principle.

The bridge principle in the Translation Studies literature has been called a 'text-type' (Holmes 1988: 74–6; Laviosa-Braithwaite 2001: 277–8; Neubert and Shreve 1992; Reiss 1981). A text-type is like a genre, except it has widespread institutional recognition and pertains to structural features of texts that exceed what is usually understood under the heading of a 'genre'. Examples of text-types include the philosophical text, the novel and the scholarly paper on natural science, and text-types can include among them sub-text-types: biology or chemistry texts may be sub-types in the natural sciences.

In acknowledging that texts come in types, we are not committed to the notion that a single text is characterizable by only one type – nor are we committed to some sort of functionalism as early defenders claimed (Reiss 1981). Plato's *Republic*, for instance, seems equally a great work of literature and of philosophy, and acknowledging text-types brings us to this appreciation. Rather the utility of acknowledging that texts come in types is to allow us to *choose* a type as the *governing type* in translation, which allows us to treat contrary text-type features of a text as contributing to the governing type's objectives. A text so viewed through the lens of a type that we elect as the governing type may be called a *work*: something whose translatable content is determined by the governing type.

If we choose to read Plato's *Republic* as primarily an example of philosophy, we then treat the poetic, dramatic, comedic, historical and empirical-scientific aspects of the text as contributing to its philosophical objectives. The ST so understood would be a work of philosophy that we can thereby translate into a TT. Our goal is to reproduce a TT that has the same text-type features of the ST including the subservient features: hence the literary and other text-type features of the text (what we identified as subsidiary types) would be reproduced in so far as they aid the philosophical objectives of the text (which we chose as the governing type). But the reason we have to choose just one type as the governing type is that there can be conflicts between differing types in a text that come to light in translation: type$_1$ of a text may render the literal, linguistic meaning salient, while type$_2$ brings attention to its pragmatic features, such as implicature. As noted in the literature, and in our previous investigation, we often cannot preserve both in translation – translation is a series of 'moves, as in a game', where 'every single move is influenced by the knowledge of previous decisions' (Levý 2000). In choosing one type as the governing type, we decide in advance how such conflicts are to be resolved. There may hence be multiple treatments of the same text as differing works that result in differing translations, but, as these were produced according to differing text-type considerations, they do not conflict. Correlatively, there may be multiple alternate translations of the same work that are, by virtue of the single *governing type* under which they were produced, equivalent.

A text-type, one that we elect as the *governing type*, serves as a protocol for designating features – pragmatic and semantic – of an ST to be preserved in a TT. Moreover, in so far as we are able to recreate a TT that has the relevant text-type features of the ST, we can call upon the text-type as providing rules for the preservation of content that show how it is that the TT is a genuine translation of the ST. So, looking back on our example of translating texts from Tamil that contain familial terms such as 'Periyamma', the invocation of text-types as a mediating principle in translation shows that there is no absolute answer to the question of what the correct translations of such terms are: rather the question of whether 'aunt' will do for 'Periyamma' has to be judged relative to the type that we elect as the governing type. It may be that in certain works, 'aunt' is the best translation for 'Periyamma', while in others, 'big mother' would be preferable, given the text-type theoretic objectives. But either way, the right translation will be determined not by fiat, nor on the basis of its effect on the audience, but by what is salient in an ST understood via the governing type.

Looking back on our example of purely pragmatic translation from the ST Bible into the TT Quran, we can see why this is implausible. It is hard to imagine a text-type that would license this type of transition – though *a priori* we cannot rule out that in the translation of some texts, perhaps texts of comedy, fiction or drama, it may be that the pragmatics of an ST Bible quotation necessary for the objectives of the governing type is best served by a quote from the Quran in the TT, given the target language and audience. If, for instance, the intelligibility of a prayer by the audience is crucial for the intelligibility of a work of drama, the purposes of translation would be served by using a prayer that the TT audience could identify, which may not be what the ST audience would easily identify.

Yet it may seem that we are back to the absurdity that led us to a dissatisfaction with *P*, choosing translations on the basis of pragmatics that are not in any straightforward sense equivalent to the ST. But our set of theoretical resources is now richer, for we can invoke the governing text-type to show that the pragmatics of the TT should in some important and non-trivial sense reflect those of the ST. Relative to the text-type considerations, we could identify duly produced translations as being derivations of the ST. But, no doubt, the dissatisfaction can be reframed again too: the problem with pairing parts of the TT with parts of the ST on the basis of pragmatic considerations is that we are helping ourselves to features of a text that are by definition context-bound. So there is no obvious sense – even with a bridge principle – to the idea that we can preserve the pragmatics of an ST in translation.

A solution to this problem has been defended at length in response to the usual criticisms about the feasibility or determinacy of translation in Translation Studies and philosophy (Ranganathan, 2007, 2011). This solution is to treat the translatable content of a work – a text viewed through the lens of a governing type – as having a distinct kind of meaning: textual meaning, which is the meaning of the work from the perspective of this governing type. And just as literal meaning has uses that go beyond literal meaning (irony and metaphor, for instance), so too does textual meaning function pragmatically beyond the scope of its textual significance. But it is only textual meaning, according to this solution, that we preserve in translation. For example, 'Plato's forms' and 'Plato's ideas' are inter-translations in philosophy not because they share a linguistic meaning or because the pragmatics of 'form' or 'idea' in wider English are the same (one can say 'that's a great idea!', but 'that's a great form!' is infelicitous), but because they share the same pragmatics relative to the text-type of philosophy. The common (governing) text-type use of these phrases yields a textual meaning, which can be shared by an analogous construction in another language – a target resource use that a translator may even need to institute if no previous usage is available. It may be that the pragmatics of such a translation end up being culturally infelicitous and perhaps even jarring for the target audience (especially if their philosophical intuitions are anti-Platonic). But this is not the fault of the translation, for the wider cultural pragmatics of the ST are not anything that the translator always has to preserve. If they are relevant in specific cases, they contribute to a certain textual meaning, which comes apart from wider pragmatic considerations in translation.

As meaning transcends context while pragmatics does not, textual meaning is something that we can preserve in translation. Textual meaning preserves the constituent literal-semantic and pragmatic features of a text in so far as their use is highlighted by the governing text-type (including subsidiary-type uses). Textual meaning preserved in translation would pass the test of validity: if an ST of a certain textual meaning is true, then the corresponding TT with the same textual meaning would also be true. The difficulty is that in endorsing this approach we renounce trying to translate textual pragmatics – the practical role that a work enjoys in its source culture in the absence of governing-type considerations. But we get to this austere position by understanding how the pragmatics of the text relative to a governing type is a distinct kind of meaning: textual meaning.

Main research methods

Mere adherence to M (assuming that linguistic meaning is what M preserves) would produce TTs that are unintelligible in proportion to their pragmatic divergence from the pragmatics of the ST. Mere adherence to P would yield absurd results. Thinking about translation as something that takes works under a governing type as objects avoids both problems, for such translation treats the governing type as determining how a TT can be equivalent to a ST (relative to that type) – and while the resulting TT may not always be culturally felicitous, it can be understood if the target audience has knowledge of the relevant type. It follows that linguistic competence in an SL and a TL are insufficient to produce an acceptable translation. One needs knowledge not only of the relevant source and target semiotic systems but also the relevant text-types. In one respect, we should not be surprised. Linguistic competence in English is not sufficient to understand most English texts of philosophy, chemistry or even poetry. Except for the odd prodigy, it takes an introduction into a text-type to render such texts intelligible. But we now see why it is not because we lack linguistic knowledge that reading chemistry, poetry or philosophy for the first time is difficult – in the cases of philosophy and poetry, novices usually know most if not all the words used. Until we understand a text-type, we are unable to evaluate how the semiotic resources of a text are *used* to express textual meaning, and our failure to appreciate textual meaning renders such texts opaque. In the case of many challenging types of text, whether law, philosophy, empirical sciences or mathematics, it often takes years of study to appreciate the type in question – we learn about the type by being challenged to understand several works of the same type. What they have in common is the type, and this is what we learn about via long-term, advanced study.

But as translating by types involves electing one as a governing type while relegating contrary types to subsidiary roles, it would seem that translators need to specialize not only in a type but also have knowledge of types that play subservient roles relative to one's chosen type. It would seem, then, that the kind of knowledge that translators share is very general, and that we should avoid overgeneralizing strategies of translation based on narrow areas of translation research (Snell-Hornby 1988: 14). What translators have in common is the need to select a governing type and understand the role of subsidiary types. The kind of rules that emerge from the specific constellation of types will depend upon the ranking of types.

The importance of type theoretic knowledge has not been lost on translators, who often specialize in specific types of text. Indeed, it would seem that it behoves translators to familiarize themselves with text-types in order to apply them in translation. Most philosophy is translated by professional philosophers (Large 2014), and this is not an accident – who else would be able to figure out what is to be translated where philosophy is concerned? Yet it appears that we have a new challenge – one that requires research: the individuation of a type.

We can put the problem thus. To translate philosophy, for instance, we need to appreciate the text-type of philosophy. But philosophers disagree about what philosophy is. If we require some type of agreement on what the type of philosophy is in order to locate it, then there are apparently as many text-types of philosophy as there are schools of philosophy, or even individual contributions to philosophy. Thus we are in danger of trivializing the idea of a 'type' of text that is philosophy, for our effort to locate it may lead us to regard each individual philosophical work as belonging to its own *sui generis* type.

A similar problem has been identified by Hans-Georg Gadamer (1990): as 'poetry', 'science' and 'philosophy' are merely words in our Western cultural and linguistic tradition, we have grounds to be sceptical not only that works from other cultures exemplify poetry, science and philosophy, but also that we have any means to adjudicate whether they do.

One promising solution that shows how text-types can be individuated despite these difficulties is to identify text-types with disciplines, as explored in the Indian tradition. According to Patañjali's 200 CE *Yoga Sūtra*, yoga, or 'discipline', is a practice that we can undertake from differing perspectives, which thereby enables us to isolate content for inquiry (for a philosopher's tranlsation of this text, see Patañjali 2008). The content so identified is objective in the sense that it is not determined from a single perspective but is converged upon from differing perspectives. Contemporary disciplines, such as mathematics or philosophy, are examples of such practices that we can undertake from differing theoretical vantage points, from which we can triangulate on objects of research. This approach allows us to identify a discipline in the face of controversy, for the discipline is what renders the controversy intelligible: it allows us to take differing sides in a debate. For example, the discipline of philosophy, on this account, is not beholden to any individual perspective on what philosophy is, but rather this discipline is the procedural aspect of engaging in philosophical disagreement that individual perspectives have in common and thus provides a common foundation upon which to build competing structures and thereby disagree about what philosophy is without talking past one another. Hence a discipline such as philosophy, so understood, cannot be rejected because the question of what counts as philosophy is controversial: the discipline makes the controversy possible. In identifying a discipline, we have thereby identified the text-type of philosophy.

Recommendations for practice

'Translation' is a term often used loosely. We have had occasion to distinguish *interpretation* and *localization* from translation. An ST that is interpreted into a TT preserves truth as the interpreter sees it. An ST that is localized into a TT serves a function desired by the commissioner of the localization. A translation of an ST into a TT can and often has to preserve errors – either, for example, as evidence or because we are not sure what is true in many cases of translation. P sheds light on both interpretation and localization, but we also need M in order to avoid the absurd results of merely preserving pragmatics in translation.

We have also discussed Quine's 'indeterminacy of translation', but, with the idea of text-type meaning in hand, it is worth another look. According to Quine, even at the limit of all possible empirical evidence, there would still be competing and incompatible, yet equally acceptable, translations of any given text (Quine 1960: 27). But a textual approach can avoid this concern. Quine's emphasis on empirical evidence is another way of talking about fixing translation by way of paring contextual word usage in the SL and TL – what Quine called 'analytical hypotheses' (Quine 1960: 68). This is a version of P. Given the trouble associated with P, we can see how it is that Quine can generate a sceptical conclusion in the face of all the empirical evidence: translations according to P are translations that violate validity, and derivations that are invalid can produce conclusions that are not consistent with their premises (such as p, therefore not p). Hence there is no guarantee of consistency between STs and TTs on this account, and hence no guarantee of the consistency of competing TTs – even and especially on the basis of the pragmatic (empirical) evidence. But in switching to a text-type, we identify textual meaning to be translated and the translation of text-type theoretic meaning ensures that resulting TTs have the same text-type meaning as the ST: STs and TTs will always be consistent with each other, and competing TTs produced by the same text-type procedure would be equally consistent – no room for indeterminacy here as a matter of equally supported, inconsistent translation. Hence the first order of business of a translator (whom we assume to be knowledgeable both about the relevant semiotic systems (languages included) and about types) when confronted with a text to translate, is to:

(1) designate one type as the governing type,

and then:

(2) identify subsidiary types and their instrumental roles.

The designation of the governing type in a translation is a choice, and one with consequences. If we choose, say, to read a journal article in chemistry as dramatic fiction, our efforts to translate it will be frustrated, for we will not be able to identify a plot. Hence the choice of a governing type can either be acceptable or not. An acceptable choice for a governing type reveals to us something about the structure of a work as a semantic totality. It does not follow from this that acceptable choices will always reveal the workings of subsidiary types at play: some works are poorly written and a translator might have to contend with translating an imperfect work. But evaluating the merits of a work as a contribution to the literature is something only possible once we identify a governing type and look for subsidiary types. And we can always draw a distinction between cases where we have merely misunderstood the governing type of a work, and when we are confronted with a poorly written work: in the latter case, we see its faults relative to the governing type, while in the former, we see ourselves at fault for incorrectly reading the text via a certain candidate type.

We can next look at:

(3) isolation of translation units.

Translation units are the smallest parts of a text to be treated as indivisible. In some cases, these may be words (especially technical terms), in other cases, sentences, and in others yet, whole passages. Such units are salient in light of (1) and (2).

Finally, what remains is:

(4) the recreation of the work in a target semiotic system by way of (1), (2) and (3).

We know we have succeeded when, translation unit for translation unit, the constituents of the units play the same role relevant to the governing and subsidiary types.

Future directions

As we have seen, ideas from non-Western contexts can shed light on problems in translation theory. A largely underexplored future direction is to look to ideas from outside of the tradition in which puzzles about translation are generated for their solutions – solutions we learn about by translation.

Related topics

Wittgenstein; Quine; Davidson; Derrida; translation theory and philosophy; equivalence; meaning; the translation of philosophical texts.

Further reading

Hickey, L. (Ed.) 1998. *The Pragmatics of Translation*. Toronto: Multilingual Matters. (Collection of articles from translation theorists on the relevance of pragmatic considerations to translation. It draws from the famous pragmatics-first theories of the day.)

Olohan, M. 2015. *Scientific and Technical Translation*. Abingdon: Routledge. (A recent example of text-type specific translation research.)

Salmon, Nathan U. 2005. 'Two Conceptions of Semantics'. In *Semantics vs. Pragmatics*, edited by Zoltán Gendler Szabó, 317–28. Oxford; New York: Clarendon Press; Oxford University Press. (A classic description of the difference between semantic-first and pragmatic-first approaches in philosophy.)

Simms, Karl (Ed.). 1997. *Translating Sensitive Texts: Linguistic Aspects*. Amsterdam: Rodopi. (SENSITIVE TEXTS is an example of a class of texts, not a kind. The collection includes articles that explore functionalist strategies.)

References

Austin, John Langshaw. 1955. *How to Do Things with Words*. In *William James Lectures. 1955*. 2nd edition. Cambridge: Harvard University Press, 2000.

Bassnett, Susan. 2002. *Translation Studies*. 3rd edition. London; New York: Routledge.

Davidson, Donald. 1996. 'A Nice Derangement of Epitaphs'. In *The Philosophy of Language*, edited by Aloysius Martinich, 465–75. New York: Oxford University Press. Original edition, Oxford.

Firth, John Rupert. 1964. *The Tongues of Men, and Speech*. London: Oxford University Press.

Frege, Gottlob. 1892. 'Über Sinn Und Bedeutung'. *Zeitschrift für Philosophie und philosophische Kritik* 100: 25–50, Translated as 'On Sense and Reference' by M. Black in *Translations from the Philosophical Writings of Gottlob Frege*, P. Geach and M. Black (eds. and trans.). Oxford: Blackwell, 3rd ed., 1980.

Gadamer, Hans-Georg. 1990. 'Culture and the Word'. In *Hermeneutics and the Poetic Motion Translation Perspectives V*, edited by Dennis J. Schmidt, translated by Dennis J. Schmidt, 11–24. Binghamton: SUNY.

Grice, Paul. 1961. 'The Causal Theory of Perception'. *Proceedings of the Aristotelian Society Supplement* Supplementary Volume 35: 121–52.

Grice, Paul. 1975. 'Logic and Conversation'. In *Syntax and Semantics 3: Speech Acts*, edited by Paul Cole and Jerry Morgan, 41–58. New York: Academic Press.

Holmes, James S. 1988. 'The Name and Nature of Translation Studies.' In *Translated!: Papers on Literary Translation and Translation Studies*, 67–80. Amsterdam: Rodopi.

Kripke, Saul A. 1980. *Naming and Necessity*. Cambridge, MA: Harvard University Press.

Large, Duncan. 2014. 'On the Work of Philosopher-Translators'. In *Literary Translation: Redrawing the Boundaries*, edited by Jean Boase-Beier, Antoinette Fawcett and Phillip Wilson, 182–203. Basingstoke: Palgrave Macmillan.

Laviosa-Braithwaite, Sara. 2001. 'Universals of Translation'. In *Routledge Encyclopedia of Translation Studies*, edited by Mona Baker and Kirsten Malmkjær, 288–91. London; New York: Routledge.

Levý, J. 2000. 'Translation as a Decision Process'. In *Translation Studies Reader*, edited by L. Venuti, 148–59. London; New York: Routledge.

Monk, Ray. 1990. *Ludwig Wittgenstein: The Duty of Genius*. London: Jonathan Cape.

Neubert, Albrecht, and D. Rothfuss-Bastian. 2003. 'Text Parameters in the Light of Translation Pragmatics'. In *Textologie und Translation*, edited by E. Hajicova, P. Sgall, H. Gerzymisch-Arbogast, Z. Jettmarova, A. Rotkegel and Dorothee Rothfuß-Bastian, 189–202. Tübingen: Gunter Narr Verl.

Neubert, Albrecht and Gregory M. Shreve. 1992. 'Translation as Text'. In *Translation Studies 1*. Kent, OH: Kent State University Press.

Nida, Eugene Albert. 1964. *Toward a Science of Translating, with Special Reference to Principles and Procedures Involved in Bible Translating*. Leiden: E.J. Brill.

Ogden, Charles Kay and Ivor Armstrong Richards. 1923. *The Meaning of Meaning: A Study of the Influence of Language Upon Thought and of the Science of Symbolism*. San Diego: Harcourt Brace Jovanovich.

Patañjali. 2008. *Patañjali's Yoga Sūtra,* Translation, Commentary and Introduction by Shyam Ranganathan. In *Black Classics*. New Delhi: Penguin Black Classics.

Quine, Willard Van Orman. 1960. *Word and Object*. Cambridge, MA: MIT Press.

Ranganathan, Shyam. 2007. *Translating Evaluative Discourse: The Semantics of Thick and Thin Concepts*. York University, Department of Philosophy (PhD dissertation). www.collectionscanada.gc.ca/obj/thesescanada/vol2/002/NR68573.pdf.

Ranganathan, Shyam. 2011. 'An Archimedean Point for Philosophy'. *Metaphilosophy* 42 (4): 479–519.

Récanati, Francçois. 2010. *Truth-Conditional Pragmatics*. Oxford; New York: Clarendon Press.

Reiss, Katharina. 1981. 'Type, Kind and Individuality of Text: Decision Making in Translation'. *Poetics Today* 2 (4): 121–31.

Russell, Bertrand. 1921. *The Analysis of Mind*. London: Allen and Unwin.

Salmon, Nathan U. 2005. 'Two Conceptions of Semantics'. In *Semantics Vs. Pragmatics*, edited by Zoltán Gendler Szabó, 317–28. Oxford; New York: Clarendon Press; Oxford University Press.

Snell-Hornby, Mary (Ed.). 1988. *Translation Studies: An Integrated Approach*. Amsterdam; Philadelphia: John Benjamins.

Szabó, Zoltán Gendler. 2006. 'The Distinction between Semantics and Pragmatics'. In *The Oxford Handbook of Philosophy of Language*, edited by Ernest LePore and Barry C. Smith, 361–92. New York: Oxford University Press.

Vermeer, Hans J. 1989. '*Skopos* and Commission in Translational Action'. In *Readings in Translation Theory*, edited by Andrew Chesterman, translated by Andrew Chesterman, 173–87. Helsinki: Oy Finn Lectura.

Wittgenstein, Ludwig. 1958. *Philosophical Investigations*. Translated by G.E.M. Anscombe. 2nd edition. New York: Macmillan.

13
Culture

Sergey Tyulenev

Introduction

Culture is one of the most problematic concepts in the humanities. Different people define it differently. Even worse, its very ontology remains debatable. Does culture really exist or is it a Western construct forced upon the rest of the world? If culture does exist, where is it located? Is it a set of observable patterns of human activities? Or is it in the minds of people? Or is it some sort of superorganic phenomenon, existing independently of individual members of a collectivity and imposing its dictates upon them?

Despite these fundamental doubts and its elusive essence, culture is one of the central concepts in the humanities and various approaches to studying it thrive and proliferate. The paradox of the concept was pithily expressed by a leading anthropologist of the twentieth century, Clifford Geertz (1926–2006): 'Though ideational, [culture] does not exist in someone's head [thus, being too private and difficult to reach and generalize]; though unphysical, it is not an occult' – rather it is an 'acted document' which is 'written not in conventionalized graphs of sound but in transient examples of shaped behavior' ([1973] 1993: 10).

As a working definition for what follows, culture is understood as an integral part of human social existence, as 'ways of acting, thinking and feeling which are transmitted from generation to generation and across societies through learning, not through [biological] inheritance' (Albrow 1999: 6).

An analysis of cultural aspects of translation has to take into consideration, first, individual translators' cultural commitments (whether conscious or sub-/semi-/unconscious) and, second, since culture is an intrinsically social, that is, collective, phenomenon, interactions of translation and culture and their interdependencies. Importantly, in both perspectives, cultural aspects of translation or the translator are socially determined and this has its epistemological and methodological repercussions – that is, the primacy of the sociological stance over the psychological and the derivative nature of the latter from the former (Tyulenev 2014: 17).

Culture is a set of values and ideas shared by a collectivity and one of the major factors making that collectivity more than just a gathering of individuals. One of the earliest theorists of culture, Wilhelm Wundt (1832–1920), emphasized that such aspects of culture as language, religion and custom are 'those mental products which are created by a community' and are 'inexplicable in terms merely of individual consciousness, since they presuppose the reciprocal action of many' ([1912] 1916: 3). In the German-American anthropologist Franz Boas' (1858–1942) words, '[w]e must understand the individual as living in his culture; and the culture as lived by individuals' (1989: xx). Individuals are introduced into a culture, through the process of enculturation – that is, absorbing the culture in which they are brought up. The culture then governs their behaviour: they may conform to or reject it or partly the former and partly the latter, but their culture constitutes the very framework of their experiences and actions. Culture is so deeply interiorized that the selection of available behavioral options is 'only exceptionally conscious and rational' (Kluckhohn 1949: 26).

The notion of culture has a long and controversial history, which is responsible for several critical issues still relevant today. Among the most important issues are: defining culture; the question of why culture is one of the key notions in the humanities and, since we are concerned with translation, also in Translation and Interpreting Studies (TIS); and, finally, how to demarcate cultural and social aspects of translation and culturally and sociologically informed approaches in translation research.

Defining culture

There is a broad range of definitions of culture. When in the early 1950s two American anthropologists, Alfred Louis Kroeber (1876–1960) and Clyde Kluckhohn (1905–60), took stock of the definitions of the term 'culture' and its synonym 'civilization' which were in circulation, they discovered no fewer than 164 (Kroeber and Kluckhohn 1952). All of those definitions, despite their differences and various emphases, agree that culture is somehow opposed to nature or biology, captured in the phrase 'nature vs. nurture'.

Culture is associated with everything human; culture is seen as the dividing line between the human species and the rest of the animal kingdom and indeed the entire universe. In the words of Kroeber, '[c]ulture is the special and exclusive product of men, and is their distinctive quality in the cosmos' ([1923] 1948: 8). This shows why culture is so important in the humanities: it can be safely called the principal uniquely human phenomenon. Although some animals do manifest ways of organizing their social life, which may remind us of human culture, the extent is never comparable to what culture means for human society. In sociology and anthropology, culture has been considered a human 'substitute for the instincts whereby most other living creatures are equipped with the means for coping with their environment and relating to one another' (Inkeles 1964: 66). The human mind is 'wired' for culture; without culture we would not be what we are both as a species and as individuals (Pagel 2012). Culture is thus 'a truly human existence that goes beyond the merely "natural" condition of animals' (Scott 2011: 11).

Let us look at the main directions in defining culture:

(1) The first and literal meaning of the term 'culture' comes from the Latin term 'colere' which means 'to till' or 'to cultivate' as in 'to till/cultivate land'. In this sense, the term is still used in agriculture when one speaks of cultivation of plants, their 'culture', or in biology to mean artificial media with nutrients in which bacteria or tissue cells are grown.

Based on the literal meaning, a series of metaphorical meanings developed and these are used whenever human culture is discussed. The underlying rationale for all the definitions of human culture has always been some degree of 'the tempering of man's "natural" instincts and desires by an arbitrary imposition of will' (Wagner [1975] 1981: 21).

Culture

(2) It is possible to speak about the culture of an individual. As one can cultivate land, one can cultivate one's mind, faculties, manners etc. and thereby develop one's culture.

(3) Consequently, the term 'culture' can be understood as arts and skills – that is, what is seen as the highest human achievements, as opposed to the rest of the human mundane material existence. Famously, Matthew Arnold (1822–88) described culture as 'a pursuit of our total perfection by means of getting to know [. . .] the best which has been known and said in the world' ([1869] 1932: 6). It is in this sense that the term is used when one speaks of 'men of culture'. This usage, although it persists, is largely dismissed nowadays as elitist ('culture in the "opera-house" sense': Wagner [1975] 1981: 21), sexist and less useful in anthropology and sociology as well as in other humanities, such as cultural studies (where such notions as pop culture or mass culture are included into culture) and TIS.

(4) The notion has been applied not only to individuals but also to entire collectivities. Some societies were seen as having a higher level of culture than others (referred to as 'primitive' or 'barbaric'). Within one and the same society, groups were compared in terms of how 'cultured' they were (in sense (3) above) and what contribution, if any, they were making to the overall culture of their society.Especially widespread, such understanding of the term 'culture' was implied when 'cultured', European or Western, nations were opposed to 'primitive' or 'savage', almost always non-European, nations. This was done by European nations, who put themselves higher than the nations with which they came into contact during the age of great geographical discoveries (the fifteenth to the eighteenth centuries). Today, this usage is largely deprecated as colonialist (Said 1994).

In this meaning, one can speak of a culture or cultures (plural). Boas was the first to start using the term 'culture' in the plural, referring to differences between different peoples and advocating a relativistic approach to studying cultures. The relativistic approach questions the comparison of different cultures in terms of superiority/inferiority. Rather, it is claimed, cultures should be appreciated on their own terms. In this sense one speaks of, say, the Hungarian culture or the Kazakh culture.

The term 'culture' was also used to mean collective identities. Cultures were understood as having a sort of collective physiognomies (Apollonian or Dionysian, megalomaniac or paranoid, as the American anthropologist Ruth Benedict (1887–1948) described some of the cultures she studied (Benedict [1934] 1989)). This approach was, however, criticized as essentialist – that is, making the entire collectivity look uniform, akin to stereotypification. While scientists no longer understand cultures as collective personalities, different collectivities are usually stereotyped by other collectivities in this or that way, and these stereotypes are studied today in imagology (Leerssen n/d; Doorslaer, Flynn and Leerssen 2016).Translation is one of the platforms which allow different cultures to meet, although not always unproblematically. For example, national cultures, referred to as the 'spirit' (*Geist* or *esprit*) of a nation, were seen by Wilhelm von Humboldt (1767–1835) as crystallized in great works of literature. He wrote that languages 'first reach into the usual habits of life, after which they can be improved on *ad infinitum* into something nobler and more complex by the spirit of the nation that shapes them' (cited in Levefere 1992: 137). Humboldt believed that it was this spirit that was virtually untranslatable, precisely because different nations have distinctly different spirits.

(5) Contributions considered among the highest human achievements (sense (3) above) are said to belong to world culture – that is, to the culture of humanity as a whole.

To register and protect world culture is the purpose of UNESCO. The UNESCO Operational Guidelines for the Implementation of the World Heritage Convention include in world culture monuments (architectural works, monumental sculptures and paintings) and ensembles of monuments and sites that are works of humanity or the combined works of nature and of humanity (WHC 2015: IIA, 45, Article 1). In a comparable but not necessarily similar way, the applicability of the concept of culture is studied in the context of this globalizing world of ours (Featherstone 1996). Such approaches consider cultural processes, which 'transcend the state-society unit and can therefore be held to occur on a trans-national or trans-societal level' (ibid.: 1). These are so-called 'third cultures' – that is, 'conduits for all sorts of diverse cultural flows which cannot be merely understood as the product of bilateral exchanges between nation-states' (ibid.). The concept of culture is applied to a sociological view of the world as a social system (Wallerstein 2004). It is possible to think about such global cultural phenomena as economic and financial flows in the global market with its stock exchanges operating internationally, information flows coordinated by mass media or ideas gaining international currency, such as democracy, peace etc. (see Arjun Appadurai's contribution to Featherstone 1996: 295–310).

(6) The term 'culture' in its most encompassing meaning denotes the way of life of a society, including material, intellectual and spiritual phenomena. Edward Tylor defined culture as 'that complex whole which includes knowledge, belief, art, morals, law, custom, and any other capabilities and habits acquired by man as a member of society' (1871: 1). This meaning is closely associated with the notion of (human) civilization. It is believed that in Europe during and after the Enlightenment (reaching its apogee in the eighteenth century), as religion was giving way to secular knowledge, culture or civilization came to replace it as the repository of ultimate values. An interesting instance of this is found in how John Ray, an Egyptologist, describes the Rosetta Stone, one of the most popular objects in the British Museum:

> For a part of its history in the museum it was displayed without a glass cover, so that visitors could touch its surface. Nowadays this is not encouraged, but the museum has enterprisingly placed a replica in the King's Library for those who feel the need to run their hands over the inscriptions. It is as if this ancient piece of granite has become the modern version of a religious relic. Religious relics in the Middle Ages were a centre for the tourist industry, and they spawned replicas and souvenirs. The stone is no exception. There are postcards, facsimiles, booklets and imitations everywhere on sale. [. . .] Such things are the takeaway equivalents of the pieces of cloth which have touched a famous icon or a bone of one of the Apostles.
> (2008: 4–5)

An object of culture is treated as a religious object.

(7) Finally, Talcott Parsons (1902–79), a leading sociologist of the twentieth century, suggested considering culture as part of studying society and thus using the term 'culture' more rigorously and in connection with other phenomena of human social existence. When working on his theory of social action, Parsons singled out three aspects contributing to social behaviour ([1951] 1959) – physical, social and ideational. The physical component belongs to the realm of the biological and psychological in social actors taken as individuals. The social is to do with interactions of individual actors (the root of the words 'society' and 'social' comes from the Latin word 'socius',

meaning a companion or ally, implying a relationship between two or more people) and with the formation and existence of various institutions. The ideational element is the domain of ideas and values transmitted by means of symbols, rituals and other conventionalized practices, which inform social actions. This ideational realm is what Parsons suggested denoting by the term 'culture'. He suggested dividing labour in the social sciences: the individual component should be studied by psychologists, acts and interactions should be studied by sociologists, while ideas and values – that is, culture – should be studied by anthropologists.

Although such neat division of labour never worked, Parsons' inscription of culture into the overall structure of human society turned out to be productive. Despite the ambiguity of the term 'culture', Adam Kuper sees the notion as a success story in the humanities:

> [W]hile other venerable concepts have mostly faded out of the social science discourse, even a postmodernist can talk unselfconsciously about culture (in quotes if necessary, but still . . . Compare the fate of personality, social structure, class, or, most recently, gender). Indeed, culture is now more fashionable than ever. Other disciplines have taken it up, and a new specialty, cultural studies, is devoted entirely to it.
>
> (2000)

There are several features about the notion of culture, which make it a convenient concept (and this also helps us appreciate its importance in the humanities). Notably, it is sufficiently capacious to theorize differences between peoples and social groups without falling into anything as controversial as the notion of race: culture is learned, not part of the biologically transmitted genetic material. At the same time, while allowing us to talk about difference, the notion also allows us to talk about what all humans share – human culture (vs. nature).

Culture and translation

To appreciate further the significance of the concept of culture in the social sciences in general and in TIS in particular, it is helpful to remember the place of culture in society as theorized in sociology following in the footsteps of Parsons. Culture is seen as a repository of ideas and values which the individual makes his or her own in the process of enculturation. As a sum total of interactions of the individual with their family and various social institutions, typically beginning with schools in modern societies and continuing with their professional environments all the way to their death, society mediates between social actors and the cultures with which they come in contact. Society is, thus, a translating agent itself. In this sense, it is possible to speak of intergenerational translation, when sons and daughters learn how to be socialized humans from their parents and their superiors (Habermas [1970] 1988: 146).

Bronislaw Malinowski (1884–1942) theorized society as having basic and derived needs. Basic needs are immediate physiological needs of human individuals and their collectivities. These needs are met by establishing social institutes. For example, the human need to reproduce is met by a system of kinship. Derived needs are those which develop in order to prescribe individual actors' behaviour in order to meet basic needs – for instance, rules of marriage are established which offer individuals choices as regards their reproduction.

Translation functions as a mechanism of making the individual aware of the institutes embodying derived needs so that he or she can meet his or her basic needs. However, the term 'translation' should be understood broadly, not only as a mechanism of interlingual communication. Jakobson's ([1959] 2012: 127) tripartite classification of translation types is helpful here. According to it, translation can be

- intralingual (explaining one word with other ones, typical in unilingual dictionaries: e.g. 'integrate is to combine one thing with another');
- interlingual (between different languages, e.g. between Russian and English);
- intersemiotic (between one sign system into another, for instance making a film version of a book, thus translating from a verbal sign system into an audiovisual sign system).

In the individual's enculturation, intersemiotic and intralingual types of translation are especially important. A newly born baby learns a language by correlating extraverbal reality in general and signs in particular (gestures or facial expressions) with words and simple phrases, and intersemiotic translation is the mechanism making this correlation possible. Later, the child acquires more complex vocabulary by being told what a 'difficult' word means with the help of 'simple' words; this is re-wording, or intralingual, translation. Translation is, therefore, an indispensable part of enculturation, helping humans to meet their basic need of growth.

Translation is also a key social mechanism in meeting one of the basic human needs – communication (not listed by Malinowski 1944: 91). Communication is ubiquitous in human society; without communication humans cannot become human (see the phenomenon of so-called feral children, like Mowgli, Rudyard Kipling's memorable character) and find it hard to survive (see Daniel Defoe's Robinson Crusoe, who clearly had a need for companionship). That is why to be a hermit is always an exceptional superhuman religious feat.

Humans communicate diatopically (across space), diachronically (across time), diastratically (across social classes), diamesically (across different media) and diaphasically (across different stylistic registers). Indeed, we communicate even intrapersonally – that is, with(in) ourselves. Friedrich Schleiermacher wrote in 1813 that translation is an indispensable mechanism enabling communication between people speaking different languages or dialects, between different social groups ('classes') and between compeers who differ in 'opinions and sensibility'; moreover, 'we must sometimes translate our own utterances after a certain time has passed, would we make them truly our own again' ([1813] 2012: 43).

Edward Sapir (1884–1939) considered means of communication in society and catalogued 'the primary communicative processes of society' (1949: 104–5). The most basic ones are language and gesture (in the broadest sense: a manipulation of any visible and movable part of the body). There are also two more communicative processes, according to Sapir: the imitation of overt behaviour – that is, doing what others do – and social suggestion of a way of acting, whether in a conformist or rebellious fashion. Sapir provides an example of churchgoing, which a person may initially do simply by overtly imitating others' behaviour. Later, the person may rebel against this socially imposed custom, yet even the rebellion is socially suggested in the sense that it is done against the background of the socially offered option. Sapir adds:

> The importance of the unformulated and unverbalized communications of society is so great that one who is not intuitively familiar with them is likely to be baffled by the significance of certain kinds of behavior, even if he is thoroughly aware of their external forms and of the verbal symbols that accompany them. *It is largely the function of the artist to make articulate these more subtle intentions of society.*
>
> (1949: 106, emphasis added)

Interpreters' and translators' work also includes mediating extraverbal as well as verbal types of communication with all their cultural subtlety (Poyatos 1997).

Sapir goes on to discuss three main classes of secondary techniques of facilitating primary communicative processes (1949: 106–7): (1) language transfers are facilitated by writing or Morse code, which allow us to speak where actual speaking is impossible (over space or time); (2) symbols, such as wigwagging, railroad lights, bugle calls in the army etc., help to communicate, avoiding among other things the verbosity and ambiguity of natural languages, in special technical situations; and (3) certain physical conditions and devices are created to enable or extend communication (railroad networks or telecommunication allow communication between people who otherwise would not be able to communicate).

Strangely, Sapir does not discuss translation as one of the ways to enable/facilitate communication, yet when he writes about the globalization of human communication through the development of the secondary techniques, he (in the very last paragraph) cannot avoid the problem of the diversity of world languages:

> The import of the obstacles [to communication] in the modern world is undoubtedly the great diversity of languages. The enormous amount of energy put into the task of translation implies a passionate desire to make as light of the language difficulty as possible. In the long run it seems almost unavoidable that the civilized world will adopt some one language of intercommunication, say English or Esperanto, which can be set aside for denotive purposes pure and simple.
>
> (1949: 109)

Translation is mentioned (only mentioned!) by Sapir, then, when he talks about the diversity of languages as an obstacle to the modern world's communication. It is probably because he nursed his hope for one international language that he did not consider translation among the means of communication, one of which it undoubtedly is.

Translation (in a broader sense) is an important means of communication both within a society and between societies. Intrasocietally, translation helps people communicate intralingually and coordinate their verbal and non-verbal behavior; translation is also a mechanism of transmitting culture to the individual via society, and culture is the very substance of what translation does in society for all of its individual members (society translates its cultural values to individuals in the process of enculturation). Intersocietally, translation is an indispensable means of crossing linguistic and cultural boundaries (more on this dimension of translation's cultural function shortly). Yet, paradoxically, until recently, translation was hardly ever factored into discussions of inter- and intercultural communication, at best only tangentially (Sapir's discussion is a typical example).

The importance of translation for culture works the other way round: culture is important for translation and for TIS. One of the major 'turns' which signified a departure from predominantly linguistic approaches to the study of translation is dubbed the 'cultural turn' (Bassnett and Lefevere 1990: 4). After the initial period of theorizing translation primarily as an interlingual transfer, it was realized that translation needed to be considered also in the context of intercultural exchange. A variety of cultural aspects of translation started being discussed, and culture gained the status of an important factor influencing translation.

Intercultural functioning of translation

Cultures, the realm of ideas and values, were understood early as hybrids. At the end of the nineteenth century, Adolf Bastian (1826–1905) insisted that cultures, like races, are never pure as they are products of not only their own evolution but also of diverse interactions with other cultures (Kuper 2000). Sometimes cultures learn from other cultures what they consider to be better practices or ideas for more efficiently adapting to their natural or sociopolitical environment. For instance, eighteenth-century Russia aspired to be one of the most influential European powers and borrowed from Western Europe in order to boost its economy and have a better army and navy (Tyulenev 2012). Yet the picture is more complex. First, it is not always cultures at less advanced stages of development that borrow. For example, European colonists of North America learned to cultivate corn from Native Americans (Lowie [1917] 1966: 67–8). Second, what is borrowed is not necessarily of immediate utilitarian significance as is the case with converting to adventitious creeds and religions or accepting foreign aesthetical values (adapting extraneous styles of clothes or trends in the arts). The cultural exchange, thus, is a complex network of mutual exchanges (Tyulenev 2012: 95–6, note 40).

Borrowing is omnipresent in the history of human cultures. Although cultures are stable, they are influenced sometimes quite radically by contacts with other cultures (Boas [1928] 2004: 132–67). Robert H. Lowie (1883–1957) analysed such phenomena as psychology, racial differences and geographical environment from the point of view of their responsibility for cultural change. He concluded that all ethnographic evidence points to contact of peoples as the principal stimulus of cultural evolution (1966: 66–97).

Alexander Goldenweiser (1880–1940) argued that since the dawn of human history, cultures develop through borrowings from one another:

> [It is a] universal fact that any local culture, however firmly rooted in its own physical environment, depends upon other cultures for numerous articles of need, use, or luxury, brought in through barter, war, or chance, as well as for ideas, customs, rituals, myths, and what not, which percolate from individual to individual, or from tribe to tribe, in the course of their historic contacts, whether regulated or not.
>
> (1937: 448)

If so, it is necessary to study the dynamics of cultural change (Boas [1938] 1965: 4) and, one must add, mechanisms of cultural exchange.

The latter aspect of the evolution of cultures is especially important for TIS, with its focus on translation as a mechanism of intercultural communication (more on this shortly). Generally, translation is underplayed in the humanities or reduced to interlingual transfers. For instance, Kroeber admitted that '[t]he speech faculty makes possible the transmission and perpetuation of culture', that 'language helps bind societies together' ([1923] 1948: 9) and that the role of translation is that of interlingual mediation.

TIS studies translation as a factor of both cultural evolution and intercultural exchange, especially from the 1970s onwards, when, from previously accentuating translation as a linguistic process, translation came to be considered principally in its cultural aspects. A translated text (source text) as well as a translating text (target text) came to be viewed as the verbalized products of their respective sociocultures. For instance, in *skopos* theory, elaborated by German translation scholars Katharina Reiss (1923–) and Hans Vermeer (1930–2010) (Reiss and Vermeer [1984] 2014), both the source and target texts were discussed in terms of their functions and corresponding stylistic characteristics. The *skopos* theorists claimed that translation had to be studied in the context of its intended function (or goal, hence the name *skopos*, which in Greek means 'goal') in the target culture. A business contract is a legal document and it is drawn up differently in different languages; it has to be translated in such a way that its legal function would be reflected, hence the translator should use the style and linguistic features (legal formulae and terminology) of the target culture rather than follow those of the original (see 'Current Contributions and Research' below).

Translation issues are realized to be of paramount importance in anthropology and ethnography as well, especially in their methodologies. Geertz wrote that ethnographic accounts inevitably carry 'signatures' of their authors (1988: 9), because ultimately the anthropologist is translating non-academic accounts and, often, foreign narratives into academic and Western idioms (ibid.: 130).

Sometimes ethnographic research is explicitly referred to as a study of the translation of culture. This is, for instance, the title of a collection of essays in honour of the eminent anthropologist E. E. Evans-Pritchard (1902–73) – *The Translation of Culture* (Beidelman 1971). For Evans-Pritchard himself, translation was primarily a process in which semantic problems were to be resolved (1965). Semantic problems, to be sure, are of primary concern for an ethnographer who constantly faces the challenge of explaining a culture expressed to him/her in one language by means of another language. Evans-Pritchard's and similar uses of the term 'translation' may be responsible for or, at least, indicative of why broadening the term 'translation' from interlingual exchange to intercultural transfer occurred: translating the semantics of cultural terms was reconsidered as translating the semantics of entire cultures. With the emergence of a discipline which sees its focus in translation as interlingual process – that is, TIS – the usages of the term 'translation' in broader senses, known as 'cultural translation', have been seen as endangering – hollowing out – the term 'translation' in the narrow sense of interlingual transfer (see review of criticisms in Sturge [1998] 2009). Discussing Homi K. Bhabha, Anthony Pym calls cultural translation 'translation without translations' ([2010] 2014: 144).

Yet in present-day anthropology, there have been attempts to take into account translation theories as developed in TIS (e.g. Rubel and Rosman 2003). Similarly, TIS borrows ideas from anthropology (and other social sciences) which help it theorize and practise translation in new ways. A prime example is the notion of thick translation. The entire ethnographic endeavour was called by Geertz 'thick description' ([1973] 1993). He borrowed the concept from Gilbert Ryle and applied it to ethnographic methodology, explaining that unlike 'thin description', which amounts to naming observed phenomena, 'thick description' interprets them. He gives an example of somebody contracting the eyelids on one of their eyes (this is a thin description tantamount to naming the action). A thick description would be saying that the person experiences an involuntary twitch or is signalling something (winking). Thick descriptions are the object of ethnography; it studies

> a stratified hierarchy of meaningful structures in terms of which twitches, winks [. . .] are produced, perceived, and interpreted, and without which they would not [. . .] in fact exist, no matter what anyone did or didn't do with his eyelids.
> (Geertz [1973] 1993: 7)

This interpretive rendering of phenomena of one culture into another was borrowed by translation scholars, especially those championing postcolonial approaches. In his famous article 'Thick Translation', originally published in 1993, Kwame Anthony Appiah, writing about translation in academic environments where students are introduced to literary works of different peoples and different periods, argued:

> A thick description of the context of literary production, a translation that draws on and creates that sort of understanding, meets the need to challenge ourselves and our

students to go further, to undertake the harder project of a genuinely informed respect for others.

([1993] 2012: 341)

The notion of thick translation was later applied to theorizing translation in similar postcolonial contexts (e.g. Cheung 2007) and in translating 'the other', understood in a more generalized inclusive fashion (e.g. in discussing feminist translation, Wolf 2003).

Current contributions and research

Culture as a notion has played an important role in the evolution of TIS. Initially, TIS almost entirely concentrated on studying linguistic properties of translation; translation was mostly defined as an interlingual transfer. Later, it was realized that translation was much more than toggling between words and phrases of one language and another. Words represent cultures. One of the major schools of thought of the 1970s and 80s which insisted on broader conceptualizations of translation as an intercultural phenomenon was the above-mentioned translation functionalism developed in Germany, the key representatives being Reiss, Vermeer, Justa Holz-Mänttärri and Christiane Nord. The functionalists emphasized translation as a means of communication, and texts were viewed in terms of their functions in source and target sociocultural contexts. The functionalists saw translation as an intercultural activity which was supposed to adapt source texts to new cultural environments, if necessary, modifying them quite radically. Language was seen as an instrument of expressing meanings. The translator was viewed as an expert in intercultural communication.

Translation was also considered against the cultural backdrop of its production in polysystem theory, elaborated originally by Itamar Even-Zohar and his followers in Tel Aviv, Israel. This school developed ideas of Russian formalism which theorized national literary systems as complex structures, including not only 'high' literature but also 'lower', or less sophisticated, literary genres (popular, children's literature etc.). All these literary genres were considered as systems (that is, networks of literary products written according to specific conventions, e.g. Bildungsroman, detective novel) within the entire national literary polysystem, or a system of systems (*poly-* meaning *multi-*).

In literary studies, translations were one of the less noticeable and less studied forms of national literary systems. Yet, as was shown by the scholars of the Tel Aviv School and, later, by a number of followers in the Low Countries (hence, another name of this approach: Tel Aviv–Leuven School), translation can be an important system in the national literary polysystem. In some periods, translation moves centre stage in the national polysystem; sometimes, it can be less influential, yet it is always there and contributes to the dynamic of the overall polysystem.

Another important tenet of the Tel Aviv–Leuven School is that translation is a fact of the commissioning (mostly, target) culture. It follows that translation should be studied taking into consideration the sociocultural backdrop of the commissioning culture, which may manipulate a given source text while translating it. Hence, another name of the school – the 'manipulation' school (see the title of an important collection of papers – *The Manipulation of Literature: Studies in Literary Translation*, Hermans 1985).

It will be noted that in the cultural turn, the term 'culture' was mostly (but not always) understood in sense (3) above. For instance, in their introduction to an influential collection of essays, *Translation, History and Culture*, Susan Bassnett and André Lefevere saw the goal of their volume as 'trying to rethink the role of translation in literary studies' (1990: 1).

Yet a broader understanding of the term 'culture' (senses (6) and (7): culture as a way of life of a society and culture as a domain of ideas and, hence, ideologies) began to influence TIS research. That is why in Bassnett and Lefevere's collection, we find contributions on feminist and postcolonial issues of translation.

This view of translation as part and parcel of the commissioning culture led to a next, logical step – taking into consideration a number of issues which were seen as socially determined. The French-Canadian translation scholar Annie Brisset was among the pioneers of what she termed the sociocritical approach to the study of translation. She proceeded from the premise that translation as a discursive act is 'fundamentally bound to the time and place of its realization' ([1990] 1996: 3). It is, therefore, important, while examining and assessing a translation, to take into account the institutional constraints that influence(d) the translation (ibid.: 4).

The cultural turn blossomed into a rich area of research into various cultural influences on translation and translation's influences on culture. Applications of the principles of the critical discourse analysis (Mason 2003) considered the interaction of language and ideology in intercultural communication. In the wake of postcolonialist approaches in the humanities, translation was studied as practised at the crossroads where the colonizer met the colonized. It was perhaps one of the major paradigms of analysis which debunked the hitherto widespread naïve view of translation as a bridge-builder. In the colonialist contexts, as it was shown, translation could be used by one culture to dominate another (Cheyfitz 1991). Yet translation could be used to turn the tables and resist various forms of colonialism or other forms of ideological subjugation (Spivak 1993: 179–200).

Main research methods

One of the main achievements of the cultural turn in TIS was opening possibilities for descriptive, rather than prescriptive, research. This development was primarily caused by turning to historiographical research into translation. The main purpose of previous theorizations of translation was working out a set of rules or principles which had to be observed by translators or by automatic translation programmes (in machine translation) in order to produce translations of a required quality. Obviously, when one speaks of translation as it was practised or theorized in past periods, the main goal was to describe what actually happened rather than what should have happened.

Methodologically, the new approach required radical changes. Notably, the notion of equivalence came to be reconsidered or completely renounced. Translation, as it turned out, was not always about achieving equivalence or at least not equivalence understood narrowly as linguistic correspondence of units of the source text with units of the target text. Outside translator training environments where linguistics-based prescriptivism reigns supreme (Venuti 2012: 391), the methodology of the study of translation shifted from comparison of a source text with its renderings into other languages to attempts to understand how a particular rendering of the source text was/is influenced by the target culture from the moment of the selection of the source text (the questions asked are: who selected it and why?) through the process of translation (who translated it and how? What determined the choice of the translator(s)? According to what principles, whether verbally formulated or implied, was the translation carried out?) to the reception of the target text in the target culture.

This type of methodology paved the way to more socioculturally contextualized approaches to studying translation. Translation praxis and theory have been studied in their natural social 'habitat'. Methodologically, this means that every instance of translation and every translating agent or an agent influencing the translation process (e.g. the commissioner, publisher, editor etc.) are to be viewed sociologically. Methods may be quantitative – for example, translation flows are studied (Casanova 2002; Heilbron 1999). It will be noted that qualitative methods are as important, yet they are applied in such a fashion that individual cases are examined as part of a larger sociocultural picture. This larger picture includes the place translated texts occupy in a particular culture (Even-Zohar 1990; Bassnett and Lefevere 1990); or translation is viewed as an interface of dominated and dominating cultures (Israel 2006); or the roles that translation plays in realizing various cultural policies, such as being a factor enriching the target culture (Berman 1984), helping to form a cultural identity (Brisset [1990] 1996; Gentzler 2008) or cultural gatekeeping, participating in different forms of censorship (Merkle 2010), are examined.

Recommendations for practice

The main pitfall in discussing cultural aspects of translation has so far been a largely commonsensical understanding of the notion of culture leading to uncritical applications of the term. Therefore, the translation student has to define the notion of culture whenever embarking on a project focusing on cultural (in whichever meaning of the term) aspects of translation/interpreting.

It should also be remembered that cultural aspects are always related to collectivities. It is necessary, therefore, if the focus of research is on culture, to consider case studies or individual translators and translations as typical or atypical against the background of the cultures which constitute their backdrop (see 'Main Research Methods').

Future directions

Among the possible future directions of culturological research into translation, the following can be suggested. It is productive to speak about translation in the context of the travelling of ideas between cultures (sense (4)). Virtually any case of interlingual translation is an instance of the exchange of ideas. There have been attempts to identify possible scenarios (Even-Zohar 1990: 47; Tyulenev 2014: 36–40). More research is needed to develop these models.

Translation plays an important part in creating and appreciating different nations' contributions to world culture (see sense (5) above). There have been projects which focused on translation as a major mechanism of collecting humanity's cultural treasury, such Goethe's ideas about *Weltliteratur* [world literature] (Berman 1984: 87–110), but this role of translation so far remains understudied.

Intralingual translation between a national culture and its subcultures is yet another area for research. Cultures as understood on a large scale (sense (4)) can be divided into smaller cultures or subcultures. For instance, Soviet culture had many subcultures and each social class can be seen as having its own culture – for example, the intelligentsia or the working class. Translation must play a role in mediating between cultures and their subcultures and between one subculture and other subcultures. What this role may be is still to be investigated.

As applied to translation one could speak of a professional culture of translation which is formed collectively by all professional translators worldwide, translation theorists and academic translator training programmes, which become especially influential with the internationalization of student populations in virtually all regions of the world, student and academic exchange programmes etc. Yet one can speak of national translation subcultures and translation amateur subcultures (Nord 1991). What are the relations between the translation culture, national translation (sub)cultures and amateur translation (sub)cultures?

Translation can and should be studied as a mechanism of social enculturation (individual <> society <> culture: sense (7) above). Such direction of research invites us to define translation in a broader sense – as not only interlingual but also intralingual (within one and the same language) and intersemiotic (between various media).

Translation and a new techno-human culture is a nascent domain of research. In 1958, Felix M. Keesing wrote that 'the *machine age* or *industrial revolution* of modern times certainly must be placed as a "second" great period of cultural dynamics' (1958: 103). He suggested calling this new 'world-wide phase of cultural growth "modern civilization" by contrast with the earlier "civilization", or "Western civilization"' with its 'strong fresh tendency which is culturally centripetal, bringing peoples and cultures at the ends of the earth into contact' (1958: 104). To appreciate translation's place in the modern civilization, TIS needs to go beyond its preoccupation with the interlingual type of translation, mostly limited to regional and bilingual case studies. A promising direction of research is examining translation's behaviour in multilingual, multicultural and multisemiotic environments and processes. A step towards this goal is an attempt to establish a comparative branch within TIS which will help to overcome various forms of its present-day compartmentalization and centrifugal tendencies (Tyulenev and Zheng 2017).

Related topics

Current trends in philosophy and translation; context and pragmatics; meaning; the translation of philosophical texts; translating feminist philosophers; machine translation; literary translation; philosophy of translation.

Further reading

Kuper, A. (2000) *Culture: The Anthropologists' Account*, Cambridge, MA and London: Harvard University Press. (A thorough study of the evolution of the term 'culture' and its meanings in several traditions.)

Jenks, C. (2005) *Culture* [second edition], London and New York: Routledge. (A short yet comprehensive and updated introduction to the notion of culture.)

Bassnett, S. and A. Lefevere (eds) (1990) *Translation, History and Culture*, London: Cassell. (A foundational text of the cultural turn in TIS.)

References

Albrow, M. (1999) *Sociology: The Basics*, London and New York: Routledge.
Appiah, K. A. [1993] (2012) 'Thick Translation', *Callaloo*, 16: 808–19. (A reprint in Venuti 2012, 331–43).
Arnold, M. [1869] (1932) *Culture and Anarchy*, Cambridge: Cambridge University Press.
Baker, M. (ed) (2010) *Critical Readings in Translation Studies*, London and New York: Routledge.
Bassnett, S. and A. Lefevere (eds) (1990) *Translation, History and Culture*, London: Cassell.
Beidelman, T. O. (ed) (1971) *The Translation of Culture*, London: Routledge.
Benedict, R. [1934] (1989) *Patterns of Culture*, Boston: Houghton Mifflin Company.
Berman, A. (1984) *L'épreuve de l'étranger. Culture et traduction dans l'Allemagne romantique*, Paris: Gallimard.
Boas, F. (ed) [1938] (1965) *General Anthropology*, Boston: D. C. Heath and Company.
Boas, F. (1989) 'Introduction', in Benedict, xix–xxi.
Boas, F. [1928] (2004) *Anthropology and Modern Life*, New Brunswick and London: Transaction Publishers.

Brisset, A. [1990] (1996) *A Sociocritique of Translation: Theatre and Alterity in Quebec, 1968–1988*, translated by Rosalind Gill and Roger Gannon, Toronto: University of Toronto Press.

Casanova, P. (2002) 'Consécration et accumulation de capital littéraire: La traduction comme échange inégal', *Actes de la recherche en sciences sociales*, 144: 7–20. (An English translation in Baker 2010, 287–303.)

Cheung, M. (2007) 'On Thick Translation as a Mode of Cultural Representation', in D. Kenny and R. Kyongjoo (eds), *Across Boundaries: International Perspectives on Translation Studies*, Seoul: Sookmyung Women's University, 22–36.

Cheyfitz, E. (1991) *The Poetics of Imperialism: Translation and Colonization from the Tempest to Tarzan*, New York and London: Oxford University Press.

Doorslaer, L. van, P. Flynn and J. Leerssen (eds) (2016) *Interconnecting Translation Studies and Imagology*, Amsterdam and Philadelphia: John Benjamins.

Evans-Pritchard, E. E. (1965) *Theories of Primitive Religion*, London: Oxford University Press.

Even-Zohar, I. (ed) (1990) 'Polysystem Studies', special issue, *Poetics Today*, 11, 1.

Featherstone, M. (ed) (1996) *Global Culture: Nationalism, Globalization and Modernity*, London: SAGE Publications.

Geertz, C. (1988) *Works and Lives: The Anthropologist as Author*, Stanford, CA: Stanford University Press.

Geertz, C. [1973] (1993) *The Interpretation of Cultures*, London: Fontana Press.

Gentzler, E. (2008) *Translation and Identity in the Americas: New Directions in Translation Theory*, London and New York: Routledge.

Goldenweiser, A. (1937) *Anthropology: An Introduction to Primitive Culture*, London: George G. Harrap & Co. Ltd.

Habermas, J. [1970] (1988) *On the Logic of the Social Sciences*, translated by S. W. Nicholsen and J. A. Stark, Cambridge, MA: MIT Press.

Heilbron, J. (1999) 'Towards a Sociology of Translation: Book Translations as a Cultural World System', *European Journal of Social Theory*, 2, 4: 195–212. (Reprint in Baker 2010, 306–16.)

Hermans, T. (ed) (1985) *The Manipulation of Literature: Studies in Literary Translation*, London: Croom Helm.

Inkeles, A. (1964) *What Is Sociology? An Introduction to the Discipline and Profession*, Englewood Cliffs, NJ: Prentice-Hall.

Israel, H. (2006) 'Translating the Bible in Nineteenth Century India', in T. Hermans (ed), *Translating Others*, Vol. 2, Manchester: St. Jerome, 441–59. (Reprint in Baker 2010, 176–90.)

Jakobson, R. [1959] (2012) 'On Linguistic Aspects of Translation,' in L. Venuti (ed) *The Translation Studies Reader* [third edition], London and New York: Routledge, 126–31.

Keesing, F. M. (1958) *Cultural Anthropology: The Science of Custom*, New York: Rinehart & Company, Inc.

Kluckhohn, C. (1949) *Mirror for Man: The Relation of Anthropology to Modern Life*, New York: Whittlesey House.

Kroeber, A. L. [1923] (1948) *Anthropology: Race, Language, Culture, Psychology, Prehistory*, London: George G. Harrap & Co. Ltd.

Kroeber, A. L. and C. Kluckhohn (1952) *Culture: A Critical Review of Concepts and Definitions*, Cambridge, MA: Published by the Museum.

Kuper, A. (2000) *Culture: The Anthropologists' Account* [Kindle edition], Cambridge, MA and London: Harvard University Press.

Leerssen, J. (n/d) www.imagologica.eu/ (accessed 8 April, 2016).

Levefere, A. (ed) (1992) *Translation/History/Culture: A Sourcebook*, London and New York: Routledge.

Lowie, R. [1917] (1966) *Culture and Ethnology*, New York and London: Basic Books, Inc.

Malinowski, B. (1944) *A Scientific Theory of Culture and Other Essays*, Chapel Hill, NC: University of North Carolina Press.

Mason, I. (2003) 'Text Parameters in Translation: Transitivity and Institutional Cultures', in E. Hajicova, P. Sgall, Z. Jettmarova, A. Rothkegel and D. Rothfuß-Bastian. (eds), *Textologie und Translation*

(Jahrbuch Übersetzen und Dolmetschen 4/2), Tübingen: Narr, 175–88. (Reprinted in Venuti 2012, 399–410.)
Merkle, D. (ed) (2010) 'Censorship and Translation within and beyond the Western World', special issue, *TTR*, 23, 2.
Nord, C. (1991) 'Scopos, Loyalty, and Translational Conventions', *Target*, 3, 1: 91–109.
Pagel, M. (2012) *Wired for Culture: The Natural History of Human Cooperation*, London: Allen Lane and Penguin Books.
Parsons, T. [1951] (1959) *The Social System*, Glencoe, IL: The Free Press.
Poyatos, F. (ed) (1997) *Non-Verbal Communication and Translation: New Perspectives and Challenges in Literature, Interpretation and the Media*, Amsterdam and Philadelphia: John Benjamins.
Pym, A. [2010] (2014) *Exploring Translation Theories*, London and New York: Routledge.
Ray, J. (2008) *The Rosetta Stone and the Rebirth of Ancient Egypt*, London: Profile Books.
Reiss, K. and H. J. Vermeer [1984] (2014) *Towards a General Theory of Translational Action: Skopos Theory Explained*, translated by C. Nord and M. Dudenhöfer, London and New York: Routledge.
Rubel, P. G. and A. Rosman (eds) (2003) *Translating Cultures: Perspectives on Translation and Anthropology*, Oxford and New York: Berg.
Said, E. W. (1994) *Culture and Imperialism*, London: Vintage Books.
Sapir, E. (1949) *Selected Writings of Edward Sapir in Language, Culture, and Personality*, ed. by David G. Mandelbaum, London: Cambridge University Press.
Schleiermacher, F. [1813] (2012) 'On the Different Methods of Translating', translated by S. Bernofsky, in L. Venuti, 43–63.
Scott, J. (2011) *Conceptualising the Social World: Principles of Sociological Analysis*, Cambridge: Cambridge University Press.
Spivak, G. (1993) *Outside in the Teaching Machine*, London and New York: Routledge. (Reprint in Venuti 2012, 312–30.)
Sturge, K. [1998] (2009) 'Cultural Translation', in M. Baker and G. Saldanha (eds), *Routledge Encyclopedia of Translation Studies* [Kindle edition], London and New York: Routledge.
Tylor, E. (1871) *Primitive Culture: Researches into the Development of Mythology, Philosophy, Religion, Art, and Custom*, Vol. 1, London: Murray, Albemarle Street.
Tyulenev, S. (2012) *Translation and the Westernization of Eighteenth-Century Russia: A Social-Systemic Perspective*, Berlin: Frank & Timme.
Tyulenev, S. (2014) *Translation and Society: An Introduction*, London and New York: Routledge.
Tyulenev, S. and B. Zheng (eds) (2017) 'Towards Comparative Translation Studies', special issue, *Translation and Interpreting Studies*, 12, 2.
Venuti, L. (ed) (2012) *The Translation Studies Reader*, London and New York: Routledge.
Wagner, R. [1975] (1981) *The Invention of Culture*, Chicago and London: University of Chicago Press.
Wallerstein, I. (2004) *World-Systems Analysis: An Introduction*, Durham, NC: Duke University Press.
WHC (2015) http://whc.unesco.org/en/guidelines/ (accessed 15 January, 2016).
Wolf, M. (2003) 'Feminist Thick Translation: A Challenge to the Formation of Feminist Cultural Identity?', *Tradução e Comunicação*, 12: 115–31.
Wundt, W. [1912] (1916) *Elements of Folk Psychology: Outlines of a Psychological History of the Development of Mankind*, translated by E. Leroy Schaub, London: George Allen and Unwin.

14
Equivalence

Alice Leal

14.1 Introduction

The issue of equivalence amongst languages has enjoyed different statuses in translation studies (TS) since it emerged in the 1950s – most notoriously in Roman Jakobson's and Jean-Paul Vinay and Jean Darbelnet's works – as one of the cornerstones of translation practice, translator training and translation criticism (Snell-Hornby 1988: 18–19; Windle and Pym 2011: 16; Leal 2012: 39). Numerous intricate equivalence typologies appeared in the following decades in an attempt to systematise the concept and produce a tool to assist practising translators, train aspiring translators and assess translation quality. Some of the most renowned examples include Eugene Nida's, Werner Koller's and Otto Kade's typologies (Leal 2012: 41–2).

Equivalence remained in the spotlight at least until the paradigm shift of the early 1980s, whereby Hans Vermeer and Katharina Reiß's functionalist approach moved the focus away from equivalence between source and target texts to the *skopos* of the translation – that is, the purpose that it was intended to fulfil in the target culture. Referring to Vermeer's *skopos* theory, Mary Snell-Hornby explains that

> [w]ith this approach a translation is seen in terms of how it serves its intended purpose, and the concept of translation, when set against the former criterion of source-language (SL) equivalence, is more differentiated and indeed closer to the realities of translation practice.
>
> (Snell-Hornby 2006: 53)

Today, equivalence is either seen sceptically, as the unachievable goal responsible for the negativity associated with translation, or used as a blanket concept that simply describes an – however unrealistic – ideal relationship between source and target texts (Leal 2012: 39, 43–4).

Lying beneath the surface of these different outlooks on equivalence are different notions of language, which in turn are largely taken for granted in the works where they emerge. Indeed, if we look at some of the equivalence typologies mentioned above, little is said about the functioning of language itself; instead, equivalence is presented almost as a natural property shared by all languages. Steiner (1998: 290) reminds us that 'theory of translation' has always treated the issues of 'the nature of the relations between "word" and "sense" (...) as trivial or resolved or of another jurisdiction'. This, he adds, does not necessarily amount to TS being negligent or unsophisticated. Rather, a 'mature' theory of translation would *'presum[e]* a systematic theory of language (...), [b]ut the fact remains that we have no such theory of language' (1998: 294).

However, when we look to philosophy of language (PL) to understand how the concept of equivalence amongst languages may have developed from antiquity until today, the opposite seems to apply. In other words, with a few exceptions, numerous thinkers have dedicated themselves to explaining the functioning of language but not to proving whether there can be equivalence amongst languages. Therefore in this chapter we will concentrate on several all-time notions of language in PL to infer consequences as far as equivalence is concerned. In order to achieve this, the distinction made by Steiner in *After Babel: Aspects of Language and Translation* (1998) between so-called universalist and relativist theories of language will be of utmost importance.

For Steiner (1998: 76–7), in PL there have been 'two radically opposed points of view', namely 'one [which] declares that the underlying structure of language is universal and common to all men' and one which 'holds that universal deep structures are either fathomless to logical and psychological investigation or of an order so abstract, so generalized as to be well-nigh trivial': hence a universalist and a monadist or relativist matrix respectively. For universalists, 'translation is realizable precisely because those deep-seated universals, genetic, historical, social, from which all grammars derive can be located and recognized as operative in every human idiom, however singular and bizarre its superficial forms' (1998: 77). Monadists or relativists, in turn, understand translation as a 'convention of approximate analogies, a rough-cast similitude' (1998: 77). Steiner stresses that neither of these matrices exist in an entirely pure form; most theories of language will, to some degree, present traces of both simultaneously (1998: 77–78).

How can we use Steiner's dichotomy to understand equivalence amongst languages? If we took universalism and monadism or relativism (henceforth simply 'relativism') as two extreme, self-excluding poles, universalism would presuppose a notion of language that allows for perfect one-to-one equivalence – not only between two languages or between sign and thing but, firstly and more importantly, between language and the world (Ricoeur 2006: 17). There would be a common, public source of meaning shared by all natural tongues, so words and sentences from a given language A and a given language B that led to the same meanings would be equivalent. 'Pure relativists' in turn would deny the existence of a common, stable source of meaning; rather, meaning would be generated in language use and would vary so dramatically from language to language that equivalence would not only be impossible but also irrelevant.

For the sake of the argument, matters have been generalised in the previous paragraph. Yet, as Steiner stresses, the dichotomy universalism versus relativism is by no means watertight and both tendencies are present in most theories of language *at once*. Indeed, any postmodern reflection is aware of the fact that dichotomies in the sense of self-excluding poles are a fallacy. The objective here is thus to look into different theories of language in terms of traces, symptoms of these universalist and relativist matrices.

It will become clear that predominantly universalist theories tend to strive to find or to create a stable, reliable source of meaning. In other words, they aim to unlock the mystery of the functioning of language, to find its lost origin, or to create a logical system, an ideal language to rid natural tongues of their elusive character. The search for this 'lost link' can ultimately be understood as the search for objective translatability and equivalence amongst languages (Steiner 1998: 251–2, 318). For Jacques Derrida (1997: 3), these approaches – in all their diversity – can be labelled 'logocentric', mostly because they 'assig[n] the origin of truth in general to the logos'. Strict equivalence ineluctably entails some form of logocentrism (and it has taken multiple forms, as we will see in the next sections).

Similarly to Steiner, Paul Ricoeur sees the paradox of human language as follows. Our 'universal ability [is] contradicted by its fragmented, scattered and disorganised execution', which leaves us with two 'paralysing alternatives', namely 'the diversity of languages' is such that untranslatability ensues or languages share a 'common fund', which puts us either on the '*original*' or on the '*universal* language' tracks (2006: 12). These 'paralysing alternatives' will permeate this chapter; we shall return to their 'paralysing' character in Section 6 below.

One last remark before we embark on this journey. This chronological overview of different notions of language – and their respective consequences for equivalence – devised by various Western thinkers should ultimately be a source of insight for TS. As Wilson (2016: 6) puts it, '[t]o turn to a discipline outside one's own is frequently seen as a vital strategy for theorists in the humanities'. And the link with philosophy should go beyond the ones suggested by Pym (2007: 24), namely (1) that translation has been used as a metaphor by philosophers; (2) that we make use of philosophical discourse in our discourse on translation; and (3) that the translation of philosophical texts is a key subject in both disciplines. The link proposed here, following Derrida's argument below, is one of strict dependence – translation is philosophy and philosophy is translation:

> What does the philosopher say when he is being a philosopher? He says: What matters is truth or meaning, and since meaning is before or beyond language, it follows that it is translatable. (...) The origin of philosophy is translation or the thesis of translatability, so that wherever translation in this sense has failed, it is nothing less than philosophy that finds itself defeated.
>
> (Derrida 1985: 120)

14.2 The classical paradigm: language as representation and the legacy left for Saussure

The idea of an all-embracing *logos* as the source of human language goes back to Heraclitus and Parmenides (Braun 1996: 5–8; Hoffmann 2003: 27). For them, language is *logos*, as the place where word and reality represent each other univocally. The *logos* remains constant and is an irrevocable part of our being, thanks to which we are able first to think and then to speak (Braun 1996: 7). Speech is the direct representation of thought; the former is secondary, derivative of the latter. The function of language is thus reduced to one of reference, of representation of reality. What was in the spotlight, then, was not language but the *logos*, the source of and condition for the existence of language (Braun 1996: 5).

Plato confirms, especially in his *Cratylus* (fourth century BC), this notion of language as a mere representation tool. However, he admits that language does not reflect reality perfectly; it is not fully faithful to reality and hence should not to be trusted – so much so that, for him, knowledge lies outside the realm of language: it precedes language (Partee 1972: 114). Plato does not seem to come to a definite conclusion as to whether language obtains its meaning through nature or through convention, though he does appear to suggest that 'the correctness of names takes precedence over custom' (Partee 1972: 117; Plato 1921: 386, 435). This 'correctness' is to be found in the natural origin of language – that is, etymology – in the 'name-givers', who named everything according to nature (Plato 1921: 411a, 436c). Further, according to Partee (1972: 122), Plato believes that 'present language seems to be a corruption of an original fidelity to nature' and that '[n]ames have been so twisted that the original language might appear to be a barbarous tongue to present speakers' (Plato 1921: 397). As Partee (1972: 132) explains, '[Plato] admits that custom reigns over certain provinces of language' but, at the same time, 'refuses to dignify any human convention as a universal'.

Also in Plato's *Sophist*, language is understood as an imitation of the world; it is 'truth-knowing and truth-speaking' (Nye 1998: 3). In this work, Plato does not propose a clear-cut distinction between speech and thought but, rather, asserts – very much like his predecessors – that speech is the representation of thought, that thought is the 'conversation of the soul with itself' (Plato 1921 263e). Unlike his predecessors, however, he stresses that language and *logos* are not the same (Braun 1996: 9); instead, he associates the *logos* either with speech or with an idea of a 'gathering of elements', of composition, such as the spelling of a word (Hoffmann 2003: 29).

Aristotle develops Plato further and shifts the focus further away from the *logos*. Particularly in his *De Interpretatione*, he argues that what remains constant and is the same for all individuals are prelinguistic, mental impressions in our minds. Further, these impressions correspond to reality in a natural way and hence guarantee the validity and safe recovery of meaning (Braun 1996: 10; Modrak 2001: 20–1). Signs in turn do not refer directly to reality but to these mental impressions, and the equivalence between both is established conventionally, traditionally (Braun 1996: 10–11; Modrak 2001: 13–14). In other words, spoken words are like 'affections of the soul', and these affections match things in the world; there is a 'likeness' between meaning and reality (Modrak 2001: 13). Aristotle explains that 'spoken sounds are symbols of affections in the soul, and written marks symbols of spoken sounds' (Aristotle [1963] 2002: 16a3), confirming the hierarchy of thought–speech–writing. Moreover, coming closer to the question of equivalence, Aristotle maintains that

> just as written letters are not the same for all humans neither are spoken words. But what these are in the first place signs of – affections of the soul – are the same for all; and what these affections are likenesses of – actual things – are also the same.
> (Aristotle [1963] 2002: 16a3)

This quotation summarises not only Aristotle's theory of language but also the concept of language generally attributed to the classical paradigm.

The classical paradigm is hence commonly associated with the idea that thought comes first and is independent from language, whereas language is secondary, derivative of thought. Also, written words are secondary to spoken words. Understandably, this notion of language tends to be dismissed as simplistic and superficial. However, newer readings, particularly of Aristotle's works, such as the one proposed by Deborah K. W. Modrak (2001), reveal that there are significantly more intricacies to his theory of language than meet the eye. By looking at his entire oeuvre and scrutinising numerous cognitive aspects of his reflections on language, she argues, for instance, that these 'affections of the soul' can be understood both as universal and individual (Modrak 2001: 248). In other words, these sensory representations that we have in our minds, however individual, carry universal content in them, and this universal content allows communication to take place. So in Steiner's vein, we could claim that even Aristotle's universalism was not fully without relativism.

Traditionally, however, these classical theories of language are referential and universal. What varies is the source of universalism – the stable source from which meaning stems and which remains constant across all languages. Whereas Heraclitus and Parmenides focused on the *logos*, Plato found the source of meaning in etymology and in the essence, the nature of things – according to which the givers of names named everything in the world. Aristotle emphasised the importance of the mental representations of the world that inhabit our minds, the 'affections of the soul', as he called them, which in turn represent reality in our minds.

We could therefore argue that within the classical paradigm, truly understanding an utterance or written text entailed searching for this stable source of meaning – be it the *logos*, the essence and nature of words, or the mental representations of things in the world. It entailed, in other words, finding equivalence between the source of meaning – *outside language* – and the spoken and then the written word. Let us not overlook the importance of this 'outside language', for language was seen then as a mere tool for representation. In effect, in the *Cratylus* (Plato 1921: 439b) we read that '[h]ow realities are to be learned or discovered is perhaps too great a question for you or me to determine; but (...) they are to be learned and sought for, not from names but much better through themselves than through names'.

If we embrace Steiner's thesis that reading and speaking in general are acts of translation (1998: 49–50), it is easy to extend this notion of equivalence inside a single language to interlingual translation. Indeed, in Partee's view, Plato believed that '[m]inor differences in sounds and syllables count for little; the languages of different countries point to a common truth'; also, '[i]f the meaning or essence remains the same, we can alter freely a few syllables or individual sounds' (Partee 1972: 120, 122).

Many have claimed that the belief in equivalence in TS stems from the classical paradigm – particularly from the traces of the classical paradigm that remained in Saussure's structuralism (Derrida 1997: 29–44; Rodrigues 1999: 186; Lages 2007: 211; Leal 2014: 81–94). On the one hand, Saussure did break away from the classical tradition of direct association between a word and the corresponding perception of reality in the world by emphasising that languages are not mere lists of terms, and that there is no reality, no pre-established ideas before and outside language. In other words, Saussure claimed that there is no essence beyond words governing them, and that each language articulates its own meanings. On the other hand, he did keep the watertight oppositions signifier–signified and speech–writing, overvaluing speech and everything that binds a sign to its sound (Derrida 1997: 30–44; Leal 2014: 87–9). Again, to return to Steiner, universalism and relativism go hand in hand, but because of the abovementioned dichotomies that remained the cornerstones of Saussure's theory of language, he tends to be associated with universal, transcendental meanings. Furthermore, it seems to have been this notion of sign and language that underpinned the concept of equivalence as it emerged in TS in the mid twentieth century. Let us now look into different reactions to the classical paradigm in order to understand its legacy and its effect on current notions of language and equivalence.

14.3 Reactions to the classical paradigm: an important interstice from Isocrates to Humboldt

For many contemporary thinkers, it makes little sense to speak of thorough theories of language or of a philosophy of language before the nineteenth century. In effect, numerous anthologies in PL open with Gottlob Frege – see, for instance, Soames (2010) and Lee (2011). However, this does not mean that there is a hiatus as far as reflection on language and our discussion on equivalence here are concerned. Nye (1998), for example, includes excerpts by Jean-Jacques Rousseau and John Locke in her anthology before moving on to Frege. Braun (1996) goes further and underlines the important role played by Isocrates, Cicero, William of

Ockham, Jakob Böhme, Thomas Hobbes, Francis Bacon, John Locke, Gottfried W. Leibniz, Giambattista Vico, George Berkeley, David Hume, Johann G. Hamann, Johann G. Herder and Wilhelm von Humboldt in developing a philosophy of language. For Braun (1996: 12), there were two main streams of reaction to the classical paradigm, namely nominalism (Ockham, Bacon, Hobbes, Locke and later Berkeley and Hume) and rationalism (especially Leibniz).

In short, nominalist thinkers associated language with mental, private ideas and went against the classical paradigm by defending three theses: (1) that signs do not represent things in themselves but, rather, these ideas that we have of the world; (2) that the same signs do not necessarily lead back to the same private ideas in two different people or situations; and (3) that language does not reduce to the *logos* and is not secondary to it (Braun 1996: 11–12). Discussing Locke, Nye (1998: 3–4) explains that 'there are no metaphysical forms, only ideas in individuals' minds', and that it is thanks to Locke that we begin to ask questions such as: 'if the choice of a sign is conventional and if ideas are private entities accessible only to the person who has them, how is common meaning possible?'; and 'does language create reality, or does language reflect reality?' (Locke 1998: 18–19). Locke does not propose a way out of this dilemma, but the denial of metaphysical forms, of a stable and external source of meaning, obviously puts into question the 'classical' notion of equivalence discussed in the previous section as relativism starts to emerge. Nevertheless, let us not forget that 'nominalism' comprises widely different approaches. Bacon's, for example, clearly had more universal aspirations than Locke's (Steiner 1998: 208). What we should bear in mind here is that nominalism sows the seed of relativism in that it 'is a protest against any sort of metaphysics' (Rorty 2000: 23).

In contrast to nominalist thinkers, rationalist thinkers see language as a means to perception – that is, language is necessary for one to be able to think and to perceive the world. Leibniz claims that language is intersubjective (and communication is possible) because beneath the surface of every tongue lies a universal language, which in turn follows strict logical-mathematical principles, the so-called *characteristica universalis* [universal characteristic] (Steiner 1998: 73; Braun 1996: 14). Therefore with rationalism we go back to the classical paradigm in terms of a predominantly referential function of language. Leibniz nonetheless goes further than his predecessors and devises the *characteristica universalis* as well as a *scientia generalis* [universal science], whereby the latter represents universal knowledge (Braun 1996: 15). As far as equivalence is concerned, this return to the classical paradigm not only reaffirms the possibility of perfect equivalence amongst languages, but it also lends equivalence, even if only aspiringly, a scientific character. With the reflections of rationalist thinkers, the dreams both of a universal language and of a rigid and strictly logical way to systematise natural languages are born. At the same time, as Steiner (1998: 78) reminds us, Leibniz need not be exclusively associated with the universalist matrix as he stresses that language is 'not the vehicle of thought but its determining medium', and that tongues 'differ as profoundly as nations do'. In other words, in his quest to systematise the universal semantic system inherent to every tongue and hence establish the source of perfect equivalence amongst all natural languages, he was aware of the unique character of each language – a glimpse of the relativist matrix that casts a shadow over the possibility of equivalence.

Going back to Braun's list of thinkers who left their imprint on PL, the reader will have noticed that a few do not belong to either nominalism or rationalism. Braun stresses that they – Isocrates, Cicero, Böhme, Vico, Hamann, Herder and Humboldt – all went against the classical notion of language, each in their own way. Due to space constraints, we cannot take a closer look at these thinkers' theories, but let us make a few considerations as far as equivalence is concerned.

Isocrates and Cicero go against the classical paradigm in that they emphasise that language is not static, not a mere vehicle to describe things. Also, for them, language and thought are inseparable, and so are language and culture – Cicero in particular advocates that language is derived from culture and *simultaneously* creates culture. The *logos* is no longer the bearer of truth; instead, the truth reveals itself through the synthesis of linguistic wealth [*copia verborum*] and world knowledge [*scientia copiae rerum*], a process which takes place when we use language (Braun 1996: 19–21). So the universalism attributed to the classical paradigm is questioned, making equivalence amongst languages slightly more complicated but certainly not impossible.

Vico follows Cicero and reasserts equivalence whilst going against the classical paradigm. He devises a metaphysics of perception, whereby language is a mode of thought and a product of fantasy. It is hence pre-logic and its origins trace back to myth and fantasy. The real world is the world of language as a human creation, so there is always congruence between word and object, linguistic expression and reality (Braun 1996: 22–3).

Böhme and Hamann too criticise the classical paradigm and make an even stronger claim for universalism, for they advocate that language is a reproduction of the word of God. Speaking and understanding (and translating) are hence tasks that involve recovering God's word, the *Ursprache* [original language] hidden in every natural language (Steiner 1998: 80; Braun 1996: 22, 24–6). The belief in the *logos* – this time a mystical, divine *logos* – returns and nurtures the belief in equivalence amongst languages.

From yet another perspective, Herder can be said to make a claim for equivalence as well. For him, thought is linguistic. Unlike Kant, he contends that there is no reason without language. Similarly to Vico and Hamann, he places emphasis on the origin of language and claims that different tongues are part of a single whole (Braun 1996: 26). Steiner argues that Herder 'never shook himself free of the enigma of the natural or divine origin of language' (1998: 81), and it is his reliance on this enigma that lends his theory of language a universalist touch. On the other hand, Herder stresses 'the irreducible spiritual individuality of each language' (Steiner 1998: 81) as well as the fact that each language reflects the world in its own particular way – which obviously compromises the claim for equivalence.

Steiner reminds us that 'the short years between Herder's writings and those of Humboldt are among the most productive in the history of linguistic thought' (1998: 82). He goes on to mention thinkers (such as William Jones, Friedrich von Schlegel and Madame de Staël) who anticipate Humboldt's work on language – and for Steiner (1998: 82–3), Humboldt is one of a few thinkers who actually contributed something new and comprehensive to the debate on language. In many ways, these thinkers pave the way to out-and-out linguistic relativism, which culminated in the Sapir–Whorf hypothesis (see Section 5).

For Braun (1996: 27), Humboldt's chief contribution was to understand language not as a means to achieving an objective but as the objective in itself. Steiner in turn considers Humboldt's notion of the 'third universe' to be key – that is, a space between 'the phenomenal reality of the "empirical world" and the internalized structures of consciousness' (1998: 85). Humboldt's concept of language, when seen solely through this perspective, is thus universal. His renowned circular argument nonetheless is clearly relativist – that 'civilization is uniquely and specifically informed by its language; the language is the unique and specific matrix of its civilization' (Steiner 1998: 88). In other words, different languages engender different worldviews in ways that cannot under any circumstances be considered equivalent. In Steiner's view, it is this duality, along with Humboldt's lack of 'demonstrable proof' and 'verifiable concepts' (1998: 88, 89), that makes these theories not incisive enough. Both Braun and Steiner agree that numerous language theories – both relativist and universalist – stem from Humboldt. Here Braun (1996: 28) lists pragmatism, the contemporary notion of transcendental philosophy of language, structural linguistics (from Saussure to Chomsky) and the work of Sapir and Whorf, who in his view proved Humboldt's reflections empirically. Steiner (1998: 89–91) focuses on the impact that Humboldt had on Cassirer, Trier and Weisberger, but also on Sapir and Whorf. We will look at the influence that Humboldt exerted on future theories of language, both universalist and relativist, in the next two sections.

14.4 Linguistic turn and pragmatic turn: the various faces of universalism

As mentioned above, PL as we know it today begins in the late nineteenth and early twentieth centuries, when it developed chiefly in two directions. The first can be summarised as the radicalisation of the modern sign theory in the sense of *characteristica universalis* associated with a predominantly empirical language theory – without being a mere repetition of the classical paradigm (Braun 1996: 29). The second, on the other hand, is marked by the rediscovery of the historical-pragmatic dimension of language and is responsible for the pragmatic turn in philosophy of language. The former can be labelled more 'equivalence-friendly', the latter less so. However different these two tendencies may be, their similarities united them in the so-called linguistic turn in philosophy. In other words, both hold that language and thought cannot be separated. More importantly, both understand that all philosophical problems are, first and foremost, linguistic problems and that philosophy is, in reality, language criticism (Braun 1996: 29).

Frege, Steiner reminds us (1998: 140–1), relied heavily on the classical paradigm and on 'Platonic idiom' and defended the thesis that there must be an external, timeless and constant source of meaning somewhere – a 'third realm'. Access to this realm would be the key to equivalence amongst languages. As Soames (2010: 12–13) puts it when explaining Frege's notion of language: 'senses, including the thoughts expressed by sentences, are public objects available to different thinkers. (...) It is this that is preserved in translation'. In other words, Frege radicalised Leibniz's project, aiming to improve the incompleteness and inexactness of natural tongues through a logical language to represent thought with mathematical precision. Both Soames (2010: 20) and Nye (1998: 4) stress the important role that Frege played in taking the classical notion of language further and sowing the seeds of analytic philosophy. As far as equivalence is concerned, the duality pointed out by Steiner remains relevant. Whilst Frege paved the way to a more sophisticated, scientifically minded and mathematical notion of equivalence, his findings led to the questioning of the very premises that would allow for equivalence in the first place. Let us now see how this duality manifests itself in different currents associated with analytic philosophy.

Analytic philosophy is characterised both by the strictly logical analysis of language and by the search for some sort of ideal language. It 'has been among the most influential [currents] in modern philosophy' (Steiner 1998: 212) and stems from that Platonic notion that natural tongues are deceptive and treacherous – hence the need for a rigorously constructed meta-language for philosophical propositions. Any progress made in this way would directly lead to progress as far as equivalence is concerned. The analytic project could be interpreted, from the point of view of TS, as an attempt to render equivalence achievable precisely by freeing natural tongues of their elusive character – as mentioned in Section 1.

Following Frege, Bertrand Russell set out to create an ideal, logical and, most importantly, formally correct language so that it could finally fulfil its sole purpose of *representing* things

(Braun 1996: 34–5). For him, 'to use a name is not to describe an object, but simply to refer to it', because 'language is a vehicle for expressing one's thoughts, rather than a social institution' (Soames 2010: 29–30).

The early Ludwig Wittgenstein advanced analytic philosophy with his thesis that behind all tongues lies a universal language with a general logical form, which in turn sets the limits of our world (Wittgenstein 1922: 5.6-5.641; Braun 1996: 36). For Steiner, both Russell's and Wittgenstein's early works can be described as a 'correspondence theory' in which 'language is (...) a one-to-one picture of the world [and] propositions "are like" the things they are about' (1998: 219–20). Therefore, both for Russell and for the early Wittgenstein, equivalence should be a matter-of-fact property of natural languages. Indeed, in *Tractatus* 3.343 we read that '[d]efinitions are rules for the translation of one language into another. Every correct symbolism must be translated into every other according to such rules. It is this which all have in common' (Wittgenstein 1922).

Rudolf Carnap took analytic philosophy in a different direction, referred to as logical empiricist and positivist or also as Ideal Language philosophy (Steiner 1998: 217; Braun 1996: 39). As Soames puts it, Carnap advanced 'analyticity – labelled logical truth – and synonymy – labelled logical equivalence' (2010: 43). Most importantly, however, Carnap worked on a strict and purely logical metalanguage for philosophical propositions. Beneath the surface of Ideal Language philosophy – and of analytic philosophy as a whole – was the hope of doing away with the deceitful character of natural languages, to find a solution to the old Platonic dilemma (a hope that lives on today – Rorty 2000: 22). This in turn would solve the equivalence enigma, making the 'transfer' amongst languages clearer, more objective and scientifically verifiable. However, in order to understand a sign, we inevitably need to resort to other signs – Derrida's *différance*, discussed in Section 6 – and this severely impairs the project of establishing a trustworthy and constant source of truth and meaning – be it a metalanguage, an artificial language or a 'third realm' outside language.

Ordinary Language philosophy emerges, then, as a response to Ideal Language philosophy and represents the historical-pragmatic turn that philosophy of language took in the twentieth century, as noted above. Others refer to it as the pragmatic or pragmatic-hermeneutic turn because, unlike Ideal Language philosophers, whose approach was solely logic-oriented, Ordinary Language philosophers focus on the pragmatic aspects of language, on its actual and multifaceted use by speakers. In other words, there is no longer any normative wish to regulate some sort of ideal language, nor is there a logic that precedes language (Braun 1996: 39–41). As Steiner asked, even though both currents agreed that philosophical problems stemmed from the elusive character of natural languages, '[h]ow can we construct an ideal language without first describing accurately and exhaustively the procedures and confusions of ordinary discourse?' (1998: 217–18).

The influence of the later Wittgenstein (of the *Philosophical Investigations* ([1953] 2009)) on Ordinary Language philosophy is undeniable. According to Wilson, in Wittgenstein:

> [l]anguage is shown to be constituted by its activities, so that we can speak of language-games (...) (*PI* 23); a language-game only makes sense against a form of life (*PI* 19); concepts are seen as blurred and linked by family resemblance, rather than as essential (*PI* 67), grammar can be both surface and depth (*PI* 664); meaning is physiognomy because the meaning of an utterance depends on the words that we choose to use (*PI* 568); it becomes more important to look than to think (*PI* 66); it is possible to make a surveyable representation, a description of what has been seen (*PI* 122).
>
> (Wilson 2016: 102)

It is as Braun (1996: 40) stresses: the later Wittgenstein has a lot in common with Humboldt, as both claim that meaning is to be found in the use of language, in its rules, in the community that uses it – hence meaning is language immanent and is to be understood pragmatically. This great shift in Wittgenstein's notion of language is highly symbolic of the duality universalism–relativism proposed by Steiner. From the *Tractatus* to the *Investigations*, there is a movement from the possibility of perfect equivalence to its impossibility. Wilson (2016: 42–3) summarises the shift as far as translation is concerned:

> Translation becomes an exercise in anthropology. The translator must forsake the crystalline beauty of the world of the *Tractatus*, where translating from one language to another would be a matter of substitution, an exercise in calculus (*TL-P* 3.343), for the 'rough ground' of the world of the *Investigations*, where meaning has to be investigated case by case in the world of everyday transaction (*PI* 107).

Ordinary Language philosophy was developed by John Searle and J. L. Austin in particular (Braun 1996: 42). Austin proposed the concept of 'performative utterances', stressing the performative character – as opposed to the referential character – of language (Austin 1998). These performative utterances, which do not simply describe or evaluate reality but, rather, create action, are at the heart of his speech act theory. By classifying utterances according to their locutionary (i.e. 'a certain sentence with a certain sense and reference'), illocutionary (i.e. 'utterances which have a (conventional) force', such as 'informing, ordering, warning') and perlocutionary (i.e. 'what we bring about *by* saying something, such as convincing, persuading, deterring') force, Austin concluded that all possible utterances have illocutionary force (Austin 1975: 109).

Departing from the conviction that speech acts follow rules and are intentional, Searle systematised Austin's speech act theory, intensifying the pragmatic turn by depicting language as action and placing emphasis on speakers' intentions (Braun 1996: 42; Leal 2014: 124). Searle explains that

> [s]trictly speaking, whenever we talk about the metaphorical meaning of a word, expression, or sentence, we are talking about what a speaker might utter it to be, in a way that departs from what a word, expression or sentence actually means. We are therefore talking about possible speaker's intentions.
>
> (1979: 77)

Rosemary Arrojo and Kanavillil Rajagopalan's discussion of Searle's theory of language (2003: 113) is particularly relevant to our reflections on equivalence. In their view, Searle's theory of meaning rests upon a linguistic dogma whereby signs *naturally have literal meanings*. This firm belief in literalness manifests itself especially clearly in three moments in Searle's writings: (1) Searle's disagreement with Austin as far as illocutionary acts are concerned; (2) his disagreement with Keith Donnellan's propositions about the issue of reference; and (3) the combination of Grice's pragmatics and the speech act theory, which in turn led to the notion of indirect speech acts. For Arrojo and Rajagopalan (2003: 120), these three key moments are underpinned by a universalist notion of meaning as a stable, constant source objectively available to all speakers at all times.

In terms of equivalence, Ordinary Language philosophy embraces the duality universalism–relativism proposed by Steiner. Its pragmatic character generally speaks against equivalence; if language is action and depends on its ordinary use by speakers, it is impossible to determine 'the' meaning of a given sign or sentence and then proceed to find its equivalent in another language (Braun 1996: 44). On the other hand, however, meaning is perceived more as public than as private commodity, to use yet another important dichotomy from Steiner (1998: 207–15) to which we will come back in Section 7. For this reason, Ordinary Language philosophy could be seen as equivalence-friendly because, as Arrojo and Rajagopalan assert of Searle, if we believe in the possibility of constant, literal meanings that are publicly available to everyone, equivalence between two languages would be a natural next step (let us remember here the notion of 'logocentrism' as used by Derrida, mentioned in Section 1).

As Braun explains (1996: 44), speech act theory paved the way both to Paul Grice's theory of conversation implicatures and Jürgen Habermas' theory of communicative action and universal pragmatics. Grice's implicatures refer to the discrepancies between what a speaker *means* to say and what the speaker's utterance *actually* means. His theory of meaning (Grice 1957, 1968, 1969) in all its diversity (Chapman 2005: 1–9) relies heavily on the notions of intention and literal meanings. For this reason, his contribution leads to similar conclusions, as far as equivalence is concerned, to the ones drawn apropos of Ordinary Language philosophy.

As for Habermas, he ties his notion of meaning not to intention but to the acceptability of speech acts (2003: 232–3). There is an important shift from the perspective of the speaker (Grice's intention) to a more global, intersubjective perspective. What does this mean for equivalence? Looking into Habermas' theory of truth and knowledge (Habermas 1999), he avoids the age-old problem of the referential character of language by stating that a proposition is true if it accurately represents the reality to which it refers in the real world *but not in a metaphysical way*. Instead, his epistemological realism is grounded on pragmatics (Habermas 2003: 343–81), which, at first glance, might appear to speak against the possibility of equivalence amongst languages. Again, let us remember the later Wittgenstein, who shows that there can be no purely semantic meaning because utterances are bound to their respective contexts. However, Habermas' pragmatics is *universal* in the sense that it attempts to stipulate *universal conditions* for mutual understanding. Therefore language users in general – regardless of the individual tongues spoken – share these conditions for mutual understanding. Does this strengthen the case for equivalence or, as Steiner puts it in relation to linguistic universals (1998: 110–11), simply describe common traits of natural languages which, nevertheless, are a far cry from point-by-point correspondences between them? We will come back to this question in Section 7.

14.5 Sapir and Whorf, Quine, hermeneutics: the shifts towards relativism

The twentieth century also witnessed pivotal moments in which relativism became central, undermining the possibility of equivalence amongst languages. One of these moments is represented by the Sapir–Whorf hypothesis, which Steiner names the 'Humboldt–Sapir–Whorf hypothesis' because of its affinities with Humboldt's theory of language (1998: 98, 106 – and see Braun 1996: 28). 'No two languages are ever sufficiently similar to be considered as representing the same social reality', explains Sapir (1985: 162). From this point of view, comparing languages aiming at establishing equivalence is an exercise in futility, because '[l]inguistic patterns determine what the individual perceives in his world and how he thinks about it (...) [and] these patterns vary widely' (Steiner 1998: 92). For Ricoeur (2006: 14–15), what Whorf and Sapir came up with was a 'theory of the untranslatable' because of the 'non-superimposable character of the different divisions on which the numerous linguistic systems rest' – in other words, because of the impossibility of equivalence amongst languages. Both Ricoeur and Steiner arrive at the conclusion that, if the Sapir–Whorf hypothesis were entirely correct, interlingual communication and learning a foreign language would be impossible tasks – in which case bilinguals would be schizophrenics (Steiner 1998: 98; Ricoeur 2006: 15).

Willard Van Orman Quine's theory of indeterminacy of translation brought about another moment that put the equivalence project into question. Steiner (1998: 283) includes Quine in his short list of people who have made a significant contribution to translation. For him, 'the separation between semantics and pragmatics is a pernicious error' (Quine 1987: 211), thus questioning the possibility of context-free literal meanings upon which the notion of equivalence rests.[1]

Another development that constituted a shift towards relativism is that of existential hermeneutics. Until Edmund Husserl, language was not considered a condition for the possibility of perception, neither did it limit or determine perception. After Husserl, language becomes a prerequisite for self-perception and for the perception of the world. Ernst Cassirer, for example, sees language as one of the transcendental conditions for one's world experience (together with religion, art, science and myth) (Braun 1996: 47). Similarly, for Martin Heidegger we only exist and understand our existence in language. Braun (1996: 50) thus speaks of a pragmatic hermeneutic turn, whereby the universality of reason is left behind and pluralism and relativism become more prominent.

Hans-Georg Gadamer develops Heidegger's reflections further and stresses the transcendental function of language: language is neither the depiction of an already given, language-free world, nor is it a manipulable sign system. Language does not refer to something external but obtains its meaning from within itself, in itself. Things become clear only in language because everything is conditioned by language – nothing exists outside it. For Braun (1996: 50–1), we can speak of a dialogic-pragmatic turn – 'dialogic' because things can only acquire meaning and be defined in language, so they may have a meaning for me, but in dialogue this meaning is faced with the meaning of the other, and the boundaries of understanding melt into each other, making mutual understanding possible. Meaning is hence constructed and redefined in each and every communicative situation. The growing interest in Walter Benjamin's 1923 'The Translator's Task' in the second half of the twentieth century underlines this 'reversion to hermeneutic[s]' (Steiner 1998: 250).

Steiner draws insight particularly from Heidegger but also from Benjamin to devise his 'hermeneutic motion' in translation (1998: 312–435), a way of depicting the process of translation that sheds light on our discussion on equivalence. He calls it a 'hermeneutic of trust' (1998: 319). Confronted with a text to be translated, Steiner explains, we are 'pu[t] off balance' by that 'a-prioristic movement of trust', so we 'lean towards it', we 'encircle and invade cognitively'; we then 'come home laden, thus again off-balance', because we took 'from "the other"' and added 'to our own', making the system 'off-tilt' (1998: 316). So trust leads to violence, to invasion, which in turn leads to embodiment. The fourth movement of the hermeneutic act, 'restitution' in and through translation, 'must compensate (...) if it is to be authentic' (1998: 319, 316). In it 'a new synthesis emerges' which 'belongs integrally to neither language' but is 'charged with currents of meaning more universal' than the two tongues in question (1998: 349).[2]

Comparing the translator's quest to Antigone's trespassing on the sphere of the gods, Steiner suggests that the translator 'does violence to the divinely sanctioned division between languages (what right have we to translate?) but (...) affirms, through this rebellious negation, the final, no less divine, unity of the *logos*' (1998: 349). Equivalence is hence not an *a priori* possibility – translating has little to do with finding equivalent words in another language or accessing a stable source of meaning outside language. Equivalence is nonetheless achieved, established through translation, thanks to which we can 'rebelliously affirm the unity of the *logos*'. This is relativism with that hint of universalism necessary for an everyday task like translating not to descend into chaos. Indeed, Ricoeur proposes the epithet 'despite everything' – translation is a 'despite everything' task (2006: 18). We will come back to the similarities between Steiner and Ricoeur in the next section.

14.6 Contemporary thought: equivalence in postmodern discourse

Contemporary philosophy has refined and attacked the notions of language (and of equivalence) discussed thus far in different ways. As Best and Kellner (1991: 18–20) explain, the domination exerted by Marxism, existentialism and phenomenology in the 1950s and 60s was gradually replaced by the 'linguistically-oriented discourses of structuralism', which in turn aimed at 'objectivity, coherence, rigour and truth'. Poststructuralism emerged as an attack on these structuralist, scientific pretensions which not only 'attempted to create a scientific basis for the study of culture' but also 'strove for the standard modern goals of foundation, truth, objectivity, certainty and system' (Best and Kellner 1991: 20; Leal 2014: 24–8; in many ways, this battle against scientism is ongoing – see Rorty 2000). In this sense, poststructuralist discourse has made pivotal contributions, particularly to the relativist matrix discussed here, though not as a unified front but, rather, as individual developments with numerous common traits but also important differences. Indeed, the notions of difference, disagreement and heterogeneity are key in poststructuralist discourse (Lyotard 2003: 6; Leal 2014: 302–10), hence the difficulty for any unified account of trying to represent it. Therefore let us concentrate on two thinkers who have developed the relativist matrix further in different ways: Derrida and Ricoeur (whose disagreements have resulted in heated debates – see Joy 1988).

In the 1960s, Derrida radicalised the linguistic turn by claiming that 'there is nothing outside of the text' (1997: 158). So not only did he acknowledge that all philosophical questions are, first and foremost, linguistic questions, questions about language and in language, but he also attributed our entire existence to language, to a 'system of writing' from which there is no escape (1997: 30–44). As Glendinning (2004: 6) puts it,

> [l]anguage has come to the centre of every philosophical problematic because everything that seemed solidly to render its status as essentially *un*problematic, everything that had assured us that it *is* what we thought it *should* be, namely the system of signification of an order of pure intelligibility (classical 'meaning'), an order traditionally grasped in terms of the divine word or *logos*, has begun to melt into air.

As mentioned above, because of Derrida's notion of philosophy and translation as one, the key concepts that pervade his oeuvre are all relevant to our discussion on equivalence: *différance*, trace/track and double bind are probably the most obvious ones. *Différance*, the 'misspelt' French word, refers to meaning as a process of both deferring (one sign leads to another sign ad infinitum) and differentiating (signs are told apart by their differences to other signs) (Derrida 1967: 297–305). Trace/track plays a central role in the process of *différance*, as signs refer to what they are not, to an absence made present; they 'carry' with themselves the traces of other signs, not references to 'reality' – signs are but traces of other signs (Derrida 1997: 66–7, my emphases). From this perspective, the origin or source to which signs are believed to refer – and which in turn works as the very basis for the notion of equivalence amongst languages – is a non-origin. There is no 'outside-language' or 'outside-the-text' to which to anchor signs.

Does this mean that equivalence is impossible for Derrida? He often refers to equivalent words in different languages (see, for example, 1997: 134). This is where the double bind comes into play: understanding, and hence translating, entails translatability and untranslatability simultaneously. We cannot help but establish a relation with others, translate them, make them our own, but *at the same time* we cannot help but maintain their otherness, their alterity – they are, after all, untranslatable. It is as though, for Derrida, every attempt to establish equivalence would entail a movement towards appropriation and a movement towards understanding that full appropriation is impossible. Accordingly, he sees translation as 'regulated transformation' and not as 'some "transport" of pure signifieds from one language to another' (Derrida 1981: 20). Translatability ensures the survival of the text – that is, the possibility of this 'regulated transformation' allows the text to live on, even before translation, simply as the transformation through which any text goes when we read it. However, total translatability (or total equivalence) would cause the text to disappear, whereas total untranslatability (the impossibility of equivalence) would lead to the immediate death of the text (Derrida 1979: 102–3). Foran (2012: 81) summarises this point as follows: 'language must be unique and self-referential in that it cannot be totally subsumed into another language, yet it must also be able to reach beyond itself to another linguistic entity'. So Derrida's 'solution' to Ricoeur's 'paralysing alternatives', mentioned in Section 1 and discussed in the next paragraph, is to live with both *simultaneously*. Indeed, he later says: 'I don't believe that anything can ever be untranslatable – or, moreover, translatable' (Derrida 2001: 178).

Ricoeur's notion of linguistic hospitality also encompasses the duality translatable–untranslatable but in a different way from Derrida's (Ricoeur does not care much for this dichotomy, as we will see – Ricoeur 2006: 14). 'Linguistic hospitality' is the space where we give up the hope of filling 'the gap between equivalence and total adequacy' and enjoy both 'the pleasure of dwelling in the other's language' and 'the pleasure of receiving the foreign word at home, in one's own welcoming house' (2006: 10). As mentioned in Section 1, because Ricoeur feels that the dichotomy translatable–untranslatable leaves us with nothing but the 'paralysing alternatives' of universalism or relativism, he proposes that we focus on the dichotomy 'faithfulness versus betrayal' instead (2006: 14).

Ricoeur posits that in order to criticise a translation effectively, we would have to compare source and target texts to a third text, 'the bearer of the identical meaning, supposed to move from the first to the second' (2006: 34). However, as argued above, no theory of language has ever managed to locate or (re)create this 'third place', and therein lies the 'paradox' of translation, asserts Ricoeur, for equivalence is always and only 'supposed equivalence' because there is no 'demonstrable identity of meaning' (2006: 22) – '[a]n equivalence without identity', he says (2006: 22). So a good, faithful translation 'can only aim at supposed equivalence', which in turn leads him to the conclusion that *equivalence is never a priori because it is produced by translation* (2006: 34–5). This conclusion takes us back to Steiner's hermeneutic motion discussed at the end of Section 5. Instead of choosing to live in a relentless double bind between translatability (and the possibility of equivalence) and untranslatability (and the impossibility of equivalence), as Derrida does, Ricoeur (similarly to Steiner) prefers to work with the notions of 'supposed equivalence' and 'equivalence without identity'. Steiner too reminds us of the impossibility of verifying equivalence, for 'to demonstrate the excellence or the exhaustiveness of an act of interpretation and/or translation is to offer an alternative or an addendum', but '[t]here are no closed circuits in natural language, no self-consistent axiomatic sets' (1998: 428).

For Derrida, the first non-logocentric notions of language emerge here, in poststructuralist discourse. To give up the *logos* means to abandon the quest for a stable source of meaning – an 'identity of meaning' in Ricoeur's words – and one such abandonment entails the rejection of equivalence as well. Yet, as we have seen, neither Ricoeur nor Derrida do away with equivalence completely. As Christopher Norris puts it in relation to Derrida, poststructuralism resides in driving the Saussurean project to its limit and challenging (*but not fully abandoning*) its premises whilst keeping 'logical rigour' (Norris [1982] 2002: 30, 145). Relativism and universalism come together yet again.

14.7 Closing remarks on an open question

Let us end our journey here with three more reflections proposed by Steiner in *After Babel*, namely on the question of whether meaning is private or public (1998: 169–215), on the issue of the elusive character of language (1998: 215–47) and, finally, on the question of intimacy (1998: 47–50).

The dilemma surrounding the public or private character of meaning is probably as old as the debate on language itself, as we have seen in Section 2, and has permeated reflection on language since. The more public meaning is, the more likely it is for equivalence amongst languages to be realisable. In Modrak's reading (2001: 248), this dilemma is already formulated in Aristotle, for whom our 'affections of the soul' are universal but carry individual content as well. Similarly, Wittgenstein insists that meaning must be *predominantly* public if language is to communicate anything ([1953] 2009: 256–314). Humboldt, on the other hand, contends that beneath the surface of language use lie largely private entities. Commenting on Humboldt, Steiner proposes the image of 'an iceberg largely under water', and goes on to conclude that '[m]eaning is at all times the potential sum total of individual adaptations' and that 'all communication "interprets" between privacies' (1998: 181, 206, 207).

In Steiner's view, this 'private language' dilemma fuelled the quest for precisely the opposite: 'unambiguous and universal codes of communication' (1998: 208), as we have seen in Sections 3 and 4. Even though this quest has achieved little in terms of establishing 'universal codes of communication' and the unequivocal possibility of equivalence, Steiner insists that we should not 'diminish the importance of the public elements of language' because '[i]f a substantial part of all utterances were not public (...), chaos (...) would follow' (1998: 214, 215).

What does Steiner's conclusion say of natural languages and of the possibility of equivalence amongst them? It says that our languages encompass large amounts of idiosyncrasies, preventing them from being properly systematised – which in turn makes strict equivalence impossible. Indeed, commenting on some of the more logical approaches discussed in this chapter, Steiner asserts that 'the logician is out of sorts from the start' because language has little to do with logic (1998: 225). There is nothing in language that prevents us from uttering out-and-out nonsense, lies, counter-factual hypotheticals, conditionals; quite the opposite: it equips us with the tools to say all that, to '*say anything*' (Steiner 1998: 227). This happens because '[t]he directly informative content of natural speech is small', so we speak about what *is not*, what *might be*, etc., and this is one of our 'greatest (...) tools by far' (Steiner 1998: 231, 234). Steiner sees the 'looseness' of natural languages as an evolutional advantage 'crucial to the creative functions of internalized and outward speech', so that 'new worlds are born between the lines' (1998: 238, 239). Steiner therefore advocates that we should have little to do with truth postulates and logical systematisations, with language as *code*, *information* and *communication*, for language is also about what is *not* said, what is concealed and blurred, what is said 'only partially, allusively or with intent to screen' (1998: 240). Thus the elusive character of language need not be seen as a hindrance to the development of objective notions like equivalence and verifiably good translations but, rather, as the very reason why there are so many languages in the first place and why translation is possible. It is as Friedrich Nietzsche explains in his seminal 'On Truth and Lying in an Extra-moral Sense' (Nietzsche 1989: 246–57): the lack of correlation between reality and language, along with our ability to say anything, calls for the existence of multiple languages.

Caught between these key dichotomies – universalism–relativism, public–private, translatability–untranslatability – the postmodern reader cannot help but be wary of self-excluding opposites. Derrida's suggestion seems particularly fitting for practising translators: aware of the impossibility of total translatability, total equivalence, we cannot help but strive for it when we translate. If we let ourselves get carried away by the second terms in these dichotomies, we might feel discouraged to translate or even to communicate at all. At the same time, as translators we must be aware of the moments of aporia associated with the first terms of these dichotomies and understand equivalence *as a construct made possible by translation* rather than as a prerequisite for translation to take place or as an all-embracing measure to assess translation quality. As for translation theorists and translator trainers, insisting on equivalence – as well as on any notion of unequivocal identity of meaning – as an *a priori*, universal parameter is not only naïve but also potentially unethical, given the negative consequences these views have brought about: the low status of translators in society and the overall sense of failure commonly associated with translation (Leal 2014: 273–4, 297–8).

One last remark on future perspectives and the question of 'intimacy'. Machine translation – which largely amounts to the ability of a computer to establish equivalence between two languages – has progressed a lot in recent years, along with neuroscience and neurolinguistics. Indeed, current research in neuroscience suggests that aspects of Chomsky's theory of universal grammar may find confirmation in the functioning of the human brain (Ding et al. 2016). However, the question formulated by Steiner in the 1970s and mentioned at the end of Section 6 remains: will this progress towards one side of our dichotomies (universalism, public, translatability) ever be substantive enough to lead to the systematisation of languages and the establishment of direct equivalence amongst them? If so, Steiner says, 'the immense diversities of languages (. . .) can be interpreted as a direct rebellion against the undifferentiated constraints of biological universality. In their formidable variety "surface structures" would be an escape from rather than a contingent vocalization of "deep structures"'(1998: 300).

In light of this scenario, I would like to leave the reader with Steiner's reflection on the notion of intimacy as 'confident, quasi-immediate translation' thanks to which 'the external vulgate and the private mass of language grow more and more concordant' (1998: 48). Intimacy may help strengthen the equivalence-friendly sides of the dichotomies discussed here – universalism, public, translatability. Has globalisation and the omnipresence of the internet brought about a new notion of intimacy – some sort of 'cyber intimacy' that brings together individuals from different parts of the globe? Take platforms such as Facebook, which is available in the exact same format in dozens of languages. Future research might bring contributions in this area, showing how the virtual revolution (Krotoski 2013) has affected the age-old notions of equivalence and translatability.

Notes

1 For more on this, refer to Chapter 7, this volume.
2 See Chapter 16, this volume, for a discussion of the feminist critique of Steiner's imagery.

Related topics

Heidegger; Wittgenstein; Benjamin; Gadamer and Ricoeur; Quine; Davidson; Derrida; translation theory and philosophy; context and pragmatics; culture; linguistics; meaning.

Further reading

Foran, Lisa (ed.), 2012. *Translation and Philosophy*. Bern: Peter Lang. (This collection explores the links between translation and philosophy, featuring celebrated theories of language by, for example, Hegel, Derrida and Ricoeur, but also by less well-known thinkers, such as Ikkyū Sōjun.)

Leal, Alice, 2012. 'Equivalence'. In Yves Gambier and Luc van Doorslaer eds. *Handbook of Translation Studies Volume 3*, Amsterdam and Philadelphia: John Benjamins. This chapter presents a brief summary of the issue of equivalence in TS.

Nye, Andrea, 1998. *Philosophy of Language: The Big Questions*. Malden and Oxford: Blackwell. (An anthology that features numerous classic texts on PL, from Plato to Donald Davidson, along with clarifying introductory remarks by the editor).

Steiner, George, [1975] 1998. *After Babel: Aspects of Language and Translation*. Oxford: Oxford University Press. (This book offers a comprehensive and detailed overview of reflections on language and translation from all eras).

References

Aristotle, [1963] 2002. *Categories and De Interpretatione* (transl. J. L. Ackrill). Oxford: Clarendon Press.

Arrojo, Rosemary and Kanavillil Rajagopalan, [1992] 2003. 'A Crise da Metalinguagem: Uma Perspectiva Interdisciplinar'. In Rosemary Arrojo ed. *O Signo Desconstruído: Implicações para a Tradução, a Leitura e o Ensino*. Campinas: Pontes, 57–62.

Austin, John L., [1970] 1998. 'Performative Utterances'. In Andrea Nye ed. *Philosophy of Language: The Big Questions*. Malden and Oxford: Blackwell Publishers Ltd, 126–31.

Austin, John L., 1975. *How to Do Things with Words*. Cambridge, Massachusetts: Harvard University Press.

Best, Steven and Douglas Kellner, 1991. *Postmodern Theory: Critical Interrogations*. New York: The Guilford Press.

Braun, Edmund, 1996. *Der Paradigmenwechsel in der Sprachphilosophie*. Darmstadt: Wissenschaftliche Buchgesellschaft.

Chapman, Siobhan, 2005. *Paul Grice: Philosopher and Linguist*. Houndmills: Palgrave Macmillan.

Derrida, Jacques, 1967. *L'écriture et la Différence*. Paris: Éditions du Seuil.

Derrida, Jacques, 1979. 'Living on / Border Lines' (transl. James Hulbert). In Harold Bloom ed. *Deconstruction and Criticism*. New York: The Seabury Press, 75–176.

Derrida, Jacques, [1972] 1981. *Positions* (transl. Alan Bass). Chicago: University of Chicago Press.

Derrida, Jacques, [1982] 1985. *The Ear of the Other: Otobiography, Transference, Translation* (transl. Peggy Kamuf). Lincoln and London: University of Nebraska Press.

Derrida, Jacques, [1967] 1997. *Of Grammatology* (transl. Gayatri Chakravorty Spivak). Baltimore and London: Johns Hopkins University Press.

Derrida, Jacques, 2001. 'What is a "Relevant" Translation?' (transl. Lawrence Venuti). *Critical Inquiry* 27, 2, 174–200.

Ding, Nai, Lucia Melloni, Hang Zhang, Xing Tian and David Poeppel, 2016. 'Cortical Tracking of Hierarchical Linguistic Structures in Connected Speech'. *Nature Neuroscience* 19, 158–64.

Foran, Lisa, 2012. 'Translation as a Path to the Other: Derrida and Ricoeur'. In Lisa Foran ed. *Translation and Philosophy*. Bern: Peter Lang, 75–87.

Glendinning, Simon, 2004. 'Language'. In Jack Reynolds and Jonathan Roffe eds. *Understanding Jacques Derrida*. London and New York: Continuum, 5–13.

Grice, Herbert Paul, 1957. 'Meaning'. *The Philosophical Review* 66, 3, 377–88.
Grice, Herbert Paul, 1968. 'Utterer's Meaning, Sentence Meaning, and Word Meaning'. *Foundations of Language* 4, 3, 225–42.
Grice, Herbert Paul, 1969. 'Utterer's Meaning and Intentions'. *The Philosophical Review* 78, 2, 147–77.
Habermas, Jürgen, [1998] 2003. *On the Pragmatics of Communication* (transl. Thomas McCarthy, Jeremy Gaines, Doris L. Jones et al.). Cambridge: Polity Press.
Habermas, Jürgen, 1999. *Wahrheit und Rechtfertigung*. Berlin: Suhrkamp.
Hoffmann, David, 2003. '*Logos* as Composition'. *Rhetoric Society Quarterly* 33, 3, 27–53.
Joy, Morny, 1988. 'Derrida and Ricoeur: A Case of Mistaken Identity (and Difference)'. *Journal of Religion* 68, 4, 508–26.
Krotoski, Aleks, 2013. *Untangling the Web: What the Internet is Doing to You*. London: Faber & Faber.
Lages, Susana K., [2002] 2007. *Walter Benjamin: Tradução e Melancolia*. São Paulo: Edusp.
Leal, Alice, 2012. 'Equivalence'. In Yves Gambier and Luc van Doorslaer eds. *Handbook of Translation Studies Volume 3*. Amsterdam and Philadelphia: John Benjamins, 39–46.
Leal, Alice, 2014. *Is the Glass Half Empty or Half Full? Reflections on Translation Theory and Practice in Brazil*. Berlin: Frank & Timme.
Lee, Barry (ed.), 2011. *Philosophy of Language: The Key Thinkers*. London and New York: Continuum.
Locke, John, [1960] 1998. 'Of Words'. In Andrea Nye ed. *Philosophy of Language: The Big Questions*. Malden and Oxford: Blackwell Publishers Ltd, 18–23.
Lyotard, Jean-François, [1997] 2003. *Postmodern Fables* (transl. Georges van der Abbeele). Minneapolis and London: Minnesota University Press.
Modrak, Deborah K. W., 2001. *Aristotle's Theory of Language and Meaning*. Cambridge: Cambridge University Press.
Nietzsche, Friedrich, [1873] 1989. 'On Truth and Lying in an Extra-moral Sense'. In Sander L. Gilman, Carole Blair and David J. Parent eds. and transl. *Friedrich Nietzsche on Rhetoric and Language*. New York, Oxford: Oxford University Press, 246–57.
Norris, Christopher, [1982] 2002. *Deconstruction: Theory and Practice*. London and New York: Routledge.
Nye, Andrea, 1998. *Philosophy of Language: The Big Questions*. Malden and Oxford: Blackwell Publishers Ltd.
Partee, Morris H., 1972. 'Plato's Theory of Language'. *Foundations of Language* 8, 1, 113–32.
Plato, 1921. *Cratylus / Sophist. Plato in Twelve Volumes*, Vol. 12 (transl. Harold N. Fowler). Cambridge, Massachusetts: Harvard University Press; London: William Heinemann Ltd.
Pym, Anthony, 2007. 'Philosophy and Translation'. In P. Kuhiwczak and K. Littau eds. *A Companion to Translation Studies*. Clevedon, Buffalo, Toronto: Multilingual Matters, 24–44.
Quine, Willard Van Orman. 1987. *Quiddities: An Intermittently Philosophical Dictionary*. Cambridge, Massachusetts: Harvard University Press.
Ricoeur, Paul, 2006. *On Translation* (transl. Eileen Brennan). London and New York: Routledge.
Rodrigues, Cristina C., 1999. *Tradução e Diferença*. São Paulo: UNESP.
Rorty, Richard, 2000. 'Being that Can Be Understood Is Language'. In *London Review of Books* 22, 6, 21–9.
Sapir, Edward, [1949] 1985. *Selected Writings of Edward Sapir in Language, Culture and Personality*, David G. Mandelbaum ed. Berkeley, Los Angeles, London: University of California Press.
Snell-Hornby, Mary, 1988. *Translation Studies: An Integrated Approach*. Amsterdam and Philadelphia: John Benjamins.
Snell-Hornby, Mary, 2006. *The Turns of Translation Studies: New Paradigms or Shifting Viewpoints?* Amsterdam and Philadelphia: John Benjamins.
Soames, Scott, 2010. *Philosophy of Language*. Princeton and Oxford: Princeton University Press.
Steiner, George, [1975] 1998. *After Babel: Aspects of Language and Translation*. Oxford: Oxford University Press.

Wilson, Philip, 2016. *Translation after Wittgenstein*. London and New York: Routledge.
Windle, Kevin and Anthony Pym, 2011. 'European Thinking on Secular Translation'. In Kirsten Malmkjær ed. *The Oxford Handbook of Translation Studies*. Oxford: Oxford University Press, 7–29.
Wittgenstein, Ludwig, 1922. *Tractatus Logico-Philosophicus* (transl. C. K. Ogden). London: Kegan Paul, Trench, Trubner & co. ltd.; New York: Harcourt, Brace & Company, Inc.
Wittgenstein, Ludwig, [1953] 2009. *Philosophical Investigations* (transl. G. E. M. Anscombe, P. M. S. Hacker and J. Schulte). Chichester: Wiley-Blackwell.

15
Ethics

Joanna Drugan

Introduction

The first edition of the standard English-language reference work for the discipline, the *Routledge Encyclopedia of Translation Studies* (1998), had no entry under 'Ethics'; the term did not even figure in the index. The substantially revised and augmented 2009 edition corrected this omission, with Moira Inghilleri and Carol Maier contributing an article on the topic. Their introduction suggested Inghilleri and Maier would pay attention to the practice of translation and interpreting: 'Ethical practice has always been an important issue for translators and interpreters, though historically the focus of concern has been the question of fidelity to the spoken or written text' (2009: 100). Yet their entry was actually concerned with summarising the best-known theoretical reflections on translation ethics, notably the contributions of leading (mainly European/US) scholars Baker, Berman, Chesterman, Levinas, Pym, Spivak and Venuti. The entry concludes with a call to 'shift the debate from questions of impartiality and loyalty to questions of justice', and to fix where possible on 'the instrumental and utopian social and political goals that translation and interpreting can help to adjudicate' (2009: 103). Other landmark reference works in Translation Studies continue to address ethics only within articles on other topics where it is relevant, such as 'Courtroom Interpreting' or 'Translator Training' (e.g. *The Oxford Handbook of Translation Studies*: Malmkjær and Windle (2011)).

For a handbook of *Translation Studies and Philosophy*, though, ethics must be a central concern. Translation is a topic of strong theoretical interest *for* philosophers working on ethics or language, but it is also a practice which *affects* philosophy (philosophers rely on translations to read canonical works on ethics, for instance) and one which itself involves ethical decision-making by those doing the interpreting and translating. Given this complex relationship between ethics and translation, clarity matters. Perhaps unusually for academics, or indeed translators, Inghilleri and Maier nonetheless gave no definition for the term 'ethics' in their discussion, though of course they were only considering the subject as it related to Translation Studies and might have believed a shared working understanding could be taken as read. The present chapter, in a collection directed at both philosophers and translation scholars, will start from the definition provided by Roger Crisp in the *Routledge Handbook of Philosophy* (1998).

Crisp divides the general topic of ethics into three parts: (1) ethics and meta-ethics, (2) ethical concepts and ethical theories and (3) applied ethics. As well as being an area of philosophy, *ethics* broadly refers to the 'systems of value and custom instantiated in the lives of particular groups of human beings' and more specifically to one in particular of these 'systems', morality, which involves 'notions such as rightness and wrongness' and moral principles. *Meta-ethics* refers to the attempt to 'articulate what constitutes ethics or morality'. It is related to other areas of philosophy and to the question of whether philosophy even has a contribution to make to ethics. In Crisp's view, 'once we have some grip on what ethics is, we can begin to ask questions about moral principles themselves' – that is, *ethical concepts and theories* such as duty, moral judgement, autonomy and ethical relations to others; but also, at a broader level, topics discussed since ancient times such as *eudaimonia*. Crisp translates *eudaimonia* as 'happiness', though others have suggested 'flourishing', 'welfare', 'well-being' or the 'happy/blessed/good life' – an illustration of the central role played by translation in the very discussion of ethics. Crisp's third category, *applied ethics*, has been around since ancient discussions of how philosophy might apply to 'real life' but became more prominent in modern philosophy from the 1960s, with increasing attention paid to contemporary practical issues, including professional ethics.

Elements of Crisp's definition are apparent throughout the development of Translation Studies as a discipline and the growing attention it has paid to ethics. This history will now be outlined chronologically, highlighting key works and scholars. Following this chronological account, the next section of the chapter will identify the main ethical themes and concerns which have attracted attention in Translation Studies thus far.

Ethics in Translation Studies: historical development and key figures

Translation Studies is a young discipline, even if interpreting and translation have taken place for millennia. Edwin Gentzler locates the establishment of the academic discipline in Belgium and Holland in the early 1970s (2014: 14), with the period between the Second World War and the 1960s representing a 'pre-discipline' which paved the way for its emergence. Gentzler takes care to acknowledge that this is the picture for Western Translation Studies, and that 'translation probably began as "discipline" within international trade' in Chinese, Persian, Turkic, Greek, Roman, Indian and other languages thousands of years earlier (2014: 14). This chapter will focus on Translation Studies in Gentzler's modern sense, as an object of academic study in universities, in industrialised and mainly capitalist countries. It seems important in ethical terms to acknowledge this and other limitations, particularly in this chapter. The author only has access to academic work on ethics and translation published in English or French and is a mother tongue speaker of (Scottish) English working in the UK. Like any other account of ethics in relation to translation, this summary is a partial one which is inevitably influenced by the available and well-known earlier scholars who worked, or were translated then published, in my languages. This need to acknowledge one's own influences (and influence) has begun to attract attention in Translation Studies in recent years. In relation to research ethics, for instance, Mellinger and Hanson (2017: 13–21) stress that research in translation and interpreting risks bias, error and incompleteness given the dominance of Western, Educated, Industrialized, Rich and Democratic (WEIRD) populations, both among researchers and in research samples. The convenient WEIRD acronym has no M for Male, but gender ought to be acknowledged too. Few female scholars are cited in accounts of work on ethics from the early days of Translation Studies, an absence which is all the more striking when we note modern female researchers' enthusiastic engagement with the theme. Among others, André Lefevere (1992) has argued that handbooks such as this one play a role in creating and sustaining the canon. As Siri Hustvedt points out in relation to literary works, 'the idea of a book's "greatness", its inclusion in the canon of Western literature, necessarily affects a person's reading of the book' (2017: 444). The following whistle-stop tour does retell the established story of ethics and Translation Studies but attempts to bring it up to date and weave in new voices with the more diverse developments in the discipline since the 1990s.

Before the 1970s, significant 'pre-discipline' debates of relevance for ethics centred around the importance, desirability or impossibility of linguistic equivalence or fidelity in work such as that by Jakobson (1959) on translatability or, often, by those translating religious texts such as the Bible translator and Christian scholar Nida (1964). As the young discipline grew across Europe and the US, religious and literary translation attracted the bulk of scholarly attention. Different positions on the emerging Translation Studies concepts of formal, dynamic and pragmatic equivalence were partly driven by ethical considerations, notably for translators of religious texts. Israeli polysystemists Even-Zohar (1979) and Gideon Toury (1978) emphasised ideas of dominance and competition in literatures and genres and between translated and non-translated works. French-American literary theorist George Steiner drew on hermeneutics to reflect on translation issues with a clear ethical dimension such as trust, resistance and 'aggression' (1975).

By the mid 1980s, theorists increasingly addressed questions of ethics directly as such. Functionalists focused on ideas such as the 'ethics of service', where service was variously to the translation brief, commission or client (Reiss and Vermeer 1984/2013). Inspired by the work of the German theorist Friedrich Schleiermacher, French translator Berman (1984/1992) argued that translation necessarily involved 'deforming tendencies' and failed to present '*l'Autre en tant qu'Autre*' (the Other as Other), a powerful image to which later scholars would return in their reflections on whether translation could be ethical, while Theo Hermans edited a landmark collection of essays on the 'manipulation' of literature and the 'marginal' position of translation (1985) in which several contributions reflected on questions of ethics in relation to literary translation. Lawrence Venuti's body of work on translator (in)visibility and the desirability of highlighting differences between different cultures and languages also drew explicitly on ethical arguments to make his case (1986). At the decade's end, the collected work of Levinas (1989) kindled a new discussion of the translator as an agent with ethical responsibility, who ought to act ethically in encounters with the Other, following its publication in new English translations.

With the 1990s, a broader range of voices began to be heard in the discipline, introducing fresh linguistic and cultural perspectives and drawing out new aspects of ethics in relation to translation theory and practice. From Canada, Luise von Flotow (1991) and Sherry Simon (1996) continued the focus on literary translation but introduced a combination of post-structuralist theory and feminism to question ethical aspects of translation practice in relation to gender. Postcolonial translation theorists including the Bengali scholar Gayatri Spivak (1987) drew on deconstructionist ethics and social activism to frame translation in both ethical and political terms. Brazilian comparative literature specialist Arrojo (1994) joined Venuti in directly challenging the marginalisation of the translator, using an appeal to ethics to argue for authorial recognition for translators. A number of landmark works examining interpreting practice also began to be published during this decade, highlighting the ethical challenges and importance of such interactions (e.g. Wadensjö 1998/2013). By the turn of the century, the Finnish scholar Koskinen had made the link between the growing body of work on post-modern approaches, ethics and translation, stressing the importance of ethics when founding assumptions in the discipline were being brought into question: 'Ethics is needed precisely at that point when the explanatory power of fidelity peters out' (2000: 20).

One of the pivotal 'turns' in the development of Translation Studies as a discipline was associated with calls for a 'return to ethics' around the time of the new millennium. A 2001 special issue of the leading journal *The Translator*, edited by Anthony Pym, argued that significant changes in society, science and technology required new reflection on the relation between translation and ethics. As well as Pym's own introductory call, Andrew Chesterman's contribution suggested four 'theoretical models' for ethical translation practices (representation, service, communication and norms) and outlined a stirring *Proposal for a Hieronymic Oath* (2001: 139–54). Increasing globalisation, massive growth in translation and associated ethical questions were also the focus for Irish theorist Cronin (2003), while questions of ethics and translation in relation to conflict, resistance and social change were addressed by Baker (2006) and Inghilleri (2005). Interest in ethical aspects of translation and interpreting mushroomed around this time and in the decade that followed, with edited collections and special issues of journals directly addressing the topic, including a special issue of the French language journal *TTR* in 2004, Sandra Bermann and Michael Wood's collection of essays on *Nation, Language and the Ethics of Translation* (2005), a special issue of *The Translator* on 'non-professionals' translating, edited by Luis Pérez-González and Şebnem Susam-Saraeva and including a sustained focus on ethical considerations of activist and non-professional practice (2012), and Mona Baker and Carol Maier's special issue of the *Interpreter and Translator Trainer* devoted to ethics in training contexts (2011). Other recent scholarship has explored translation and the translator in relation to questions of ethical concern, such as empowerment and inclusion (Tymoczko 2007), activism and commitment (Boéri 2008), development (Marais 2014), ecology (Cronin 2016), justice (Inghilleri 2012) and migration (Inghilleri 2017). Nor has the focus on literary translation and ethics been lost among this recent blossoming of interest, with the new English translation of earlier work on ethics, politics and poetics by Meschonnic (2011) bringing his ideas to a wider readership, for example.

In contrast to the early focus on ethics in relation to literary and religious translation by a small number of Western European scholars, the first two decades of the twenty-first century have witnessed the extension of concern to a wider range of ethical issues as well as the beginning of a project to 'decentre' Translation Studies (Wakabayashi and Kothari 2009), with debates featuring more diverse contributors from a wider range of cultures, nations and languages. In this, developments in relation to ethics in Translation Studies have mirrored those in related disciplines such as Communication Studies (Rao and Wasserman 2007). Also in contrast to the early focus on the translation of literary and sacred texts has been a stronger new focus on professional translation and interpreting practice as a legitimate topic of scholars' concern. Heike Walker's translation of Anthony Pym's (1997) lectures at the *Collège international de philosophie* in Paris, *On Translator Ethics*, focuses attention on 'the translator's professionalism in philosophical terms' (Pym 2012: 2). Rebecca Tipton's and my special issue of *The Translator* suggesting the new theme of 'Translation, Ethics and Social Responsibility' (2017) is an attempt to consider how an important debate in applied ethics, on social responsibility and corporate social responsibility, might apply to translation, while Tipton's 2017 collection, edited with Carmen Valero-Garcés, brings sustained attention to ethics in relation to public service interpreting and translation. Along with work by Mustapha Taibi and Uldis Ozolins on community translation (2016), these offer new perspectives on an areas of translation practice which have previously been neglected by researchers and where ethical challenges are prominent.

Ethical themes and questions in translation theory and practice

The next section summarises the main ethical themes and concerns which have been the focus of attention in Translation Studies thus far but also includes the professional practice of translation and interpreting. The initial emphasis in the academic discipline was firmly on ethical considerations when translating literary and religious texts. Researchers later went on to tackle a wider range of issues and challenges in relation to translation theory but also began to devote serious attention to professional practice. Theoretical developments were thus occurring alongside greater deontic attention to ethics in the translation and interpreting profession. This reflected the spread of the academic discipline of Translation Studies and the concurrent growth of what was increasingly described as the language-services industry. From the 1990s, an increasing number of professional associations for translators and interpreters were established internationally and, like most such bodies, they saw part of their role as codifying, and sometimes regulating, ethical professional conduct.

This section thus moves on to the latter two categories identified in Crisp's 1998 account of ethics: *ethical concepts and theories* and *applied ethics*; but it also challenges his separation of the two. It is difficult to conceive of a discussion of ethical concepts and theories in relation to translation which entirely excludes applied ethics, because there are critical links between the interpreting and translation professions and Translation Studies. Academics naturally look to professional practice to inspire, inform and test theoretical reflections on translation ethics. The relationship is not one-sided or parasitical, though. Translation Studies has made an important contribution to the profession, and this is perhaps particularly true in relation to ethics. Notably, academics bring a less directly engaged or partial perspective and an understanding of the historical and philosophical context which can illuminate difficult debates in the industry, whether these are emerging current challenges or perennial problems which can be better understood by taking the long view. They can examine professional codes critically, comparatively and independently of the associations which draw them up. Importantly, they educate students of translation and interpreting about ethical aspects of practice and thus have a significant role, and ethical responsibility, in the future ethical development of the professions.

Chesterman (1993: 1) has previously pointed out the risks in such academic engagement, railing at 'the long tradition of confusion in translation studies, between descriptive and prescriptive aims'; it is significant that he targeted this criticism precisely at scholarly work on translation ethics. This confusion is arguably also endemic in philosophical ethics, of course. Ethics has long been concerned with 'the advocacy of particular ways of living or acting', as Crisp recognises in his discussion of ethical concepts and theories (1998). The main themes which have attracted the attention of philosophers through the centuries, according to Crisp, will now be used as a framework to structure the following snapshot of ethical themes and questions as they relate to translation. The aim is to present a broad-brush descriptive account while acknowledging that there is an inherent danger of prescribing or reinforcing what is worthy of attention in the study of ethics, philosophy and translation.

At the heart of ethics since Greek philosophers enquired into *eudaimonia* ('happiness' in Crisp's preferred translation) has been 'the question of what makes for a human life that is good for the person living it' (ibid.). Crisp acknowledges this long history in Western ethics but focuses more directly on the modern tradition of consequentialism – that is, 'we are required by morality to bring about the greatest good overall'. Depending on how we define 'the good', this leads to a wide range of views about how we ought to live or act. Theories of the good or the good life (and their opposites, 'the bad'/evil) are present in Translation Studies in discussions of topics such as translator responsibility and agency, the ethics of translating religious or missionary texts, translation in situations of conflict, translator and interpreter conduct in ethically challenging contexts and the roles and responsibilities of educators. Translation theorists have differed on what constitutes the good in relation to translation decision-making and practice just as philosophers have for other domains or areas of life. This has been a particularly rich source of inspiration and debate in interpreting studies (Wadensjö 1998/2013; Angelelli 2004a).

Crisp goes on to oppose consequentialist views (based on ideas of 'the good') to deontological ones (based on ideas of 'the right'). He explains the difference by pointing to deontological theories' claims that 'we should keep a promise even if more good overall would come from breaking it' (1998). A parallel might be seen here to debates in Translation Studies around such ideas as the tension between the translator's moral agency and duty of impartiality (see, for example, Chesterman's (2015) critique of Inghilleri's work, contrasting deontic and utilitarian approaches). Crisp situates a later reaction in philosophical ethics against consequentialist and deontological ethics, and a return to ancient Aristotelian notions of the virtues during the second half of the twentieth century, when philosophical attention turned to the elaboration and analysis of virtues and related concepts (for example, charity, honour, integrity, prudence, trust, truthfulness). In Translation Studies too, consideration of such virtues can be observed in the attention devoted to broader themes including charity (attention to pro bono, volunteer and community translation), integrity (in relation to social justice and social responsibility, for instance) or issues of trust and truthfulness.

In all the above, it is clear how intimately Translation Studies' focus on ethics is intertwined with examples and illustrations from translation practice, and it is indeed in relation to applied ethics that Crisp's illustrations correspond most directly to debates in Translation Studies. While recognising that ethics has always been applied to real life, he focuses in his account on philosophical ethics since the 1960s and the interest in 'detailed discussion of particular issues of contemporary practical concern' (1998). The areas of medicine (particularly issues involving life and death) and advances in science and technology (particularly information technology, risk and the responsibilities of scientists), both highlighted by Crisp, have drawn substantial attention from both academics and practitioners in relation to translation ethics. In relation to medicine, first, it is unsurprising that this profession, with its more developed ethical infrastructure and training, has provided a rich source of reflection in relation to translation ethics. Interpreters and translators who work in the medical domain are engaging with a profession where ethics is considered deserving of serious attention and where ethical challenges are often acute. In relation to advances in science and technology, second, issues of applied ethics have been the focus of work in Translation Studies on ethical integration of new technologies such as machine translation and speech recognition; the impact on translation quality and access of emerging technologies; ownership of translation resources in relation to their exploitation by technology providers; and, indeed, the role of translation in ethical communication of scientific discoveries and knowledge across languages.

Crisp situates the more recent development in applied ethics of such detailed discussion of particular issues in medicine or technology as part of a wider movement involving research into the ethical requirements of particular occupations, including some which have previously not been subject to much philosophical attention (Crisp mentions business, journalism, law and sport). In Translation Studies too, there has been a similar development of a more outward-looking approach, with academics increasingly considering how those from a range of professions who rely on translators and interpreters are affected by this interaction, the ethical dimensions of such connections and the impact on users and intermediaries of all kinds. In this, work in Translation Studies reflects a preoccupation in philosophical ethics with human relationships, between individuals but also between society, state and individuals. Here, Crisp mentions such familiar themes as the ethics of the market (see the work by Abdallah (2011), Cronin (2003, 2016), Gentile (2017) and others on the broader political and economic context in which translation is commissioned, performed, financed, accessed and used). Other topics he suggests under the area of human relationships may not thus far have been the focus of significant attention in Translation Studies, but there is a body of emerging work on such areas as the ethics of sexuality in relation to translation (work on 'queering' Translation Studies or the ethics of translating pornography) which suggests this picture is changing. One significant site of human impact which has increasingly been a focus for philosophical ethics is the planet and those who live on it or will live on it in future. Again, while not all of the areas Crisp highlights under this heading appear to be directly relevant for a discussion of ethics in relation to translation, some of the themes he suggests are also drawing the attention of researchers in Translation Studies, such as development ethics, ecological philosophy, obligations to future generations and sustainability, particularly in relation to technology.

Notably absent from Crisp's main themes and areas, however, are some of the dominant debates in Translation Studies, particularly in relation to applied ethics. Naturally, Crisp could not cover all areas of importance in philosophical ethics in his relatively brief *Handbook* chapter, and his selection is necessarily subject to his own inherent biases and focus as well as those of his discipline; this is something he recognises from the outset. However, the difference in focus between Crisp's selection for philosophy and the ethical issues which have dominated discussion in Translation Studies might perhaps illuminate what is distinctive or of unusual significance in relation to translation ethics. Most obvious among the key areas in which the Translation Studies focus on ethics seems somehow distinct from that of philosophical ethics (at least in Crisp's presentation of that field) is the more sustained deontological focus in relation to the translation and interpreting professions. This is to be expected given the more direct link between Translation Studies and one related set of professional activities, something which does not exist for academic philosophy and any single profession. Ongoing work makes clear this firm connection between the practice and theory of translation. Academics have drawn on novel research methodologies to be able to investigate professional interpreting or translation ethics *in situ* (e.g. Angelelli's 2004b study of healthcare interpreting in US hospitals, with an emphasis on ethics), but practitioners too have played an important part in studying and analysing the nature of translation and interpreting duties or obligations (for instance, practising translator Chris Durban devoted a chapter to a detailed applied discussion of 'Ethics' in her 2010 guide, with Eugene Seidel, to how to become a *Prosperous Translator*). Professional associations such as the American Translators Association have developed training and accreditation programmes in relation to ethics with a clear deontological emphasis, while researchers including the Canadian Julie McDonough Dolmaya (2011) have paid ongoing attention to codes of ethics or Continuing Professional Development requirements in relation to ethics.

The deontological focus has not been limited to professional practice of translation and interpreting, though. It is also particularly apparent in wide-ranging discussions of the ethics of provision by non-professionals of all types (O'Hagan 2011). Translation and interpreting are unregulated activities in most countries, so that untrained, unqualified (and often unpaid) providers are commonly used (Taibi and Ozolins 2016). Even where translators and interpreters are subject to some degree of formal registration or have access to training and qualifications, there are inevitably substantial exceptions where professional providers are not an option. This is due to factors such as the high number of languages now needed, many of which do not have any corresponding formal qualifications or even agreed written forms; fluctuating demand for some language pairs making professional practice unviable; and the cost of provision. This challenging context has been exacerbated by soaring demand for information globally in the internet age. The large numbers of unqualified or *ad hoc* translation providers, such as child language brokers and volunteer bilinguals, are frequently pressed into service in natural emergencies, conflicts and other high-stakes situations, where ethical decision-making can be particularly fraught or demanding but where no training or support are available. A significant body of work has focused on the ethical issues related to these sorts of non-professional translation and interpreting from a deontological perspective. Important themes explored here include: the ethics of translating out of the mother tongue into rare languages, and from 'dominant' to 'less dominant' languages; ethical considerations for trained professionals working alongside non-professional providers; the role and duties of interpreter and translator trainers; ethical challenges for non-professional providers and their clients in particular settings such as courts or police work; and the role of translation in language preservation and social inclusion. This is another area where the close ties between the academic discipline and translation and interpreting practice have been significant. Notorious miscarriages of justice and tragedies have been attributed in official reports internationally to inadequate provision of translation and have led to academic reflection on the ethical duty to prevent their recurrence.

The ethical issues seen as important by philosophers, according to Crisp, and in Translation Studies are marked by differing levels of emphasis on technology. While Crisp indicates that the ethical implications of technological developments have been an important theme for philosophers, they have been more prominent in debates on translation ethics. The ethical implications of emerging technologies have increasingly been the focus of work in relation to interpreting, too, as speech recognition and remote-video interpreting technologies have developed and begun to be used more widely. The rise of machine translation (MT) and the concomitant focus on post-editing and translation quality have regularly been considered in terms of their ethical implications for a range of affected parties including translators, language-service providers, software developers and end users. Scholars have studied the ethical dimension of related human deskilling, issues of confidentiality and ownership of intellectual capital or products, and the appropriate use and limits of technologies such as MT and computer-assisted translation tools. Ethical aspects of human–machine interaction have drawn increasing attention as the technologies have become more pervasive and sufficiently reliable to be integrated in professional workflows, in at least some conditions. The impact of technology on interaction *between* humans has been an important topic too. Debate here has centred on the ways different players in the production and use of translation have agency, influence or power, and how the increasing reliance on technological tools is affecting this picture. Others have directed attention to translator/interpreter relationships with clients, users and other affected parties when the technology has a greater role and impact.

Many of these questions about ethical aspects of new technologies are difficult to separate from broader sociocultural issues. Technological developments have occurred alongside, and played a part in, major ongoing shifts in social structures, migration patterns, trade, information and employment. The world is increasingly connected. Pym has argued (2001) that a key factor in the 'return to ethics' in Translation Studies has been growing acknowledgement of the importance of intercultural communication in this context and of communication being about much more than language. Translation Studies, as an 'inter-discipline', has drawn here on related developments across a rich array of other academic fields including business ethics, communication ethics and sociology. The 'social' and 'cultural' turns in Translation Studies emphasised differing cultural understandings of ethical behaviour and different historical traditions and conceptions of ethics, for example, though there continues to be frustratingly little communication across languages and intellectual traditions on this point, at least in Western Translation Studies. That a discipline concerned with translation continues to communicate overwhelmingly in one *lingua franca*, English, is in no small way ironic, but it also raises important questions in relation to ethics. Who is published, read and cited in Translation Studies, whether in relation to ethics or any other topic of interest to the discipline? What does this mean for power, access to information, education and the future ethical development of both the academic discipline and the translation industry? Such questions are increasingly considered worthy of attention. Work on language and rights, translation policy in a changing political climate and the effects of market conditions on translation provision and democracy has often invoked broad ethical concepts such as fairness, justice and trust. The move away from the 'conduit' model of interpreting towards a more engaged or even activist participation in translated encounters has been framed in terms of ethical responsibility or duty, as have calls for translator visibility, engagement and social or political activism. In this view, the translator is inevitably implicated in political and ethical terms and bears responsibility for his or her choices and behaviour, whether at the level of the individual assignment or, more broadly, in the resulting impact on society. Translation Studies is a discipline which places text at its centre, so it is not surprising that scholars have turned to narratives and texts of various kinds to understand and guide difficult ethical choices. Mona Baker's introduction of a narratological approach (2006), based on developments in Communication Studies, offers one novel way to understand the reasoning behind ethical decision-making in translation. Codes of practice have also been an important area of study, though they are recognised as insufficient guides, as they are unable to include all possible situations, even if a single ethical response were feasible. Key concepts in the codes such as accuracy, confidentiality and impartiality require interpretation and are likely to be understood differently. Moreover, the various codes sometimes contradict or undermine one another, and may come into conflict with higher-level ethical duties such as safeguarding, so the ongoing exercise of informed ethical judgement by practising interpreters and translators is essential.

Informed exercise of ethical judgement by academics has also been the topic of some debate in Translation Studies in recent years, whether in their roles as public intellectuals (for example, around interpretations of the Israel boycott in relation to Translation Studies events, publications and scholars) or in relation to research ethics when working across languages and cultures. There are manifold possibilities for conflicting ethics or different ethical understanding in such endeavours. Some scholars have adopted a deontological approach here, setting out in some detail recommended ways of working ethically as Translation Studies researchers. Such attempts call to mind the limits of translator codes of conduct, however. Translation Studies is an inter-discipline which draws on multiple other disciplinary perspectives, all with their own approaches to ethics, in order to examine translation, an area of practice which itself encompasses all industries and types of human communication; as such, ethical conduct is unlikely ever to be satisfactorily codified or static. There is still no agreement on the central question of whether translation can ever be ethical (since it involves compromise and betrayal of either source or target text) or is an ethical act par excellence, enabling communication and understanding across languages and cultures where there would otherwise be none.

Conclusion and future directions

The blossoming of research on translation ethics has if anything underscored the gaps in knowledge. Chief among these is the need for broader perspectives to illuminate ethical issues and approaches. As in philosophy (e.g. Park 2013), work on ethics in Translation Studies has neglected important bodies of knowledge from different linguistic or cultural perspectives. Chinese, Japanese, Russian and other strong ethical traditions remain conspicuous by their absence in relation to translation, at least in Western Translation Studies, yet the skills to translate canonical works are unusually available in this discipline. Translations with informed commentaries might provide fresh insights from long-standing traditions. A broader array of perspectives in other terms is also likely to be fruitful: this might mean discussing work by academics in philosophy and Translation Studies from a wider range of backgrounds (for instance, in terms of age, culture, gender, language, sexuality or social class). But it might also mean including the perspectives of far more other parties in translated encounters: users and readers of all kinds, clients and commissioners, those affected by translation and those who cannot access translation when they need it.

The social and political context in which translation and interpreting are commissioned and performed is also likely to carry on raising important ethical questions. Ongoing technological and environmental developments will continue to affect translation and interpreting in unpredictable ways with unforeseen ethical implications. High levels of migration and our increasingly diverse societies involve ethical issues as well as cultural, economic, linguistic, political and social ones, and all these factors will continue to interact in complex new ways. Researching these areas will not be straightforward, and research conduct will continue to merit serious reflection. Crisp's distinction between ethics and applied ethics does not hold true for translation, where the boundaries between academic theory and professional practice are more fluid. Translation Studies is likely to continue to look to other disciplines with established ethical training and support, such as medicine or social work, for inspiration and understanding of how to achieve a helpful balance between theory and practice. The developing conversation between philosophy and Translation Studies offers a rich source of data (translation ethics as a topic of study), methods of analysis and helpful support: philosophy can bring an informed understanding of ethics to bear on translation theory and practice, and assist Translation Studies in making connections between translation, other professions and other academic disciplines.

Related topics

Translation theory and philosophy; culture; equivalence; feminism; the translation of philosophical texts; mysticism, esotericism and translation; toward a philosophy of translation.

Further reading

Inghilleri, Moira. 2008. 'The Ethical Task of the Translator in the Geo-political Arena', *Translation Studies* 1 (2): 212–23. (An account of the relationship between the social, the *ethical* and the *political*, based on military linguists' translations in the context of the 'war on terror', this highlights many of the current debates in Translation Studies.)

Koskinen, Kaisa. 2000. *Beyond Ambivalence: Postmodernity and the Ethics of Translation*. Tampere: University of Tampere. (An informative critical discussion of some of the leading contributions in Translation Studies, notably the work of Pym and Venuti in relation to ethics.)

Meschonnic, Henri. 2011. *Ethics and Politics of Translating*. Translated and edited by Pier-Pascale Boulanger. Amsterdam/New York: John Benjamins. (An engaged and thoroughly illustrated explanation of what it might mean to translate ethically.)

Pym, Anthony. 2001. 'The Return to Ethics in Translation Studies'. In *The Return to Ethics*, edited by Anthony Pym, special issue of *The Translator* 7 (2): 129–38. (Includes Pym's call for renewed attention to ethics, and Chesterman's proposal for a 'Hieronymic Oath'.)

References

Abdallah, Kristiina. 2011. 'Towards Empowerment. Students' Ethical Refections [sic] on Translating in Production Networks'. *The Interpreter and Translator Trainer* 5 (1): 129–54.

Angelelli, Claudia. 2004a. *Revisiting the Interpreter's Role: A Study of Conference, Court, and Medical Interpreters in Canada, Mexico, and the United States*. Amsterdam/Philadelphia: John Benjamins.

Angelelli, Claudia. 2004b. *Medical Interpreting and Cross-Cultural Communication*. Cambridge: Cambridge University Press.

Arrojo, Rosemary. 1994. 'Fidelity and the Gendered Translation'. Special issue of *TTR: Traduction, Terminologie, Rédaction* 7 (2): 147–63.

Baker, Mona, ed. 1998. *Routledge Encyclopedia of Translation Studies*. London/New York: Routledge.

Baker, Mona. 2006. *Translation and Conflict: A Narrative Account*. London/New York: Routledge.

Baker, Mona, and Carol Maier, eds. 2011. 'Ethics and the Curriculum: Critical Perspectives'. Special issue of *The Interpreter and Translator Trainer* 5 (1).

Berman, Antoine. 1984/1992. 'Translation and the Trials of the Foreign', translated by Lawrence Venuti. Reproduced in Lawrence Venuti, ed. 2000. *The Translation Studies Reader*. London/New York: Routledge: 284–97.

Bermann, Sandra and Michael Wood, eds. 2005. *Nation, Language and the Ethics of Translation*. Princeton/Oxford: Princeton University Press.

Boéri, Julie. 2008. 'A Narrative Account of the Babels vs. Naumann Controversy: Competing Perspectives on Activism in Conference Interpreting'. *The Translator* 14 (1): 21–50.

Chesterman, Andrew. 1993. 'From "Is" to "Ought". Laws, Norms and Strategies in Translation Studies'. *Target* 5 (1): 1–20.

Chesterman, Andrew. 2001. 'Proposal for a Hieronymic Oath'. *The Translator* 7 (2): 139–54.

Chesterman, Andrew. 2015. 'Review of Moira Inghilleri, *Interpreting Justice. Ethics, Politics and Language*'. *Target* 27 (2): 313–18.

Crisp, Roger. 1998. 'Ethics'. In *Routledge Encyclopedia of Philosophy Online*. Routledge, doi: 10.4324/9780415249126-L132-1. www.rep.routledge.com/articles/overview/ethics/v-1.

Cronin, Michael. 2003. *Translation and Globalization*. London/New York: Routledge.

Cronin, Michael. 2016. *Eco-Translation: Translation and Ecology in the Age of the Anthropocene*. London/New York: Routledge.

Drugan, Joanna, and Rebecca Tipton, eds. 2017. *Translation, Ethics and Social Responsibility*. Special issue of *The Translator* 23 (2).

Durban, Chris, and Eugene Seidel. 2010. *The Prosperous Translator: Advice from Fire Ant and Worker Bee*. FA&WB Press.

Even-Zohar, Itamar. 1979. 'Polysystem Theory'. *Poetics Today* 1 (1/2): 287–310.

Gentile, Paula. 2017. 'Political Ideology and the De-Professionalisation of Public Service Interpreting: The Netherlands and the United Kingdom as Case Studies'. In *Ideology, Ethics and Policy Development in Public Service Interpreting and Translation*, edited by Rebecca Tipton and Carmen Valero-Garcés. Bristol: Multilingual Matters, 63–83.

Gentzler, Edwin. 2014. 'Translation Studies: Pre-Discipline, Discipline, Interdiscipline, and Post-Discipline'. *International Journal of Society, Culture and Language* 2 (2): 13–24.

Hermans, Theo, ed. 1985. *The Manipulation of Literature: Studies in Literary Translation*. London/Sydney: Croom Helm.

Hustvedt, Siri. 2017. *A Woman Looking at Men Looking at Women: Essays on Art, Sex and the Mind*. London: Sceptre.

Inghilleri, Moira. 2005. 'Mediating Zones of Uncertainty: Interpreter Agency, the Interpreting Habitus and Political Asylum Adjudication'. *The Translator* 11 (1): 69–85.

Inghilleri, Moira. 2012. *Interpreting Justice: Ethics, Politics and Language*. London/New York: Routledge.
Inghilleri, Moira. 2017. *Translation and Migration*. London/New York: Routledge.
Inghilleri, Moira, and Carol Maier. 2009, 'Ethics'. In *Routledge Encyclopedia of Translation Studies*, London/New York: Routledge, 100–4.
Jakobson, Roman. 1959. 'On Linguistic Aspects of Translation'. Reproduced in Lawrence Venuti, ed. 2000. *The Translation Studies Reader*. London/New York: Routledge, 113–19.
Koskinen, Kaisa. 2000. *Beyond Ambivalence: Postmodernity and the Ethics of Translation*. Tampere: University of Tampere.
Lefevere, André. 1992. *Translation, Rewriting, and the Manipulation of Literary Fame*. London/New York: Routledge.
Levinas, Emmanuel. 1989. *The Levinas Reader*, edited by Sean Hand. Oxford: Basil Blackwell.
Malmkjær, Kirsten, and Kevin Windle, eds. 2011. *The Oxford Handbook of Translation Studies*. Oxford: Oxford University Press. http://dx.doi.org/10.1093/oxfordhb/9780199239306. 013.0016.
Marais, Kobus. 2014. *Translation Theory and Development Studies: A Complexity Theory Approach*. New York/Abingdon: Routledge.
McDonough Dolmaya, Julie. 2011. 'Moral Ambiguity: Some Shortcomings of Professional Codes of Ethics for Translators'. *JoSTrans: The Journal of Specialised Translation* 15: 28–49.
Mellinger, Christopher D., and Thomas A. Hanson. 2017. *Quantitative Research Methods in Translation and Interpreting Studies*. London/New York: Routledge.
Meschonnic, Henri. 2011. *Ethics and Politics of Translating*. Translated and edited by Pier-Pascale Boulanger. Amsterdam/Philadelphia: John Benjamins.
Nida, Eugene A. 1964. *Toward a Science of Translating. With Special Reference to Principles and Procedures Involved in Bible Translating*. Leiden: E. J. Brill.
O'Hagan, Minako, ed. 2011. *Translation as a Social Activity. Community Translation 2.0*. Special issue of *Linguistica Antverpiensia* 10.
Park, Peter. 2013. *Africa, Asia and the History of Philosophy: Racism in the Formation of the Philosophical Canon 1780–1830*. Albany, NY: SUNY Press.
Pérez-González, Luis, and Sebnem Susam-Saraeva, eds. 2012. 'Nonprofessionals Translating and Interpreting: Participatory and Engaged Perspectives'. Special issue of *The Translator* 18 (2).
Pym, Anthony. 1997. *Pour une éthique du traducteur*. Arras/Ottawa: Artois Presses Université/Presses d'Université d'Ottawa.
Pym, Anthony. 2001. 'The Return to Ethics'. Special issue of *The Translator* 7 (2).
Pym, Anthony. 2012. *On Translator Ethics: Principles for Mediation between Cultures*, translated by Heike Walker. Amsterdam/Philadelphia: John Benjamins.
Rao, Shakuntala, and Herman Wasserman. 2007. 'Global Media Ethics Revisited: A Postcolonial Critique'. *Global Media and Communication* 3 (1): 29–50.
Reiss, Katharina, and Hans J. Vermeer. 1984/2013. *Grundlegung einer allgemeinen Translationstheorie*. Tübingen: Niemeyer; translated by Christiane Nord as *Towards a General Theory of Translational Action*. Manchester: St. Jerome.
Simon, Sherry. 1996. *Gender in Translation: Cultural Identity and the Politics of Transmission*. London/New York: Routledge.
Spivak, Gayatri Chakravorty. 1987. *In Other Worlds: Essays in Cultural Politics*. London: Methuen.
Steiner, George. 1975. *After Babel*. Oxford: Oxford University Press.
Taibi, Mustapha, and Uldis Ozolins. 2016. *Community Translation*. London/New York: Bloomsbury.
Tipton, Rebecca, and Carmen Valero-Garcés. 2017. *Ideology, Ethics and Policy Development in Public Service Interpreting and Translation*. Bristol: Multilingual Matters.
Toury, Gideon. 1978. 'The Nature and Role of Norms in Translation'. Reproduced in Lawrence Venuti, ed. 2000. *The Translation Studies Reader*. London/New York: Routledge: 198–211.
Tymoczko, Maria. 2007. *Enlarging Translation, Empowering Translators*. Manchester: St. Jerome.
Venuti, Lawrence. 1986. 'The Translator's Invisibility'. *Criticism* 28 (2): 179–212.

von Flotow, Luise. 1991. 'Feminist Translation: Contexts, Practices and Theories'. *Traduire la théorie: TTR* 4 (2): 69–84.
Wadensjö, Cecilia. 1998/2013. *Interpreting as Interaction*. London/New York: Routledge, originally published by Addison Wesley Longman.
Wakabayashi, Judy, and Rita Kothari, eds. 2009. *Decentering Translation Studies: India and Beyond*. Amsterdam/Philadelphia: John Benjamins.

16
Feminism

Valerie Henitiuk

Introduction: an exchange of words and women? Mitiarjuk and *Sanaaq*

In the early 1950s, a 23-year-old Inuk[1] named Mitiarjuk (1931–2007) is asked by a Catholic missionary newly arrived in her northern Quebec settlement of Kangirsujuaq to draw up lists of words and phrases to help him learn the Inuit language. This creative and independent-minded woman quickly grows bored with her limited, not to mention culturally foreign task. The more or less passive role of furthering someone else's goals is rejected in favour of a more equitable co-production of knowledge. In what in fact constitutes a striking act of self-assertion, Mitiarjuk takes up the valuable tool of syllabic writing that she has only just acquired (and which complements her considerable oral narrative skills) and instead begins conceptualizing and writing out stories. The original priest moves on, others take his place, but Mitiarjuk continues to express herself, over the space of some two decades. *Sanaaq* would eventually comprise 48 interlinked episodes concerning a young widow (who remarries early in the story), her daughter, and their small community in the 1920s, detailing the period of initial contact between Inuit and missionaries, the imposition of a market economy, and the impact of government intervention that would forever alter their lifestyle. Profoundly impacted also over that time period has been Inuit language use, along with traditional expressions of gender and gender roles, sexuality, and naming, as we will see below, all reflected in meaningful ways in the translations (along with their paratexts) of Mitiarjuk's text.

Sanaakkut Piusiviningita Unikkausinnguangat – the full title reads literally 'a fictional story about the old ways of Sanaaq and her family' – was first published in its original Inuktitut only in 1984, with the close involvement of Bernard Saladin d'Anglure, a Sorbonne-trained anthropologist who founded the seminal journal *Inuit Studies* in 1977 and is well known for his work on shamanism and the 'third gender', or 'third social sex', among Inuit. He was made aware of Mitiarjuk's initial stories as early as 1956, through contact with the priest who had collected them. By 1962 (Saladin d'Anglure 2002: 9), he had taken them up as his doctoral project, under the general direction of none other than Claude Lévi-Strauss, often called the father of modern anthropology. Saladin d'Anglure encouraged Mitiarjuk to carry on writing, eventually himself shaping her work for publication in both Inuktitut and, almost twenty years later, his own French version. It would take yet another decade before English-language readers finally gained access to this significant woman-authored, minority-language text, through Peter Frost's 2014 relay translation.

The late-twentieth- and early-twenty-first-century emergence on the world stage of successful Inuit-Canadian women such as the artist Kenojuak or environmental leader Sheila Watt-Cloutier may suggest a sudden shift from more typically subordinate positions. However, Inuit culture has always valued female roles, in terms of contributing vital skills to their community and passing along accumulated wisdom (see, e.g., Jackson 1996 [1994]: 39).[2] *Sanaaq* itself readily challenges a wide range of preconceptions that readers, whether Inuit or *qallunaat*, may hold. In its author we have a woman who never attended school but would go on to become an important educator, particularly of her people's language. Mitiarjuk had from childhood mastered both masculine and feminine life skills: as the eldest child in a family with no sons, she had been taught hunting and fishing along with traditional sewing and other homemaking techniques. Further, contrary to the customary practice of brides joining the husband's family, her own marriage was uxorilocal. This atypically gendered upbringing coupled with her well-developed creative abilities (Mitiarjuk's talent as a soapstone sculptor is also appreciated) allowed her to offer an engrossing as well as uniquely comprehensive record of the day-to-day life of all members of her community, both male and female, so it is no surprise that Saladin d'Anglure showed an early interest in her writing and went on to produce a French translation and eventually to have his student produce an English one. And, finally, she creates a literary work: *Sanaaq* has been called 'the first Inuit novel ever written' (see the publisher's website at https://uofmpress.ca/books/detail/sanaaq), despite the fact that Mitiarjuk herself would never have read a novel nor indeed any works of literature other than those of an ecclesiastical nature at the time she began to write. Although there are various positive (even impressive) aspects to her life story, this author's agency and voice are problematized throughout her text's translation journey.

The involvement of the Church in Mitiarjuk's life and writing is far from irrelevant to my concerns here, given her early adoption of Catholicism, not to mention the long, closely intertwined history of translation studies with biblical translation. Feminists have highlighted the male-centred language and tropes of established religion in order to demonstrate its often misogynist nature, and they have insisted on more inclusive language in modern versions of the Bible (see, e.g., Simon 1996: 124–31 and von Flotow 2000); recent scholarship has also looked at gender inclusivity in the Qur'an (see, e.g., Hassen 2011).

In *After Babel*, George Steiner describes the work of Levi-Strauss as being based on social structures understood 'as attempts at dynamic equilibrium achieved through an exchange of words, women and material goods' (Steiner 1975: 302). While the reference here is to the workings of an entire society, the notion of words and women being passed between and among the men or institutions who hold the balance of power is also directly relevant to an understanding of the fate of women writers in translation. It is important to bear in mind that Frost had previously been Saladin d'Anglure's MA student and, having no Inuktitut, worked exclusively from his former supervisor's French translation. This unique woman's text comes to English-language readers exclusively through two successive and closely connected (white) male translators, neither of whom is a literature specialist, much less possesses a background in either translation studies or women's studies. Saladin d'Anglure has enjoyed a long and distinguished anthropological career, with his translation and other writings being grounded in that specific expertise and backed by the academic establishment he so effectively represents. Although Frost is an experienced and conscientious French-English academic translator, his own formal training has also been in anthropology (personal correspondence). Complicating matters in an interesting and important way, Saladin d'Anglure positions himself in all of his research as a passionate reader of gender on various levels. While not intending to dismiss the very real contributions of either of Mitiarjuk's existing translators, it is worthwhile to consider how the text might read were English-language readers to have access through a more direct route, or one less influenced by a single authority, or one more explicitly informed by feminist theory, or even – dare I suggest – through an actual female lens.

The way in which the newly literate Mitiarjuk deliberately and determinedly assumes her role as preserver/transmitter of cultural memory for her own community stands in stark contrast with the more typically imposed role of native informant in anthropological research. In crafting her own response to the priest's original request, Mitiarjuk turns the tables on what Talal Asad has characterized as the 'asymmetrical tendencies and pressures in the languages of dominated and dominant societies' (1986: 164). She prefers to use her mother tongue to create not long lists of isolated, deracinated, decontextualized words and phrases but instead coherent stories about the types of people and settings she recognizes; she rejects a unidirectional relationship in which she would play the passive, voiceless native. Mitiarjuk immediately puts her new tool of literacy to specific, almost idiosyncratic use to expand its reach and power rather than slavishly doing what is asked of her by the *qallunaaq* priest, erstwhile figure of absolute authority.

This is of course not to deny that power hierarchies and patriarchal institutions and practices exist and are deeply implicated in the fate of her text. As I discussed in 'Translating Woman: Reading the Female through the Male', citing Annette Kolodny, reading is a learned social process,

> an activity heavily influenced by what we are taught and the type of texts to which we are exposed: 'We read well, and with pleasure, what we already know how to read, and what we know how to read is to a large extent dependent on what we have already read' [...].
> (Henitiuk 1999: 473)

My concern here is with the way this particular Inuit woman's text has or has not been read and transmitted, because her mediators are not only not women but also not well versed in feminist critical theory, thus untrained in how to read women's writing and what specifically to read for, both what is written and the often meaningful silences between.

Any translation necessarily involves manipulation (Hermans 1985), conscious as well as unconscious choices that affect the resulting text and thus how it reaches a new readership – this is not intended as criticism along the lines of *traduttore traditore* (i.e. the omnipresent 'the translator is a traitor' theme) but is simply descriptive of the act's essential nature. What may well elude readers of these two published translations of *Sanaaq* is the centrality of the protagonist's experience *as a woman* and thus her experience of and reaction to patriarchal attitudes and power hierarchies. Mitiarjuk describes, for instance, such gendered life crises as having to reject an unwanted and overly insistent suitor; an unmarried pregnant woman being rejected by the Church; and the eponymous heroine being beaten by her husband, so badly that she must be sent thousands of kilometres south to the hospital for several weeks. Presumably such episodes are what led the *Times Literary Supplement* reviewer to describe Mitiarjuk's book as 'an even rarer marginal literature' than might be expected, namely, 'feminist Inuit fiction' (Anon. 2014: 32). But *Sanaaq* is made available to non-Inuktitut-speaking readers exclusively by a male, highly privileged *qallunaaq* academic – whether at one or two removes (since Frost is in effect translating Saladin d'Anglure rather than Mitiarjuk herself) – and thus the opportunity for a more feminocentric reading is lost. In Saladin d'Anglure's postface from 2002, he acknowledges that his author provides 'an original female viewpoint on Inuit life and psychology' and goes on to lament that this is 'too often described by men and by people from outside Inuit culture who have underestimated the contribution of women and ignored their viewpoint' (translated in Frost 2014: xvii). How ironic, then, is the fact that both her translators are men, and men from outside that culture, although Saladin d'Anglure admittedly knows Inuktitut and has spent a considerable amount of time in Inuit communities. Further, it is hard not to notice the absence of Mitiarjuk's own voice in all of the paratextual matter (reproduced, in English, in Frost's version) in his French translation, despite their close working relationship over a period of four decades.

Feminism and translation

The foundational work of Sherry Simon (1996) and Luise von Flotow (1997) on the intersection of gender and translation, now some twenty years old (itself drawing on earlier essays by, e.g., Godard 1984, Lotbinière-Harwood 1991, Levine 1991 and Arrojo 1994), continues to inspire scholars working on a wide range of theories, texts and contexts (see, e.g., Mezei 1986, Chamberlain 2000 [1988], Henitiuk 1999, Sardin 2009 and von Flotow 2011). Translators informed by feminist thought have brought to light a wealth of previously unknown women's writing from around the globe. Feminists have usefully addressed what it means to be a woman translator, in cases where the source author is male and his text explicitly or even implicitly misogynous, but also where the source author is female and previous critical response has been unfairly dismissive or even non-existent. Further, translation itself has rightly been proposed as a means for resisting overly restrictive social constructions and thus for re-evaluating and challenging the status quo. Translation (or retranslation, as the case may be) in such cases functions as a critical act that offers the possibility of 'recontextualizing the ideology of the original text' (Levine 1991: 3) as well as of its reception. It has been argued that, since women have always had to 'translate' a hostile patriarchal discourse in order to express experiences unrepresented in mainstream literature, they are uniquely sensitive to the role language plays in constructing power relations as well as meaning. This leads to the notion that women occupy a privileged space from which to critique the limits of a given discourse, especially one based on harmful binaries, and to articulate previously silenced views. Based on these and related ideas, a variety of ways have usefully been explored of increasing awareness of women, women's writing and how it has been read and mediated.

Authority and originality remain highly gendered concepts, informed by questions of difference and dominance, and because of their double marginalization, women translators may be well positioned to write and act transgressively. Feminist translation can function and indeed has functioned as both critique and creative innovation. Translation has sometimes been likened to rape, to an act of colonizing brutality perpetrated on a text: a translator must capture and penetrate the original in order to possess it (see, e.g., Lotbinière-Harwood 1991 and Arrojo 1994; also see Mezei 1986 and 1988 on 'translation as betrayal' and Henitiuk 1999 and 2015 on male translators' deliberate or inadvertent stifling of women's voices and themes). This rhetorical figure, while seeming to preclude women from successfully translating anything at all, has nonetheless proven to have great subversive potential. Feminist translators have paradoxically located their challenge to patriarchal oppression in aggressive appropriation of an otherwise recalcitrant text.

The fact that translation has traditionally been conceived of as a lesser act of procreation or reproduction than the autonomous production that an original text may represent necessarily problematizes many of the positive connections suggested above and underscores a range of complex political implications (see, e.g., Chamberlain 2000 [1988], discussed below). Throughout history, women have often turned to translating precisely because they have been barred from direct authorship. This then raises questions central to both feminism and translation, about voice, visibility, gatekeeping, autonomy, agency, and so on.

In the 1970s, the women's movement and subsequent feminist debate over socially constructed sex roles gave rise to new conceptions of gender as a set of conventional behaviours and characteristics that function to create an individual and limit that individual's identity as either masculine or feminine. The focus during that initial paradigm (again, for both feminism and feminist translation studies) was on biased treatment of women within a patriarchal culture and society, and the onus (certainly by the 1980s) was on women translators as well as writers to correct the then prevalent representation of their sex. A second paradigm, dating from the 1990s, rejected simple binary oppositions and destabilized gender itself as a meaningful category. Since then, the emphasis has been on diversity (of sexual orientation, class, ethnicity, race, and so on), underscoring the range of socio-political factors that construct gendered identity. Translation itself began to be understood as a performative act, with serious attention being paid to how contingency and instability are encoded in language.

If Western society has only recently come to understand that gender is, rather than a reductive binary, in fact a continuum (almost as plural as are feminisms), long-established Inuit culture and beliefs may have been more fluid on this topic. As suggested above, a major theme of Saladin d'Anglure's career-long research has concerned what he terms 'le troisième sexe social des Inuit' [the third social sex among Inuit], which he argues inherently troubles any simplistic gender duality. In Inuit culture, it was, for example, a common practice to raise children according to the gender of their namesake,[3] rather than their biological sex; Saladin d'Anglure also describes a traditional belief that a foetus could change its sex at birth (*sipiniq*). On a perhaps more straightforward level, he points specifically to our author as among those whose gender is less easily classified:

> À Kangiqsujuaq (au Nunavik) par exemple, il y avait Mitiarjuk, une femme inuit qui avait tout appris de la chasse et du maniement du kayak ou du traîneau à chiens avec son père, souvent malade, qu'elle suppléa jusqu'à son mariage (il n'y avait pas de garçon dans sa fratrie), quand Naalak, son mari, accepta de venir vivre chez ses beaux-parents et d'être le pourvoyeur de la famille.
>
> (Saladin d'Anglure 2007: 167)

> In Kangiqsujuaq (in Nunavik), for example, there was an Inuit woman named Mitiarjuk, who had learned all about hunting and how to manage a kayak or a dogteam from her father, who was often ill and whom she replaced as the family's provider until her marriage (there were no boys among the siblings), when her husband Naalak agreed to come live with his in-laws and assumed that role.
>
> (translation mine)

As is common in colonial contexts worldwide, missionaries worked quickly to put a stop to many traditional practices, imposing marriage customs and gender roles prevalent in the colonizing, hegemonic culture.

Feminism and translation studies

Possibly owing to this country's history of both colonization and official bilingualism, Canadians (especially within Quebec) have played a significant role in elaborating feminist approaches to translation studies, with groundbreaking work produced by Barbara Godard, Susanne de Lotbinière-Harwood, Annie Brisset, and others. Much of this early writing emphasized a profoundly creative practice that experimented with translating not only French/English but also masculine/feminine, and resisted any single solution. In place of a strictly linear path toward the logical, correct interpretation, there is a strong underscoring of the playfulness of a multivalent translation process and what it has to say about the ever shifting relations between cultures and between the sexes. In particular, Godard's coinage of the term 'womanhandling' posited a 'feminist translator, affirming her critical difference, her delight in interminable re-reading and re-writing, [who] flaunts the signs of her manipulation of the text [. . .]' in a bid to challenge and even replace the stereotypical view of a translator as 'modest, self-effacing' (1990: 91). In place of such stereotypes we find the translator as an active participant in creating meaning (Godard 1990: 94), who, by performing the complexity of gender, opens up space for new feminist readings. Sherry Simon's 1996 *Gender in Translation: Cultural Identity and the Politics of Transmission* and Luise von Flotow's *Translation and Gender: Translating in the 'Era of Feminism'*, published only one year later, build on this work and remain essential reading. Von Flotow's 2011 collection *Translating Women* and her subsequent 2016 volume *Translating Women: Different Voices and New Horizons* (co-edited with Farzaneh Farahzad) bring the discussion up to date, with essays addressing women in their varied roles as authors, characters, and translators.

Lori Chamberlain's influential 1988 article, 'Gender and the Metaphorics of Translation', details how the inferior status of both women and translation has given rise to metaphors that are overtly sexualized and inherently biased. Drawing on notions of fidelity as a conceptual framework, coinages such as the seventeenth-century 'les belles infidèles' [lit. the beautiful unfaithful ones; note that 'belles' is a feminine noun], which suggests that only the ugly can be counted on to be faithful, not only characterize translations as untrustworthy but also point to a misogyny underlying the theoretical discourse. Aggressive, male-dominated imagery can be identified from St. Jerome, who describes the translated text as a slave captured and brought home in triumph, through George Steiner, who conceptualizes translation as invasion, extraction, even penetration (1975: 303), and beyond. Even our discipline's most basic terms of 'source' and 'target' language/literature suggest doing violence to a text: as translator Gregory Rabassa once reminded us, targets are typically understood at something one shoots at in order to kill (1989: 5). As has been underscored in various venues, there are many other possible images and approaches to conceiving of the translation process that could prove more fruitful. For example, alternative metaphors such as 'a song sung in harmony, a dance of approximation, sub-version, a twin voice, good sabotage, a clearing of mist, an erotic engagement, a spiritualization, a coupling' (Ouriou 2010: 3) offer very different ways of understanding both the process and product of translation and could point to elements that our own standard terminology may have blocked from view.

Sex and sexuality comprise a developing sphere of interest in translation studies. See, for example, the range of essays in Santaemilia (2005) and Larkosh (2011) (von Flotow 2009 provides a helpful overview as well) that explore important theoretical gaps in prior research on translation and gender, including the (re)negotiation of sex, gender, and translation, along with taboos and censorship, and point out intersectionality with race and ethnicity. The same criticism that was levelled at feminism in earlier decades, namely that of being almost exclusively white, Western, and middle-class and thus caught up with a particular, limited set of concerns, can be applied to translation studies. The discipline is now being challenged to be more inclusive, to incorporate, draw from, and work with texts, scholars, and approaches originating in many parts of the world beyond Western Europe and North America. One reason it is helpful to focus on an Inuit text in a chapter on feminism and translation is that this serves as a salutary reminder that even within these hegemonic geographic regions there exist cultures and languages, not to mention gender identities, that have also long remained largely unknown to translation studies.

(In)visibility and naming

Translation by definition makes visible but, as with any implicitly political act, rarely in a fully unproblematic way. Someone has to select texts and authors, from specific languages and cultures, to be translated. Someone has to produce the translation, into another specific language, and then someone has to agree to publish it. With all the pressures arrayed against them, including the low likelihood of even being given the chance to write, how many female authors have texts that actually get translated, through which mediators, and for what purposes, ostensible or otherwise? It is neither a simple nor transparent matter to counter the long-standing effects of linguistic, cultural, economic, and gendered obscurity.[4] Further, despite the very best of intentions, where the power differential is as extreme as in the case of an unschooled Inuk and a Sorbonne-trained academic, there is a very real risk of oppressively 'speaking for' the Other.[5]

An example of a woman author with close connections to the top of the hierarchy being rendered in an overly simplistic and deeply unsatisfactory way may be helpful here. In recent years, scholars have detailed the problematic translation history of Simone de Beauvoir's *Le deuxième sexe* [The Second Sex] (see, e.g., Simons 1983 and Bogic 2010 and 2011). The argument is that, despite its undeniable and ongoing global influence, this 'bible of feminism' (see, e.g., Rodgers 1998: 59) has been radically decontextualized and thus diminished when translated into English. The initial English translation, a bestseller for Knopf (only four years after its original 1949 publication) by zoologist Howard M. Parshley, has served as the basis for much feminist (not to mention anti-feminist) thinking and action, despite the fact that it is an abridged (by approximately 10 per cent) and decidedly partial reading. The publisher was keen to have a version it felt would be accessible to an American public, which had been primed by the recent appearance of the Kinsey Report on male sexuality to be interested in learning about female sexuality. It was assumed from the outset that US readers would be impatient of the French philosopher's more nuanced arguments, and thus Parshley was directed to excise significant sections and themes, shaping the English-language version in particular ways. A long-awaited new translation by Constance Borde and Sheila Malovaney-Chevalier, Paris-based English teachers and authors of various textbooks for English as a Second Language and of cookbooks, whose previous translation experience was slight, appeared in 2009. The general consensus is that the retranslation is not an improvement (see, e.g., Bogic 2011). If even key books by such respected intellectuals as de Beauvoir suffer such a fate, this does not bode well for translation of women writers more generally.

At least we do have two readings of *The Second Sex* in English, however flawed, and since the original exists in a widely spoken language, comparisons can be readily made. The case of texts in minority or lesser-taught languages is even less promising, in that they are typically granted only one chance at being rendered into a given major language. Whether that publication is a failure or a success, the odds of the market demanding another version or a champion stepping forward to insist on it are slim.

A close analysis of translators' attitudes as expressed in prefaces, introductions, and notes usefully reveals the gendered ways that readers have been led to understand and respond to female authors, often with a negative impact on the reader's reception and experience of a text. Due attention to the mediation involved in a specific image of author and work being offered up for consumption helps us bear in mind the inherently untransparent nature of the act of translation. These paratexts tend to function implicitly if not explicitly to reveal aims and objectives as well as biases (see, e.g., Henitiuk 2011).

It is not unusual to find women authors characterized as less skilled or more culturally/ politically naïve than they actually are. Note that Mitiarjuk went on to publish almost two dozen booklets (primarily pedagogical resources) and was part of the team that produced Lucien Schneider's important Inuktitut–French dictionary; she was also awarded an honorary doctorate from McGill University. Yet although Saladin d'Anglure acknowledges many of these facts, overall he presents her as coming out of nowhere, unconnected to other work going on at the same time, including literary production by other Inuit. Neither is it inconsequential that the copyright to both his French translation and Mitiarjuk's original Inuktitut version is held by the anthropologist, or that even the English translation is presented as something akin to a co-written production (interestingly, no biographical or other information is provided on Frost, which only underscores Saladin d'Anglure's role).

Saladin d'Anglure also characterizes Mitiarjuk as spontaneously producing a novel, which is problematic on two additional levels. First, there has been a long-standing tendency in various times and places to categorize women's writing into particular, often devalued genres, and, second, is *Sanaaq* in fact a novel? In Mary Eagleton's introduction to the 'Gender and Genre' section of her 1996 *Feminist Literary Theory: A Reader*, she reminds us that women in the Western literary tradition have always had or been seen to have a special relationship with the novel (Eagleton 1996 [1986], 137–43). Its development in the late eighteenth and early nineteenth century is closely tied to middle-class women, both positively (i.e. white, middle-class women were able to write in the privacy of their homes) and negatively (i.e. the genre lacked status and was deemed to require less intellectual rigour than other genres such as poetry). Feminist critics have famously challenged dismissive evaluations of women novelists and their literary production, not to mention their female readerships (see, e.g., excerpts from Moers, Armstrong, Mitchell, Jacobus, and Felski in Eagleton's *Reader*). Therefore any translation that so identifies an Inuk woman's prose must in some way address this gendered history and context and be examined with a critical eye. Saladin d'Anglure himself introduces his author's work as 'un roman atypique' [an atypical novel] (2002: 5) and argues that he was obliged to give it 'la forme et la fluidité d'un roman pour grand public' [the shape and flow of a novel for general readers] (ibid.: 11), which should and does give pause. In any case, as Martin (2014) has rightly noted, Mitiarjuk's book (whether in the original or either of its translations) may not look to readers like any other novel they've ever seen, being instead 'a long work of prose fiction restrained in its exploration of the characters' psyches'. As such, we may find that it fundamentally challenges expectations as much generic as ethnocentric.

I have written elsewhere about some challenges involved in the translation and circulation of classical Japanese women writers, whose works form that country's literary canon and, through translation, are read globally. The fact of female authorship cannot be separated from an understanding and appreciation of their work without the risk of misrepresenting both Japanese and world literary history. While there are now numerous translations in various languages, perhaps none has truly done justice to their masterpieces; it is no accident that virtually all of the translators for these authors have been men. In the case of Sei Shōnagon, of the some fifty versions of her *Pillow Book* that exist in European languages, only a handful have been by women (Henitiuk 2012). My 2008 article 'Going to Bed with Waley: How Murasaki Shikibu Does and Does Not Become World Literature' (Henitiuk 2008) posits

Virginia Woolf as the absent, impossible translator of *The Tale of Genji*. The argument is that Woolf's reading, had we access to such a thing, might have opened up for English-language readers an entirely other – not to mention immensely enriched and enriching – conception of both author and work.

Women writers have often circulated in the public sphere only through somewhat camouflaged identities – note, for instance, that both Murasaki Shikibu and Sei Shōnagon are sobriquets – and Inuit naming has its own peculiar history. Saladin d'Anglure provides his author's name in full as Salomé Mitiarjuk Attasi Nappaaluk. Traditionally, Inuit are given a single non-gender-specific name, usually that of someone who has recently died, although they often use kinship terms instead of proper names among themselves. When missionaries began baptizing new converts in the latter half of the nineteenth century, most Inuit were given Christian names. Then, in the early twentieth century, the government of Canada assigned each Inuk a 'disk number' in the form of a dog tag they were to wear around their necks at all times. In the 1960s, the government initiated what is known as 'project surname', which forced family names – usually those of a father or grandfather – on all Inuit. Therefore *Sanaaq* is frequently catalogued under Nappaaluk, and many news stories or other sorts of entries about our author use that name. Valerie Alia's extensive research in what she terms 'political onomastics' offers various examples of Inuit women expressing dismay and incomprehension at being suddenly told they bear the name of their husband's grandfather (see, e.g., Alia 2005: 264). Traditional naming practices, however, have in fact carried on underground, beyond the reach of the patriarchal institutions of power and control. Interestingly, despite its undeniable ethnographic interest, Saladin d'Anglure ignores this history entirely in his preface and postface, and the cover of both the English and French translations provide Mitiarjuk's given and family names without comment. (The 1984 publication in Inuktitut, with its bilingual cover, gives the author's name as Mitiarjuk Nappaaluk in the French title but Mitiarjuk alone in her language.)

'But there's one that I don't name': sexuality, censorship, and elision

The role of both anthropologists and translators is to interpret unfamiliar works, cultures, and traditions, by definition that which may initially prove impenetrable to readers. In her important study of how these two disciplines intersect, Sturge (2014) quotes Clifford Geertz as rightfully pointing out that an anthropologist cannot count on shared knowledge and thus 'is faced with the unattractive choice of boring his audience with a great deal of exotic information or attempting to make his argument in an empirical vacuum' (Geertz 1973: 36). Inuit having a unique and complex culture, even today only very partially known by *qallunaat*, a significant amount of explanation, paraphrase, or other forms of mediation by external experts is generally deemed essential for comprehensibility. Such mediation can also, however, readily take the form of elision and censorship, which constitutes a third option: the silencing of troublesome or poorly understood voices or themes.

Particular choices made by Mitiarjuk and by translators on her behalf are important and worthy of attention, and I would like now to tease out one intriguing example of (self-) censorship. In a passage halfway through the book in which a traditional game played with small animal bones is described, our author takes pains to name all of the bones each character manages to obtain: for example, some are shaped like dogs, known as *qimminguat*, some like seals, *nassinguaq*, and others like women, *arnanguat*. Mitiarjuk's narrator also comments: 'ilangalli uqannginakku' (Nappaaluk 1984: 127), which is rendered in two different ways by Saladin d'Anglure in his 1969 PhD dissertation. We first find a gloss of the Inuktitut as 'mais certains d'entre eux, je ne les dis pas' [but some of them, I don't say] (Saladin d'Anglure 1969, vol. 2: 166), and then in the anthropologist's 'free translation' (ibid., vol. 1: 265) as: 'mais il y en a un parmi eux que je ne nomme pas' [but there's one of them that I don't name; in the Inuktitut original, the direct object here is in fact singular, not plural, so the initial gloss would appear to be in error[6]]. The translation is accompanied by Saladin d'Anglure's 'ethnographic commentary' on the facing page explaining that there are three bones called *ussulutuq* [or *utsulutuq*], or 'vulva' (ibid., vol. 1: 264), and that the author opts not to name them since she was at that time writing for a priest.

The postface of Saladin d'Anglure's full French translation of *Sanaaq* includes a section titled 'Le fond de l'oeuvre et le non-dit qui l'entoure', or 'the content of the work and all that remains unsaid'. Here he explains that it was only at his prompting back in 1965 that Mitiarjuk had clarified the name of that particular bone, that she had in fact originally concluded the list of bones by writing: 'il y en a encore un dont je n'ose pas donner le nom' [there is still one whose name I don't dare give] (Saladin d'Anglure 2002: 280). And in the body of Saladin d'Anglure's published translation, in place of the original self-censorship, we find a straightforward bilingual rendering of the full list:

> des *qimminguat* (figures de chien [dog figurines]), un *aquviartulutuq* (figure de personne accroupie [figurine of a person kneeling]), un *sappa* (coffre à bagages [storage box]), une *qulliq* (lampe à huile [oil lamp]), un *kaivvasuk* (figure d'adolescent [figurine of an adolescent]), un *illaulusuk* (figure de fœtus [figurine of a fetus]), un *utsulutuq* (figure de vulve [figurine of a vulva]) et un *kuutsitualik* (figure de déhanché [figurine of a disabled person]).
>
> (2002: 170)

One can well imagine that by 2002 it was no longer the case that the priests were her primary readers, or perhaps the times had simply become somewhat less prudish, but something important is lost here. To my mind, what is significant throughout this exchange is not only how aware Mitiarjuk was of her readership but also how she insists on the integrity of the cultural practice being described, even at a time when she feels unable to name all its parts. For instance, in her initial writing she could easily have entirely omitted any mention of the bone with the awkward name/shape but opted not to do so, thus paradoxically ensuring that it is kept in plain sight.

At first glance, the English version appears to go full circle, restoring on some level the original's coyness, with the body of the text reading simply and (to the vast majority of readers) opaquely: 'a *qimminguat*, an *aquviartulutuq*, a *sappa*, a *qulliq*, a *kaivvasuk*, an *illaulusuk*, an *utsulutuq* and a *kuutsitualik*' (Frost 2014: 121). Unlike the French version, the English defines all Inuktitut terms only in the glossary found at the back of the book, whether at Frost or his publisher's behest. For the term in question, we find if we flip the pages: 'little bone, figurine of a vulva' (ibid.: 221). Further, Saladin d'Anglure's separate preface and postface have been combined into a single foreword (again, it is unclear whether this was the choice of the translator or the publisher), which means that English readers who begin at the beginning are in effect told to watch for this reference as they read on. So far so good, but the manner in which the heading of this section has been rendered in English brings us up short. Frost gives this as: 'Content and Implicit Surrounding Details' (Frost 2014: xii). A tremendous amount of ink has been spilt in feminist criticism from Simone de Beauvoir to Hélène Cixous to Julia Kristeva to Nicole Brossard about everything that may be left unsaid/unspoken in women's writing and the multiple, complex reasons for such silences.

Accordingly, to render the expression 'non-dit' by the anodyne 'implicit details' is, if not disingenuous, at the very least cloth-eared.

Despite the strong, central roles women traditionally held in Inuit communities, censorship and especially self-censorship nonetheless do have particular valences for women. McGrath (1997) explains how, in order to circumvent cultural taboos against women calling attention to themselves, most female Inuk autobiographers record only their childhoods, or wait until advanced old age before attempting to write about their lives. It is possible that Mitiarjuk used these stories of Sanaaq and her daughter Qumaq to fictionalize her own childhood, allowing her to describe her life as a woman while avoiding violation of a taboo. The lack of cultural background for understanding Inuit writing in general and for seeing culture-specific patterns can result in inaccurate translation, not to mention unfairly negative appraisals of literary quality, and this is only exacerbated where texts authored by women are concerned. As McGrath rightly notes, even if it is sometimes relatively easy to see and appreciate the narrative structure of a man's text, based on well-known legends, other reference points may be 'almost entirely overlooked because we are unfamiliar with the bulk of Inuit folklore' (1997: 226). And the case of women's writing is even more dire:

> It could well be that Inuit women use patterns of narrative that are not as easily recognized, or that are unknown outside the culture because the majority of non-Inuit who recorded Inuit oral literature were male missionaries and male anthropologists who had no interest in or access to the female domain.
>
> (McGrath 1997: 226)

In another, earlier reference to Geertz, Elaine Showalter suggests that '[a] genuinely "thick" description of women's writing would insist upon gender and upon a female literary tradition among the multiple strata that make up the force of meaning in a text' (1988: 350). Although this feminist critic is not speaking of translation per se, her comment certainly applies to a linguistic activity intrinsically concerned with textual analysis and interpretation. A politically informed and intentional reader of this literature could potentially offer a version that brings out and analyses layers of the text hitherto downplayed – layers that include not only literary but also explicitly gendered aspects. A review of the specific text that concerns us here, written by Inuk scholar Norma Dunning, helpfully underscores how 'the violence laid upon Sanaaq [during the beating by her husband] changes the tone of the story' (2014: 271).

I have written elsewhere about the dangers of male translators being blind to feminocentric discourse systems (see, e.g., Henitiuk 1999), and the array of male mediators (i.e. three different missionaries; Saladin d'Anglure himself; his initial doctoral supervisor, Jean Melaurie; his research director, Levi-Strauss; his publisher, Alain Stanké; and, finally, his student Frost) with their hands all over Mitiarjuk's text is far from a minor point in this literary translation historiography. Regardless of the fact that something of great value has been accomplished in actually making *Sanaaq* available to be read outside of Inuit communities, certain aspects of this text's mediation from Inuktitut through French to English are inherently problematic. It is clearly essentialist and wrong to claim that one must be biologically female to translate accurately the voice of a woman author (see Kinloch 2007 on whether one must be gay to translate a gay author). Nonetheless, an awareness of the issues brought into the debates around gender and translation over the last few decades should surely be considered imperative to a full reading of this early and rare fictional text authored by a female Inuk. Anything short of full, and fully sensitive, engagement has a direct, and negative, impact on the journey this text takes on its way into the hands of its English-language audience, limiting their experience as readers.

Conclusion

Since quite early in the discipline's history, translation studies scholars have been exploiting the premises of feminist theory and practice to argue for a more nuanced and sophisticated understanding of language and culture in general and the sexual politics of translation more specifically. Oppressive structures, practices, and attitudes are exposed as products of an ideology all the more insidious for remaining too long unacknowledged and unchallenged. This chapter has introduced a unique woman's text from a little-known language and culture, that of Inuit in northern Canada, in order to illustrate some of the dangers of readings that may or may not be properly informed by feminism and a full awareness of power hierarchies. In so doing, it has discussed the intersection of feminist theory with the discipline of translation studies, drawing on the particular history of Mitiarjuk's *Sanaaq* from Inuktitut through French to English in order to underscore a number of points about how silences, slippages, and places of indeterminacy in both texts and paratexts must be identified and taken seriously. Feminist translation studies is well positioned to explore these implications, to name and articulate them, and has not only taken up this challenge over the past several decades but must continue doing so.

Notes

1 Inuk is the singular form of Inuit, a term that in Inuktitut means 'the human beings'. Formerly called Eskimos (that term remains current in Alaska), Inuit are a circumpolar, traditionally semi-nomadic people living in Canada, the US, Russia, and Greenland. Non-Inuit are known as *qallunaat* (singular: *qallunaaq*), or 'heavy eyebrows' (NB: the etymology is uncertain); depending on the context, this term *qallunaat* can refer to Whites or simply anyone who is not Inuit.
2 This should not be taken to imply that Inuit women's lives were idyllic in any way; they were, for example, subject to often punishing ritual taboos (see, e.g., Aodla Freeman 1996 [1994]): 249, on the 'very heavy' rules traditionally prescribed for young women, and on the fact that women in general were required to be 'patient and to work without ever complaining'). Many traditional stories, including the widely told tale of Sedna, reference women who either refuse to marry or choose to flee their husbands.
3 As discussed below, traditional Inuit names are not gender-specific.
4 For a compelling argument about inclusion as it relates to this very volume of essays, see Carolyn Shread's chapter on 'Translating Feminist Philosophers' (Chapter 20, this volume).
5 My own implication, as a *qallunaaq* scholar, in the overweening authority so readily assumed by Saladin d'Anglure and others in the earlier generation of Inuit studies must of course be acknowledged, with a view to foregrounding the importance of intersectionality for feminist translation studies.
6 I am indebted to Marc-Antoine Mahieu, of INALCO, for this and many other helpful clarifications of the Inuktitut.

Related topics

Translating feminist philosophers.

Further reading

Santaemilia, José, ed. *Gender, Sex and Translation: The Manipulation of Identities*. Manchester: St. Jerome, 2005. (This volume explores gendered and sexual identities and their relationship to ideologies and power hierarchies.)

Sardin, Pascale, ed. *Traduire le genre: femmes en traduction*. Special issue of *Palimpsestes* 22, 2009. (This special issue offers ten case studies of works and writers in French and English, from the eighteenth century to the present, bringing a gender-oriented approach to translation and transcultural studies.)

von Flotow, Luise, ed. *Translating Women*. Ottawa: University of Ottawa Press, 2011. (A diverse collection of essays that provides a much needed update on the foundational texts related to gender and translation from the late twentieth century; the contributors variously and innovatively apply feminist theory to the study and practice of translation.)

von Flotow, Luise and Farzaneh Farahzad, ed. *Translating Women: Different Voices and New Horizons*. London: Routledge, 2016. (This collection continues the important work of von Flotow 2011, examining the impact of 'Western' feminism on translation in other cultures.)

Acknowledgements

This research was supported by the Social Sciences and Humanities Research Council of Canada.

Social Sciences and Humanities Research Council of Canada   Conseil de recherches en sciences humaines du Canada   Canada

References

Alia, Valerie. 'Inuit Names: The People Who Love You'. In *Hidden in Plain Sight: Contributions of Aboriginal Peoples to Canadian Identity and Culture*. Eds. David R. Newhouse, Cora J. Voyageur, and Dan Beavon. Vol. 1. Toronto: University of Toronto Press, 2005. 251–66.

Anon. Review of Peter Frost's English translation of Mitiarjuk's *Sanaaq*. 'On the Margins'. *Times Literary Supplement* (March 21, 2014): 23.

Aodla Freeman, Minnie. 'Traditional and Contemporary Roles of Women'. In *Inuit Women Artists: Voices from Cape Dorset*. Eds. Odette LeRoux, Marion E. Jackson, and Minnie Aodla Freeman. 2nd edition. San Francisco: Chronicle Books, 1996 [1994]. 248–50.

Arrojo, Rosemary. 'Fidelity and the Gendered Translation'. *TTR* 7.2 (1994): 147–63.

Asad, Talal. 'The Concept of Cultural Translation in British Social Anthropology'. In *Writing Culture: The Poetics and Politics of Ethnography*. Eds. James Clifford and George E. Marcus. Berkeley: University of California Press, 1986. 141–64.

Bogic, Anna. 'Uncovering the Hidden Actors with the Help of Latour: The "Making" of *The Second Sex*'. *MonTI (Monographs in Translation and Interpreting)* 2 (2010): 173–92.

Bogic, Anna. 'Why Philosophy Went Missing: Understanding the English Version of Simone de Beauvoir's *Le deuxième sexe*'. In *Translating Women*. Ed. Luise von Flotow. Ottawa: University of Ottawa Press, 2011. 151–66.

Chamberlain, Lori. 'Gender and the Metaphorics of Translation'. In *The Translation Studies Reader*. Ed. Lawrence Venuti. London and New York: Routledge, 2000 [1988]. 314–29.

Dunning, Norma. 'Review of Peter Frost's English Translation of Mitiarjuk's *Sanaaq*'. *Inuit Studies* 38.1–2 (2014): 269–72.

Eagleton, Mary, ed. *Feminist Literary Theory: A Reader*. 2nd edition. Oxford: Blackwell, 1996 [1986].

Frost, Peter, transl. *Sanaaq. A Novel*. By Mitiarjuk Nappaaluk. Winnipeg: University of Manitoba Press, 2014.

Geertz, Clifford. *The Interpretation of Cultures: Selected Essays*. New York: Basic Books, 1973.

Godard, Barbara. 'Translating and Sexual Difference'. *Resources for Feminist Research* XIII.3 (1984): 13–16.

Godard, Barbara. 'Theorizing Feminist Discourse/Translation'. In *Translation, History and Culture*. Ed. Susan Bassnett and Andre Lefevere. London: Pinter, 1990. 89–96.

Hassen, Rim. 'English Translation of the Quran by Women: The Challenges of 'Gender Balance' in and Through Language'. *MonTI (Monographs in Translation and Interpreting)* 3 (2011): 211–30.
Henitiuk, Valerie. 'Going to Bed with Waley: How Murasaki Shikibu Does and Does Not Become World Literature'. *Comparative Literature Studies* 45.1 (2008): 40–61.
Henitiuk, Valerie. 'Prefacing Gender: Framing Sei Shônagon for a Western Audience, 1875–2006'. In *Translating Women*. Ed. L. von Flotow. Ottawa: University of Ottawa Press, 2011. 239–61.
Henitiuk, Valerie. 'Translating Woman'. *Meta* 44.3 (1999): 469–84.
Henitiuk, Valerie. 'Translating Women's Silences'. *TranscUturAl: A Journal of Translation and Cultural Studies* 7.1 (2015): 4–15. http://ejournals.library.ualberta.ca/index.php/TC.
Henitiuk, Valerie. *Worlding Sei Shônagon: The Pillow Book in Translation*. Ottawa: University of Ottawa Press, 2012.
Hermans, Theo, ed. *The Manipulation of Literature: Studies in Literary Translation*. Beckenham: Croom Helm, 1985.
Jackson, Marion E. 'The Voices of Inuit Women'. In *Inuit Women Artists: Voices from Cape Dorset*. Eds. Odette LeRoux, Marion E. Jackson and Minnie Aodla Freeman. 2nd edition. San Francisco: Chronicle Books, 1996 [1994]. 37–40.
Kinloch, David, 'Lillies or Skelfs: Translating Queer Melodrama'. *The Translator* 13.1 (2007): 83–103.
Larkosh, Christopher, ed. *Re-Engendering Translation: Transcultural Practice, Gender/Sexuality, and the Politics of Alterity*. New York: Routledge, 2011.
Levine, Suzanne Jill. *The Subversive Scribe: Translating Latin-American Fiction*. St. Paul: Graywolf Press, 1991.
Lotbinière-Harwood, Susanne de. *The Body Bilingual*. Toronto: Women's Press, 1991.
Martin, Keavy. 'Review of Peter Frost's English Translation of Mitiarjuk's *Sanaaq*'. *The Globe and Mail* (January 17, 2014): n.p.
McGrath, Robin. 'Circumventing the Taboos: Inuit Women's Autobiographies'. In *Undisciplined Women: Tradition and Culture in Canada*. Ed. Pauline Greenbill and Diane Tye. Montreal: McGill-Queen's University Press, 1997. 223–33.
Mezei, Kathy. 'Tessera, Feminist Literary Theory in English Canadian and Quebec Literature, and the Practice of Translation as Betrayal, Exchange, Interpretation, Invention, Transformation, and Creation'. In *Mapping Literature*. Eds. D. Homel and S. Simon. Toronto: University of Toronto Press, 1988. 47–9.
Mezei, Kathy. 'The Question of Gender in Translation'. *Canadian Fiction Magazine* 57 (1986): 136–41.
Nappaaluk, Mitiarjuk. *Sanaaq unikkausinnguaq*. Roman inuit par Salome Mitiarjuk Nappaaluk. Québec: Association Inuksiutiit, 1984.
Ouriou, Susan. 'Preface'. In *Beyond Words: Translating the World*. Ed. Susan Ouriou. Banff: Banff Centre Press, 2010. 2–4.
Rabassa, Gregory. 'No Two Snowflakes Are Alike: Translation as Metaphor'. In *The Craft of Translation*. Eds. J. Biguenet and R. Schulte. Chicago: University of Chicago Press, 1989. 1–12.
Rodgers, Catherine. 'The Influence of *The Second Sex* on the French feminist scene'. In *Simone de Beauvoir's The Second Sex: New Interdisciplinary Essays*. Ed. Ruth Evans. Manchester: Manchester University Press, 1998. 59–96.
Saladin d'Anglure, Bernard. *Sanaaq, Récit esquimau composé par Mitiarjuk*. Unpublished PhD thesis. Vols 1 and 2. Paris: Ecole Pratique des Hautes Etudes, 1969.
Saladin d'Anglure, Bernard, trans. *Sanaaq. Un Roman*. By Mitiarjuk Nappaaluk. Paris: Stanké, 2002.
Saladin d'Anglure, Bernard. 'Troisième sexe social, atome familial et médiations chamaniques: pour une anthropologie holiste: entretien avec Bernard Saladin d'Anglure'. *Anthropologie et Sociétés* 31 (3) 2007: 165–84.
Santaemilia, José, ed. *Gender, Sex and Translation: The Manipulation of Identities*. Manchester: St. Jerome, 2005.
Sardin, Pascale, ed. 2009. *Traduire le genre: femmes en traduction*. Special issue of *Palimpsestes* 22.
Simon, Sherry. *Gender in Translation: Cultural Identity and the Politics of Transmission*. London: Routledge, 1996.

Simons, Margaret. 'The Silencing of Simone de Beauvoir: Guess What's Missing from the Second Sex'. *Women's Studies International Forum* 6.5 (1983): 559–64.
Steiner, George. *After Babel: Aspects of Language and Translation*. Oxford: Oxford University Press, 1975.
Sturge, Kate. *Representing Others: Translation, Ethnography and the Museum*. London: Routledge, 2014.
von Flotow, Luise. 'Gender and Sexuality'. In *Routledge Encyclopedia of Translation Studies*. 2nd edition. Eds. Mona Baker and Gabriela Saldanha. London and New York: Routledge, 2009. 122–6.
von Flotow, Luise. *Translation and Gender: Translating in the 'Era of Feminism'*. Manchester: St. Jerome, 1997.
von Flotow, Luise, ed. *Translating Women*. Ottawa: University of Ottawa Press, 2011.
von Flotow, Luise. 'Women, Bibles, Ideologies'. *TTR* 13.1 (2000): 9–20.

17
Linguistics

Kirsten Malmkjær

Introduction/definitions

Linguistics is the academic discipline that investigates language in each of its major manifestations – speech, writing and signing – and in terms of each of its aspects – sound (not directly relevant in signing and writing), structure and meaning – and of its place in the society and in the individual. Like any science, linguistics works by way of an interplay between observation, description, hypothesis formation, hypothesis testing and the formulation of theories. This process is circular in the sense that once á theory is formed, it guides observation. Observation is never theory-neutral: what you think you know (your theory), along with what interests you, guides your manner of understanding what you observe and subsequently describe. What prevents the process from being viciously circular is surprise, a major player in scientific advance: If you observe something that should not be the case given what you think you know, you will typically seek for an explanation and perhaps revise your theory.

Linguistics has several sub-disciplines, which will be introduced below. As indicated above, three major, traditional subdivisions are sound, structure and meaning, but modern linguistics also deals with language in use in societies (sociolinguistics), by individuals (psycholinguistics) and in texts (text linguistics, discourse and conversational analysis, and genre analysis). In addition, historical linguistics deals with the history of languages, and comparative or contrastive linguistics is concerned with comparisons between languages, something that can be done with a focus on any of the linguistic sub-disciplines.

Philosophers have defended the relevance of linguistics to philosophy on the grounds that some philosophical problems revolve around the nature of language, and that linguistic theory may incorporate solutions to these problems (see e.g. Katz (1965). Furthermore, Higginbotham (2002: 578) points out that the detailed study of a variety of human languages has enriched philosophers' understanding of logical form.

The sounds of language: phonemics, phonetics and phonology

The sounds of language are the subject of the sub-disciplines of linguistics known as phonetics, phonology and phonemics. The international phonetic alphabet (IPA) chart (freely available from the website of the International Phonetic Association (www.internationalphoneticassociation.org/content/ipa-chart) under a Creative Commons Attribution-Sharealike 3.0 Unported License, Copyright © 2015 International Phonetic Association) lists phonemes, the smallest units of sound in language capable of causing a difference in meaning (see Barry 2006 for a discussion of the controversies surrounding this concept). These are usually represented between slashes (e.g. /p/ for the so-called bilabial plosive that is the first sound in 'pal'). Phonology is the study of how these minimal sounds combine to form syllables and words, which are usually presented within square brackets (e.g. [pal]). The rules for phoneme combination differ between languages, so even though phonemes as such may be language-independent, their realisations in words differ between languages.

One of the reasons for 'foreign accents' is that someone speaking a language that is not their language of habitual use may import into that language the phonemic habits of the language that *is* their language of habitual use. Pronunciation practice can help alleviate this and is therefore useful for interpreters (and spies and language learners). Ear training is an important part of pronunciation training, because unless you can hear how a native speaker pronounces the words of their language in natural speech, you are unlikely to be able to imitate them; and since humans are much better at hearing the distinctions that matter in their own language than they are at hearing those which do not matter in their own language, effort often needs to be made by learners to learn to perceive important distinctions between sounds in the language that they are learning. However, Brown (1977: 14) points out that eye training is equally important: 'It is immensely helpful for most listeners to see the speaker's face as the speaker is talking'; this is because the vocal stance, the shape of the lips and the movements of the tongue and mouth, contains clues to the sounds being made and the words being spoken. Trainee interpreters can therefore benefit from studying these facial/vocal stances; and the absence of these clues to meaning may be partly responsible for the faster onset of fatigue that has been identified in remote interpreting compared to situations where the interpreter is able to see the speaker (Braun 2013; Moser-Mercer 2003).

Words, clauses and sentences

The structure of words, clauses and sentences is the subject of morphology (word structure) and of syntax or grammar (clause and sentence structure). Morphology deals with the combination of morphemes, the smallest meaningful parts of language, in words, and grammar deals with how these words can combine in clauses and sentences. There are many different types of grammar, but the main division between them is between descriptive and theoretical grammars, also often referred to as a distinction between surface (or descriptive) and theoretical grammar. Surface grammars describe how a language has been and is being used in spoken and written text, although typically not beyond the sentence level (larger stretches are dealt with in discourse, genre and text analysis; see below). Theoretical grammars tend to be concerned with language structures in general and with relating the structures of individual languages to these more general structures, which, in turn, are often related to the so-called language faculty of humans. The grammars developed by the American linguist Noam Chomsky are theoretical and focused on language in the mind, whereas those developed by the British linguist Michael Halliday are predominantly descriptive and socially oriented. The distinction relates, very roughly, to one between sociolinguistics, the study of language in use in human societies, and psycholinguistics, the study of language in the individual; however, the distinction is by no means absolute; for example, Hallidayan, or systemic functional grammar, which is clearly focused on language as used by individuals in society, makes claims about the human meaning potential, a notion that is not so different from the idea of the language faculty, although the orientation of the further explanation provided in this conception of grammar is decidedly social. According to systemic functional grammar (see e.g. Halliday 1978, 1985), the human meaning potential has three main components: the ideational, or experiential, the interpersonal and the textual, which orient towards three aspects of the environment, namely 'field', what is going on (ideational or experiential), 'tenor', who is taking part (interpersonal), and 'mode', the part that the language is playing (textual). Field, tenor and mode define the 'register' of a piece of discourse – that is, the configuration of linguistic resources that groups of speakers typically associate with a situation of language use. The notion of register is closely, if not precisely, associated with the notion of genre (see below). Hallidayan grammar, or systemic functional grammar, has become immensely popular within the translation studies community, especially in China (see e.g. Zhang 2015; Webster and Peng 2017).

The smallest grammatical unit of a language is the morpheme, and morphemes may be free or bound. Free or lexical morphemes are those, like 'man', which can occur on their own. Bound, or grammatical morphemes cannot stand alone – for example, '-ly' in 'manly', 'happily' and so on. Some morphemes, such as the plural morpheme in 'men' or the past-tense morpheme in 'went' cannot be divorced from the graphic form of the word. In morphological analysis, these combinations are written as '{man} + {PLU}', and '{go} + {PAST}' respectively. Morphemes constitute or form words, and words can be classified according to their so-called 'part of speech' – strictly speaking a misnomer, since what is at issue is word classes, albeit defined with reference to their function. The parts of speech were originally defined by the Roman grammarian Priscianus Caesariensis, commonly known in English as Priscian, who, in the sixth century, adapted Greek grammar to Latin (Dinneen 1967: 114–15). For English, the *Cambridge International Dictionary of English* (1995: xiii–xviii) gives the following ten parts of speech with their main purposes:

Nouns: refer to people, things, qualities etc.
Adjectives: describe and inform about phenomena
Pronouns: can substitute for a noun(-phrase) or proper name
Determiners: are used before nouns to indicate definiteness and/or quantity
Verbs: ascribe actions or states to someone or something
Adverbs: inform about time, place, or manner of an action or state
Prepositions: indicate directionality, place and relationships between phenomena
Conjunctions: link language units (words, phrases, clauses)
Exclamations/interjections: indicate emotions or are used conventionally in greetings ('hi') or formulaically ('please')
Combining forms: add to words or parts of words to change or add meaning (prefixes and suffixes (rarely also infixes)

Other languages have other, fewer or additional word classes; for example, Danish and German both make much use of discourse particles, a category that does not exist in English (and whose uses and functions are only loosely comparable to those of the English discourse markers, like 'oh', 'well', 'now', 'then', 'you know' and 'I mean'). Interesting issues may arise from differences like this between languages that form translational pairs in a translator's work. For example, the opening clauses of Hans Christian Andersen's story, 'Nattergalen'

(1848, 'The Nightingale') contain two discourse particles next to each other, highlighted here: 'I Kina ved du **jo nok** er Kejseren en kineser' (gloss: in China know you xx xxx is emperor DEFINITE.ENDING a Chinese). In a selection of translations, these clauses are rendered as follows:

Corrin:	In China, as you probably know, the Emperor is Chinese
Dulcken:	In China, you must know, the Emperor is a Chinaman
Haugaard:	In China, as you know, the emperor is Chinese
Shaw:	In China, you know of course, the emperor is Chinese
Spink:	In China, you know, the emperor's a Chinaman

These valiant attempts reflect that 'jo' indicates that whatever is being communicated is already known by both parties, and Corrin's translation, especially, suggests that 'nok' indicates probability; but neither of these explanations of what is indicated are translations, and the expressions proffered for 'jo nok' are not as straightforwardly translations as the remaining parts of these sentences are – as suggested by the variations in the inserted clauses compared to the lack of variation (leaving aside the choice of expression of the nationality of the emperor) in the surrounding clause.

Words form groups or phrases consisting of a head and one or more pre- or post-modifiers. For example, in the nominal group or noun phrase (NP), a noun will be the head word, typically pre-modified with at least a determiner and perhaps also with one or more adjectives, and perhaps post-modified with a prepositional group as in 'The pleasant young man in the corner'. In this NP, 'man' is the head word, 'The' is a determiner and 'pleasant' is an adjective; both pre-modify 'man'; 'in the corner' is a prepositional group which post-modifies the head noun, 'man'. Phrases or groups like this form elements of clauses, which, in the English clause, are subject, verb or predicator, object, complement and adjunct. The subject and object are typically realised by a noun phrase or nominal group, the predicator by a verbal group, the complement by an adjectival or adverbial group, and the adjunct by adverbial or prepositional groups. These groups also have specific structures. Clauses form sentences, either by co-ordination, when each clause is 'free' or capable of standing alone, or by subordination, where one clause is 'bound', or 'subordinate', to the other and unable to stand alone. For example, in 'I was hiding behind a tree and I saw you' the two clauses are co-ordinated (are in parataxis), and both 'I was hiding behind a tree' and 'I saw you' could be used on its own; in contrast, in 'Hiding behind a tree, I saw you' the first clause, 'Hiding behind a tree', cannot be used on its own; it is subordinated to the second clause, 'I saw you'; the relationship between these clauses is called hypotaxis. A free clause in English must indicate tense in the verb (past or present), which 'was' does (past tense) but which 'hiding' does not do. In some languages – for example, in Chinese – the verb does not indicate time (other parts of Chinese clauses can of course do so). The English clause must also indicate definiteness, either indefinite, as in 'a tree', or definite, as in 'the tree'. In some languages, again, this is not necessary. For example, in Polish, nouns do not need to be pre-modified with a determiner. Such differences rarely cause difficulties in translating because, for example, the context is likely to contain information about time, which is indicated in English by the tense of the verb, and about participants' familiarity with objects of the discourse, which is suggested in English by determiners. Other grammatical issues, such as the positioning of verbs at the ends of some clauses in German can cause problems for interpreters, who may be forced to wait for the verb before they can begin to interpret. However, the co-text and context may suggest what the verb is going to be.

Meaning: semantics

Linguistics deals with meaning in its branch of study known as semantics, but although linguistics and philosophy share this nomenclature, the two differ radically in their approaches to the study of meaning. In philosophical semantics – at least in its analytical branch – the main task is to provide an account of what speakers know when they know meaning and of how they can come to know it (Davidson [1973] 1984: 125); but in linguistic semantics, the aim is rather to group words and relationships between words according to their meanings (which are taken to be known). For example, 'dog' is a so-called hyponym of the superordinate term, or hypernym, 'animal'; and 'gold' is a hyponym of the superordinate term, 'metal'. When attention turns to relationships between language and the world in linguistic semantics – for example, to how a dog or gold might be identified – proposals can been made about how the meanings of words can be analysed into smaller parts called components, an endeavour known as componential analysis. For example, 'man' contains the meaning components, or semantic markers, 'adult', 'human' and 'male', whereas 'woman' contains the meaning components 'adult', 'human' and 'female'; and each of these components might itself be further analysed. From a philosophical point of view, this is unsatisfactory because, as Malakoff and Lewis (1983: 190) point out, it is possible to know what they call 'the Markerese translation' of a sentence without knowing the conditions under which the sentence would be true, which is what they believe we need to know in order to approach the development of a theory of meaning. Meanwhile, linguistic semantics operates happily with combinations of componential analysis and analyses of semantic fields. For example, the field of mammals can be conceived of as organisable into increasingly finely distinguished subclasses (e.g. cats, dogs, whales . . .) and further subdivisions of these (e.g. of dogs into poodles, retrievers, boxers, setters and so on). The relationships between members of semantic fields are known as sense relations. Sense relations include sameness of meaning (synonymy), oppositeness of meaning (antonomy), the 'kind of' relation (hyponomy) and the 'part of' relation (meronymy). Among the opposites, some are gradable and others absolute. For example, 'dead' and 'alive' are in principle not gradable (it is not possible, in principle at least, to be more or less dead), whereas 'cold' and 'hot' are gradable. Synonymy is very rare in languages, because languages seem to resist it, so that if two terms should happen momentarily to mean the same, they swiftly take on different nuances or register positions. 'Deep', for example, does not mean precisely the same as 'profound', at least not if collocations and contexts of use are taken into consideration; you cannot really fall into a profound hole. Pairs like 'vixen' and 'female fox' seem to be synonymous and exchangeable in many contexts, but Frege ([1891] 1977: 23) argues that although '"2," "1+1," "3-1," "6:3" stand for the same thing . . . the different expressions correspond to different conceptions'. Of course, this raises concerning issues for the notion of translation between what we view as different languages, because in these, the forms of expressions that are considered translation equivalents (a notion that is discussed elsewhere in this *Handbook*) almost always differ; on the other hand, Frege argues elsewhere that 'The same sense has different expressions in different languages or even in the same language' ([1892] 1977: 58), and by 'sense' Frege means 'mode of presentation' ([1892] 1977: 57). Here therefore Frege appears to throw a lifeline to translators and translation scholars.

Meaning: pragmatics

A later addition to linguistics, related to semantics, is pragmatics, the study of language in use. Interest in this area is probably as great or greater in linguistics than in philosophy, and it is an area that translation studies has also found approachable. Pragmatics originated with the so-called natural-language philosophers, most of them based in Oxford, who started to look for progress in the study of meaning outside of the formalisms that had halted progress in philosophical semantics, as they saw it. The first major work in this area is the theory of speech acts developed by J. L. Austin in the 1930s and expounded in a series of twelve William James lectures that Austin gave at Harvard University in 1955. These lectures were published in 1962 under the title *How to Do Things with Words*. Here, Austin (1962: 3) reacts to what he calls 'the descriptive fallacy', according to which a declarative sentence is always used to describe something and must always be either true or false. Austin points out that many declarative sentences neither describe, report nor state but do very different things such as promising, warning and betting (Austin 1962: 5). Austin calls such utterances performatives or performative utterances, and although these may be explicit about the act that is being performed ('I bet you ten pounds that Jones will win the tournament'), many are much less explicit, as, for example, a shout of 'Fire, fire'. But this shout is just as much a warning as the explicit form, 'I warn you that there is a fire' would have been; it is simply an implicit performative. In fact, every utterance is either an implicit or an explicit performative, because it would be possible to begin every declarative utterance by saying 'I state that' or 'I declare that'. *Ergo* every utterance is a speech act. Both Austin and, later, Searle (1969) drew up lists of broad classes of speech act and of rules for their performance. For example, for promising, Searle suggests the following rules:

> A promise can only be made in an utterance that predicates a future act on the part of the speaker (you cannot promise to do something yesterday).
>
> A promise can only be made if the hearer would prefer that the speaker do what they are promising to do to them not doing it (otherwise it is more of a threat).
>
> A promise can only be made if it is not obvious to both hearer and speaker that the speaker would do the act that is being promised as a matter of course (in the case of most couples (probably), it would be odd for one of them to promise their partner not to be unfaithful to them today).
>
> A promise can only be made if the speaker intends to do the action that is being promised (otherwise the promise is not sincere, that is, not a real promise).

Clearly, knowledge of rules like these is essential for a speaker to be able to function effectively in a speech community, and they must be understood, explicitly or implicitly, by translators and interpreters. Further, speakers need to know when these rules are being exploited in what Searle (1975) refers to as 'indirect speech acts'. For example, in 'Is that your coat on the floor' spoken by a parent to a child, the child will know that one of the rules for questioning is that the speaker must not already know the answer to the question and will therefore look for a different act that the parent may be engaging in, such as reprimand. That anyone should want to use an indirect rather than a direct speech act may be due to considerations of politeness. The same indirect speech acts may not, however, function in different languages. For example, a compliment about an item of clothing may in some cultures suggest that the speaker is asking for the item to be given to them; and repeatedly answering in the negative to an offer of food, which in some cultures may simply be polite, may in other cultures result in the answerer going hungry.

Given the differences between languages that have been discussed briefly above, as well as a multitude of other differences of detail between them, the question of interlingual translatability has often been raised, along with questions about relationships between language and thought, or, more radically, between language and what people perceive as reality. Here, attention must be given to three further areas of linguistics that are of relevance to translation studies in relation to philosophy, namely sociolinguistics, psycholinguistics and text and discourse analysis.

Sociolinguistics

There have been attempts in philosophy to account for language origins with reference to one inventive individual gradually working out how it might be possible for him (or her) to share ideas with other people (see e.g. Locke [1690] 1960: Book Three, Chapter II; Bennett 1976: 137–9). In contrast, Wittgenstein ([1953] (2009): 244–71) argues that language is necessarily social. In any case, as Grayling (1982: 186) points out, it is difficult to imagine how the complexity of thought required to develop a language could be experienced by a language-less creature; it is much more likely that thought and language developed contemporarily; certainly, language as we know it is a social phenomenon, and, as such, it is the subject of sociolinguistics, the study of language in society, of how language is used among pairs and groups of speakers – for example, women (Coates 1986; Coates and Cameron 1988), teenagers (Sagliamonte 2016) or people of specific regions (Trudgill 1984). Language develops and undergoes change through interpersonal interaction, and different groupings of speakers often give rise to different varieties of the same language. In sociolinguistics, we encounter the notions of language variety according to location, the subject matter of dialectology, and according to use, the subject matter of register and genre analysis. Each of these poses interesting opportunities for creativity for translators. Dialect and accent (that is, the grammar, lexis and pronunciation used by groups of speakers in particular locations) raise questions about how one might represent the speaker of, for example, Cockney in translation, given that this particular dialect, with its distinctive accent, is very precisely defined as confined to a specific area of London: how do you 'translate' an area lying within hearing of the bells of St Mary-le-Bow into, say, Swedish? Even if a dialect, with its accent, of Swedish were chosen, it would obviously relate to quite a different geographical location. Of course, understanding (in the sense of being able to comprehend what is being said) accents and dialects is vital for interpreters, who may be required to interpret for speakers who use them. Registers – that is, the selection of language choices that given speaker groups consider appropriate to specific situations – may differ equally across languages and cultures. For example, in British academic circles it is common for students to speak to their lecturers in rather familiar terms and to call them by their first names, a practice which, in my experience, students with backgrounds in some mainland European and Middle Eastern countries find difficult to adopt. Equally, parent–child relationships and consequent speech habits differ markedly between cultures. Register differences are also at least partly responsible for the impression that some British people may form that people from certain other cultures are overly direct or abrupt or even impolite (see House 2005). These issues raise interesting philosophical questions about personality in relation to language: do we adopt a 'realist' position according to which personality is, at least momentarily, a fixed phenomenon, underlying but not affected by mode of expression, or do we adopt an 'antirealist' position according to which the surface evidence of a personality is all that there is to personality. In the former case, a person's personality, or identity, remains stable whatever language they are speaking; in the latter case, a person's personality is affected by the language they are using (for opposing views on this issue see Pavlenko 2014 and McWhorter 2014). How we answer these questions may also impact on translators' and interpreters' translation decisions: for example, if we believe that a very accurate translation of what a person has said may offend the addressee, would we be morally right or wrong if we were to take the risk of a providing a fairly free translation? These speculations take us naturally to the topic of language in the individual, the concern of psycholinguistics.

Psycholinguistics

Psycholinguistics is concerned with the organisation of language in individual brains, language processing, language impairments, the acquisition of language (by young children), bi- and multilingualism and with the learning of second and subsequent languages. Investigations of language organisation in the mind may with time yield results that speak to the interesting quasi-philosophical questions of how to distinguish one language from another, how many 'languages' an individual needs to understand to function in society and so on; and the results of investigations of modes of language learning are helpful for people devising language-teaching syllabuses, including those aimed at translators and interpreters. Individuals' emotional and political attachment to their languages are also interesting and informative topics to study in quests for understanding feelings of belonging and national loyalties; implicit or, indeed, explicit understandings of these associations have at times led conquerors to impose their language on the conquered and to forbid or minimise the use of the conquered people's own language. In this respect, there is clearly considerable overlap between socio- and psycholinguistics.

Language impairments can have surprising effects on translation and interpreting. Ardila (2018: 277) reports that:

> Idiosyncratic disturbances in the ability to translate have been documented in aphasic patients. Paradis, Goldblum and Abidi (1982) analyzed two patients … [who] alternately suffered severe word-finding difficulties in one language while remaining relatively fluent in the other. They retained good comprehension in both of their languages at all times. They were able to translate correctly and without hesitation from the language they could speak well at the time into the language unavailable for spontaneous use, but were unable to translate from their temporarily poor language … into the language they could speak quite well at the time. Aglioti, Beltramello, Girardi and Fabbro (1996) reported a bilingual patient … [whose] mother tongue was Venetian, whereas her L2 was standard Italian. The patient had more difficulties when translating into her mother tongue than into her second language.

As he points out, this finding is surprising if we assume, as is often done, that it is easier to translate into one's mother tongue than out of it. Ardila (ibid.) adds that:

> In language therapy it has been documented that recovery of a word in one language usually generalizes to the other language for cognate words (e.g., English 'fruit', Spanish 'fruta'), but not for non-cognate terms (e.g., English 'pencil', Spanish 'lápiz') (Roberts and Deslauriers 1999) suggesting that cognate words have a common brain representation in bilinguals. However, this cognate effect is variable across patients (Hughes and Tainturier 2015) probably depending upon the specific patient's bilingualism characteristics.

For translation and interpreting, an immensely interesting observation is that whatever form of bilingualism a person may present – it may be bilingualism from birth or bilingualism as the result of later learning; and it may be balanced bilingualism, where both languages are known equally well insofar as that can be established, as opposed to a situation where one language is known better or used more habitually than the other – bilingualism does not come with a guaranteed ability to translate (Toury 1984). This is important for translation studies insofar as it attests to the fact that translation and interpreting are special skills, something confirmed in Valdés' (2003) study of young interpreters, all of whom were bilinguals but only some of whom enjoyed and/or excelled in interpreting; on the other hand, it raises difficult quasi philosophical and ethical questions about the notion that every normal adult speaks their language perfectly: are some people (even monolinguals) in fact especially gifted linguistically? And if they are, wherein does their giftedness lie? And does the extra activity of translating that some bilinguals excel in go some way to explaining or, more accurately, justifying claims that language learning is good for the intellect generally? Generalisations in these politically and culturally sensitive areas are not to be made lightly.

As far as language processing is concerned, findings in translation studies research show that reading for translating is different from reading for comprehension (Schaeffer et al. 2017); it takes more time to read for translation, as people fixate for longer on words in the source text, leading to an overall longer gaze time in the case of reading for translation than in the case of reading for comprehension. As Lykke Jakobsen and Jensen (2008: 116) point out, this suggests that 'a fair amount of pre-translation probably enters into the reading of a text as soon as it is taken to be a source text for translation'. Hypotheses concerning the control that bilinguals and translators have of the activation of their languages may be made as a result of this type of research; and it is possible that the differences referred to above between comparable bilinguals' translating ability may at least partly be a matter of such control.

Genre analysis, text linguistics and discourse and conversational analysis

Genre analysis, text linguistics and discourse and conversational analysis are concerned with the organisation of language into stretches of text that are recognised as befitting particular situations or serving specific social or professional purposes.

Genre analysis

Of these phenomena, genre is the more specialised insofar as a genre, in the technical sense developed by Swales (1990), is a grouping of texts that are 'owned' by so-called discourse communities (Swales 1990: chapter 2 and *passim*). A discourse community is a community that is held together by its special interests, which are catered for by the genres it owns, rather than by co-location, as in the case of traditional communities. Therefore the genres owned by the discourse community are especially important, not only for the exchange of information but for the very existence of the community. Nevertheless, a genre that is common to different cultures may differ considerably in how it is realised or shaped linguistically between them. For example, a genre as simple as the greeting may have highly culture-specific realisations, and this raises questions for translators. When a German or Austrian speaker wishes someone 'grüß Gott' (roughly 'God bless you'), the most suitable translation into English is often a simple 'hello', because the function of greeting is served by this expression in (many forms of) English; but if the speaker is, for example, a monk, 'God bless you' might be equally or more suitable. This highlights the extent to which translators rely on aspects of context, as well as the extent to which 'meaning', at least if understood in terms of the effect utterances have on the world, is dependent on the same.

Swales (1981, 1985, 1987, 1990) developed a type of genre analysis intended to cast light on the conventions governing academic writing in English. For academic article introductions, he initially (1981) identified four so-called moves: (1) establishing the field, (2) summarising previous research, (3) preparing for the present research and (4) introducing the present research. Later, the two first moves were collapsed into one called 'Handling previous research', and scholars have further refined Swales' model or produced models of their own, more or less on the same, move-based principle, which was influenced by the type of discourse analysis developed by John Sinclair and Malcolm Coulthard at the University of Birmingham in the 1970s and 1980s (see below). The aim of Swales' genre analysis was to provide more linguistically precise information about how native speakers of a language structure texts of various genres, and how they signal to their readers that a particular move or section has ended and another begun, than had been provided by, for example, contrastive rhetoric (e.g. Kaplan 1966), which had a tendency to lapse into more or less metaphorical claims about linear versus circular ways of thinking and constructing arguments. As far as translation and interpreting are concerned, as suggested above, genre differences across cultures challenge translators to decide whether to implement radical changes in translation in order to make a translation conform to the conventions that govern its genre in its destination culture, or whether to risk a translation that replicates the conventions of the source text but which may therefore seem alien to its readership.

Text linguistics

Shreve (2018: 165) defines texts as 'units of language larger than a single sentence, typically comprised of several written sentences or spoken utterances grouped together in a particular sequence'. He does not distinguish between text and discourse or between utterance and sentence, whereas here, I distinguish between the analysis of written text (text linguistics) and the analysis of spoken discourse (discourse and conversational analysis). Text analysis can be used to develop text typologies according to shared formal and perhaps also semantic features of texts, and so-called 'text grammars' of rules for combinations of these features have been proposed (see e.g. Van Dijk 1977, 2004). In translation studies, text linguistics has influenced Hatim and Mason (1990), Neubert and Shreve (1992) and Alexieva (1994) (see Shreve forthcoming). As Shreve (forthcoming) points out, if the seven standards of textuality identified by de Beaugrande and Dressler (1981: 3) are indeed standards that must be met in order to ensure text-ness, then they must be met by translations, too. The standards are cohesion, coherence, intentionality, acceptability, informativity, situationality and intertextuality, and a translator needs to be aware of them, whether or not he or she intends to apply them in a translation in the same way, as far as is possible, as they have been applied in the source text. Many decisions in this regard will be determined by the genre conventions that may obtain in the two cultures at issue and which may differ between them. For example, Clyne (1987: 213) finds that German books and articles commonly include a so-called *Exkurs*, a digression in which information that may help readers move through the argument is provided. Mauranen (1992, 1993: 3) shows that Finnish writers of academic texts tend to situate their main thesis later in their text than Anglo-American writers do, while Graves (1997: 235) identifies a marked preference for indirect speech acts of warning on Canadian cigarette packets (e.g. 'Smoking can kill you') compared to direct warnings on American versions (e.g. 'Surgeon General's Warning: Smoking Causes Lung Cancer, Heart Disease, Emphysema, and May Complicate Pregnancy'). He also finds significant differences between marketing letters sent to US addresses and to English-speaking Canadian addresses

(1997: 237). For example, letters sent to American readers tended to begin with the rather familiar greeting, 'Dear Friend', probably seeking to minimise the distance between sender and receiver, whereas letters addressed to Canadians did not include this feature of form (the greeting) but came straight to the point with an expression like 'I am writing to ask you ... '. (1997: 243–4).

Discourse and conversational analysis

Three major, rather different types of analysis of spoken language in natural settings developed from the 1970s onwards: conversational analysis (Sacks, Schlegloff and Jefferson 1974), the analysis of discourse (Sinclair and Coulthard 1975) and discourse analysis (Brown and Yule 1983).

According to the sociological approach adopted by Sacks *et al.*, conversations are structured in terms of turns:

> the existence of organized turn-taking is something that the data of conversation have made increasingly plain. It has become obvious that, overwhelmingly, one party talks at a time, though speakers change, and though the size of turns and ordering of turns vary; that transitions are finely coordinated; that techniques are used for allocating turns ... and that there are techniques for the construction of utterances relevant to their turn status'.
>
> (Sacks, Schlegloff and Jefferson 1974: 699)

They note that the sets of conventions they identify as governing turn-taking, turn-allocation, turn-construction and turn-transitions seem to hold for Thai, New Guinea creole 'and for an undetermined number of languages in the competence of a substantial number of linguists' (Sacks, Schlegloff and Jefferson 1974: 700, note 10). The conventions are that (1) speaker-change occurs; (2) overwhelmingly, one party speaks at a time; (3) where overlaps occur, they are brief; (4) transitions between turns mostly occur without gaps or overlap or with slight gaps or slight overlaps; (5) the order of turns varies; (6) the size of turns varies; (7) conversation length is not fixed in advance; (8) what parties say is not fixed in advance; (9) relative distribution of turns is not specified in advance; (10) the number of parties in a conversation can vary; (11) talk can be continuous or discontinuous; (12) turn-allocation techniques are used; (13) turns can consist of different linguistic units such as a word or a sentence; and (14) 'Repair mechanisms exist for dealing with turn-taking errors and violations; e.g. if two parties find themselves talking at the same time, one of them will stop prematurely, thus repairing the trouble' (Sacks, Schlegloff and Jefferson 1974: 700–1). The point of these observations is (i) to stress that conversations differ from other speech events like meetings, interviews and ceremonies, where, for example, turn-size and speaker selection may be predetermined; and (ii) to cast light on the nature of conversation, because 'all sorts of scientific and applied research use conversations' (Sacks, Schlegloff and Jefferson 1974: 701–2). The main unit of analysis in this approach is the adjacency pair, a pair of utterances, each by a different speaker, of which the first sets up an expectation that the second will be of a particular type. For example, a question is likely to be followed by an answer, although, as Burton (1980: 142) points out, a challenge like 'why do you want to know?' is also possible. This draws inter-speaker relationships into the analysis, potentially, insofar as challenging linguistic behaviour may relate to power relationships, and this is also a feature of the method of analysis of discourse developed by Sinclair and Coulthard (1975).

The method of analysis of discourse developed by Sinclair and Coulthard arose out of a research project entitled 'The English Used by Teachers and Pupils', which was sponsored by the UK Social Sciences Research Council between 1970 and 1972 (Sinclair and Coulthard 1975: 1). Sinclair and Coulthard chose the classroom setting for their analysis because they suspected that (1975: 4) 'Desultory conversation was perhaps the most sophisticated and least overtly rule-governed form of spoken discourse and therefore almost certainly not the best place to begin'. In classrooms, in contrast, the teacher is clearly in control of the discourse. The approach is more 'grammatical' than conversational analysis in its focus on 'the organization of linguistic units above the rank of the clause' (Sinclair and Coulthard 1975: 1), and the units it operates with are called moves. The moves are organised in a rank scale like the one that Halliday (1961) presented for grammar. In a rank scale, the unit at the lowest rank has no structure within its own level; for example, at the level of grammar, the morpheme is the smallest unit and can only be divided into units operating at the level of phonology. The unit at the highest rank itself becomes a unit at the lowest rank in another rank scale. So the sentence, which is the highest rank at the level of grammar, ought to become the unit at the lowest rank of the scale of discourse, in its functional guise as an utterance. However, an utterance turn, to borrow a term from conversational analysis, often seemed too complex to function as the smallest unit in discourse. For example, in the teacher utterance 'To keep you strong. Yes. To keep you strong. Why do you want to be strong?' (Sinclair and Coulthard 1975: 21) there seems to be a boundary between the part that is a response to something a pupil has said and the question at the end, which elicits a new pupil turn. Each of these two phenomena is a move. Moves themselves are composed of acts and form exchanges, and the rank scale for classroom discourse is Lesson – Transaction – Exchange – Move – Act. Each of these, except for Act, has a structure at the level of discourse, although the Lesson is an unordered series of transactions. The typical teaching exchange is composed of an Initiating move, a Response move and a Feedback move, and this core, IRF structure was found to be common in many other types of discourse – for example, doctor–patient discourse (Coulthard and Ashby 1975), drama dialogue (Burton 1980) and courtroom discourse (Harris 1984; Mead 1985), although there are variations on the basic three-part structure (Stubbs 1983: chapter 7).

Unlike the conversation analysts and the analysts of discourse, Brown and Yule (1983) do not offer a particular analytical framework; indeed, they distance themselves from 'the formal approach' in favour of a focus on language functions, of which they identify two, the transactional and the interactional, which correspond to the dichotomies between the representative and the expressive (Bühler 1934), the referential and emotive (Jakobson 1960) and the ideational and interpersonal (Halliday 1970; Brown and Yule 1983: 1). They label their own approach both 'primarily linguistic' and 'pragmatic', and they draw on insights from sociolinguistics, psycholinguistics, philosophical linguistics and computational linguistics in order to put 'the speaker / writer at the centre of the process of communication' (1983: x and ix). Theirs is an immensely wide-ranging account of 'how people use language to communicate with each other' (1983: 270), and it introduces the analyst to issues pertaining to context, topic, staging, information structure, cohesion and coherence.

These developments in linguistics away from an exclusive occupation with the written sentence and towards enhanced interest in conversations in natural settings happened against the background of the work of the so-called natural-language philosophers discussed above (Austin 1962; Searle 1969; Grice 1975; Sarangi and Coulthard 2000: xvii). They belie claims made in the past that linguistics has nothing to offer translation studies because of its narrow focus on sentences and its neglect of longer stretches of naturally occurring text

Linguistics

(Snell-Hornby [1988] 1995: 14–15), and it is interesting to see the harmonious co-existence of the two disciplines in the contributions to Malmkjær (2018).

Historical perspectives

Given that the starting date for modern linguistics is commonly considered to be around 1916 and that it lies with Saussure's move away from the historical study of language (diachronic linguistics) to the study of language at a moment in time (synchronic linguistics), translation studies is something of an upstart in comparison, if we date the latter to the 1970s, the decade that saw the seminal conference at which James Holmes named the nascent discipline (Third International Congress of Applied Linguistics, Copenhagen, 21–6 August 1972; a version of Holmes' paper, entitled 'The Name and Nature of Translation Studies' is included in Venuti (2004: 180–92)). But then, in comparison with Western philosophy, linguistics itself is a veritable Johnny-come-lately. Copleston (1962: 38) cites Thales of Miletus (c. 624–546 BC) as among the earliest Western philosophers proper, and Eastern philosophy has a history of several thousand years (see Harrison 2013).

Before Holmes' naming act, however, several scholarly and/or practical works on translation had been published, which acknowledged, whether in their titles or in their content, a debt to, or at least an influence from, linguistics. Vinay and Darbelnet ([1958] 1995) adopted a comparative stylistic approach to 'a methodology for translation' (subtitle) between:

> two linguistic structures: two lexicons, two morphologies; but also, and perhaps above all ... two particular viewpoints of life which inform these languages or which result from them: two cultures, two literatures, two histories and two geographies, in short ... two different natures.
>
> (Vinay and Darbelnet [1958] 1995: 4)

Whereas Vinay and Darbelnet thus confine themselves to providing a method for translating between French and English, albeit fairly well generalisable to other language pairs, Catford (1965) and Nida (1964) consider their own approaches more general. Nida's plentiful examples derive from his experience as a Bible translator, which may have influenced his approach to an extent, but Catford is indebted to none but Halliday (1961), at least not explicitly. Catford (1965) receives short shrift from Snell-Hornby ([1988] 1995: 20) on the grounds that he 'bases his approach on isolated and even absurdly simplistic sentences ... as well as on isolated words', and it is true that there are few extended examples in his book. Nevertheless, it is worth bearing in mind that Catford, acknowledging his debt to Firth (1957), whose interest in context is legendary, takes as his starting point 'a consideration of how language is related to the human social situations in which it operates' (Catford 1965: 1), and that Toury, one of the most important and influential scholars to have graced translation studies in the twentieth century, starts his famous reconsideration of the notion of translation equivalence with reference to Catford's general definition of that phenomenon (Toury 1980: 37). Nida fares better under Snell-Hornby's scrutiny because of his experience as a Bible translator but is still taken to task for his interest in equivalence (Snell-Hornby [1988] 1995: 18–19), a concept which Snell-Hornby herself buries under the cloak of 'text (re)production' ([1988] 1995: 79). Nida (1964: 60) embraces Chomsky's (1957, 1961) generative grammar 'based on minimal kernel constructions and numerous transformations' with its emphasis on transformations, a metaphor which Nida applies to translation, 'for in translating from one language into another he [the translator] must ... attempt to describe the mechanisms by which the total message is decoded, transferred, and transformed into the structures of another language'. It is worth noting, though, that Chomsky himself is emphatic that his theory 'does not imply that there must be some reasonable procedure for translating between languages' (1965: 30). Nida (1964: 8) explains that the 'fundamental thrust' of his work

> is of course linguistic, as it must be in any descriptive analysis of the relationship between corresponding messages in different languages. But the points of view are by no means narrowly linguistic, for language is here viewed as but one part of total human behaviour, which in turn is the object of study of a number of related disciplines.

Nida is perhaps best known for the distinction he drew between formal and dynamic equivalence (1964: 159): 'Formal equivalence focuses attention on the message itself, in both form and content ... In contrast, a translation which attempts to produce a dynamic ... equivalence is based upon the 'principle of equivalent effect" (see also Chapter 14, this volume: 'Equivalence').

A more recent application of linguistic theory to translation studies is Halverson's (2003) of Langacker's Cognitive Grammar (1987). Cognitive grammarians think of grammar as meaningful, as Hallidayans do, and as reflecting human beings' ability to understand situations in different ways. This approach, however, has not enjoyed widespread appeal within the translation studies community of scholars.

Critical issues and topics

In addition to the tensions hinted at above between Snell-Hornby and other translation theorists, and those that have occasionally been perceived to exist between Hallidayan and Chomskyan syntax, Gutt's (1990, 1991) application to translation of Sperber and Wilson's theory of relevance ([1986] 1995) has also caused a degree of consternation. Announced provocatively in a translation studies journal as 'A Theoretical Account of Translation – Without a Translation Theory', Gutt's thesis is that the concept of relevance suffices to account for all matters translational. Sperber and Wilson distinguish between literal language use, which they consider 'assertive', and non-literal language use, which they consider 'interpretive' ([1986] 1995: 228–9). The latter includes speech and thought report and also, in Gutt's view (1990: 147) translations. According to Sperber and Wilson, the human cognitive system is programmed to seek and provide for relevance, and relevance is measured in terms of 'the greatest possible cognitive effect for the smallest possible processing effort' (Sperber and Wilson [1986] 1995: vii). According to Gutt, translators also apply this principle, and therefore relevance theory suffices to account for all translational phenomena. However, as Tirkkonen-Condit (2002: 194) points out, 'Translation scholars ... are interested in explaining what is unique to translation', and clearly switching from one language to another is a major translational phenomenon not shared by other instances where a text is to a greater or lesser degree based on another, such as 'summarising, reviewing, paraphrasing'. It is difficult to imagine how the specificities that accrue to translation because of its bilinguality can be accounted for by a theory that ignores it.

Related topics

Context and pragmatics; equivalence; meaning.

Further reading

De Beaugrande, R. A. and Dressler, W. U. 1981. *Introduction to text linguistics*. London: Longman. (One of the seminal works in text linguistics, explaining the nature of textuality and introducing the seven standards.)

Federici, F. M. (ed.) 2011. *Translating Dialects and Languages of Minorities*. Oxford: Peter Lang. (Contains eleven contributions which deal with translation-related sociolinguistics issues in a number of languages.)

McCabe, A. *An Introduction to Linguistics and Language Studies*. Sheffield: Equinox Publishing. (Introduces methods of analysing and understanding language from various theoretical perspectives within linguistics, including phonetics, phonology, conversation analysis, morphology, syntax and semantics, with exercises and questions for reflection.)

Sedivy, J. 2014. *Language in Mind: An Introduction to Psycholinguistics*. Oxford: Oxford University Press. (Introduces the central questions and approaches in psycholinguistics.)

Quirk, R. 1985. *A Comprehensive Grammar of the English Language*. London: Longman. (A fairly theory-neutral, primarily descriptive grammar that will provide much more detail about grammatical items, concepts and notions than it has been possible to provide here.)

References

Aglioti, S., Beltramello, A., Girardi, F. and Fabbro, F. 1996. 'Neurolinguistic and follow-up study of an unusual pattern of recovery from bilingual subcortical aphasia'. *Brain* 119 (5): 1551–64.

Alexieva, B. 1994. 'Types of texts and intertextuality in simultaneous interpreting'. In M. Snell-Hornby, F. Pöchhacker and K. Kaindl (eds) *Translation Studies: An Interdiscipline*. Amsterdam: John Benjamins, 179–87.

Ardila, A. 2018. 'Language disorders, interpreting and translation'. In K. Malmkjær (ed.) *The Routledge Handbook of Translation Studies and Linguistics*. London: Routledge, 267–80.

Austin, J. L. 1962. *How to Do Things with Words*. Oxford: Oxford University Press.

Barry, W. J. 2006. 'Phoneme'. In E. K. Brown (ed.) *Encyclopedia of Language and Linguistics*, vol. 9. Amsterdam: Elsevier, 345–50.

Bennett, J. 1976. *Linguistic Behaviour*. Cambridge: Cambridge University Press.

Braun, S. 2013. 'Keep your distance? Remote interpreting in legal proceedings: A critical assessment of a growing practice'. *Interpreting* 15 (2): 200–28.

Brown, G. 1977. *Listening to Spoken English*. London: Taylor and Francis.

Brown, G. and Yule, G. 1983. *Discourse Analysis*. Cambridge: Cambridge University Press.

Bühler, K. 1934. *Sprachtheorie*. Jena: Gustav Fischer.

Burton, D. 1980. *Dialogues and Discourse: A Sociolinguistic Approach to Modern Drama and Naturally Occurring Conversation*. London: Routledge and Kegan Paul.

Cambridge International Dictionary of English. 1995. Cambridge: Cambridge University Press.

Catford, J. C. 1965. *A Linguistic Theory of Translation: An Essay in Applied Linguistics*. Oxford: Oxford University Press.

Chomsky, N. 1957. *Syntactic Structures*. Berlin: Mouton & Co.

Chomsky, N. 1961. 'Some methodological remarks on generative grammar'. *Word* 17: 219–39.

Clyne, M. 1987. 'Cultural differences in the organisation of academic texts'. *Journal of Pragmatics* 11: 211–47.

Coates, J. 1986. *Women, Men and Language*. London: Longman.

Coates, J. and Cameron, D. (eds) 1988. *Women in Their Speech Communities*. London: Longman.

Copleston, F. C. 1962. *A History of Philosophy: Volume I, Greece and Rome, Part I, New Revised Edition*. Garden City, NY: Image Books.

Coulthard, M. and Ashby, M. C. 1975. 'Talking with the doctor'. *Journal of Communication* 25 (3): 240–7.

Davidson, D. [1973] 1984. 'Radical interpretation'. Reprinted in *Inquiries into Truth and Interpretation*. Oxford: Clarendon Press, 125–39, from *Dialectica* 27 (1973): 313–28.

Dinneen, F. P. 1967. *An Introduction to General Linguistics*. New York: Holt, Rinehart and Winston.

Firth, J. R. 1957. *Papers in Linguistics 1934–1951*. London: Oxford University Press.

Frege, G. [1891] 1977. 'Function and concept'. An address given to the Jenaische Gesellschaft für Medicin und Naturwissenschaft, 9 January, 1891. Reprinted in P. Geach and M. Black (eds) *Translations from the Philosophical Writings of Gottlob Frege*. Oxford: Basil Blackwell, 21–41.

Frege, G. [1892] 1977. 'On sense and reference'. First published in *Zeitschrift für Philosophie und philosophische Kritik*, vol. 100 (1892), 25–50. Reprinted in P. Geach and M. Black (eds) *Translations from the Philosophical Writings of Gottlob Frege*. Oxford: Basil Blackwell, 56–78.

Graves, R. 1997. "Dear Friend' (?): Culture and genre in American and Canadian direct marketing letters'. *The Journal of Business Communication* 34 (3): 235–52.

Grayling, A. C. 1982. *An Introduction to Philosophical Logic*. Malden, MA: Harvester Press.

Grice, H. P. 1975. 'Logic and Conversation'. *Syntax and Semantics*, vol. 3, P. Cole and J. Morgan (eds). New York: Academic Press.

Gutt, E. A. 1990. 'A theoretical account of translation – without a translation theory'. *Target* 2 (2): 135–64.

Gutt, E. 1991. *Translation and Relevance: Cognition and Context*. Oxford: Basil Blackwell. Second edition (2000). Manchester: St. Jerome.

Halliday, M. A. K. 1961. 'Categories of the theory of grammar'. *Word* 17: 241–92.

Halliday, M. A. K. 1970. 'Language structure and language function'. In J. Lyons (ed.) *New Horizons in Linguistics*. Harmondsworth: Penguin, 140–65.

Halliday, M. A. K. 1978. *Language as Social Semiotic*. London: Edward Arnold.

Halliday, M. A. K. 1985. *An Introduction to Functional Grammar*. London: Edward Arnold.

Halverson, S. L. 2003. 'The cognitive basis of translation universals'. *Target* 15 (2): 197–292.

Harris, S. 1984. 'Questions as a mode of control in magistrates' courts'. *International Journal of Sociology of Language* 49: 5–27.

Harrison, V. 2013. *Eastern Philosophy: The Basics*. London: Routledge.

Hatim, B. and Mason, I. 1990. *Discourse and the Translator*. London: Longman.

Higginbotham, J. 2002. 'On linguistics in philosophy, and philosophy in linguistics'. *Linguistics and Philosophy* 25(5/6): 573–84.

House, Juliane. 2005. 'Politeness in Germany: Politeness in GERMANY?'. In L. Hickey and M. Stewart (eds) *Politeness in Europe*. Clevedon: Multilingual Matters, 13–29.

Hughes, E. and Tainturier, M. 2015. 'The cognate advantage in bilingual aphasia: Now you see it, now you don't'. Frontiers in Psychology. Conference Abstract: Academy of Aphasia 53rd Annual Meeting.

Jakobson, R. 1960. 'Closing statement: Linguistics and poetics'. In T. A. Sebeok (ed.) *Style in Language*. Cambridge, MA: MIT Press, 350–77.

Kaplan, R. D. 1966. 'Cultural thought patterns in intercultural education'. *Language Learning* 16: 1–20.

Katz, J. J. 1965. 'The relevance of linguistics to philosophy'. *The Journal of Philosophy* 62 (20): 590–602.

Langacker, R. 1987. *Foundations of Cognitive Grammar 1*. Stanford: Stanford University Press.

Locke, J. [1690] 1960. *An Essay Concerning Human Understanding*. Glasgow: William Collins Sons & Ltd. Co. Second edition 1694; 1960.

Lykke Jakobsen, A. and Jensen, K. T. H. 2008. 'Eye movement behaviour across four different types of reading task'. In S. Göpferich, A. Lykke Jakobsen and I. M. Mees (eds) *Looking at Eyes: Eye-Tracking Studies of Reading and Translation Processing*. Copenhagen: Samfundslitteratur. 103–24.

Malakoff, M. and Lewis, D. 1983. 'General semantics', 189–232 in *Philosophical Papers*. New York: Oxford University Press.

Malmkjær, K. (ed.) 2018. *The Routledge Handbook of Translation Studies and Linguistics*. London: Routledge.

Mauranen, A. 1992. *Cultural Differences in Academic Rhetoric. A Textlinguistic Study*. PhD thesis, University of Birmingham.

Mauranen, A. 1993. 'Contrastive ESP rhetoric: Metatext in Finnish-English economics texts'. *English for Specific Purposes* 12: 3–22.
McWhorter, J. 2014. *The Language Hoax.* Oxford: Oxford University Press.
Mead, R. 1985. *Courtroom Discourse.* Birmingham: English Language Research, University of Birmingham.
Moser-Mercer, B. 2003. 'Remote interpreting: Assessment of human factors and performance parameters'. *Communicate!* Summer 2003. http://aiic.net/ViewPage.cfm?page_id=1125 (accessed 12/03/2016).
Neubert, A. and Shreve, G. M. 1992. *Translation as Text.* Kent, OH: Kent State University Press.
Nida, E. A. 1964. *Toward a Science of Translating: With Special Reference to Principles and Procedures Involved in Bible Translating.* Leiden: E. J. Brill.
Paradis, M., Goldblum, M. C. and Abidi, R. 1982. 'Alternate antagonism with paradoxical translation behavior in two bilingual aphasic patients'. *Brain and Language* 15 (1): 55–69.
Pavlenko, A. 2014. *The Bilingual Mind and What It Tells Us about Language and Thought.* Cambridge: Cambridge University Press.
Roberts, P. M. and Deslauriers, L. 1999. 'Picture naming of cognate and non-cognate nouns in bilingual aphasia'. *Journal of Communication Disorders* 32 (1): 1–23.
Sacks, H., Schlegloff, E. A. and Jefferson, G. 1974. 'A simplest systematic for the organization of turn-taking'. *Language* 50 (4), Part 1: 696–735.
Sagliamonte, S. A. 2016. *Teen Talk: The Language of Adolescents.* Cambridge: Cambridge University Press.
Sarangi, S. and Coulthard, M. 2000. 'Discourse as topic, resource and social practice: An introduction'. In Sarangi, S. and Coulthard, M. (eds) *Discourse and Social Life.* Harlow: Pearson, xv–xli.
Schaeffer, M., Paterson, K., McGowan, V., White, S. and Malmkjær, K. 2017. 'Reading for translation'. In A. L. Jakobsen and B. Mesa-Lao (eds) *Translation in Transition: Between Cognition, Computing and Technology.* Amsterdam: John Benjamins, 17–54.
Searle, J. R. 1969. *Speech Acts: An Essay in the Philosophy of Language.* Cambridge: Cambridge University Press.
Searle, J. R. 1975. 'Indirect speech acts'. In P. Vole and J. L. Morgan (eds) *Syntax and Semantics, 3: Speech Acts.* New York: Academic Press, 265–77.
Shreve, G. M. 2018. 'Text linguistics, translating and interpreting'. In K. Malmkjær (ed.) *The Routledge Handbook of Translation Studies and Linguistics.* London: Routledge, 165–78.
Sinclair, J. McH. and Coulthard, M. 1975. *Towards an Analysis of Discourse: The English Used by Teachers and Pupils.* Oxford: Oxford University Press.
Snell-Hornby, M. [1988] 1995. *Translation Studies: An Integrated Approach.* Revised edition. Amsterdam: John Benjamins.
Sperber, D. and Wilson, D. [1986] 1995. *Relevance: Communication and Cognition.* Oxford: Basil Blackwell.
Stubbs, M. 1983. *Discourse Analysis: The Sociolinguistic Analysis of Natural Language.* Oxford: Basil Blackwell.
Swales, J. M. 1981. *Aspects of Article Introductions.* Aston ESP Research Reports, no. 1. Birmingham: Language Studies Unit, University of Aston.
Swales, J. M. 1985. 'English language papers and authors' first language: Preliminary explorations'. *Scientometrics* 8: 91–101.
Swales, J. M. 1987. 'Utilizing the literatures in teaching the research paper'. *TESOL Quarterly* 21: 41–68.
Swales, J. M. 1990. *Genre Analysis: English in Academic and Research Settings.* Cambridge: Cambridge University Press.
Tirkkonen-Condit, S. 2002. 'Review of Ernst-August Gutt. *Translation and Relevance: Cognition and Context*'. *Target* 14 (1): 193–6.
Toury, G. 1980. 'Translated literature: System, norms performance: Toward a TT-oriented approach to literary translation'. In *In Search of a Theory of Translation.* Tel Aviv: Porter Institute, 35–50.

Toury, G. 1984. 'The notion of 'native translator' and translation teaching'. In W. Wilss and G. Thome (eds) *Die Theorie des Übersetzens und ihr Aufschlußwert für die Übersetzungs- und Dolmetschdidaktik*. Tübingen: Narr, 186–95.

Trudgill, P. (ed.) 1984. *Language in the British Isles*. Cambridge: Cambridge University Press.

Valdés, G. 2003. *Expanding Definitions of Giftedness: The Case of Young Interpreters from Immigrant Communities*. Mahwah, NJ: Lawrence Erlbaum Associates.

Van Dijk, T. A. 1977. *Text and Context*. London: Longman.

Van Dijk, T. A. 2004. 'From text grammar to critical discourse analysis: A brief academic bibliography'. www.discourses.org/From%20text%20grammar%20to%20critical%20discourse%20analysis.html (accessed 01/04/2016).

Venuti, L. (ed.) 2004. *The Translation Studies Reader*. London, New York: Routledge, 180–92. Second edition.

Vinay, J. P. and Darbelnet, J. [1958] 1995. *Comparative Stylistics of French and English: A Methodology for Translation*, trans. and ed. by J. C. Sager and M. J. Hamel from *Stylistique compare du français et de l'anglais*. Paris: Les editions Dedier. Amsterdam: John Benjamins Publishing Co.

Webster, J. J. and Peng, X. (eds.) 2017. *Applying Systemic Functional linguistics: The State of the Art in China Today*. London: Bloomsbury.

Wittgenstein, L. ([1953] 2009). *Philosophical Investigations*. trans. G.E.M. Anscombe, P.M.S. Hacker and J. Schulte. Chichester: Wiley-Blackwell.

Zhang, M. F. (2015). *Functional Approaches to English–Chinese Translation*. Beijing: Foreign Languages Press.

18
Meaning

Rachel Weissbrod

Introduction

The purpose of this chapter is to map the different and often clashing approaches to the relationship between translation and meaning and introduce some of their main representatives. It will address the following approaches: (1) translation is capable of transferring meaning; actually, this is what translation is about; (2) translation cannot transfer meaning; (3) meaning is not what translators are supposed to transfer; (4) translators are authorized to create meaning rather than transferring it; (5) Translation Studies is not about meaning.

18.1 Translation is capable of transferring meaning; actually, this is what translation is about

18.1.1 Sense for sense

The transfer of meaning as the essence of translation can be traced back to ancient Greece. For the Greek, translation meant charging words in the target language with meanings extricated from words in the source language (Chesterman 2016: 20–1). In the Roman era, this issue became part of the debate between the proponents of literal vs. free translation. The latter was preferred by Cicero:

> I decided to take speeches written in Greek by great orators and to translate them freely, and I obtained the following results: by giving a Latin form to the text I had read I could not only make use of the best expressions in common usage with us, but I could also coin new expressions, analogous to those used in Greek, and they were no less well received by our people as long as they seemed appropriate.
>
> (Cicero in Lefevere 1992: 46–7)

In the fourth century, St. Jerome – the translator of the Vulgate – introduced the 'sense for sense' approach, in contrast to the 'word for word' tradition. In his words: *non verbum e verbo sed sensum de sensu* (in Malmkjær 2005: 3). St. Jerome found this practice fitting for the translation of secular writings:

> I admit and confess most freely that I have not translated word for word in my translations of Greek texts, but sense for sense, except in the case of the scriptures in which even the order of the words is a mystery.
>
> (St. Jerome in Lefevere 1992: 47)

St. Jerome restricted the freedom of the translator to the transfer of the original sense. According to Robinson (2001: 87–8), proponents of the 'sense for sense' approach did not give up faithfulness to the source. They were interested in the transfer of meaning but believed that it necessitated liberty from the exact wording of the source and consideration of textual units larger than the word. This idea is still prevalent today and characterizes, for example, the Paris school of interpreting identified with Danica Seleskovitch (Malmkjær 2005: 88). Nevertheless, the 'sense for sense' approach is often linked with free translation (Munday 2016: 32). As a way to transfer meaning, it does not rule out the possibility that 'word for word' too can serve this end. In the above quotation, St. Jerome admits that in the Bible even the syntax is a mystery. If meaning is not necessarily detached from form, as he implies, then both 'sense for sense' and 'word for word' can be utilized to transfer it.

18.1.2 Roman Jakobson – translation is the transfer of meaning

For Jakobson, translation is not merely capable of transferring meaning; the transfer of meaning is what translation is about. Jakobson's starting point is that meaning is an attribute of linguistic signs; objects and phenomena outside language do not have meaning. Using the word 'cheese' as an example, he takes issue with Bertrand Russell (Russell 1950). According to Russell, a person who has no acquaintance with cheese cannot understand the meaning of the word. Jakobson disagrees. To understand the meaning of a word, one does not have to experience what it stands for; evidently, people understand the meaning of words such as 'nectar' and 'ambrosia', even though they have never dined with the gods on the Olympus. To understand the meaning of a word, one has to translate it: 'the meaning of any linguistic sign is its translation into some further, alternative sign' (Jakobson 1959: 232). Translation can take three forms (1959: 233). One can transmit the meaning of linguistic signs in the same language (intralingual translation, also referred to as paraphrase), in another language (interlingual translation, or translation proper) or in another sign system (intersemiotic translation, or transmutation). Though Jakobson offers a very wide view of translation, it is noteworthy that the only way of transmitting meaning to which he refers as 'translation proper' is translation between 'historical-natural languages' (Petrilli 2003: 18). According to Hermans (1997: 17), his terminology reveals his unease with his own theory. From another perspective, Toury (1994) criticized the lack of intrasemiotic translation in Jakobson's mapping. Translation can take place between non-linguistic texts, or entities, such as pictures or musical works, but Jakobson does not pay heed to these possibilities.

Two generalizations that Jakobson makes support his claim that meaning is transferrable. The first is that 'languages differ essentially in what they *must* convey and not in what they *may* convey' (Jakobson 1959: 236). Languages are capable of expressing the cognitive experience of their speakers, and if there is a deficiency, various means such as loan-translations, neologisms and semantic shifts can be employed to enlarge the linguistic repertoire. One of the examples Jakobson gives is 'electrical horse-car' for a tram, used by Russian speakers who looked for words to refer to a new experience. However, languages 'force' their speakers to express what can remain unuttered in other languages. For example, they must distinguish between male and female in situations in which speakers of other languages do not have to make such a distinction. In Russian, objects and abstract phenomena have a grammatical gender: death, for instance, is a female, and this in Jakobson's view deeply affects the way Russian speakers think of death. In making this claim, Jakobson (1959: 234) quotes Benjamin L. Whorf, alluding to what has become known as the Sapir–Whorf hypothesis (Whorf 1956: 213–14). According to this hypothesis, languages shape and not just reflect their speakers' conceptions of the surrounding world.

Jakobson's second generalization is that equivalence exists between entire messages rather than single code-units (and one may add: linguistic or other, such as visual elements in a picture). It may be difficult to find an equivalent for every code-unit in the original utterance, or text, but messages 'may serve as adequate interpretations of alien code-units or messages' (Jakobson 1959: 233). Jakobson does not speak explicitly of compensation mechanisms in translation (when loss of meaning in one place is compensated in another place; see Newmark 1988: 90), but this is what his generalization leads to.

Despite his belief that meaning can be transferred, Jakobson is aware of the limits of translatability and gives some examples:

> But in jest, in dreams, in magic, briefly, in what one would call everyday verbal mythology and in poetry above all, the grammatical categories carry a high semantic import. In these conditions, the question of translation becomes more entangled and controversial.
>
> (Jakobson 1959: 236)

In other situations, however, the transmission of meaning is possible and, as mentioned, this process can involve semiotic systems other than language. In this 1959 essay, Jakobson laid the foundations for a wide and flexible conception of translation. His approach opened many paths of research, including the study of intra-systemic and intralingual translation (Even-Zohar 1990; Göpferich 2007; Zethsen 2007; Karas 2016), adaptation (Weissbrod 2004; Kohn and Weissbrod 2012; Cattrysse 2014) and the transfer of models (Even-Zohar 1990). The latter refers to the possibility of transferring 'recipes' for the creation of texts, not necessarily by means of translating concrete individual texts (Sela-Sheffy 2000; Weissbrod 2004).

18.1.3 Eugene A. Nida and Charles R. Taber – 'kernels' and 'surface structure'

In a section called 'Definition of translating' in an article about Bible translations (Nida 1966), Nida offers a definition 'which is in accord with the best traditions of Biblical scholarship' (1966: 16) and suits the purpose of Bible translation – to make the addressee of the translated text respond to it in ways which are similar to those in which the addressee of the source text responded to it. According to this definition, 'translating consists in producing in the receptor language the closest natural equivalent to the message of the source language, first in meaning and secondly in style' (ibid.). Nida expects the translator to aspire to the 'closest' equivalence possible – he acknowledges that absolute correspondence is unattainable. By 'natural' he expresses his objection to what Lawrence Venuti would refer to thirty years later as 'foreignization' (Venuti 2008/1995). Nida also acknowledges that 'equivalence in both meaning and style cannot always be retained' (Nida 1966: 16). Giving precedence to meaning over style, he asserts that if 'one must be abandoned for the sake of the other, the meaning must have priority over the stylistic forms' (ibid.).

Years later, definitions of this kind will be criticized for their essentialism and prescriptivism (Toury 2012: 26). Nida, however, does not merely define the optimal translation but goes on to suggest how to achieve the ends of such a translation – namely, to transmit meaning in the first place and style in the second place. To explain the optimal process of translating, that will yield the optimal translation, Nida – in collaboration with Taber (Nida and Taber 1969) – differentiates between two methods of translating.

The first method consists of:

> setting up a series of rules which are intended to be applied strictly in order and are designed to specify exactly what should be done with each item or combination of items in the source language so as to select the appropriate corresponding form in the receptor language.
>
> (1969: 33)

This one-stage process is based on the application of rules to the surface structure of the language. The term 'surface structure', which has developed in the framework of Transformational Grammar (Chomsky 1957, 1965), refers to what is overtly spoken or written. The process is considered to be best accomplished through an intermediate, neutral, universal linguistic structure – whether natural or artificial.

The second method, which Nida and Taber obviously prefer, consists of three stages: (1) analysis of the surface structure of the source; at this stage, the translator looks into the meaning of the words and combinations of words, and the grammatical relations between them; (2) transfer, in which the analysed material is transferred in the translator's mind from the source language to the target language; and (3) restructuring of the transferred material in order to produce an acceptable translation in the target language. This method is more complicated but Nida and Taber believe that it leads to more adequate results and helps the translator cope with the ambiguities in the surface structure. Such ambiguities can be found not only at the level of words and their combinations but also in grammatical constructions. One and the same grammatical construction may have different meanings, depending on the context. For example, in English the structure 'X of Y' does not have the same meaning in 'the will of God' (that is, God has a will) and 'the city of peace' (that is, a city where peace prevails). The fact that some languages can use nouns to refer to what Nida and Taber call 'events' ('God loves', but also: 'God is love') and other languages cannot is another obstacle.

To deal with such ambiguities, the translator is advised to transform the surface structure into 'kernels' (another concept developed in Transformational Grammar). Kernels are 'the basic structural elements out of which the language builds its elaborate surface structures' (Nida and Taber 1969: 39). They are clearer and less ambiguous than the surface structure. The procedure is possible because of the distinction between objects, events, abstracts and relations. Kernels are created by expressing objects as nouns, events as verbs ('God loves' rather than 'God is love'), abstracts as adjectives and adverbs, and relations as prepositions and conjunctions. Every language has no more than six to twelve kernels that underlie its more complex and elaborate surface structures. At the level of kernels, the proximity of languages to each other is maximal. Transforming surface structures into kernels thus ensures an accurate translation. To justify the time and effort required, Nida and Taber make an analogy between the translation process and the crossing of a river: rather than crossing it anywhere, it is better to walk along the bank until one finds a place where the water is shallow and passing is safe (1969: 34).

However, translation is not supposed to stop at the level of kernels, because the style is embedded in the surface structure. One and the same kernel may be realized in stylistically different surface structures which are language-dependent. After replacing source kernels by target kernels, the translator is expected to create new surface structures so as to reconstruct in the target language the subtle stylistic features of the source text. This is consistent with the above-quoted definition of translating as an act that does not neglect style but gives precedence to the transfer of meaning.

18.2 Translation cannot transfer meaning

18.2.1 Willard Van Orman Quine – 'the indeterminacy of translation'

Quine (see Chapter 5, this volume), a prominent analytic philosopher, used translation to illustrate his ideas about meaning in general. He was primarily interested in 'radical translation' – translation from a hitherto unknown language. In radical translation, meaning can only be discovered by observing the speaker's behaviour, since there are no dictionaries or bilingual interpreters to rely on (Quine 1960: 26–30; 1969: 45). The linguist may try to develop a system for translating the native's language by producing a translation manual (Quine 1960: 27, 71). However, the contents of the manual are merely hypotheses. Quine refers to this uncertainty as the 'inscrutability of reference' which results in the 'indeterminacy of translation' (Quine 1969: 37, 45). He distinguishes between 'radical translation' and translation from an already known source language, whether related to the target language or not. If the source and target languages are kindred, translation is aided by the resemblance of cognate word forms; if they are unrelated, the translator can use 'traditional equations' (Quine 1960: 28). Translation which is not 'radical' yet cannot transfer meaning is the concern of Catford (1965).

18.2.2 John C. Catford – 'textual equivalence' and 'formal correspondence'

In *A Linguistic Theory of Translation* (1965), Catford argues that the source text and the target text cannot have the same meaning: 'An SL [source language] text has an SL meaning, and a TL [target language] text has a TL meaning' (1965: 35). Catford refers to Firth (1957), defining meaning as 'the total network of relations entered into by any linguistic form' (Catford 1965: 35). These relations are of two kinds: formal and contextual: 'By *formal relations* we mean relations between one formal item and others in the same language' (ibid.). The relations between grammatical units in the rank scale of a certain language (e.g., morpheme, word, group, clause and sentence in English) can serve as an example: 'By *contextual relations* we mean the relationship of grammatical or lexical items to linguistically relevant elements in the situations in which the items operate as, or in, texts' (1965: 36). For example, in English one can say 'I have arrived', clarifying that there is a single speaker (rather than two or more); but there is no need to tell the gender of the speaker. One element in the situation (single or plural?) is linguistically relevant, and another (male or female?) is not. Both formal and contextual relations are language-dependent and can, at best, be approximated in translation.

To illustrate his argument further, Catford refers to the words *a-cho* and *a-yas* in Burushaski, one of the languages of Pakistan (1965: 39–40). When translated into English, both of them will probably be replaced by 'my brother'. But in Burushaski, a male uses *a-cho* when he refers to his brother, and a female uses *a-yas* when referring to her brother. The language reflects the point of view of the speaker in a way that has no parallel in English. For Catford, this proves his point: the possibility of finding fitting textual equivalents does not imply that meaning has been transferred.

The translation problem posed by *a-cho* and *a-yas* can also be addressed through the notion of 'conceptual voids' (Weizman 2010). In Translation Studies, a void is a linguistic item in the source language that has no equivalent in the target language (Dagut 1981; Ivir 1987). On the face of it, *cho* and *yas* for 'a brother' are not voids, because English speakers are acquainted with the phenomenon of having a brother and do not lack linguistic signs to refer to it. Yet, as Catford claims, the translation only approximates the source in terms of meaning, and this can be explained with the assistance of Elda Weizman's theory of voids. Based on the 'triangle of reference' described by Ogden and Richards (1923), Weizman differentiates between three kinds of void, depending on their focus: the sign, its referent and the conception that links them in the speaker's mind. The latter is referred to as a 'conceptual void'. The differentiation between *cho* and *yas* imply that in Burushaski, having a brother is a different experience for males and for females. Thus, *cho* and *yas* can be considered conceptual voids. Though Weizman deals with single voids, she suggests shifting the focus to entire semantic fields. Concepts regarding time, space, emotions, family, etc. find their place in semantic fields which are organized differently in every language, depending on the shared experiences of its speakers. The idea of semantic fields that are not quite the same in different languages can indirectly support Catford's claim that meaning is language-specific and thus untransferrable.

However, if – as Catford insists – translation is not capable of transferring meaning, then what does it transfer? Catford's answer can be found in his concept of 'textual equivalence' – the equivalence between textual units in the source and target texts. Textual equivalence is an empirical phenomenon, discovered by comparing SL and TL texts. 'A textual equivalent is any TL text or portion of text which is observed [...] to be the equivalent of a given SL text or portion of text' (Catford 1965: 27). In order to recognize textual equivalence, Catford suggests that the translator should –

> systematically introduce changes into the SL text and observe what changes if any occur in the TL text as a consequence. A *textual translation equivalent* is thus: *that portion of a TL text which is changed when and only when a given portion of the SL text is changed.*
> (1965: 28)

One example is the English text 'My son is six', the equivalent of which in French is 'Mon fils a six ans' [My son has six years]. If one changes the English text into 'Your daughter is six', the TL text will become (in the formal/plural form) 'Votre fille a six ans' [Your daughter has six years]; 'The changed portion of the TL text (Mon fils/Votre fille) is then taken to be the equivalent of the changed portion of the SL text (My son/Your daughter)' (ibid.).

Catford's concept of 'textual equivalence' served the need to show that the source and target text can be equivalent even though they do not share the same meaning. However, his theorizing was severely criticized for its circularity – translation consists of textual equivalence, and textual equivalence is what translation consists of (Snell-Hornby 1988: 19). His argumentation also seems to contain a contradiction. On the one hand, he regards textual equivalence as an empirical phenomenon discovered by comparing SL and TL texts – not a dictate or a recommendation by the researcher. On the other hand, he does delineate, in advance, the borderlines of textual equivalence by stating the necessary conditions under which it can take place. In his view, SL and TL texts or items are translation equivalents when they are interchangeable in a given situation: 'The TL text must be relatable to at least some of the situational features to which the SL text is relatable' (Catford 1965: 49). More generally speaking, Catford looks at translation as a linguist. For him, textual equivalence is a means to evaluate the proximity or distance between languages. Fittingly, one of his key terms is 'formal correspondence': 'A formal correspondent is any TL category which may be said to occupy, as nearly as possible, the "same" place in the economy of the TL as the given SL category occupies in the SL' (1965: 32). If the languages are close, textual equivalence will reflect the formal correspondence between them. If they are remote, textual equivalence will not reflect any formal correspondence. In his wording: 'the degree of divergence between textual equivalence and formal correspondence may perhaps be used as a measure of typological difference between languages' (1965: 33). Since the publication of *A Linguistic Theory of Translation* in 1965, Translation Studies has moved from linguistics to new areas of interest (Snell-Hornby 2006). However, the belief that translation does not involve the transfer of meaning persists, though it takes new forms.

18.2.3 Paul Ricoeur – the 'third text'

Ricoeur (see Chapter 6, this volume) comes from a different intellectual world – French hermeneutics – and he is often associated and compared with Jacques Derrida (see, e.g., Pirovolakis 2010). However, he shares with Catford both the belief that translation does not transfer meaning and the conviction that this does not hinder translation. Looking at the diversity of languages on every possible level, Ricoeur regards it as a symptom of the human condition: 'this is how we are, this is how we exist, scattered and confounded' (Ricoeur 2006: 19). In light of this diversity, a perfect transmission of the original meaning in translation is inconceivable: meaning cannot be 'extracted from the unity it shares with the flesh of words' (2006: 38).

Ricoeur takes his argument one step further when he claims that adequacy is not just beyond reach: it cannot be measured at all. In order to compare the source and target texts one has to abstract the meaning of the original and rewrite it as a third text in either a natural or an artificial language. And this, Ricoeur claims, cannot be done. If readers, critics or researchers try to use another translation as the third, mediating text, it is more than probable that this translation too will prove inadequate; and if they try to create such a third text themselves ('retranslate after the translator': 2006: 10), they are bound to suffer the same pitfalls as the previous translator of the text. And yet Ricoeur acknowledges that translation has served as a means of human communication since the dawn of civilization. The solution to the paradox lies in his definition of translation as 'equivalence without adequacy' (ibid.). While adequacy means a perfect matching between the source and target texts, which is beyond reach, equivalence refers to the actual relationship between them; it is '*produced* by translation rather than *presupposed* by it' (2006: 35). Acknowledging that translation is equivalence without adequacy leads to the axiom which is at the core of Ricoeur's philosophy of translation: if translation exists, it has to be possible (2006: 15). Interestingly, his distinction between equivalence and adequacy is very similar to Toury's (see Section 5.2), though they belong to quite different intellectual worlds (Toury 2012; Weissbrod 2009).

18.3 Meaning is not what translators are supposed to transfer

18.3.1 Walter Benjamin – 'the pure language'

The most prominent representative of the idea that the transfer of meaning is not the main task of the translator is probably Benjamin (1997/1923; see Chapter 3, this volume). Benjamin presented his ideas about translation in 'The Translator's Task' – first published in 1923 as an introduction to his translation of Baudelaire's poems into German.

Benjamin's starting point is that translation is a distinctive mode characterized by its orientation toward language in its totality (1997/1923: 159). This orientation is what makes translation different from, but not inferior to, original writing. While a poetic work is concerned with 'certain linguistic structurings of content' (ibid.), translation 'ultimately has as its purpose the expression of the most intimate relationships among languages' (1997/1923: 154). Therefore, to say that a translation reads like an original (an ideal represented for example by John Dryden:1992/1697) is not a compliment.

The translations that Benjamin cherishes replace only the words of the source text but retain the original syntax at the expense of the transmission of meaning (Benjamin 1997/1923: 160–1). The accumulation of translations which echo the original language will eventually lead to the formation of a pure language, free from the burden of meaning – a vision rather than an attainable goal. The nearest example is holy scripture, 'in which meaning has ceased to be the watershed dividing the flow of language from the flow of revelation' (1997/1923: 165).

Nowadays, Benjamin's ideas are a source of inspiration for postmodernist and poststructuralist thinkers. Largely through commentaries on 'The Task of the Translator', poststructuralist thinkers like Jacques Derrida and Paul de Man explode the binary opposition between 'original' and 'translation' which underwrites the translator's invisibility (Venuti 1992: 6). In the context of Cultural Studies, Bhabha (1990) used Benjamin's essay to develop his ideas about 'cultural translation', in which the encounter is between cultures rather than languages, resulting in their fusion and hybridity.

18.4 Translators are authorized to create meaning rather than transferring it

18.4.1 Roland Barthes, Jacques Derrida, Lawrence Venuti – the instability of meaning

As early as 1968, Barthes challenged the idea that a text has a fixed stable meaning produced by the author:

> We know now that a text consists not of a line of words, releasing a single 'theological' meaning (the 'message' of the Author-God), but of a multi-dimensional space in which are married and contested several writings, none of which is original: the text is a fabric of quotations, resulting from a thousand sources of culture [...] the writer can only imitate an ever anterior, never original gesture; his sole power is to mingle writings, to counter some by others, so as never to rely on just one.
>
> (Barthes 1989/1968: 52–3)

The responsibility for producing meaning lies with the reader:

> a text consists of multiple writings, proceeding from several cultures and entering into dialogue, into parody, into contestation; but there is a site where this multiplicity is collected, and this site is not the author, as has hitherto been claimed, but the reader.
>
> (1989/1968: 54)

The idea that the text does not contain any stable meaning was further developed by Derrida (1985, 1997/1967) and de Man (1986). For Derrida, this instability is an inevitable result of the rift between signifiers and signified. Signifiers lead to other signifiers, creating an endless chain: 'There are no final meanings that arrest the movement of signification' (Culler 2007: 188). The signified is deferred, though the movement from one signifier to another leaves, on each move, a trace, or *restance*, in a sort of resistance to the utter disappearance of meaning (Levy 1997: 123).

In translation, the idea that meaning is unstable led to a shift of focus from the source text as a 'coherent expression of authorial meaning' (Venuti 1992: 7) to its translatability in the sense that Benjamin (1997/1923) attached to this term – that is, being worthy of translation (Venuti 1992: 7). The source is conceived as the site of multiple and divided meanings which is replaced – in the translation – by a new set of multiple and divided meanings (1992: 8). A simple correspondence of meaning between the source and target text is thus impossible (ibid.). Rather than reconstructing the source, the translation supplements it (1992: 10). As we have seen, the claim that meaning cannot be transferred in translation was already made in the 1960s – for example, by Catford (1965) – but in poststructuralism it entailed a new conception of the role of the translator as one who 'inventively joins in the production of meaning' (Venuti 1992: 12). As a producer of meaning, the translator is no longer subordinate to the author. For Venuti, this is the rationale behind his call for visibility – of the translator as a personality, and the translation as a text. The latter is no longer expected to conceal its foreign origin by displaying a fluent and readable façade (Venuti 1992, 2008/1995).

18.4.2 Luise von Flotow – feminist approaches to translation

Feminist approaches to translation and the translations that they trigger illustrate the role of the translator as the producer of meaning. According to Flotow (1991), two of the main sources of these approaches are second-wave feminism - feminist activity originating in the US in the 1960s (Whelehan 1995) – and poststructuralism, represented, for example, by Derrida (1985). The poststructuralist insistence on the 'relativity in meaning' (Flotow 1991: 80) encouraged translators to manifest their creativity, experiment with the texts under translation and even 'abuse' them.

Flotow discusses three strategies used in feminist translation: supplementing, prefacing and footnoting, and 'hijacking' (1991: 74). Supplementing takes place when the source language is criticized in the source text for its patriarchal or sexist characteristics. The intervention in the translation is intended to turn the critique of the source language into a critique of the target language. To illustrate this strategy, Flotow quotes *La nef des sorcières* [The Witches' Ship], a dramatic work produced by a group of feminist writers in Quebec in 1976. The original reads: 'Ce soir, j'entre l'histoire sans relever ma jupe' (1991: 69). A traditional translation into English would be: 'This evening I'm entering history without pulling up my skirt'. However, Flotow suggests that a feminist translator may choose to accentuate the message: 'This evening I'm entering history without opening my legs' (1991: 70). The second translation with its 'shock effect' manifests an aggressive and creative approach to translation.

Prefacing and footnoting are another form of feminist intervention (1991: 76). By using this strategy, feminist translators reflect on their work and stress their active presence. They may also use the first strategy (supplementing) and accompany it by their own explanations (1991: 77). Thus, they participate in the creation of meaning. However, this is a mild intervention compared with the third strategy, 'hijacking'. The term is used by Flotow neutrally or positively, but it actually derives from a critical attack on feminist translation by a Montreal journalist: 'the translator [. . .] is so intrusive at times that she all but hijacks the author's work' (Homel 1990 in Flotow 1991: 79). The three strategies differ in their treatment of the source text. What they share is the replacement of 'notions of fidelity and truth, transparency and definitive meaning in translation' by 'supplementation, experimentation, interference and "transformance"' (1991: 82).

18.4.3 Suzanne Jill Levine – subversive translation

The strategy referred to as 'hijacking' (Flotow 1991) can be illustrated by *Infante's Inferno*, the English version of the semi-autobiographical novel *La Habana para un Infante Difunto* [Havana for a Deceased Infant] by the Cuban writer Guillermo Cabrera Infante (1984/1979). The translator Suzanne Jill Levine found the novel, which tells about the narrator's youth in Havana, annoyingly sexist: 'The *Inferno*'s Infante [a pun combining the author's name and the Spanish word for 'infant'] mocks women and their words' (Levine 1992: 82). She hesitated whether to translate it: 'Where does it leave a woman as translator of such a book? Is she not a double betrayer, to play Echo to this Narcissus, repeating the archetype once again?' (1992: 83). On the face of it, she could either refrain from translating the work, or translate it with no revision on the ground that the author is responsible for what he has written, or moderate or delete the sexist expressions. Levine however chose a fourth path: she exaggerated the sexist utterances, turning them into an object of ridicule. The translation is therefore both a sexist text and a parody of such a text, as the following example illustrates:

> When the Havana narrator makes the jaded statement 'no one man can rape a woman', the infernal translator undermines this popular myth with the book's own corrosive mechanism of alliteration and writes: 'no wee man can rape a woman'.
>
> (ibid.)

The translator mocks the chauvinist cliché that women are willing victims. By replacing 'one' with 'wee' she insinuates that rape is out of the question only when very small men ('wee') or women ('wee man') are concerned (see also Flotow 2016: 27).

The following are more manifestations of the same strategy:

> Verbal logic supplants fidelity when 'fines de siglio' is translated not as 'turn of the century' but as the 'gay nineties,' or when 'Amor Propio' (the title initiating a chapter in praise of masturbation) is translated not as *amour-propre*, 'Self-Esteem' or 'Self-Love,' but as 'Love Thyself.' (After all, the Bible is the book of books!) And the text continues to metamorphose blasphemously into another text when the following chapter (about the narrator's pursuit of women in movie theatres) is titled 'Love Thy Neighbor' instead of 'False Love,' a literal translation of the Spanish saying 'Amor trompero' (the original chapter title).
>
> (1992: 83–4)

By 'gay nineties', the translator insinuates that this was the decade of homosexuals, thus exaggerating the author's sexism. Masturbation is referred to in a Biblical elevated language, which ridicules its praise by the narrator. The pursuit of women in the movie theatres of Havana is similarly ridiculed by the incongruous style. Levine's 'hijacking' of Infante's book takes to the extreme the idea that the translator is a producer of meaning no less than the author. At the same time, it raises ethical questions regarding the responsibility of the translator towards the author, on the one hand, and the target readers, on the other hand – all the more so in the case under consideration because feminism is represented by a member of the American cultural hegemony (see Nord 1997: 123–8, Pym 2001 on ethics in translation).

18.5 Translation Studies is not about meaning

18.5.1 Leo Hickey – perlocutionary equivalence

Hickey (1998) approaches translation from the perspective of pragmatics. Based on Austin (1962), he makes use of the concept of 'speech acts' and the distinction between 'locution', 'illocution' and 'perlocution'. The concept of speech acts derives from the idea alluded to in the title of Austin's book that people can do things with words – make requests, command, apologize, etc. Locution refers to what the speaker says, illocution to the speech act performed and perlocution to the effect upon the reader or hearer. Hickey expects translation to create a perlocutionary equivalence – that is, to reconstruct, in the translation, the potential of the source text to create a certain effect (or more than one) upon the addressee. In his opinion, even understanding – which is a change in the addressee's state of mind – can be considered a perlocutionary effect. There are three ways to achieve perlocutionary equivalence, and Hickey assumes that translators manoeuvre between them, taking into consideration the kind of text that they translate. The first is marking – the translator acts as a mediator between the source text and the target addressee, and marking exposes the act of mediating, either overtly, by stating that the text is a translation and mentioning the translator's name, or more subtly – for example, by using foreign measures or forms of address. The second is exegesis – providing background information. Hickey's concept of exegesis seems to approximate to what Translation Studies refers to as explicitation (Blum-Kulka 1986; Englund Dimitrova 2005). He claims that there is an equilibrium – the more marking is used, the less exegesis is needed and vice versa. The third way is recontextualization – straying from the original locution and changing the entire context to achieve perlocutionary equivalence. As mentioned, Hickey links the translator's use of marking, exegesis and recontextualization with the type of text under translation. Marking is required in legal texts, since translators are not supposed to familiarize the source text and change the terminology that it uses. In literary translation, both marking and exegesis are weak. One does not need either to mark the source as foreign or explain it extensively, because, in Hickey's opinion, the literary world is universally oriented even when it is embedded in a specific culture. Moderate marking and exegesis will suffice to enable the addressee to have an aesthetic experience similar to the one that the readers of the source had.

In translating humorous texts, the translator's task is to make the addressee identify some incongruity, which is the foundation of humour (Hickey 1998). Exegesis will spoil the humour, because the addressee is supposed to respond immediately and at the same time to the incongruity encountered and to the possible congruity that could exist. Retaining the humour may require a drastic deviation from the source – for example, a joke based on an English idiom will have to be replaced by a joke based on a French idiom. Marking is irrelevant in the translation of humour because recontextualization entails anchoring the text in a new local or neutral context (ibid.). Hickey's work and the concepts and terminology that he uses manifest the possibility of conceptualizing translation without dealing with meaning.

18.5.2 Gideon Toury – functional equivalence and norms

Some of the terms used by Toury (2012) are quite similar to those used by Catford (1965), but he uses them in a very different way. Toury, like Catford, uses the term 'formal correspondence'. However, while Catford employs it to assess the distance between languages, Toury looks at the translated text itself: formal correspondence means that the target text resembles the source text in its formal properties, thus manifesting source-language transfer (Toury 2012: 272).

Another term shared by Toury, Catford and many other scholars in the field of Translation Studies is 'equivalence' (see Chapter 11, this volume). As mentioned above, Catford (1965) regards 'textual equivalence' as an empirical fact: a textual equivalent is any TL text or portion of text which replaces SL text or portion of text (Catford 1965: 27). Nida and Taber (1969) have used a similar term, 'dynamic equivalence', for a different purpose: 'Dynamic equivalence is [...] to be defined in terms of the degree to which the receptors of the message in the receptor language respond to in substantially the same manner as the receptors in the source language' (1969: 24). For example, if the target culture is not acquainted with snow, and has no word for it, the snow referred to in the idiom 'white as snow' can be replaced by another referent which is recognized as white, or pure. Toury uses a similar term, 'functional equivalence', to express a different idea. Functional equivalence means that the 'textual functions' of the source text – that is, the network of inner relations between its components – are reconstructed in the translation (Toury 2012: 304). If there is functional equivalence between the source and target text, the translation is adequate. Using Itamar Even-Zohar's definition, Toury describes an adequate translation as 'a translation which realizes in the target language the textual relationships of a source text with no breach of its own [basic] linguistic system' (Even-Zohar 1975: 43, quoted in Toury 2012: 79).

As one of the founders and proponents of Descriptive Translation Studies, Toury does not make any value judgement about adequate translation. Integrating it into his theory of norms, he regards it as norm-dependent. If adequacy is undesirable and acceptability is preferred, the original relations will undergo changes so as to adapt the translation to the target-culture norms. In his seminal book from 2012, Toury uses the word 'meaning' occasionally; but his conceptualization of translation does not depend on it. According to his notion of 'assumed translation', translations are 'all utterances in a [target] culture which are presented or regarded as translations' (2012: 27). His objection to pre-fixed definitions of translation entails, by necessity, disagreement with the view of translation as the transfer of meaning (Jakobson 1959; Nida 1966). At the same time, his view of translation as a flexible historical phenomenon clashes with the idea that translation, as a rule, cannot or should not transfer meaning (Catford 1965; Benjamin 1997/1923).

Despite the huge differences between Toury and Hickey, it is noteworthy that both of them base their conceptualization of translation on concepts other than 'meaning'. In other words, they do not put 'meaning' centre stage. In this, they differ, for example, from Catford (1965), Ricoeur (2006) and Benjamin (1997/1923), who deal extensively with meaning even though Catford and Ricoeur claim that it cannot be transferred in translation and Benjamin regards it as negligible in the translator's work.

18.6 Conclusion

It is noteworthy that most of the thinkers concerned do not define meaning. Quine (1960, 1969) takes care to limit his observations to 'stimulus meaning' – the meaning which one deduces from the response of the native speaker to a certain situation. Catford (1965) employs the definitions made by Firth (1957). Others let the concept of meaning remain elusive and evasive. This should make one cautious in drawing conclusions and making comparisons, all the more so given that they talked about meaning in different languages: Latin, French, German, English and more.

With this reservation in mind, the conclusion of this chapter is that the transmission of meaning – if the concept is at all relevant to the research paradigm or school of thought under consideration – can be conceived as possible/necessary/impossible/irrelevant; viewpoints change over time and depend on the translator's agenda. The concept of meaning can thus be a way to map Translation Studies.

Ricoeur seems to represent all the thinkers and approaches discussed in this chapter in claiming that 'since there is such a thing as translation, it certainly has to be possible' (Ricoeur 2006: 15). Beyond this axiom, they differ greatly. The disagreement between them cannot be always explained in terms of the time of writing. Catford (1965), who insists that translation does not convey meaning, and Jakobson (1959) and Nida and Taber (1969), who stress the opposite, may have developed their ideas in different intellectual contexts, but there is no significant time gap between them.

Despite the differences, there are some ideas – 'memes' in the terminology of Chesterman (2016) – that can be detected in different eras and contexts. The relationship between meaning and form is manifest in two opposing 'memes' – one regards meaning as separate from form, and the other sees them as inseparable. The 'sense for sense' approach, which regards sense as distinct from form, was introduced by St. Jerome in the fourth century. In the twentieth century, it can be traced in the writings of Jakobson (1959), who believes that meaning can be delivered by different signs, belonging to different languages and sign systems. This 'meme' is also at the basis of the differentiation between meaning and style, or surface structure, made by Nida and Taber (1969). Benjamin likewise regards meaning and syntax as separable (Benjamin 1997/1923), though his willingness to retain the syntax and give up the meaning in translation sets him apart from the 'sense for sense' group. Conversely, the conviction that meaning and form are inseparable links the ancient 'word for word' tradition with Catford (1965) and Ricoeur (2006), though, in their case, it leads to admitting that translation cannot convey meaning; the translator must make do with 'textual equivalence' or 'equivalence without adequacy' respectively.

If we take the factor of time into consideration, it seems that the most significant change, associated with postmodernism and post-colonialism, concerns the role of the translator. Rather than asking if the translator is able to deliver the meaning of the source, as Jakobson, Catford and Nida and Taber do, postmodernist thinkers such as Venuti (1992, 2008/1995) regard the translator as the producer of meaning. Accordingly, translators are called to make themselves visible rather than hide their presence by domesticating the source and using a fluent style which eliminates the act of mediation (ibid.). The change in the status of the translator entails a licence to use translation in order to promote a political agenda, as one can learn from Levine's feminist translation of Cabrera Infante's novel (Levine 1992).

Based on this example, one may suggest that every theoretical and philosophical approach to the issue of meaning has implications for translation as a practice. This is self-evident when the researcher acts like a guide, as Nida and Taber (1969) as well as Hickey (1998) do, or has an explicit agenda, which applies to Venuti (1992, 2008/1995). However, even research conducted in the framework of Descriptive Translation Studies has implications for translation as a practice. For example, by bypassing the issue of meaning and stressing the role of norms in translation, Toury (2012) calls attention not just to the constraints which force themselves on the translator but also to his or her freedom to choose.

This chapter has addressed the ideas of translation scholars, linguists and philosophers. Some of them – for example, Catford and Quine, or Toury and Ricoeur (Weissbrod 2009) – seem to conduct a dialogue even though they belong to different disciplines and the dialogue did not take place in reality. In other examples, the dialogue is more than imaginary (see Chapter 9, this volume, on Wittgenstein for a philosophical approach to meaning that is becoming influential). In both cases, however, their significance to each other and mutual enrichment are evident.

Related topics

Benjamin; Gadamer and Ricoeur; Quine; Derrida; translation theory and philosophy; equivalence; feminism; toward a philosophy of translation.

Further reading

Barthes, R. 1989/1968. 'The Death of the Author', in *The Rustle of Language*, tr. by R. Howard. Berkeley and Los Angeles: University of California Press, pp. 49–55. (Barthes' article marks the point of reversal when – in literary criticism – the responsibility for the creation of meaning has shifted from the author to the reader. This obviously has implications for the translator as a reader.)

Chesterman, A. 2016. *Memes of Translation: The Spread of Ideas in Translation Theory* (revised edition). Amsterdam and Philadelphia: John Benjamins. (Chesterman surveys the development of translation theory through the prism of 'memes' – ideas that spread. Meanwhile, he discusses the attitude to 'meaning' in various theoretical approaches.)

Lefevere, A. (ed.) 1992. *Translation/History/Culture: A Sourcebook*. London and New York: Routledge. (This collection of historical sources from Roman times to the 1920s, translated into English from a variety of languages, includes some of the most important statements on meaning (or sense) in translation by St. Jerome, Dryden, Schleiermacher and many more.)

References

Austin, John L., 1962. *How to Do Things with Words*. Oxford: Clarendon Press.

Barthes, Roland, 1989/1968. 'The Death of the Author', in *The Rustle of Language*, tr. Richard Howard. Berkeley and Los Angeles: University of California Press, pp. 49–55.

Benjamin, Walter, 1997/1923. 'The Translator's Task', tr. Steven Rendall. *TTR* 10:2, pp. 151–65.

Bhabha, Homi K., 1990. 'The Third Space', in *Identity: Community, Culture, Difference*, Jonathan Rutherford (ed.). London: Lawrence and Wishart, pp. 207–21.

Blum-Kulka, Shoshana, 1986. 'Shifts of Cohesion and Coherence in Translation', in *Interlingual and Intercultural Communication*, Juliane House and Shoshana Blum-Kulka (eds.). Tübingen: Gunter Narr, pp. 17–35.

Cabrera Infante, Guillermo, 1984/1979. *Infante's Inferno*, tr. Suzanne Jill Levine. New York: Harper & Row.

Catford, John C., 1965. *A Linguistic Theory of Translation*. Oxford: Oxford University Press.

Cattrysse, Patrick, 2014. *Descriptive Adaptation Studies: Epistemological and Methodological Issues*. Antwerp and Apeldoorn: Garant.

Chesterman, Andrew, 2016. *Memes of Translation: The Spread of Ideas in Translation Theory* (revised edition). Amsterdam and Philadelphia: John Benjamins.

Chomsky, Noam, 1957. *Aspects of the Theory of Syntax*. Cambridge, MA: MIT Press.

Chomsky, Noam, 1965. *Syntactic Structures*. The Hague: Mouton.

Culler, Jonathan, 2007. *On Deconstruction: Theory and Criticism After Structuralism*. Ithaca: Cornell University Press.

Dagut, Menachem, 1981. 'Semantic "Voids" as a Problem in the Translation Process'. *Poetics Today* 2: 4, pp. 61–71.

de Man, Paul, 1986. 'Conclusions: Walter Benjamin's "The Task of the Translator"', in *The Resistance to Theory*. Manchester: Manchester University Press, pp. 73–105.

Derrida, Jacques, 1985. 'Des tours de Babel', in *Difference in Translation*, tr. Joseph F. Graham. Ithaca and London: Cornell University Press, pp. 165–207.

Derrida, Jacques, 1997/1967. *Of Grammatology*, tr. Gayatri Chakravorty Spivak. Baltimore: Johns Hopkins University Press.

Dryden, John, 1992/1697. 'On Translation', in *Theories of Translation: An Anthology of Essays from Dryden to Derrida*, Rainer Schulte and John Biguenet (eds.). Chicago and London: University of Chicago Press, pp. 17–31.

Englund Dimitrova, Birgitta, 2005. *Expertise and Explicitation in the Translation Process*. Amsterdam and Philadelphia: John Benjamins.

Even-Zohar, Itamar, 1975. 'Decisions in Translating Poetry: Baudelaire's Spleen in Hebrew Translation of Lea Goldberg'. *Ha-Sifrut* 21, pp. 32–45. [In Hebrew.]

Even-Zohar, Itamar, 1990. 'Translation and Transfer'. *Polysystem Studies* (a special issue of *Poetics Today*) 11:1, pp. 73–8.

Firth, John Rupert, 1957. *Papers in Linguistics 1934–1951*. London: Oxford University Press.

Flotow, Luise von, 1991. 'Feminist Translation: Contexts, Practices and Theories'. *TTR* 4:2, pp. 69–84.

Flotow, Luise von, 2016. *Translation and Gender: Translating in the 'Era of Feminism'*. London and New York: Routledge.

Göpferich, Susanne, 2007. 'Translation Studies and Transfer Studies: A Plea for Widening the Scope of Translation Studies', in *Doubts and Directions in Translation Studies*, Yves Gambier, Miriam Shlesinger and Radengundis Stolze (eds.). Amsterdam and Philadelphia: John Benjamins, pp. 27–40.

Hermans, Theo, 1997. 'Translation as Institution', in *Translation as Intercultural Communication: Selected Papers from the EST Congress, Prague 1995*, Mary Snell-Hornby, Zuzana Jettmarová and Klaus Kaindl (eds.). Amsterdam and Philadelphia: John Benjamins, pp. 3–20.

Hickey, Leo, 1998. 'Perlocutionary Equivalence: Marking, Exegesis and Recontextualisation', in *The Pragmatics of Translation*, Leo Hickey (ed.). Clevedon: Multilingual Matters, pp. 217–32.

Homel, David, 1990. 'Lise Gauvin Astutely Explains Quebec to Outsiders'. *The Gazette* (April 21).

Ivir, Vladimir, 1987. 'Procedures and Strategies for the Translation of Culture'. *Translation across Cultures* (a special issue of *Indian Journal of Applied Linguistics*) 13:2, Gideon Toury (ed.), pp. 35–46.

Jakobson, Roman. 1959. 'On Linguistic Aspects of Translation', in *On Translation*, Reuben A. Brower (ed.). Cambridge, MA: Harvard University Press, pp. 232–9.

Karas, Hilla, 2016. 'Intralingual Intertemporal Translation as a Relevant Category in Translation Studies'. *Target* 28:3, pp. 445–66.

Kohn, Ayelet and Rachel Weissbrod, 2012. '*Waltz with Bashir* as a Case of Multidimensional Translation', in *Translation, Adaptation and Transformation*, Laurence Raw (ed.). London and New York: Continuum, pp. 123–44.

Lefevere, André (ed.), 1992. *Translation/History/Culture: A Sourcebook*. London and New York: Routledge.

Levine, Suzanne Jill, 1992. 'Translation as (Sub)Version: On Translating Infante's Inferno', in *Rethinking Translation – Discourse, Subjectivity, Ideology*, Lawrence Venuti (ed.). London and New York: Routledge, pp. 75–85.

Levy, Ze'ev, 1997. *'Bikoret ha-Logotsentrism shel Derrida ve-Lévinas ve-Hashlakhoteyha al Hora'at ha-Philosophya'* [The Criticism of Logocentrism by Derrida and Levinas and its Implications for the Teaching of Philosophy], in *Khinukh be-Idan ha-Siakh ha-Postmoderni [Education in the Era of Postmodern Discourse]*, Ilan Gur-Ze'ev (ed.). Jerusalem: The Magness Press, The Hebrew University, pp. 121–33. [In Hebrew.]

Malmkjær, Kirsten, 2005. *Linguistics and the Language of Translation*. Edinburgh: Edinburgh University Press.

Munday, Jeremy, 2016. *Introducing Translation Studies: Theories and Applications*. London and New York: Routledge.

Newmark, Peter, 1988. *A Textbook of Translation*. New York: Prentice Hall.

Nida, Eugene A., 1966/1959. 'Principles of Translation as Exemplified by Bible Translating', in *On Translation*, Reuben A. Brower (ed.). New York: Oxford University Press, pp. 11–31.

Nida, Eugene A. and Charles R. Taber, 1969. *The Theory and Practice of Translation*. Leiden: Brill.

Nord, Christiane, 1997. *Translating as a Purposeful Activity: Functionalist Approaches Explained*. Manchester: St. Jerome.

Ogden, Charles Kay and Ivor Armstrong Richards, 1923. *The Meaning of Meaning: A Study of the Influence of Language Upon Thought and of the Science of Symbolism*. New York: Harcourt, Brace and World.

Petrilli, Susan, 2003. 'Translation and Semiosis. Introduction', in *Translation Translation*, Susan Petrilli (ed.). Amsterdam: Rodopi, pp. 17–37.

Pirovolakis, Eftichis, 2010. *Reading Derrida and Ricoeur: Improbable Encounters between Deconstruction and Hermeneutics*. Albany: New York University Press.

Pym, Anthony (ed.), 2001. *The Return to Ethics* (a special issue of *The Translator*) 7:2.

Quine, Willard Van Orman, 1960. 'Translation and Meaning', in *Word and Object*. Cambridge, MA: MIT Press, pp. 26–79.

Quine, Willard Van Orman, 1969. 'Ontological Relativity', in *Ontological Relativity and Other Essays*. New York: Columbia University Press, pp. 26–68.

Ricoeur, Paul, 2006. *On Translation*, tr. Eileen Brennan. London and New York: Routledge.

Robinson, Douglas, 2001. 'Free Translation', in *Routledge Encyclopedia of Translation Studies*, Mona Baker (ed.). London and New York: Routledge, pp. 87–90.

Russell, Bertrand, 1950. 'Logical Positivism'. *Revue Internationale de Philosophie* 4:11, pp. 3–19.

Sela-Sheffy, Rakefet, 2000. 'The Suspended Potential of Culture Research in TS'. *Target* 12:2, pp. 345–55.

Snell-Hornby, Mary, 1988. *Translation Studies: An Integrated Approach*. Amsterdam and Philadelphia: John Benjamins.

Snell-Hornby, Mary, 2006. *The Turns of Translation Studies: New Paradigms or Shifting Viewpoints?* Amsterdam and Philadelphia: John Benjamins.

Toury, Gideon, 1994. 'A Cultural-Semiotic Perspective', in *Encyclopedic Dictionary of Semiotics*, vol. 2: N–Z, Thomas A. Sebeok (ed.). Berlin and New York: Mouton de Gruyter, pp. 1111–24.

Toury, Gideon, 2012. *Descriptive Translation Studies – and beyond* (revised edition). Amsterdam and Philadelphia: John Benjamins.

Venuti, Lawrence, 1992. 'Introduction', in *Rethinking Translation – Discourse, Subjectivity, Ideology*, Lawrence Venuti (ed.). London and New York: Routledge, pp. 1–17.

Venuti, Lawrence, 2008/1995. *The Translator's Invisibility: A History of Translation*. London and New York: Routledge.

Weissbrod, Rachel, 2004. 'From Translation to Transfer'. *Across Languages and Cultures* 5:1, pp. 23–41.

Weissbrod, Rachel, 2009. 'Philosophy of Translation Meets Translation Studies: Three Hebrew Translations of Kipling's "If" in Light of Paul Ricoeur's "Third Text" and Gideon Toury's "Adequate Translation"'. *Target* 21:1, pp. 58–73.

Weizman, Elda, 2010. 'Voids Revisited: An Issue in Translation Studies and its Implications for the Study of the Hebrew language', in *Hebrew: A Living Language*, Rina Ben-Shahar, Gideon Toury and Nitsa Ben-Ari (eds.), vol. 5. Tel Aviv: Hakibbutz Hameuchad and the Porter Institute, Tel Aviv University, pp. 201–17. [In Hebrew.]

Whelehan, Imelda, 1995. *Modern Feminist Thought: From the Second Wave to 'Post-Feminism'*. New York: New York University Press.

Whorf, Benjamin L., 1956. *Language, Thought, and Reality: Selected Writings of Benjamin Lee Whorf*, John Carroll (ed.). Cambridge, MA: MIT Press.

Zethsen, Karen Korning, 2007. 'Beyond Translation Proper – Extending the Field of Translation Studies'. *TTR* 20:1, pp. 281–308.

Part III
The translation of philosophy

19
The translation of philosophical texts

Duncan Large

Introduction

No philosophical tradition is an island: philosophy is an inherently multicultural and multilingual discipline. Many philosophers have had (or deliberately acquired) the linguistic equipment to understand philosophical texts written in languages other than their own, but in most cases the reception of foreign-language philosophy has depended on translations. Indeed, some philosophers would hardly have had any reception at all without translations (how many of Kierkegaard's readers outside Scandinavia read him in the original Danish?).[1] This chapter will address some of the specific questions associated with the translation of philosophical texts. After a historical overview of some of the key translations that have changed the course of the development of philosophy, I will focus on three questions: 'why translate philosophy?', 'who translates philosophy?' and 'how to translate philosophy?'.

Historical perspectives

The history of philosophical translation in the west begins in the first century BCE with Roman translations and adaptations of Greek philosophy into Latin, and the creation of a new philosophical vocabulary in order to do so. As in most other cultural spheres, Roman philosophy exhibits a self-conscious and deferential desire to emulate prestigious Greek models (Seele 1995). Lucretius' (*c.* 99–*c.* 55 BCE) epic didactic poem *De rerum natura* [On the Nature of Things] seeks to introduce Roman readers to Epicurean philosophy through a free adaptation of Epicurus' Περὶ Φύσεως [Peri Physeos: On Nature] with an admixture of paraphrase and translation (Clay 1983; Sedley 1998). Rather than simply importing Greek words, with technical terms he is self-consciously innovating in order to create a philosophical vocabulary in Latin, through neologisms, calques, extensions of the meaning of existing words and other strategies. The poem itself explains the poet's predicament and blames it on the rudimentary state [*egestas*] of the Latin language:

> Nor does it fail me that discoveries – obscure and dark –
> Of Greeks are difficult to shed much light on with the spark

> Of Latin poetry, chiefly since I must coin much new
> Terminology, because of our tongue's dearth and due
> To the novelty of subject matter
>
> (Lucretius 2007: 10)

Lucretius' contemporary Cicero (106–43 BCE) faced the same problem and adopted the same solution but from a more combative position. He was translating Greek oratory and philosophy (Epicurus, Xenophon, Plato, Aristotle) into Latin for an elite, educated (i.e. Greek-speaking) readership of free-born males who could be expected to be familiar with the source texts in their original language. In other words, at the outset of Western philosophy translation the modern expectation that a text needed to be translated because it could not be understood in the source language did not apply. In his dialogue *Academica* [On Academic Scepticism, 45 BCE] Cicero explicitly raises the question of the need for Latin translations at all under such circumstances, when his fictional collocutor the lexicographer Varro asks:

> For since I saw that philosophy had been most carefully expounded in Greek, I judged that any of our people who had an interest in this, if they were learned in the teachings of the Greeks, would sooner read Greek writings than ours, and if on the other hand they hated the sciences and systems of the Greeks, they would not care even for philosophy, which cannot be understood without Greek learning.
>
> (White 2015: 117, adapted)

In response to such sceptics and nay-sayers, Cicero translates as a stylistic exercise, in order to develop the expressive potential and analytical precision of the Latin language and to prove wrong those (such as Lucretius) who regretted the supposed poverty of the Latin language in relation to Greek by demonstrating instead the copiousness [*abundantia*] of a Latin lexis which could, as required, be exploited for philosophical purposes. Cicero uses multiple Latin translations for the single Greek term κατάληψις [catalepsis] – *cognitio, perceptio, comprehensio* – but whereas earlier commentators denigrated this practice for its looseness, Georgina White (2015: 99–115) argues that this is a deliberate and habitual strategy asserting the relative superiority of Latin over Greek. Cicero was also unashamedly neologistic, coining terms such as *essentia, evidentia, humanitas, perspicuitas* and *qualitas*, which would become mainstays of the Latin-language philosophical tradition.

After the classical period the transmission of Greek philosophy in the Latin West was very desultory. For around 800 years Plato was known almost exclusively through Calcidius' early fourth-century translation of the *Timaeus*, and Boethius' early sixth-century translations of Aristotle's works on logic were the only significant portions of his canon available to Christendom till the twelfth century. Anglo-Saxon England saw a golden age of translation into the vernacular (Stanton 2002), with King Alfred looking to establish Old English as a literary language in the later ninth century and taking the lead himself through translations of religious and philosophical works, including the first fifty psalms and the most popular philosophical work of the period, Boethius' *Consolation of Philosophy* (Discenza 2005). In general, philosophy translations into European vernacular languages were relatively few in the medieval period, but Boethius was a notable exception and attracted other celebrity translators including Notker Labeo (Old High German, *c.* 1000), Jean de Meun (Old French, thirteenth century) and Geoffrey Chaucer (Middle English, late fourteenth century) (Hoenen and Nauta 1997). Beyond Christendom, though, in late-eighth-century Baghdad the Abbasid Caliph Harun al-Rashid established the House of Wisdom, which, over the next century and a half, developed into not only the largest library in the world but the home of an ambitious translation project to translate (and retranslate) classics of science and philosophy from Greek (often via earlier Syriac translations) and Sanskrit into Arabic in great quantities (Lyons 2009; Al-Khalili 2011). As Dimitri Gutas argues, the significance of the Graeco-Arabic translation movement 'lies in that it demonstrated for the first time in history that scientific and philosophical thought are international, not bound to a specific language or culture' (Gutas 1998: 192).

Translations of Aristotle into Arabic by Al-Kindī and his circle in Abbasid Baghdad gave a decisive impetus to the development of a specifically Islamic philosophy or *falsafa* (Adamson 2007; Alwishah and Hayes 2015). The 'Recovery of Aristotle' in the West came a good deal later and spanned roughly a century from the mid twelfth to mid thirteenth centuries. Scholars working from Arabic and Byzantine Greek sources (in Toledo and elsewhere) translated most of the 'Corpus Aristotelicum' into Latin, leading to the rise of medieval Aristotelianism. At the same time, Latin translations of the Arabic-language Muslim philosophers Averroes and Avicenna were placed on the curriculum in the new universities of thirteenth-century Europe, and Averroist thought would persist into the Renaissance and beyond (Akasoy and Giglioni 2013). In the fifteenth century the European Renaissance was also initially fuelled by a spate of new Latin translations of Aristotle (Copenhaver 1988); the number of Renaissance humanists translating Plato was much smaller, but foremost among them was Marsilio Ficino, whose *Complete Works of Plato* in Latin (1484) fuelled Renaissance neo-Platonism.

In the sixteenth century works of classical philosophy also began to be translated into European vernacular languages for the first time in significant quantities (Demetriou and Tomlinson 2015). Just as Lucretius and Cicero, 1600 years earlier, had aimed to establish a philosophical tradition in Latin through translation, now the same impulse led Bible translator Antonio Brucioli (*c.* 1498–1566) to translate Aristotle into Italian (Bianchi, Gilson and Kraye 2016). In 1540 the French humanist Étienne Dolet (1509–46) published the first European treatise on translation (Worth 1988) and lumped French together with 'Italian, Spanish, German, English, and other vulgar tongues' as 'languages not yet established in the field of art' (Dolet 1992: 28), but in sixteenth-century France 'under Francis I, enrichment of the French language became national policy' (Copenhaver 1988: 84). This led to such high-quality philosophical outputs as Dolet's own French Cicero (1542) and Plato (1544), Jacques Amyot's French Plutarch (1559, 1572) and Louis Le Roy's French Plato (1551–63). In contemporary England Nicholas Grimald published the first English translation of Cicero's popular *De Officiis* (1556) (Jones 1998), and several key works of Stoic philosophy appeared: James Sandford translated Epictetus' *Manual* (1567, from the French), Arthur Golding (translator of Shakespeare's Ovid) translated Seneca's *De Beneficiis* (1578) and Méric Casaubon the *Meditations* of Marcus Aurelius (1634). Philemon Holland (1552–1637) translated Plutarch's *Moralia* (1603), but the best-known Renaissance English translation of Plutarch was Sir Thomas North's version of the *Parallel Lives* (1579, from Amyot's French) – best known because it too would be used by Shakespeare.

The other well-known example of an English philosophical translation used by Shakespeare, John Florio's version of the *Essayes* of Montaigne (1603), is a notable example of the first wave of philosophical translations *between* European vernacular languages, which would also include the first translations of Machiavelli – whom Shakespeare may have read in one of the four manuscript versions available in English by the close of the sixteenth century (Petrina 2009; De Pol 2010). The European Renaissance was indeed a golden age of translation, and this included the first major translations from non-European languages, too, notably thanks to the work of Jesuit missionaries in translating Chinese classics, bringing them to the attention of Western readerships (and packaging them as philosophy rather than religion). The Italians Michele Ruggieri (1543–1607) and Matteo Ricci (1552–1610) translated classic works of Confucianism and neo-Confucianism into Latin, and Jesuit philosophical Sinology culminated in the late seventeenth century with the publication of *Confucius Sinarum Philosophus* (Couplet 1687), a Latin anthology that included versions of three of the *Four Books* (the *Great Learning*, the *Analects* and the *Doctrine of the Mean*) together with a biography of Confucius, edited by Flemish Jesuit Philippe Couplet. The Daoist classic *Tao Te Ching* – now one of the most translated texts after the Bible – was first translated into a Western language (again, Latin) *c.* 1720 by the French Jesuit Jean-François Noëlas (1669–1740). All this translation activity laid the groundwork for the considerable interest in China displayed by writers of the European Enlightenment such as Leibniz, Voltaire and Vico (Davis 1983; Perkins 2004; Harvey 2012; Mungello 2013; Brandt and Purdy 2016).

More overtly colonial European expansionism in the eighteenth and nineteenth centuries brought close contact with the philosophical cultures of India and Egypt. Whereas European understanding of the latter needed to wait till after Champollion's decipherment of hieroglyphic script in 1822 (the first translation of the ancient Egyptian *Book of the Dead* was Karl Richard Lepsius' German version from 1842), the opening up of India and its colonial exploitation by the East India Company from 1757 led to fruitful cultural contact by the end of the eighteenth century, such as the first translation into a European language of the *Bhagavad Gita* by the Orientalist Charles Wilkins (1785) and the development of the Indo-European-language hypothesis (1786) by his colleague in the Asiatick Society of Bengal William Jones (Franklin 2011). The emergence of Indology, Orientalism more generally and comparative religion as academic disciplines by the turn of the nineteenth century, especially in Germany and France, led to another golden age for translation in German Romanticism. In 1808 Friedrich Schlegel prepared the way with his *Über die Sprache und Weisheit der Indier* [On the Language and Wisdom of the Indians] containing a partial translation of the *Bhagavad Gita* into German, but it was his brother August Wilhelm who – as well as being the 'Schlegel' in 'Schlegel-Tieck', the standard German set of Shakespeare translations – held the first chair of Indology in Germany (at the University of Bonn). A. W. Schlegel founded the scholarly journal *Indische Bibliothek* (1820–30) and set up a Sanskrit printing press, which he used to publish the first Sanskrit text in Europe, the *Bhagavad Gita*, in 1823 with his own Latin translation. The publication attracted a lot of interest in intellectual circles: Wilhelm von Humboldt gave two lectures on the text at the Royal Prussian Academy of Sciences in Berlin in June 1825 and June 1826, and it was the publication of these lectures in the *Schriften der Berliner Akademie* in 1827 that led Hegel to publish a substantial review in his periodical *Jahrbücher für wissenschaftliche Kritik*, in which he radically altered his earlier view on the significance of Indian philosophy (Herling 2006; Karyekar 2014; Rathore and Mohapatra 2017).

The first European-language translation of a Hindu text was a two-volume Latin retranslation and commentary of a Persian translation of fifty *Upanishads*, published in 1801–2 by Abraham Hyacinthe Anquetil-Duperron (1731–1805), the first professional French Indologist (Anquetil-Duperron 1801–2; cf. Anquetil 2005). It was this edition that Arthur Schopenhauer encountered in March 1814 when he borrowed it from the library in Weimar; he subsequently bought and heavily annotated his own copy, which he considered his favourite book and which was to have a profound impact on the development of his own philosophy (Cartwright 2010: 265–76). Schopenhauer's follower Nietzsche inherited a favourable view of Indian philosophy from his mentor (Parkes 1991). He had at least some familiarity with the *Avesta* (which had been available since 1771 in Anquetil-Duperron's

French translation (Anquetil-Duperron 1771)), and his respect for the historical Zoroaster led to his adopting 'Zarathustra' as his mouthpiece in *Also sprach Zarathustra* [Thus Spoke Zarathustra, 1883–5] (Rose 2000; Brobjer 2008: 65–6). Nietzsche was a close personal friend of the leading Indologist (and fellow Schopenhauerian) Paul Deussen and read his groundbreaking translation of the *Brahma Sutras* on its publication in 1887 (Deussen 1887). Nietzsche's reading of Louis Jacolliot's French translation of the *Law of Manu* that same year (Jacolliot 1876) led directly to the favourable comments on Manu that he incorporated into his late texts *Twilight of the Idols* and *The Antichrist* (Elst 2008), which, in turn, led Nietzsche's correspondent the Swedish writer August Strindberg to write a novel on Nietzschean themes with the title *Tschandala*, first published in 1889 (in a Danish translation by Peter Nansen).

Another scion of German academic Indology, the distinguished Sanskritist F. Max Müller, began to translate the *Upanishads* while studying under F. W. J. Schelling in Berlin in the 1840s, but he moved to Britain, where he would become Oxford's first Professor of Comparative Philology in 1868 and the leading British mediator of Indian culture. Müller was renowned for his edition of the *Rig-Veda* (Müller 1849–74) and as general editor of the monumental fifty-volume series of translations *The Sacred Books of the East* (Müller 1879–1910; see also Molendijk 2016 and Davis and Nicholls 2017), which was inaugurated with his own translation of the *Upanishads* (Müller 1879–84). Müller's series included six volumes of *The Sacred Books of China* (1879–91), which were all translated by his prolific colleague the Scottish Sinologist James Legge, Oxford's first Professor of Chinese (Girardot 2002). While a missionary in Hong Kong, Legge had previously completed a five-volume bilingual edition of *The Chinese Classics* (1861–72), which was published in London by Nicholas Trübner, who would go on to publish many more philosophical translations in his collections 'English and Foreign Philosophical Library' (from 1877) and 'Trübner's Oriental Series' (from 1878). Not that the nineteenth-century translational traffic between Europe and the East was all one way: there was an influx of Western philosophy *into* Japan in the late Tokugawa period and especially after the Meiji Restoration of 1868, leading to what is described by Yūjirō Nakamura as a philosophical 'culture of translation' in Japan even now (cited in Blocker and Starling 2001: 2; see also Mayuko 2017). At the turn of the twentieth century in China, Yan Fu (1854–1921), father of modern Chinese translation theory, was introducing secular Western thought through highly influential translations of Thomas Huxley, Adam Smith, Herbert Spencer, John Stuart Mill and Montesquieu (Delisle and Woodsworth 2012: 209–12).

Within Europe, the development of British Idealism in the second half of the nineteenth century was bolstered by early English translations of Kant and Hegel (Mander 2011). In the twentieth century, to name just a few of the most prominent examples of translation-led cross-cultural philosophical fertilisation, translations of Wittgenstein and the Vienna Circle fuelled the development of logical positivism and analytic philosophy of language in the English-speaking world, while in France the phenomenological tradition developed through translations of Husserl and Heidegger (Large 2014: 187). The post-War vogue for existentialism was fed by English-language translations of Sartre and Camus, and the later spread of 'continental' philosophy to the English-speaking world was only possible thanks to myriad translations of French structuralist, poststructuralist and postmodernist texts. Now the textual movement is going the other way, with the rapid spread of Anglo-American analytic philosophy translated into other European languages reversing the flow of the previous fifty years and reflecting the rapid increase in continental European interest in analytic philosophy over the last thirty years.

In the twenty-first century we have an embarrassment of riches: the philosophical canon is available in multiple translations and expanding all the time with the advent of university courses in 'world philosophy'. Substantial series such as 'Cambridge Texts in the History of Philosophy' (CUP) and 'International Library of Philosophy' (Routledge) in the UK, the 'Philosophical Classics' series from Dover and Hackett in the US and, in Germany, Felix Meiner Verlag's 'Philosophische Bibliothek' (publishing since 1868, currently with 506 titles) keep translated philosophy titles in print, and smaller presses cater for new translated trends (e.g. L'Éclat, Ithaque and Agone for analytic philosophy in France). The last two decades have seen an explosion of online publication, too, with out-of-copyright translations available from gargantuan e-text collections like Project Gutenberg (www.gutenberg.org) and the Perseus Digital Library (www.perseus.tufts.edu), and philosophy-specific sites such as Early Modern Texts (www.earlymoderntexts.com), the Marxists Internet Archive (www.marxists.org) and Historic Analytic (www.hist-analytic.org). Such freely available resources are supplemented by subscription services such as the Loeb Classical Library (www.loebclassics.com), and with the rise of open-access publishing even in-copyright translations are becoming freely available.

Critical issues and topics, 1): why translate philosophy?

Revisiting Cicero's question from the start of philosophy translation in the West – what is its purpose? – I would like to analyse five possible responses.[2] First, philosophy translation (generally speaking) arises from the intention – on the part of a translator, publisher or other translation commissioner – simply to make a work or body of philosophy available to a new readership who lack command of the source language. This is what Chantal Wright terms the 'humanist case for translation' (Wright 2016: 19–30), and while it may sound like disinterested cultural mediation, it is usually motivated by at least an intercultural scholarly interest in promoting an alternative world view, and often a good deal more than that, amounting to the advancement of colonialist and other ideological agendas. Lawrence Venuti writes of the 'ethnocentric violence of translation' (Venuti 1995: 41), and Nietzsche before him writes of Roman poets translating roughshod over their Greek forebears, in an age when 'to translate meant to conquer' (Nietzsche 1992: 69). Examples of this approach range from Cicero advancing his political agenda (Baraz 2012) and the Abbasids looking to assert intellectual primacy over the Byzantines and Persians to state-sponsored translations of Marx and Engels published in Soviet Moscow by Progress Publishers and disseminated worldwide.

A second major aim in philosophy translation has been to use translation as a vehicle for exegesis of the philosophy itself, clarifying ambiguities and resolving cruces through translation choices (in addition to any editorial apparatus that might also be provided). Again, this can seem harmless – for example, in the mid twentieth century J. L. Austin translating Frege for teaching purposes (Frege 1950) – but all translation is more or less overt interpretation, whether consciously or not, and this applies to philosophy as to any other text type. In his translations of Plato, for example, 'Cicero engages in the philosophical interpretation and correction of his original text' (White 2015: 206), and in his *Timaeus* 'Cicero is able to subtly manipulate the original Platonic source text to emphasise the similarity of its thought to the doctrines of Pythagoreanism' (White 2015: 304–5). Almost two millennia later another distinguished Plato translator, Benjamin Jowett, openly admits that his general aim 'has been to represent Plato as the father of Idealism' (Plato 1875, II: 19). Often translators have to wrestle with a term which is ambiguous in the source language and can have multiple translations, resolving the dilemma by opting for one alternative over another – for example, Peter Adamson (2016) points out that Arabic translators of Aristotle had to choose between two different words to translate *eidos*, depending on whether they thought it meant 'form' or 'species'. English translators of Hegel's *Phenomenology* (1807) find themselves in a similar quandary when faced with the notorious shibboleth *Geist* and end up priming the reader for very different readings of the text by translating the title with either 'mind' (Hegel 1910) or 'spirit' (Hegel 1977). Venuti gives the example of Elizabeth Anscombe's version of Wittgenstein's *Philosophical Investigations* (1953) and, by analysing lexical choices such as 'philosophical problems arise when language *goes on holiday*' at *PI* 38 for 'die philosophischen Probleme entstehen, wenn die Sprache *feiert*', points out how Anscombe's translation assimilated Wittgenstein to domestic philosophical taste (Venuti 1998: 107–15). The stakes can be very high indeed with such manipulations (Hermans 1985): in his lectures on Parmenides, Heidegger describes the Latin translation of Greek terms for 'being' as a kind of ontological original sin:

> What is decisive is that the Latinization occurs as a *transformation of the essence of truth and Being* within the essence of the Greco-Roman domain of history. This transformation is distinctive in that it remains concealed but nevertheless determines everything in advance.
>
> (Heidegger 1992: 42)

For Heidegger, the creation and adoption of a Latin philosophical vocabulary determined a very different (and in his view baneful) course for the historical development of philosophy itself.

Third, irrespective of the nature and quality of the translation, the infusion of new ideas and forms has invariably had a reinvigorating impact on indigenous philosophical traditions. Reception has usually followed a common path, from translation and commentary to imitation and emulation, to adaptation and syncretistic fusion with native traditions. Such was the case with Al-Kindī and his circle in Baghdad, who made the translation of Aristotle into a springboard for developing a distinctive Islamic philosophy; likewise the Kyoto School in twentieth-century Japan was a response to contact with nineteenth-century German thought, synthesised with Asian traditions (Davis 2014). It has been the case over the history of philosophy with all the various translation-led 'neo-philosophies' (neo-Aristotelianism, neo-Platonism, neo-Hegelianism, etc.), which pass from a revival of interest in an earlier philosopher or movement to a new style of thinking. In some cases the impact has been minor (Nietzsche adopting the word *Tschandala* to supplement his already extensive multilingual vocabulary of abuse); in others it has been more profound (Schopenhauer's descriptions of the workings of the 'Veil of Maya'). In any event, in this way translation can be genuinely productive even when the target-language philosophy which results is based on poor translations, misunderstandings, skewed or partial (decontextualised) interpretations, or creative misreadings – witness the impact of Alexandre Kojève's Hegel on twentieth-century French philosophy (Dale 2014), or the post-War success of Simone de Beauvoir's *Le deuxième sexe* [The Second Sex] in the English-speaking world despite the patent inadequacies of the 1953 translation by entomologist Howard Madison Parshley (Bogic 2011).

An important consideration for many of the translators reviewed above, from Lucretius and Cicero to King Alfred and Étienne Dolet, was the desire to enrich a fledgling vernacular at a crucial point in its emergence as a literary language, to oblige one's language to think about the world differently. With the emergence of European literary vernaculars in the Renaissance period, Italian, French, Spanish and English were initially prominent and German was rather slower off the mark, but German developed in the course of the eighteenth century – that is, *after* Leibniz, who wrote mainly in Latin and French – to become the European language of philosophy *par excellence*, largely through the work of Christian Thomasius (1655–1728) and Christian Wolff (1679–1754). Eric Blackall writes that 'Wolff's German terminology translates into the natural speech material of his day the meaning of the Latin concepts, or of the new distinctions which he is introducing' (Blackall 1959: 33). Just as Cicero championed Latin over Greek, now Wolff believed that German was a better language for scholarship than Latin (Blackall 1959: 37). In turn, 'his works were the first scholarly works in German to be translated into several languages' (Blackall 1959: 47), and it was Wolff who by such means prepared the way for Kant in the next generation to forge a new vocabulary once again.

A fifth benefit from philosophy translation is developing and extending the philosophical horizons of individual translators. Many apprentice philosophers have produced translations of philosophical works at the beginning of their careers as a way of cutting their teeth and then gone on to greatness (Large 2014). Not that they are necessarily translating for publication or circulation – they might be translating out of sheer intellectual curiosity, for personal pleasure or for other distinctly personal motives, as with the sixty-year-old Queen Elizabeth I, who translated Boethius into early modern English at Windsor Castle in 1593 as a projection of intellectual power and in order to earn the respect of her courtiers for the speed with which she worked (Benkert 2001).

Critical issues and topics, 2): who translates philosophy?

This brings us to the question of who translates philosophy. In the history of philosophy translation, a figure like Elizabeth I has always been an exception – and not just because she was a ruling monarch or a woman but because she was a non-specialist. Philosophy is a very specialised literary genre with (for the most part) a specialised readership. It has always been regarded as one of the most demanding kinds of translation, requiring specialist technical knowledge. As early as 1531 the Spanish humanist Juan Luis Vives argued: 'The works of Aristotle will be badly translated by a man who is not a philosopher and those of Galen by a man who is not a doctor' (Vives 2002: 92). Such an argument resembles the parallel claim that poetry translation needs to be done by poets, but – as with poetry – it doesn't necessarily follow that the strongest, most original exponents of the art will produce the best translations. For example, J. L. Austin's translation of Frege's *Foundations of Arithmetic* has been criticised by its more recent translator, Dale Jacquette:

> Austin's translation has served to introduce several generations of students to Frege's ideas, and has endeared itself to its readers for its fluidity and charm. Frege himself, unfortunately, is not quite as charming as Austin's translation portrays, and Austin does not always faithfully represent or seem to perfectly understand certain of Frege's German idioms. It is worth remembering that Austin's translation was originally prepared as lecture notes for students, and that Austin was not otherwise known as having a special interest in German literature or philosophy.
>
> (Jacquette 2016: v)

Many of the world's greatest philosophers have translated the works of others and translated them well, whether cutting their teeth in a philosophical apprenticeship or as established figures (Large 2014). Philosophy translators have often not been philosophers of the first rank themselves, though, nor have they necessarily been academics (e.g. the autodidact Nietzsche translator R. J. Hollingdale, whose day job was as an editor for the *Guardian* newspaper). Some significant modern philosophical translations have been carried out by jobbing professional literary translators (e.g. Ralph Manheim's Heidegger 1959 or Shaun Whiteside's Nietzsche 1993), but these constitute exceptions. After all, no translator makes a great deal of money out of translating philosophical texts: they do not turn into bestsellers, as a rule, and any aspiring professional translator will need to make their living mostly by other means. As a result most modern philosophy translations are carried out by moonlighting academics (who do not need the money), to support their pedagogy or the development of their research careers – what Alastair Hannay, surveying Kierkegaard translations, calls 'not professional translators but scholars who have felt a rapport with the writing and feel impelled to bring [it] to the notice of contemporaries' (Hannay 2013: 387).

The perceived difficulty of philosophy translation has lent it an undoubted prestige, which goes some way to explaining its attraction over the years to high-class amateur translators such as King Alfred and Queen Elizabeth I. In the historical period other women philosophy translators have been few, given their exclusion from the universities. Notable Enlightenment translations by women include the German translations of Bayle, Leibniz and Hobbes by Luise Gottsched (Brown 2012: 48–60), the English Epictetus of Elizabeth Carter (1717–1806) (Agorni 2005) and the French translation of Adam Smith's *Theory of Moral Sentiments* by Sophie de Condorcet (1764–1822); then in the nineteenth and early twentieth centuries stand-outs include Harriet Martineau's (1802–76) Comte, George Eliot's Spinoza and Feuerbach, the *Bhagavad Gita* of Annie Besant (1847–1933), Helen Zimmern's (1846–1934) Nietzsche, the Plato translations of Ellen Francis Mason (1846–1930) and Elizabeth Haldane's (1862–1937) Descartes and Hegel. In the post-War period many significant contributions have been made by women translators: for example Suzanne Bachelard, Françoise Dastur, Monique Wittig and Françoise Wuilmart in the French-speaking world, and in the English-speaking world Elizabeth Anscombe, Hazel Barnes, Seyla Benhabib, Mary J. Gregor, Peggy Kamuf, Susanne Langer, Gayatri Chakravorty Spivak, Joan Stambaugh and Barbara Stoler Miller.

Critical issues and topics, 3): how to translate philosophy?

In the light of the rich history of practical philosophy translation work detailed above, it may seem surprising that theorists of translation have so often concluded that philosophy is untranslatable (Large 2018). The history of reflection on the translation of philosophy has been dominated by the question of translation difficulty, and it has been widely recognised that philosophical texts pose a particular challenge to the translator, comparable to translating scripture or poetry. Kant in English translation, say, is not 'the same' as Kant in German; no one-to-one equivalence is possible, and the failure to achieve exact correspondence in the translation of philosophical terms has often led to purist cries of untranslatability. Barbara Cassin's recent *Dictionary of Untranslatables* (Cassin 2014) is (for the most part) a dictionary of concepts, and what commentators usually mean when they call philosophy untranslatable is its rigorous conceptual language, for that is what marks the specificity of philosophy (and, with it, philosophy translation) in the first place. But technical terms will often have agreed equivalents in a target language (e.g. Kantian *Anschauung* = 'intuition'), even if such agreement is by no means always reached and can in any case mask a great deal of approximation. Philosophy is a broad domain which encompasses many other kinds of language: as Jonathan Rée puts it, 'the arts of philosophical writing overlap in many ways with the practices of storytelling' (Rée 2001: 227), and those texts which place a greater emphasis on exploiting the expressive potential of a particular natural language (e.g. through frequent use of metaphor and other rhetorical tropes) often pose translation difficulties which are at least as great. It may be essential to work out the precise meaning of, say, *sophrosune* [prudence, temperance] in the classical canon, but in poring over concepts it is easy to forget that, as Leonardo Bruni was pointing out as early as the fifteenth century,

> Aristotle himself and Plato were, I may say, the very greatest masters of Literature, and practiced a most elegant kind of writing filled with the sayings and maxims of the old poets and orators and historians, and frequently employed tropes and figures of speech that have acquired idiomatic meanings far different from their literal meanings.
> (Bruni 2002: 58)

As with poetry translation, though, the greater the difficulty, the more opportunity for adventurousness and experimentation. At the outset of vernacular traditions, as we have seen (Lucretius and Cicero, Chaucer, Wolff and Kant), translators placed in a position of maximal foreign exposure have responded with considerable creativity and ingenuity, by importing foreign vocabulary wholesale, perhaps, or creating conceptual neologisms and calques. Nor did this stop with the first wave of translations: in 1855 the nineteen-year-old John Meiklejohn writes in the 'Translator's Preface' to his new English translation of Kant's *First Critique*:

> it has been found requisite to coin one or two new philosophical terms, to represent those employed by Kant. It was, of course, almost impossible to translate the Kritik with the aid of the philosophical vocabulary at present used in England.
> (Meiklejohn 1855: xii)

Something similar occurs in the twentieth century with Spivak's Derrida (1976) – it is not just at the start of a vernacular tradition that a philosopher can choose to neologise rebarbatively and ask questions of the translator('s creativity).

Derrida coined the French term *déconstruction* as a calque on Heidegger's German terms *Abbau* and *Destruktion* (Derrida 1985: 86–7), and Heidegger's own writings are determinedly neologistic – not because he is at the start of a vernacular tradition of philosophising, but because he is deliberately turning his back on the tradition and starting again with (German) language's relation to a thinking of Be-ing. Generations of Heidegger translators have met the challenge of his language more or less successfully, but Heidegger translation reached a crisis with the publication of the first English translation of the *Beiträge* at the turn of the millennium. Parvis Emad and Kenneth Maly's highly controversial translation of *Beiträge zur Philosophie (Vom Ereignis)* as *Contributions to Philosophy: From Enowning* (Heidegger 1999) took Heideggerian neologising to a new extreme. They approached the text with a hyperbolic reverence, intent (in true Heideggerian fashion) on bringing out/forging etymological resonances, even (in fact, generally) at the expense of the sense of the target language standard. Earlier in the twentieth century, following Carnap, English-language analytic philosophy had pilloried Heidegger's 'nothing noths' as the epitome of empty metaphysics (even if that precise phrase was never published as a translation of 'Das Nichts selbst nichtet'), but this was something else again:

> Time-space is the enowned encleavage of the turning trajectories [*Kehrungsbahnen*] of enowning, of the turning between belongingness and the call, between abandonment by being and enbeckoning (the enquivering of the resonance of be-ing itself!).
> (Heidegger 1999: 260)

Simon Blackburn was not impressed by the mystical/mystificatory tone of this translation and published a damning review (Blackburn 2000), but even fellow Heideggerians thought Emad and Maly had gone too far. Richard Polt (himself a distinguished Heidegger translator) comments:

> the translators have resorted to neologisms too often. I prefer to use established English words while allowing their connotations to adapt to a new context. Heidegger himself usually adopts normal words (such as *Ereignis* and *Wesen*), so that even though these words gain new meanings in his experiments, they retain a connection to the old. Language opens fresh horizons by drawing creatively on its own heritage – not by breaking with it.
>
> (Polt 2013: 9)

The controversy eventually resulted in the publication – by the same publisher (Indiana University Press) – of a new, more conservative translation by Richard Rojcewicz and Daniela Vallega-Neu as the 'official' translation for the Heidegger *Gesamtausgabe* in English (Heidegger 2012). As in this case, retranslations have often been drier, more dutiful and tended to err on the side of literalness – although that is not to say that, as with the King James Version of the Bible, there are not also readers who prefer an earlier translation for literary or other reasons (e.g. Meiklejohn or Kemp Smith's translations of Kant's *First Critique* over the more recent versions by Pluhar or Guyer and Wood). Unusually, in the case of Heidegger's *Contributions*, the publisher does not consider the second translation to have superseded the first, and the two versions are both still in print, offering the aspirant reader a choice between two very different translation strategies (see Chapter 3, this volume).

Conclusion: future directions

Heidegger in English has become the 'poster boy' for creative style in philosophy translation. David Farrell Krell's 1975 translation of Heidegger's essay 'The Anaximander Fragment' – which includes sentences like 'The surmounting of disorder properly occurs through the letting-belong of reck' (Heidegger 1975: 47) – is cited approvingly by Venuti as his example *par excellence* of an experimental translation style which at the same time accords with Heidegger's own 'poetising' translation strategy (Venuti 1998: 119–22). Employing the concept of 'the remainder, the collective force of linguistic forms that outstrips any individual's control and complicates intended meanings' (Venuti 1998: 108), Venuti concludes with a call to arms for philosophy translators to be more creative:

> The translation of philosophical texts can be improved, and the issue of translation productively introduced in philosophical interpretation, if translators take a more experimental approach to their work. [...] However unpredictable the remainder may ultimately be, it nonetheless requires translators to respond creatively to the stylistic pressures exerted by the philosophical project of concept formation.
>
> (Venuti 1998: 122)

It would seem to me that not very many other philosophers lend themselves to being translated in the way Venuti recommends. The kind of experimental translation strategy practised by many of Heidegger's English translators is licensed by the source-text author's creativity with language in the first place, putting the translator in the same position as the translator of some of Heidegger's favourite poets (notably Friedrich Hölderlin), whose style he was ultimately imitating.[3] Experimental translation strategies have been most successful and appropriate with poetic material, or with highly opaque, self-reflexive prose like Joyce's *Finnegans Wake* (O'Neill 2013; see also Tawada 2013), so it is not surprising if they have had their most signal successes with philosophy at the more poetic end of the stylistic spectrum (another example is Peter Glassgold's Boethius 1994). Generally speaking, though, the kind of fireworks available from Krell or Emad and Maly are not available for other philosophers, and because of the nature of the subject matter, philosophical translators have tended to prioritise terminological precision and consistency above all else. In this respect it is surprising that translators (and their publishers) have not exploited more the hypertextual possibilities available online. Kevin C. Klement's innovative 'Side-by-Side-by-Side Edition' of Wittgenstein's *Tractatus* sets the original German alongside the two standard English versions, the Ogden (or Ogden/Ramsey) translation (1922) and the Pears/McGuinness translation (1961): the result is undoubtedly hugely helpful to the scholar, but the translations themselves are unchanged.

Be that as it may, Venuti's starting point is that translation is not often enough thematised within philosophical study, and that can be addressed – the translator can be made more visible – even without flamboyantly drawing attention to the translatedness of 'foreign philosophy' through furiously foreignising translations. For all too long commentators have been regretting translation loss, but one of the important aspects of the impact of translation studies on philosophy has been an increased willingness to acknowledge possibilities of translation gain and always to expect translation difference. The ultimate interest of a project like Barbara Cassin's *Dictionary of Untranslatables* (Cassin 2014) lies not so much in drawing attention once again to the straw man that is the supposed untranslatability of philosophical concepts but in fostering a greater recognition of the extraordinary intellectual achievement that is actually involved in the translation of philosophical texts.

Notes

1 Spanish novelist and philosopher Miguel de Unamuno, for one, thought it worth the effort (Collado 1962). Adorno – who wrote a dissertation on Kierkegaard (1989) – didn't.
2 Though not exactly an aim of philosophy translation, one of the unintended consequences down the years has been preserving the translated philosophy from not just neglect but oblivion. Lucretius' poem is used as a means of recovering lost texts by Epicurus (Clay 2000), and Cicero's translations of Aristotle are used as a source for reconstructing the Greek (White 2015: 212–30). A number of Aristotle's works have come down to us only because of their Arabic translations (Alwishah and Hayes 2015), and many otherwise lost Sanskrit texts have been preserved in translation in Tibetan and Chinese (Hung and Pollard 1998).
3 Emad and Maly's earlier translation of Heidegger's lectures on Hegel's *Phenomenology* (Heidegger 1988) is much more conventional, as befits a source-text style that is itself a good deal less free-wheeling than in Heidegger's unpublished notebooks. Likewise Frank O. Copley's translations of Cicero (1967) are much less exuberant and adventurous than his versions of Catullus from a decade earlier (1957).

Related topics

Nietzsche; Heidegger; Wittgenstein; Derrida; current trends in philosophy and translation; equivalence; translating feminist philosophers; Shelley's Plato; translating Kant and Hegel; translating Derrida; Levinas: his philosophy and its translation.

Further reading

Large, Duncan, 'On the Work of Philosopher-Translators', in Jean Boase-Beier, Antoinette Fawcett and Philip Wilson (eds), *Literary Translation: Redrawing the Boundaries* (Houndmills and New York: Palgrave Macmillan, 2014), 182–203. (A study of the way many major philosophers have, like poet-translators, developed their own distinctive style through translating the works of others.)

Rée, Jonathan, 'The Translation of Philosophy', *New Literary History*, 32/2 (2001), 223–57. (The best single article on this topic: a superb treatment of many of the issues raised by the translation of philosophy, with plenty of examples.)

Venuti, Lawrence, 'Philosophy', in *The Scandals of Translation: Towards an Ethics of Difference* (London and New York: Routledge, 1998), 106–23. (A leading translation theorist calls for a more experimental style of philosophy translation, with impressive analyses of translations of Wittgenstein and Heidegger.)

Young, Robert J. C., 'Philosophy in Translation', in Sandra Bermann and Catherine Porter (eds), *A Companion to Translation Studies* (Chichester: Wiley Blackwell, 2014), 41–53. (A lucid account of some of the key issues in the historical encounter between philosophy and translation, by one of the leading postcolonialist theorists.)

References

Adamson, Peter, *Al-Kindī* (Oxford and New York: Oxford University Press, 2007).

Adorno, Theodor W., *Kierkegaard: Construction of the Aesthetic*, ed. and trans. Robert Hullot-Kentor (Minneapolis: University of Minnesota Press, 1989).

Agorni, Mirella, 'A Marginal(ized) Perspective on Translation History: Women and Translation in the Eighteenth Century', *Meta*, 50/3 (2005), 817–30.

Akasoy, Anna and Guido Giglioni (eds), *Renaissance Averroism and Its Aftermath: Arabic Philosophy in Early Modern Europe* (Dordrecht: Springer, 2013).

Al-Khalili, Jim, *The House of Wisdom: How Arabic Science Saved Ancient Knowledge and Gave Us the Renaissance* (New York: Penguin, 2011).

Alwishah, Ahmed and Josh Hayes (eds), *Aristotle and the Arabic Tradition* (Cambridge: Cambridge University Press, 2015).

Anquetil, Jacques, *Anquetil-Duperron: premier orientaliste français* (Paris: Presses de la Renaissance, 2005).

Anquetil-Duperron, Abraham Hyacinthe (ed. and trans.), *Zend-Avesta, ouvrage de Zoroastre*, 3 vols in 2 (Paris: N. M. Tilliard, 1771).

Anquetil-Duperron, Abraham Hyacinthe (ed. and trans.), *Oupnek'hat (id est Secretum tegendum)*, 2 vols (Strasbourg: Argentorati, 1801–2).

Baraz, Yelena, 'The Gift of Philosophy: The Treatises as Translations', in *A Written Republic: Cicero's Philosophical Politics* (Princeton, NJ and Woodstock: Princeton University Press, 2012), 96–127.

Bianchi, Luca, Simon Gilson and Jill Kraye (eds), *Vernacular Aristotelianism in Italy from the Fourteenth to the Seventeenth Century* (London: Warburg Institute, 2016).

Blackall, Eric A., 'The Language of Philosophy', in *The Emergence of German as a Literary Language 1700–1775* (Cambridge: Cambridge University Press, 1959), 19–48.

Blackburn, Simon, 'Enquivering', *The New Republic*, 30 October 2000, 43–8.

Blocker, H. Gene and Christopher L. Starling, *Japanese Philosophy* (Albany: State University of New York Press, 2001).

Boethius, *The Poems from 'On the Consolation of Philosophy', Translated Out of the Original Latin into Diverse Historical Englishings Diligently Collaged by Peter Glassgold* (Los Angeles: Sun & Moon Press, 1994).

Bogic, Anna, 'Why Philosophy Went Missing: Understanding the English Version of Simone de Beauvoir's *Le deuxième sexe*', in Luise von Flotow (ed.), *Translating Women* (Ottawa: University of Ottawa Press, 2011), 151–66.

Brandt, Bettina and Daniel Leonhard Purdy (eds), *China in the German Enlightenment* (Toronto, Buffalo and London: University of Toronto Press, 2016).

Brobjer, Thomas H., *Nietzsche's Philosophical Context: An Intellectual Biography* (Urbana and Chicago: University of Illinois Press, 2008).

Brown, Hilary, *Luise Gottsched the Translator* (Rochester: Camden House, 2012).

Bruni, Leonardo, 'On the Correct Way to Translate', trans. James Hankins, in Douglas Robinson (ed.), *Western Translation Theory from Herodotus to Nietzsche*, 2nd edn (Manchester and Northampton: St. Jerome, 2002), 57–60.

Cartwright, David E., *Schopenhauer: A Biography* (Cambridge: Cambridge University Press, 2010).

Catullus, Gaius Valerius, *The Complete Poetry*, trans. Frank O. Copley (Ann Arbor: University of Michigan Press, 1957).

Cassin, Barbara (ed.), *Dictionary of Untranslatables: A Philosophical Lexicon*, trans. S. Rendall, C. Hubert, J. Mehlman, N. Stein and M. Syrotinski, ed. E. Apter, J. Lezra and M. Wood (Princeton and Oxford: Princeton University Press, 2014).

Cicero, Marcus Tullius, *On Old Age; and On Friendship*, trans. Frank O. Copley (Ann Arbor: University of Michigan Press, 1967).

Clay, Diskin, *Lucretius and Epicurus* (Ithaca and London: Cornell University Press, 1983).

Clay, Diskin, 'Recovering Originals: *Peri Physeos* and *De Rerum Natura*', *Apeiron*, 33/3 (2000), 259–71.

Collado, Jesús-Antonio, *Kierkegaard y Unamuno: la existencia religiosa* (Madrid: Gredos, 1962).

Copenhaver, Brian P., 'Translation, Terminology and Style in Philosophical Discourse', in Charles B. Schmitt and Quentin Skinner (eds), *The Cambridge History of Renaissance Philosophy* (Cambridge and New York: Cambridge University Press, 1988), 77–110.

Couplet, Philippe (ed.), *Confucius Sinarum Philosophus, sive, Scientia Sinensis Latine Exposita* (Paris: Daniel Horthemels, 1687).

Dale, Eric Michael, 'Hegel and Kojève', in *Hegel, the End of History, and the Future* (Cambridge and New York: Cambridge University Press, 2014), 80–110.

Davis, John R. and Angus Nicholls (eds), *Friedrich Max Müller and the Role of Philology in Victorian Thought* (London and New York: Routledge, 2017).

Davis, Walter W., 'China, the Confucian Ideal, and the European Age of Enlightenment', *Journal of the History of Ideas*, 44/4 (1983), 523–48.

Delisle, Jean and Judith Woodsworth (eds), *Translators Through History*, 2nd edn (Amsterdam and Philadelphia: John Benjamins, 2012).

Demetriou, Tania and Rowan Tomlinson (eds), *The Culture of Translation in Early Modern England and France, 1500–1660* (Houndmills and New York: Palgrave Macmillan, 2015).

De Pol, Roberto (ed.), *The First Translations of Machiavelli's 'Prince': From the Sixteenth to the First Half of the Nineteenth Century* (Amsterdam and New York: Rodopi, 2010).

Derrida, Jacques, *Of Grammatology*, trans. Gayatri Chakravorty Spivak (Baltimore and London: Johns Hopkins University Press, 1976).

Derrida, Jacques, *The Ear of the Other: Otobiography, Transference, Translation*, ed. Christie V. McDonald, trans. Peggy Kamuf (New York: Schocken Books, 1985).

Deussen, Paul (ed. and trans.), *Die Sūtra's des Vedānta, oder die Çārīraka-Mīmāṅsā des Bādarāyaṇa nebst dem vollständigen Kommentare des Çaṅkara* (Leipzig: Brockhaus, 1887).

Discenza, Nicole Guenther, *The King's English: Strategies of Translation in the Old English 'Boethius'* (Albany: State University of New York Press, 2005).

Dolet, Etienne, 'Extracts from *De la manière de bien traduire d'une langue en autre* ("On the Way of Translating Well from One Language into Another")', in André Lefevere (ed.), *Translation/History/Culture: A Sourcebook* (London and New York: Routledge, 1992), 27–8.

Elst, Koenraad, 'Manu as a Weapon against Egalitarianism: Nietzsche and Hindu Political Philosophy', in Herman W. Siemens and Vasti Roodt (eds), *Nietzsche, Power and Politics: Rethinking Nietzsche's Legacy for Political Thought* (Berlin and New York: De Gruyter, 2008), 543–82.

Franklin, Michael J., *Orientalist Jones: Sir William Jones, Poet, Lawyer, and Linguist, 1746–1794* (Oxford and New York: Oxford University Press, 2011).
Frege, Gottlob, *The Foundations of Arithmetic: A Logico-Mathematical Enquiry into the Concept of Number*, trans. J. L. Austin (Oxford: Basil Blackwell, 1950).
Girardot, Norman J., *The Victorian Translation of China: James Legge's Oriental Pilgrimage* (Berkeley, Los Angeles and London: University of California Press, 2002).
Gutas, Dimitri, *Greek Thought, Arabic Culture: The Graeco-Arabic Translation Movement in Baghdad and Early 'Abbāsid Society (2nd–4th/8th–10th Centuries)* (London and New York: Routledge, 1998).
Hannay, Alastair, 'Translating Kierkegaard', in John Lippitt and George Pattison (eds), *The Oxford Handbook of Kierkegaard* (Oxford: Oxford University Press, 2013), 385–401.
Harvey, David Allen, 'The Wisdom of the East: Enlightenment Perspectives on China', in *The French Enlightenment and Its Others: The Mandarin, the Savage, and the Invention of the Human Sciences* (Basingstoke: Palgrave Macmillan, 2012), 41–68.
Hegel, G. W. F., *The Phenomenology of Mind*, trans. J. B. Baillie (London and New York: Macmillan, 1910).
Hegel, G. W. F., *The Phenomenology of Spirit*, trans. A. V. Miller (Oxford: Clarendon Press, 1977).
Heidegger, Martin, *An Introduction to Metaphysics*, trans. Ralph Manheim (New Haven: Yale University Press; London: Oxford University Press, 1959).
Heidegger, Martin, 'The Anaximander Fragment', trans. David Farrell Krell, in *Early Greek Thinking*, trans. David Farrell Krell and Frank A. Capuzzi (New York: Harper & Row, 1975), 13–58.
Heidegger, Martin, *Hegel's Phenomenology of Spirit*, trans. Parvis Emad and Kenneth Maly (Bloomington and Indianapolis: Indiana University Press, 1988).
Heidegger, Martin, *Parmenides*, trans. André Schuwer and Richard Rojcewicz (Bloomington and Indianapolis: Indiana University Press, 1992).
Heidegger, Martin, *Contributions to Philosophy (From Enowning)*, trans. Parvis Emad and Kenneth Maly (Bloomington and Indianapolis: Indiana University Press, 1999).
Heidegger, Martin, *Contributions to Philosophy (of the Event)*, trans. Richard Rojcewicz and Daniela Vallega-Neu (Bloomington and Indianapolis: Indiana University Press, 2012).
Herling, Bradley L., *The German Gita: Hermeneutics and Discipline in the German Reception of Indian Thought, 1778–1831* (New York and London: Routledge, 2006).
Hermans, Theo (ed.), *The Manipulation of Literature: Studies in Literary Translation* (London: Croom Helm; New York: St. Martin's Press, 1985).
Hoenen, Maarten J. F. M. and Lodi Nauta (eds), *Boethius in the Middle Ages: Latin and Vernacular Traditions of the 'Consolatio Philosophiae'* (Leiden: Brill, 1997).
Hung, Eva and David Pollard, 'Chinese Tradition', in Mona Baker (ed.), *Routledge Encyclopedia of Translation Studies* (London and New York: Routledge, 1998), 365–76.
Jacolliot, Louis (ed. and trans.), *Les législateurs religieux: Manou, Moïse, Mahomet* (Paris: Lacroix, 1876).
Jacquette, Dale, 'Preface', in Gottlob Frege, *Foundations of Arithmetic*, trans. Dale Jacquette, 2nd edn (London and New York: Routledge, 2016), v–vi.
Jones, Howard, *Master Tully: Cicero in Tudor England* (Nieuwkoop: De Graaf, 1998).
Karyekar, Madhuvanti Chintamani, 'Hegel and the Latin *Bhagavadgītā* (1823): A Critique of Understanding and Translating the Foreign', in Federico M. Federici and Dario Tessicini (eds), *Translators, Interpreters, and Cultural Negotiators: Mediating and Communicating Power from the Middle Ages to the Modern Era* (Houndmills and New York: Palgrave Macmillan, 2014), 155–72.
Large, Duncan, 'On the Work of Philosopher-Translators', in Jean Boase-Beier, Antoinette Fawcett and Philip Wilson (eds), *Literary Translation: Redrawing the Boundaries* (Houndmills and New York: Palgrave Macmillan, 2014), 182–203.
Large, Duncan, 'The Untranslatable in Philosophy', in Duncan Large, Motoko Akashi, Wanda Józwikowska and Emily Rose (eds), *Untranslatability: Interdisciplinary Perspectives* (New York and London: Routledge, 2018), 50–63.

Legge, James (ed. and trans.), *The Chinese Classics: with a Translation, Critical and Exegetical Notes, Prolegomena, and Copious Indexes*, 5 vols (Hong Kong: Legge; London: Trübner, 1861–72).

Legge, James (ed. and trans.), *The Sacred Books of China*, 6 vols (Oxford: Clarendon Press, 1879–91).

Lucretius, *The Nature of Things*, trans. A. E. Stallings (London: Penguin, 2007).

Lyons, Jonathan, *The House of Wisdom: How the Arabs Transformed Western Civilization* (New York and London: Bloomsbury, 2009).

Mander, W. J., *British Idealism: A History* (Oxford and New York: Oxford University Press, 2011).

Mayuko, Uehara (ed.), *Philosopher la traduction/Philosophizing Translation* (Nagoya: Chisokudō, 2017).

Meiklejohn, J. M. D., 'Translator's Preface', in Immanuel Kant, *Critique of Pure Reason*, trans. J. M. D. Meiklejohn (London: Henry G. Bohn, 1855), xi–xv.

Molendijk, Arie L., *Friedrich Max Müller and the 'Sacred Books of the East'* (Oxford and New York: Oxford University Press, 2016).

Müller, F. Max (ed.), *Rig-Veda-Sanhita: The Sacred Hymns of the Brahmans, Together with the Commentary of Sayanacharya*, 6 vols (London: W. H. Allen, 1849–74).

Müller, F. Max (ed.), *The Sacred Books of the East*, 50 vols (Oxford: Clarendon Press, 1879–1910).

Müller, F. Max (ed. and trans.), *The Upanishads*, 2 vols (Oxford: Clarendon Press, 1879–84).

Mungello, D. E., 'European Acceptance of Chinese Culture and Confucianism', in *The Great Encounter of China and the West, 1500–1800*, 4th edn (Lanham: Rowman & Littlefield, 2013), 91–122.

Nietzsche, Friedrich, 'On the Problem of Translation', trans. Peter Mollenhauer, in Rainer Schulter and John Biguenet (eds), *Theories of Translation: An Anthology of Essays from Dryden to Derrida* (Chicago and London: University of Chicago Press, 1992), 68–70.

Nietzsche, Friedrich, *The Birth of Tragedy Out of the Spirit of Music*, trans. Shaun Whiteside, ed. Michael Tanner (Harmondsworth: Penguin, 1993).

O'Neill, Patrick, *Impossible Joyce: Finnegans Wakes*, 3rd edn (Toronto, Buffalo and London: University of Toronto Press, 2013).

Parkes, Graham (ed.), *Nietzsche and Asian Thought* (Chicago and London: University of Chicago Press, 1991).

Perkins, Franklin, *Leibniz and China: A Commerce of Light* (Cambridge: Cambridge University Press, 2004).

Petrina, Alessandra, *Machiavelli in the British Isles: Two Early Modern Translations of 'The Prince'* (Farnham: Ashgate, 2009).

Plato, *The Dialogues of Plato*, ed. and trans. Benjamin Jowett, 5 vols (Oxford: Clarendon Press, 1875).

Polt, Richard, *The Emergency of Being: On Heidegger's 'Contributions to Philosophy'* (Ithaca and London: Cornell University Press, 2013).

Rathore, Aakash Singh and Rimina Mohapatra, *Hegel's India: A Reinterpretation, with Texts* (New Delhi: Oxford University Press, 2017).

Rée, Jonathan, 'The Translation of Philosophy', *New Literary History*, 32/2 (2001), 223–57.

Rose, Jenny, 'Thus Spoke Nietzsche', in *The Image of Zoroaster: The Persian Mage through European Eyes* (New York: Bibliotheca Persica Press, 2000), 173–94.

Schlegel, August Wilhelm (ed.), *Bhagavad-Gita* (Bonn: Weber, 1823).

Schlegel, Friedrich, *Ueber die Sprache und Weisheit der Indier: Ein Beitrag zur Begründung der Alterthumskunde; Nebst metrischen Übersetzungen Indischer Gedichte* (Heidelberg: Mohr und Zimmer, 1808).

Sedley, David, *Lucretius and the Transformation of Greek Wisdom* (Cambridge: Cambridge University Press, 1998).

Seele, Astrid, *Römische Übersetzer: Nöte, Freiheiten, Absichten. Verfahren des literarischen Übersetzens in der griechisch-römischen Antike* (Darmstadt: Wissenschaftliche Buchgesellschaft, 1995).

Stanton, Robert, *The Culture of Translation in Anglo-Saxon England* (Cambridge: D. S. Brewer, 2002).

Strindberg, August, *Tschandala*, trans. Peter Nansen (Copenhagen: I. H. Schubothe, 1889).

Tawada, Yoko, *Portrait of a Tongue: An Experimental Translation*, trans. Chantal Wright (Ottawa: University of Ottawa Press, 2013).

Venuti, Lawrence, *The Translator's Invisibility: A History of Translation* (London and New York: Routledge, 1995).
Venuti, Lawrence, 'Philosophy ', in *The Scandals of Translation: Towards an Ethics of Difference* (London and New York: Routledge, 1998), 106–23.
Vives, Juan Luis, 'Practice in Writing', trans. Foster Watson, in Douglas Robinson (ed.), *Western Translation Theory from Herodotus to Nietzsche*, 2nd edn (Manchester and Northampton, MA: St. Jerome, 2002), 92.
White, Georgina Frances, unpublished PhD diss., 'Copia verborum: Cicero's Philosophical Translations' (Princeton University, 2015).
Wittgenstein, Ludwig, *Philosophical Investigations*, trans. G. E. M. Anscombe (Oxford: Basil Blackwell, 1953).
Worth, Valerie, *Practising Translation in Renaissance France: The Example of Étienne Dolet* (Oxford: Clarendon Press, 1988).
Wright, Chantal, *Literary Translation* (London and New York: Routledge, 2016).

Webography

Adamson, Peter, 'Arabic Translators Did Far More Than Just Preserve Greek Philosophy', 4 November 2016. https://aeon.co/ideas/arabic-translators-did-far-more-than-just-preserve-greek-philosophy
D'Ancona, Cristina, 'Greek Sources in Arabic and Islamic Philosophy', *Stanford Encyclopedia of Philosophy*, 2017. https://plato.stanford.edu/entries/arabic-islamic-greek/
Benkert, Lysbeth, 'Translation as Image-Making: Elizabeth I's Translation of Boethius's *Consolation of Philosophy*', *Early Modern Literary Studies*, 6/3 (January 2001), 2.1–20. https://extra.shu.ac.uk/emls/06-3/benkboet.htm
Davis, Bret W., 'The Kyoto School', *Stanford Encyclopedia of Philosophy*, 2014. https://plato.stanford.edu/entries/kyoto-school/
Early Modern Texts. www.earlymoderntexts.com/
Historic Analytic. www.hist-analytic.org/
Loeb Classical Library. www.loebclassics.com/
Marxists Internet Archive. www.marxists.org/
Perseus Digital Library. www.perseus.tufts.edu/
Project Gutenberg. www.gutenberg.org/
Wittgenstein, Ludwig, *Tractatus Logico-Philosophicus*, ed. Kevin C. Klement. https://people.umass.edu/klement/tlp/

20
Translating feminist philosophers

Carolyn Shread

Introduction: blowing up the master house

Translation both illuminates and obscures. Contemporary French philosopher Catherine Malabou's articulation of *plasticité* (2009) is exemplary of this process, for in English it sheds a key facet. Plasticity expresses the ability to mould or take form; however, the French term also resonates with *plasticage* – that is, explosion. After all, form is also produced by destruction. Like the explosive potential hidden in plasticity, this chapter not only attests to a re-forming of philosophy by feminists in their work and translations but also sits like a bomb in a book all of whose named philosophers are men.

To dispense, from the start, with a misleading elision of woman and feminist, we should note that not all feminists are women. Rather, feminism is an intellectual perspective, often combined with an active commitment to changing women's oppression, open to everyone. However, in this *Handbook*, quite typically, only one of the fourteen men is a feminist and the rest can be said to be in the service of, and subject to, patriarchy. To restate the point, and expand it to allow for gender fluidity that goes beyond a man/woman binary, feminist philosophers are thinkers anywhere on the gender spectrum whose philosophy is largely informed by the knowledge and experiences of women. Qualifying philosophy as feminist acknowledges the male bias prevalent in philosophy. Feminist philosophers respond to the lived experience of patriarchy through a myriad of emancipatory moves that range from the act of speaking as a woman in a male-dominated context to proposing alternative philosophical schemas. We shall move swiftly here from a singular feminism to the plural form to recognize that these diverse expressions work against the multiple instantiations of the global institutions of patriarchy. These feminisms are as varied as the historical and geographical manifestations of male hegemony and are defined and governed by their own, specific, local priorities and analyses rather than any universal formula.

As a point of access to this tremendous diversity, this chapter posits that there is a special relation between its three terms – translating – feminist – philosophers – such that together they offer solutions to Audre Lorde's astute diagnosis that 'The Master's Tools Will Never Dismantle the Master's House' (Lorde 1984: 110). Indeed, no. Feminists use DIY and, when necessary, the explosive plasticity that lies within all the languages of our translations to unsettle foundations that have left too many, for too long, homeless.

Translating feminist philosophers

In the *Companion to Translation Studies* entry 'Philosophy in Translation' Robert Young points out that 'It comes as something of a shock to realize that Descartes never actually wrote the words "cogito ergo sum"... [it] was the invention of Descartes' translator. Descartes himself, writing in French, offered the more humble "je pense, donc je suis"'[I think therefore I am] (Berman and Porter 2014: 41). It is equally shocking to think through the implications of Bracha Ettinger's insight that contrary to the long-standing and widespread adoption of Descartes's cogito, 'the moment of birth doesn't have to represent a mental barrier' (Ettinger 1994: 50). Instead of finding the indubitable foundation of that paradigmatically discrete Western rational subject standing tall and all alone, we would then start with the subjectivity-as-encounter that Ettinger describes in her matrixial model. In Ettinger's feminist philosophy 'Several comes before the One' (Ettinger 1992: 200) and our house has many thresholds. The consequences of this rethinking suggest that our origin lies more in an originary state of translation than in the autonomy and heroic originality that novelist and critic Nancy Huston describes as definitive of the *Professeurs de désespoir* [professors of despair] (2004). Ettinger's proposal is just one instance exemplifying any number of interventions that challenge an unquestioned male, Western bias by offering an alternative philosophical approach. To cite another example, contrary to debates and assumptions about equivalence in translation studies, Sonia Alvarez and Claudia de Lima Costa draw on Amerindian perspectivism to define translation as an equivocation that 'does not seek to find correspondences between different worldviews' precisely because 'while there may be a single representation [...] the referent can be multiple' (Castro and Ergun 2017: 121–2). These then are just two of the multifarious ways in which a dominant Western, male conception is contextualized and decentred by including a wider range of thinkers.

The first task to attend to therefore is the surplus that this chapter presents vis-à-vis a *Handbook* that addresses the two disciplines of philosophy and translation studies by adding the third element: feminism. What does a feminist do to the two terms, and why is feminism otherwise excluded by default? Robin May Schott has a useful answer for our DIY project: she claims that 'feminism helps philosophy do its job better' (Schott 2007: 44). That sounds helpful, and certainly a good starting point for a new house, since the old one is collapsing and insufficient. New materials, such as Kimberlé Crenshaw's intersectional methodology that insists that a black woman needs to be seen at the intersection of the categories of both race and gender, to name just one influential contribution, make for structures that are better because they account for complexity (Crenshaw 1989). While Crenshaw's intervention, that builds on the brief but incisive foundation of the 1977 Combahee River Collective statement, dates from nearly forty years ago, the sophisticated analysis of the functioning of interlocking oppressions by Black feminist thought is still as relevant as ever, as shown by the recent republication of the statement in Keeanga-Yamahtta Taylor's edited presentation and interviews, *How We Get Free: Black Feminism and the Combahee River Collective* (2017).

In developing these tools, we therefore need to be wary of the 'add and stir' danger discussed by Karen Warren in *An Unconventional History of Western Philosophy* (2009). Presenting '2,600 Years of the History of Western Philosophy *Without Women*' – one of several anthologies of feminist philosophy in English published around the millennium – Warren insists 'one cannot just "add women and stir" them into an otherwise unchanged conception and curriculum of philosophy' (Warren 2009: 8). Echoing our opening image of the plastic explosive, Warren posits that 'attempts to add women and stir produce something more like an explosion than an integrated mixture' (9). We undertake the dangerous enterprise of restructuring the very foundations of philosophy and then build with different materials, aesthetics and ethics – to name only some of the premises. Such a project is characterized as 'radical' by the authors of *The Cambridge Companion to Feminism in Philosophy* (2000), but so be it. Unlike Miranda Fricker and Jennifer Hornsby, whose attempt to integrate feminism in the less hospitable tradition of analytical rather than continental philosophy I support, but whose reasonableness seems unnecessarily modest, I propose a *radical* chapter on 'Translating Feminist Philosophers' because the implications of this concatenation are, I believe, truly radical.

The heuristic fiction grounding this chapter is as follows: *feminist philosophers think in every language and culture*. Thus, elaborating on Schott's point that philosophy is improved by feminism, this *Handbook* indicates that translation studies too can help philosophy do its job better by allowing it to learn from and engage with places beyond its borders. Our dilemma is that our topic is too vast to afford an overview, let alone any attempt at a comprehensive approach. Instead, our gesture will be to present an inclusive, illustrative selection of feminist philosophers as they disseminate their own conceptions of philosophy via translation.

Acknowledging that the tug towards feminist philosophy might detract from the actual translations and those who do the translating – still viewed in a generally utilitarian manner – we will appeal to translation to narrow the vast topic of feminist philosophers. Our focus is the field of *translation* – be it the translators themselves, the translations they produce, or the way their work is read. In so doing we remain true to one of the main commitments of translation studies: rendering the translator a visible agent, and the product a material artefact whose specific objectives, particular conditions of creation and varying impact upon reception are all worthy of examination. In the next section a historical glimpse of 'translating feminist philosophers' recalls our axiom *feminist philosophers think in all places* and adds: *they have done so at all times*.

Some historical perspectives on the 'oxymoron problem'

The eight volume *Encyclopedia of Philosophy* (Edwards 1967) needed a supplement (Borchert 1996). Why? Because, as Linda Lopez McAlister explained, it 'didn't contain a single article about a woman' (McAlister 1996: viii). For some thirty years after its publication, this authoritative source stood as a gatekeeper in English, silencing the contributions of women philosophers over the centuries in every area. Eventually, with the publication of the *Supplement* in 1996, these omissions began to be corrected. But the lacunae had already been noted, and in 1981 Mary Ellen Waithe began directing the collaborative task of what became the four volume *History of Women Philosophers* (Waithe 1987) – inspired by her encounter with Beatrice Zedler's translation of Gilles Ménage's 1690 *Historia mulierum philosopharum*, or *History of Women Philosophers* (1984). Once again in English it became increasingly apparent that feminist philosophy had a history – I say once again and specify English since this amnesia is cyclical and linguistically bound: there are earlier periods and places where the history of feminist philosophers was more evident. Moments of erasure are not absolute; rather, they are culturally and historically determined. Waithe's project is relevant to our interests in that she frequently acknowledged the importance of translation as integral to a more inclusive history. Likewise, the Society for the Study of Women Philosophers has, from the start, emphasized translation as an essential part of the restoration stage that works alongside recovery efforts. This scholarly and pedagogically inspired research has produced both online resources and other publications such as the recent DVD and book *Busted! A Pictorial History of Women Philosophers from Antiquity to the Twenty-first Century*. All these projects valorizing translation are in line with the point Penelope Deutscher makes in her introduction to the *Hypatia* special issue on *Contemporary French Women Philosophers:* 'Translation practices are one of the most significant means of establishing women philosophers as recognized and important thinkers. Not to translate is to designate the interest of the writer in question local and temporary' (Deutscher 2000: 4). Given that the Western philosophical tradition has always relied on translations to access its founding texts, it is clear that a dependence on translation is central to the discipline and, moreover, to whatever canon is construed. If we are to develop a global conception of feminist philosophy and its histories, this will require a study of the dense and complex network of translation, re-translation, delayed translation and non-translation between any number of language combinations.

That philosophy has been entangled with translation from the start is evident even within the limited scope of the three European modern languages used primarily by the elected philosophers of this handbook: German, English and French. As stated earlier, this selection of philosophers re-inscribes a history of philosophy without women. Although my remit is to discuss *translating* feminist philosophers, I cannot begin to analyse translations of their work that do or do not exist without acknowledging the way in which any circulation of feminist philosophy is interrupted by what Eileen O'Neill dubbed the 'oxymoron problem' – that is, one cannot be both a woman and philosopher.

In Kourany's (1998) *Philosophy in a Feminist Voice*, O'Neill's important chapter 'Disappearing Ink: Early Modern Women Philosophers and Their Fate in History' parses the perceived contradiction between philosopher and woman before offering the counter-evidence of an impressive catalogue of feminist philosophers. O'Neill's avowed goal is to 'overwhelm you with the presence of women in early modern philosophy' (1998: 32) and that she does. To repeat just some of her incantation: Laura Bassi defended theses at the University of Bologna in 1732 to become the first woman to hold a lectureship at a European University; Sor Juana Inés de la Cruz contributed to theological debates in Mexico as a woman in the seventeenth century; Madeleine de Scudéry's work was 'reprinted and translated until the end of the eighteenth century' (1998: 22); Margaret Cavendish Duchess of Newcastle, Viscountess Anne Conway, Mary Astell, Lady Marsham, Catherine Trotter Cockburn, Judith Drake, Catherine Macaulay and Mary Wollstonecraft all wrote important philosophical texts in English; while Gabrielle Suchon, Anne Dacier, Madame de Lambert and Olympe de Gouges philosophized primarily in French. Many of these thinkers were also translators – for instance, Sophie de Grouchy, Marquise de Condorcet, who not only brought Adam Smith into French but also developed his *Theory of Moral Sentiments* by appending eight letters refining his conception of the origin of sympathy (Brown 2000). If the names listed are not immediately familiar to modern-day philosophers, O'Neill argues, it is not because they were unknown in their time. Rather, she identifies several factors that produced an erasure: 'the alignment of the feminine gender with the issues, methods, and styles that "lost out", together with a good deal of slippage between gender and sex, and the scholarly practice of anonymous authorship for women' (36). Disciplinary, social, political and material factors were thus responsible for the production of 'woman philosopher' as oxymoron.

O'Neill's analysis is complemented by several aspects that emerge from the slight, classroom-ready selection of seven *Women Philosophers of the Early Modern Period* (1994) prepared by Margaret Atherton in a deliberate attempt to reintroduce women philosophers to the academic curriculum through their engagements with the now better-known philosophers of their time. This research prompts us to think through the implications of unequal education practices and the exclusion of women from scholarly institutions in the period that followed the wider possibilities for women offered by earlier monastic culture, for, as Atherton explains, 'only rarely was a woman able to acquire the training necessary to enter into philosophical discussion, whose full participation required a knowledge of Latin and French or English' (1994: 2). Women philosophers therefore depended, even more than their male colleagues, on translation as a mode of access to knowledge. Moreover, if we observe the flowering of feminist philosophers during early modern Europe, it may in part be ascribed to the new norm of publishing in the vernacular. For while some privileged individuals such as Princess Elisabeth of Bohemia were able to learn Latin and Greek, or even, like Anne Dacier, publish translations along with her commentary on Marcus Aurelius, many others, such as Lady Cavendish, relied on translations to read Descartes since she knew neither Latin nor French. Translation is often closely allied to a redistribution of access – and consequently all the more policed. On the other hand therefore, at this point, it was actually the gradual absence of dependence on translation due to the increased use of the vernacular that opened up closed books to new readers. There are many other fascinating stories of language barriers and transfers in this context, but I'll close with an interesting case discussed by Atherton in which women's work is transmitted via translation:

> Anne Conway's treatise, *The Principles of the Most Ancient and Modern Philosophy* [...] is said to have been prepared for publication and translated into Latin [...] This Latin treatise was subsequently retranslated into English, and published in England in 1692. Anne Conway's original English version being lost, this retranslation was published by Peter Loptson in 1982.
>
> (1994: 47)

A significant and specific domain in publishing, translation has always been a critical gateway for the archiving and dissemination of work by feminist philosophers.

Other material practices that have impacted women philosophers include norms such as the use of anonymity or pseudonyms. O'Neill mentions G. S. Aristophile, the pseudonym that consigned Gabrielle Suchon to oblivion (26). This example is symptomatic of the larger impact of 'enforced discontinuity' diagnosed by Gerda Lerner in her chapter 'Why So Few Women Philosophers?' (Lerner 2000: 9). Lerner's point, informed by her research as author of *The Creation of Patriarchy* (1986), is that a lack of sustained narrative related to women philosophers is detrimental to the creation and transmission of larger systems. Destroying the links that ensure continuity, the non-recognition, including non-translation, of feminist philosophers interrupts both the establishment of traditions of intellectual thought and the contestation derived from alternative philosophies that can only be brought into contact with one another through translations.

Returning from the history of European philosophy to the point from which I write, I should explain that this chapter is framed by my work as one of French contemporary philosopher Catherine Malabou's many translators. While I refute the teleological conceit that views the present place or moment as a culmination, I acknowledge that having translated five of her books is a touchstone experience that situates my comments. Consequently, as a rebuttal to the oxymoron with which we began to articulate the erasure of feminist work in many historical accounts of European philosophy, I'll close this section with reference to an essay in Malabou's *Changing Difference: The Feminine and the Question of Philosophy* (2011) entitled 'Woman's possibility, philosophy's impossibility.' In this account of her career as a philosopher, Malabou exposes the violence she, like so many other women, suffers, and is determined to ask, 'Ain't I a philosopher?' (140).

Critical issues and topics: 'I do more translating / Than the Gawdamn UN'

The critique and dissatisfaction with dominant philosophical histories, narratives and doxas described in the European context above is echoed by contemporary thinkers working in other places, some of whom go further, naming the effect of their exclusion 'epistemicide'. This is the phenomenon Brazilian Black feminist philosopher Djamila Ribeiro discussed in an interview for the online blog Afropunk, saying 'we still have a long way to go to combat what black feminists call "epistemicide", the murder of our epistemes, as if black women don't produce knowledge' (Boateng 2016). We note that Ribeiro's accusation is amplified because the original Portuguese is also available in English. Translation offers a means of survival and expression of solidarity for feminist philosophy. It is part of the process that follows Boaventura de Sousa Santos's conviction that 'there is no global justice without global cognitive justice' (Santos 2006: 14). It is to this type of translational support for the emergence of feminist voices in philosophy that I now turn.

Before discussing translations of feminist philosophy, however, we must ask the preliminary question: who is translating? We have established that feminist philosophy might be written by a man, although it is more often the work of women, but what about the translators? Lori Chamberlain's foundational article for feminist translation, 'Gender and the Metaphorics of Translation' (1988) deconstructed the established feminization of the translator, along with the many negative or subservient assumptions the associated metaphors communicated. Concurrent with this critique of a devalorization of translation that parallels that of women, strategies of feminist translation were developed in response. What has subsequently been identified as the Canadian school of feminist translation emerged, including Godard (1989), de Lotbinière-Harwood (1991), Simon (1996) and von Flotow (1997b), many of whom were involved in disseminating feminist work in translation, although not all feminist translation concerned feminist texts. Feminist translation produced not only a range of strategies, many of them interventionist, claiming agency for the translator, but also a body of critique. To cite one example, von Flotow, one of the strongest champions of these approaches, wrote about their limitations in 'Mutual Pun-ishment? Translating Radical Feminist Wordplay: Mary Daly's "Gyn/Ecology" in German' (1997a) in response to Erika Wisselinck's 1980 translation. Beyond the Canadian context, which von Flotow (2006) subsequently defined as a specific moment, feminist translation continues to prompt creative and assertive approaches by translators. In my own work as a feminist translator, this involves not only how I translate but also, perhaps even more importantly, what I choose to translate. A symbol of how this commitment manifests is that when I wrote 'Ain't I a philosopher?' I brought Malabou's 'Philosophe, ne le suis-je donc pas du tout moi-même?' [literally, Am I, myself, not a philosopher at all?] into more than the English language: I brought it into proximity with one of the hallmark voices of feminist thought in the US context by echoing Sojourner Truth's famous (1851) speech 'Ain't I a Woman?' – a speech, it should be noted, that bore the traces not of the Southern dialect of its transcription but, rather, an accent derived from the Dutch she spoke exclusively until age nine.

Another option open to feminist philosophers is self-translation. This technique is probably more widespread than imagined. Sigrid Weigel argues that in the case of Hannah Arendt, the impact of German and English versions in the reception of her work is underestimated. She explains: 'The specific bilingual character of Arendt's work is still a largely obscure phenomenon that has not yet attracted adequate attention. It means that any dialogue or symposium on Arendt in which German and English readers and scholars participate refer to two quite different works by the same author – mostly without the participants being aware of it. In general the 'German Arendt' is regarded as an intellectual whose philosophical thoughts are shaped through metaphors and poetic language whereas the 'American Arendt' is a more political thinker' (Weigel 2012: 73). Aside from the textual complexity or equivocation due to the coexistence of translational versions, feminist philosophers writing in postcolonial contexts might find the experience of translating oneself very familiar. While this area has been analysed to some extent, the specific impact for our topic invites further research.

Recognizing that translators rarely work in a void, but more often within a framework defined by financial considerations, it would be naive not to acknowledge the impact funding has on determining who translates and which work circulates. For instance, describing the manufacture of 'French feminism' by North American academia, Claire Goldberg Moses explains: 'Their well-financed publishing ventures may explain why *Psych et po* became the best known of the MLF groups among feminists abroad' (Goldberg Moses 2003: 267). Similarly, Dongchao Min argues that 'transnational links around development funding played a fundamental role in pushing Chinese women's studies into particular ways of connecting with the international track in the 1990s' (Min 2014: 586). Thus, for instance, in this moment in the Chinese context, the Ford Foundation's funding dictated, to a large degree, who and what to translate. To answer the questions 'who is translating feminist philosophers?', 'which feminist philosophers are translated?' and 'who is supporting the translation of feminist philosophers?' systematically would require a vast body of research, one beyond the confines of this chapter. For present purposes, we will move on to an analysis of some of the results of translators' work.

I propose that in response to the erasure that feminist philosophers frequently suffer, translation opens three pathways for establishing their work: as a method of canonization and institutionalization via the recognition and promotion that is translation; as a means of forging alliances with receptive audiences beyond an initial context, sometimes through a pairing with established authorities, sometimes as an innovative force; and as a travelling escape either from an environment that would quash the voice of the feminist philosopher or as a reformulation, including reuse, in new contexts. Of course, many other aspects could be discussed, but these three strategies are widespread. We will explore their ramifications along three, somewhat winding, pathways.

While O'Neill's focus was on the forgetting of a history of feminist philosophers, another type of erasure concerns the foundational role translations themselves have played for these bodies of thought. I should preface the next example with the caveat that here the concept of 'philosophy' itself is pressured by the activist agenda that informs feminism, but I will not legislate on the line between the feminist movement and the discipline (even reimagined) of philosophy. Emek Ergun's analysis 'Translational Beginnings and Origin/izing Stories: (Re)Writing the History of the Contemporary Feminist Movement in Turkey' offers a cautionary tale for the tendency in canon creation to repress translations in favour of 'native' texts. Ergun re-examines the history of feminist thought in Turkey to reveal the way that the characterization of the Women's Circle – a group established in 1983 dedicated explicitly to feminist translation – tends, in retrospect, to eclipse its translational role in favour of a local 'authentic' identity. Arguing against accounts that celebrate indigenous feminism at the expense of 'the generative mechanisms of translation and contributive labor of translators' (Ergun 2017: 51), Ergun's example is significant for insisting that feminist philosophy recognize its translations as constitutive. This example illustrates the delicate tightrope walk between the influence, not to say imperialism, of Western feminist texts and the unique trajectories of Turkish feminism; the solution is not to privilege one at the expense of the other but to recognize their mutual and shared role in developing feminist thought. Indeed, this insight might be one of the major contributions of translation studies to feminist philosophy. One way that Ergun makes her point regarding the foundational impact of translations is at the level of feminist discourse. She explains that *cinsel taciz* [sexual harassment] is now so assimilated to Turkish that a member of the Women's Circle admitted 'I don't know how many women today would say that "sexual harassment" is a translation from another language' (2017: 45). Without dismissing the significant consequences of power differentials, Ergun's analysis of the prejudices that result in a repression of the critical role played by translation indicates an unwillingness to acknowledge either the innovative effects of translation or our shared and interconnected feminist histories. However, these histories are being uncovered in every domain as both translation studies and feminism gain ground. Emblematic of this mutual agenda, the recent publication of works such as the edited volume *Feminist Translation Studies: Local and Transnational Perspectives* (Castro and Ergun 2017) continue to promote the goal of its subtitle not only through individual interventions but also by using collaborative methodologies, as exemplified in 'A Cross-Disciplinary Roundtable on Feminist Politics of Translation' (2007: 111–36), included in the collection, where nine thinkers work together with a view to practising the way in which 'translation assists us in recognizing and creating commonalities (not sameness) with others' (2007: 121).

In addition to challenging canons, one strategy for overcoming nationalist prejudices that interrupt the acknowledgement, transmission and promotion of translation is institutionalization, notably through transnational organizations. Such institutionalization flags the centrality of translation practices that occur constantly at an informal level, for, as Kate Rushin wrote in her eponymous poem cited in *This Bridge Called My Back: Writings by Radical Women of Color*: 'I do more translating / Than the Gawdamn UN' (Moraga and Anzaldúa's [1981] 2015: xxxiii). Beyond dominant monolingual groups, translation has always been a necessary reality and an important survival strategy – both in daily life and for the life of philosophical ideas.

Translation practices common in multilingual contexts also exist in some institutional structures. In 2007 UNESCO sponsored the founding of the International Network of Women Philosophers. An online directory of women philosophers created as a part of this effort is divided into five regions (Africa, Arab States, Asia and the Pacific, Europe and North America, Latin America and the Caribbean) and uses the six official languages of UNESCO (Arabic, Chinese, English, French, Russian, Spanish). In addition to international assemblies, the network launched an online journal in 2011. So far two issues have been published: the inaugural 2011 'Squaring the Circle', available in English and French (Cassin, Balibar and Collin 2011) and a 2013 issue on the 'Arab Spring as seen by Women Philosophers', published in French and Arabic (Cassin, Balibar and Gendreau-Massaloux 2013). Initiatives such as this formalize and promote transnational exchanges through an explicit commitment to a translational practice.

Another institutional structure that could be mentioned is the *Centre d'études et de recherches féminines en Islam* (CERFI, also known as the Center for Women's Studies in Islam) in Morocco (Laghzali 2017). Founded in 2010, it seeks to develop a transnational understanding of Islamic feminism in multiple languages. I include this example to push again at our notion of what exactly feminist philosophy entails, asking what is its relation to religion? Stella Sanford's comment that philosophy is 'the most tightly policed discipline in the humanities' in contradistinction to 'the transdisciplinary practice of feminist theory' (Sandford 2015: 159) – and, I would add, translation studies – is indicative of the pressures on the object of our enquiry. Translations done at CERFI might provide some answers – or prompt more questions, including the relation between disciplines and institutions.

In an entirely different context, but addressing analogous issues, Claudia de Lima Costa asks 'By what means and through which institutionalities do feminist concepts/discourses/practices gain temporary (or even permanent) residence in different representational economies?' (Alvarez et al. 2014: 25). Her intention is to emphasize that such migrations and naturalizations occur regularly, not always according to the most evident power hierarchy but also via the production of new forms by subaltern receiving environments. Other twentieth-century structures that counter Western hegemonies include the 1955 Bandung Conference of newly independent Asian and African states and the resulting series of Afro-Asian Writers Conferences. Liu (2014) has emphasized the importance of relating the histories of these types of alliance as part of a global framework for interpreting translational connections. In her recent research, Liu has explored translational exchanges between India, Russia and China. Thus, while the majority of the translations I discuss in this chapter have English as either source or target language, this is a reflection of who I am and where I am writing from rather than the multifarious connections that exist between the languages of the world.

Considering institutions in the Anglo-American context brings to mind the scholarly journal *Hypatia: A Journal of Feminist Philosophy*, begun in 1984 with a special issue dedicated to Simone de Beauvoir, the year after *Radical Philosophy* published a special issue on 'Women, Gender and Philosophy'. Over the last thirty years, *Hypatia* has been a beacon for feminist philosophers in the Anglophone world and has served to recognize and disseminate the work of philosophers from several other languages through translation. Special issues include *French Feminist Philosophy* (1989), *Eastern European Feminisms* (1993), *Contemporary French Women Philosophers* (2000), *Contemporary Feminist Philosophy in German* (2005) and a forthcoming *Cluster on Latina Feminist Philosophy*. The website includes advice on 'Where to Publish Feminist Philosophy' and the journal seeks to promote increasingly diverse feminist thought. These examples of routes for creating new canons that include feminist philosophers respond to contemporary challenges to found historical narratives and share resources across languages and cultures as an alternative to the 'continuity of commentary [that] links one male philosopher to another' (Tougas and Ebenreck 2000: xvi). This approach leads me to our second pathway: strategies that insert feminist thought into the frameworks of existing disciplines through strategic alliances.

The opening rhetoric of this chapter, with its reference to explosive plasticity, might alarm those committed to more moderate forms of change, and indeed we can call on all the forms of alteration available in the effort to give feminist philosophers their due. Pairings with established authorities – as proposed by Atherton's *Women Philosophers of the Early Modern Period*, where Princess Elisabeth of Bohemia corresponds with Descartes, Lady Masham corresponds with Leibniz and Catherine Trotter Cockburn entertains *A Defense of Mr. Locke's Essay of Human Understanding* – are also an effective mode of transformation. A testimony to this approach is offered by Lisa Bergin in her report on teaching Chicana feminist philosopher 'Gloria Anzaldúa's *Borderlands/La Frontera* and René Descartes's *Discourse on Method*' (Bergin 2000). Bergin explains the enriched pedagogic effect of juxtaposing 'René Descartes's unitary consciousness and Gloria Anzaldùa's *mestiza* consciousness' (2000: 139). Parallel to Descartes's use of the vernacular in place of Latin, Anzaldúa's use of 'a mixture of languages, mostly Tex-Mex, Spanish and English' (2000: 140) offers a particularly powerful translational resource in a single text. Bergin's commentary on how this pairing rendered her teaching more relevant and compelling is also significant for her observation about how it increased her effectiveness as a 'short female graduate student who looks younger than she is': 'Part of what helped me establish authority as a philosophy teacher was that I was teaching women as philosophers' (2000: 145). Returning to the image with which this chapter began, Bergin concludes that 'giving them authority gave me authority [. . .] and so helps me to call philosophy home' (ibid.).

The didactic potential of translation is explored by another teacher of feminist philosophy seeking an effective strategy: Kanchuka Dharmasiri describes her experience in Sri Lanka in 'Voices from the *Therīgāthā*: Framing Western Feminisms in Sinhala Translation' (2017). Dharmasiri explains how, negotiating very different linguistic and cultural contexts, she deployed the familiar – 'selected verses from *Therīgāthā*, accounts by Buddhist women dating from the fourth century B.C.E.' (2017: 175) – as a mechanism to defuse negative responses to Western feminist texts. Skillfully bringing Subhā's 'painted doll' in the *Therīgāthā* into conversation with Wollstonecraft's 'angel in the house' from *Vindication of the Rights of Women* (1792), Addhakāsī to Simone de Beauvoir's *Le deuxième sexe* (1949) and Somā to Judith Butler's contemporary texts on gender as performance and subversion, Dharmasiri weaves together feminist concerns through time and space. The authority of *Therīgāthā* grants these new, foreign translations a hearing and opens a space of possible dialogue between different bodies of work. Like Bergin, a pedagogic goal informs this strategy, since Dharmasiri is seeking to correct the disadvantages experienced by students in the Sinhala stream at the University of Peradeniya, as compared to those in the English stream, because, as she explains, there is 'a distinct gap in learning' depending on whether or not students have access to primary reading material. In this gap lie the stakes of translation for feminist philosophers.

Within the translation gap we find an additional issue identified by French philosopher Barbara Cassin, amongst others, in her comments on the use of a pivot language (Cassin 2011: 25–42). In interview, Cassin explains the effect of dominant languages, notably English, as an intermediary for translations into a third language. A typical example is Howard Pashley's 1953 English translation of *The Second Sex*, which 'was the only source text for most Chinese translations' (Haiping 2017: 159). This issue affected not only the Chinese translations, for, as Anna Bogic has explained, the English version also served as a source text for the Persian translation, 'doubtless with major implications' (2011: 153). Quite aside from questions that have been raised about how de Beauvoir's *philosophical* contribution was obscured in the first English translation (Simons 1983; Moi 2002) and the philosophical competency of Constance Borde and Sheila Malovany-Chevallier for the 2009 re-translation (von Flotow 2012; Daigle 2013), the pivot, or relay, language factor has significant consequences for the transmission of de Beauvoir's existentialist thought.

Perhaps of even more serious concern is the generalized use of English as a relay language for machine-translation protocols used by tools such as Google Translate. One basic problem is that current algorithms default to the masculine. At this point, Google Translate systematically offers 'his' for the French possessive adjective '*son*', although in fact it means either 'his', 'her' or 'its' depending on the context. For the corpus-based algorithm it is effectively only '*sein*' [breast] that will produce a 'her'; apparently everything else belongs to him ... While I cannot discuss these issues further here, a chapter on translating feminist philosophers cannot ignore the consequences of the increasing prevalence of online, automatic translation that currently uses sexist algorithms and more often than not depends on English as pivot language. At this point it would be disingenuous not to acknowledge the way in which English acts in this chapter, if not as a pivot language, then as the language in which this chapter is written and the pin around which most of my argument turns. Such are my limitations, along with my privileging of French as my second language. Written in different languages, 'translating feminist philosophers' would tell different stories. With this in mind, we move on now to our third pathway, namely translation travelling, either as salvational escape or as recycling, for the feminist philosopher.

Carolyn Shread

Translation produces many effects, as feminist translation studies theorists Kathy Mezei, Sherry Simon and Luise von Flotow demonstrate in *Translation Effects: The Shaping of Modern Canadian Culture* (2014). Perhaps the single most powerful of these effects is the selection and promotion of work from one culture in another. While such selections are often held to be representative of their source culture, they may say more about the host culture. Given the minute percentage of work that is translated, any single translation cannot but fail to fully convey a foreign context. This point is made very clearly in the example analysed by Goldberg Moses in 'Made in America: 'French Feminism' in Academia' (2003). She describes the role of the US-based journal *Signs* and anthologies such as Marks and Courtivron's *New French Feminisms* (1980) in enthroning a trinity composed of Hélène Cixous, Julia Kristeva and Luce Irigaray in US academia in the 1980s. Their work met the needs of US feminists at that point but did not by any means represent the range of feminisms in France, as de Beauvoir objected, saying the anthology 'gives a totally distorted image of French feminism' (1984: 235). The fact that in this selection of texts for the US the 'materialist critique stays home' (Pheterson 1994: 262) is important and valid, but I would argue that it is not so much the translations per se that should be criticized. Given the odds, almost any translation is a translation to be celebrated for its very existence. We need to examine our conception of what exactly we expect translation to do once it is taken as only a part of a much larger whole. Goldberg Moses's case study allows us to understand translation as what Maria Tymoczko has argued is a metonymic, rather than metaphoric, process (1999). In analysing such translational metonyms, a sociological approach emphasizes that the manufacturing process Goldberg Moses describes is not solely the responsibility of the rogue translator but rather the construction of the larger networks in which they are embedded. Drawing on Bruno Latour's Actor–Network Theory, Bogic illustrates this point with regard to the denunciations of Parshley's translation of *The Second Sex*. Bogic presents and analyses the translator's correspondence with Knopf publishers to show that he did not work alone and that responsibility for decisions that shaped the translation should be shared amongst all the participants in the process (2010).

Even as we use translation studies to better understand and frame translations of feminist philosophers that exist, we must also focus on those that do not. For instance, Liu notes that 'few translations or studies of early Chinese feminists and their writings exist in English', but this should not occlude the fact that 'the birth of Chinese feminism was an event of global proportions' (2013: 4). A body of work on what de Lima Costa calls 'The Traffic in Theories' (2007) has identified, first, the unequal roles attributed within the trade and, second, the unequal directions of exchanges. She draws on Chilean cultural critic Nelly Richard, who identifies inequities in substance such that 'while the academic center theorizes, it expects the periphery to supply case studies' (de Lima Costa 2007: 169). Beyond this observation, we could cite any number of complaints about the lack of reciprocity in translation exchanges. A sample might begin with Hélène Cixous's criticism (which was subsequently at least partially corrected): 'We translate what American women write, they never translate our texts' (Marks and de Courtivron 1980: ix) and include Gertrude Postl, who introduces the *Hypatia* issue on *Contemporary Feminist Philosophy in German* with the comment 'the topics, the names, and the titles regularly debated in Vienna were strikingly absent from any feminist discussion in the United States', while 'the main texts by U.S. feminist philosophers are for the most part translated into German' (Postl 2005: viii, xiv), and Rajkumar Eligedi, who, in his dissertation on 'Translating Feminism into Telugu: A Socio-Historical Study of Agents', observes that 'while the journey of feminist knowledge from English to Telugu appears to be vibrant, the travel back did not happen at the same pace' (Eligedi 2015: 7). Moreover, on the question of pivot languages raised earlier, Eligedi notes that 'the travel of feminist knowledge as mediation is entirely through the medium of English [...] even in the case of other neighboring languages like Kannada, Malayalam, and Tamil to Telugu and from Telugu into other Indian languages' (2015: 7). Yet even as we level the accusation of Western feminist philosophy as cultural imperialism, theorists such as de Lima Costa warn against the assumptions underlying such an interpretation. She cites John French's argument that a 'simplistic model of US domination/imposition and subaltern submission/complicity is empirically and theoretically wrongheaded. It erases the process of local appropriation while vastly exaggerating the power and influence that US-based notions have had' (French 2003: 376). This view finds support in Min's article 'Toward an Alternative Traveling Theory', where she recognizes that 'gender theory has flowed far more easily from the North to the South or from the West to the East' and yet warns, citing recent China–Nordic country exchanges as an example, 'there are many more invisible discursive trajectories that link the development of gender theories and movements in the world that have so far been ignored' (2014: 584–5). Thus, while from the US perspective, the work of the Chinese Society of Women's Studies appears to reinforce a narrative that 'feminism developed specifically out of western thought, and now is spreading to other countries and cultures' (Min 2008: 83), this narrative is challenged by Chinese scholars. The invisible threads of an infinite number of translations weave a far tighter and more complex web than the lines evident from any single vantage point. Such has been one of the challenges of writing this chapter: my object, even as I sense it is there, for the most part eludes me. Perhaps the greatest step forward I can take is to assert what I cannot but surmise, given the conditions of women and the human propensity to think: *feminist philosophers think in every language and culture.*

If feminist philosophers have always thought, they have not done so according to the same conceptual schemas. Countering a Kantian confidence in universal categories, feminist philosophers help diversify the foundations and structures of philosophy. Translation studies is in a privileged position to both illustrate and refine our understanding of this process, for just as translation itself is a cluster concept, so too is feminism. In *Enlarging Translation, Empowering Translators* (2007), drawing on Ludwig Wittgenstein's description of family resemblances or partial similarities across a variable set of exemplars, Maria Tymoczko introduces 'cluster concept' as a means to explain the multiplicity of understandings of translation. An example of both translation and feminism as cluster concepts is found in *The Birth of Chinese Feminism: Essential Texts in Transnational Theory* (2013), in which Lydia Liu, Rebecca Karl and Dorothy Ko offer important new narratives to an Anglophone history of feminism by introducing key Chinese texts, starting with Jin Tianhe's *The Women's Bell* (1903), and key figures such as anarchist feminist translator He-Yin Zhen, editor of the journal *Natural Justice* from 1907 to 1908, who lived and worked in Japan while introducing her ideas to China. Such historical facts serve not only to establish a more complete account globally but also, critically, alter our conception of how feminist philosophy lives and travels in translation.

Recognizing the mobility capital enjoyed by the conceptual frameworks of certain cultures at particular times is a development of what Edward Said described as 'traveling theory' (1983) and Mieke Bal explored in *Traveling Concepts in the Humanities: A Rough Guide* (2002). These approaches are supported by many recent studies, including research projects like 'Traveling Concepts in Feminist Pedagogy: European Perspectives' (Sandford 2015: 163), linked to the Athena Network Project, a grassroots transnational feminism organization, and the Leverhulme Trust-funded international network Translating Feminism: Transfer, Transgression, Transformation (1945–90), based at the University of Glasgow from 2016.

Coalitions between feminist philosophers and translation studies have forged new visions for the task of translation, as Min explains:

> Rather than focusing on whether a particular concept of theory has been translated 'correctly' so as to maintain a certain essence, Boaventura de Sousa Santos (2006) [...] points out that the recognition of a diversity of understandings in different contexts may allow for fruitful dialogue.
>
> (Min 2014: 590)

As stated at the beginning of this chapter: translation, feminism and philosophy form a powerful trio and together help to dismantle the master's mansion before beginning on the project of reassembling a village full of homes for all peoples.

This power has not always been recognized. Recounting the challenges of transdisciplinarity, Sandford notes that 'in the English-speaking world, mainstream philosophy resisted feminism, and one of its main tactics was to deny that feminist philosophy was in fact "philosophy" at all' (2015: 173). Amongst other tensions, philosophers have not always accepted the activist commitments of feminist thought. The dependence of philosophy on translation has also been neglected as an area of study. Established philosophy has often been loath to engage in the type of work von Flotow and Scott describe in 'Gender Studies and Translation Studies: "Entre braguette" – Connecting the Transdisciplines' (2016). And yet I might easily have written this entire chapter through a focus on the translation of just two words whose philosophical import is explosive: sex and gender.

It is impossible to write on the translation of feminist philosophy without acknowledging sex–gender as one of the most powerful and surprising tools in the box. This topic has been studied in depth – for instance, by Braidotti (2002) working in the European context or Thayer (2002), whose 'incisive study of North–South travels of the concept' presented 'more politically progressive appropriations of gender' in Brazil (de Lima Costa 2007: 181). These studies of central concepts in feminist philosophy teach us that aside from translation limits, one of the reasons that feminist philosophies remain partially opaque even when they manage to escape or expand into new contexts is what Liu terms the 'translingual precariousness of analytical categories' (2013: 11). As a case in point, Liu presents the Chinese term *nannü* [man and woman; male/female] as a 'more enabling analytical category', one which exceeds the sex–gender problematic that structures many Western theorizations. She explains:

> He-Yin Zhen insists that feminists must take *nan* and *nü* together as a single conceptual dividing mechanism rather than focusing on '*nü*-woman' or on 'difference' per se. The notion of *nü* cannot possibly be captured outside of the originary structural distinctions introduced by the binary opposition of *nannü*.
>
> (2013: 20)

The working through of binaries that was so productive in the context of deconstructive philosophy is complemented here by an entirely different approach.

Liu's work is worth spending time with, since she brings clarity to our three terms: translating – feminist – philosophers. She argues that 'at stake is not linguistic incommensurability' but instead in conceiving 'He-Yin Zhen's category in comparative terms and in so doing, to question not only Chinese usage but also theoretical categories used in the English language' (2013: 11). She explains how He-Yin Zhen's use of *nannü* exceeds 'gendered social relations between man and woman' to reference 'the relationship of the past to the present, of China to the world, of politics to justice, of law and ritual to gendered forms of knowledge, interaction and social organization' (2013: 10). Hence, if feminist philosophy proves one point, it is that categories may cluster but they are not universal.

This 'more comprehensive rubric than "sex–gender"' (2013: 10) may be more easily understood from other places in the world. Abosede George's short but ground-shifting article 'He-Yin Zhen, Oyěwúmi, and Geographies of Anti-Universalism' illustrates the way in which 'gender' manifests as a non-universal category. Furthering Liu's analysis of He-Yin Zhen's *nannü* as one that 'entangles class, generational, moral, ritual, and sexual subjugation' (2015: 186), George also discusses how Oyěwúmi (1997, 2011) problematizes the category of 'gender' in Western discourses from a West African perspective by explaining that in Yoruba culture 'age' is the determining category. She describes how Oyěwúmi develops 'a theory of generational difference as the fundamental axis of social difference in late nineteenth and early twentieth-century Yorubaland' (2015: 186). George also contributes an explanation of how it is that a Western notion of 'gender' has travelled so far, clarifying that it was not 'the absence of competing understandings' but rather the 'comfortable embrace that the European conception of women received in far-flung parts of the world, from audiences as diverse as liberal feminists in China to Yoruba masculinities in West Africa' (2015: 188). Certainly, a material and historical understanding of why such an embrace occurred will help explain the trajectories, and precarity, of different conceptual schema.

From this sprawling section on critical issues, which has moved from who translates feminist philosophers along the three twisting pathways of canonization, alliance and travelling effects, we now move to a concise, highly selective analysis of current contributions in which I abandon any attempt to survey the lay of many lands in favour of a concrete suggestion of three feminist philosophers, whose work, at the very intersection of translation studies, might lay claim to the honor of an individual chapter in this *Handbook*: Judith Butler, Gayatri Chakravorty Spivak and Barbara Cassin. Needless to say, there are many other candidates, and I am all too aware of those who are excluded by my choice, which is, of course, determined not so much by their importance or contribution as by where I sit.

Current contributions and research: three candidates for individual entries

I have argued that the three terms – translating – feminist – philosophers – have an especially valuable relation. One place that these three terms interrelate productively is in the conception of 'cultural translation' as presented by contemporary American feminist philosopher Judith Butler, who builds on Homi Bhabha's use of the term and its meaning in critiques such as Tejaswini Niranjana's *Siting Translation: History, Post-Structuralism and the Colonial Context* (1992). Butler suggests a resolution to long-standing dilemmas about the apparent incompatibility of the universal, particular and singular by explaining that the process by which universality is articulated with the particular or singular excluded is not dialectical but rather translational: 'Without translation, the very concept of universality cannot cross the linguistic borders it claims in principle, to be able to cross' (2000: 35). Butler's argument is indicative of the way in which translation has moved from a marginal area of study into a transdisciplinary space in which we know we cannot do without it. As Kimberly Hutchings explains in her discussion of Butler's response to the conflict between cosmopolitan and communitarian approaches to ethics in a translational framework, 'it is not a matter of subsuming all languages under a meta-language but of forging common ground across different languages, or of recognizing the limits of mutual intelligibility' (2013: 25). In the context of philosophy, the process of recognizing culture as inherent to translation produces schema capable of engaging with a less homogenously defined world. Translation thus becomes an essential component to political philosophy and, moreover, the grounds for democracy.

In moving from translation to cultural translation, we must make sure, as Sherry Simon insists, battling other fields that have co-opted translation, that translation retain its connection to the fact of language. Citing Harish Trivedi's warning that 'cultural translation has become a way for cultural studies theorists to appropriate "translation" – without learning the languages' (Buden et al. 2009: 210), Simon wrestles the dialogic back from monolingualism. We cannot afford to have language evacuated from translation. Or, to put it another way, 'global' must be far more than global English.

Prior to her focus on 'cultural translation', Butler's contribution as a feminist philosopher deeply committed to dislodging the resistance of philosophy to feminism was evident in texts such as 'Can the "Other" of Philosophy Speak?' (2004). Preceding this work, her influential *Gender Trouble: Feminism and the Subversion of Identity* (Butler 1990) intersects with the earlier discussion of the dissemination of the concept of gender globally through her highly influential rescripting of gender as a performative category.

Our question, following Butler's echo of Gayatri Chakravorty Spivak's 'Can the Subaltern Speak?' (1988), might then be what language do these others of philosophy speak? And who translates them? These are the questions that lay the groundwork for Dorothy Ko and Wang Zheng's claim in the opening to *Translating Feminisms in China* (2007) that 'feminism is always already a global discourse, and the history of its local reception is a history of the politics of translation'. No feminist philosophy translator can read this statement without hearing one of the founding texts of feminist translation practice, Spivak's (1992) 'The Politics of Translation', and indeed Spivak is my second proposal for a candidate warranting an individual chapter.

In Spivak we find a feminist philosopher deeply committed to the practice of translation. Not only the translator of Jacques Derrida's *Of Grammatology* (1976), she is also the translator of Indian author Mahasweta Devi, beginning with *Imaginary Maps* in 1995. Reflecting on her role as translator, Spivak laid out a feminist ethics for translators, grounded in love and insisting that translators must have a 'tough sense of the specific terrain of the original' and an 'intimate knowledge' (1995: 180) of the source language and culture. Spivak continues to challenge, through a postcolonial lens, many of the assumptions that circulate within the North American academia in which she works, maintaining, through activities in her native India and around the world, an enduring engagement with translation that is practical as much as it is theoretical.

My third vote for an individual chapter – the one that blows away the elected, the one I find inconceivable is not on the list – is Barbara Cassin. In her capacity as editor for the French *Vocabulaire européen des philosophies: Dictionnaire des intraduisibles* (2004), which became, ten years later in English, *Dictionary of Untranslatables: A Philosophical Lexicon*, Cassin undertakes an encyclopedic project to 'chart the geography of philosophy' (Young 2014: 48). Collaborating with 150 contributors, the dictionary takes some 400 individual philosophical terms – truth, subject, *Dasein* . . . – parsed in more than twelve languages. Each term is presented in parallel with different languages with an accompanying commentary on its history, uses and meaning through multiple languages. We have here a veritable genealogy of philosophy's building materials. As Cassin explains it:

> In order to find the meaning of a word in one language, this book explores the networks to which the word belongs and seeks to understand how a network functions in one language by relating it to the networks of other languages.

(2014: xvii)

The result is a *pavé*, a doorstopper of a book, with over 1,300 pages devoted to the complex multilingualism out of which philosophy is woven. As if the venture were not sufficiently ambitious – but, also, who could resist the temptation? – Cassin's *Vocabulaire* has been translated not only into English but also Ukrainian, Russian, Portuguese, Romanian, Spanish, Greek and Arabic, with no doubt more to come. Each version has prompted not only culturally determined pruning but also the drafting of new terms and specialist articles in inset boxes. For instance, the English dictionary added an entry on 'gender', written by Judith Butler, as well as one on 'planetarity', by Gayatri Chakravorty Spivak. This monument of twenty-first-century philosophy, with its proliferating, rhizomic structure, places translation studies and the practice of translation firmly as the cornerstone of philosophic thought. Cassin's book, and the translations it continues to inspire, is the epitome of the meeting of translation studies and philosophy that this *Handbook* seeks to circumscribe – and yet that it ignores.

Cassin's work has brought the issue of the 'untranslatable' to the forefront. In her 'Introduction' she explains this term that has been widely misunderstood and misused: 'to speak of untranslatables in no way implies that the terms in question [. . .] are not and cannot be translated: the untranslatable is rather what one keeps on (not) translating' (2014: xvii). The intense focus on language and translation that this philosophical meditation provokes interrupts the long-standing habit of treating translation in an instrumental way, as if content could be extracted from words and live without them. Instead, Cassin's achievement is to demonstrate, concretely, that translation is 'a form of philosophizing with differences' (2015: 145) and that philosophy cannot do without it.

This chapter opened with Malabou's plasticity, including the explosiveness it harbours. In a recent article Cassin described the energy generated by the *Dictionary* project, acknowledging that 'the gesture it represented is no longer under my control' (2015: 145). Cassin uses the Greek term *energeia* – an eruptive force – to describe the linguistic encounter that is translation. Once philosophy recognizes that it sits within this plastic space, it will be better prepared to welcome the innovation that comes not only from feminist philosophers but from translation itself. Beyond Cassin's initial two goals of challenging both Globish and an ontological nationalism invested in the *génie des langues*, or innate genius of a given language, she finds the nesting of energies at work produced by translation as it denationalizes language. She ends with a 'practical plea' remembering the fundamental point made by Hannah Arendt: 'all languages are *learnable*' (2015: 156–7). This pedagogically oriented conclusion returns us to plasticity in the neuroscientific context that inspires Malabou: our brains are plastic (2008) even when they are blue and not entirely our own (2017). Thanks to neuroplasticity, not only are we capable of learning languages and translating, but we can also transform our philosophical schema.

Future directions: the future is plastic

Plastic as we are, we are also bound by our languages, translations and human ability to process ideas. This chapter has wavered between an awareness of its vast scope, an ambition to open up 'translating feminist philosophers' to the whole world in all its complex interactions, and the necessarily limited sightlines of its author. The wavering between we/our and I/my throughout the analysis conveys the ambivalent sense of belonging to a movement – that of translators and feminist philosophers – while also recognizing my limitations. When I write 'we', who are we? Certainly not all women, and yet I do not feel that I speak and write alone. Without speaking for others, I speak with them and invite them to speak with me, in every language and through interpreters and translations when we reach our limits.

I suggested that feminism helps philosophy do its job better, as does translation studies, but the question remains, as Kourany puts it: 'What is philosophy good for?' (1998: 3). Kourany's concern is that 'much of the philosophy most Western philosophers engage in and teach and study [. . . is] unhelpful to everyone, but especially unhelpful to women' (ibid.) due to the biases it perpetuates. This brings us to the point Michèle Le Doeuff made in regard to such objections from feminists vis-à-vis philosophy: 'Sexist segregation seems of slight importance compared with the massive exclusion that has caused philosophy to remain the prerogative of a handful of the learned' (1977: 2). By introducing class and elitism into the matrix of intersectional critique, Le Doeuff goes beyond questions of erasure to the phenomenon of exclusion through mechanisms such as non-recognition and non-translation. Here, for instance, Liu's work challenging liberal feminism's assumptions that suffrage, sexuality and rights are the priorities for a feminist agenda provides an alternative. For He-Yin Zhen, it is the invisible labour of women that must be analysed through categories such as *shengji* [livelihood]. Liu explains how this Chinese intervention helps 'elucidate [. . .] "woman" as a transhistorical global category – not of subjective identity but of structured unequal social relations' (2013: 9). Thus, when Naomi Zach asks that we 'think through the implications of intersectionality' (2007: 193), her challenge involves rethinking the very categories of the current Anglo-American 'race, gender, class, sexuality, nationality, ability' mantra by calling on translation. To do so would encourage us to include language, too, as an intersectional difference and a site for human rights. In this expansive gesture, philosophy's uses increase, and it is good for more than just the happy few.

I look forward to the day that 'feminist philosopher' does not connote woman, that it assumes its role as a view that promotes human values by ensuring that no person anywhere on the gender spectrum, and whatever their sexuality, is subordinated to another. One of the future directions I encourage is a building and integrating of feminist philosophy by men. In so saying I acknowledge that one very important feminist philosopher in French is a man: Jacques Derrida. Our one feminist on the list. As Elizabeth Grosz put it in a remembrance: 'With the exception of John Stuart Mill [. . .] Derrida is really the first (male) philosopher for whom feminism is essential if philosophy is to be undertaken properly' (2005: 88). Feminist philosophy thus starts with the deconstruction of the oxymoron. Yes, I, a feminist, a woman, I am a philosopher. We are philosophers. In every place, time and language we are truly plastic – able to give and receive form but also to shape with destructive explosion. In our plasticity, we translate our transformations.

Related topics

Derrida; feminism.

Further reading

Godayol, P. (2013) 'Gender and Translation' in C. Millán and F. Bartrina (eds) *The Routledge Handbook of Translation Studies*, New York: Routledge, 173–85. (A useful overview of the field of gender and translation that offers a good sample of foundational texts and emerging questions.)

Liu, L., R. Karl and D. Ko (2013) *The Birth of Chinese Feminism: Essential Texts in Transnational Theory*, New York: Columbia University Press. (A valuable analysis of translation in the context of the history of feminist thought in China.)

O'Neill, E. (1988) 'Disappearing Ink: Early Modern Women Philosophers and Their Fate in History' in J. Kourany (ed.) *Philosophy in a Feminist Voice: Critiques and Reconstructions*, Princeton, NJ: Princeton

University Press. (This article offers an excellent overview of some of the significant women philosophers in the Western tradition and an explanation for their disappearance from histories of philosophy by the nineteenth century.)

References

Alvarez, S., C. de Lima Costa, V. Feliu, R. Hester, N. Klahn and M. Thayer (2014) *Translocalities/ translocalidades: Feminist Politics of Translation in the Latin/a Americas*. Durham and London: Duke University Press.

Atherton, M. (1994) *Women Philosophers of the Early Modern Period*, Indianapolis, IN: Hackett Publishing Company.

Bergin, L. (2000) 'Gloria Anzaldúa's *Borderlands/La Frontera* and René Descartes's *Discourse on Method:* Moving Beyond the Canon in Discussion of Philosophical Ideas' in C. Tougas and S. Ebenreck (eds) *Presenting Women Philosophers*, Philadelphia: Temple University Press, 139–45.

Berman, S. and C. Porter (2014) *Companion to Translation Studies*, London: John Wiley & Sons.

Boateng, R. (2016) 'Interview: Brazilian Black Feminist Philosopher Djamila Riberio on Intersectionality and the Black Feminist Movement', tr. R. Batista, Afropunk, posted by The Race Card, 25 February. www.afropunk.com/profiles/blogs/interview-brazilian-black-feminist-philosopher-djamila-ribeiro-on (accessed 6 July 2016).

Bogic, A. (2010) 'Uncovering the Hidden Actors with the Help of Latour: The "Making" of *The Second Sex*' in *MonTU. Monografías de Traducción e Interpretación* 2, Alicante: University of Valencia, 173–92.

Bogic, A. (2011) 'Why Philosophy Went Missing: Understanding the English Version of Simone de Beauvoir's *Le deuxième sexe*' in L. von Flotow (ed.) *Translating Women*, Ottawa: University of Ottawa Press, 151–66.

Borchert, D. (ed.) (1996) *Encyclopedia of Philosophy. Supplement*, New York and London: Macmillan Reference, Simon & Schuster Macmillan.

Braidotti, R. (2002) 'The Uses and Abuses of the Sex/Gender Distinction in European Feminist Practices' in G. Griffin and R. Braidotti (eds) *Thinking Differently: A Reader in European Women's Studies*, London: Zed Books.

Brown, K. (2000) 'Madame de Condorcet's Letters on Sympathy' in C. Tougas and S. Ebenreck (eds) *Presenting Women Philosophers*, Philadelphia: Temple University Press, 225–37.

Buden, B., S. Nowotny, S. Simon, A. Bery and M. Cronin (2009) 'Cultural Translation: An Introduction to the Problem, and Responses', *Translation Studies* 2:2, 196–219.

Butler, J. (1990) *Gender Trouble: Feminism and the Subversion of Identity*, New York: Routledge.

Butler, J. (2000) 'Restaging the Universal: Hegemony and the Limits of Formalism' in L. Butler and S. Žižek (eds) *Contingency, Hegemony, Universality: Contemporary Dialogues on the Left*, London: Verso, 11–43.

Butler, J. (2004) *Undoing Gender: Philosophy Outside of Philosophy*, New York: Routledge.

Cassin, B. (ed.) (2004) *Vocabulaire européen des philosophies: Dictionnaire des intraduisibles*, Paris: Seuil.

Cassin, B. (2011) 'Intraduisible et mondialisation' in M. Oustinoff (ed.) *Traduction et mondialisation*, Paris: CNRS Éditions, 25–42.

Cassin, B. (ed.) (2014) *Dictionary of Untranslatables: A Philosophical Lexicon*, ed. E. Apter, J. Lezra and M. Wood, tr. S. Rendall, C. Hubert, J. Mehlman, N. Stein and M. Syrotinski, Princeton, NJ: Princeton University Press.

Cassin, B. (2015) 'The Energy of Untranslatables: Translation as a Paradigm for the Human Sciences', tr. M. Syrotinski, *Paragraph* 28:2, 145–58.

Cassin, B., F. Balibar and F. Collin (2011) 'Squaring the Circle', *Journal of the International Women Philosophers* 1, 6–9.

Cassin, B., F. Balibar and M. Gendreau-Massaloux (2013) 'Printemps arabes, printemps durables', *Revue des Femmes Philosophes* 2–3, 8–9.

Castro, O. and E. Ergun (eds) (2017) *Feminist Translation Studies: Local and Transnational Perspectives*, London: Routledge.

Chamberlain, L. (1988) 'Gender and the Metaphorics of Translation', *Signs: Journal of Women in Culture and Society* 13:3, 454–72.

Crenshaw, K. (1989) 'Demarginalizing the Intersection of Race and Sex: A Black Feminist Critique of Antidiscrimination Doctrine, Feminist Theory and Antiracist Politics', *University of Chicago Legal Forum* 1:8, 139–67.

Daigle, C. (2013) 'The Impact of the New Translation of *The Second Sex*: Rediscovering Beauvoir', *Journal of Speculative Philosophy* 27:3, 336–47.

de Beauvoir, S. (1949) *Le deuxième sexe*, Paris: Gallimard, tr. Howard Pashley (1953) *The Second Sex*, New York: Knopf.

de Lima Costa, C. (2007) 'Unthinking Gender: The Traffic in Theory in the Americas', *Feminist Philosophy in Latin America and Spain*, Amsterdam: Rodopi, 167–86.

de Lotbinière-Harwood, S. (1991) *Rebelle et infidèle. La traduction comme ré-écriture au feminine / The Body Bilingual*, Montreal/Toronto: Éditions remue-ménage/The Women's Press.

Derrida, J. (1976) *Of Grammatology*, tr. G. Spivak, Baltimore, MD and London: Johns Hopkins University Press.

Deutscher, P. (2000) '"A Matter of Affect, Passion and Heart": Our Taste for New Narratives of the History of Philosophy', *Hypatia: Special Issue on Contemporary French Women Philosophers*, 15:4, 1–17.

Devi, M. (1995) *Imaginary Maps*, tr. G. Spivak, New York: Routledge.

Dharmasiri, K. (2017) 'Voices from the Therīgāthā: Framing Western Feminisms in Sinhala Translation' in O. Castro and E. Ergun (eds) *Feminist Translation Studies: Local and Transnational Perspectives*, London: Routledge, 175–93.

Edwards, P. (1967) *Encyclopedia of Philosophy*, New York: Macmillan.

Eligedi, R. (2015) 'Translating Feminism into Telugu: A Socio-Historical Study of Agents'. https://ejournals.library.ualberta.ca/index.php/TC/thesis/view/33 (accessed 17 January 2017).

Ergun, E. (2017) 'Translational Beginnings and Origin/izing Stories: (Re)Writing the History of the Contemporary Feminist Movement in Turkey' in L. von Flotow and F. Farahzad (eds) *Translating Women: Different Voices and New Horizons*, New York: Routledge, 41–55.

Ettinger, B. (1992) 'Matrix and Metramorphosis', *Differences: A Journal of Feminist Cultural Studies* 4:3, 176–208.

Ettinger, B. (1994) 'The Becoming Threshold of Matrixial Borderlines' in G. Robertson et al. (eds) *Travellers' Tales: Narratives of Home and Displacement*, London: Routledge, 38–62.

French, J. (2003) 'Translation, Diasporic Dialogue, and the Errors of Pierre Bourdieu and Loïc Wacquant', *Neptala: Views from the South* 4:2, 375–89.

George, A. (2015) 'He-Yin Zhen, Oyěwúmi, and Geographies of Anti-Universalism', *Comparative Studies of South Asia, Africa and the Middle East*, 35:1, 183–8.

Godard, B. (1989) 'Theorizing Feminist Discourse/Translation', *Tessera* 6, 42–53.

Goldberg Moses, C. (2003) 'Made in America: "French Feminism" in Academia' in R. Célestin et al. (eds) *Beyond French Feminisms*, New York: Palgrave MacMillan, 261–84.

Grosz, E. (2005) 'Derrida and Feminism: A Remembrance', *Differences: A Journal of Feminist Cultural Studies*, 16:3, 88–94.

Haiping, L. (2017) 'Manipulating Simone de Beauvoir: A Study of Chinese Translations of *The Second Sex*' in L. von Flotow and F. Farahzad (eds) *Translating Women: Different Voices and New Horizons*, New York: Routledge, 159–71.

Huston, N. (2004) *Professeurs de désespoir*, Arles: Actes Sud.

Hutchings, K. (2013) 'Universalism in Feminist International Ethics: Gender and the Difficult Labor of Translation' in J. Browne (ed.) *Dialogue, Politics and Gender*, Cambridge: Cambridge University Press, 81–106.

Kourany, J. (1998) *Philosophy in a Feminist Voice: Critiques and Reconstructions*, Princeton, NJ: Princeton University Press.

Laghzali, B. (2017) 'The Translation of Islamic Feminism at CERFI in Morocco' in L. von Flotow and F. Farahzad (eds) *Translating Women: Different Voices and New Horizons*, New York: Routledge, 207–22.

Le Doeuff, M. (1977) 'Women and Philosophy', tr. D. Pope, *Radical Philosophy* 17, 2–11.
Lerner, G. (1986) *The Invention of Patriarchy*, Oxford: Oxford University Press.
Lerner, G. (2000) 'Why Have There Been So Few Women Philosophers' in C. Tougas and S. Ebenreck (eds) *Presenting Women Philosophers*, Philadelphia, PA: Temple University Press, 5–14.
Liu, L. (2014) 'The Eventfulness of Translation: Temporality, Difference and Competing Universals', *Translation: A Transdisciplinary Journal* 4, 147–70.
Liu, L., R. Karl and D. Ko (2013) *The Birth of Chinese Feminism: Essential Texts in Transnational Theory*, New York: Columbia University Press.
Lorde, A. (1984) 'The Master's Tools Will Never Dismantle the Master's House' in *Sister Outsider: Essays and Speeches by Audre Lorde*, Berkeley, CA: Ten Speed Press, 110–13.
Malabou, C. (2008) *What Should We Do with Our Brain?*, tr. S. Rand, New York: Fordham University Press.
Malabou, C. (2009) *Plasticity at the Dusk of Writing: Dialectic, Destruction, Deconstruction*, tr. C. Shread, New York: Columbia University Press.
Malabou, C. (2011) *Changing Difference: The Feminine and the Question of Philosophy*, tr. C. Shread, Cambridge: Polity Press.
Malabou, C. (2017) *Métamorphoses de l'intelligence: Que faire de leur cerveau bleu?* Paris: Presses Universitaires de France/Humensis [tr. C. Shread (forthcoming) *Morphing Intelligence: From IQ Measurement to Artificial Brains*, New York: Columbia University Press].
Marks, E. and I. de Courtivron (1980) *New French Feminisms: An Anthology*, Amherst, MA: University of Massachusetts Press.
McAlister, L. (ed.) (1996) *Hypatia's Daughters: Fifteen Hundred Years of Women Philosophers*, Bloomington and Indianapolis, IN: Indiana University Press.
Ménage, G. (1984) *History of Women Philosophers*, tr. B. Zedler, New York: University Press of America [1690 *Histoira mulierum philosopharum*].
Mezei, K., S. Simon and L. von Flotow (2014) *Translation Effects: The Shaping of Modern Canadian Culture*, Montreal: McGill-Queen's University Press.
Min, D. (2008) 'What about Other Translation Routes (East–West)? The Concept of the Term "Gender" Traveling into and throughout China' in K. Ferguson and M. Mironesco (eds) *Gender and Globalization in Asia and the Pacific: Method, Practice, Theory*, Honolulu: University of Hawai'i Press, 79–98.
Min, D. (2014) 'Toward an Alternative Traveling Theory', *Signs: Journal of Women in Culture and Society* 39:3, 584–92.
Moi, T. (2002) 'While We Wait: The English Translation of The Second Sex', *Signs: Journal of Women in Culture and Society* 27:4, 1005–35.
Moraga, C. and G. Anzaldúa [1981] (2015) *This Bridge Called My Back: Writings by Radical Women of Color*, Albany, NY: SUNY Press.
Niranjana, T. (1992) *Siting Translation: History, Post-Structuralism and the Colonial Context*, Berkley, CA: University of California Press.
O'Neill, E. (1988) 'Disappearing Ink: Early Modern Women Philosophers and Their Fate in History' in J. Kourany (ed.) *Philosophy in a Feminist Voice: Critiques and Reconstructions*, Princeton, NJ: Princeton University Press.
Oyěwúmi, O. (1997) *The Invention of Woman: Making an African Sense of Western Gender Discourses*, Minneapolis: University of Minnesota Press.
Oyěwúmi, O. (2011) *Gender Epistemologies in Africa: Gendering Traditions, Spaces, Social Institutions, and Identities*, New York: Palgrave MacMillan.
Pheterson, G. (1994) 'Group Identity and Social Relations: Divergent Theoretical Conceptions in the United States, the Netherlands, and France', *European Journal of Women's Studies* 1, 257–64.
Postl, G. (2005) 'Introduction: Contemporary Feminist Philosophy in German', *Hypatia*, 20:2, viii–xvi.
Said, E. (1983) *The World, the Text and the Critic*, Cambridge, MA: Harvard University Press.
Sandford, S. (2015) 'Contradiction of Terms: Feminist Theory, Philosophy and Transdisciplinarity', *Theory Culture & Society*, 32: 5–6, 159–82.

Santos, B. (2006) *The Rise of the Global Left: The World Social Forum and Beyond*, London: Zed.
Schott, R. (2007) 'Feminism and the History of Philosophy' in L. Alcoff and E. Kittay (eds) *The Blackwell Guide to Feminist Philosophy*, Malden, MA and Oxford: Blackwell Publishing, 43–63.
Simon, S. (1996) *Translation and Gender. The Politics of Cultural Transmission*, London and New York: Routledge.
Simons, M. (1983) 'The Silencing of Simone de Beauvoir: Guess What's Missing from *The Second Sex*', *Women's Studies International Forum*, 6:5, 559–64.
Spivak, G. (1988) 'Can the Subaltern Speak?' in C. Nelson and L. Grossberg (eds) *Marxism and the Interpretation of Culture*, Champaign, IL: University of Illinois Press, 271–312.
Spivak, G. (1992) 'The Politics of Translation' in M. Barrett and A. Phillips (eds) *Destabilizing Theory: Contemporary Feminist Debates*, Stanford, CA: Stanford University Press, 177–200.
Taylor, K.-Y. (ed.) (2017) *How We Get Free: Black Feminism and the Combahee River Collective*, Chicago: Haymarket Books.
Thayer, M. (2002) 'Traveling Feminisms: From Embodied Women to Gendered Citizenship' in M. Burawoy (ed.) *Global Ethnography: Forces, Connections and Imaginations in a Transnational World*, Berkeley, CA: University of California Press, 203–33.
Tougas, C.T. and Ebenreck, S. (eds) (2000) *Presenting Women Philosophers*. Philadelphia: Temple University Press.
Truth, S. (1851) 'Ain't I a Woman?' Women's Convention, Akron, Ohio, 28–9 May.
Tymoczko, M. (1999) *Translation in a Postcolonial Context. Early Irish Literature in English Translation*, Manchester: St. Jerome.
von Flotow, L. (1997a) 'Mutual Pun-ishment? Translating Radical Feminist Wordplay: Mary Daly's "Gyn/Ecology" in German', *Traductio*, 45–66.
von Flotow, L. (1997b) *Translation and Gender. Translation in the 'Era of Feminism'*, Manchester and Ottawa: St. Jerome and University of Ottawa Press.
von Flotow, L. (2006) 'Feminism in Translation: the Canadian Factor', *Quaderns: Revista da traduccío* 13, 11–20.
von Flotow, L. (2012) 'Translating Women: From Recent Histories and Re-translations to «Queerying» Translation, and Metramorphosis', *Quaderns: Revista da traduccío* 19, 127–39.
von Flotow, L. and J. Scott (2016) 'Gender Studies and Translation Studies: "Entre braguette" – Connecting the Transdisciplines' in Y. Gambier and L. van Doorslaer (eds) *Border Crossings: Translation Studies and Other Disciplines*, Amsterdam: John Benjamins, 349–74.
Waithe, M. (1987) *A History of Women Philosophers*, Dordrecht: Kluwer Academic Publishers.
Warren, K. (ed.) (2009) *An Unconventional History of Western Philosophy: Conversations Between Men and Women Philosophers*, Lanham, MD: Rowman & Littlefield.
Weigel, S. (2012) 'Sounding Through – Poetic Difference – Self-Translation: Hannah Arendt's Thoughts and Writings between Different Languages, Cultures, and Fields' in E. Goebel and S. Weigel (eds) *'Escape to Life' German Intellectuals in New York. A Compendium on Exile after 1933*, Berlin and Boston, MA: Walter de Gruyter, 55–79.
Young, R. (2014) 'Philosophy in Translation' in S. Berman and C. Porter (eds) *Companion to Translation Studies*, Chichester: John Wiley & Sons, 41–53.
Zach, N. (2007) 'Can Third Wave Feminism be Inclusive? Intersectionality, Its Problems and New Directions' in L. Alcoff and E. Kittay (eds), *The Blackwell Guide to Feminist Philosophy*, Oxford: Blackwell Publishing, 193–207.

21
Shelley's Plato

Ross Wilson

Introduction

This chapter considers translations of Platonic texts by the English poet, political campaigner, and essayist Percy Shelley (1792–1822). Two questions immediately arise. First, why Plato? The history of translations of Plato is, to be sure, rich terrain for the student of the relation between philosophy and translation because, in Plato's case, translation and philosophical reception are remarkably intertwined. Marsilio Ficino's translation into Latin of and commentary upon Plato's works, first printed in 1484, represents a crucial moment in the recuperation of Plato during the Renaissance (the 1588 text, published at Lyons, is available online: Ficino 1588). Ficino's revival of Platonism and Neo-Platonism via his translation and commentary was recuperative not only in the sense that it restored the esteem of Plato, long considered a mere precursor to Aristotle, whose pre-eminence over his teacher was marked during the Middle Ages: Ficino developed a version of Plato not straightforwardly or simply present in Plato's texts as they stood. Ficino's work was translation in the strict sense that it rendered Plato's writings into Latin, but also in the broader sense that the Platonic corpus was taken up and reinterpreted as part of the development of a new philosophical direction. Christopher S. Celenza puts the matter well when he states that

> Ficino lived in an era when interpretive exegesis represented a form of philosophical composition. [...] [His] enterprise of translation was as much designed to render the texts themselves from Greek into Latin as it was to translate Plato, and indeed the entire 'ancient theology' of which Plato had been the prime representative, into the cultural idiom of the late medieval and Renaissance world in which Ficino found himself.
> (Celenza 2015: §2.3)

While the first translation of Platonic dialogues into English seeks to emphasise in its 'Epistle Dedicatory' its endeavour to cut through differing interpretations of Plato's texts, including Ficino's (Anon 1675: vii–ix), Ficino was a vital source for Shelley (Nelson 2007: 101). Moreover, the first complete translation of Plato into English, undertaken by Thomas Taylor and incorporating earlier eighteenth-century translations by Floyer Sydenham, was deeply invested in the Neo-Platonic tradition (Taylor 1804). Translation was undertaken by Ficino and by Taylor in both the strict sense and in a much broader sense. Translation, for them, was not just the rendering of Plato's Greek into Latin, in Ficino's case, or English, in Taylor's, but involved in doing so the calibration of emphases, the deployment of idiom, and the flexing of terminology to advance a particular interpretative reading.

Translation in this broad yet vital sense is crucial to Plato's texts in themselves. As is well known, the majority of Plato's works revolve around the character (if that is the right word) of Socrates and his various interlocutors. As is likewise well known, the historical Socrates, inspirational teacher as he evidently was, nevertheless left no writing. So, Socrates' oral teaching undergoes translation by Plato into a medium that it did not originally countenance. Furthermore, translation in this sense – transference, quotation, reprising, even ventriloquism – is crucial on yet more layers to a number of Plato's dialogues. Both of the Platonic dialogues translated in full by Shelley – and it is upon these that this chapter will concentrate – concern translation in this broad sense, in one case explicitly (the *Ion*), in the other implicitly, by means of narrative framing (the *Symposium*). That Shelley should have chosen to translate the *Ion* is readily understandable. It is readily understandable on the simplest level because, along with Book X of the *Republic*, the *Ion* contains Plato's most thoroughgoing reflection on the status of poetry and its interpretation. Advancing a theory of inspiration and its mediation, the *Ion* suggests that poetic composition is the result of the transference – a key Shelleyan term (Hogle 1988) – of an original divine impulse from god to poet – and thence, in fact, to the poet's interpreters or 'rhapsodes'. Moreover, the *Ion*'s emphasis on the centrality to poetry of inspiration as opposed to learning accords somewhat with Shelley's ideal of poetry as, in the words of his poem 'To a Sky-Lark', 'profuse strains of unpremeditated art' (Shelley 2002: 304). It is important to remember that 'unpremeditated' is not the same as 'unmediated', which announces a difference from the view of poetry as wholly non-rational that Ion, in response to Socrates' questioning, subscribes to. It is also worth noting, by the way, that speech, expression, etc. are frequently described as 'unpremeditated' in Shelley's translations of Plato, including where such a translation stretches the meaning of the Greek: both Pausanias and Socrates in the *Symposium* describe their speeches on the topic of Love as 'unpremeditated' (Shelley 1930: 179 and 193), where the Greek differs in the two cases and in neither evokes the specifically psychological connotations of 'unpremeditated'.

The mechanism of translation – of the transference and transposition of inspiration from divine source to poetic recipient to rhapsodic interpreter – at work in the *Ion* is not only, however, the explicit subject-matter of Plato's dialogues, as it is in that dialogue. The narrative of the *Symposium* is framed in such a way as to remove the initial speaker, Apollodorus, from what he is narrating: he is recounting a recounted account of a conversation. Despite the temptation of seeing Plato as the self-appointed amanuensis of Socrates, this kind of distancing framing is prevalent in his work, such that many speakers are relaying what they have at second or third hand, and many narrative frames have fuzzy rather than sharp edges. Richard Hunter, in his commentary on the *Symposium*, attests to Plato's 'persistent concern to advertise and problematize the fictional status of his dialogues' (Hunter 2004: 22). The form that this concern takes in the *Symposium* in particular is a bewildering series of narrative transferrals. The narrator, Apollodorus, is in one sense not the narrator at all but the retailer, so to speak, of an already retold narrative. Developing a comparison between the *Symposium* and Homeric epic – representative works, one might imagine, on opposite sides of the ancient quarrel between poetry and philosophy (of which more later) – Stanley Rosen strikingly remarks that '[w]hereas Homer's song is guaranteed by the divine Muses, Plato's readers are dependent upon the memories of singularly unheroic disciples' (Rosen 1987: 6). Suspect as the poets may be from a Platonic perspective, Plato's narratives themselves are based on a still shakier foundation. And before we, the readers, presume that we at least are firmly anchored and clearly identified, it has to be recalled that we are hardly addressed directly, that we, rather, overhear the dialogue in its multiple layers.

Critical issues and topics

We will return to the specific difficulties of translating the *Symposium* when we turn to Shelley's own encounter with that text. Here it is necessary to emphasise that translation in the broad sense – of oral teaching into written work, of the narrative of one narrator into the mouth of another – is thus philosophically vital to Plato's dialogues. But we must not lose sight, of course, of the considerable philosophical significance of translation in the strict sense. In a wide-ranging essay, John Logie, for example, has tracked the influence of twentieth-century literary-theoretical considerations on the translation into English of a number of Plato's texts, chiefly the *Phaedrus*, the *Apology*, and the *Gorgias* (Logie 2004). The abstract to Logie's article claims that '[c]lose readings of passages addressing "books" and "authors" in 20th Century renditions of Plato's dialogues reveal highly variable translations' (Logie 2004: 47). The key terms of that claim, 'books' and 'authors' – both kept at arm's length with scare-quote tweezers – of course turn out to be highly provisional, since Logie is able to show that the translations, for example, of ποιητοῦ (poiētou) as 'author' or βιβλίον (biblion) as 'book' are not shared by all twentieth-century translators of Plato into English. (Logie focuses on English translations of Plato subsequent to Benjamin Jowett's, which, while not the first complete translation of Plato into English, remains a landmark in the modern reception of Plato in English (Marshall 1881 and Mustain [no date]).) Logie gives evidence from work in Greek philology and the history of the ancient world – especially Eric Havelock's seminal *Preface to Plato* (1963) – for the rejection of the identification of a βιβλίον (biblion) with (what we would recognise as) a book. But at the same time Logie seeks to base his examination of the translation of such terms in a much broader consideration of twentieth-century literary theory and history. He aims to show that the critique of the category of authorship is felt to necessitate different choices of translation where earlier in the century it was felt that 'author' would suffice. Logie points to groundbreaking historical work like Elisabeth Eisenstein's 1979 *The Printing Press as an Agent of Change* and the development of its thesis in the work of Martha Woodmansee, as well as to the literary-theoretical critique of authorial intentionality and writerly authority advanced by figures as different as W.K. Wimsatt and Monroe Beardsley, Roland Barthes, Jacques Derrida, and Michel Foucault. What Logie makes abundantly clear is that the history of twentieth-century translations of Plato can be closely tied to the history of twentieth-century reflection on questions of authorship and literary creation more broadly – questions that were, of course, already central to the Platonic corpus. Different possibilities in translation are allowed for by historical uncertainty concerning whether, for example, a βιβλίον (biblion) did or did not at all resemble what we call a book, but such uncertainties are not finally decisive without the influence of theoretical and philosophical considerations.

Less concerned with the influence on translations of Plato of, so to speak, external philosophical considerations, Christina Hoenig nevertheless focuses on a translational crux of central thematic concern in Plato's work. Emphasising the significance of Cicero's and Calcidius' interpretations of Plato, rather than of twentieth-century English translations as Logie does, Hoenig examines the meaning of εἰκος λόγος (eikos logos) in Plato's *Timaeus*. This phrase is especially important in the Platonic context in view of its usual translation as a 'probable' or 'likely' account and given Plato's concern to differentiate λόγοι (logoi), as it were, epistemologically. Echoing Logie's emphasis on the importance of philosophical and literary-theoretical positions in relation to specific questions of translation, Hoenig is able to show that the translation of εἰκώς λόγος (eikos logos) as *probabile* [probable] and *veri simile* [verisimilar] proffered by Cicero is testament to his own scepticism and hence to the sceptical character of his Platonism: the investigative method advocated by Cicero 'thus served to establish a viewpoint that was "probable" or "convincing"' (Hoenig 2013: paragraphs 14–15). In her somewhat more intricate account of the translation of εἰκος λόγος (eikos logos) by the fourth-century writer Calcidius, of whom very little is known (Reydams-Schils 2000), Hoenig nevertheless likewise emphasises that Calcidius' choice reflects a much broader set of philosophical commitments. So, in this case, Calcidius' rendering of εἰκος λόγος (eikos logos) as *mediocris explanatio* [middle, or even mundane, explanation] is explained by the prominence given in Calcidius' commentary on the *Timaeus* to the fact that its topic is physics rather than theology (Hoenig 2013: para 33). The *Timaeus* is thus found – that is to say, translated so as – to contain the systematic separation of physics and theology to which later Platonists, such as Calcidius, subscribe.

It is clear from Logie that late-twentieth-century cultural and intellectual history, as well as literary theory, have (gradually) disabled historically suspect translations. No more is Plato full of 'authors' and 'books' in the wake of Eisenstein, Barthes, and others. Hoenig, comparably, traces the translational choices of Cicero and Calcidius to their specific philosophical investments. Translations of Plato have involved, then, not just the translation of philosophy but also the philosophising of translation.

In turning to consider Shelley's reading and translating of Plato, moreover, we must also consider the degree to which Plato is not only a philosophical but also a literary or poetic writer. As we have already seen, the *Symposium*, the main text translated by Shelley, manipulates multiple narrative voices and perspectives; it is, in other words, literarily as well as philosophically virtuosic. Crucially, Shelley refused to recognise a distinction between philosophy and poetry:

> The distinction between poets and prose writers is a vulgar error. The distinction between philosophers and poets has been anticipated. Plato was essentially a poet – the truth and splendour of his imagery and the melody of his language is the most intense that it is possible to conceive. He rejected the measure of epic, dramatic, and lyrical forms, because he sought to kindle a harmony in thoughts divested of shape and action, and he forbore to invent any regular plan of rhythm which would include, under determinate forms, the various pauses of his style.
>
> (Shelley 2002: 514)

The otherwise near-identical opening two sentences of this passage effect between them a deft rhetorical twist in the chiastic inversion of 'poets'–'prose writers'–'philosophers'–'poets'. But then the real achievement of this verbal arrangement is, of course, precisely to make us wonder whether it is in fact a chiasmus: after all, both sentences question the too ready identification of 'prose writers' with 'philosophers' and, moreover, the differentiation of both from 'poets'. In any case, Shelley's description of Plato as 'essentially a poet' is not empty praise. Rather, Shelley specifies quite clearly that Plato is a poet thanks to his splendid imagery and, perhaps more significantly, the intensity of his linguistic melody, which, though it eschewed the metrical forms of particular poetic genres, is nevertheless strikingly rhythmical.

Shelley's estimation of Plato as a poet is, crucially, given in his 'A Defence of Poetry' (written 1821, first published 1840) very shortly after he expressed his scepticism with regard to translation. Contrary to the understanding of words as merely conventionally related to what they signify – promulgated, for instance, by John Locke – Shelley insists that sounds are related both to other sounds and to thoughts, before going on to declare that such relations make translation problematic:

> Hence the language of poets has ever affected a certain uniform and harmonious recurrence of sound, without which it were not poetry, and which is scarcely less indispensable to the communication of its influence, than the words themselves without reference to that peculiar order. Hence the vanity of translation; it were as wise to cast a violet into a crucible that you might discover the formal principle of its colour and odour, as seek to transfuse from one language into another the creations of a poet. The plant must spring again from its seed or it will bear no flower – and this is the burthen of the curse of Babel.
>
> (Shelley 2002: 514)

It might be objected that Shelley is talking here about poetic composition and that philosophical works would thus be exempt from this sceptical view of translation. Timothy Webb claims in the still standard treatment of Shelley and translation that '[s]o long as Shelley was concerned with communicating facts or ideas, translation was a perfectly adequate process' (Webb 1976: 24). But as we have just seen, Shelley's view of Plato (as Webb acknowledges) involves the suspension of a clear distinction between poetry and philosophy, as does, incidentally, his view of a quite different thinker, Francis Bacon (Shelley 2002: 514–15). Moreover, it is clear from Shelley's fragmentary reflection 'On Learning Languages' that 'facts' are not allied to 'ideas' but are as much juxtaposed to them, in all their variety, as to poetry:

> The generous and inspiring examples of philosophy and virtue you desire intimately to know and feel, not as mere facts detailing names and dates and motions of the human body, but clothed in the very language of the actors – that language dictated by and expressive of the passions or principles which governed their conduct. Facts are not what we want to know in poetry, in history, in the lives of individual men, in satire or in panegyric.
>
> (Shelley 1993: 164)

The lack of distinction between 'philosophy and virtue', on the one hand, and 'poetry', etc., on the other, is fundamental to Shelley's conception of the linguistic character of each discipline. But Shelley's avowal of the identity amongst philosophy, poetry, history, biography, satire, and panegyric, in opposition to 'facts', entails, for him, that works in translation are afflicted by 'worthless and miserable inadequacy', are 'undelightful and uninstructive', a situation for which the only remedy, Shelley tells the imagined recipient of his advice, is 'four years [. . .] to be consumed in the discipline of the antient languages, and those of modern Europe which you only imperfectly know' (Shelley 1993: 164).

In offering this advice, Shelley is likely developing an argument advanced by William Godwin in his essay 'Of the Study of the Classics', in which Godwin emphasises the necessity of knowing more than one language:

> But it is perhaps impossible to understand one language, unless we are acquainted with more than one. It is by comparison only that we can enter into the philosophy of

language. It is by comparison only that we separate ideas, and the words by which those ideas are ordinarily conveyed. It is by collating one language with another, that we detect all the shades of meaning through the various inflections of words, and all the minuter degradations of sense which the same word suffers, as it shall happen to be connected with different topics. He that is acquainted with only one language, will probably always remain in some degree the slave of language.

(Godwin 1797: 43)

The 'philosophy of language' is deftly poised between being philosophical reflection on language and the philosophy that belongs to language, that language makes possible. Godwin goes on to put it beyond doubt that his insistence on knowing various languages is not a concern so much with the capacity for framing utterance in them but with the development of the individual understanding:

He that is not able to call his idea by various names, borrowed from various languages, will scarcely be able to conceive his idea in a way precise, clear and unconfused. If therefore a man were confined in a desert island, and would never again have occasion so much as to hear the sound of his own voice, yet if at the same time he would successfully cultivate his understanding, he must apply himself to a minute and persevering study of words and language.

(Godwin 1797: 47)

Godwin's stress on the importance of learning languages – a salutary reminder in the context of twenty-first-century education policy in Anglophone countries – is, indeed, a precursor to Shelley's own insistence that serious study of multiple languages is necessary to access 'generous and inspiring examples of philosophy and virtue'. Godwin does not comment explicitly on translation, although it is plausible to suppose that his argument is subtended by the conviction that translations are unreliable and that, in particular, Classical works must be read in their original languages. And yet, in emphasising that it is 'by collating one language with another' that the fullest range of meaning is arrived at, Godwin's account necessitates active comparison between different languages.

Comparably, it would at first appear that Shelley's own translations of Plato fly in the face of his explicit critique of translation in 'A Defence of Poetry'. Like Godwin, he believes in the need to learn languages in order properly to access key literary and philosophical works. But also like Godwin, his privileging of language learning at the expense of translation is not perhaps as emphatic as it may initially appear. We should pause, that is, before categorising Shelley's remarks as involving an outright rejection of translation, vain as it may be in the case of poetry. Translation as transfusion is certainly to be rejected, as it had already been, incidentally, in the 'Epistle Dedicatory' to the first (anonymous) translation of Platonic dialogues (the *Apology* and the *Phaedo*) into English. There the translator emphasises her/his otherwise plain style but defends the occasional nod to elegance:

a Translator ought to be allowed competent liberty to use such words, phrases and figures of speech, as he shall judge most fit, as well to conserve the beauty and elegance of the original conception, as to symbolize and suit with the argument; and this lest his style become pedantique and flat, and the Matter it self be debased, as the best Wines lose their Spirit by transfusion from vessel to vessel.

(Anon 1675: xiii–xiv [no page numbers given in the text])

The teetotal Shelley may not have appreciated this comparison (it is highly unlikely, by the way, that he knew this translation; Notopoulos (1949: 30–6) gives an account of translations of Plato available to Shelley). Nevertheless, for Shelley, too, the image evoked by transfusion entails a view of the relation between intellectual content and linguistic expression that he rejects. But the concluding image to the passage in which Shelley remarks on 'the vanity of translation' suggests that the work of poets may be disseminated, so to speak, in languages other than its original: 'The plant must spring again from its seed or it will bear no flower – and this is the burthen of the curse of Babel'. The final phrase here is significantly ambiguous. On the one hand, 'the burthen of the curse of Babel' is simply the burdensome task of translation consequent upon God's decision to baffle the overweening collective projects of humanity. On the other hand, the context suggests a more promising reading: a 'burthen', or burden (of which the former is simply an old spelling), is also '[w]hat is borne by the soil; produce, crop' (*OED Online* 2016: 'burden/burthen, n.'), which, given that the metaphorical context ('seed', 'flower') is a horticultural one, allows for a distinctly positive view of the prospects for poetic transference between languages.

To be sure, the requirements for a successful translation are still extraordinarily high. Not everyone is capable of providing a suitable growing medium for the seed of poetry, as Shelley's remark, recorded by Thomas Medwin, would imply:

> There is no greater mistake than to suppose [. . .] that the knowledge of a language is all that is required in a translation. He must be a poet, and as great a one as his original, in order to do justice to him.
>
> (Medwin 1913, cited in Webb 1976: 26)

In the case of the *Symposium*, the bar for adequate translation would seem to have been set especially high. Writing over half a century after Shelley, Benjamin Jowett prefaced his translation of Plato's text with the following revealing observations:

> Some writings hardly admit of a more distinct interpretation than a musical composition; and every reader may form his own accompaniment of thought or feeling to the strain which he hears. The Symposium of Plato is a work of this character, and can with difficulty be rendered in any words but the writer's own. There are so many half-lights and cross-lights, so much of the colour of mythology, and of the manner of sophistry adhering – rhetoric and poetry, the playful and the serious, are so subtly intermingled in it, and vestiges of old philosophy so curiously blend with the germs of future knowledge, that agreement among interpreters is not to be expected.
>
> (Jowett 1892: 524)

In one way, the *Symposium* is superabundantly full, overflowing with mythology, rhetoric, poetry, old philosophy, and future knowledge. But in another way, in calling forth 'his own accompaniment of thought or feeling' from every reader, it seems to demand supplementation, never arriving at a definitive version. (Erik Satie's *Socrate*, incidentally, sets to music part of Alcibiades' praise of Socrates from Victor Cousin's translation of the *Symposium* (1822–4); Leonard Bernstein's *Serenade (after Plato's 'Symposium')* is an instrumental work.) Like Jowett, and as we would expect from Shelley's description of Plato as a poet, Shelley emphasises what we might envisage as the musicality of the *Symposium* and, again like Jowett, the difficulty with which – owing to that very musicality – it is translated. The first time he mentions his own translation he remarks in a letter to John and Maria Gisborne that

'I am employed just now having little better to do, in translating into my fainting & inefficient periods the divine eloquence of Plato's Symposium' (Shelley 1964: 20). In a later letter, this time to Leigh Hunt, Shelley reflects more broadly, and again negatively, on the enterprise of translation as such, and on this occasion anticipates the other metaphorical aspect of Jowett's description – namely, its emphasis on the colour and luminescence of the *Symposium*:

> With respect to translation, even I will not be seduced by it [. . .]. I have only translated the 'Cyclops' of Euripides when I could absolutely do nothing else – and the 'Symposium' of Plato, which is the delight and astonishment of all who read it; I mean the original, or so much of the original as is seen in my translation, not the translation itself.
>
> (Shelley 1964: 153)

It is high time to turn to Shelley's translation of the *Symposium* itself, the title of which he chose also, unusually, to translate (as *The Banquet*). Shelley's treatment has, of course, been subject to much discussion, including in Notopoulos' (1949) and Wallace's (1997) explorations of Shelley's Platonism and in O'Neill's (2004) and Nelson's (2007) extensive discussions of the *Symposium* translation itself. (Robinson's overview of Shelley's translations confines itself to his poetic translations, while acknowledging that his version of the *Symposium* was one of his 'most ambitious translations' (2006: 107).) Wallace testifies to the fact that, unlike earlier translators of Plato (see Taylor 1804), Shelley did not straighten, as it were, the amorous homosexual partnerships discussed in the dialogue by substituting female for male partners. Nevertheless, he was keen to downplay the role of physical attraction between men, rendering their relationships much more intellectual than they are at points in Plato. As Wallace comments, 'it is revealing that even in a translation which flaunts its grainy realism and documentary objectivity, elements of authorial censorship and bowdlerization are evident' (Wallace 1997: 106). O'Neill offers a strongly appreciative reading of 'one of [Shelley's] most intricate and still relatively neglected masterpieces' (O'Neill 2009: 67), drawing attention to the delicacy and ingenuity of Shelley's prose in his translation of Plato. Emphasising Shelley's responsive and yet creative impulse in contrast, in particular, to Jowett's somewhat more 'plodding' translation (ibid.: 57), what is central for O'Neill's estimation is the fact that 'Shelley is alive in his translation to Plato's overall scenario of philosophical quest' (ibid.: 61). O'Neill certainly has an eye to the relation of Shelley's text to Plato's Greek, but the most thorough account of Shelley's individual translational (and mistranslational) choices is Nelson (2007). Nelson, like O'Neill, appreciates Shelley's translation as the work of a masterful writer but also as the 'culmination' of a tradition of Neo-Platonism stretching back through Thomas Taylor to Plotinus (also translated by Taylor) and Ficino, on whom Shelley frequently relied in composing his translation. In particular, Nelson ascribes the success of Shelley's translation to its recognition of the importance of the interplay in the *Symposium* between 'concrete detail and abstract ideals' (Nelson 2007: 102), an interplay that is the result of Shelley's Neo-Platonic tendencies, whereby the transcendent is emphasised, counterpoised by the materialism with which his idealism is tempered. The bulk of Nelson's treatment, however, focuses on Shelley's various omissions, additions, and alterations, of which she provides a fairly comprehensive catalogue. Hence there are 'shortcuts and mistranslations', many of them the result of Shelley translating Ficino instead of Plato, many others imaginative embellishments of Shelley's own, and some simple errors and instances of carelessness (ibid.: 105–10); there are also, of course, 'bowdlerizations' (ibid.: 110–16), already attested, as we saw, by Wallace (1997: 106); and then there is the intriguing category of Shelley's attempts to dignify Plato's humour (Nelson 2007: 116–21).

The most significant of these, perhaps, is a result of Shelley's 'enthusiasm' for the poetically inclined Agathon, whom Plato frequently sees, as Nelson persuasively argues, as funny. I follow Nelson's practice (2007: 120) in the quotation below of printing Shelleyan additions to this description of Love in bold, taking the text of the *Symposium* from Plato (1925) and citing it hereafter according to Stephanus references (in this case, 197e) rather than page numbers:

> the best, the loveliest [omitting ἡγεμὼν (hēgemōn), 'leader']; in whose footsteps everyone ought to follow, celebrating him excellently in song, and bearing each his part **in that divinest harmony** which Love sings **to all things which live and are**, soothing the troubled minds of Gods and men.
>
> (Shelley 1930: 192)

The matter of Shelley's omission can be dealt with fairly easily, though Nelson does not address it. Shelley, that is, may well have thought that 'in whose footsteps everyone ought to follow' makes sufficiently clear that Love is to be followed, without making Love (as Plato admittedly does) a ἡγεμὼν [hēgemōn], which Shelley may well have wished to avoid in the post-revolutionary context in which he wrote, although 'hegemon' itself is first attested in English in 1829, seven years after Shelley's death, and 'hegemony', though attested in 1567, does not take hold in English until later in the nineteenth century (*OED Online* 2016: 'hegemon, n.' and 'hegemony, n.'). Shelley's 'in that divinest harmony' adds a further layer of desription and evaluation to ᾠδῆς [ōdēs] (Plato 1925: 197e), 'song' or 'ode', and 'to all things which live and are' both anticipates the πάντων θεῶν τε καὶ ἀνθρώπων [pantōn theōn te kai anthrōpōn] ('all things divine and human') in the following clause, reinforcing the importance of the audience for Love's song to this passage, as well as introducing a characteristically Shelleyan concern with the nature of, and potential differences between, living and being (Wilson 2013).

In addition to those departures from, or tendentious renderings of, Plato identified by Nelson, we may, to be sure, consider that Shelley's 'private person' (Shelley 1930: 172, 188) for ἰδώτην [idōtēn] (Plato 1925: 178d) seems to betray an understanding of the relation between persons and the state schooled by social-contract theory and hence is somewhat anachronistically deployed in the Platonic context. Likewise, while it is necessary to translate ἰατρικῆς [iatrikēs] (ibid.: 176d) so as to mark it out as 'medicine' in the general, disciplinary sense rather than in the sense of a remedy or drug (φάρμακον [pharmakon]), Shelley's 'science of medicine' (Shelley 1930: 169) perhaps indulges his early-nineteenth-century enthusiasm for the emergence of medicine as a science in a recognisably modern sense – somewhat at the expense, here, of Eryxmachus' emphasis specifically on practice. And to say that through Love 'the Muses discovered the arts of literature' (ibid.: 191) is a tendentious rendering of Μοῦσαι μοθσικῆς (Mousai mothsikēs) (Plato 1925: 158) – which I think we can probably forgive the poet.

Of course, each of these in some ways questionable renditions is at the same time forgivable, as are those (as she acknowledges) catalogued by Nelson. I want to focus, however, on one instance of a Shelleyan translation that Nelson views as a 'shortcut' with regard to a contrast difficult to render in English (and which I have discussed briefly elsewhere (Wilson 2013: 10–11). In his speech on Love, Phaedrus has been arguing that an army comprised of mutual lovers would be especially effective because those in love would prefer any pain or hardship to suffering disgrace in the eyes of their beloved. He cites in particular the Homeric example of Achilles, who not only avenged and honoured 'his beloved Patroclus' (Shelley 1930: 173; Plato 1925: 105 opts for the less euphemistic 'his lover Patroclus' for τῷ ἐραστῇ Πατρόκλῳ [tō erastē Patroklō]) to the extent that he was willing 'not to die for him merely, but to disdain and reject that life which he had ceased to share' (Shelley 1930: 173). Nelson (2007: 106) sees this as an evasion of the difficulty raised in Plato's text by the distinction between ὑπεραποθανεῖν [huperapothanein] and ἐπαοθανεῖν [epaothanein], which she, in circumlocutory mode, renders as the difference between 'not only to die for him [as he might have, were Patroclus alive]' and 'even to die after him who had already deceased' (ibid.). For Nelson, Shelley shifts the emphasis to Achilles' emotional state, adding 'a vivid sense of "disdain" not present in the Greek' (ibid.). But this is to rush, rather, to a decision about what is present in the Greek, when the meaning of the distinction between ὑπεραποθανεῖν [huperapothanein] and ἐπαοθανεῖν [epaothanein] is precisely what is at issue. Shelley's solution need by no means be viewed as a shortcut or a deflection of a difficult translation into mere characterisation, however colourful; it may just as well be the result of serious philosophical reflection on why someone should wish to sacrifice himself for his friend when that friend is already dead. To Lear's fundamental and intractable question at the end of a play Shelley esteemed as 'the most perfect specimen of the dramatic art existing in the world' (Shelley 2002: 519) – 'Why should a dog, a horse, a rat, have life, / And thou no breath at all?' (Shakespeare 1997: 5.3. 282–3) – Shelley, effectively, has Achilles add 'And why should I?'. Reflection on the question that Lear asks is helpful, in fact, for the translational difficulty that Shelley is facing. One potential consquence of Lear's despairing question is the realisation that since it is now had by creatures such as dogs, horses, and rats, rather than his beloved daughter, life itself is diminished and hardly worth the living. Indeed, the conception of friendship adumbrated in Plato's works is a key concern for Shelley. In a rare moment of explict criticism of Plato, Shelley makes the following comment in his translation of a short passage on grief from the *Republic*:

> Do we assert that an excellent man will consider it anything dreadful that his intimate friend, who is also an excellent man, should die? – By no means, (*an excessive refinement*).
> (Shelley 1930: 261)

Shelley's parenthetical response to Plato here is in keeping with his translation of the *Symposium*, in that it registers Shelley's own interest in friendship but recognises the centrality of this concern to Plato's philosophy. Shelley also criticises here the excessively unemotional manliness advocated at this point of the *Republic*. It thereby brings out a real distinction between these different moments in Plato's work, to which Shelley was acutely alive as both reader and translator of that philosopher–poet.

Future directions

There are two main 'future directions' that this chapter might end by pointing out. First, of course, translations of Plato into English have been legion since Shelley's effort and show no sign of abating. Since there have been many excellent translations of Plato's dialogues, with different interpretative emphases and approaches to translation, this is a good thing. I briefly discussed Jowett above, but in the last thirty years alone there have been seven translations of the *Symposium* into English: Nehamas and Woodruff (1989); Allen (1991); Sharon (1998); Waterfield (1994); Benardete (2001); Gill (1999); and Howatson (2008). Those by Nehamas and Woodruff (1989) and Waterfield (1994) have attracted particular praise (see Hunter (2004: 137) and, on Waterfield, Pender (1995)). Rowe's (1998) edition, like the Loeb Classical editions, is a facing-page translation with extensive notes and commentary. Moreover, as we have seen, interest in the history of the translation of Plato has increased, especially as part of the exploration of the Neo-Platonic tradition, but there is still much work to do here, despite the helpful and suggestive interventions of Logie (2004) on twentieth-century translations into English and Hoenig (2013) on later Classical receptions and translations of Plato. One direction that work might take is comparative: to consider the different stakes and strategies of translations of Plato into different languages, in different national and literary contexts. Comparison of Schleiermacher's (1817–28) and Cousin's translations of Plato with Taylor's, Shelley's, and even Jowett's would not only entail a rich account of the different philosophical priorities at work in these authorships and literary/national contexts but would enable a broad comparative account of philosophical translation to be developed.

What of Shelley in particular? Recent years, again, have brought a marked increase in work on his translations. Perhaps the most promising direction for future work on Shelley and translation is in fact that suggested by Robinson (2006), who, however, explicitly excludes the *Symposium* translation from his consideration. Robinson claims that '[a] careful reading of Shelley's translations in relation to his own poems, in fact, may lead one to posit "translation", for him, as the essential visionary act of poetry itself and perhaps a definition of Shelley's Romantic poetics' (2006: 108). But there is significant evidence, some of it cited by Robinson himself (e.g., on Wordsworth; 2006: 105), that such a view of translation was important not just for Shelley but for other Romantic writers; and, further, as we have seen in this chapter, translation was not just important for Romantic poetry and poetics but for philosophy more widely. Promising indications notwithstanding, there is still considerable progress to be made in investigating these avenues.

Related topics

Schleiermacher; the translation of philosophical texts; literary translation; mysticism, esotericism and translation.

Further reading

Hoenig, C. (2013), 'Εικὼς λόγος: Plato in Translation(s)', *Methodos*, 13, doi: 10.4000/methodos.2994. Available at: http://methodos.revues.org/2994 [accessed: 15 July 2016]. (This article focuses on the different translations of the phrase εικὼς λόγος (eikōs logos) from Plato's *Timaeus* in Cicero and Calcidius. From this deliberately narrow starting point, Hoenig then helpfully draws out the different philosophical priorities of Cicero and Calcidius and the degree to which they are reflected in their translational decisions.)

Logie, J. (2004), 'Lost in Translation: The Influence of 20th Century Literary Theory on Plato's Texts', *Rhetoric Society Quarterly*, 34 (1): 47–71. (Logie's article argues that translations of Plato into English in the twentieth century have clearly been affected by changing views concerning authorship. Focusing in particular on cultural history and literary theory, Logie carefully tracks changing priorities through a number of twentieth-century translations of Platonic texts.)

Mustain, J. [no date], *A Brief History of Translations: The Development of Translations into the English Language, Especially of the Works of Plato*, Palo Alto, CA: Stanford University. Available at: www.hermes-press.com/translations1a.htm [accessed: 12 July 2016]. (A useful and brief account of the history of translations of Plato in England and into English by the Curator of Rare Books at Stanford University. Informative about the first authentic translation of Platonic dialogues into English, as well as subsequent translations.)

Nelson, S. (2007), 'Shelley and Plato's *Symposium*: The Poet's Revenge', *International Journal of the Classical Tradition*, 14 (1/2): 100–29. (This is a thorough treatment of Shelley's departures from the Greek in his translation of the *Symposium*. Nelson does not merely censure Shelley's questionable translations, however, but accounts for them under a number of different headings (shortcuts, embellishments, and the like). Helpfully gives the relevant passages of Greek along with the sections of the Shelley text under discussion.)

O'Neill, M. (2009), 'Emulating Plato: Shelley as Translator and Prose Poet'. In A.M. Weinberg, and T. Webb, eds. *The Unfamiliar Shelley*, Farnham: Ashgate, pp. 239–56. (Along with O'Neill's earlier article (2002), this chapter in an important book on hitherto relatively neglected aspects of Shelley's authorship is a signal treatment of Shelley's Plato from a leading contemporary Shelleyan. O'Neill offers an appreciative close reading of Shelley's translation of the *Symposium* and argues for the importance of Shelley's Platonic translations to his work as a whole.)

References

Allen, R.E. (tr) (1991), *The Symposium*, New Haven, CT: Yale University Press.

Anon. (tr) (1675), *Plato his Apology of Socrates, and Phædo or Dialogue Concerning the Immortality of Mans Soul, and the Manner of Socrates his Death: Carefully Translated from the Greek, and Illustrated by Reflections Upon Both the Athenian Laws, and Ancient Rites and Traditions Concerning the Soul, therein Mentioned*, London: Printed by T.R. & N.T. for James Magnes and Richard Bentley.

Benardete, S. (tr) (2001), *Plato's Symposium*, Chicago: University of Chicago Press.

Celenza, C.S. (2015), 'Marsilio Ficino'. In E.N. Zalta, ed. *The Stanford Encyclopedia of Philosophy*, Palo Alto, CA: Stanford University. Available at: http://plato.stanford.edu/archives/sum2015/entries/ficino/ [accessed: 12 July 2016].

Cousin, V. (tr) (1822–4), *Oeuvres de Platon*, Paris: Bossanges frères et al, vol. 13.

Ficino, M. (1588), *Divini Platonis Opera Omnia*, Lugduni [Lyons].

Gill, C. (1999), *The Symposium*, London: Penguin.

Godwin, W. (1797), *The Enquirer: Reflections on Education, Manners, and Literature*, London: Printed for G.G. and J. Robinson.

Havelock, E. (1963), *Preface to Plato*, Oxford: Blackwell.

Hoenig, C. (2013), 'Εικὼς λόγος: Plato in Translation(s)', *Methodos*, 13, doi: 10.4000/methodos.2994. Available at: http://methodos.revues.org/2994 [accessed: 15 July 2016].

Hogle, J.E. (1988), *Shelley's Process: Radical Transference and the Development of His Major Works*, Oxford: Oxford University Press.

Howatson, M.C. (2008), *The Symposium*, Cambridge: Cambridge University Press.

Hunter, R. (2004), *Plato's 'Symposium'*, Oxford: Oxford University Press.

Jowett, B. (tr) (1892), *The Dialogues of Plato* [third edition], Oxford: Clarendon Press, vol. 1.

Logie, J. (2004), 'Lost in Translation: The Influence of 20th Century Literary Theory on Plato's Texts', *Rhetoric Society Quarterly*, 34 (1): 47–71.

Marshall, E. (1881), 'Translations of Plato', *Notes and Queries*, s6–IV (101): 454.

Mustain, J. [no date], *A Brief History of Translations: The Development of Translations into the English Language, Especially of the Works of Plato*. Palo Alto, CA: Stanford University. Available at: www.hermes-press.com/translations1a.htm [accessed: 12 July 2016].

Nehamas, A. and Woodruff, P. (trs) (1989), *Symposium*, Indianapolis: Hackett.

Nelson, S. (2007), 'Shelley and Plato's *Symposium*: The Poet's Revenge', *International Journal of the Classical Tradition*, 14 (1/2): 100–29.

Notopoulos, J. (1949), *The Platonism of Shelley: A Study of Platonism and the Poetic Mind*, Durham, NC: Duke University Press.

OED Online (2016), Oxford: Oxford University Press. Available at: www.oed.com/ [accessed: 12 July 2016].

O'Neill, M. (2004), '"The Whole Mechanism of the Drama": Shelley's Translation of the *Symposium*', *Keats–Shelley Review*, (18): 51–67.

O'Neill, M. (2009), 'Emulating Plato: Shelley as Translator and Prose Poet'. In A.M. Weinberg and T. Webb, eds. *The Unfamiliar Shelley*, Farnham: Ashgate, pp. 239–56.

Pender, E. (1995), 'Review of Robin Waterfield (tr)', *Symposium: A New Translation, The Classical Review*, 45(2): 437.

Plato (1925), 'Symposium', tr by W.R.M. Lamb, *Plato III: Lysis, Symposium, Gorgias*, Cambridge, MA: Harvard University Press, pp. 80–245.

Reydams-Schils, G. (2000), 'Calcidius'. In L.P. Gerson, ed. *The Cambridge History of Philosophy in Late Antiquity*, pp. 498–508. Available from: Cambridge Histories, doi: 10.1017/CHOL9780521764407.034 [accessed: 13 July 2016].

Robinson, J. (2006), 'The Translator'. In T. Morton, ed. *The Cambridge Companion to Shelley*, Cambridge: Cambridge University Press, pp. 104–22.

Rosen, S. (1987), *Plato's 'Symposium'* [second edition], New Haven, CT: Yale University Press.

Schleiermacher, F.D.E. (tr) (1817–28), *Platons Werke*, Berlin: In der Realschulbuchhandlung, vol. 3.

Shakespeare, W. (1997), *The Riverside Shakespeare* [second edition], ed. by G. Blakemore Evans *et al.* Boston: Houghton Mifflin.

Sharon, A. (tr) (1998), *Plato's Symposium*, Newburyport, MA: Focus.

Shelley, P. (1930), 'The Banquet of Plato'. In R. Ingpen and W.E. Peck, eds. *The Complete Works of Percy Bysshe Shelley*, vol. 7, New York: Gordian Press, pp. 163–220.

Shelley, P. (1964), *The Letters of Percy Bysshe Shelley*, ed. F.L. Jones, Oxford: Clarendon Press, vol. 1.

Shelley, P. (1993), 'On Learning Languages [written 1816; first published 1840]'. In E.B. Murray, ed. *The Prose Work of Percy Bysshe Shelley*, Oxford: Oxford University Press, vol. 1, p. 164.

Shelley, P. (2002). 'A Defence of Poetry [written 1821; first published 1840]'. In D.H. Reiman and N. Fraistat, eds. *Shelley's Poetry and Prose: Authoritative Texts, Criticism* [second edition], New York: Norton, pp. 478–508.

Taylor, T. (tr) (1804), *The Works of Plato, viz. his Fifty-Five Dialogues, and Twelve Epistles, Translated from the Greek; Nine of the Dialogues by the Late Floyer Sydenham, and the Remainder by Thomas Taylor*, London: Printed for Thomas Taylor, by R. Wilks, and sold by E. Jeffery, and R.H. Evans.

Wallace, J. (1997), *Shelley and Greece: Rethinking Romantic Hellenism*, Houndmills: Palgrave.

Waterfield, R. (tr) (1994), *Symposium*, Oxford: Oxford University Press.

Webb, T. (1976), *The Violet in the Crucible: Shelley and Translation*, Oxford: Clarendon Press.

Wilson, R. (2013), *Shelley and the Apprehension of Life*, Cambridge: Cambridge University Press.

22
Translating Kant and Hegel

Nicholas Walker

Introduction

In the Hegelian tradition of thought all appeals to immediacy, to the immediately given, are often regarded as a forgetting – as a kind of natural illusion that arises from the deceptive familiarity in which all previous material and cultural labour has sunk into oblivion or quasi-oblivion. This also applies to the often unregarded or underappreciated hermeneutic labour of intellectual mediation and transmission that is 'translation'. In this regard it is possible to forget or ignore the achievements which have already helped to build up a tradition of reception, one from which we can learn, with which we can engage and productively disagree. And it is equally possible to forget the distinctive challenges confronted by pioneers in an intellectual terrain that was once unfamiliar and in some respects profoundly alien. Indeed the linguistic acclimatization or incorporation of the foreign may eventually appear so successful that it acquires a spurious self-evidence which lets us forget we are dealing with mediated texts at all.

Peter France has pointed out that 'ordinary readers and students of literature' all too often

> act as if in reading a translation they were reading – perhaps with some loss of intensity – the original. (In the same way, it is not unknown for philosophers to discuss the ideas of Descartes or Kant as if they had written in English).
>
> (2000: xx)

It might be argued that philosophers, especially those for whom hermeneutics is still a largely unknown country, are particularly prone to this illusion, and this in spite of the assumption that what Richard Rorty called the 'linguistic turn' has exercised an irreversible effect on almost all contemporary thought. In this connection it is curious to note that although recent years have seen a proliferation of 'dictionaries' and 'handbooks' dedicated to specific authorships, these sometimes give little or no information about the original vocabulary of the thinker concerned. This can easily lead to vague and potentially confusing generalizations based on the conflation of quite different terms in different authorships.[1]

In a standard reference work we read under the first entry 'abandonment': 'A rhetorical term used by existentialist philosophers such as Heidegger and Sartre to describe the absence of any sources of ethical authority external to oneself [...]' (Honderich 1995: 1). This is a possible though certainly contestable translation of one of a number of different terms (sometimes themselves translations or purported equivalents) used by different philosophers in different languages (*die Geworfenheit, la déréliction, l'abandono, thrownness* etc.). The inevitable compression required by such generalizations (and the entry offers an excellent succinct account of what is indeed a central issue in modern continental philosophy) immediately alerts us to the intertextuality which is as characteristic of philosophical texts as it is of 'literary' ones – though whether the language of those whom A. J. Ayer once described as 'novelist philosophers' is ultimately more 'rhetorical' in a pejorative sense than that of logical positivism or analytical philosophy is another question.

Translating Kant

If we begin at the beginning, in the first few decades of the nineteenth century, before any kind of translation tradition has been established, we can see that the earliest translators in some ways enjoyed certain advantages over their successors. The relative lack of temporal distance between the publication of the original works and the earliest attempts to translate them meant it was possible to presuppose certain shared expectations with regard to literary and intellectual cultural products in a 'contemporary' period in spite of the differing vernaculars in which the relevant works of thought or literature found initial expression. Thus a sensitivity to register favoured the 'elevated' style that was deemed appropriate for works of serious import in the field of philosophy, religion, and the sciences in general. This sense of rhetorical formality – compared with the less varied and more informal styles favoured today – may appear particularly unfamiliar and disconcerting to modern readers. The relative proximity of the earliest translations to the works they rendered also allowed for the ready reproduction of a variety of other textual features, over and above tone and register, which are now often regarded as adaptable at will to much more recent and increasingly standardized conventions of print style, layout, orthography, and punctuation, many of which are dictated by largely commercial considerations.

We have to speak of 'relative' proximity here since there may be considerable distance between distinct literary and philosophical cultures which inevitably affects the character and rapidity of the reception of foreign works of whatever genre. This is particularly relevant for the Anglophone reception of Kant on account of the significant historical differences within the European 'Enlightenment' (a word with an interesting history of its own that significantly post-dates – like the expression 'German Idealism' – the period of modern European culture to which it is usually applied). The earlier phase of the German Enlightenment was associated with the names of Leibniz, Wolff, and Baumgarten, and indeed the later phase associated with contemporaries of Kant himself, such as Lessing and Moses Mendelssohn, was strongly marked by a metaphysical rationalism rooted in the Aristotelianism of the 'Schools' and a critical but sympathetic relation to the tradition of natural theology and natural-law jurisprudence. This contrasts significantly with both the style and substance of the principal French and British contributions to Enlightenment thought. In Britain the leading figures of the empiricist tradition after Bacon typically espoused the vernacular tongue as an eloquent medium of philosophical expression (though Hobbes also published in Latin to ensure a continental readership), eschewing or radically adapting the use of the older technical and scholastic terminology with its plethora of definitions and demonstrations. Such language remained strongly associated with the established forms of religious thought and natural theology still propagated in a university context but towards which those empiricist thinkers who largely worked outside of academic institutions and adopted a strongly naturalistic approach were sceptical or expressly hostile. Kant's mature philosophy, from 1781 onwards, can naturally be regarded as an attempted mediation between the competing claims of the rationalist and empiricist traditions, while rejecting their common premise that there was essentially one primary source of knowledge (whether reason or sensible experience). Although his position was radically sceptical or destructive in relation to the pretensions of traditional metaphysics, it emphatically upheld our 'metaphysical interest' in the ultimate questions of morality and religion in a quite new way. The twofold thrust of Kant's project finds exemplary expression in his claim that while his new approach provides definitive justification for the truth claims of scientific knowledge in relation to the empirical world, it simultaneously counters 'that unbelief [...] which wars against morality' and enjoys 'the inestimable benefit that all objections to morality and religion will be forever silenced' since 'critique alone can sever the root of materialism, fatalism, atheism, free-thinking, fanaticism, and superstition' (B xx; B xxxi; B xxxiv). The sometimes baroque mode of expression in which Kant formulated his critical philosophy could hardly be more different from that of the great empiricists, for in developing his new approach Kant drew heavily on an established lexicon of philosophical terminology and subscribed to a demanding conception of philosophy as a systematic 'Science' par excellence – a complete interrelated body of grounding principles rather than an author aggregate of empirical findings or isolated claims (B 860) – while radically recasting that tradition and redeploying established terms in new ways, as with the word 'transcendental' itself, now specifically defined by Kant in contrast with the tradition of dogmatic or 'transcendent' metaphysics (A 11–A 12). Kant was well aware of the abstruse and seemingly scholastic character of his own language and of the considerable problems it caused to his first German readers and some of the leading minds of the age. These difficulties of style and substance are proverbial. J. B. Barnard, the first translator of the third *Critique* into English, confessed to finding the style of the work 'repulsive' and added: 'Kant was never careful of style, and in his later years he became more and more enthralled by those technicalities and refined distinctions which deter so many from the Critical Philosophy' and which 'encumber every page, and [...] are a constant source of embarrassment to the unhappy translator' (Kant 1892: x) In an expository work which appeared only a few years after the first *Critique* and appears to have received Kant's imprimatur the author writes:

> With respect to both the novelty and treatment of its subject matter, this work is wholly original and with respect to the penetrating acuteness of mind and almost inaccessible profundity which characterizes it throughout, it is almost the only one of its kind. [...] Nevertheless this important work has the peculiar fate that almost everyone complains about its impenetrable obscurity and unintelligibility.
>
> (Schultz [1785] 1995: 3)

And no doubt thinking of distinguished contemporaries such as Moses Mendelssohn, he added that 'even for the majority of the learned public it is as if it consisted solely of hieroglyphs' (ibid.: 5). It must also be remembered that the use of the German vernacular for the expression of complex scientific and philosophical thought was a relatively recent development, for Kant's great predecessors such as Leibniz and Wolff had availed themselves of French or Latin for their most serious writings, intended for a broad European readership, and Kant himself had earlier published a number of substantial works in Latin. The language of the 'Schools', and Kant's considerable knowledge and deep appreciation of Latin literature more generally, had left an indelible mark on his own idea of a philosophical prose, which was never intended to emulate a 'popular' style. (It seems appropriate that the earliest recorded translation of the first *Critique* was a Latin version of the text.[2]) Not only do juridical metaphors famously play a crucial role in Kant's conception of a self-instituted 'tribunal of reason', but his concentrated mode of expression, so anxious to avoid possible ambiguity and include the requisite qualifications at every point in order to ensure the necessary precision, has almost nothing to compare with it in a modern context outside the genre of the 'law report' (Heine called this Kant's 'chancellery language').

When the young Arthur Schopenhauer first visited Britain in 1803, and on subsequent visits as an independent man of letters, he was singularly unimpressed by the contemporary intellectual culture. Although we might not instantly think of Schopenhauer as a typical Enlightenment spirit, he found a country 'wrapped in an Egyptian darkness', too influenced by ecclesiastical institutions and respectful of religious orthodoxy, and scandalously unfamiliar with the groundbreaking thought of 'Father Kant', as German writers were already describing the founder of the Critical Philosophy in the early nineteenth century. He even proposed to remedy this lamentable situation by offering to translate Kant's first *Critique* and several other key texts into English himself, or at least to collaborate on such a project with an English-speaking scholar. With remarkable optimism and faith in his own linguistic abilities Schopenhauer offered in 1829 to translate the first *Critique*, the *Prolegomena*, and the third *Critique*, estimating he would be able to complete the *Prolegomena* in three months and the *Critique of Pure Reason* in a year, including explanatory notes of his own. Although this never came to pass, it might have been instructive to see how Schopenhauer would translate the term *Vorstellung* – variously rendered in the nineteenth century as 'idea', 'presentation', or 'representation' – which is so central both to Kant's work and his own. In fact the reception and translation of Kant's writings had begun many years before, albeit in an understandably tentative and intermittent way, and well before any of the three *Critiques* were available in English.[3] It is worth noting that the earliest translations focused on Kant's moral and religious thought (such as the *Groundwork for the Metaphysics of Morals* and *Religion within the Bounds of Reason Alone*) – although these texts are obviously difficult to interpret precisely without constant reference to the foundations laid out in detail in the first two *Critiques* in particular – and even included certain pre-critical works that reflect a radically superseded stage in the evolution of Kant's thought (such as *The Only Possible Ground for the Demonstration of the Existence of God* of 1762, which was translated in 1836 and appeared together with a version of Kant's important critical text of 1783, the *Prolegomena to Any Future Metaphysics*). The relative delay in translated reception of the foundational critical works of Kant, especially the first *Critique*, which appeared nearly fifty years after its original publication in 1781, is significant in light of the fact that at the beginning of the nineteenth century knowledge of German was not at all common amongst the educated classes or those with specific interests in philosophy, theology, natural science, or in the emerging disciplines (anthropology, history of myth and religion, historical linguistics and comparative philology) that would only come to be regarded as 'cultural sciences' over a century later (not least under the influence of German hermeneutic philosophy, strongly marked by Kantian and post-Kantian idealism). It was mainly through the efforts of literary figures such as Coleridge, Scott, and Carlyle that German literature and philosophy was mediated to British culture in the first instance. In George Eliot's *Middlemarch*, set around 1830, the Reverend Casaubon, of the older generation, laboured on ancient and classical sources in his fruitless quest for 'the key to all mythologies', but a decade or two later he would also have been poring over the works of the Schlegel brothers, Wilhelm von Humboldt, Friedrich Creuzer, Jacob Grimm, and Schelling.

When the early translators approached Kant's dense and terminologically complex texts for the first time, it was not as if the philosophical English of the day offered no appropriate resources for the task. (It is worth remembering, however, that many of the philosophical terms and descriptive labels so common today were either completely unknown, extremely rare, or used in quite different senses in the late eighteenth and early nineteenth century: 'epistemology', 'theory of knowledge', 'philosophy of mind', 'philosophy of religion', 'heteronomy', 'rationalism', 'realism', and even 'idealism' – the latter coming into use largely as a result of Kantian and post-Kantian German philosophy.) It was possible to take over or adapt much of the existing philosophical language, ascribing some new and quite specific meanings in the Kantian context to words such as 'idea', 'intuition', 'perception', 'cognition', 'representation', 'understanding', and 'apperception'. Certain older equivalents, perhaps surprising to us today, such as 'perception' or 'forms of perception' for *Anschauung* and *Anschauungsformen*, which do not precisely capture Kant's distinctions (between sensuous intuition itself, sensations in particular, and the more advanced conceptual level of perception), result from the fact that established meanings did not always sit well with Kant's usage – 'intuition' often being understood in the sense of direct intellectual apprehension of self-evident truths or as a kind of 'contemplation' or visual 'beholding', whereas *Anschauung* in Kant, with reference to *human* experience, refers to hyletic data of all kinds and the dimension of receptivity or sensibility itself. The word 'idea' could be detached from its psychologistic and empiricist use and restricted to a new specific sense (with the requisite Platonic echoes) and the general word 'representation' deployed, amongst other things, for the 'ideas and impressions' dear to the empiricist tradition. Some early commentators recommended the long-established word 'intellect' as a translation of Kant's *Verstand* as distinct from 'reason' in its highest sense (*Vernunft* as the faculty of the unconditioned), which was not in itself implausible since earlier thinkers had often distinguished lower and higher senses of the rational faculty in a *metaphysical* context. But given Kant's debt to the empiricist tradition and Hume in particular and his rejection of the traditional metaphysical conception of reason altogether, it was not so surprising that most translators and commentators adopted the cognate word 'understanding' for the ordinary exercise of our human cognitive powers in relation to perceptual experience (and Kant constantly uses words such as *Menschenverstand* and *Menschenwesen* in the specifically critical context).

A key question in translating a writer such as Kant is the need to establish a consistent and perspicuous set of lexical equivalents for the numerous essential concepts that are defined contrastively with one another (intuition and concept, transcendent and transcendental, thinking and knowing) and are expressly deployed in a precise sense that cannot adequately be captured by recourse to a variety of ordinary words with an inevitably indeterminate semantic range. In some ways Kant was deliberately conservative when it came to employing an established philosophical terminology, even when he intended to bestow a new significance on such traditional terms. Thus he did not favour the deliberate creation of neologisms or the resuscitation of archaic forms if the inherited terminology could be adapted appropriately.[4] This does not mean, however, that he was at all unaware of the rich resources of so-called 'ordinary' language (a problematic enough concept in itself, but here understood to mean language that has not been terminologically regularized or methodically stipulated) or indeed of powerfully affective or religious language, especially when it came to discriminating phenomenologically between subtly different but closely related forms of experience in the context of ethics and aesthetics – for example, words such as *Neigung* (inclination), *Gesinnung* (disposition), *Achtung* (respect), *Ehrfurcht* (reverence), *Geheimnis* (mystery), *das Angenehme* (the agreeable), *Wohlgefallen* (delight), and *Gunst* (favour).

The first complete English translation of Kant's first *Critique*, by Francis Haywood, appeared anonymously in 1838 and in a second revised version under the translator's name in 1848. This was a conscientious attempt on the part of a general scholar rather than a professional philosopher or specialist in Kant's thought. He had indeed communicated with Schopenhauer on the idea of a joint translation, although this came to nothing, and indeed it is difficult to imagine a frictionless collaboration with a thinker with such singular and emphatic views on the correct reading of Kant. Although many translations in the nineteenth century were presented with very little in the way of added footnotes, annotations, or glossaries – the kind of editorial supplements that are now common in translated philosophical texts – Haywood did provide some elucidatory notes and an 'explanation of terms' with a list of the key German expressions, their English equivalents, and corresponding definitions compiled, the translator tells us, 'in accordance with the best commentators'. Apart from the obviously uncontroversial ones, a good number of his renderings of Kantian terms either became the established ones or have been re-employed in modern times – 'intuition' (*Anschauung*), 'understanding' (*Verstand*), 'to cognize' (*erkennen*), 'cognition' (*Erkenntnis*), 'to represent' (*vorstellen*), 'representation' (*Vorstellung*) – while some Germanic-sounding compound phrases such as 'understanding-conceptions' (*Verstandesbegriffe*) have fallen by the wayside. It is worth noting that Haywood 'naturally' took the second edition of the first *Critique* as the obvious source text for translation without saying anything about the substantial differences between that one and the first edition of 1781, surely mindful of the enormous labour that would be involved in identifying all these changes and perhaps misled by Kant's considerable understatement on the title page of the 1787 edition that his text had merely been 'improved here and there' (whereas Schopenhauer would have insisted – like Heidegger later but for quite different reasons – that the first edition was a more radical and powerful statement of the central insights of the critical philosophy). One curious detail in Haywood's 'explanation of terms' perhaps reveals the extent to which, as those who read widely in eighteenth and nineteenth literature and philosophy will readily recognize, the predominantly male authors of the period were constantly if problematically aware of gender issues in matters of style and language: Kant seems to use the grammatically neuter and feminine forms of the noun *Erkenntnis* (knowledge or cognition) interchangeably, but his English translator avers that the feminine form involves a suggestion of caprice or subjectivity that is supposedly absent from the more 'objective' use of the neuter form. (While there is much to be said of the persistent metaphorics of sexual difference in leading thinkers of this period, such as Rousseau or Fichte, it seems to me that *Erkenntnis* or *erkennen* in Kant invariably signifies a strict conception of objectivity and universality in contrast to *Meinung*, or 'opinion', although *das Erkenntnis* is still used in German in specifically juridical contexts, like 'cognizance' in its specialist legal use).

After a second translation of the 1787 edition of the first *Critique* (Kant 2003), which was widely regarded as achieving a rather more natural and fluent style in English, though retaining much the same translations of Kant's basic vocabulary, in 1881 the versatile and bilingual scholar Max Müller produced a centenary translation in two volumes which in some respects anticipates the editorial approaches adopted today. Müller took the first edition of 1781 as his basic text but also included the significant changes introduced to the second edition as supplements, along with a long historical introduction to Kant's thought by another author. Instead of providing a separate glossary, Müller introduced the original German in brackets in the main text at the first occurrence of Kant's central philosophical terms so they could be appreciated in context. His primary concern was to provide a very readable version with the sensitivity of a native speaker to those idiomatic turns of phrase and important points of emphasis, often indicated by enclitics and adverbial expressions, which had sometimes eluded his predecessors. Such attention to what should not be regarded as 'mere' points of style was certainly to be welcomed since lack of expertise in this regard can often make a dense philosophical text much harder to follow in translation even when there are no egregious cases of downright semantic error or grammatical misunderstanding. This is something that has not always sufficiently been recognized by modern translators who are so exercised by so-called 'literal' fidelity to a text that they are often unwilling to 'unpack', or disambiguate, where required. A grammatically gendered language such as German, and one that favours substantivized verbal forms and telegraphic compound phrases, may be much clearer in the original than it can seem in an otherwise technically 'correct' translation that is reluctant to spell out the antecedents of now ambiguous subject and relative pronouns, or rephrase complex sentences with a plethora of subordinate periods.

Translating Hegel

By the time Müller's centenary edition appeared, the influence of post-Kantian developments in German thought had long since made themselves felt too. In a couple of striking essays published in the Westminster Review in 1838 and 1840 the leading British thinker of the age, John Stuart Mill, drew attention to the antithesis between the empirical outlook of Bentham and the romantic mentality of Coleridge. Mill here expressed a desire for a more concrete and more comprehensive philosophy that would do justice to every dimension of human experience beyond immediate utilitarian concerns, uniting the interests of science with the needs of culture and the demands of the moral spirit but without relapsing into a discredited metaphysics or a religious orthodoxy increasingly at odds with the claims of modern scientific and historical consciousness. In relation to that antithesis he wrote that 'whoever could master the premises and combine the methods of both would possess the entire English philosophy of the age'. Many of the thinkers who eventually became so influential in the second half of the century, within the broad spectrum of the British idealist tradition that is often described as broadly Hegelian in inspiration, would see these words as an unwitting prophecy of the mediating philosophy they strove to develop in order to overcome what they saw as the persisting and disabling dualisms bequeathed by earlier thought, including Kantian philosophy unless it too was subjected to immanent critique and dialectical reconstruction. Nonetheless, the reception of Kant itself had already opened the way to the post-Kantian movements from the 1870s onwards which now claimed to build upon the critical philosophy while contesting its apparently sceptical or agnostic implications and questioning its conception of the limits imposed on human thought with regard to reality itself. The appropriation of the Hegelian tradition would play a central role in establishing the remarkable influence, if not exactly the hegemony, of 'idealist' thought in the principal centres of university life and intellectual culture in Britain up until the Great War. After considerable initial resistance, this movement succeeded in challenging what T. H. Green, one of its pioneers, called the 'national tradition' that had been impressively exemplified by Mill.[5]

The first translation of a complete 'work' by Hegel was not really a work at all.[6] In 1857 John Sibree, friend of the young Marianne Evans, translated the *Philosophy of History* from a posthumously published text that had been edited and put together on the basis of student transcripts of Hegel's lectures in Berlin in the 1820s (Sibree [1857] 1861). The style of the translation is rather free and florid by contemporary standards, and although it cannot be said fundamentally to misrepresent 'popular' lectures already couched in an exoteric language that deliberately makes use of traditional religious images, it is particularly easy to misinterpret in a naively theological way without constant reference to the foundational systematic works in which Hegel attempts to present his immanent criticisms of alternative positions, to ground his fundamental categories, and to exhibit their specific relation to concrete fields of experience. The translation teems with capitalized nouns, not itself unusual in texts of this period, such as *Spirit, Providence, Divine Wisdom, Ultimate Design, Theodicy* etc., which hector and weary the reader who does not already know how to treat them with caution and 'translate' them (again, as it were) into the appropriate conceptual register. Hegel's 'Introduction' is the only part based on an autograph manuscript (the part which has been retranslated more than once in modern times), but Sibree's version of the rest of the substantial text is unfortunately still the only one available of this volume of Hegel's *Werke* as published in 1840.

Hans-Georg Gadamer has defended the austere view that strictly speaking Hegel only wrote two major philosophical books, the *Phenomenology of Spirit* and the *Science of Logic*, everything else being a summary condensation, more detailed concrete extension, or application of the philosophy to specific fields (i.e. the *Encyclopaedia of the Philosophical Sciences*, the *Philosophy of Right*, and the voluminous posthumously edited lectures on art, religion, world history, and history of philosophy). In fact all of the nineteenth-century translations of Hegel were concerned with these historically influential texts, while the *Phenomenology* and the *Science of Logic* had to wait until 1910 and 1929 respectively.

The first book published about Hegel in English was J. H. Stirling's *The Secret of Hegel* of 1865 (Sterling [1865] 1990), a strange work that conferred a certain eccentric celebrity on its author.[7] What is principally of interest here is not so much Stirling's panlogistic reading or counter-intuitive claim that Hegel is 'the thinker of Christianity' but the striking translations he offered of excerpts from the beginning of Hegel's *Logic* and his discussions of Hegel's language. Stirling was not afraid to stretch the possibilities of standard English, to create new words, or bring out buried etymological connections in a way that is sometimes reminiscent of the poetry of Gerard Manley Hopkins or of contemporary efforts to capture the distinctive idiom of the later Heidegger. His quest for semantic plasticity and a vigorous literalness led to translations such as 'there-being' for *Dasein*, the 'vocations of being' for *Seinsbestimmungen*, 'ordeal' for *Ur-teil* (usually 'judgement') and 'be-ënt' for *seiend*, and to curious Latinisms and Greekisms such as 'existency', 'talification', 'essentity', 'hetereity', and 'heterization' (for *Anderssein* and *Anderswerden*, or 'becoming-other'). In his quest to emphasize the self-conscious and all-encompassing character of what Hegel calls the Concept in the singular (*der Begriff*), Stirling reverted to an older Latinism of the English Platonic tradition and used the capitalised term 'the Notion', and this less happy innovation proved so influential that it prevailed in almost all subsequent translations of Hegel until fairly recent times. His other innovation was not universally adopted but has remained in use to this day. With the famous Hegelian use of *Aufhebung* and *aufheben* – the verb means to 'lift' in the sense of elevating and doing away with – Stirling resisted his etymological proclivities (*up-heaval*) and chose the archaic inkhorn words 'sublation' and 'sublate'. Hegel liked to use quite ordinary words instead of a special Latinized terminology where possible: *aufheben* is a common enough word, especially in the negative sense, and indeed Kant had used it this way in his famous remark that he had found it necessary to 'limit' or 'suspend' reason to make room for faith. But it has been argued that the fact that 'sublate' is almost unintelligible in itself may be an advantage, in that it immediately alerts us to the double meaning that Hegel intended.

There is another well-known problem that comes into view when we consider the efforts of another important translator and commentator on Hegel in this period. William Wallace produced fairly free but often eloquent versions of two thirds of the Hegelian system as expounded in summary form for use in lectures as the *Encyclopaedia of the Philosophical Sciences*. Wallace had no doubt in the age of now fully autonomous natural sciences that the 'philosophy of nature' was the most obsolete dimension of his thought, but he believed that the richness of Hegel's interpretation of the individual and social life of the mind in history and culture, in art, religion, and philosophy was his true legacy. It is often claimed that Hegel appealed to so many thinkers in Britain at this time precisely because he appeared to furnish a philosophical legitimation of religion when it seemed increasingly exposed to radical challenge both from the advances of natural science and historical criticism. Yet, after Stirling at any rate, British idealists realized that speculative idealism involved a major reconstruction rather than apologetic justification of traditional inherited forms of religious thought. In several essays appended to his translation of the encyclopaedia *Philosophie des Geistes* Wallace took pains to explain what Hegel did and did not mean by *Geist*, and signalled his understanding of the question by translating the work as *Hegel's Philosophy of Mind*. Precisely because the word 'spirit' was still so freighted at the time with religious and specifically Christian associations, Wallace wished to underline the way Hegel's thought represented an expressly *modern* revival of Aristotelian 'psychology' in a vastly expanded context that went far beyond what the period understood as 'mental philosophy', or the 'moral sciences', to include the subject matter of what in Germany would soon be called the *Geisteswissenschaften*. Wallace claimed that to translate Hegel's key word *Geist* as 'spirit' throughout 'would carry us over ... into the proper land of religiosity' (1894: 1) too quickly or exclusively, just indeed as Hegel had emphasized to his students that *Geistigkeit* (spirit as 'mindedness', to use a current term) had nothing to do with otherworldly *Spiritualismus*.

In this regard Wallace was followed by J. B. Baillie, who published his version of *The Phenomenology of Mind* in 1910 (Baillie 1931), perhaps Hegel's most challenging work from the perspective of translation. As we can see from his 'Introduction', the translator adopted a version of the British idealist approach to Hegel, and did not scruple to preface each chapter and various key sections with a summary of the unfolding argument as he took it to be. He moves from 'mind' to 'spirit' (or rather 'Spirit') when he reaches the social and cultural order, though the reader may later be disconcerted to encounter 'the' Absolute Spirit with the definite article, as if to underline the thought that Hegel's Absolute, however immanent to human experience, is more compatible with theism than almost any contemporary interpreter would be tempted to conclude. Nonetheless, whether we share Baillie's own reading or not, the translation is a work of quality and evidently the fruit of very careful consideration. The translator turns some of the most convoluted passages into intelligible English without simply relinquishing the literary and dramatic qualities of this remarkable text. There is perhaps a hermeneutic lesson here regarding the way that committed translations may still prove illuminating in many respects even when we do not endorse the translator's ultimate view of the author in question. Good translations may encourage or facilitate the work of understanding and interpretation (where very poor ones render it all but impossible), but they cannot replace or predetermine that work, for the *original* texts themselves – and what better examples are there than the writings of Kant and Hegel? – continue to provoke and perplex their native readers as much as they do those who read them in translation.

Modern responses

It was suggested that the general reception of Kant was not helped by the relative delay in translating all three of the *Critiques*, although in the second half of the nineteenth century the leading figures in philosophy and theology who were directly interested in German idealist thought were well acquainted with the texts in the original – namely, writers such as T. H. Green, B. Bosanquet, A. C. Bradley, F. H. Bradley, and H. H. Joachim. It is perhaps regrettable that those most highly regarded for their style (such as Joachim and F. H. Bradley, much admired by Eliot), or later writers in the idealist tradition such as R. G. Collingwood or M. Oakeshott, did not venture to translate any key German works (but then F. H. Bradley's attitude to German philosophical style was profoundly ambivalent, and he once claimed that all German thinkers should have been forced to express themselves in French to ensure greater clarity). Benjamin Jowett, famous in his time for his translations of Plato and his part in the debates regarding theological modernism, had strongly encouraged the study of German philosophy and indeed translated some of Hegel, although none of this was published. But the interpretation of Kant himself was itself soon caught up in – or prematurely overtaken by – the growing interest in his philosophical successors and the widespread feeling amongst the newer generation that Kant's monumental work was still a half-completed 'revolution in our mode of thought' (to use his own expression) – not a stopping-place but an essential stepping-stone in the evolution of what Bosanquet called 'concrete idealism' (the idea of an immanent path 'from Kant to Hegel' had thus been embraced by the British idealists at the time when in Germany itself the rallying cry was rather 'Back to Kant' after the alleged excesses of post-Kantian idealism).[8]

But a fundamental change in the philosophical atmosphere that could already be sensed before the Great War was certainly hastened and intensified by it – namely, the emphatic reassertion of the empiricist tradition in the emerging analytical philosophy that also drew on other recent developments in continental philosophy, especially in logic and the methodology of the natural sciences. In hindsight it came to look as if the 'spell' of German idealist philosophy in its post-Kantian form had been broken rather suddenly, encouraging in part a turn to the seemingly more modest claims of the Kantian tradition and an attempt to clarify relations between them and the newer philosophical developments. Significant changes in the cultural and intellectual climate may well be one of the factors that prompt the desire to revisit translations of canonical texts in the context of new interpretive approaches, but another is the cumulative effect of a body of existing translations where the greater availability of a greater range of texts by a given author casts new light on the earlier stages of reception and modifies the understanding of the corpus in question. In addition the emergence of comprehensive critical editions which not only attempted to establish a more reliable text but dramatically increased the amount of material accessible (whether supposedly marginal or 'early' works or previously unpublished writings in the form of correspondence, lecture courses, notes and drafts etc.) provided a richer context for works already known and prompted new translations. The first attempts to produce truly critical comprehensive editions of Kant and Hegel date from the early 1900s; the nineteenth-century edition of Hegel's *Werke* omitted everything previously unpublished, however substantial, if it was deemed early or merely 'on the way' to the 'System', but it included often problematic compilations and conflations of Hegel's lecture courses from different years based on student transcripts. The critical re-editing of the latter materials over the last few decades has led to a wave of efficient retranslations with some significant differences from earlier translations based on older source texts.

In this context Norman Kemp Smith's translation of the first *Critique* ([1929] 1933) was a significant contribution to the renewed study of Kant 'in his own right' in the interwar period and far beyond, not least because of its confident tone and accomplished literary style. Kemp Smith reflected the intellectual culture of the time in not deigning to translate the Latin quotations that adorn the text, but he did footnote certain textual issues and provide the original German in some specific cases. It was the first English version that attempted, even if with certain problems, to introduce the variant passages of the A edition alongside the B edition in a single volume in a way that helped the reader to identify the relevant differences, while also providing marginal pagination to the German source text. It is not unusual for new translations to justify themselves by reference to the real or alleged problems of earlier attempts, even if precise details of those problems are not always forthcoming. Kemp Smith did not deny his debt to earlier translators, but he suggested that they had not sufficiently engaged in the kind of 'thorough study' of Kantian philosophy that was a prerequisite for adequate translation.[9] What he did share with many of his predecessors, however, was a recognition of the rhetorical dimension of these texts and the ability to produce perspicuous and even elegant versions of the complex grammatical periods frequently encountered in Kant's prose, even if he did not scruple to break down some of Kant's most serpentine sentences for the sake of clarity. There are practical and stylistic points involved here. On the one hand, it is the minimum obligation of a translator not to *introduce* unnecessary obscurities which are not endemic to the original but easily arise in translation unless the referents of pronouns are spelt out by repeating subject terms or rearticulating an especially tortuous sentence (technically speaking, a 'sentence' in German prose of this period can be half a page long or more, consisting of a host of main and subordinate clauses separated by semi-colons). On the other hand, one stylistic feature of Kant's writing is the way that he may clinch or epitomise the argument of an extremely dense preceding passage by offering an untypically succinct formulation, and such contrasts should be preserved in translation. But in addition to all this there are also semantic problems which immediately point to fundamental interpretive philosophical issues, and here Kemp Smith's 'thorough study' of Kant – he produced one of the two principal Anglophone commentaries on the first *Critique* – has not spared his own translation from subsequent criticism. An evident problem for the translator with any philosophical text is obviously the occurrence of linguistic doublets where the source language may have two common words which largely correspond to one in the target language or vice versa, and which in the context of 'ordinary' language use are not strictly distinguished from one another or not yet terminologically defined in terms of a specific contrast. Thus in many contexts we would capture both *erkennen* and *wissen* by 'to know', and *Erkenntnis* by 'knowledge' or 'act of knowledge' (coming to know or recognize something rather than simply being 'affected' or having sensations or feelings), and we would render *Gegenstand* and *Objekt* alike by 'object'. On the other hand, the word *Glauben* would naturally be rendered in English by 'belief' in an epistemic context or 'faith' in a religious one. Another fundamental term in Kant which he acknowledges is difficult to define precisely because it is so all-encompassing is *Vorstellung*, usually rendered by 'representation' or 'presentation', which in its broadest sense denotes any kind of mental content or modification, from the most rudimentary level of sensory experience through feeling and perception to empirical and *a priori* concepts and 'Ideas'. In his lectures and certain published texts Kant would often indicate the Latin equivalent for his key concepts, although this does not automatically justify us in adopting an English word directly derived from the same Latin word as the best translation.

When it was pointed out earlier that the 'consistent' deployment of key terms is a desideratum of Kant translation this was not intended to suggest this is a simple matter of establishing a rigid grid of lexical equivalents, and the early translators were often sensitive to the difficulties arising from the question of whether the 'same' word is in fact functioning in every context as the same technical term. And given the general intellectual, social, and religious culture they inhabited, different in so many ways from our own and closer to that of Kant or Hegel, they were mindful of the resonance of words that enjoyed a life and history of their own long before they were appropriated and redeployed by philosophy – a central word such as *Bestimmung*, for example, which beyond the purely logical context of 'determination' plays such an important role in the moral and political philosophy of Kant as the inalienable human vocation or 'calling', with its significant semantic links to the dimension of *Stimme* [voice] and *Stimmung* [attunement]. That is perhaps an obvious case where a single word displays clearly different (though not unrelated) senses and would be translated differently according to context. But there are harder and more indeterminate cases. Kemp Smith did not generally distinguish between *wissen* and *erkennen* since he saw that Kant was fundamentally concerned with what we can *know* about the world and ourselves, and about 'the last things' pertaining to our own soul and to God, the ultimate questions to which we can never be 'indifferent'. Kant uses *Wissen* more rarely than the form *Erkenntniss*, and the translator prioritized the common verb 'knowledge' (which can signify what is known and the act of knowing) for the latter rather than adopt what was then a rather fusty academic word from the past such as 'cognition'. But many modern translators have embraced it because Kant indicated that *cognitio* was its Latin equivalent, it can be used in the plural like the German *Erkenntnisse*, and above all it permits us to retain 'knowing' for *wissen* and for the body of knowledge that constitutes 'science' [*Wissenschaft*]. If we insist on consistency then every instance of the German word will be translated as 'cognition', however inappropriate that may sound: the striking opening sentence of the 1781 'Preface' will invoke 'one species of our cognitions' when Kant refers to the (actual or presumed) knowledge that metaphysics once promised to provide, while 'the call to reason to undertake anew the most difficult of all its tasks' will now concern 'self-cognition' rather than 'self-knowledge'. With *Gegenstand* and *Objekt* there are passages where Kant seems to use them interchangeably, but also, as is well known, places where he draws a significant distinction between them. Earlier translators of Kant and Hegel sometimes attempted to mark the deployment of different German words with a single natural English equivalent by highlighting one of the terms through eye-catching capitalization ('object' and 'Object'), but this may seem to lend undue emphasis on one of a pair of terms which is not always being distinguished from the other, or is distinguished but is not necessarily prioritized. Modern translations tend instead to footnote the cases where the less common German term (here *Objekt*) appears or expressly marks a distinction. The case of *Vorstellung* is interesting because the word is ubiquitous in Kant and central in the work of his successors down to Schopenhauer, acquiring new significations in the process. Kant inherited the word from the academic tradition as a vernacular equivalent to *representatio* but extended and employed it in his own way. In the nineteenth century it was sometimes translated as 'presentation', especially in the context of psychological discussions of so-called mental imagery and of proto-phenomenological analyses of subjective life as a 'stream of presentations'. In recent times a considered case has been made for this rendering in the Kantian context on the grounds that 'representation' may too readily suggest 'representationalist' theories of knowledge and perception strongly associated with the kind of realist and empiricist accounts that Kant was challenging. The proposal has not widely been taken up, not least perhaps because 'representation' has become so entrenched in the translation tradition, but, more importantly, because *Vorstellung* in Kant, like a host of other terms, arguably functions as a kind of dummy term which is progressively vested with meaning, or rather meanings, only in the course of his analysis of experience as a whole and in the context of all his other evolving terms. Extensive consideration could be given to any of these terms in their own right, and to some extent it has been.[10] More recent times have seen a proliferation in translations of all Kant's major texts and of the numerous shorter but crucial essays on history, religion, and politics. Of particular significance is the emergence of ambitious projects for coordinated translations of all the philosophical writings along with other relevant materials.[11] The considerable advantage of these modern editions lies in the way that they provide extensive introductions, explanatory notes, and detailed glossaries that allow the reader to see the translation choices that have been made and thus to form a judgement about the possible limits of consistent or standardized approaches as applied to a specific text or across a whole range of texts. Books which provide detailed cross-referenced information about the philosophers' original terms, their history, etymology etc. are an indispensable resource, irrespective of the explications offered, for identifying and exploring the key passages and contexts to which translators have responded in different ways. It can also be extraordinarily illuminating to consult leading dictionaries, lexicons, and indeed grammars from the time of the philosophers concerned, as long as we do not expect such sources, in a naively historicist way, to resolve our linguistic-interpretive questions. Apart from the fact that such sources, like older dictionaries generally, often exhibit an inevitable lag in registering recent or emerging uses, significant philosophical texts, no less than literary ones, can enrich or reshape existing language with new forms, or indeed reinvigorate it with apparently obsolete or archaic ones.[12]

During the interwar period and for a good while after it the philosophical climate in the UK remained deeply inhospitable to Hegel, if not in the same degree to Kant. A significant change first began to manifest itself, though more in the humanities and social sciences, from the 1960s and eventually ushered in a surprising renewal of interest in this half-forgotten tradition. The new Hegel generally seemed less 'metaphysical' than the Hegel enshrined by British idealism and was initially approached mainly in relation to social and political philosophy and Critical Theory. A new translation of the *Phenomenology* by Arthur Miller, which appeared in 1970 (Miller [1970] 1977), still reflected that older approach in some ways, retaining 'the Notion' for Hegel's *Begriff*, but otherwise exhibited a fluent and literate style. Various errors have been detected (as there were in the first edition of Baillie's version), and some have felt the style is too elegant in places to capture the knotty intransigence of the original. A number of excellent versions of major previously untranslated essays of Hegel followed, along with the *Aesthetics* (the older version of which was particularly unreliable), two versions of the once despised *Philosophy of Nature*, and in recent years a series of careful translations of extensive lecture manuscripts and transcripts on a new textual basis. It is worth remarking that in a culture where institutional religion is far less of an obvious presence, 'spirit' returned instead of 'mind' in Miller's *Phenomenology* and has since largely established itself as the favoured translation of *Geist* in most contexts. The issue of consistency in rendering key terms is duly acknowledged in the most sensitive modern translations without being fetishized as such (although one can still encounter dispiriting counter-examples such as 'the Tree of Cognition of Good and Evil'). It is also to be welcomed that the entrenched convention of using 'the Notion' for *Begriff* has finally been laid to rest (in this regard the major continental translations of Hegel saw no need to appeal to anything but the standard vernacular equivalent for 'concept'). One important issue which inevitably arises for contemporary translations and interpretations of older texts generally is linguistic sensitivity to questions of gender and whether or not it is advisable to furnish 'improving' interventions in this regard. If one believes that this issue is indeed philosophically significant (given the arguable connections between the masculine noun *der Geist* and traditional monotheism, for example, or indeed the masculinist bias that is manifest in Hegel's treatment of sexual difference within the alleged universality of 'spirit'), it seems that translated texts should generally be left to exhibit the sometimes problematically or ambiguously gendered features of the originals so that we in principle can address the significance or otherwise of the connections between linguistic-grammatical gender and substantive cultural and historical conceptions of gender (where there are intriguing grey areas of overlap and conceptual 'interference'). It is one thing to translate *der Mensch* or *die Menschheit* into the more acceptable contemporary language of 'the human being' and 'human kind' rather than 'man' and 'mankind', perhaps another to render *Gott selbst* as 'Godself' as has been done in an otherwise scrupulous and excellently presented translation (Hodgson 1985).

Concluding remarks

While recognizing the considerable advances represented by many modern editions that aim to become the 'standard' translations, one would still hope there is room for contributions of a different character: for revisiting or revising older translations, for example, or for exploring alternative approaches alongside the generally prevailing ones. I am thinking here of the opportunities for producing self-contained translations of key sections in difficult philosophical works which pay very close attention to the rhetorical character and the specific linguistic details of the text while providing a detailed commentary on the vocabulary and the structure of the argument. Such concentrated translations can be extremely illuminating for understanding a philosophical authorship even though they cannot necessarily be generalized for a whole work or range of works where the relevant parameters for translation are much broader. Nor should we forget the kind of creative 'translation-commentary' of key texts that was provided by Alexandre Kojève (1947) and was designed to make us look at a familiar text in a quite new way.

We do not wish to be forced to answer the tacit question: do we want an accurate and consistent translation or do we want a flexible one that is sensitive to the expressive possibilities and historical dimensions of language? The dialectical answer would be: both, even if this is a counsel of perfection. We are also sometimes encouraged as translators to be contemporary, accessible, and readable, although fundamental aspects of the style and substance of a philosophical text may be at odds with contemporary expectations and not particularly accessible in character, even if all such works desire, in their own way, to be read. There is an untimeliness to certain works which is not a mark of irrelevance or obsolescence and need not be shunned or minimized. Adorno was irked by the title of a once famous book by Benedetto Croce on *What is Living and What is Dead in the Philosophy of Hegel*, not just because it implies we can cleave truth from error, insight from ideology, in a clean and clinical fashion, but because it suggests that we today directly furnish the unquestioned measure for the object and need not allow it to question us in its potential strangeness and unfamiliarity. This has implications for the practice of translating the illustrious dead. The pianist Sviatoslav Richter once said that when playing he was not unaware of the immediate audience out there, but if he was *too* aware of it, he would lose concentration on the work to be communicated, on the demands of the thing itself.

Notes

1 I remember one animated but fruitless argument at an academic conference which turned on the alleged inconsistency of Adorno in readily deploying the concept of 'authenticity' in his own work while deploring it in that of Heidegger, although it is a question of two different words in the original texts: *Authentizität* and *Eigentlichkeit* respectively.
2 Friedrich Gottlob Born, an ardent supporter of Kant, produced a four-volume Latin translation which included the first two *Critiques*, the *Prolegomena*, and a large number of Kant's key works and later essays, under the title *Opera ad philosophiam criticam*. The *Critique of Pure Reason* had already been translated into French and Italian before the first English version appeared in 1838. On the European continent, publication in Latin continued in the academic context well into the middle of the nineteenth century. Hegel's first work to be published under his own name, along with a series of paradoxical dialectical theses, was the notorious *Dissertatio philosophica de orbitis planetarum* of 1801. As late as 1841 Kierkegaard had to petition the King of Denmark

to be allowed to submit his dissertation *The Concept of Irony with Continual Reference to Socrates* in his native tongue.

3 The history of some of the earlier discussions and translations can be indicated in brief: F. A. Nitzsch, a disciple of Kant, delivered lectures in London on the Critical Philosophy (1795); a 1797 translation of J. J. Beck's *Principles of Critical Philosophy* by Richardson (1797); A. F. M. Willich published *Elements of Critical Philosophy* (1798); Richardson published an abridged 1798 translation of Kant's 1793 book on religion under the title *Religion within the Sphere of Naked Reason* (1799); Kant's *Metaphysics of Morals* was translated by Richardson (1799); the *Prolegomena to Any Future Metaphysics* by the same translator (1819); Richardson later published a version of *The Only Possible Demonstration of the Existence of God*, along with his version of the *Prolegomena* (1836); *Groundwork for the Metaphysics of Morals* by Semple (1836); *Religion within the Boundary of Pure Reason*, also by Semple (1838). The first translation of the first *Critique* by Francis Haywood appeared anonymously in 1838 as the *Critick of Pure Reason*, with a second augmented edition in 1848; some of Kant's works on moral philosophy appeared in *Kant's Theory of Ethics*, translated by T. K. Abbott in 1873, and an abridged translation of the *Critique of Practical Reason* (Part II, along with Part I of Kant's book on religion: 'On Radical Evil'), also by Abbott, was published in 1879; J. H. Bernard's version of the *Critique of Judgement* followed in 1892 (Kant 1892). Two other translations of the first *Critique* appeared before the turn of the century: that by J. M. D. Meiklejohn in 1855–60 (Kant 2003) and the more famous version by Max Müller in two volumes in 1881 (1902), an updated version of which is now available (Kant 2007, edited and revised by Marcus Weigelt).

4 See, for example, his remarks in the first *Critique* (A 312–13/B 369–70):

> Despite the great wealth of our languages, the thinker often finds himself at a loss for the expression which exactly fits his concept, and for want of which he is unable to be really intelligible to others or even to himself. To coin new words is to advance a claim to legislation in language that seldom succeeds; and before we have recourse to this desperate expedient it is advisable to look about in a dead and learned language, to see whether the concept and its appropriate expression are not already there provided. [...] For this reason, if there be only a single word the established meaning of which exactly agrees with a certain concept, then, since it is of great importance that this concept be distinguished from related concepts, it is advisable to economize in the use of the word and not to employ it, merely for the sake of variety, as a synonym for some other expression, but carefully to keep to its own proper meaning.
>
> (Kemp Smith [1929] 1933: 309–10)

5 In the *Encyclopaedia Logic* Hegel alluded sarcastically to the notoriously empirical bent of British thought, saying that in England the name of philosophy 'goes down as far as the price-lists of instrument makers', and he delighted in quoting an English newspaper advertisement for a recent book: *The Art of Preserving the Hair on Philosophical Principles* (Wallace and Miller 1971: 11). The new German developments were initially mediated indirectly through meagre manuals and handbooks of modern philosophy, sometimes in notoriously free or wayward translations. Apart from the suspicions rooted in the empiricist tradition, there was considerable complementary resistance from the side of orthodox religion. One of the earliest public references to Hegel in English appears in G. W. Tenneman's *Manual of the History of Philosophy* (1832: 468), which tells us that

> speculative philosophy has been altogether neglected by the English [...] Their national pride has at all times inclined them to concern themselves little about the philosophical pursuits of other nations, and, with few exceptions, they have attempted nothing by the path of abstruse and painful research.

But the translator – Arthur Thompson – reassures the reader that he decided to omit all those passages 'that appeared to militate against revealed religion rather than to alter [sic.] or soften them'. In 1835 a leading religious philosopher of the time, Dugald Stewart, ominously referred to post-Kantian idealism as 'the New German School' in much the same way that musical traditionalists would soon refer to the startling innovations of Liszt and Wagner.

6 The principal Hegel translations from the earlier period of reception may be indicated here in chronological order: *Philosophy of History*, translated by Sibree ([1857] 1861); the *Encyclopaedia Logic*, translated by Wallace ([1830] 1975); *History of Philosophy*, translated by E. S. Haldane and

F. Simpson (1892–6); *Encyclopaedia Philosophy of Mind*, translated by Wallace (1894); *Philosophy of Religion*, translated by E. B. Speirs and J. B. Sanderson (1895); *Philosophy of Right*, translated by S. W. Dyde (1896); *Phenomenology of Mind*, translated by J. Baillie (1910, 1931); *Science of Logic*, translated by W. H. Johnson and L. G. Struthers (1929); *Philosophy of Fine Art*, translated by F. P. B. Osmaston (1920).

7 In the 1840s Ludwig Feuerbach had interpreted the 'secret' of Hegel quite differently, in a humanist-materialist key, by suggesting that the *Geheimnis* (secret or mystery) of theology and speculative philosophy was 'anthropology'. The left-Hegelian tradition had already been introduced to English readers by George Eliot's important translation of D. F. Strauss's *The Life of Jesus* in 1846 and Feuerbach's *The Essence of Christianity* in 1854 (the only book she published under her real name, Marian Evans).

8 Many of the first expositions of Kant in English were written from a Hegelianizing perspective, such as J. H. Stirling's *Textbook to Kant* ([1881] 1993), J. Watson's *The Philosophy of Kant Explained* (1888), and Edward Caird's substantial commentary *The Philosophy of Kant* (1889).

9 Müller had set a very high bar when he said: 'What I am convinced of is that an adequate translation of Kant must be the work of a German scholar' who has the advantage over anyone 'who has derived his knowledge of the language from grammars and dictionaries only'. Of course, by 'scholar' he did not mean a 'professional philosopher' (doubtless mindful of the fact that none of the great modern thinkers before Kant had been a professional philosopher in the contemporary sense).

10 Gram (1982) gives a good idea of the thorny issues surrounding the translation of some of Kant's most basic terms, even if the solutions suggested do not always convince; see also the critical discussion of these issues in Scarpitti and Möller (1996). The essay is also a corrective against a complacent tendency to regard most of the early translators as little more than enthusiasts or gifted amateurs who were insufficiently 'rigorous'. The difficulty with some recent translations, on the other hand, springs in part from the professional division of labour, which means that modern practitioners do always not read very much in the source language beyond the field of technical philosophy and are relatively unfamiliar with the history of the language itself and the broader literary and cultural context in which the German philosophers wrote.

11 *The Cambridge Edition of the Works of Immanuel Kant*, edited by Paul Guyer and Allen Wood, Cambridge University Press (Kant 1998); a comparable project along similar editorial principles has recently begun for Hegel under the title *The Cambridge Hegel Translations*, edited by Michael Baur, Cambridge University Press.

12 See Caygill (1995) and Inwood (1992).

Related topics

The translation of philosophical texts; toward a philosophy of translation.

Further reading

Burbidge, J. W. (2001) *Historical Dictionary of Hegelian Philosophy*, Lanham, MD: The Scarecrow Press, Inc. (Useful source book with cross-referenced entries on key terms with a bilingual glossary.)

Kainz, H. P. (1994) *Hegel's Phenomenology of Spirit. Selections translated and annotated by H. P. Kainz*, Pennsylvania, PA: The Pennsylvania State University Press. (Contains a preface with observations on some of the problems of translating Hegel.)

O'Malley, J. J. et al. (eds) (1973) *The Legacy of Hegel*, The Hague: Nijhoff. (Contains a chapter specifically discussing the issue of translation.)

Royce, J. (1901) 'Hegel's Terminology', in: J. M. Baldwin (ed.), *Dictionary of Philosophy and Psychology*, New York: Macmillan. (An early discussion of aspects of Hegel's language.)

References

Abbott, T.K. (1873) *Kant's Theory of Ethics*, London: Longmans, Green & Co.

Beck, J.S. (1797) *The Principles of Critical Philosophy, selected from the works of Emmanuel Kant*, tr. J.J. Richardson, London [?] and Hamburg: B.G. Hoffman.

Caygill, H. (1995) *A Kant Dictionary*, London: Blackwell.
France, P. (2000) *The Oxford Guide to Literature in English Translation*, Oxford: Oxford University Press.
Gram, M. (ed.) (1982) *Interpreting Kant*, Iowa, IA: University of Iowa Press.
Haywood, F. (1848) *Critick of Pure Reason* from the original of I. Kant, London: W. Pickering.
Hodgson, P. C. (ed.) (1985) *Hegel. Lectures on the Philosophy of Religion*, vol. III, Berkeley, CA: University of California Press.
Honderich, T. (ed.) (1995) *The Oxford Companion to Philosophy*, Oxford: Oxford University Press.
Inwood, M. (1992) *A Hegel Dictionary*, London: Blackwell.
Kant, I. (1892) *Critique of Judgement*, tr. J. H. Barnard, New York: Dover.
Kant, I. (1998) *Critique of Pure Reason*, tr. P. Guyer and A. W. Wood, Cambridge: Cambridge University Press.
Kant, I. (2003) *Critique of Pure Reason*, tr. J.M.D. Meiklejohn, New York: Dover.
Kant, I. (2007) *Critique of Pure Reason*, tr. M. Weigelt, London: Penguin.
Kemp Smith, N. [1929] (1933) *Immanuel Kant's Critique of Pure Reason*, London: Macmillan.
Kojève, A. (1947) *Introduction à la lecture de Hegel*, Paris: Editions Gallimard.
Miller, A. A. [1970] (1977) *Hegel's Phenomenology of Spirit*, Oxford: Oxford University Press.
Richardson, J. (1799) (2 vols.) *Essays and Treatises*, London: William Richardson.
Richardson, J. (1819) *Prolegomena to Every Future Metaphysic*, London: Simpkin & Marshall.
Richardson, J. (1836) *Of the Celebrated Immanuel Kant, translated from the German with a Sketch of his Life and Writings*, London: n.p.
Scarpitti, M. A. and Möller, S. (1996) 'Verschlimmbesserung: Correcting the Corrections in Translations of Kant', *Semiotica* 111–1/2: 55–73.
Schultz, J. [1785] (1995) *Exposition of Kant's Critique of Pure Reason*, tr. J. C. Morrison, Ottawa: University of Ottawa Press.
Semple, J.W. (1836) *The Metaphysics of Morals*, Edinburgh: Thomas Clark.
Semple. J.W. (1838) *Religion within the Bounds of Pure Reason*, Edinburgh: Thomas Clark.
Sibree, J. (tr.) [1857] (1861) *Lectures on the Philosophy of History by G. W. F. Hegel*, London: Henry G. Bohn.
Sterling, J.H. [1865] (1990) *The Secret of Hegel* [new edition], Bristol: Thoemmes.
Sterling, J.H. [1881] (1993) *Textbook to Kant*, London: Routledge.
Tenneman, G.W. (1832) *A Manual of the History of Philosophy*, tr. A. Johnson, Oxford: D. A. Talboys.
Wallace, W. (tr.) [1830] (1975) *Hegel's Logic*, Oxford: Oxford University Press.
Wallace, W. (tr.) (1894) *Hegel's Philosophy of Mind*, Oxford: Clarendon Press.
Wallace, W. and Miller, A.V. (trs) (1971) *Hegel's Philosophy of Mind*, Oxford: Oxford University Press.
Willich, A.F.M. (1798) *Elements of the Critical Philosophy*, London: T.N. Longman.

23
Translating Derrida

Oisín Keohane

23.1 Introduction

The Jacques Derrida (1930–2004) that most readers know is Derrida-in-English, and because of what I will call 'Anglobalisation', this will likely not change in the coming decades. The reception of Derrida thus cannot be disentangled from his English translators nor his English-language readership. The significance of this language for Derrida can be recalled by noting that several of his texts were in fact available in English some years before they were available in French (because Derrida encouraged translations of his works to be published before the so-called original-language texts). One can also observe that translations of Derrida's texts into English arguably hold the distinction of being among the best instances of philosophical translation in the twentieth century, even if some are, without doubt, problematic. Furthermore, Derrida has attracted a very wide range of translators in English, rather than being reliant on a small group. Some of these translators have also become influential as theorists in the field of 'translation studies'. Such scholars thus not only write about translation: they combine the activity of writing about Derrida with translating his works, something relatively rare when it comes to translators of other philosophers. Two such key figures who translated Derrida and who are widely credited with having inspired and influenced the field of 'translation studies' are Gayatri Chakravorty Spivak, who translated, in 1976, the second full 'book' of Derrida's to be translated into English – *Of Grammatology* – and Lawrence Venuti, who translated, in 2001, Derrida's 'What Is a Relevant Translation?'.

But though there are now dozens of Derrida's texts translated into English, and we will likely have a new translation of Derrida every few years for the next few decades due to the publication of his seminars, translating Derrida can still be a fraught and difficult business. The latest public controversy concerns Spivak's 2016 retranslation of Derrida's *Of Grammatology* and Geoffrey Bennington's review of it (the subject of Section 4). Such controversies potentially reveal a lot about the enterprise of translation. Indeed, the very fact that the controversy is about a retranslation (rather than simply a translation) has its own import, and it can be noted more generally that several of Derrida's texts, especially his shorter compositions, conference addresses and articles, have been retranslated, usually by different hands, in a relatively short amount of time. I highlight this because while retranslating philosophical works is nothing new, we still tend to have only one English translation of major twentieth-century philosophical works, such as Adorno's *Negative Dialectics* and Husserl's *The Crisis of European Sciences and Transcendental Phenomenology*. Derrida, while being widely acknowledged to be difficult to translate, has had many translators to translate him, to try their hand and be inventive, rather than leave his work – like so many others, who do not always deserve this unhappy fate – on the shelf, untranslated. This is the paradox of translation that Derrida discusses numerous times: the paradox that the text that provokes the most sustained attempt to translate it is often the text held to be in some sense difficult, or even impossible, to translate.

It should also be noted that translating Derrida into English poses its own unique set of circumstances. This is because some scholars claim that English is currently a vehicle of linguistic imperialism (Phillipson, 2009) or Globish (Cassin, 2014). To emphasise how linguistic issues are intertwined with globalisation, I prefer to speak of 'Anglobalisation', which names a process too complicated to be either simply opposed or praised. 'Anglobalisation' refers to the growing globalisation of English as well as the ways in which English itself has had an impact on globalisation. The latter is as important as the former, since most theories of globalisation, no matter how they understand globalisation – be it, for example, as fundamentally an economic, cultural, technological, political or philosophical process – usually neglect issues pertaining to language and translation. 'Anglobalisation' also impacts philosophy, because English has risen to become, by the end of the twentieth-century, the most common language used to translate texts of philosophy. In China, for instance, as of 2002, seven of Jacques Derrida's books were 'available in Chinese translation, [but] only two come directly from the original French' (Zhang 2002: 141). The others, the majority, were translated from the English translations. They were thus translations of translations. 'Anglobalisation' is therefore not only important because increasingly more philosophical works are being published in English, but also because more works are translated from English, even when they were not originally written in English. In other words, the most commonly translated language in the publishing industry now is English. The power of writing philosophy in English – and it is precisely a question of power and of what is commonly called 'language politics' – is not only that you can be read by an Anglophone, but that your work is much more likely to be translated. But even when works are not written originally in English, English is still used as a so-called pivot, or bridge, language in translation. English is thus being used as an intermediary language for translation between other languages – to translate between any pair of languages A and B, one translates A to the pivot language P, then from P to B. This is done so that the combinations of languages involved are linear rather than quadratic, minimising the language competencies needed to translate. In sum, English is the language that would translate all other idioms. Derrida himself was increasingly aware of this fact and made statements about the rise of English from the 1980s to his death in 2004. See, for instance, his comments on English in his first UNESCO talk, 'The Right to Philosophy from the Cosmopolitical Point of View' (2002a), his 1994 piece 'Faith and Knowledge' in *Acts of Religion* (2002b) and his 1999 talk 'Globalization, Peace and Cosmopolitanism' in *Negotiations* (2002c).

Another major issue in translating Derrida is that Derrida's seminars (which are estimated to contain over 14,000 pages of material) are currently being published and translated by the University of Chicago Press (they have published five volumes in translation so far). The decision to edit the unpublished seminars led to the formation of an editorial team for the Derrida Seminars Translations Project (DSTP), which began its work in 2006. This team assembles a group of well-known scholars of Derrida's thought: Geoffrey Bennington (Emory University, US), Marc Crépon (École Normale Supérieure, France), Thomas Dutoit (Université Lille-III, France), Peggy Kamuf (University of Southern California, US),

Michel Lisse (Université catholique de Louvain, Belgium), Marie-Louise Mallet (independent scholar, France) and Ginette Michaud (Université de Montréal, Canada). The group's varied institutional and linguistic make-up is significant, and reflective of Derrida's global reach, as it notably comprises members of institutions in both official monolingual French countries (France) and official bilingual countries (Belgium, Canada), as well as one country which does not have an official language at federal level, but whose many states do, often making English their official language (US). Thus, while early Derrida translation was often a solitary process, nowadays, as well as scholars continuing to translate texts by Derrida on their own, there is the DSTP, which works, to at least some degree, collectively. The DSTP does not, however, seek to control how other translators translate Derrida (though this accusation will in fact be launched by none other than Spivak). This raises interesting questions of authority and of any possible, or desired, standardisation between Derrida's many published works.

Derrida also knew a number of his translators personally and counted many of them as friends, such as Geoffrey Bennington, Peggy Kamuf, Michael Naas, Avital Ronell, Elizabeth Rottenberg, Nicholas Royle, Gayatri Chakravorty Spivak, Samuel Weber and David Wills. This usually led to the translators consulting with Derrida about specific choices they had made. This is frequently acknowledged as such by the translator's foreword. Moreover, Derrida, in several of his texts (such as 'Living On: Borderlines' in *Parages*), pre-empts his translators by directly addressing them in the text and wondering, out loud, as it were, how they will translate a given word or passage, and at other times, he appears to give instructions to his translator ('Force of Law'). This both raises the stakes of translation and makes the issue of translation more visible. Finally, if we take what Derrida says about translation seriously, then we need to read him in French *and* in other languages, including English. In other words, the translated texts will not be lacklustre substitutes for whoever cannot read French but works that have the power to make us think about Derrida's work differently.

23.2 Historical perspectives

The first translation of Derrida into English dates from 1967 (it was an extract from *Speech and Phenomena*). This was followed by 'The Ends of Man' in 1969, translated by Edouard Morot-Sir et al. and 'Structure, Sign and Play' in 1970, translated by Macksey and Donato. A few other papers followed in the 1970s, as well as the first book-length English translation of Derrida – David B. Allison's translation of *Speech and Phenomena* in 1973. In 1976, Spivak released her aforementioned translation of Derrida's 1967 *De la grammatologie*, which had already been translated into Italian in 1969 and German in 1974. Finally, in 1977, Samuel Weber and Jeffrey Mehlman translated 'Signature Event Context'. This phase is characterised by translators who were not former students of Derrida (though Spivak was a former student of Paul de Man), who were not necessarily familiar with all his published work up until that date and who mostly translated a single work by Derrida rather than multiple volumes.

I thus want to suggest that we group the translations from 1967 to 1977 together as the first phase of Derrida-in-English, since this phase would open with Derrida's first ever English translation and close with one of his most influential texts, which later would give rise to the so-called Searle–Derrida debate in the mid 1980s. I also want to note the particular importance of Spivak's translation in this period. There have been numerous reactions to Spivak's *Of Grammatology*. One of the reasons so many have commented on it is that this translation is widely acknowledged to have had the single biggest influence any translation of Derrida has had on the reception of Derrida's work in the Anglophone world. This is partly due to its translator's preface. As Anthony Pym observes, 'Spivak's preface, with its partial recommendation of frivolity, its autobiographical style and eminently literary location, did what it could to ensure that Derrida would not be accepted among mainstream English-language philosophers' (Pym 2012: 127–8). Jonathan Rée, on the other hand, states that

> Derrida's multilingualism has had an electrifying effect on philosophical translation from French into English. The carelessness of the early renderings of Sartre and Merleau-Ponty would never be tolerated in translations of Derrida, especially after Gayatri Spivak's brilliant version of *De la Grammatologie*, published in 1976. Spivak brought to French philosophical translation the same scrupulousness that could already be expected in translations from German; and although her work met with some incredulity on its appearance, it now has the status of a kind of classic.
>
> (Rée 2001: 237)

However, Rée goes on to offer some criticisms of Spivak, noting that one disadvantage of what he calls Spivak's

> petrified scrupulousness is that comparatively unpretentious originals, with their feet more or less touching the linguistic ground, get levitated by the process of translation into showy exhibitions of near incomprehensibility. After Spivak, indeed, readers seem to have developed a positive relish for philosophical translations that do not make much sense, and translators do not always escape the suspicion that they sophisticate their work with an extra dash of unintelligibility, just to gratify the public taste.
>
> (Rée 2001: 237–8)

To complicate matters further, there are in fact three editions of Spivak's *Of Grammatology*, there is the original one from 1976, the corrected edition from 1997 and the revised edition from 2016. To put this into context, in 2011, the editors of *Reading Derrida's Of Grammatology* (Sean Gaston and Ian Maclachlan) point out that while Spivak (who contributed to the volume they had assembled) belonged to a remarkable generation of scholars 'who began the daunting task of translating Derrida into English', even the corrected version completed by Spivak in 1997 still contains 'errors and confusions'. They thus state that 'one could take this project [that is, the very book they are editing] as the call for a "new translation" of *De la grammatologie*' (Gaston and Maclachlan 2011: xxv). Five years later, in January 2016, the new translation appeared, the fortieth-anniversary edition, published by Johns Hopkins University Press. This anniversary edition also featured a new introduction by Judith Butler and a new afterword by Spivak herself. I will discuss this particular publication in more detail in Section 4, since it marks a contemporary watershed moment in translations of Derrida.

Moving past 1977, we can perhaps identify a second phase of Derrida-in-English, from 1978 to 1987, when Alan Bass, the most prominent translator in this phase, published all his translations of Derrida, beginning with *Writing and Difference* (1978) and ending with *The Postcard* (1987). Bass also retranslated several influential papers first published in English in the 1970s in *Margins of Philosophy* (1982), such as 'Signature Event Context' and 'Différance'. The other prominent translators in this phase would be Barbara Johnson, who translated 'Fors' in 1976 (revised in 1986) and *Dissemination* in 1981, and John P. Leavey, who translated *The Archeology of the Frivolous* in 1980 and *Glas* in 1986. I noted before that translators often posed questions to Derrida about his works to improve their translations. Bass has commented that, when translating *The Postcard*, this mostly occurred via letters with

Derrida, with whole pages of annotations sent back to Bass, but it also meant occasionally meeting to discuss the text. This phase is all the more distinctive in that it is the only phase where it becomes the norm for translators of Derrida to produce a substantial 'translator's introduction' to their translations, ranging from sixteen to twenty-two pages. Bass provides a 'translator's introduction' to *The Postcard* that includes a glossary of French words, beginning with A and ending with V, writing that

> many [of the words listed] do not function as switch points or levers in English. Most of these words have been left in French or somewhere in the text: thus, it is likely that if you find a French word in the text, you will find an entry on it here. Other words have not necessarily been left in French, but have seemed to require an entry.
>
> (Bass 1987: xiii)

In addition, in his translator's introduction to *Writing and Difference*, Bass writes:

> The question arises – and it is a serious one – whether these essays can be read in a language other than French [...] The translator, constantly aware of what he is sacrificing, is often tempted to use a language that is a compromise between English as we know it and English as he would like it to be in order to capture as much of the original text as possible. This compromise English, however, is usually comprehensible only to those who read the translation along with the original. Moreover, despite Derrida's dense and elliptical style, he certainly does not write a compromise French. It has been my experience that however syntactically complex or lexically rich, there is no sentence in this book that is not comprehensible in French – with patience. Therefore, I have chosen to try to translate into English as we know it.
>
> (Bass 2001 [1978]: xv–xvi).

In this passage, Bass explains his translation strategy. One can observe that his emphasis on what needs to be sacrificed means he does not mention what can also be gained in the transaction of translation rather than simply lost. He also speaks of 'compromise English', something presumably in between English as we know it and English as we would like it to be, which makes it sound like it is closer to being a deficient form of English, something suboptimal, rather than something that can positively develop the English language in innovative ways. Accordingly, he chooses to defend his translation strategy – namely, his decision to translate into English as we know it – rather than write what he describes as 'compromise English'. Bass notably does not clarify here what the first-person plural ('as *we* know it') means in this context; is the 'we' referring to all English speakers or only to so-called first-language speakers, or, even more narrowly, to a certain group of first-language speakers – namely, English speakers trained in philosophy? Matters are left unclear. However, one positive outcome of Bass' translator's introduction is that we know where he stands, because he states it so directly. This will be less clear with translators that come after Bass, in what I describe as the third and fourth phase of translating Derrida. Johnson, in her translator's introduction to *Dissemination*, states that she will offer parallel texts (namely, Philippe Sollers' letter to Derrida and a text entitled 'Mimique', in both French and English) 'in lieu of a theory of translation' (Johnson 2004 [1981]: xx). But, unlike Bass, she does not speak (solely) of sacrifices when it comes to translating Derrida but instead of serendipity and positive effects accruing from the English translation. She thus writes: 'One might almost believe, for instance, that, with its recurring emphasis on weaving and seeing, *Dissemination* had been waiting all along for the English homonymy between "sow" and "sew" to surface' (ibid.). She adds:

> To translate an author so excruciatingly aware of the minutest linguistic differance [she replicates Derrida's neographism, but without the accent] is an exercise in violent approximation. On the one hand, one must try to find an English equivalent not only for what Derrida says but also for the way in which his text *differs* from its own statements and from standard French usage. But on the other hand, these microstructural differances cannot be privileged at the expense of the text's power to *intervene* in the history of philosophy and criticism. Nonetheless, since Derrida's most striking intervention is precisely his way of reworking writing, I have generally tried to align my English with Derrida's disseminative infidelity to French rather than reduce his French to the statement of a thought *about* dissemination. Hence, every weapon available – from Latin to neologism to American slang – has been mobilized to keep the juggling-puns in the air'.
>
> (ibid. xviii–xix)

She thus thinks that any translation will be a 'violent approximation' and that it will have to pay attention to how Derrida's idiom differs from 'standard French usage'. Johnson's comments highlights Derrida's creativity with French itself and how this has inspired her, in turn, to use what she describes as 'every weapon available'. She proceeds to name three such 'weapons' – the Latin language, neologisms and American slang. This juxtaposition of the old (Latin) and the new (American slang) stands out, and points to how she wants to capture his scholasticism as well as what we might think of as his ability to cultivate a form of intimacy with the reader. Derrida-in-English for Johnson would thus resemble a character like Professor Bertram Potts, a fictional lexicographer in Howard Hawks' *Ball of Fire* (1941), who begins the movie as a clichéd stuffy professor unable to leave his study or his books but who develops, by the end of the movie, a keen interest in American slang and a disseminative infidelity to English. What Johnson highlights in sum is the importance of so-called non-standard usage alongside what was historically considered prestigious (the use of Latin) or proper to English. The second phase of translation is hence characterised by translators who were much more familiar with Derrida's work as a whole, who sometimes were former students, who also translated multiple works of Derrida's and who produced substantial translator's introductions, providing an outline as to what they perceive the key translation issues to be.

The third phase I would identify extends from 1988 to 2009, when the first volume of Derrida's seminars was published. A list of prominent translators in this phase would include: Geoffrey Bennington, Pascale-Anne Brault, Peggy Kamuf, Michael Naas, Elizabeth Rottenberg and David Wills. It might also be noted that most of Derrida's translators worked individually up until this point; one characteristic of this phase is the number of co-translations produced. This is most notable in the co-translations by Pascale-Anne Brault and Michael Naas, who have jointly translated seven of Derrida's books – *The Other Heading* (1992), *Memoirs of the Blind* (1993), *Resistances of Psychoanalysis* (1998), *Adieu* (1999), *Rogues* (2005), *Learning to Live Finally* (2007) and *Athens Still Remains* (2010a). The other co-translations worth noting would be those of Geoffrey Bennington, whose first few translations were co-translations (*Truth in Painting* with Ian McLeod, in 1987, and *Of Spirit* with Rachel Bowlby, in 1989), but who has since translated on his own, as well as those of Peggy Kamuf and Elizabeth Rottenberg, who mostly have translated Derrida on their own but who teamed up to translate both volumes of

Psyche (2007/2008). This phase is characterised by a further emphasis on translators who were much more familiar with Derrida's work as a whole, who again were mostly former students of Derrida's and who also translated multiple works by Derrida rather than a single work. In this phase, the so-called translator's introduction, utilised so effectively by Bass and Johnson, mostly disappears or is dramatically reduced to being an explanation of how the text came about rather than a substantial discussion of translation issues.

Finally, the fourth phase of Derrida-in-English would be from 2009 to the present. The list of prominent translators in this phase would include the same names as the third phase; however, this time, they would be working under the umbrella of the DSTP, beginning to publish the seminars of Derrida, which span from 1959 to 2003. As of 2017, five English translations have been published – *The Beast and the Sovereign*, Volume 1 (2009), *The Beast and the Sovereign*, Volume 2 (2011), *The Death Penalty*, Volume 1 (2013), *Heidegger: The Question of Being and History* (2016) and *The Death Penalty*, Volume 2 (2017). In this phase, we also begin to see retranslations of early major works first translated in the 1970s, such as Leonard Lawlor's retranslation of *La Voix et le Phénomène* into *Voice* and *Phenomena* (2010b) and Spivak's *Of Grammatology* (2016). This phase is further characterised by a more collective sense of identity among the translators with the creation of the DSTP in 2006 and its annual summer workshops in Caen, France, which houses some of Derrida's papers at *L'Institut mémoires de l'édition contemporaine* (IMEC).

In their joint foreword to the translation of *The Death Penalty*, Bennington and Kamuf state that 'Additional translators' notes have been kept to a minimum'. This strategy is neither explained nor justified, but the fact it is included as a statement at all is telling. It reveals that they recognise that translator's notes are necessary, but that in their own view they must be kept to a minimum, that they must be controlled in number – neither too little nor too much. This seems to be in contrast to the style Bass developed in the 1980s. Bennington and Kamuf add that:

> Translating Derrida is a notoriously difficult enterprise, and while the translator of each volume assumes full responsibility for the integrity of the translation, as series editors we have also reviewed the translations and sought to ensure a standard of accuracy and consistency across the volumes.
>
> (Bennington and Kamuf 2012: viii)

This highlights how the DSTP works collectively, even if, as they note, each translator of a given volume assumes full responsibility for the integrity of their own translation.

I have so far named a number of the most influential translators. However, a more comprehensive list of Derrida's translators would include the following names: David B. Allison, Gil Anidjar, Derek Attridge, Alan Bass, Jennifer Bajorek, Andrew Benjamin, Geoffrey Bennington, Ruben Berezdivin, Rachel Bowlby, Beverley Bie Brahic, Pascale-Anne Brault, Eduardo Cadava, Mary Ann Caws, George Collins, Peter Connor, Giacomo Donnis, Mark Dooley, Thomas Dutoit, Jeff Fort, Joseph F. Graham, Barbara Harlow, Marian Hobson, Michael Hughes, James Hulbert, Christine Irizarry, Barbara Johnson, Peggy Kamuf, Leonard Lawlor, John P. Leavey, Ned Lukacher, Jr., Phil Lynes, Christie V. Macdonald, Ian McLeod, Mary Louise Mallet, Jeffrey Mehlman, Patrick Mensah, Laurent Milesi, Edward P. Morris, Jan Plug, Eric Prenowitz, Michael Naas, Catherine Porter, Jan Plug, Mary Quaintance, Richard Rand, François Raffoul, Avital Ronell, Elizabeth Rottenberg, Christine Roulston, Gayatri Chakravorty Spivak, Anne Tomiche, Peter Pericles Trifonas, Lawrence Venuti, Samuel Weber, David Wills, Joshua Wilner and David Wood.

Oisín Keohane

23.3 Critical issues and topics

The following is a non-exhaustive list that illustrates a number of critical issues when it comes to translating Derrida into English.

1. Lexical issues in his texts, such as families of words, cognate words.
2. Syntactical issues, such as Derrida's frequent use of French reflexive verbs to indicate autoaffection, or phrases which due to their syntactical structure can have more than one meaning, such as *tout autre est tout autre* (this phrase will be examined in depth below).
3. Idioms, such as *donner raison à l'autre* [to concede that the other is right] or *donner la mort* [to put to death, but more literally, to give or grant death]. Derrida often uses idioms and reflects on them, and the very notion of the *idion* (its Greek etymon), in many of his writings.
4. Translating a text by Derrida written in several languages (which eradicates the foreign effect inside the original), such as translating Derrida's use of non-French words or passages in his French texts.
5. Translating the English words that appear in Derrida's texts and so words in the so-called target language, which are thus effaced, notable examples being 'double bind' or 'speech act'.
6. Homographs in his texts: words which do not belong to one language – famous examples in Derrida's work include the word 'or' (which can be read as an English word or as a French word; if the latter, it is a conjunction as well as an adjective [golden] and noun [gold]). Another example is the word 'car' that Derrida uses in *The Postcard* ('Car la chose est un véhicule en translation'), which can be read as an explanation of what the first word, 'car', means in English, so that Derrida's sentence could be translated as 'Car: the thing is a vehicle in translation' (note, though, that the common word for translation in French is *traduction*; *translation* in French usually refers to movement and traffic, to a form of transfer). Alternatively, the word 'car' can be treated as a French conjunction meaning 'because', so that Derrida's sentence would be translated as 'because the thing is a vehicle in translation'). Finally, all of this takes place against the backdrop of a reflection on notion of the thing, *das Ding*, a famous philosophical topos since Kant (later echoes of which are found in Heidegger and Lacan).
7. Homophones in his texts: words that sound (almost) the same in a given language, such as *des tours* [towers] and *détour* [detour] in French, or *sans* [without] and *sang* [blood].
8. Words that can be read as having antithetical meanings, such as *hôte* [guest or host] or *partage* [share or divide].
9. Performative issues in his texts – see for instance Derrida's analysis of Descartes' 'if I am writing in French [*si j'écris en français*]' in the *Eyes of the University*, which highlights how translation also involves issues of logic, since if you translate *j'écris en français* into English ('I am writing in French') you change its truth value from true to false.
10. Derrida's (re)translations of non-French-language texts into French, especially the texts of Heidegger, which he often alters or translates himself entirely (sometimes because they were not yet available in French).
11. Derrida's own translation suggestions for famously difficult terms to translate in other philosophers, such as his suggestion of using the French word *relève* to translate

Aufhebung (a difficult term to translate, because it means both conservation and negation, a fact famously exploited by Hegel).

12. Derrida's instructions or suggestions to his translators in the texts being translated. In 'Force of Law', Derrida writes out English words that translate a French phrase. For instance, he follows 'la violence conservatrice' with a parenthetical remark offering the English translation 'law-preserving violence'. Similarly, 'faire la loi' is followed by 'making the law'. In the same text, he also presents a passage from Walter Benjamin's *Zur Kritik der Gewalt* [*Critique of Violence*] three times, first his own French translation, then in the original German, then Edmund Jephcott's English translation. Mary Quaintance, in her translation of 'Force of Law', gives Benjamin's text a translation entirely different from the one Derrida supplies, and ignores the instruction to translate '*la violence conservatrice*' into 'law-preserving violence'; she displays Derrida's instruction, together with her rebellion against it. Translators need to think about whether they want to obey or disobey Derrida's instructions if they are present and their reasons for doing so.
13. Derrida's self-instructions in the texts being translated and the difference between translating something which is going to be read out loud instead of simply being published. For instance, in 'Force of Law', first delivered as a conference address in New York, Derrida wrote the following: 'C'est ici un devoir, je dois *m'adresser* à vous en anglais (à prononcer en français puis en anglais en soulignant *adresse*)') ['This is an obligation, I must *address* myself to you in English (to be spoken in French, then in English, emphasizing *address*)']. Quaintance chose not to translate this self-instruction by Derrida but instead enacts it. Moreover, she omits this self-instruction not only in the version read out loud by Derrida that day in New York but also in the published English version, where she might have chosen to do something different. Her published translation thus conveys her response to Derrida's instruction rather than the instruction itself.
14. The gender of the French terms that he uses, such as *la voile* [sail], *le voile* [veil], or pluralisation, *les voiles* (which makes the gender undecidable, meaning it can be either or both).
15. When to include Derrida's French in an English translation, either by leaving it untranslated or by inserting it in parentheses.
16. Neographisms or neologisms created by Derrida, such as 'différance' or 'désistance' or 'Sarl' or 'hostipitalité' or 'destinerrance' or 'mondialatinisation'.
17. The layout of the page, especially when this is crucial to a text, such as *Glas*, which is divided into two columns, one on Genet and the other on Hegel. Derrida also interrupts these columns with what he calls judases (a judas in French, as in English, can refer to a spyhole), pockets of words that spill out beyond the column, resulting in sentences and even words being disrupted in those columns.
18. The use of punctuation marks, such as hyphens, parentheses, dashes, colons, where these are (typo)graphically important to the text and are not reducible to instructions on how to read the words they space out.
19. The ways that Derrida subverts as much as employs the French language.
20. The way Derrida does not always write full sentences but sometimes incomplete syntagms.
21. That translators possibly keep in mind what Derrida had to say about translation.

Another way of tracking some of the critical issues in translating Derrida is to track how a given phrase has been retranslated by numerous translators. Accordingly, I will examine the phrase *tout autre est tout autre*, used frequently by Derrida in his publications from the 1990s until his death. Derrida, writing about the phrase in *The Gift of Death*, says:

> The essential and abyssal equivocality, that is, the play of the several senses of *tout autre est tout autre* or *Dieu est tout autre*, is not, in its literality (that of French or Italian, for example), universally translatable according to a traditional concept of translation. The sense of play can no doubt be translated by a paraphrase in other languages; but not the formal economy of the slippage between the two homonyms that can here be called singularly my own [. . .] We have here a kind of Shibboleth [. . .] like a secret in one's so-called natural or mother tongue.
>
> (Derrida 2008: 88)

- Peggy Kamuf, in *Specters of Marx* and in *Without Alibi*, translates it as: 'every other is altogether other'. She translates it again, in a translator's note to *Specters of Marx*, which includes the original French expression, as 'altogether other is every other', and, in *Without Alibi*, she translates once again, as well as leaving it untranslated without parentheses: 'the same and altogether other: *tout autre est tout autre*, every other is altogether other the same'.
- John P. Leavey, in *On the Name*, translates it as: 'any other is totally other'. He includes the French in parentheses.
- Thomas Dutoit, in *Aporias*, translates it as: 'every other is completely other'. He includes the French in parentheses.
- George Collins, in *Politics of Friendship*, translates it as: 'The altogether other, and *every other (one) is every (bit) other*'. In a translator's note, he provides the French and states that he follows David Will's translation in the first edition of *The Gift of Death*.
- Eric Prenowitz, in *Archive Fever*, includes the French without parentheses and then translates it as: 'every other is every other other, is altogether other'.
- Samuel Weber, in 'Faith and Knowledge', translates it as: 'every other is utterly other'. He includes the French in parentheses.
- Patrick Mensah, in *Monolingualism of the Other*, translates it as: 'the entirely other is entirely other'. He does not include the French.
- Pleshette DeArmitt and Kas Saghafi, in 'Aletheia', translate it as: 'every other (one), the wholly other, is every (bit) other'. They include the French in parentheses.
- David Wills, in *The Gift of Death*, translates it as: 'Every other (one) is every (bit) other'. He includes the French in parentheses and leaves a chapter title with this heading untranslated.
- Pascale-Anne Brault and Michael Naas, in 'Of Responsibility – Of the Sense to Come', translate it as: 'every other is every (bit) other'. They include the French in parentheses.

Different strategies are deployed here to translate these deceptively easy five French words, which can also be counted, using the type/token distinction, as three words, since two words are repeated (*tout* and *autre*). In French, *tout* can be a both an indefinite pronominal adjective [some, someone, some other one] and an adverb [totally, absolutely, radically]. The way Derrida has written it means we can read it both ways. Moreover, as Derrida notes, if the first *tout* is an indefinite pronominal adjective, then the first *autre* becomes a noun and the second, most likely, an adjective.

In the English translations provided above, the translations range from using five words, the same as the French, to eleven, more than double the amount of French words, to capture the various senses at stake. All ten translations noticeably use the word 'other' at least twice (some use it three times), to capture the double use of *autre* by Derrida. However, only four translations use a word to translate *tout* twice, namely Mensah, who uses 'entirely' twice, DeArmitt and Saghafi, who use 'every' twice in their tripartite 'every/wholly/every', Wills, who uses 'every' twice, and Brault and Naas, who also use 'every' twice. The other translators all choose to translate the double *tout* differently in the same phrase: 'every/altogether,' 'any/totally,' 'every/completely,' 'altogether/every,' and 'every/utterly'.

Most of the translations also use one clause to translate it, but some use three, and four of the translations resort to parentheses for the words 'one' and 'bit' to capture more than the one meaning at stake. Finally, one translator (Collins) uses the conjunction 'and' instead of the copula 'is' to capture the homophone between *est* [is] and *et* [and] in French, and two (Collins and Mensah) use the definite article to mark out what they call 'the' other. What is fruitful here is that several strategies have been deployed to capture the various intricacies involved in the French. We need not be disappointed that no one is clearly better than all the others. What we need to do in each case is work out what effect their translation has had and why it was suggested.

Another way to differentiate the various translations is to compare how they incorporate a tautological reading with a heterological reading, since Derrida's point is to make both readings possible at the same time, and in fact he writes it in such a way that one is not only able to read it both ways but *must* do so.

A tautological reading of *tout autre est tout autre* stresses that every other is (equally) every other. It highlights the quality of sameness by means of similarity – saying the same thing twice over. Any other can be replaced by any other, because all are equally other. No one is more other, more unique, than another. This is the logic of substitution. Anyone or anything can be replaced, but this replacement guarantees that all others are equally other.

The other reading that is possible is the heterological reading. On this reading, *tout autre est tout autre* is stressing that every other is all, completely, or entirely, other. It highlights the quality of difference by means of dissimilarity – saying something different, even when using the same set of words. No other can be replaced by another, because all are singular and irreplaceable. Every other is thus singularly other, and so unique. This is the logic of non-substitution. No one (or no thing) can be replaced, for everyone (or everything) is singular.

We have seen that a number of translators have tried to capture both readings by translating *tout* in at least two separate ways: 'every/altogether', 'any/totally', 'every/completely', 'altogether/every' and 'every/utterly'. Some, such as Wills, have tried to capture both readings by inserting words in parentheses: 'every other (one) is every (bit) other'. Will's translation also keeps the 'XY is XY' structure if one ignores the words in parentheses, elegantly finding a way to keep the structure of the original while making possible a heterological reading. However, one could also argue that this translation prioritises the tautological reading over the heterological one, unlike Derrida's French formulation, since it is the heterological one that is in parentheses and is thus positioned as second in the order of readings, since the words in parentheses are optional, unlike the words outside of parentheses, which enable the tautological reading. Again, this shows us the use of different translations, all of which have their different merits. We can deem all these translations reasonable, as they all have their justifications, though we might prefer some above others. This raises the question of consistency. Should Derrida's translations in English in the future all use the same locution to translate *tout autre est tout autre*? I would argue that they should not, and that leaving the French in parentheses is enough to mark a placeholder for those wishing to keep track of the phrase in Derrida's writings, such as in his seminars.

23.4 Current contributions and research

In March 2016, Geoffrey Bennington published an 8,000-word review (which is itself noteworthy, given that lengthy reviews of translations are infrequent in prestigious publications) of Spivak's new translation of *Of Grammatology* in the *Los Angeles Review of Books*, entitled 'Embarrassing Ourselves'. In its final footnote, it states that the DSTP has written collectively to Johns Hopkins University Press asking that this new translation be withdrawn, pending approved revision. Bennington in this article points out how the new translation is not only not an improvement on the previous editions but is in fact even more flawed.

Bennington gives numerous examples to show how systematic the problems are, but I will only focus on one, where he shows how Spivak has mistranslated Derrida's use of French verb *solliciter* in one famous passage. In the original 1976 edition, Spivak translated this as 'destroy', while in the new 2016 edition she translates it twice, both times differently. In the main body of the text, she translates *solliciter* as 'be interested in', while later in the volume, in the 'Afterword' to the new edition, quoting the exact same passage again, she translates it as 'put a strain on'. So, one can now compare the three translations proposed by Spivak: her original 1976 translation and her two translations in the 2016 edition:

1. The movements of deconstruction do not destroy [*solliciter*] structures from the outside (1976).
2. The movements of deconstruction are not interested in [*solliciter*] structures from the outside (2016).
3. The movements of deconstruction do not put a strain on [*solliciter*] structures from the outside (2016 – 'Afterword').

What is odd, as Bennington points out, is that the translation from the main body of the 2016 text is misleading and has little justification, while the translation in the 'Afterword', which offers a much better translation, does not explain why it differs from the translation in the main body of the text (even if translators do sometimes uses different translations for the same word, it is highly unusual to translate the same sentence differently in the same volume at different points without explanation). To draw out the significance of these differing translations, Bennington notes the use of the French word *solliciter* in some of Derrida's earliest published texts, such as 'Force and Signification' and 'La différance', as well as from Derrida's 1964 seminars on Heidegger by Derrida (which were translated in 2016). Bennington also notes that Derrida himself discusses the word in several publications and regularly glosses it as a shaking movement [*citare*] of the whole [*sollus*], or totality, and that the word has a connection with the Heideggerian notion of *Destruktion*. Bennington thus calls *solliciter* a 'signature term' of Derrida's. Whether this is true or not, it seems that Spivak's translation of *solliciter* as 'not interested in' is not only difficult to understand as a translation of the French, but it loses the vibrancy of the French – and it is a question of vibrancy, of resonance, of shaking things up – that Derrida was interested in.

What is even more revealing, though, is how Spivak responded to Bennington's piece at the UK launch of the new edition, held at Birkbeck, University of London, which can be seen on YouTube (Birkbeck, University of London 2016).

I will be quoting her words, but one should keep in mind that she is, for the most part, improvising and speaking on the spot. Her initial response does not downplay, but in fact highlights, her own lack of training in the language she is translating (though Bennington brings this up nowhere in the review). She states: 'I don't know any French; this is completely accepted by me and others, including my students. I am not hiding behind any knowledge of French. I am not a French PhD. I am not a native speaker'. Leaving aside what she might mean by the enigmatic claim of 'hiding behind any knowledge of French', she usefully brings up the issue of what qualifies one to translate a given language, if anything. She explicitly raises two standard paths and denies having access to them, namely training in the language (all the way up to PhD level) and being raised in that language (and so being a so-called native speaker of that language). But rather than use this to explain any deficiencies in the translation, she suggests this gives her a different status to other Derrida translators, a status that she thinks many of the other translators cannot, or will not, accept. Spivak thus speaks of herself as an outsider, or someone identified as an outsider by others: someone who did not go through the usual channels of legitimation (from geographical origin to linguistic professionalisation). Her status as a translator is all the more noteworthy given that she has been institutionally involved in the promotion of translation studies at third-level institutions. She founded the MFA in translation in the Department of Comparative Literature at the University of Iowa just before publishing her translation of Derrida, and she has been widely praised for her Bengali-to-English translations of authors such as Ram Prashad Sen and Mahasweta Devi, winning a prize from the National Academy of Literature in India for translating the latter.

She thus carries a great deal of authority and prestige as a translator, both as a practitioner and as a theorist (if we can distinguish these activities in translation), so what she discusses next in the Birkbeck interview is significant – she speaks of and critiques the idea of 'correctness' in translation. She does this by first praising the DSTP but, referring to the group of Derrida translators discussed earlier, such as David B. Allison, Alan Bass, and Barbara Johnson, argues that the translations they produced, each with their distinct histories, should not be 'demolished and made correct'. She thus suggests the DSTP has exceeded its mandate by commenting on translations of Derrida other than those of the seminars, acting as if their task were the monitoring or even policing of all Derrida translations. Having praised the pre-DSTP translators of Derrida, she then proceeds to distinguish *good* translations, which she thinks is a legitimate judgement, from *correct* translations, which she does not view as legitimate: 'I think it is a mistake to think that any good translation can be a correct translation'.

To illustrate her point, she shows the Birkbeck audience three published translated pages from three different texts, each of which contains a plethora of handwritten annotations that address translation points. Her three pages derive from three different sources, the first a page from Hegel (specifically A. V. Miller's translation of the *Phenomenology of Spirit*), the second a page from Marx (specifically one of the volumes of *Capital* translated by Ben Fowkes) and the third a page from Lacan (specifically Bruce Fink's translation of *Écrits*). The point of the demonstration is to show that 'good translations', which she considers all the translations above to be, are imperfect and can always be improved upon – to show that there are always other ways of proceeding, but that this does not make translations any less valuable or, indeed, good. This is odd as a response to Bennington's criticism in his article, given that Bennington would readily agree with this. He launches his critique not because he thinks there are such things as perfect translations which are held to be (by him or the community at large) correct, but because Spivak has made basic mistakes. The issue is thus not about which translation of a given word or sentence or syntagm is better in the circumstances, but something more fundamental, namely good scholarship and basic accuracy. While many things can be translated more than one way, there are some ways which are simply incorrect, because they fail to meet the basic standards of good interpretation.

Spivak thus seems, at best, to misunderstand Bennington's point and, at worst, to misrepresent him (as if he were the one who thought that there was only one correct way to translate things). This is all the more remarkable given that she thinks there is one 'huge mistake' in the translation of Marx she shows, which, she states, is not 'pardonable, because Marx is trying to say something which is obliterated by that mistake, and I don't know if it is deliberate [...] one can hardly miss that [mistake]'. Spivak thus thinks that while Bennington's critique is uncharitable, and confuses good translation with correct translation, in her own criticisms of other translations she can claim that the translator's mistake might have been nothing less than deliberate, due to its obviousness, and she deems such a mistake not 'pardonable'.

23.5 Recommendations for practice

Many of the Heidegger translations by Indiana University Press have a glossary of German words at the back of the text. A particularly excellent example of this is in Reginald Lilly's translation of Heidegger's *The Principle of Reason*. He includes a German–English glossary first and then an English–German glossary. Finally, he adds a list of various cognate words that are particularly important in Heidegger's text. Such a list of cognate words, and a French–English as well as English–French glossary, might be helpful in future editions of Derrida's texts.

23.6 Future directions

This is a tricky issue when writing about Derrida, since Derrida in his writings from the 1990s emphasises the to-come [*avenir*], as opposed to the future [*futur*] – and, to some extent, what is most interesting about the future of Derrida and the future of Derrida-in-English is that which we cannot foresee or predict, the events that will occur that are not seen on the horizon. Nevertheless, mentioning some issues seem justified. The first concerns which other retranslations of Derrida might we profit from, in the wake of Spivak's new translation and Lawlor's retranslation. The second concerns the need to translate all of Derrida's published writings (since some small pieces remain unpublished). The third comes from the kind of English that is used in translations of Derrida. Historically speaking, most translations of Derrida have been translated into an idiom that resembles American English or, more rarely, British English. Since most speakers of English nowadays are not so-called native or first-tongue speakers, there is an argument that the kind of English that Derrida might be translated into be expanded, so that it resembles another kind of English altogether. This move could positively estrange Derrida's tone and work even further, opening new resonances and linguistic possibilities. However, publishers would have to accept a wider category of English than they currently do, since publishers usually insist on a given standard, which is something closer to a so-called national variety of English.

Third, there is also a small number of texts by Derrida that were published bilingually, with the French on one side and English on the other, such as *Spurs* (which in its first publication featured four languages: French, English, Italian and German – the latter two languages were omitted in the English publication). It would be particularly interesting if this multilingual publishing avenue was explored by Galilée, the French publisher of so many of Derrida's writings, including his seminars, for one major consequence of an English-language press incorporating the French is that it lessens the needs to buy a French edition. Since one might wish, for very good reasons, to continue to support non-English publishers, it might be beneficial to reverse the position, so that the French publication already included an English translation. This, of course, would be controversial, especially in France, as English as the language of translation would still be privileged, but I believe that this is better than the alternative, where non-English publishers suffer economically due to 'Anglobalisation'.

The fifth and final issue, connected to the fourth, is how to promote non-English languages while promoting the rightful place of translation in the age of 'Anglobalisation'. We need to work out how to pay attention to the non-English *and* praise the English-language translators who find inventive and creative ways to translate the text into English. It is not a question of choosing the translation over the so-called original or vice versa. The choice that faces us is not about emphasising the French and never reading Derrida in English, nor is it simply reading Derrida in English all the time and forgetting about the French idiom that he so loved. This raises the question of linguistic justice: how to promote the fair use of language in the age of 'Anglobalisation'.

Related topics

Nietzsche; Heidegger; Benjamin; Gadamer and Ricoeur; Derrida; Levinas: his philosophy and its translation.

Further reading

Jacobson, Arthur J. (2005) 'Authority: An *homage* to Jacques Derrida and Mary Quaintance', *Cardozo Law Review*, 27.2, 791–800. (This article explores how Mary Quaintance deals with Derrida's instructions on how to translate him in 'Force of Law'.)

Venuti, Lawrence (2012) 'Translating Derrida on Translation: Relevance and Disciplinary Resistance' in *Translation Changes Everything: Theory and Practice*, London and New York: Routledge. (One of the most famous scholars of translation studies discusses his experience of translating Derrida.)

Lezra, Jacques (2015) 'This Untranslatability Which is Not One', *Paragraph*, 38.2, July 2015, 174–88. (In this article, Lezra, responding to Derrida's *Monolingualism of the Other*, in both the French edition and the English translation, outlines how Derrida disrupts a notion of mathematical identity in translation.)

Davis, Kathleen (2001) *Deconstruction and Translation*, Manchester: St. Jerome Publishing. (This was the first book-length treatment of translation from a perspective indebted to Derrida.)

References

Bass, Alan (1987) 'Translator's Introduction: L before K', in Jacques Derrida, ed., *The Postcard: From Socrates to Freud and Beyond*, tr. Alan Bass, Chicago: University of Chicago Press, vii–xxx.

Bass, Alan (2001) [1978] 'Translator's Introduction', in Jacques Derrida, ed., *Writing and Difference*, tr. Alan Bass, London: Routledge, ix–xxiii.

Bennington, Geoffrey (2016) 'Embarrassing Ourselves', *Los Angeles Review of Books*, 20 March.

Bennington, Geoffrey and Peggy Kamuf (2012) 'Foreword to the English Edition', in Jacques Derrida, ed., *The Death Penalty*, Volume 1, tr. Peggy Kamuf, Chicago: Chicago University Press.

Birkbeck, University of London (2016) 'Politics of Deconstruction: Gayatri Chakravorty Spivak and Oscar Guardiola-Rivera in Conversation', available at: www.youtube.com/watch?v=28zoswK4zF0 (accessed 1 May 2017).

Cassin, Barbara (2014) *Sophistical Practice: Toward a Consistent Relativism*, New York: Fordham University Press.

Derrida, Jacques (1982) *Margins of Philosophy*, tr. Alan Bass, Chicago: University of Chicago Press.

Derrida, Jacques (1992) *The Other Heading: Reflections on Today's Europe*, tr. Pascale-Anne Brault and Michael B. Naas, Bloomington, IN: Indiana University Press.

Derrida, Jacques (1993) *Memoirs of the Blind: The Self-Portrait and Other Ruins*, tr. Pascale-Anne Brault and Michael B. Naas, Chicago: Chicago University Press.

Derrida, Jacques (1998) *Resistances of Psychoanalysis*, tr. Peggy Kamuf, Pascale-Anne Brault and Michael B. Naas, Stanford, CA: Stanford University Press.

Derrida, Jacques (1999) *Adieu to Emmanuel Levinas*, tr. Pascale-Anne Brault and Michael B. Naas, Stanford, CA: Stanford University Press.

Derrida, Jacques (2002a) 'The Right to Philosophy from the Cosmopolitical Point of View', in *Ethics, Institutions, and the Right to Philosophy*, ed. and tr. Peter Pericles Trifonas, Lanham: Rowman & Littlefield, 1–18.

Derrida, Jacques (2002b) 'Faith and Knowledge: The "Two Sources" of Religion at the Limits of Reason Alone', in Gil Anidjar, ed., *Acts of Religion*, tr. Samuel Weber, New York: Routledge, 42–101.

Derrida, Jacques (2002c) 'Globalization, Peace and Cosmopolitanism', in *Negotiations: Interventions and Interviews, 1971–2001*, tr. E. Rottenberg, Stanford, CA: Stanford University Press, 371–86.

Derrida, Jacques (2005) *Rogues: Two Essays on Reason*, tr. Pascale-Anne Brault and Michael B. Naas, Stanford, CA: Stanford University Press.

Derrida, Jacques (2007) *Learning to Live Finally*, tr. Pascale-Anne Brault and Michael B. Naas, Basingstoke and New York: Palgrave Macmillan.

Derrida, Jacques (2007/2008) *Psyche: Inventions of the Other*, tr. P. Kamuf and E. Rottenberg, Stanford: Stanford University Press.

Derrida, Jacques (2008) *The Gift of Death*. 2nd edition, tr. David Wills, Chicago: Chicago University Press.

Derrida, Jacques (2010a) *Athens Still Remains: The Photographs of Jean-François Bonhomme*, tr. Pascale-Anne Brault and Michael B. Naas, New York: Fordham University Press.

Derrida, Jacques (2010b) *Voice and Phenomenon: Introduction to the Problem of the Sign in Husserl's Phenomenology*, tr. Leonard Lawlor, Evanston, IL: Northwestern University Press.

Derrida, Jacques (2016) *Of Grammatology*. 40th anniversary edition, tr. Gayatri Chakravorty Spivak, Baltimore, MD: Johns Hopkins University Press.

Gaston, Sean and Ian Maclachlan (eds) (2011) *Reading Derrida's Of Grammatology*, London and New York: Continuum.

Hawks, Howard (1941) *Ball of Fire*, Goldwyn Productions.

Johnson, Barbara (2004) [1981] 'Translator's Introduction', in Jacques Derrida, ed., *Dissemination*, tr. Barbara Johnson, London and New York: Continuum, vii–xxxv.

Phillipson, Robert (2009) *Linguistic Imperialism Continued*. London: Routledge.

Pym, Anthony (2012) *On Translator Ethics: Principles for Mediation Between Cultures*, tr. Heike Walker, Amsterdam and Philadelphia: John Benjamins Publishing Company.

Rée, Jonathan (2001) 'The Translation of Philosophy', *New Literary History*, 32.2, 223–57.

Zhang, Ning (2002) 'Jacques Derrida's First Visit to China: A Summary of His Lectures and Seminars', *Dao*, 2.1, 141–62.

24
Levinas
His philosophy and its translation

Bettina Bergo

Introduction: *temimut,* or faithfulness to the letter of the text

Emmanuel Levinas (1906–95) has come to be known as the contemporary philosopher of responsibility and creator of a new, fundamental ethics. Most interesting is that his responsibility does not entail prescription ('you ought') and it is not normative in the sense of directing our conscious will. It is rooted in the emotional impact that the gaze of another person has on me in the immediacy of our encounter. As such, and after his first treatise *argued* the point of the radical otherness of the other person, Levinas's *magnum opus* of 1974 explored the 'moods' of ethical summoning by the other. Taken together, the two great works (*Totality and Infinity*, 1961, and *Otherwise than Being or Beyond Essence*, 1974) argue for the intersubjective – or from the other person *to* me – ground for our 'interest' in ethical questions like the good, for the others. But the 'ground' here is not a typically philosophical one; it is affective and does not begin in me. Moreover, unlike today's ethical intuitionism, this is not a way of seeing that is inculcated through education. Unlike today's neo-Kantian ethics, this is not a foundation that one can deduce by eliminating empirical qualities from a moral principle to bring to light its *a priori* or pre-experiential dimension. These are but a few of the remarkable novelties in Levinas's thought.

Levinas's work poses a number of difficulties to the translator, which I will review in what follows. In the first place, he is not so much writing *in* French, a language he associated with the Enlightenment, as *through* French. His first languages were Hebrew and Lithuanian, followed by Russian, French, and German. As a child in Kaunas, he studied the Bible. It was only three decades later that he would plunge into the Talmud. Now, biblical Hebrew and that of the fourth-century Talmud are not *one* language, but registers, idioms. Their styles are different; complex because they run, each in their respective ways, a gamut between mytho-poetics, epic narration, legal discussion, psalmody and wisdom literature. This is important because translating Levinas's philosophy demands that we keep in mind Hebrew concepts from the Bible, 'Greek' concepts from phenomenology and Levinas's idiosyncratic French. To take one significant example, Annabel Herzog reminds us that the 'sincerity' with which 'I' respond to the other who confronts me is already a translation at two removes: from *sincérité*, but also, and primordially, from the Hebrew *temimut*, 'innocence', 'integrity' (Herzog 2014: 140–1).

Philosophical translators know that their undertaking is overdetermined. Jonathan Rée has documented the difficult 'translation' of Greek concepts into Cicero's Latin, and then into Scholastic Latin via a detour through Arabic (Rée 2001: 245–50). In English, even the transparent English of Locke found it had to accommodate Greco-Latin technical terms like *substantia*, short of forging an equally problematic 'Saxon' idiom with awkward 'translations' like 'upholding' or 'standing under'. Rée points out that 'Locke's apologetic Latinity has dominated philosophical English ever since... and although the great English philosophical writers... were multilingual, they all preferred to use the English they *inherited* from Locke' (Rée 2001: 249).

Translating Levinas urges that we respect his own technical terms, given the resonances they have with Hebrew, but also given that his work is an ongoing dialogue with Hegel, Husserl, and Heidegger. That is, Levinas is explicitly conversing with, and criticizing, idealist dialectics, classical phenomenology, and ontology as first philosophy. If only for that reason – and the fact that philosophical texts carry an extraordinary sedimentation of traditions, some in conflict, some cross-fertilizing each other – my first priority in translating Levinas has been faithfulness to the letter of his text. This immediately poses two problems: preciousness and exoticism. Translating French into English means moving out of a language that constantly negotiates Latin roots fully familiar to French speakers. Some of these roots came into English with the Normans, creating a 'double language' in which the Saxons ate lamb and oxen, while their conquerors consumed mutton and beef. When English speaks from the heart, it demands 'freedom'; when it theorizes, it ponders 'liberty'. Hence the ongoing problem of preciousness due to Latin roots. Exoticism also results from an over-zealous preservation of Latinisms in the many cases where a Saxon root would be clearer than and as hard-hitting as the original was.

Greater difficulties await translators who value style (as we all do), notably because the later Levinas contests Martin Heidegger's priority of 'Being' through 'performative' choices like dropping the verb 'to be' from many of his discussions. This creates long parataxes designed to reproduce the 'situation' of bearing witness to the encounter with the other, like a breathless accounting for oneself. This choice must be preserved, although it is close to impossible to hold subjects and predicates together without reintroducing the verb 'to be' in English. Remaining faithful to the letter and style of Levinas's text thus carries risks beyond the linguistic cosmopolitanism of most French philosophical works.

Another difficulty is found in the motivation underlying Levinas's later works. Stated inadequately, his motivation arises from two pressing questions: how to write philosophy 'after Auschwitz', to paraphrase Adorno (Adorno 2000: 210)? Or again: what is left of philosophy after the systematic and legal destruction of over six million people? And indeed, how to bring the ethical 'message' of the biblical prophets into a phenomenology that enquires into its experiential source? If we suppose this is a reductive expression of Levinas's rationale, then recall his answer when pressed by Christian Chabanis in 1982 to ground his conception of responsibility to the other: 'Starting from the Holocaust, I think of the death of the *other* man; I think of the *other* man, for whom – and I don't know why – one can already feel like a survivor, responsible' (Levinas 1995: 166, emphasis added). As much as they involve protracted debates with phenomenology and hermeneutics, Levinas's texts are inspired by events to which they bear witness, directly and performatively, or indirectly. The centrality of responsibility, and later of 'substitution' (cf. *temimut*), places extraordinary emphasis on certain intersubjective *affects* that 'I' undergo spontaneously and in situations where another suffers. Edmund Husserl's phenomenology had already discussed *Einfühlung* [empathy], defining it as spontaneous and passive affect. But Husserl's crucial influence on

Levinas also proved limited. Phenomenology 'constituted' the other as 'like me', starting from *my* gaze. Levinas stepped outside the framework of phenomenology by arguing that the other person is never wholly constituted the way objects can be. The other remains enigmatic to me; her force does not awaken empathy so much as provoke a response. The implications are significant: some intersubjective affects give rise to uncalculated acts of generosity and self-sacrifice, but they do not start from *my* initiative. As such they are epistemologically unverifiable, as if eccentric to phenomenological method. We can only bear witness to such 'events', describing them from a first-person perspective and thereby losing the origin in the other.

Bearing witness is not foreign to philosophy. However, as a style it requires recourse to performative registers of language. These are not so difficult to translate in and of themselves. Yet, in Levinas, these registers are said to rest on a consciousness that is pre-intentional, pre-reflective; these registers must therefore convey the transitive, open desire that motivates the witness – in suffering or in passion – to speak. Phenomenology might call this consciousness 'horizonal'. I would call it a pre-text, something impelling the witness's saying-to us.

This brings me to a third point, which intimately concerns the first two (faithfulness to the letter and to style): it is something like the density of language, or the unceasing crossing of what structuralism called the paradigmatic and the syntagmatic axes – that is, the cognitive sources of sentences and active construction of sentences themselves. When Jacques Derrida pondered this density of language, he observed that he never spoke but one language. Yet he also could not speak *one* language. If this curious antinomy can be 'translated', then we gain a glimpse into another fundamental difficulty of translation: the 'language' that 'I' speak is not the set of words codified in a dictionary, it is an *idiom* that I (as singular speaker, as *idios*) can and cannot make my own. As an idiom, it always outstrips my communicative intentions, and I can never appropriate it the way I do an object, even one communally held. Often, it is not *one* language but many. This is eminently the case for Levinas, whose 'idiom' weaves Lithuanian, Russian, French, Hebrew, and German together, opening questions of linguistic identity, performative authority, and even authorship (all of which are concepts in the semantic universe of *auctoritas*). It similarly raises dilemmas of a text historically and semantically overdetermined like Levinas's *Otherwise than Being*, which attempts to express the conditions of what it states, to set into words that which motivates their expression (Levinas 1974). By this point in my text, we can see that we have moved beyond basic questions of translation. Yet this third 'psychological' question has actually stepped back or beneath the two initial questions of faithfulness to the text and respect of style.

Problems of faithfulness to the letter of the text

It is a commonplace that we should remain as close to the letter of a philosophical text as possible. One reason for this is that we may not recognize the depth of debate to which a single technical term refers. Some translators have chosen a natural English over the complexities of the philosophical jargon so often characteristic of continental philosophy. But Levinas is fully conscious of his hybrid style and, as I indicated, he uses form as though it were the content of arguments he made elsewhere. Moreover, he is steeped in Russian literature. We must feel the cultures of Gogol and Dostoevsky, among others, but also of the great rabbi of Vilna, Chayyim of Volozhin, who wrote *The Soul of Life* (2012), and finally 'humanist' strains of Talmudic interpretation inherited from his teacher, Monsieur Shushani (Malka 1994, 2002: 138–41). Therefore, it would be a mistake to try to 'naturalize' Levinas's French, which does not mean that textual hybridity should obscure understanding. Rée speaks of producing an English translation both 'unnatural and faithful' to the original (Rée 2001: 228). Because Levinas's textual heterology deliberately impacts his philosophy, we must make do with a significant element of apparent exoticism, notably where he is enacting his response to another as if it were immediate, *here and now*. As to preserving the sedimentation of concepts and traditions, this is often the stock and trade of philosophical translation (Rée 2001: 233–4).

Since French readers confront the problem of exoticism in Levinas's text almost the way English readers do, naturalizing amounts to obscuring his rhetoric. As I pointed out, by reinserting the verb 'to be' into Levinas's parataxes, the translator is making an indirect *philosophical* point: the primacy of the copula and its omnipresent transparency. Eliding the verb cannot eliminate 'being', as existence or Heideggerian question. However, it is an ingredient in Levinas's thematic focus on the other person, whether understood as the face that speaks to me, or the memory that I carry within. Here style must cede to all the elements composing the arguments, including the indirect ones. In another sense, Levinas has created his own paratactic style that performs what is the ultimate task remaining for philosophy: bearing witness to the human context in which it can arise, if only as responsibility or a promise to speak to someone. When Levinas constructs arguments, as he does explicitly in *Otherwise than Being*, chapter 1 (Levinas 1991: 3–20), there is no difficulty translating them. But the challenge at the level of his performative utterances is to convey the affects associated with being called upon or singled out. The language of witnessing carries almost more affect than predication (Lyotard 1988: §§ 110, 134–5), in which case we must not force the text didactically to make more sense than it already does.

Sensitivity to the fact that tone and rhetoric have philosophical consequences means grasping that *they* too determine whether an argument proves probative and even whether arguments that are highly condensed or incomplete will move us. In philosophy as in literature, a fundamental act of faith must be elicited then cultivated between reader and author. This is more than a matter of consistency of arguments. As much as I would like, I do not subscribe to Gadamer's definition of understanding as the 'fusion of horizons', unless said 'fusion' be itself asymptotic and often unstable (see Gadamer 2004: 305).

Problems of respect of style

As we have seen, there is a tension between literality and a strong respect of style. This tension is not always present, the two may complement each other. Nevertheless, the effect of style is the creation of tone, which, as Kierkegaard understood better than most, largely determines the reception of a text. He went so far as to say that we cannot properly evaluate an idea if it is presented in a style that corrupts it. An idea or event that should be presented seriously must not be forced into a style that is comical, tragic, much less 'objectivist' or 'positivistic'. In 1844, Kierkegaard pondered this after the scandal provoked by his *Diary of a Seducer*, which had been read by a public ignorant of its profound irony; in writing *The Concept of Anxiety* (1980), he changed tones. He was now seeking the right voice in which to explore sin as a real question. It could no longer be a matter of irony, much less of theological piety or scientific curiosity. Indeed, when read by psychology, sin loses its experiential intensity and all its paradoxes and becomes an object of science. When translated into metaphysics, sin changes into an object of speculation. Sin's aporetic quality – as 'determined' through the affect of anxiety over my possibilities, and then 'freely' realized in a 'free' leap – evaporates in metaphysical arguments. Ideas like sin thus depend on the tone in which they are expressed, and tone proves to be the great challenge to a translator who must watchfully adjust style to the voice of the author.

Interestingly, style is both an action and its outcome. There is a reciprocity between style of execution and style of what is produced. The first-century Roman historian Pliny the Elder urged that style denoted *ways* of painting and the *stilus*, which spread the wax colours on a surface, was the material technology through which style was forged (1857: 250 n. 10). In fourteenth-century France, the *stille* was both the *poinçon à écrire* [a writing brush] and the little rod mounted atop a sundial, which indicated the hour of the day. Objects termed *stille* concerned the means of production and the orientation and conditions under which communication transpired, even communication of the time of day. Technology, technique and their manifestations, material and immaterial, coexisted in reciprocity. While Kierkegaard argued that there is no understanding without the proper tone, in philosophy style equates to conviction. It is no mere patina that one layers upon one's language. But philosophy is not just logic; when it is *phenomeno*-logy, as the description of what our moving bodies perceive in the world, then philosophy must embrace the literary, despite the objections of some. Philosophy then becomes, to paraphrase Nietzsche, a 'dramatisches *Urphänomen*' [a fundamentally dramatic phenomenon] (Nietzsche 1993: 43). By this he meant that philosophy unfolded as a staging of select phenomena with a view to seeing them clearly, and by extension, to understanding what it means to hear them better as well. All of this depends strictly on obtaining the right style.

The recognition that style has ontological density and virtually creates worlds we are talking about, finds itself caught up in yet another tension: the all too contemporary question of 'originalism' implies a static text and style, whose transparency offers itself only to readers who consider themselves unbiased by interpretation. When we attempt to reproduce the style (or insist on remaining close to the letter of the text), we produce, in the idiom of translation, a creature that may not have much equivalency with the original language. In the case of Levinas, then, my initial priority often carries more weight than the second one, though this has not spared me hermeneutic perplexities, themselves also philosophical. For the underlying question is whether the configuration of literality and style do get us closer to something like the original intentions of the author. That question admits many disputable answers. Context and related texts help us, but never definitively set forth the intentions, and certainly not the vast intellectual sedimentations, of the author and the life of his or her mind.

Toward an 'otherwise than being'

In regard to Levinas's two great works, it is particularly difficult to translate *Otherwise than Being* because there is precisely a tone that appears sometimes imperative, sometimes obsessed with mourning. This tone is woven into and continuously overflows the argumentative structures of chapters 2, 4, and 5. It is not so much a suffering that somehow starts from the *individual* Levinas as it is the suffering recurring out of what he saw and heard, as though this suffering were a-subjective and contagious like trauma. The tone of the work is inward-looking, and ongoingly resistant to arguments that would reduce it to existentialism or force it into dialogue with the thinkers of ontological difference. To be sure, Heidegger's influence was considerable, notably because, for him, Being reveals itself precisely thanks to those *Stimmungen* [moods/tones] that open our access to it and to the meaning of our own being (Heidegger 1962: 172–9). Heidegger thus extends Kierkegaard's emphasis on tone and truth, although he does not bear witness to alterity the way Levinas does.

As I indicated, Levinas's witness is prepared by arguments in chapter 1 of *Otherwise than Being*. The first and most important of these is that there is a kind of temporality specific to the intersubjective affect (pleasure or pain) that comes to me from the other who faces me. By the later work, this other is translated into an affective alterity so potent that it interrupts the flowing time-consciousness that defined Husserl's phenomenological subjectivity at the transcendental level (Husserl 1991: 77–9). Yet even this argument is continually disrupted by Levinas's enactment of the 'ethical' interruption that prompts his gesture of bearing witness of it *to* someone. Still, the arguments are clear: affective time does not unfold as a pure flow, as an ordered sequence. Affective time is not a plurality of events moving in a forward direction (Husserl's 'rectilinear multiplicity', Husserl 1991: 120). Rather, affective time repeats like a traumatic memory, which renews suffering though it may have no object. And the argument continues: if, for phenomenology, consciousness is fundamentally structured by the flow of time, which integrates *all* lived experience in its passing, even as it preserves the places or times of each event that flows back thanks to time indices, then the experience of suffering occurs in this flow *and* overflows it. Suffering and trauma return, 'obsessively'. Levinas writes: 'Obsession is not consciousness, nor a species or a modality of consciousness, even though it overwhelms the consciousness that tends to assume it' (Levinas 1974: 139, 1991: 87). But trauma is not 'narcissistic'; enduring trauma concerns the suffering of another person. We might document such a claim with psychological studies of trauma, and then venture that our philosopher was traumatized... by the murder of his family and friends. But if we do we will thereby lose the point of the argument. That is, if all that we 'know' – that is, what *is* – is conditioned by phenomenology's foundational flow of experienced 'time', which is a time more basic and embodied than the socially constructed time of clocks and calendars, then Levinas's traumatizing 'moments' and their repetitions, which do not just *flow on*, interrupt our consciousness *and* our ability to grasp think about existence in that moment. This claim is of profound philosophical interest because it sets the origin of philosophical questioning in the other person and in what escapes our cognitive grasp of him or her. Moreover, it complexifies Husserl's linear time-consciousness by insisting on an intersubjective time indissociable from certain affects. While trauma interrupts thanks to both its intensity and its lack of identifiable *reason*, its lack of 'why', it is pre-eminently induced in one who witnesses the suffering or destruction of another person. In that sense, trauma is not part of ordinary experience but may befall anyone. What we learn from it concerns the quality of our connection to another person, which 'is' otherwise than 'Being' when 'Being' denotes everything that-is. If Being unfolds, in Heidegger, as the temporalization of the being that we are, as *Da-sein* or open insertion in the world, then the implications of intersubjective trauma contest Being as closure and totality.

Levinas's polemical claim clearly proves challenging for two reasons. First, nothing should be outside of what-is, including trauma. Second, the implication for Levinas's argument is peculiar because it means that he *cannot assert* this 'experience' of suffering for-another, or before-another person, as a fact of existence. Levinas's suffering here might be compared to a pure tone, indeed to Heidegger's argument about the verbality of being ('the red reddens' is processual; Be-ing has no 'subject'), except that Levinas proposes that his tone *attaches to* Be-ing's dynamism, like an ad-verb ('*autrement*' [otherly]). Or, as he says, it is like 'the music in Xenakis' *Nomos Alpha pour Violoncelle Seul*... which bends the notes and method into qualities like adverbs. Every quiddity becomes a mode, the strings and woods passing into sonority' (Levinas 1974: 71, 1991: 41 translation modified). The task then, for Levinas as for the translator, is to convey the performance of this bending of notes as if language could be tonal, and where the tone corresponds to affects attaching to intersubjective encounters and memory – whether we qualify them psychologically as traumatic or simply as a disturbing incident.

Levinas's adverbial forms would have the kind of unperceived 'force' that a performative may have in J. L. Austin's sense of the illocutionary speech act (e.g. 'please listen, I am speaking to you'; cf. Austin 1962: 98–101), or in John Searle's sense of 'expressive' illocutionary acts that always carry a specific attitude toward a statement, such as regret, remorse or shared joy (Searle 1976: 4–5). Such speech acts concern address and the way intersubjective connections are established. In Levinas we find similar 'declarations', which, as illocutionary acts, alter a state of affairs and create new interpersonal reality. For example, 'The meeting was adjourned' or 'The defendant is found guilty' – becomes an interruption in Levinas: 'And I still interrupt the ultimate discourse in which all the discourses are stated in saying it to one . . . situated outside the said that the discourse says' (Levinas 1974: 264, 1991: 170). His peculiar performative consists in making an argument in a text into a confession to the reader. This is one of Levinas's techniques for bearing witness in his text as if *to you, here and now*.

Levinas makes use of the illocutionary force of performatives, inherent in the sheer *fact* of declaring (the meeting was ongoing, it is now adjourned; I am writing this, but I am speaking to you and it concerns you and your own life), *or* expressing the intention of promptly enacting the deed that is the illocutionary act itself. We do not lose sight of the literary artifice in Levinas. Yet it is effective as it moves between a declarative form ('The discussion I am presently holding at this very moment . . .' [Levinas 1974: 264, 1991: 170, translation modified]) and an expressive form ('To be oneself, otherwise than being, to be dis-interested, is to carry the misery and the failure of the other' [Levinas 1974: 185, 1991: 117, translation modified]).

Levinas and multilingualism

Levinas apportions his many languages according to function: Hebrew, for Torah and Talmudic reflection; Russian for home life but also for literary examples; German for phenomenology and hermeneutics; and French for the idiom of *his* philosophy. What are the implications of this multilingualism for his thought? Derrida's point that we have but one language and it is not ours, holds true (Derrida 1998: 25). But as Derrida added, Levinas does not 'inhabit' a *Muttersprache* [mother tongue] the way Hannah Arendt did with German (Derrida 1998: 84–5). His inhabitation is distributed, and only French plays the role of Enlightenment language. Before discussing other psychological and cultural implications of multilingualism, we should enquire what these many languages mean for translation.

Of course translation is a commerce in multilingualism. Other than remaining faithful to the letter of the text, with its accompanying difficulties, is there a way effectively to translate philosophies proceeding on dynamic distributions of languages and concepts? That is, in translating what are already translations, we must preserve context, perspectival shifts, and even interpretations. This can only be done by knowing the work of the philosopher well – and by being familiar with the theses he or she contests or adopts. Thus, in addition to being sensitive to semantics, connotation, and the relationship between overarching structure, its design and its performance, we need to be minimally specialized in a given philosophy. But here, and like the later Derrida, Levinas is writing 'Greek-Jew', he is 'translating' the biblical prophets' justice-teaching into a phenomenology of its origin in the address of the other person. He is offering a secular trans-lation while keeping the 'religious' expression as if in reserve.

Rée offers an illuminating example of this kind of difficulty. The translator of Sartre's *Esquisse d'une théorie des émotions* stayed close to the letter of the text. So much so that he translated the idiomatic *il n'est pas indifférent que* [it is important] as 'it is not a matter of indifference' (Rée 2001: 234). Thereupon, he translated *réalité humaine* by 'human reality', which might have found a lighter, more elegant expression were it not for the fact that the term was not so much Sartre's own as the echo of a work he was criticizing. The philosopher Henry Corbin had used the term in his work *Qu'est-ce que la métaphysique?* itself echoing Heidegger's Being-there. Indeed, this much questioned translation, *réalité humaine*, was subsequently used in the Portuguese version of Heidegger's *Being and Time*, thereby reviving debates around the meaning of *Dasein* Now, despite the fact that *Dasein* is more about the open 'site', that we are, of activity in the world, the expression *réalité humaine* hung on, following sinuous semantic paths through many Latinate languages. Here, it was not so much a matter of 'Greek-Jew' as of 'Latin-German'. As Rée points out, 'Philosophical translation is never bilateral . . . other, ulterior, languages keep drawing up a seat at the linguistic table' (Rée 2001: 235). But the lesson remains: faithfulness to the letter of the text may protect us from flattening the many semantic associations and tonal colors of a text. That also implies sometimes translating against one's common sense.

Take the text of the prophet Ezekiel, for example. Appropriate because this prophet of exile is surely the most poetic of these great allegory makers. Further, Ezekiel bears witness to the fury of Adonai against the faithless of Israel. To that end he is commanded to imbibe the scroll of judgement which unfolds before him like the face of the other. The translation of André Chouraqui, faithful to the Hebrew, integrates the most concrete and disorienting terms precisely from the original.

> Make chains: yes, the earth if filled with the judgement of bloods, / the city fills with violence. / I call forth the worst nations, they inherit of their houses. / I interrupt the spirit of the implacables, the powerful; / their sanctuaries are profaned. / Fright comes. They ask for peace, and nothing! / Damn upon damn will come, rumour upon rumour shall be. / They will seek the contemplation of the inspired, / but the torah is lost for the priests, counsel for the elders.
>
> (Ezekiel 7: 23–7)

Every biblical translation entails interpretation. The Chouraqui edition opens a window that allows us to see the roots of the Hebrew words and syntax. He is unruffled by uncanny usage, and it works. Indeed, the success of this translation depends on the sedimentation of prior versions. For here, the value of naturalism gives way to a brutal encounter with a little-mediated original. The voice of Adonai consists in repeated invectives and accusations. How then to extract a message of justice that is not vengeance? Clearly, from context (which means, for Levinas, the entire Bible) and from commentary, from Talmud. Jewish hermeneutics is fully aware of this, as we will soon see.

But suppose the idiom Derrida identifies as his 'one language' represented the dilemma of the translator. One language does not mean a private language, much less that all utterances will be somehow cross-contaminated by other idioms and registers. And yet . . . considering his situation of ongoing 'translation', first as a francophone incapable of writing Hebrew or Arabic, and possessing shards of Berber, Derrida extended his claim into an aporia: '1. One never speaks but a single language, 2. One never speaks a single language' (Derrida 1996: 21). In the first place, we have the impression of 'possessing' a language ('I call it my home, and I experience it as such . . . ' [Derrida 1996: 13]). This home language is the implicit one into which we translate other languages, spoken or written. Yet Derrida reminds us that the sedimentations of translations, which are our sedimentations, our 'reservoir' of meanings (cf. Husserl 2001: 227), imply a certain 'idiopathy' for each of us; this one language we possess is our 'idiom', though it is not private. Yet this idiom is never pure (Derrida 1996: 23), any more than a language is pure. This destabilizes all our hierarchies of languages, dialects, idioms, or *patois* (though Derrida is fully aware of linguistics' arguments distinguishing them). Together, the two propositions imply that I am always both the author and not the author, the translator and not the translator of my utterances; together, they urge that the 'language' in which 'I' speak is no purer than my notion of myself in my *id*-entity. This echoes Levinas's ongoing struggle with the illusion of totalization in philosophy; there is neither pure thought, pure being nor pure logic. For Derrida, 'it is impossible to count languages', notably once 'the One of a language, which escapes any arithmetical accounting, is never determined' (Derrida 1996: 55). Thus he can add, 'I have but one language, and it is not my own' (Derrida 1996: 13).

Aside from the obvious claim that I neither fully possess a language nor could claim that it somehow *belongs* to that idiom in which I learned to say 'I', this suggests something translators know well: the translation (and with it models of adequation between languages) is as essential as it is impossible. Derrida equates this less with semantics than with tone:

> If I have always trembled before that which I could say, it was because of the tone . . . and not the content [*fond*]. And that which, obscurely and as if despite myself, I sought to imprint, giving or loaning it to others as to myself, to myself as to the other . . . I believe that in all things, it is with the *rhythm* that I risk everything, for everything.
> (Derrida 1996: 81, emphasis added)

Tone thus includes rhythm and together they are what 'speaks', like Kierkegaard's moods, before we have so much as unfolded the argument – indeed, before we know the 'milieu' in which we understand! This is what Chouraqui preserves of the prophets, the obsessive rhythm of the voice of Adonai; this is what passes through Levinas's parataxes. Tone is clearly central to witnessing, and Levinas has set all his French 'monolingualism' in service to this uncanny performative dimension. For example:

> Exposure precedes the initiative – that a voluntary subject might take – of exposing itself. For the subject finds no place for itself, even in his own volume, nor in the night. He opens himself in space but is not-in-the-world. The restlessness of breathing, the exile in oneself, the in-itself without rest . . . is a *panting, a trembling of substantiality, a within the Here* – a passivity of exposure that does not manage to take form . . . . *But the relation to the air through which are formed and uttered, the experiences expressed in these truths, are not in turn an experience* . . . .
> (Levinas 1974: 276–7, 1991: 180–1, translation modified)

As if panting under the trauma of investiture, Levinas enlists the 'images' of space, air, breathing, and exile to the passive affect he calls *le Dire* [the saying], that innocence and integrity expressed by *temimut*. Here and elsewhere, the language is strange but recognizable. However, affect is carried strictly by tone and rhythm, which reflect the sincerity of the witness and an exasperated attempt *to say*; almost in the way Ezekiel 'translates' the invectives of Adonai. In both cases, the words run on – even run out of breath. Without these tones and rhythms, witnessing becomes declaratives and descriptions, and Levinas's adverbial '*autre-ment*' slides back into Heidegger's Being, into predication and totalization.

I tremble to imagine what translating *Otherwise than Being* must have felt like for Alphonso Lingis. Notoriously untranslatable – above all in his tone – Levinas, like Derrida, resists translation, just as they both resist the reduction of their witness and arguments. This is not a facile resistance. 'Not that I am cultivating the untranslatable', writes Derrida.

> Nothing is untranslatable if one so much as accords oneself the time of the effort [*le temps de la dépense*] or the expansion of competent discourse... But 'untranslatable' remains – should remain... the poetic economy of the idiom, the one that is important to which counts for me, for I would die even more quickly without it... there where a formal given 'quantity' always fails to restore the singular event of the original...
>
> (Derrida 1998: 56, translation modified)

Not an otiose resistance, then: it is an invitation to recognize waters beneath the waters, the affective preconditions of the text (Levinas 1982: 95–6; 1998a: 56–7).

Translating Levinas's hermeneutic 'reduction' to a common root of signifying

The singular event that is the original poses yet another problem in Levinas. Because he unequivocally adopted French as *the* 'language of philosophy' (Derrida 1996: 111 n.), and because the subtlest nuance of 'idioms', including Hebrew, had to find or forge a place in this 'Greek', there ought to be no insurmountable problem with the contents of what is *said*. But as we have seen, the translation of tone and rhythm is, in Levinas, also that of conveying the intersubjective affect at the root of responsibility. That is why Levinas himself performs the first act of translation on his *own* thought, using a hermeneutic reduction of words said [*le Dit*], designed to reveal the underlying affective process of the saying [*le Dire*]'. I believe he adopted this strategy from Heidegger, whose ontology was itself firstly hermeneutic. Heidegger's was the self-interpretation of (our) existing as that open site (the *Da-*) in which our 'worlds' unfold in different moods, authentic and inauthentic. His initial task entailed translating the silent speech or call of Being to us. This curious translation proceeded through the suspension or 'reduction' brought about by moods like anxiety, joy, or boredom. That is, just as moods color the way we perceive our worlds, they incite us to set aside our concern with objects and events therein. In short, we find in both Heidegger and Levinas projects of expressing that which overflows everyday language, through affects that open access for us to an extra-thematic 'X'. The latter takes up the affective suspension to ask what lies beneath my concern for another person, and sometimes my ongoing mourning of their suffering and demise. He came to call this 'ground' 'the saying' [*le Dire*]. It is affective and 'sensible', that is, embodied and *between* me and the other.

> In sensibility the qualities of perceived things turn into time and into consciousness... has not sensibility already been *said* then? Do its qualitative variations not make the *how* of the verb stated in it understood [as in Heidegger's hermeneutics]? Do not the sensations in which the sensible qualities are lived resound *adverbially* and, more precisely, as adverbs of the verb 'to be'?
>
> (Levinas 1974: 61, 1991: 35)

By using an utterly new reduction to affects or 'sensibility' – one that digs beneath Husserl's cognitive intentionality *and* Heidegger's hermeneutics of moods that 'unveil' Being, Levinas is effectively *translating* a flesh and blood body in the situation of facing another person. Conscious awareness (Husserl) and existence, or Being (Heidegger) are still 'with us' (i.e., 'the qualities of perceived things turn into time [as flowing consciousness]') (Levinas 1974: 61, 1991: 35). Yet the process called Being is doubled by qualities that inflect it in different ways. These 'qualities' – finding an appropriate language for them means uncovering something not-yet-conscious and so, not yet 'existing', are themselves comparable to tone and rhythm. They 'condition' existence, but they are expressed neither by nouns or verbs. Literature, notably poetry, seems to have understood and utilized this – consider the unique language of Mallarmé's *Hérodiade* or Paul Celan's poems turning into breath in *Atemwende* [Breathturn]. The problem – which Nietzsche called, throughout his career, the 'great falsification' (Nietzsche 1967: 36–8, 1989: 247–52) created by grammar and predication – is *translating* intersubjective sensibility as it plays out in rhythms and tones largely unattended to, not to mention the unanticipated performatives. '*But then if they [the sensations] could be surprised on the hither side of the said, would they not reveal another meaning?*' (Levinas 1974: 61, 1991: 35)?

The performatives that cross through his late work are like an invitation to translate backwards, from utterances to their affective condition: 'unsaying the said' (Levinas 1974: 19, 70, 1991: 7, 40). This shows how the immediacy and simplicity of witnessing, what Levinas calls the *kerygma*-quality underlying all language, prove to be as difficult to nail down as their expression (their translation from the body) is open to doubt. Levinas took French for the universal language of philosophy, as we have seen. Yet *his philosophy* is drama, poem, and at times lamentations. Again, it is a translation of what philosophy calls a pre-condition – maybe even a transcendental pre-condition – even as it flatly refuses being integrated into (Kantian *or* Husserlian) logics of conditions of possibility. The criticism Levinas raises against Husserl challenges the abstraction of the latter's formalism, notably that of homogeneously flowing time-consciousness; then later and above all, Husserl's 'standing-streaming' [*stehend-strömend*] that is 'the consciousness in which *all events* flow, sediment, and from which neither perception nor our subtle apperception (awareness of self) ever escapes' (Levinas 1974: 9–23, 1991: 8–19).

We have seen similar undertakings, even beyond literature. Freud was uncomfortable with reifications of the unconscious (Freud 1991: 121–5), he knew that access to the part of the unconscious created by repression of affective conflicts was possible only through traces, dreams, and neuroses, like words forgotten, slips of the tongue, the 'composite' people and places of dream-life. Access required dialogue and analytic interpretation, precursive to the task of translation, which ultimately only the subject could do. Like Levinas's adverbial affects, *this* problem precedes translation of words and sentences. Yet it returns when we confront the original text and later when the cultural heritage of the new language attempts to accommodate the linguistic and extra-linguistic preconscious of the author.

Translating silence and the 'negative sentence' of affects

This dimension of witnessing did not escape a reader sensitive to the disturbance felt by the victims who brought Holocaust denier and 'historian' Robert Faurisson to trial in 1979 for racial defamation. Called to prove that the gas chambers both existed and operated, the survivors were caught in the double-bind of explaining how one might be both a victim of the gas chambers and still alive today. Facing the positivist, juridical language into which they were challenged to 'translate' their experience and that of their loved ones, the victims were caught up in what Jean-François Lyotard calls a performative '*différend*'. Lyotard explains: 'the differend is the unstable state and the instant of language wherein something that ought to be able to be set into sentences cannot yet be so. This state entails the silence that is a *negative sentence*, but it also appeals to sentences [still] possible in principle. *What we ordinarily call a feeling* [affect] *points toward this state*' (Lyotard 1983: 29, my translation and emphasis). I will return to the question of silence and negative sentence. Note for now that a similar problem of translation inhabits Levinas's text and, I would venture, with Lyotard, that the only way of securing something indemonstrable – much less giving voice to such a feeling – is by repeatedly bearing witness to it and, in Levinas's case, by witnessing with parataxes, hyperbolic expressions, and self-interruption. If it were simply a matter of replaying classical phenomenology's descriptions of intersubjective *Einfühlung* (empathy), then there would not be the '*différend*' that, Levinas recalls, encourages the return of scepticism or doubt (Levinas 1974: 163–5). Nevertheless, and unlike Lyotard's project, Levinas witnesses from a first-person perspective rather than describing (from a third-party perspective) a blocked confrontation between two parties (the differend). Levinas chooses to speak out of the singularity of his experience in all its passivity:

> As if set under a blazing sun, supressing in me every shadowy corner, every residue of mystery, every *arrière-pensée*... I am a witnessing—or a trace, or a glory—of the Infinite, breaking with the bad silence protected by [Plato's] secret of Gyges.
> (Levinas 1998: 75, translation modified)'

This means the bad silence that Plato associates in the *Republic* with the shepherd, Gyges, who discovered a ring that made him invisible, allowing him to hide from others at will. Thus, for Levinas, bearing witness to an experience that emotionally overflows argumentative grammars (abstract subjects and predicates) is bearing witness to what Levinas calls in-finite 'experience' of intersubjective sensibility.

If we suppose that this is just God-talk, then we have reduced Levinas's witness to some religious ontology. Did Heidegger not argue persuasively that ontology and religion stand opposed, or that theology betrays ontology (Heidegger 1962: 73–5, 1974: 54–5)? More important than this is breaking 'the bad silence', whether it be that which lies at the depths of subjectivity (as with Gyges and his magic ring), or the silence of not being able to find the words by which to state one's 'experience'. To be a witness, beyond the responsibility of our assuming the first-person position, is to fold what we call our 'inside' as if 'outside', to open out those inner sufferings we prefer to hold far from the light of day. This amounts to 'translating' a feeling into something that never fully enters an intentional act. Consequently, the 'translation' here (as in Lyotard's victims' dilemma) is always suspect – something from which the translation from one language into another will also suffer. Levinas asks, 'How does the saying differ from an act beginning in a conquering and voluntary ego, its *signifying*, an act transforming itself into being, its 'for the other' taking a hold in identity?' (Levinas 1991: 153, translation modified). One answer was provided by Derrida who repeatedly expressed Levinas's *le Dire* [the saying] as a fundamental promise made to an other.

> As soon as I open my mouth, I have already promised, or sooner, sooner still, the promise has seized the *I* who promises to speak to the other, to say something, to affirm or confirm [something] by his word... This promise is older than I. This is what appears impossible, as the theoreticians of speech acts would say: like all authentic performatives, a promise must be made in the present.
> (Derrida 1987: 547, my translation)

In the speech from which this quote is drawn, Derrida was invited to address the *question* of negative theology. He spoke at length of a promise or a pre-condition – and its paradoxes.

> Before or rather within a *double bind: how [do I] avoid speaking*, since I have already begun to speak and always already begun to promise to speak. That I might already have

begun to speak, or rather that the trace at least of a word might have preceded this one, is what we cannot deny. *Translate*: *we cannot but deny it*'.

(Derrida 1987: 549)

Following Levinas closely, Derrida translates an intersubjective affect as a pre-reflective promise. The sceptics' denial he mentions comes from various places: from a charge of irrelevance ('there are always conversations going on, they are not preceded by a promise'); the question of a ground or first gesture ('let us focus on what is said, rather than some conception of what preceded it *in your mind*'); or a demand for transparency ('how would you *know* that you promised anything, when your interlocutor invited you first and you merely responded?'). These objections beg the question that everything is always already conscious or 'about' something. Yet they indicate that the pragmatic *translation* of Derrida's apparent commonplace sets it straightaway into an antinomy. I would argue that the contradiction has as much to do with the openness of interpretation, *and translation*, as it does with Levinas's core element of intersubjective existence: the unstated promise to respond that is immediately elicited in face-to-face confrontations. This immediacy, however we translate it, comes to be so fundamentally a part of our affective lives that the later Levinas will assign it the trope of 'obsession'.

Infinite translation as a task: Jewish approaches to the Torah

The question of a promise and of hermeneutic openness brings us back to bearing witness to an affect that overflows both ordinary intuition and categorical understanding. Translation as witness and communication would be an infinite process of conveying an in-finite 'experience'. Nevertheless, what Levinas calls 'infinite' is not the same in Christian negative theology and in Jewish approaches to the Torah and the Talmud. Bearing witness in *Otherwise than Being* should be read as the translation of rabbinical reading practices into phenomenological philosophy. How to understand this? In Judaism, readings (translations) of the Torah entail four levels, expressed in the initials of the word *Pardes* [paradise]: *pshat*, the literal reading; *remeze*, the allegorical reading; *drash*, the haggadic or moral meaning, and *sod*, the mystical signification. The reasons for this perspectivism are many, but must be read in the context of a Jewish conception of history and the absent God. It entails an orientation toward the future, that of awaiting the coming of a messiah (who is not God) and knowing that the messiah will never come. This sets the future up as an imperative ('Continue to wait!') but also as a confidence that knowingly destabilizes itself.

As Levinas observes, translating the *Tractatus Sanhedrin* (98b): the voice of Ullah proclaims, 'may the Messiah come, but may I not see him', to which Rabbi Yossi responds, 'may he come, and may I deserve the favour of sitting next to the shadow of his mule's manure' (Levinas 2010: 122, my translation). Again, the messiah does not come, but that neither closes down the openness of the future nor justifies abandoning the waiting. Moreover, if we allow the premise that the Torah is a revealed text, then translating it entails setting secular, or non-Jewish words in place of the 'holy' ones. How, then, to translate such words (many of which precisely bear witness)? Marlène Zarader ventures, ironically, 'under one condition only: provided the new word adds nothing to the text, provided it limits its presentations to *delivering* the text' (2006: 92).

This again recalls my value of remaining as close to the text as possible. Yet it quickly falls into a sceptical dilemma: how could one possibly urge, much less show, that *the* text has been *delivered* (and how, to echo Derrida, does one ever do anything but this)? Moreover, what becomes of the translator, or the reading 'subject' in such a delivery effort? Drawing from David Banon's *La lecture infinie* (Banon 1987), Zarader reminds us that the Jewish tradition, which is 'through and through an exegetical' one (2006: 93) and thus ongoingly concerned with trans-lation – that is, moving voices and texts among each other – solved the dilemma early on with a distinct conception of the interpreter (translator). The latter should not be compared to the 'classical position of the reader'. Instead, she or he is 'the indispensable partner, the interlocutor of a text that speaks only in this dialogue' (Zarader 2006: 92). In treating the Torah as a spoken word, a word proffered in and as a promise, no doubt, translation (interpretation) belongs from the outset both to dialogue and to our hearing it.

The implications of this may seem extreme, as there are surely better and worse translations. However, as Betty Rojtman has argued, Hebrew as a language without vowels (added later to certain texts) *requires* the vocalization provided by the reader, and thereby the textual performance assured by him or her. Like the

> score for a song, whose vowels determine the diction, always actualized, always taken up again and different from itself, the Torah is presented as a call by the text itself, which bears witness – even in its typographical 'blank white spaces' – to a 'void' in which the meaning finds its inspiration.
>
> (Rojtman 1998: 2–3; Zarader 2006: 93)

This 'void', which Rojtman qualifies as processual and temporarily 'filled' by sound, argues that each reader, each translator, will – indeed, must – approach the text as interlocutor *and* as re-creator. Hardly controversial, one might respond, but hardly an assurance of the aforementioned completeness or fidelity. Yet the argument has scarcely begun: 'if we want, in effect, the task of the interpreter [translator] not to be subjective, while being resolutely active, we must declare that there is nothing in the interpretation that is not already in the text' (Zarader 2006: 94). Now, given the Jewish conception of the future as open, the implication is that the text 'already contains, albeit in a latent mode, all the elements that will [ultimately] be discovered in it' (Zarader 2006: 94, translation modified).

Interpretation, like translation, would thus face the task of teasing out elements present in a latent mode in its text. It would confront the responsibility of realizing potentialities. This is less a call to hermeneutic activism than it is the recognition that in each translation something will (continue to) be lacking, the work of the translator proceeding *according* to her or his level of linguistic, cultural, hermeneutic, and 'auditory' competence. The perspectivism and futural emphasis here addresses the charges of scepticism, which, as Levinas is fond of saying, arise *as a positive thing* (Levinas 1974: 261). Scepticism would contest arguments that proceed as though truth could be stated once and for all, or as if philosophy could forge a monolithic and transparent order. However, many interpretations and even translations have proven to be possible, this in-finity is multiply attested and still open. Gershom Scholem recounts the parable that the Torah reveals itself uniquely to each of its readers, and that, since Sinai, it is different at various ages. Thus, in the (Kabbalistic) age in which we stand, one letter is missing or incomplete. It may reappear in the next cosmic age at the same time that a letter, presently perceived, vanishes (Scholem 1996: 80; Zarader 2006: 94). This allegory casts light on the *here and now* of Levinas's witness, as it does on time conceived as the moment of hearing-interpretation (translation) in light of an open future: each one to whom the witness is addressed participates in its actualization. *That* is one sense of Levinas's 'substitution' (one letter for another, one witness for another, but always *for* the others), and it entails the promise or responsibility of which Derrida and Levinas both speak.

> That means that Jewish hermeneutics is marked by a double 'supplement'. On the one hand, it is not [so much] a matter of making a sense appear that was, on first glance, hidden, but rather of giving oneself to an 'inexhaustible quest', to a 'perpetual movement'. On the other hand, this movement consequently is more than an act of knowledge, more even than a cast of mind. It becomes something like a way of existing. In this way the Jewish tradition can define itself... as an 'infinite reading'.
>
> (Zarader 2006: 95)

This open movement does not mean that 'anything goes' in translating. Taken together with the norm of faithfulness to the text, it intensifies the responsibility of the translator. Translators find themselves obliged to provide a reading faithful to the letter and the style of the text, knowing that such a project will succeed *and* fail. The aforementioned question of competence thus stands in parallel with the four planes of reading (*Pardes*). It is not a matter of translating Levinas's *philosophy* as allegory, or mysticism; but neither is it one of focusing just on the literal meaning. It is a matter of realizing that, in his performatives, bearing witness is open, 'more than an act of knowledge', and that it will be multiply heard (or not heard! cf. Levinas 2009: 233 no. 1–2). Indeed, even where there seems to be no 'hearing', no force of conviction, the addressee (translator) may find a 'letter' hitherto undiscovered. Again, not so much Gadamer's fusion of horizons as ongoing encounters in which we cannot be sure that two horizons, supposedly given, ever merge. This is 'the idea ... of a text that is open ... in its own most being, awaiting a future' (Zarader 2006: 96). It clearly expresses the task of the translator who confronts Levinas.

Again, nothing of this diminishes the force of our responsibility. It is, rather, the sharpest acknowledgement of the finitude of the translator (interpreter) and of their capacities, *just as it is* the call to textual ethics. One might even venture that Levinas's 1961 *Totality and Infinity* sets the interpretable alterity of the Torah into the context of a phenomenology of the face, where the face is pure expression rather than a phenomenon or object (Levinas 1961). Simply to assert that the face is 'expression is to urge that one has "understood" something, passively and *in the moment* of responding, before one has recognized "the colour of his eyes"'(Levinas 1995: 85):

> To renounce the psychagogy, demagogy, pedagogy [that] rhetoric involves is to face the Other, in a true conversation. Then this being is nowise an object, he is outside all grasping. This detachment from all objectivity means, positively, for this being, his presentation in the face, his *expression*, his language .... The relation of conversation is necessary to 'let him be' ...'.
>
> (Levinas 1961: 42–3, 1998: 70–1, my translation)

Does this amount to saying that Levinas's ethical responsibility has set the Torah in the place of a human other? The more interesting question would rather be: *how* would the Torah and the other person 'flow together', and what is it in the human experience – call it intersubjective life lived from within – that nourishes the hermeneutics just described? What is it moreover, in first-person experience, that gave rise to a monotheism in which *hearing* a word, a dialogical word, had priority over *seeing* 'the God'? These questions may best be left open to avoid reification or dogmatism, but they stand at the root of what Derrida deemed, translating Joyce with irony, 'Greek-Jew is Jew-Greek'. They are, then, a matter of translating into a philosophy largely unconcerned with its non-Greek sources, ideas that return to it from a host of thinkers, explicitly or implicitly. Levinas, Derrida, and Zarader, among others, set about 'to translate' these sources back into phenomenology. In so doing, they develop an expanded, and deeply philosophical, sense of what translation might be. 'It is clear that this theory of translation – still judged 'hallucinatory' today – breaks radically with the habitual comprehension of what a text is' (Zarader 2006: 97).

Conclusion

It is crucial to grasp, when reading or translating Levinas, that Jewish hermeneutics enquires into an open text, not into its author. Whether this concerns qualities of the author, the nature of his or her existence, or of his or her inscrutable will, is secondary to listening to a text and to its ongoing realization. This is well known, of course. Yet less well known is the implication for Levinas's phenomenology. Because Judaism is not preoccupied with *theo*-logy, the position of the other remains open, an empty space. Thus, when the other addresses me, it is perfectly admissible to ascribe humanity to that other. But it is just as admissible to conceive the address as coming from a word, a voice, as in Ezekiel's witness. This is why in chapter 2 of *Otherwise than Being*, Levinas seeks a reduction unheard of in classical phenomenology, one leading back to something like a common root of iterative performance *and* object constitution. In the 1974 work, his bearing witness to obsession, or to what he calls 'the other-in-the-same', is a kind of word or concept, so we might suppose that, as such, the root of language requires our recourse to words, to language. It is not, however, just any text, but the justice 'text' of the biblical prophets. In that respect, the prophetic utterance – from whomever it came – has priority in *Otherwise than Being*. Put simply, prophetic performances are not visions of future events the way Greek seers foretold what was to come to their public. Ezekiel is not Cassandra. The function of the Hebrew prophet is to summon a community to justice. Nevertheless, the implication of the reduction might also be that human experience, at the affective level that concerns Levinas, contains the seed that elicits both prophetic saying and a response to an other in the world. That would be the ultimate meaning, and ambiguity, of his *le Dire* [the saying]. What this implies for the translator is simultaneously a recognition of finitude, and the continual balancing of tone and textual letter. The lesson that Scholem, Banon, Rojtman, Goldwyn (2015), and Zarader teach us is that each translation will bring its specific letter into a universal discourse that includes the philosophical. This lesson should provide the translator with as much hope as it does anxiety.

Related topics

Heidegger; Derrida; ethics; the translation of philosophical texts; translating Derrida; translation, mysticism and esotericism.

Further reading

Banon, D. (1987). (*La lecture infinie: Les voies de l'interprétation midrashique*. Paris: Le Seuil. For French-language readers, this accomplished study of Midrash discusses the four meanings of interpretation, and translation. The work includes a 'Preface' by Levinas.)

Herzog, A. (2014). 'Levinas and Derrida on Translation and Conversion', *Prooftexts*, Vol. 34: 127–46. (For a sensitive discussion of the intricacies of translating Levinas and Derrida, this recent article affords us insight into important Hebrew concepts underlying Levinas's sometimes unconventional vocabulary.)

Rée, J. (2001). 'The Translation of Philosophy', *New Literary History*, Vol. 32, No. 2: 223–57. (This historic and trans-cultural discussion of translating philosophical texts is clear and comprehensive; an indispensable reading of the implications of philosophy's conceptual cosmopolitanism.)

Rojtman, B. (1998). *Black Fire on White Fire: An Essay on Jewish Hermeneutics from Midrash to Kabbalah*. Trans. S. Rendall. Berkeley: University of California Press. (Coming out of comparative literature, Rojtman's text focuses on the evolution and ambiguities of demonstrative pronouns in Bible and mysticism. Her attention to the speculative, or hidden, level of interpretation (and its translation) clarifies a characteristic tension between openness and orthodoxy in Jewish hermeneutics.)

References

Adorno, T. (2000). 'Cultural Criticism and Society (1951)' in *The Adorno Reader*. Ed. B. O'Connor. Oxford: Blackwell Publishers, pp. 195–210.

Austin, J. L. (1962). *How to Do Things with Words: The William James Lectures (1955)*. Oxford: Clarendon Press.

Chayyim of Volozhin. (2012). *The Soul of Life: The Complete Neffesh Ha-Chayyim*. Trans. L. Moskowitz. Teaneck, NJ: New Davar Publications.

Derrida, J. (1987). 'Comment ne pas parler: Dénégations' in *Psyché, inventions de l'autre*. Paris: Galilée.

Derrida, J. (1996). *Le monolinguisme de l'autre. La prothèse d'origine*. Paris: Galilée.

Derrida, J. (1998). *The Monolingualism of the Other, or: The Prosthesis of Origin*. Trans. P. Mensa. Stanford: Stanford University Press.

Freud, S. (1991). 'The Unconscious' in *General Psychological Theory: Papers on Metapsychology*. Ed. P. Rieff. New York: Collier Books Macmillan Publishing, pp. 109–46.

Gadamer, H. G. (2004). *Truth and Method*. Trans. J. Weinsheimer and D. G. Marshall. London: Continuum.

Goldwyn, E. (2015). *Reading between the Lines: Form and Content in Levinas' Talmudic Readings*. Pittsburgh: Duquesne University Press.

Heidegger, M. (1962). *Being and Time*. Trans. J. Macquarrie and E. Robinson. New York: Harper & Row.

Heidegger, M. (1974). 'The Onto-Theological Constitution of Metaphysics' in *Identity and Difference*. Trans. Joan Stambaugh. New York: Harper and Row, pp. 42–74.

Husserl, E. (1991). *On the Phenomenology of Internal Time Consciousness*. Trans. J. Barnett Brough. Dordrecht: Kluwer Academic Publishers; *Husserliana*, Vol. X.

Husserl, E. (2001). *Analyses Concerning Passive and Active Synthesis: Lectures on Transcendental Logic*. Trans. A. Steinbock. Dordrecht: Springer; *Husserliana*, Vol. XI.

Kierkegaard, S. (1980). *The Concept of Anxiety*. Trans. and ed. R. Thomte. Princeton: Princeton University Press.

Levinas, E. (1961). *Totalité et infini, essai sur l'extériorité*. The Hague: Martinus Nijhoff.

Levinas, E. (1974). *Autrement qu'être ou au-delà de l'essence*. The Hague: Martinus Nijhoff.

Levinas, E. (1982). *De Dieu qui vient à l'idée*. Paris: Vrin.

Levinas, E. (1991). *Otherwise than Being, or: Beyond Essence*. Trans. A. Lingis. Dordrecht: Kluwer Academic.

Levinas, E. (1995). *Ethics and Infinity: Conversations with Philippe Nemo*. Trans. R. A. Cohen. Pittsburgh: Duquesne University Press.

Levinas, E. (1998). *Totality and Infinity: Essay on Exteriority*. Trans. A. Lingis. Pittsburgh: Duquesne University Press.

Levinas, E. (1998a). *Of God who Comes to Mind*. Trans. B. Bergo. Stanford: Stanford University Press.

Levinas, E. (2009). *Carnets de captivité et autres inédits*, Vol. I. Eds. R. Calin and C. Chalier. Paris: Bernard Grasset.

Levinas, E. (2010). 'Textes messianiques' in *Difficile liberté, Essais sur le judaïsme*. Paris: Livre de Poche.

Lyotard, J. F. (1983). *Le différend*. Paris: Éditions de Minuit.

Lyotard, J. F. (1988). *The Differend: Phrases in Dispute*. Trans. G. Van Den Abbeele. Minneapolis: University of Minnesota Press.

Malka, S. (1994). *Monsieur Chouchani: L'énigme d'un maître du XXe siècle*. Paris: Jean-Claude Lattès.

Malka, S. (2002). *Emmanuel Lévinas: la vie et la trace*. Paris: Jean-Claude Lattès.

Nietzsche, F. (1967). *On the Genealogy of Morals/ Ecce Homo*. Trans. W. Kaufmann. New York: Vintage Books.

Nietzsche, F. (1989). 'On Truth and Lying in an Extra-Moral Sense (1873)' in *Friedrich Nietzsche on Rhetoric and Language*. Eds. S. L. Gilman, C. Blair, and D. J. Parent. Oxford: Oxford University Press.

Nietzsche, F. (1993). *The Birth of Tragedy out of the Spirit of Music*. Trans. S. Whiteside. London: Penguin Books.

Pliny the Elder. (1857). *The Natural History of Pliny*, Vol. VI. Trans. J. Bostock and H. T. Riley. London: Henry G. Bohn.

Rojtman, B. (1998). *Black Fire on White Fire: An Essay on Jewish Hermeneutics from Midrash to Kabbalah*. Trans. S. Rendall. Berkeley: University of California Press.

Scholem, G. (1996). *On the Kabbalah and Its Symbolism*. Trans. R. Mannheim. New York: Schocken Books.

Searle, J. R. (1976). 'A Classification of Illocutionary Acts' *Language and Society*, Vol. 5, No. 1: 1–23.

Zarader, M. (2006). *The Unthought Debt: Heidegger and the Hebraic Heritage*. Trans. B. Bergo. Stanford: Stanford University Press.

Part IV
Emerging trends

25
Cognitive approaches to translation

Maria Şerban

25.1 Introduction

Cognitive approaches to translation studies are driven by three interrelated aims: to understand the structure and organization of the capacities of cognitive agents involved in processes of translation, to build better theories and models of translation, and to develop more efficient methods and programs for translator training. Meeting the goals of such a broad agenda requires the fusion of different theoretical and experimental tools, involving fields such as cognitive psychology, linguistics and artificial intelligence (AI). The current landscape of research programs that investigate the cognitive underpinnings of translation is therefore both varied and constantly developing, and covers exploratory studies that aim to carve out the very problem space for cognitive approaches to translation through to large-scale projects that promise helpful technological innovations.

In Section 2, which forms the bulk of the chapter, I describe and analyse five of the key research domains within this complex area, focusing on meaning, competence, expertise and emotion, before turning to the important and emerging area of machine translation and AI.

In Section 3, I address the question of how the field of cognitive aspects of translation should be conceptualized. My analysis shows that, unlike some 'hard' sciences, cognitive research is not driven by a 'master' theory, in this case of the psychological capacities involved in the translation process. Instead, it seems that cognitive approaches to translation are better conceptualized as a family of projects based on multiple theories that are differentially relevant for studying the translation process. Cognitive approaches, I argue, are dynamically organized around specific problems or questions that have been shaped by previous research, by well-established cognitive hypotheses and by the current theoretical and practical interests of the discipline of translation studies.

25.2 A varied landscape of cognitive approaches to translation

Broadly construed, the explanatory task of cognitive approaches to translation is to offer an account of how translators are able to create, transform and communicate meanings in various contexts by manipulating and interacting with different types of texts (Malmkjær 2012;

Malmkjær and Windle 2012). By expanding existing cognitive models of language processing and comprehension, as well as of general human capacities like learning, problem solving and decision making, cognitive scientists provide theoretical insight and practical recommendations concerning translators' choices and behaviours. Cognitive models are used to guide answers to specific theoretical and practical research questions. How are meanings assigned to specific situations and texts? Are there language or cultural universals that can serve as a basis for translation? Do machine translation programs inform us about how human translation works or do they provide an alternative that overcomes some of the limitations encountered by human translators? What kind of tools best help translators in their problem solving and decision making processes?

In order to generate good explanatory answers to these questions, existing models of cognitive capacities are calibrated and tested against relevant data. In addition to introspection, cognitive researchers deploy a host of empirical methods to collect and analyse data about the translation process. Some of these include EEG measurements, theoretical analysis, think-out-loud protocols of individual language learners and translators and of groups of translators, participant observation, tracking/logging the translation process on computer screens and eye-tracking during translation tasks. While first and second-generation cognitive studies typically work with data collected via a single empirical method, third-generation studies triangulate multiple sources of data to calibrate and confirm particular models of the cognitive capacities involved in the translation process. In addition, third-generation studies have started to combine data from translation process observation with data gathered from translation product analysis and corpus-based translation studies.

In what follows, I survey several examples of current cognitive research on translation. These short case studies will serve to illustrate (i) the differences between first, second and third-generation cognitive studies of translation, and (ii) the roles that theoretical models and specific research questions play in determining and organizing cognitive approaches to translation.

25.2.1 Cognitive perspectives on meaning in translation

Cognitive approaches conceive of the process of translation broadly as requiring that the same or similar meanings are carried from the source language to the target language. This makes theories of meaning central to explaining what cognitive capacities are involved in the translation process and how they are modulated by various physical, cultural and social factors. The variation in cognitive approaches to translation starts in how they conceptualize the notion of meaning itself. Cognitive models differ in what they take to be the locus of meaning: some models assume that meanings are the sort of things that belong to texts, to languages and even to neural patterns, while others assign meaning to specific socio-cultural interactions.

Such theoretical perspectives on the notion of meaning are associated with broader cognitive paradigms that comprise specific models of cognitive capacities, e.g., reasoning, problem solving and decision making. There are three major frameworks or paradigms that have been imported from the field of cognitive science to translation studies: the information processing, the neural networks (or connectionist) and the situated and embodied cognition frameworks (Risku 2012). Each of them implies different ways of thinking about how meaning is created and manipulated through different cognitive capacities during the translation process.

The information processing paradigm views translation as a matter of manipulating symbols in accordance with a set of well-specified rules. Relying on the analogy of a digital computer, this paradigm models human minds as manipulating and transforming internal mental symbols or representations. Mental representations are thought to be the bearers of meanings and to have causal roles in shaping human reasoning capacities and behaviours. A landmark in the development of symbolic approaches to meaning has been the introduction of componential analysis to Chomskyan generative grammar by Fodor and Katz. *The Structure of a Semantic Theory* (1963) proposed a model of meaning combining a structuralist method of analysis, a formalist system of description and a mentalist conception of meaning. Although the Katzian model is no longer the standard in contemporary semantic analyses, its lasting influence comes from the introduction of two key ideas in linguistic theorizing: the requirement of describing the structure of lexical meaning in the context of a formal grammar and the issue of the psychological reality of meaning (Geeraerts 2015: 2–3). The first idea contributed to the emergence of two contemporary ways of formalizing the semantics of natural language: computational semantics and formal semantics. The second idea has generated different theoretical positions (on a spectrum from permissive to restrictive) concerning the issue of the independence of linguistic capacities (and linguistic knowledge) from other cognitive capacities (and world knowledge).

More specifically, both ideas have informed cognitive models of translation. For instance, equivalence theories view translation primarily as a task of comparing and matching linguistic and/or mental representations (e.g., Catford 1965; Nida and Taber 1969/1982; House 1977; Snell-Hornby 1988). In broad outline, these approaches seek to establish and to represent formally general rules that govern the process of transferring meanings from source to target language (Panou 2013). Some of their most salient differences concern the issue of whether the linguistic capacities involved in the translation process (or word-knowledge) should be treated as independent or interconnected with other cognitive capacities (world-knowledge).

However, equivalence theory approaches to translation share in part the challenges that have been levelled against the adoption of the information processing paradigm in cognitive science more broadly. For instance, in light of an increasing number of cognitive studies, the symbolic computationalist framework has been criticized for offering too idealized a picture of human reasoning abilities. Rather than relying solely on semantic characteristics of mental representations, cognitive scientists have proposed that human cognitive functioning depends on emotionally loaded exemplars drawn from experience.

The emerging alternative framework models human cognitive capacities in terms of neural networks. This framework places a double emphasis on the experiential and culturally constructed nature of cognitive categorizations and on the constraints imposed by the biological brains whose function is to support and maintain specific cognitive capacities. That is, the neural networks or connectionist framework assumes that world knowledge based on individual experiences plays a key role in cognitive processes like understanding, learning and decision making. Also, against the classical symbolic view of cognition, connectionist models assume that knowledge is not stored in discrete data structures; rather, knowledge is said to be implemented across patterns of neural activation. Thus, instead of thinking of cognitive processes in terms of specific symbol-manipulating algorithms, the connectionist paradigm suggests that neural networks 'learn' to recognize regularities in the environment by having access to novel inputs and by exploiting existing connections between their nodes. It follows that the meaning of words is learned in concrete interactions with the environment at a subsymbolic level. The observed stability of meaning is the result of repetition of certain types of situations and interactions between the world and the cognitive system. Nevertheless, according to connectionist models, meaning is a constantly changing construct.

Prototype theory is one class of theories of the translation process that has been influenced by the connectionist framework. Prototype theory postulates that the translation process consists of the manipulation and transformation of experienced-based units of thought. These units are referred to as frames, scripts, schemas, scenes or scenarios. For instance, Vannerem and Snell-Hornby (1986) used the notions of scenes and frames to explain the experiential basis of text analysis and production in translation. Their model emphasized that the understanding and production of texts requires understanding the particular translation situations, which in turns determines specific expectations about the meaning and style of the source and target texts. Thus, rather than reproducing meaning structures (symbols) from one language to another, the task of a translator is better conceptualized as one of offering possibilities for the construction of meaning. According to prototype theory, translators do not just follow rules in a task of symbol manipulation, but rather engage in a complex task of integrating situation-specific inputs and internal-individual or culture-specific models (schemas, scenarios, etc.).

The connectionist paradigm thus facilitated the development of models which capture the dynamic nature of meanings manipulated in the translation task. But while prototype theory approaches accounted for the role of experience as a factor in translators' performance, they have also been criticized for neglecting (or downplaying) the social and artefact-mediated aspects of the translation task (Muñoz Martín 2010). This criticism of the sub-symbolic models of meaning and translation process made room for a third theoretical paradigm of cognitive models.

The situated and embodied cognition paradigm tries to integrate the physical, social and cultural factors that lie outside human minds and which play key roles in how cognitive capacities develop and are applied in different situations (Clark 1997). Instead of explaining cognition in terms of the recognition, reconstruction and use of mental representations or neural patterns, the situated/embodied view conceptualizes cognition in terms of an interaction between agents and their psycho-social environment. With respect to the problem of meaning, this framework entails that one cannot localize meaning on paper or in the brain, and that one should view it as a product of interaction with a particular environment. The implications of this way of viewing meaning for translation studies include: (1) placing more emphasis on the role of personality traits, emotional features and social skills of translators and (2) taking into account the structure of translators' communities and translators' training in understanding translators' behaviour and choices (Kiraly 2000; Risku 2010).

Describing the translation process in terms of problem solving and decision making has encouraged symbolic and connectionist models that seek to explain: (1) how agents overcome the problems encountered during different types of translation tasks, (2) the differences between the performance of expert and novice translators and (3) micro and macro strategies and methods that might work best for overcoming the processing difficulties met during the translation process. The situated/embodied paradigm, on the other hand, brings to light the unconscious and 'non-problematic' aspects of the translation process, such as experts' ability to interact with novel texts, how personality traits of the translator affect the product of the translation process or how the affective elements implicit in a translation context impact the end result. As a result, the situated cognition paradigm has encouraged cognitive researchers to take into account these aspects in explaining the concept of translation competence and expertise (Muñoz Martín 2010; Risku 2010).

The problem of meaning in translation generates a rich collection of models of the cognitive capacities involved in the different stages of the translation process and the internal and external factors that modulate this process. As I showed in this section, these models can differ with respect to the theoretical assumptions they make about human minds in general and the specific cognitive factors involved in the translation process. Despite this diversity, I argue there is an underlying unity to cognitive approaches to translation. Before addressing the issue of how to think about this unity, the following subsections will further exemplify the research questions raised by cognitive models of meaning in the translation process.

25.2.2 Translation competence

The question of whether translation, as a process which involves the manipulation and transformation of meanings, requires a special type of psychological competence has proven to be a fruitful research problem at the intersection between translation studies and psycholinguistics. Theories of meaning and language acquisition, as well as cognitive models of the social and cultural factors that might impact the agent's performance in translation tasks, have flourished in the past years.

For example, the PACTE project at the University Autonoma de Barcelona focuses on the development of the translation competence of both language students and experienced professional translators. Their model of translation competence comprises several submodules: the bilingual competence submodule, the extra-linguistic competence submodule, the strategic and instrumental competencies submodules, the knowledge about the translation process submodule, as well as other psycho-physiological components. The predictions yielded by the PACTE model have been tested via two longitudinal studies comparing the knowledge and skills of experienced translators with those of foreign language teachers with no experience in translation and with those of trainee translators, respectively. The outcome is a dynamical model of the translation process in which all the cognitive submodules interact in a way that integrates declarative knowledge (*know-that*) and procedural knowledge (*know-how*). In addition, PACTE's experimental results indicate a more substantial contribution of procedural knowledge to the improvement of the quality of translation (Hurtado Albir *et al.* 2014; Hurtado Albir 2017).

A similar process-orientated longitudinal study is at the basis of the TransComp project at the University of Graz. Following the development of translation competence in undergraduate translation students, the project offers the opportunity to translation researchers to model the acquisition and development of expertise, or experienced professionalism, in the field of translation. Building on the PACTE model of translation competence, the TransComp researchers posit six distinct capacities whose development leads to translation expertise: communicative competence in the source language and the target language, domain competence, and tools and research competence, translation routine activation competence, psychomotor competence and strategic competence. Measuring creativity indicators such as uniqueness, optional shift and novelty, their longitudinal study showed that the quality of translation is correlated with achieving a cognitive balance between creative problem solving and automaticity of the translation process (Göpferich, Jakobsen and Mees 2009; Göpferich, Bayer-Hohenwarter, Prassl and Stadlober 2011). While further cognitive research is required to test the empirical predictions of projects such as PACTE and TransComp, these early findings provide a 'proof of concept' for the contributions of cognitive approaches to the problem of expertise in translation.

25.2.3 Expertise in translation

While translation competence is analysed in terms of several other cognitive capacities, expertise in translation is conceptualized as (1) a permanent state of mastery reached after a substantive amount of practice *or* as (2) a process which takes place at the upper limit of translation competence. The latter perspective emphasizes the continuity between translation competence and expertise rather than the extensive amounts of practising hours required in order to reach a certain level of expertise.

More generally, cognitive research has yielded a series of categories for differentiating multiple types of expertise at work in the translation process. For instance, while some studies distinguish between translation experts and experienced non-experts, others focus on the cognitive differences between routine experts and adaptive experts. These distinctions are important because they also reflect the theoretical interest in identifying the multiple factors, such as work experience, cultural background, linguistic competence and the level of understanding of the expectations and needs of the target audience that might influence what counts as expertise in different translation contexts (Siren and Hakkarainen 2002).

In addition, these more fine-grained expertise research categories have been used to interpret the surprising findings of several empirical studies showing that expert translators do not always produce high-quality translations. One way of understanding these results is with the help of the categories of routine and adaptive experts. When an expert translator applies a routine translation approach to a novel (non-routine) task, the results might be suboptimal. The less successful translators might fall in the category of routine experts that have difficulty in adapting to novel translation tasks. In other contexts, the suboptimal results are due to the fact that the experimental translation task falls outside the professional domain in which a translator is an expert. This points to another relevant distinction between expertise and professionalism which has been applied to the field of translation.

Some cognitive studies pursue a more in-depth analysis of the process view of translation expertise and of its consequences, in particular with respect to the so-called *automaticity* question. The latter refers to the common assumption that novices have to work hard at a translation task while experts select and process the relevant information quickly and effortlessly. Cognitive research on the different stages involved in the translation process challenges this assumption, revealing the fact that given the same translation assignment experts would typically work harder and invest more time in the decision making stage of the translation. The automaticity question is a growing topic of research in cognitive psychology, indicating that we are still some way from having any definitive answers. However, the emerging models suggest that the effect of automaticity might be a robust pattern in the translation process. Thus, investigating the 'translation does not get easier' phenomenon may help refine further expertise research categories and inform translation training programs.

For a more concrete illustration of the expertise research agenda, consider the work of the network EXPERTISE coordinated by Andin F. Rydning at the University of Oslo (2001–5) and comprising a number of translation researchers and cognitive scientists from all over Europe. Members of this research network published numerous reports discussing various aspects of translation expertise. Several of these studies used Thinking Aloud Protocols (TAPs) to investigate the cognitive dimensions of translation expertise. This method requires that the translators involved in the study verbalize their translation procedures and decisions, which are subsequently analysed in parallel with their written translations. While the use of TAPs has raised a number of serious concerns and objections,[1] it has also been argued that the methodology can yield valid data if certain conditions are met during data collection and analysis (Ericsson & Simon 1984/1993; Künzli 2009). In a series of studies, Alexander Künzli has relied on TAPs to investigate the factors which directly influence the comparative evaluation of the performance of different groups of translators: expert translators and translation students (Künzli 2001), technical translators and routine translators (Künzli 2004). These preliminary studies established that linguistic background and specialist domains are key in determining expertise performance in a specific translation task. Whether and how the effect of these factors can be modulated by other contextual elements is a growing topic in translation research.

Another class of studies aimed at integrating the results of TAPs with other methods used in translation process research such as eye-tracking methods and computer keystroke logging in order to explore further the features of translators' expertise. In a series of Translog studies of experts and novices, Arnt Jakobson has triangulated these different perspectives on the translation process and succeeded in validating three important aspects of translators' expertise (Jakobsen 2003, 2005, 2011). First, he established that experts spend more time on initial orientation and final revisions. Second, experts are capable of processing longer units or segments. Finally, they have superior speed potential. In addition, Jakobson's findings can be shown to provide further support for Künzli's hypothesis that peak performance is possible only in domains in which translators are specialized.

Expertise research, and translation process research more generally, aims to identify and explain not only the cognitive but also the affective elements involved in the translation process. Thus, the problem agenda of expertise research has recently been extended by contributions from affective cognitive science, which further refine the questions and associated hypotheses about the emotional aspects of translation.

25.2.4 Emotion in the translation process

Research linking emotion to translation studies can be divided into two main strands. The more prominent strand focuses on the question of how to translate emotive language or emotional material, while the less developed component of this research agenda concerns the emotions evoked in translators and interpreters. Nevertheless, an increasing number of translation process studies point to the relevance of the latter strand of research for understanding the factors that influence translator performance as well as translator training. Thus, while not a traditional research problem in translation studies, the investigation of the emotional aspects of translation, using the resources (models, theories, methods) from affective studies, has the potential to complement current hypotheses about the organization and dynamics of how translators operate and even of how they gain expertise in a particular domain.

As noted in the previous section, a translator needs to not only to be a competent linguist, but also to know how to mediate effectively between cultures, to understand a target reader's needs and expectations in order to be able to communicate a source author's message in a successful way to target readers or to a target audience (in an interpreter's case). Being able to recognize and communicate one's own and other people's emotions guarantees a more successful intercultural communication, and thus should count as an important skill for translators and interpreters.[2] These latter aspects of a translator's competence are part of what personality psychology investigates under the label of *emotional intelligence*.

Current research on the emotional aspects of the translation process points to the existence of a robust link between creativity, emotional intelligence and translators' performance. For example, Davou (2007) focuses on the interaction of cognition with emotion in the processing of textual material. The study explores the link between creativity and emotion, suggesting that creativity is a product of the interaction between different emotional stimuli that are sent simultaneously and are capable of triggering multiple thoughts and cognitive processes. Thus, observed differences in levels of creativity among translation students or even professional translators might be explained in terms of the different emotional interpretations that the same text generates for each of them. This hypothesis seems to be supported by previous empirical observations that successful translators are typically emotionally engaged individuals who derive personal and contextual meanings from texts and create interpersonal relationships with source text authors and target readers (e.g., Boase-Beier 2006; Jääskeläinen 1999).

Different texts are also likely to elicit different emotional responses from translators, so that a legal translation will not have the same potential for emotivity as translating a love poem. Because of this, the role that emotional intelligence plays in the process will vary across translation tasks.

One fairly obvious implication of this line of research into the emotional aspects of the translation process is that the translation of texts with high emotive potential is likely to be more successfully undertaken by an emotionally intelligent translator, while texts with low emotive potential do not have the same requirement because they rely less on the ability of the translator to regulate and manage emotions. This prediction can be tested in experimental studies, which in turn will yield additional refinements of the emotional involvement hypothesis.

Similar exploratory studies have already begun to investigate the relationship between levels of emotional intelligence and individual differences among the performance of interpreters, as well as translators. Focusing on the performance of signed language interpreters, Karen Bontempo designed two studies of Auslan/English interpreters that made use of multiple psychological measurements such as self-efficacy, negative affectivity and self-esteem (Bontempo and Levitzke-Gray 2009). Her findings suggest that personality, and more specifically affective traits, have an impact on interpreters' perceptions of competence – that is, how confident they are during the interpretation or translation process. This in turn is seen as a factor that modulates the individual's capacity to carry out a specific interpretation task. In particular, emotional stability or an individual's ability to manage difficult life events and emotions has been shown to be a good predictor of interpreter competence. A series of subsequent studies, conducted by Bontempo and collaborators points to a more general hypothesis according to which individual personality differences correlate to translation outcomes. In Bontempo and Napier (2011), the researchers compared personal variables such as interpreting experience and professional qualifications with opinions about linguistic skills and competence, as well as with some self-reported personality traits. The findings show that personality modulates not only self-perceptions of translation competence but also interpretation outcomes. The researchers concluded that non-cognitive criteria should be explicitly addressed and incorporated in translators' and interpreters' education programs (Bontempo and Napier 2011; Bontempo, Napier, Hayes and Brashear 2014).

Rosiers, Eyckmans *et al.* (2011) have also used self-report measures of student translators and interpreters to investigate the relationship between levels of linguistic self-confidence, motivation and language anxiety. Their comparative study of translating and interpreting students yielded a series of differences between the two groups. They found that interpreting students rate their communicative competence higher than translation students, who in turn experience more language anxiety than interpreting students. While this study does not target explicitly the emotional traits involved in the translation process, it identifies a series of personality characteristics and attitudes that impact the translators' and interpreters' performative behaviours.

Affective research in the process of translation is still in its exploratory stage. The studies briefly reviewed earlier suggest how psychometric measures can be used to shed light on translation creativity and competence. Future generation studies in the field of translation are likely to benefit from incorporating more non-cognitive (affective) concepts and measures in their empirical and theoretical work. It is also expected that pursuing the link between emotion and translation would yield more efficient translators and interpreters training programs.

25.2.5 Machine translation

We have seen that cognitive approaches can contribute to translation studies by articulating specific models of the various cognitive and non-cognitive aspects of the human translation process. Another area of cognitive science, namely AI, focuses on the human cognitive capacities involved in translation to design and build technologies that can serve as external aids in the translation process. A series of AI projects aims to use knowledge about how the human mind and brain operate during translation tasks to construct artificial devices that would assist occasional, novice, routine and professional translators and interpreters. Thus one way to understand the broad problem agenda of machine translation (henceforth MT) is in terms of its engineering aim to develop various computational tools that may assist or even perform automatically different translation tasks. In what follows, I will briefly review some of the main research directions pursued in this field, pointing to the difficulties and limitations that MT projects have encountered along the way in their more than 60 years of history (Way 2010; Hutchins 2012).

The difficulty of making translation an automated (or semi-automated) process by designing and building an appropriate computer program is closely tied to the ways in which we conceptualize the process of translation itself. As we saw in the previous sections, translation involves an understanding of the meaning of the source text (or speech) followed by a culturally and pragmatically appropriate rendering of the given text in the target language. Abstracting away from the many factors that influence and modulate the various stages of the translation process, a simpler representation of the translation task from an AI perspective includes selecting the correct sense of each individual word and identifying the right relationship between the words as captured in the syntax of the source language. But even this simplified representation of the translation problem generates a series of hard challenges for machine translation. Three of the most common issues are lexical ambiguity, syntactic ambiguity and cultural variation. I will briefly review these challenges to MT before introducing the main methods used to overcome or avoid them.

The problem of lexical ambiguity affects what is typically conceived as the first stage of the machine translation process, namely word-sense selection. Many words have multiple meanings. These include true homonyms as well as polysemous words with more or less closely related meanings. In addition, the morphological inflections characteristic of some languages are a further source of lexical ambiguities for computer-based translation programs. Even when words from the source text are not lexically ambiguous in these ways, the translation task can still be affected by this problem if the target language contains more than one word with an appropriately related meaning. Various strategies can be used to simplify the word selection task and choose the appropriate corresponding word in the target language. Still, these strategies need to take into account another source of trouble: syntactic ambiguity. *Eating cakes can be satisfying* is an apparently innocuous sentence which can pose serious problems to an MT program. Sometimes the source and target languages allow for the same types of syntactic ambiguities, in which case the MT program might get away with not solving the syntactic ambiguity in the first place. But very often computer-assisted translations need to go through a post-editing process to check for mistakes generated by such cases of syntactic ambiguity. Finally, another common problem for an MT program is the selection of the appropriate style and register for a particular translation. While this rarely poses a problem to experienced human translators, computers make more mistakes in picking up the appropriate level of detail, register and style for a pair of languages. These problems motivate the development of rigorous evaluation and post-editing protocols that accompany computer-assisted translations.

There are two mainstream approaches that have emerged in MT research and which try to tackle the sort of translation problems listed earlier: rule-based approaches and statistics-based approaches. While basic research favours statistics-based MT methods, the majority of commercial MT systems are still based on some version of the rule-based approach. This preference reflects the fact that the rule-based approach is more robust – that is, it is easier to maintain. On the other hand, improving and perfecting the translation outputs of these systems is more resource-demanding. That is, they require both more time and more expert knowledge than statistics-based MT systems. The advantage of the latter method is that MT systems can be developed more quickly, although it is not entirely clear how they can be fine-tuned. I will return to this issue later.

An MT program based on a rule-based approach starts by analysing the individual words in a sentence. Dictionary look-up identifies the part of speech of the word and lists possible candidate translated meanings. Then the MT program seeks to determine the internal structure of each sentence, identifying syntactic relations and trying to solve lexical and syntactic ambiguities contained in the source text. If the program parses a complex sentence, it will focus on identifying its 'building blocks' at the expense of its overall structure. This explains why sometimes the partial output of MT commercial systems can seem to be on the right track and then completely fall to pieces.

The key idea behind the statistics-based approach is that a computer program can learn how to translate by parsing and analysing large amounts of data from previous translations and then computing statistical probabilities which inform the choice of translation for a new input. The statistical method in MT research relies on the existence of huge amounts of what is called *bilingual corpora* data. The analysis of this data is typically divided into two parts. In the first part, the program builds the *translation model*. That is, it analyses the data and estimates probabilities for correspondences between individual words and phrases in the two languages. This counts as the program learning word correspondences between the two languages. The second part of the program consists in learning the *target language model* by computing probabilities that certain word-sequences are legitimate in the target language. The two models constitute the 'facts' that the computer 'knows' about the source and target languages. The actual translation task is performed by the third component of the MT system which is known as a *decoder*. Its function is to take the input sentence, evaluate the various probabilities for all the individual words and phrases in the translation model, and then put these through the target language model to yield the most probable translation according to the systems' learned statistical distributions. The success of the MT systems based on this approach depends to a large extent on the quality of the data on which the programs are trained. One surprising feature of these statistical MT-systems which depend on the features of the available training data is that they may not produce the same translation for two very similar sentences. This gives rise to further research questions about the comparative evaluation of the translation outputs of a rule-based MT system and a statistical MT-system (Somers 2012).

One recent success story of the statistics-based approach to MT is the radical transformation and improvement of the Google Translate program. Based on an audacious 'neural-translation' research idea, the new program behind Google Translate uses hierarchically nested neural networks to learn statistical probabilities from massive amounts of bilingual corpora data. The main breakthrough of the Neural Machine Translation (NMT) approach is that it manages to reduce both training time and translation inference time with no cost for the quality of the output translation (Wu et al., 2016; Johnson et al., 2016). Moreover, the researchers working on the NMT program promise that further developments to the system will not be epistemically opaque and will increase the translation performance of the system much faster than with traditional rule-based MT systems. They also require minimal changes in the old architecture supporting the Google Translate program, thus avoiding the hardware costs that made some of the previous statistics-based approaches unappealing from a commercial perspective.

Researchers behind the NMT project have also claimed that their research approach provides a way of bridging the gap between human translation and machine translation (Wu et al., 2016). Although we cannot do justice to this broad problem in this review, it is important to clarify one misleading interpretation of this statement. Although the neural network approach is inspired (loosely) by the functioning of biological brains (Minsky and Papert 1969), the proposal is not that human brains and minds operate in a similar way to the 'Google brain', which parses massive amounts of data and computes statistical probabilities to improve both the speed and quality of its translation outputs, but rather, the models that constitute the NMT program are best thought as being inspired by how human brains operate. The hierarchical organization of the neural networks used in this MT project roughly resembles the nested and modular architecture of the brain, while the learning rules used by the system are more sophisticated versions of the Hebbian rule of synaptic plasticity. These general principles have encouraged researchers to describe the statistical process behind NMT as a bridge between neurobiological and AI research. That is, not only is neurocognitive research thought to provide useful resources for the improvement of the quality of NMT results, but advancements in the latter are expected to yield novel insights about the functioning of the brain.

Ongoing projects explore the potential lessons that the success of NMT might have for understanding the cognitive processes involved in human translation, but the final story will very likely be more complicated than saying that the 'Google brain' is a faithful mirror of how human brains operate in the translation process. Just as with the problem of comparing human intelligence and machine intelligence, the relationship between AI and cognitive psychological research into translation cannot be settled by merely identifying the two or by a definitive pronouncement of the demise of one or other of them.

25.3 The organization of cognitive approaches to translation

Cognitive studies of translation constitute a varied landscape of research questions and methodological strategies which seems to challenge the attempt to offer a systematic account of their contributions to translation studies. The overview offered in Section 2 supports this mosaic-like conceptualization of the field. The question is whether this topical and methodological diversity should simply be taken as a symptom of the field's current immaturity or as a more intrinsic characteristic that is likely to endure.

Traditional philosophical discussions of the structure of scientific theories (Oppenheim and Putnam 1958; Kuhn 1996) associate the maturity criterion for a scientific field with the existence of a 'master' theory or set of theoretical principles which guides its development and organization. The physical and the biological sciences are candidates for this theory-driven view of mature sciences. According to this view, the plurality of cognitive models (e.g., symbolic, connectionist, situated) of the cognitive capacities involved in the translation process is the result of the immaturity of a field that is still on the lookout for a stable theoretical framework. Such a framework would articulate the laws or stable regularities that govern the cognitive processes relevant for the analysis of the translation process.

On descriptive grounds, though, this theory-driven picture appears to offer an inadequate perspective on the organization and potential unity of cognitive approaches to translation. To begin with, recent discussions in philosophy of science suggest that the theory-driven picture of science is a poor guide for understanding even how some branches of the physical and biological sciences have developed and are currently organized. Waters (2007), Love (2013, 2014) and Sullivan (2016a, 2016b) have proposed that scientific fields as diverse as microbiology, developmental biology and cognitive neuroscience are not organized around any master biological theory. According to the perspective defended by these philosophers, the structure and progress of these well-established scientific domains should be analysed in terms of the clusters of research questions that one finds presented in textbooks and research journals.

For instance, theoretical models from cellular, molecular and evolutionary biology inform answers to explanatory questions in developmental biology. Challenging the stability or importance of the field as a whole on grounds of a lacking 'master' theory of development rests on the problematic assumption that all fields of scientific inquiry should conform to the same maturity criteria. Given the methodological diversity that characterizes science as a broad intellectual enterprise, such uniformity is unlikely and may, perhaps, even be damaging to the development of certain fields (Waters 2007; Love 2013). Thus, adopting a theory-informed and question-based perspective on science requires challenging the idea that there is only one way to think about scientific investigation and allowing the articulation of more 'local' criteria of scientific success.

Extending this perspective to cognitive approaches of translation, I propose that the absence of a unified theory points to a question-based way of thinking about the organizing structure of the field as being the most productive (Koralus and Mascarenhas 2013). The core idea is that the organization and dynamics of cognitive research in translation studies is driven by the existence of stable and broad domains of interrelated questions or *problem agendas* (Waters 2007). That is, cognitive studies of translation are organized by multiple questions clustered into problem agendas which are approached with the theoretical and methodological resources made available from different areas of cognitive science, including linguistics, psycholinguistics and AI.

One place to start unpacking this erotetic structure of cognitive studies of translation is in the textbooks, companions and handbooks which synthesize the knowledge accumulated in this area of research and present it in a way suitable for transfer to novices (e.g., Baker 2011; Baker and Saldhana 2008; Bassnett 2002; Gentzler 2001; Malmkjær & Windle 2012; Munday 2008; Pym 2010/2014; Venuti 2012). A survey of such collections reveals a series of interrelated questions about the agency involved in the translatorial action, the role of the translator as a cultural mediator, the roles and consequences of the multimodality of the translation process, the pragmatic and semantic theories of meaning developed for understanding different types of translation, the analogies and disanalogies between human and machine translation (MT), the cognitive roles and effects of the processes of translation evaluation and revision, the cognitive models used for translation training, and so on.

These and other additional themes have been explored within the different disciplines that constitute the field of cognitive science. Researchers with different backgrounds have approached these questions at various levels of *abstraction* and by taking into account different degrees of *variation* in the translation phenomena they take as their targets. Most of current research is also seeking to establish *connections* between the models and theories developed in response to some of these questions and to expand them by incorporating different accounts of the *temporal* dimension of the translation process and of its outputs.

I suggest that the landscape of cognitive approaches to translation is in fact structured around these variables (*abstraction*, *variation*, *connectivity* and *temporality*) in the sense that cognitive models and theories can be distinguished with respect to whether they target aspects of translation at a more abstract or concrete level, whether they accommodate a wider or a narrower domain of translation phenomena, whether they seek to integrate multiple models and theoretical ideas and even put them into practical models aimed at translator training programs, and whether they deal with the temporality of translation as a process and cultural product. In fact, these four variables can be used to articulate and further refine the questions pursued within different disciplines of cognitive science. Particular research problems will be formulated at a certain level of abstraction and they will exclude or presuppose a certain range of cognitive phenomena involved in translation that are temporally or atemporally (i.e., constitutively or conceptually) related to other relevant cognitive phenomena.

The problems which define the agendas (or research programs) of different cognitive approaches in translation studies can be best understood as composite lists of multiple interrelated questions, which in turn can be individuated with the help of these four analytical variables. We do not need to presuppose that these problems are *a priori* logically structured or well-defined in order to talk about their role in guiding long-term investigation in translation studies. On the contrary, thinking about cognitive scientific research in translation studies in terms of clusters of interrelated questions provides a descriptively adequate picture of the field because this erotetic structure is something that is primarily accessible to the working scientist.

To get an even broader picture of the field we can point to three further dimensions that structure the space of problems for the cognitive study of translation. These are the dimensions of *history, heterogeneity* and *hierarchy* (Love 2014). The clusters of questions or problem agendas pursued in a discipline like psycholinguistics or AI will depend to a large extent on the *historical development* of the field – that is, on the types of questions that have been historically investigated and the models that have been developed to answer to these questions. History also contributes to some degree to establishing whether a cognitive model or theory will be more or less abstract, to which other existent models it will be possible to link it and whether it could cover more or fewer kinds of translation phenomena. The *heterogeneity* dimension corresponds to the fact that problem agendas contain multiple and distinct types of questions that can be related in specific ways depending on whether they are studied from a psycholinguistic or AI perspective, for instance. In addition, these heterogeneous questions can be *hierarchically* organized, depending on either their level of abstractness or on their temporal properties (e.g., one aspect of translation can be part of or preceding another aspect, etc.). Emphasizing the *hierarchical dimension* of problem agendas reinforces our previous point that even if a scientific field is not theory-driven but only theory-informed and erotetically organized, it can still constitute a fruitful and coherent area of scientific research.

This way of understanding the organizing structure of the cognitive studies of translation has three main advantages. First, the erotetic account refers to categories that fit the language of actual research practice, thereby being descriptively adequate. Second, by emphasizing the interconnectedness of the questions pursued by cognitive scientists investigating translation phenomena the proposed framework allows for a better understanding of the dynamics of the field – that is understanding why some problems are more stable than others and how one type of problem can evolve or be transformed into a different type of problem. And finally, the erotetic view of the organization of this field of research allows for a reassessment of the value of the exploratory studies developed in the field and their role in promoting new questions and research hypotheses.

The proposed analytical framework can also be used to help disentangle the relationships between the different research projects summarized in Section 2. In each of the chosen case studies, I have tried to identify the clusters of questions around which cognitive research on translation is organized. Some questions are only very abstractly specified, whereas others target very specific issues pertaining to particular translation tasks. Both expertise research and the newer area of affective science of translation try to cover a wide variety of phenomena related to the translation process. They also take into account quite explicitly the temporal dimension of the activity of translation. The section on machine translation showed how different cognitive models can be integrated to advance the general aims of translation studies.

Overall, I claim that thinking about the organization of cognitive approaches to translation in terms of the problem agendas researchers are actually pursuing is a more productive perspective on the field of translation studies as a whole.

I have also proposed that thinking about the history, heterogeneity and hierarchical structure of the field complements the erotetic perspective. Although I have not followed any strictly historical storyline in the selection of case studies, a more abstract perspective emergences. This perspective combines the three dimensions and imposes a further organization of the research programs and studies such as those sketched in Sections 2.3 to 2.5 into three groups: first-generation, second-generation and third-generation studies. First-generation cognitive studies of translation are characterized by their exploratory character and the general research questions pursued as well as by the predominance of a single empirical research method being used. I include in this category most of the studies investigating the link between emotion and translation. Second-generation studies focus on more fine-grained research questions investigated via a single research method. Such are some of the expertise studies and the first examples of machine translation research projects. Third-generation studies typically triangulate evidence and methods to validate robust results about specific aspects of the translation phenomena. Projected studies in the affective science of translation, expertise research and machine translation research fall into this category.

The erotetic view offers a descriptively adequate account of current and future cognitive approaches to translation. Thinking about the questions that organize cognitive scientific research in translation can also shed light on the various types of challenges that face the multidisciplinary collaborations pursued in translation studies. The success of these projects depends not only on the alignment of theoretical backgrounds of the participating researchers (linguists, cognitive psychologists, computer scientists, etc.) but also on the collective determination of the problem agendas and associated questions to be pursued in a joint research project. The job of negotiating the methods, assumptions and expectations of the different disciplines becomes easier when there is a common cluster of questions on which these disciplines are supposed to meet.

Related topics

Current trends in philosophy and translation; translation theory and philosophy; meaning; machine translation.

Notes

1 Some of the most forceful criticisms concern the loose treatment of methodological issues such as the research design, data analysis and research report involved in translation studies based on the Thinking Aloud Protocols (Bernardini 2001; Eftekhari and Aminizadeh 2012).
2 In fact, the ability to understand and transfer sensitive and context-bound information, to capture the meaning of source culture texts and to have the interpersonal skills to adapt to different working situations are acknowledged by the European Commission Directorate-General for Translation as key skills of competent translation professionals.

Further reading

Klein, E. and Veltman, F. (1991) *Natural Language and Speech*. Symposium Proceedings, Brussels November 6/27. Berlin: Springer-Verlag. (An early introduction of the agenda and problems of

statistical approaches to natural language processing. Highly relevant for understanding the prospects and challenges of statistical models of machine translation.)
Koralus, P. and Mascarenhas, S. (2013) "The erotetic theory of reasoning: Bridges between formal semantics and the psychology of propositional deductive inference". *Philosophical Perspectives* 27: 312–65. (A general introduction of the principles of erotetic logic in the context of scientific reasoning. Presents the key ideas concerning the role of questions in the organization of inquiry.)
Love, A. (2014) 'The Erotic Organization of Developmental Biology'. In Minelli, A. & Pradeu, T. (eds), *Towards a Theory of Development*. Oxford: Oxford University Press 33–55. (An example of analyzing the erotetic structure of another scientific field of inquiry: developmental biology. The motivations and advantages for turning to an analysis of the structure of a field of scientific inquiry are also clearly presented in this article.)
Way, A. (2010) 'Machine Translation'. In Clark, A., Fox, C. and Lappin, S. (eds) *The Handbook of Computational Linguistics and Natural Language Processing*. Chichester: Wiley-Blackwell. (A comprehensive survey of trends in machine translation, comparing the limitations and advantages of different models.)
Geeraerts, D.(2015) 'Post-structuralist and Cognitive Approaches to Meaning'. In Keith, A. (ed) *The Oxford Handbook of the History of Linguistics*. Oxford: Oxford University Press. (Geerts' chapter offers a brief history of developments of semantics leading to cognitive approaches to meaning. It comprises also an overview of contemporary trends that emphasizes current corpus-based methodological developments relevant for translation studies.)

References

Baker, M. and Saldhana, G. (eds) (2008) *Routledge Encyclopedia of Translation Studies* (2nd ed.). London: Routledge.
Baker, M. (2011). *In Other Words: A Coursebook on Translation* (2nd ed.). London: Routledge.
Bassnett, S. (2002) *Translation Studies*. London: Routledge.
Bernardini, S. (2001) 'Think-Aloud Protocols in Translation Research'. *Target* 13(2): 241–63.
Boase-Beier, J. (2006) *Stylistic Approaches to Translation. Translation Theories Explored*. Manchester: St. Jerome.
Bontempo, K. and Levitzke-Gray, P. (2009) 'Interpreting Down Under: Signed Language Interpreter Education and Training in Australia'. In Napier, J. (ed), *International Perspectives on Signed Language Interpreter Education*. Washington, DC: Gallaudet University Press, 149–70.
Bontempo, K. and Napier, J. (2011) 'Evaluating Emotional Stability as a Predictor of Interpreter Competence and Aptitude for Interpreting'. *Interpreting* 13(1): 85–105.
Bontempo, K., Napier, J., Hayes, L. and Brashear, V. (2014) 'Does Personality Matter? An International Study of Sign Language Interpreter Disposition'. *The International Journal for Translation & Interpreting Research* 6(1): 23–46.
Catford, J.C. (1965) *A Linguistic Theory of Translation: An Essay on Applied Linguistics*. London: Oxford University Press.
Clark, A. (1997) *Being There. Putting Brain, Body, and World Together Again*. Cambridge, MA: MIT Press.
Davou, B. (2007) 'Interaction of Emotion and Cognition in the Processing of Textual Material'. *Meta* 52 (1): 37–47.
Eftekhari, A.A. and Aminizadeh, S. (2012) 'Investigating the Use of Thinking Aloud Protocols in Translation of Literary Texts'. *Theory and Practice in Language Studies* 2(5): 1039–47.
Ericsson, K.A. and Simon, H.A. (1984/1993) *Protocol Analysis: Verbal Reports as Data* (2nd ed.). Cambridge, MA: MIT Press.
Fodor, J. and Katz, J. (1963) 'The Structure of a Semantic Theory'. *Language* 39: 170–210.
Geeraerts, D. (2015) 'Post-Structuralist and Cognitive Approaches to Meaning'. In Keith, A. (ed), *The Oxford Handbook of the History of Linguistics*. Oxford: Oxford University Press.
Gentzler, E. (2001) *Contemporary Translation Theories* (2nd ed.). London: Routledge.

Göpferich, S., Jakobsen, A.L. and Mees, I.M. (eds) (2009) *Behind the Mind: Methods, Models and Results in Translation Process Research.* (Copenhagen Studies in Language 37) Copenhagen: Samfundslitteratur, 11–37.

Göpferich, S., Bayer-Hohenwarter, G., Prassl, F. and Stadlober, J. (2011) 'Exploring Translation Competence Acquisition: Criteria of Analysis Put to the Test'. In O'Brien, S. (ed), *Cognitive Explorations of Translation.* London: Continuum, 57–85.

House, J. (1977) *A Model for Translation Quality Assessment.* Tübingen: Gunter Narr.

Hurtado Albir, A., Beeby, A., Castillo, L., Fox, O., Galán-Mañas, A., Kuznik, A., Massana, G., Neunzig, W., Olalla, Ch., Rodríguez-Inés, P. and Romero, L. (2014) 'Results of PACTE's Experimental Research on the Acquisition of Translation Competence: the Acquisition of Declarative and Procedural Knowledge in Translation. The Dynamic Translation Index'. *Translation Spaces* 4 (1): 29–53.

Hurtado Albir, A. (ed) (2017) *Researching Translation Competence by PACTE Group.* Benjamins Translation Library. Amsterdam: John Benjamins Publishing Company.

Hutchins, J. (2012) 'Recent Applications of Machine Translation'. In Malmkjær, K. and Windle, K. (eds), *The Oxford Handbook of Translation Studies.* Oxford: Oxford University Press, 441–54.

Jakobsen, A. L. (2003) 'Effects of Think Aloud on Translation Speed'. *Triangulating Translation: Perspectives in Process Oriented Research* 45: 69–85.

Jakobsen, A.L. (2005) 'Investigating Expert Translators' Processing Knowledge'. *Knowledge Systems and Translation* 173–89.

Jakobsen, A.L. (2011) 'Tracking Translators' Keystrokes and Eye Movements with Translog'. In Alvstad, C., Hild, A. and Tiselius, E. (eds), *Methods and Strategies of Process Research: Integrative Approaches in Translation Studies.* Amsterdam: John Benjamins, 37–55.

Jääskeläinen, R. (1999) *Tapping the Process. An Explorative Study of the Cognitive and Affective Factors Involved in Translating.* Amsterdam: University of Joensuu Press.

Johnson, M., Schuster, M., Le, Q.V., Krikun, M., Wu, Y., Chen, Z., Thorat, N., Viégas, F., Wattenberg, M., Corrado, G., Hughes, M. and Dean, J. (2016) 'Google's Multilingual Neural Machine Translation System: Enabling Zero-Shot Translation'. arXiv:1611.04558 [cs.CL] (last accessed 23.07.2017).

Kiraly, D. (2000) *A Social Constructivist Approach to Translator Education: Empowerment from Theory to Practice.* Manchester: St. Jerome.

Koralus, P. and Mascarenhas, S. (2013) 'The Erotetic Theory of Reasoning: Bridges Between Formal Semantics and the Psychology of Propositional Deductive Inference". *Philosophical Perspectives* 27: 312–65.

Kuhn, T.S. (1996) *The Structure of Scientific Revolutions* (3rd ed.). Chicago: University of Chicago Press.

Künzli, A. (2001) 'Experts vs Novices: L'utilisation de Sources d'Information Pendant le Processus de Traduction'. *Meta* 46 (3): 507–23.

Künzli, A. (2004) 'Risk Taking: Trainee Translators vs Professional Translators: A Case Study'. *The Journal of Specialised Translation* 2: 34.

Künzli, A. (2009) 'Think-Aloud Protocols: A Useful Tool for Investigating the Linguistic Aspect of Translation'. *Meta: Translators' Journal* 54 (2): 326–41.

Love, A. (2013) 'Theory Is As Theory Does: Scientific Practice and Theory Structure in Biology'. *Biological Theory* 7: 325–37.

Love, A. (2014) 'The Erotetic Organization of Developmental Biology'. In Minelli, A. and Pradeu, T. (eds), *Towards a Theory of Development.* Oxford: Oxford University Press, 33–55.

Malmkjær, K. (2012) 'Meaning and Translation'. In Malmkjær, K. and Windle, K. (eds), *Oxford Handbook of Translation Studies.* New York: Oxford University Press.

Malmkjær, K. and Windle, K. (2012) *Oxford Handbook of Translation Studies.* New York: Oxford University Press.

Minsky, M. and Papert, S. (1969) *Perceptrons. An Introduction to Computational Geometry.* Cambridge, MA: MIT Press.

Munday, J. (2008) *Introducing Translation Studies: Theories and Applications.* London: Routledge.

Muñoz Martín, R. (2010) 'On Paradigms and Cognitive Translatology'. In Shreve, G.M. and Angelone, E. (eds), *Translation and Cognition*. Amsterdam: John Benjamins, 169–89.

Nida, E.A. and Taber, C.R. (1969/1982) *The Theory and Practice of Translation*. Leiden: E.J. Brill.

Oppenheim, P. and Putnam, H. (1958) 'Unity of Science as a Working Hypothesis'. *Minnesota Studies in the Philosophy of Science* 2: 3–36.

Panou, D. (2013) 'Equivalence in Translation Theories'. *Theory and Practice in Translation Studies* 3(1): 1–6.

Pym, A. (2010/2014) *Exploring Translation Theories*. London: Routledge.

Risku, H. (2010) 'A Cognitive Scientific View on Technical Communication and Translation: Do Embodiment and Situatedness Really Make A Difference?' *Target* 22 (1): 94–111.

Risku, H. (2012) 'Cognitive Approaches to Translation'. In *The Encyclopedia of Applied Linguistics*. doi: 10.1002/9781405198431.wbeal0145.

Siren, S. and Hakkarainen, K. (2002) 'The Cognitive Concept of Expertise Applied to Expertise in Translation'. *Across Languages and Cultures* 3 (1): 71–82.

Snell-Hornby, M. (1988) *Translation Studies: An Integrated Approach*. Amsterdam: John Benjamins.

Somers, H. (2012) 'Machine Translation: History, Development and Limitations'. In Malmkjær, K. and Windle, K. (eds) (2011), *Oxford Handbook of Translation Studies*. Oxford University Press, doi: 10.1093/oxfordhb/9780199239306.013.0029.

Sullivan, J. (2016a) 'Construct Stabilization and the Unity of the Mind-Brain Sciences'. *Philosophy of Science* 83: 662–73.

Sullivan, J. (2016b) 'Stabilizing Constructs through Collaboration across Different Research Fields as a Way to Foster the Integrative Approach of the Research Domain Criteria (RDoC) Project'. *Frontiers in Human Neuroscience*. 10: 309 doi: 10.3389/fnhum.2016.00309.

Vannerem, M. and Snell-Hornby, M. (1986) 'Die Szene hinter dem Text. Scenes-and-frames semantics' in der Übersetzung'. In Snell-Hornby, M. (ed), *Übersetzungswissenschaft—Eine Neuorientierung. Zur Integrierung von Theorie und Praxis*. Tübingen: Francke, 184–205.

Venuti, L. (ed) (2012) *The Translation Studies Reader* (3rd ed.). London: Routledge.

Waters, C.K. (2007) 'The Nature and Context of Exploratory Experimentation'. *History and Philosophy of the Life Sciences* 29: 275–84.

Way, A. (2010) 'Machine Translation'. In Clark, A., Fox, C. and Lappin, S. (eds), *The Handbook of Computational Linguistics and Natural Language Processing*. Chichester: Wiley-Blackwell, 531–74.

Wu, Y., Schuster, M., Chen, A., Le, Q.V., Norouzi, M., Macherey, W., Krikun, M., Cao, Y., Gao, Q., Macherey, K., Klingner, J., Shah, A., Johnson, M., Liu, X., Kaiser, Ł., Gouws, S., Kato, Y., Kudo, T., Kazawa, H. Stevens, K., Kurian, G., Patil, N., Wang, W., Young, C., Smith, J., Riesa, J., Rudnick, A., Vinyals, O., Corrado, G., Hughes, M. and Dean, J. (2016) 'Google's Neural Machine Translation System: Bridging the Gap between Human and Machine Translation'. arXiv:1611.04558 [cs.CL] (last accessed: 23.07.2017)

26
Machine translation

Dorothy Kenny

26.1 Introduction

Machine translation (MT) is the automatic translation of text from one human language into another. From ambitious if unpromising beginnings in the aftermath of the Second World War, MT had become ubiquitous and massively used by the first decade of the new millennium. Often lauded for its democratizing effects (Boitet et al. 2010; Goltz 2017) and its contribution to the maintenance of (online) linguistic diversity (Cronin 2013: 59), MT can be equally seen as underwriting myths of universal meaning and linguistic transparency, and symptomatic of a purely instrumentalist vision of language (see, for example, Raley 2003; Cronin 2013). Somewhat paradoxically, it is also often construed as supporting the continuing cultural hegemony of English (Raley 2003; Poibeau 2017: 168).[1] A key technology for wealthy global corporations (Poibeau 2017: 6), MT is at the same time implicated in the declining fortunes of many freelance human translators (Moorkens 2017). It is no wonder then that MT has, at times, been controversial in translation studies. It remains, however, an area of great intellectual interest, not least because the way MT developers approach their task can both reflect and help construct understandings of language, meaning and translation in the world at large (Kenny 2012a), but also because it is primarily through the interface with MT that translation studies can engage with some of the most pressing questions of our time, questions linked to the resurgence of interest in artificial intelligence, and to the future of human labour.

In this chapter we first present some basic definitions of MT and sketch its historical development from the 1940s to the present day. We then outline the main approaches to MT, before addressing some of the critical issues mentioned earlier. The chapter ends with some brief recommendations for practice recently espoused in the literature and with a very tentative look to the future.

In the definition of MT with which we opened this chapter, 'text' is understood as written text. Although automatic speech translation has become widely available, it normally draws on complementary technologies that first convert a speech signal into a written text in the same language (in a speech recognition phase), and then use conventional MT techniques to convert that written text into written text in a second, target language. The translated written output may be converted into target-language speech, again using speech synthesis technology, but the interlingual conversion phase – Jakobson's (1959) *translation proper* – even in so-called 'speech-to-speech translation' remains one in which operations are carried out solely on written language.[2] Recent experiments have, however, seen spoken language, in the form of Spanish audio files, automatically translated into English written text without prior transcription, using techniques based on artificial neural networks (Reynolds 2017). Similar techniques have also been used to integrate information from images when generating translations of written texts (see, for example, Elliott et al. 2017). In such 'multimodal' MT, however, the image is an informational input to translation, but there is little mention thus far of automatically translating the image itself, in the same way as a human translator might replace an image in a movie or a videogame, for example, with a more appropriate image in the target culture.[3]

To complicate matters further, contemporary MT is frequently embedded in complex workflows in which it sits cheek by jowl with other technologies normally considered as aids to human translation. At the same time, MT has come to rely very heavily on human translation for reasons we will address later. It has thus become commonplace to say that the lines between human translation – especially 'computer-aided' human translation – and MT are blurring (see, for example, Kenny 2012a; Doherty 2016; Moorkens 2017). Cronin (2003: 112) goes so far as to describe human translators as *'translational cyborgs* who can no longer be conceived of independently of the technologies with which they interact' (emphasis in the original). But it is worthwhile maintaining the distinction between human and MT for the moment at least, for a number of reasons. For one, only by maintaining the distinction can we do justice to the historical development of MT. From the point of view of contemporary human translators, differentiation is also vital – it is often the most recent provenance of a translation, and especially whether it comes from a machine or a human, that marks it as trustworthy or not (Karamanis, Luz and Doherty 2011). What is more, much contemporary translation does not use MT at all, and it would be highly inaccurate to conflate human and MT in such cases. Finally, for pedagogical purposes, the benefit of ontologies that make clear distinctions between concepts is obvious, even if those concepts are liable to change over time. In what follows, we distinguish between 'human translation' – a process in which a human being is the primary agent responsible for the conversion of a source-language text into a target-language text, even if that human has recourse to multiple technological tools and resources to assist in the process – and 'machine translation' – a process in which the interlingual conversion of text is carried out by a machine, even if the proper functioning of that machine relies on the labour of human beings before or after run-time. The machines in question are, of course, digital computers that run translation programs, but the term 'computer translation' (Weaver 1949) has never gained currency.

26.2 Historical perspectives

John Hutchins, the pre-eminent historian of MT, acknowledges seventeenth-century ideas about 'universal' or 'philosophical' languages as important conceptual precursors to modern interlinguas used in some MT efforts, but notes that such early proposals 'should not be considered in any way as constituting embryonic automatic translation systems' (Hutchins 2004: 11). Rather, the early history of MT begins in the 1930s, with the filing of two patents in 1933 – one by Georges Artsrouni in France, the other by Petr Trojanskij in Russia – for electromechanical devices that could be used as multilingual 'translation' dictionaries. Of the two, Trojanskij's ideas were more developed. He anticipated a three-stage architecture in which a monolingual human operator would parse a source text using a universal scheme that could capture all possible grammatical functions of words. The operator would then locate source-text words, one by one, in the part of the machine that acted as a translation dictionary, and add the relevant grammatical code for the current use of that word. The machine would output the 'equivalent' word in the target language, along with the grammatical code, information that would, in a third step, be used by a monolingual target-language speaker, to create a morphologically correct target text. Although Trojanskij anticipated a third human in the chain, namely a bilingual editor who would attend to 'meaning' and 'literary finishing', he later dropped the requirement that this person be bilingual (Hutchins 2004). Not only does Trojanskij's work thus stand as a forerunner to the three-stage MT architectures that would be developed later in the twentieth century, it also anticipates a debate on the role of bilingual humans in MT workflows, a debate that continues to this day.

Trojanskij's proposed translating machine differed, however, from the MT systems that were to come to prevalence later in the century, on one very important count: he envisaged a special-purpose translating machine. But it was general-purpose digital computers, unknown to Trojanskij at the time of his death in 1950, that were to dominate the field. Indeed, MT, or 'mechanical translation' as it was often known in its early days, has been described as probably the first non-numeric application of electronic computers (Hutchins 2000:1).

The main impetus for the subsequent early development of MT came in the form of a famous Memorandum circulated by Warren Weaver of the Rockefeller Foundation in 1949 (Weaver 1949). In it he bemoans the 'multiplicity of language' that 'impedes cultural interchange between the peoples of the earth, and is a serious deterrent to international understanding' and proposes the use of electronic computers to overcome the ensuing 'world-wide translation problem'. He sets out four possible avenues that research into computer translation could pursue, in particular to overcome the shortcomings of automatic word-for-word translation (which was becoming possible thanks to the advent of electronic dictionaries) and the challenges posed by ambiguity in natural languages. He thus proposes the use of the immediate context of a given word – effectively a short window of n words to the left or right of the word in question – to disambiguate that word. He also proposes that MT take advantage of contemporaneous work on the logical basis of language, as well as cryptographic methods developed during the Second World War, Claude Shannon's Information Theory and 'the real but as yet undiscovered universal language'. Although received by some with scepticism, including Norbert Wiener, founder of cybernetics, with whom Weaver had communicated in 1947, Weaver's ideas are credited with having sparked the first wave of MT research in the early 1950s (Hutchins 2000: 2). His Memorandum is also notable for the role it continues to play today as 'focal point for skepticism' (Mitchell 2010: 169), especially in the critical humanities, about MT and many of its attendant assumptions. Weaver's contribution has been criticised (see, especially, Raley 2003; Mitchell 2010) on many grounds, including its naïve universalism, its dichotomizing approach to language (seen either as logical and functional or alogical and literary), its perceived anglocentricity and its misguided conflation of decryption with translation.

Shortly after the circulation of Weaver's Memorandum, research programmes in MT were launched in the US and elsewhere. A key event in the early history of MT came in the guise of the first demonstration of a functioning MT system at Georgetown University on 7 January 1954. Under the guidance of Léon Dostert and in cooperation with IBM, a Russian-to-English translation system was demonstrated to the waiting press. While many of the reports of the day acknowledged shortcomings of the system, the demo was generally met with great enthusiasm, if not awe, with reporters extolling the virtues of the new 'electronic brains' and agreeing that MT systems 'capable of translating almost everything' would become available within five years (Hutchins 2006). The Georgetown demo is thus generally viewed as having triggered the first hype cycle in MT history, and instigating what was to become something of an in-joke in translation circles, namely that MT would be ready 'in five years' (Wiggins 2017).

The years following the Georgetown demo saw MT research groups spring up in the US, the Soviet Union, the UK and elsewhere. Their activities are described in detail in Hutchins (2000). Much of the American research was funded by the CIA and the military and was concentrated on Russian-to-English translation, reflecting Cold War anxieties, while research in the Soviet Union appears to have been based on a wider range of languages (Hutchins 2000: 7–8). Different teams had different priorities: some pursued the immediate goals of building and formalizing large bilingual dictionaries, while others were more interested in investigating 'the internal semantics of the human mind' (ibid: 2), but all four of Weaver's avenues of research were explored in some shape or form.

Despite the considerable practical challenges faced by MT pioneers, the years 1954 to 1959 have been characterised by Hutchins (ibid: 6) as ones of 'innovation and enthusiasm'. By 1960, however, disillusionment was beginning to set in and some research teams had already begun either to disband or to move towards other activities (Hutchins 2000: 9) .The expected benefits of integrating syntactic analysis into MT did not materialise (ibid.) and while early protagonists such as Weaver (1949) had acknowledged the problem of 'multiple meaning' in translation, but had been optimistic about solving the problem for restricted domains and through the use of micro-context, it now seemed that the machine's inability to deal with macro-context would be its downfall.

In 1960, Yehoshua Bar-Hillel argued that MT had reached an impasse, as some semantic ambiguities could not be resolved by reference to a micro-context of n words to the left or right of the ambiguous word, or even to neighbouring sentences or entire texts (Bar-Hillel 1960). Rather, what was needed was access to encyclopaedic knowledge, which computers did not have (and Bar-Hillel was sceptical that they could ever acquire all the encyclopaedic knowledge that a typical human has). Bar-Hillel concluded his survey of contemporary MT research on a pessimistic but pragmatic note:

> Fully automatic, high quality translation is not a reasonable goal, not even for scientific texts . . . Reasonable goals are then either fully automatic, low quality translation or partly automatic, high quality translation.
>
> (Bar-Hillel 1960)

The 'high quality' in 'partly automatic, high quality translation' was to be achieved by the use of human post-editors who would fix faulty MT output.

The main body blow to MT research, however, came in the form of the Automatic Language Processing Advisory Committee (ALPAC) Report in 1966. The Committee had been set up by government sponsors of MT in the US against a backdrop of mounting bills and disappointing results in MT research. The Committee famously concluded that MT was 'slower, less accurate and twice as expensive as human translation' (Hutchins and Somers 1992: 7) and that there was 'no immediate or predictable prospect of useful machine translation' (ALPAC 1966: 32). The ALPAC Report was widely criticised for being narrowly focused and short-sighted (Hutchins 1986), but the damage was done. Funding for MT research in the US and elsewhere largely dried up. The ALPAC Report remains of interest today, however, providing as it does an early example of an MT evaluation campaign, and indicating how extrinsic factors such as the then abundance of human translators and relatively low cost of their services affect the overall assessment of MT. Finally, if Weaver had been concerned in the post-War period about the need for translation to ensure 'cultural interchange between the peoples of the earth', priorities had now shifted to ensuring timely delivery of those translations, and *only* those translations, desired by certain American scientists, and for whom more and more texts were becoming available in English anyway. The Report warns in particular of the possibility of an 'excess of translation', noting that 'Translation of material for which there is no definite prospective reader is not only wasteful, but it clogs the channels of translation and information flow' (ALPAC 1966: 13).

The post-ALPAC period saw reduced levels of activity in MT in the US, but growing interest in the field in Canada, where official bilingualism had been enshrined in law in 1969 by the Official Languages Act (Canada), and in the then European Communities (now the European Union), where multilingualism was foundational and translation demands would continue to grow with successive expansions. Translation was a political imperative in such cases and a matter of citizens' rights, rather than primarily a means of monitoring a rival power's scientific knowledge, as had been the case in much of the government-sponsored MT in the US before ALPAC.

One area in which MT found a firm foothold in Canada was in the translation of weather forecasts: the Météo system stands as one of the most successful MT implementations of the twentieth century, from the point of view of its longevity – a version of the English-to-French Météo system was in service from 1977 to 2002 (Poibeau 2017: 87) – but also from the point of view of its productivity; translating up to 45,000 words a day in early the 2000s (Langlais, Gandrabur, Leplus and Lapalme 2005: 84); the quality of its output, which reached accuracy levels of 90 per cent (Hutchins and Somers 1992: 208); and the ideal nature of the use case. Weather bulletins require rapid translation, but have short shelf lives. They are also tedious for humans to translate. Crucially, they are linguistically simple and draw on a naturally restricted range of vocabulary and grammatical structures. These latter properties are what allow the language of weather bulletins to be described as a 'sublanguage'. Other sublanguages, however, proved less amenable to translation by machines (Hutchins and Somers 1992: 219).

The European Union for its part, began its long history of engagement with MT in 1976, when the then Commission of the European Communities (CEC) first started using the Systran MT system for English–French translation (other language pairs were added later). Systran's Russian–English system had been deployed by the US Air Force from 1970; it was used by NASA during the Apollo-Soyuz space mission, and would also be introduced at Euratom in 1976. Its use at the European Commission continued well into the current millennium, but was eventually discontinued in 2010. By this time the European Commission had introduced its own fully in-house MT system known as mt@ec (ECMT 2013), which was in turn superseded by another in-house system, eTranslation, in November 2017 (European Commission 2017). Systran, meanwhile, continues to provide MT services to other major clients using technology that has changed considerably since it was first developed in the 1960s.

The 1980s in general are notable for a proliferation of commercial systems, in North America and Japan in particular, some of which were designed for the emerging personal computer market, and were described as 'crude' and requiring 'hefty post-editing' by contemporary reviewers (Bédard 1989). Mainframe systems also continued to be developed for multilingual organisations or to be customised for specific clients, as in the case of Systran installations at Aérospatiale and NATO (Hutchins and Somers 1992: 9).

In most cases, unless machine translations were wanted just for 'gisting' or information assimilation purposes, post-editors were used to improve the machine's output. In the early days, post-editors simply identified and corrected faulty machine translations by hand, sometimes working with pen and paper printouts; by the 1980s word processing programs were being used for this purpose (Sereda 1982). In some cases, users attempted to pre-empt problems in automatic translation by pre-editing source texts, and some MT implementations relied on both pre-editing and post-editing (ibid.). Pre-editing sometimes involved implementing 'controlled languages' or rules that placed constraints on sentence length and the vocabulary and structures used in the source text (see Kuhn 2014). In other cases, attempts were made to improve MT as it happened. The ALPS Translation Support System was a good example of an early 'interactive' system, in which users were asked to resolve ambiguities in source texts during the MT process itself (Bateman 1985).

Addressing the state of the art in MT at the beginning of the 1990s, Harold Somers reflected on post-ALPAC, or 'second generation', MT systems and observed that despite the more principled approach they took, 'in the 20 years since ALPAC, the second generation architecture had led to only slightly better results than the architecture it replaced' (Somers 1993: 232).

An alternative to the overwhelmingly linguistics-oriented systems of the day had first been presented by a team of researchers from IBM in 1988 (Brown et al. 1988a, 1988b) and was subsequently developed in Brown et al. (1990) and Brown, Della Pietra, Della Pietra and Mercer (1993). The IBM approach was based on statistics and ideas from information theory, following a lead first proposed by Weaver in his 1949 Memorandum. Using the bilingual proceedings of the Canadian Parliament, the IBM researchers showed how probabilistic models of translation could be learned directly from such 'bitext' without the use of linguistic knowledge. The approach was initially met with incredulity (see Way 2009), but by the early 2000s statistical MT (SMT) had gathered momentum. It was helped by the growing availability of electronic bitext, but also by increasing computer power and data storage and the collaborative efforts of developers who made available open-source SMT toolkits from 1998, thus enabling the rapid development of SMT systems by research groups the world over (Way 2009; Koehn 2010a:18). As has always been the case in MT research, geopolitical and economic factors were also at play. In the aftermath of the attacks on the World Trade Center in September 2001, for example, US defence agencies stepped up funding for MT research for Arabic. The 2000s also saw increased American interest in automatic translation from Mandarin. At the same time, successive expansions of the European Union (and the recognition of Irish as an official language in 2007) meant that translation needs continued to grow: by 2004 the number of official languages in the Union had grown to 20, by 2014 it had reached 24 (DGT 2016). The wider technological environment of the 1990s and 2000s also provided space for MT research to flourish. The rapid growth of the internet, which boasted one billion users by 2005, two billion users by 2010, and three billion by 2014 (Internetlivestats 2018), was accompanied by increasing online linguistic diversity. Not only did the increasing number of multilingual web pages contribute to the growing stock of suitable bilingual data from which new statistics-based systems could learn how to translate, but the world wide web itself provided a platform from which MT could be easily delivered to millions of casual users. As early as 1997, Systran was being used to translate web pages retrieved through the AltaVista search engine (Joscelyne 1998). Google Translate was launched in 2006; by 2016 it claimed to have over 500 million users, translating an average of 1 billion words per day across 103 languages (Turovsky 2016). The means by which users could interact with the system had also diversified: integration of complementary technologies meant that speech input was now possible as was the translation of words recognised in images, for some languages at least. Third-party software developers could also integrate Google Translate functions into their applications using the Google Translate Application

Programming Interface (API). Google Translate had also built a community of users who would provide feedback to improve the system's output, in line with the trend towards a kind of participatory amateur translation culture much analysed in translation studies (see, for example, O'Hagan 2011). Other major technology companies, for example Microsoft, also developed MT systems in the 2000s, with similar multi-modal input capacity for in-house, online consumer or third-party commercial use (Microsoft 2018).

At the same time as free online MT was beginning to become a mass-consumer product in the mid to late 1990s, however, MT remained of only marginal interest to most professional translators.[4] One reason for this was undoubtedly that the output from many of the then available MT systems did not reach quality thresholds required to make it worthwhile post-editing. Another is that the market for computer aids for translators had already been largely occupied by 'translation memory', a technology that allowed efficient reuse of human translations (see Kenny 2011). First used in the software industry, translation memory tools proliferated in the late 1990s and the 2000s (Chan 2017). But while translation memory was conceived as a way of improving, among other things, the productivity of human translators, it also eventually supported efforts to increase automation in the translation industry: on the one hand, translation memory tools enabled bitext to be created in great quantities and in a format that could be easily used in SMT; on the other hand, they provided an editing environment in which MT outputs could be presented to human translators for editing alongside human translations retrieved from memory. In this way, human translation fed into MT, and MT fed into human translation.

SMT found widespread application and was generally considered state of the art for more than a decade from the mid 2000s. It dominated the research agenda and beat all other contenders in the annual MT evaluation campaigns organised from 2004 onwards (see Bojar et al. 2016; Bentivogli et al. 2016c). Performance improvements in SMT plateaued in the mid 2010s, however, and there was thus a strong incentive for research teams to explore other avenues. The breakthrough came in 2015/16 when the leading SMT systems were outperformed by a new, albeit related approach, called neural MT, or NMT (Bentivogli, Bisazza, Cettolo and Federico 2016b; Koehn 2017: 6). By the end of 2016, NMT was being deployed by major technology companies to provide translation across a variety of platforms (see, for example, Google 2016; Microsoft 2016), and other translation users and specialist MT providers had begun shifting to the new technology, assisted in their development efforts by the availability of free open-source NMT toolkits (see Forcada 2017: 302; Koehn 2017).

26.3 Main methods

Rule-based machine translation

As has already become apparent, MT has thus far relied on two main approaches: the first approach manipulates linguistic knowledge in the form of handcrafted grammatical and lexical rules. These systems, commonly known as 'rule-based machine translation' or RBMT systems, were state-of-the-art until the turn of the millennium, but rule-based systems continue to be developed and supported, especially for languages for which training data is less readily available. A well-known example of such a system is Apertium (Forcada et al. 2011).

RBMT systems are usually divided into three types: direct, transfer and interlingua (see Hutchins and Somers 1992). Direct systems, as exemplified by pre-ALPAC 'first generation' systems, used dictionary look-up to provide word-for-word translations, and then perhaps some local reordering rules to fix a limited number of obvious errors.

The direct approach was clearly limited, and the earlier-mentioned 'second generation' systems were based on the idea that a more satisfactory translation could be generated if an initial syntactic, and perhaps also semantic, analysis of source-language sentences was carried out. This analysis would result in an intermediate representation of the source sentence that would be more amenable to translation, as it would go some way towards neutralising the differences between the source and target languages. Rather than attempting to translate the surface forms of a source-language sentence, these systems would convert the more neutral 'intermediate representation' of that sentence to a similarly construed intermediate representation of a sentence in the target language, in the phase known as transfer. From the target language representation, a surface target language sentence could then be generated. This tripartite architecture involving analysis, transfer and generation, thus mirrored the workflow originally proposed by Trojanskij in the 1930s.

In interlingual systems, an analysis of the source-language sentence would be carried out in much the same way as in a transfer system, with one important exception: ideally it would culminate in a representation of the content of the source-language sentence that no longer bore traces of the source language, and from which a sentence in any target language could be generated. In other words, a true interlingua would be natural-language independent. It would involve some kind of universal notation, capable of expressing any meaning expressible in any source or target language covered by the system. But despite the efforts of a number of research teams to merely approximate an interlingua in the 1970s and 1980s (see, for example, descriptions of the Rosetta system and Carnegie Mellon University's Knowledge Based MT in Hutchins and Somers 1992, and Melby's 1995: 43–9 discussion of attempts to develop universal sememes), the approach has never been deployed on a large scale (Poibeau 2017: 32), with researchers ultimately finding it impractical and even theoretically misguided (Melby ibid.).[5]

Data-driven machine translation

The second broad approach to MT is data-driven, sometimes also called 'corpus-based'. As suggested earlier, the basic tenet of data-driven MT is that translation knowledge can be learned directly from parallel corpora (or 'bitexts'), that is, collections of source texts aligned with their human translations. Data-driven MT, like RBMT, can be divided into three subtypes: example-based MT, statistical MT and neural MT.

Simplifying greatly (for a more detailed overview, see Somers 1999), example-based MT involved the automatic identification and extraction from bitexts of equivalent, usually linguistically motivated chunks in the source and target texts. Such equivalent chunks would then be stored in a database. When a new text was to be translated, it would first have to be segmented into sentences and then chunks. If the training corpus offered no existing translation of the source sentence, then the system could resort to looking for translations of chunks of the new source sentence in the database. If adequate matches were found, their target-language equivalents were taken and 'recombined' to make a new target-language sentence. The approach thus had much in common with translation memory, and EBMT functionality was integrated into at least one translation memory tool, Déjà Vu; however, EBMT was largely eclipsed in MT research by SMT which dominated the field by the mid 2000s.

SMT, for its part, is conceived as a problem in which the system has to decide on the most probable translation for a given source sentence, based on a probabilistic model (or a combination of several models) of translation that it has learned from a parallel corpus, and on a probabilistic model of the target language, learned from a large monolingual corpus of texts in that language.[6] The 'learning' of these models is done in a phase known as 'training'. In a second phase, called 'tuning', system developers work out the optimal weight that should be assigned to each model to get the best outcome. When the system is called upon to translate a new sentence (in a third phase called 'decoding'), it generates many thousands of hypothetical translations for the input string and calculates which one is most probable, given the particular source sentence, the models it has learned and the weights assigned to them. SMT systems thus have a tri-partite architecture and involve much tuning to find the optimal weights for different models.

The original translation models proposed in the early work at IBM were based on unigrams, that is single words, but techniques were subsequently applied that could learn translations not just for single words, but for *n*-grams, that is, strings of one, two, three or *n* words that appear contiguously in the training data used. (For example 'contiguously in' is a bigram in the previous sentence; while 'contiguously in the' is a trigram.) These *n*-grams became known as 'phrases' in SMT circles, hence the description of most SMT systems as 'phrase-based SMT'.[7] Translation 'knowledge' in phrase-based SMT was thus recorded in so-called 'phrase tables' which would specify a string in the source language and a string in the target language and assign a numerical probability that the latter was a translation of the former.

The relatively limited amount of co-text used to build models, the fact that the *n*-grams are translated largely independently of each other and that they do not necessarily correspond to any kind of structural unit in linguistic theory mean that SMT systems can have difficulty handling discontinuous dependencies like that between 'send' and 'back' in the sentence 'Send your certificate of motor insurance back'.[8] They are also known to perform poorly for agglutinative and highly inflected languages because they have no principled way of handling grammatical agreement. Other problems include word drop, where a system simply fails to translate a given source word, and inconsistency, where the same source-language word is translated two different ways, sometimes in the same sentence.

Neural MT systems, like SMT systems, learn to translate from parallel corpora, but do so using very different computational methods. They use artificial neural networks, in which thousands of individual units or artificial 'neurons', analogous to neurons in the human brain, are linked to other such neurons, and the activation state of each neuron depends on the stimuli received from other neurons and the strength or 'weight' of the connections between them. As Forcada (2017: 293) points out, the activations of individual neurons do not make much sense by themselves. It is, rather, the activation states of large sets of connected neurons that can be understood as distributed representations of individual words and the contexts in which they appear, where context can refer both to source-language and target-language 'co-text'. Training a neural network for MT basically means learning the weights that will result in those distributed representations that can best ensure that the network, when called upon to translate,[9] outputs translations that are as close as possible to the 'gold standard' human translations found in the training data. Representations are not built in one go, but rather in successive 'layers', where layers are fixed-sized lists (vectors) of numerical quantities. The external layers, which correspond to inputs to and outputs from the network, are open to the human analyst's scrutiny, but intermediary layers remain 'hidden', a point to which we return again later.[10]

NMT thus shares with SMT the fact that systems learn from training data, and learning weights is similar to learning translation probabilities.[11] NMT systems, however, have a simpler, 'monolithic' architecture (see Forcada 2017: 301) and they process full sentences rather than *n*-grams. They are known to handle morphology, lexical selection and word order phenomena (including discontinuous dependencies) better than SMT (see Bentivogli,

Bisazza, Cettolo and Federico 2016b; Castilho et al. 2017), but they take much longer and much more computing power to train and usually require dedicated hardware in the form of graphical processing units (Forcada 2017). However, NMT output can include some deceptively fluent but inaccurate passages and because they sometimes translate sub-word strings (in cases where they encounter previously unseen words), NMT systems can also produce non-words in the target language.

26.4 Critical issues

Meaning

As Hutchins (2000: 2) puts it, the 'outstanding problem' of the early days of MT was meaning, 'or more precisely the differences between how different languages expressed the same objects, ideas and concepts'.[12] Rule-based MT systems are, implicitly or explicitly, inclined to see meaning as objective and residing in more-or-less discrete concepts, labelled by expressions that can in turn be combined according to the principle of compositionality and the dictates of syntax. They are thus aligned to symbolism, which has the advantage of analytical transparency, but makes RBMT prone to grounding problems[13] and problems caused by pervasive linguistic ambiguity.[14] Although there is no requirement in artificial intelligence that machines process language in the same way as humans do, RBMT has also been criticised for its cognitive implausibility (Nagao 1984).

Statistical MT, on the other hand, does not trouble itself too much with questions of meaning.[15] Its proponents tend to take it as given that the source and target texts in the parallel corpora on which MT engines are trained 'mean the same thing' – the problem of ensuring same meaning having been solved upstream by the human beings who carried out the translations in the first place. Although the phrase translation model that an SMT system learns should contain many useful pairings of source and target language *n*-grams, having no access to meaning, it might also contain many nonsensical pairings. As for the idea that SMT might somehow be cognitively plausible, Hearne and Way (2011: 206) are dismissive, opining that systems that generate target sentences 'by translating words and phrases from the source sentence in a random order using a model containing many non-sensical translations ... are not intended to be either linguistically or cognitively plausible'.

But although the pioneers of SMT made few claims about meaning, others working in the broader field of statistical natural language processing see parallels between techniques that attempt to learn about words by observing their distribution in corpora – which is what even *n*-gram-based language models can claim to do – and the view of meaning as use promoted by Wittgenstein (1968) and Firth (1957) in particular (see, for example, Manning and Schütze 1999: 17.) As the state of the art in MT shifts towards neural approaches, allusions to both Wittgenstein and Firth appear to be growing more frequent (Koehn 2017), with commentators like Poibeau (2017: 176 ff.) stressing the contribution that statistical analysis can make to our understanding of meaning.

As this description of neural MT might suggest, NMT is consistent with theories in which meaning is seen as associative, relational and distributed. If the meaning of a linguistic form is 'the total network of relations' it enters into, as Catford (1965: 35) puts it,[16] then an artificial neural network appears to be a good way to represent those monolingual syntagmatic and paradigmatic relations, as well as interlingual relations that can be learned from a parallel corpus. It is even possible to represent relations between linguistic forms and extralinguistic entities, for example images where features of such images serve to ground automatic translation.[17] Such considerations, along with the fact that NMT relies on computational techniques inspired even if only very loosely (Forcada 2017: 292; Henderson 2010: 379d) by human neurology, have no doubt encouraged much of the contemporary hype of NMT, in which 'artificial brains' are said to achieve near human performance in translation. However, many MT researchers are eager to counteract such hype (see, for example, Koehn 2016; Moorkens 2017: 471).

Opacity

Improved performance of MT has come at the price of increased opacity, with systems moving from the relative transparency of rule-based approaches, which explicitly manipulate knowledge, to the somewhat diminished transparency of statistical MT, which although initially difficult for non-statistically oriented researchers to understand (see Way 2009) was 'still comprehensible in its inner workings' (Bentivogli, Bisazza, Cettolo and Federico 2016b: 1), to the total opacity of neural MT (ibid.). That the workings of the 'hidden' layers in NMT currently defy analysis is a point that has been made by several researchers, with Koehn and Knowles (2017: 1) observing that the answer to why the training data in a given NMT system leads the system to produce particular outputs is 'buried in large matrices of real-numbered values'.

Increased opacity, an issue in many areas of machine learning (Domingos 2017), is a particular cause for concern for humans required to work with contemporary MT systems because it can limit their ability to intervene in translation workflows, thus undermining agendas of translator empowerment (Kenny and Doherty 2014). It may also increase the risk of inaccurate translation, or translation that is based on hidden biases. While relative opacity (from the point of view of human translators) remained largely due to 'technical illiteracy' (Burrell 2016) in the case of SMT and could thus be tackled through translator education (Kenny and Doherty ibid.), the opacity of many contemporary machine learning techniques is rather a property that arises from the nature of the algorithms themselves and the scale required to apply them (Burrell 2016), and so is much more difficult to solve. The problem affects MT developers as much as anyone else, however, and there is thus a strong incentive to develop better analytics for NMT (Koehn and Knowles 2017).

The relationship between human translation and machine translation

Recent advances in data-driven MT have also prompted pessimistic prognoses for the human translation profession, principally from translation industry outsiders. Brynjolfsson and McAfee (2011), for example, proffer translation as an area in which computers have 'raced ahead' of humans. The incremental improvements observed with neural MT have only served to intensify speculation in the press that the days of the human translator are numbered.[18] But such prognoses assume that MT substitutes for human translation, when it is more often the case that human translation complements MT. For one, human translators provide the data on which MT systems are trained, and they are also typically used to post-edit MT output. Although there are use cases in which 'raw' MT output is sufficient, such cases remain rare (Moorkens 2017) and industry sources claim that human post-editing of MT is one of the fastest growing sectors of the translation market (Common Sense Advisory 2016). However, concerns about deskilling and boredom among humans called upon to post-edit MT output have been raised and remuneration can be poor (see Moorkens and O'Brien 2017; Moorkens 2017).

There is also a long history in certain quarters of MT research of attempting to exclude human translators from MT workflows where 'human translators' are understood as professionals, one of whose essential attributes is that they are at least bilingual. This tendency goes back as far as Trojanskij (see earlier) and resurfaces in attempts to recast the role of the post-editor as that of a 'monolingual translator' or to enable crowdsourced 'monolingual translation' (see, for example, Koehn 2010b; Chang, Bederson, Resnik and Kronrod 2011), even if some of these efforts are motivated by a desire to achieve noble translation goals despite the unavailability of qualified bilingual humans.

In some of the more pessimistic treatments, bilingual human translators thus face extinction, boredom or irrelevance. A number of broad responses to these projections can be observed in the literature: on the one hand, human translators are advised not to try to compete with machines, but to focus their efforts on the more creative, better-paid segments of the market (Moorkens 2017); on the other hand, researchers have begun investigating how the technological environments in which human translators work can better serve their needs. Here, adaptive MT (Bentivogli et al. 2016a; Farajian, Turchi, Negri and Federico 2017), that is, MT that learns from post-editors' corrections so they are not forced to make the same edits over and over again, is seen as one of the principal ways in which translator/post-editor experience of MT can be enhanced.[19] This latter approach is favoured by commentators who seek to put human translators back at the centre of technologised professional workflows, in configurations that enable what is now being called 'augmented translation' (Lommel 2017).

26.5 Conclusion

MT has had a chequered history. At the time of writing, it has moved into a new phase, with neural approaches offering promising results, but still beset by the problems associated with most deep learning.[20] MT also remains a technology that cannot explain or take responsibility for its decisions in the way a human translator might be expected to, and it is still prone to errors that might only be spotted by an informed bilingual human. For these reasons, bilingual humans will continue to be important arbiters in professional workflows that use MT. Although MT is available for the world's most economically important languages, and languages that are of interest to certain national intelligence services, the vast majority of the world's written and spoken languages are not served by any machine translation system. In such cases, human translation or non-translation remain the only options, but in the coming years, we can expect data collection initiatives to be accelerated for languages not currently catered for by contemporary data-driven MT but that become of sufficient economic, political or strategic importance to sponsors of MT research.

Notes

1 This view stems both from Warren Weaver's (1949) strategic description of foreign texts as texts that were 'really written in English' and from the fact that Google Translate systematically used English as a pivot language in its statistical machine translation systems.
2 The term 'spoken-language translation' is used when spoken language is automatically transcribed using speech recognition technology, and the resulting transcript is then automatically translated into a written text in the target language (see, for example, Cettolo et al. 2016). It differs from speech-to-speech translation in that there is no final speech synthesis phase.
3 A well-known example of such a replacement was the substitution of green bell peppers for broccoli in the Japanese version of the Pixar movie *Inside Out*, a replacement motivated by the fact that while

American children find broccoli revolting, green bell peppers are the most despised food among Japanese children (Battersby 2015).
4 Poibeau (2017: 222) offers an interesting example of the marginality of MT to the translation efforts of the European Commission, for example. Despite the Commission's longstanding engagement with MT, in 2013 less than 5 per cent of translation at the Commission's Directorate General for Translation benefited from automation.
5 Tentative claims about the 'discovery' of interlingual representations in neural machine translation have recently been made by researchers at Google (Johnson et al. 2016), but have been met with some scepticism.
6 As Hearne and Way (2011: 206) point out, two separate formulae are available to compute the most probable translation. The first, the noisy-channel model, is a straightforward application of Bayes' theorem. The second, the log-linear model, can express the same computation as the noisy-channel model, but is more flexible.
7 The term 'phrase' here does not correspond with 'phrase' as used in much linguistic theory, and some authors – for example, Poibeau (2017) – avoid it altogether, preferring the term 'segment-based machine translation'.
8 This is one of the longer 'separations' attested in the representative sample of British English that is the British National Corpus (Gardner and Davies 2007: 345).
9 As in statistical machine translation, the translation phase in NMT is called 'decoding'.
10 In the broad field of machine learning (see, e.g., Domingos 2017), the term 'deep learning' has come to stand for the use of neural networks with multiple hidden layers.
11 Indeed, Koehn (2017: 5) sees neural MT as a type of SMT.
12 This preoccupation with expressing the 'same meaning' in translation, which is frequently repeated even in contemporary MT literature (for example, Koehn 2010a: 43), was not one that was not necessarily shared with translation theorists working outside machine translation circles, and for many of whom meanings were often language specific or not amenable to capture in static formalisms (see, for example, discussions in Kenny 2012b and Malmkjær 2011).
13 As Harnad (1990: 335) puts it: 'How can the meanings of the meaningless symbol tokens, manipulated solely on the basis of their (arbitrary) shapes, be grounded in anything but other meaningless symbols?'.
14 Ambiguity in MT arises when a word can be assigned more than one interpretation, or a string of words can be assigned more than one syntactic structure, according to the dictionaries and grammars in use. Practically every discussion of 'why translation is difficult for computers' contains a lengthy section on ambiguity. See, for example, Hutchins and Somers 1992 and Poibeau 2017.
15 The pioneers of SMT were, in fact, careful to point out that their approach 'eschews the use of an intermediate mechanism (language) that would encode the "meaning" of the source text' (Brown et al. 1988a: 1).
16 Catford's (1965) work is, of course, inspired by both J.R. Firth and M.A.K. Halliday.
17 Elliot, Frank and Hasler (2015) give the following example: 'in the German sentence "Ein Rad steht neben dem Haus", "Rad" could refer to either "bicycle" or "wheel", but with visual context the intended meaning can be more easily translated into English'.
18 Such prognoses are, incidentally, not supported by other work in labour economics. See Frey and Osborne (2017) and The US Bureau of Labor Statistics (2016), which views translation and interpreting as 'bright future' professions.
19 Other approaches rely on a version of 'interactive' MT in which the machine attempts to predict the words that the human translator is currently typing; quality estimation, in which the machine attempts to decide whether an MT output is good enough to propose to a post-editor; and better integration of MT and translation memory (Bentivogli et al. 2016a).
20 Pontin (2018) lists as the downsides of deep learning the fact that it is 'greedy' (systems require huge quantities of training data), 'brittle' (systems cannot easily cope with scenarios not encountered in their training data), 'opaque' (systems are difficult to debug) and 'shallow' (systems possess no innate knowledge or common sense).

Related topics

Current trends in philosophy and translation; translation theory and philosophy; meaning; cognitive approaches to translation.

Further reading

Poibeau, T. 2017. *Machine Translation*. Cambridge, MA/London: The MIT Press. (This book provides a very accessible, non-technical overview of machine translation, covering history, major approaches (linguistic rule-based, statistical and neural), evaluation and commercial systems.)

Forcada, M. 2017. 'Making Sense of Neural Translation'. *Translation Spaces* 6(2): 291–309. (In this journal article, Mikel Forcada, one of the pioneers of neural machine translation, explains NMT in non-mathematical terms to a translation studies audience, focusing on basic methods, typical outputs and the implications for translators and post-editors.)

Hearne, M. and A. Way. 2011. 'Statistical Machine Translation: A Guide for Linguists and Translators'. *Language and Linguistics Compass* 5/5 (2011): 205–26. (In this journal article, the authors explain SMT to a non-technical audience, describing both how language and translation models are trained, how decoding works, and how systems are tuned.)

Koehn, P. 2010. *Statistical Machine Translation*. Cambridge: Cambridge University Press. (This textbook is the standard reference for SMT. While its primary audience is students of computer science, some chapters are accessible to non-mathematical audiences. The book can be supplemented by a draft chapter on neural machine translation, updated in September 2017, and available at: https://arxiv.org/pdf/1709.07809.pdf.)

Hutchins, J. (ed.) 2000. *Early Years in Machine Translation. Memoirs and Biographies of Pioneers*. Amsterdam/Philadelphia: John Benjamins Publishing. (This edited volume contains contributions by or about the earliest researchers in machine translation, providing personal recollections not just of scientific endeavours, but also of the political and social contexts in which MT research was conducted in the 1950s and 1960s.)

References

ALPAC. 1966. *Language and Computers in Translation and Linguistics. A Report by the Automatic Language Processing Advisory Committee*. Washington, DC: National Academy of Sciences, National Research Council Publication 1416. www.mt-archive.info/ALPAC-1966.pdf

Bar-Hillel, Y. 1960. 'The Present Status of Automatic Translation of Languages'. *Advances in Computers* 1: 91–163.

Bateman, R. 1985. 'Introduction to Interactive Translation'. *Tools for the Trade: Translating and the Computer 5*. Proceedings of a conference... 10–11 November 1983. London Press Centre, Veronica Lawson (ed.). (London: Aslib, 1985): 193–7 www.mt-archive.info/70/Aslib-1983-Bateman.pdf

Battersby, M. 2015. 'Inside Out: Pixar Makes Crucial Change for Japanese Audiences by Editing out Broccoli'. *The Independent*, 24 July 2015.

Bédard, C. 1989. 'The Return of Low-Linguistics MT. PC-Translator: Can a Low Cost Machine Translator Do the Job?' *Language Technology/Electric Word*, 14 July–August 1989: 53, 57.

Bentivogli, L., N. Bertoldi, M. Cettolo, M. Federico, M. Negri and M. Turchi. 2016a. 'On the Evaluation of Adaptive Machine Translation for Human Post-Editing'. *IEEE/ACM Transactions on Audio, Speech, and Language Processing* 24(2): 388–99.

Bentivogli, L., A. Bisazza, M. Cettolo and M. Federico. 2016b. 'Neural versus Phrase-Based Machine Translation Quality: A Case Study'. In *EMNLP 2016*. arXiv:1608.04631v1 [cs.CL] 16 Aug 2016.

Bentivogli, L., M. Federico, S. Stüker, M. Cettolo and J. Niehues. 2016c. 'The IWSLT Evaluation Campaign: Challenges, Achievements, Future Directions'. In G. Rehm, A. Burchardt et al. (eds.) *Proceedings of the LREC 2016 Workshop "Translation Evaluation—From Fragmented Tools and Data Sets to an Integrated Ecosystem"*. 14–19.

Boitet, C., H. Blanchon, M. Seligman and V. Bellynck. 2010. 'MT on and for the Web'. *Proceedings of the 6th International Conference on Natural Language Processing and Knowledge Engineering (NLPKE-2010)*. www-clips.imag.fr/geta/herve.blanchon/Pdfs/NLP-KE-10.pdf

Bojar, O., C. Federmann, B. Haddow, P. Koehn, M. Post and L. Specia. 2016. 'Ten Years of WMT Evaluation Campaigns: Lessons Learnt'. In G. Rehm, A. Burchardt *et al.* (eds.) *Proceedings of the LREC 2016 Workshop "Translation Evaluation—From Fragmented Tools and Data Sets to an Integrated Ecosystem"*. 27–34.

Brown, P., J. Cocke, S. Della Pietra, V. Della Pietra, F. Jelinek, R. Mercer and P. Roossin. 1988a. 'A Statistical Approach to French/English Translation'. In *Second International Conference on Theoretical and Methodological Issues in Machine Translation of Natural Languages (TMI 1988)*, June 12–14. Pittsburgh, PA. No page numbers.

Brown, P., J. Cocke, S. Della Pietra, V. Della Pietra, F. Jelinek, R. Mercer and P. Roossin. 1988b. 'A Statistical Approach to Language Translation'. In *Proceedings of the 12th International Conference on Computational Linguistics* Vol. Budapest, Hungary, August 22–7, 1988. Budapest: John von Neumann Society for Computing Sciences, 71–6.

Brown, P., J. Cocke, S. Della Pietra, V. Della Pietra, F. Jelinek, J. Lafferty, R. Mercer and P. Roossin. 1990. 'A Statistical Approach to Machine Translation'. *Computational Linguistics* 16(2): 79–85.

Brown, P., V. Della Pietra, S. Della Pietra and R. Mercer. 1993. 'Computational Linguistics—Special Issue on Using Large Corpora: II'. 19(2): 263–311.

Brynjolfsson, E. and A. McAfee. 2011. *Race Against the Machine*. Lexington, MA: Digital Frontier Press.

Bureau of Labor Statistics. 2016. *Occupational Outlook Handbook, 2016–17 Edition: Interpreters and Translators*. Washington, DC: U.S. Department of Labor. www.bls.gov/ooh/media-and-communication/interpreters-and-translators.htm

Burrell, J. 2016. 'How the Machine 'Thinks': Understanding Opacity in Machine Learning Algorithms'. *Big Data & Society*, January–June 2016: 1–12.

Castilho, S., J. Moorkens, F. Gaspari, I. Calixto, J. Tinsley and A. Way. 2017. 'Is Neural Machine Translation the New State of the Art?' *The Prague Bulletin of Mathematical Linguistics* 108(1): 109–20.

Catford, J. C. 1965. *A Linguistic Theory Of Translation*. Oxford: Oxford University Press.

Cettolo, M., J. Niehues, S. Stüker, L. Bentivogli, R. Cattoni and M. Federico. 2016. 'The IWSLT 2016 Evaluation Campaign'. In *Proceedings of the 13th International Workshop on Spoken Language Translation*, Seattle, WA. https://workshop2016.iwslt.org/downloads/IWSLT_2016_evaluation_overview.pdf

Chan, S. 2017. *The Future of Translation Technology: Towards a World Without Babel*. London/New York: Routledge.

Chang, H., B. Bederson, P. Resnik and Y. Kronrod. 2011. 'MonoTrans2: A New Human Computation System to Support Monolingual Translation'. In *CHI '11 Proceedings of the SIGCHI Conference on Human Factors in Computing Systems*. Vancouver, BC: ACM, 1133–6.

Common Sense Advisory. 2016. 'Global Market Research Firm Common Sense Advisory Finds Post-edited Machine Translation (PEMT) Among Fastest-growing Segments of the Language Industry'. www.commonsenseadvisory.com/default.aspx?Contenttype=ArticleDet&tabID=64&moduleId=392&Aid=36546&PR=PR

Cronin, M. 2003. *Translation and Globalization*. London/New York: Routledge.

Cronin, M. 2013. *Translation in the Digital Age*. London/New York: Routledge.

DGT. 2016. 'Translation Tools and Workflow'. *Brochure*. https://publications.europa.eu/en/publication-detail/-/publication/e0770e72-afa1-4971-8824-6190512537dc/language-en

Doherty, S. 2016. 'The Impact of Translation Technologies on the Process and Product of Translation'. *International Journal of Communication* 10: 947–69.

Domingos, P. 2017. *The Master Algorithm*. London: Penguin.

ECMT. 2013. https://webgate.ec.europa.eu/fpfis/mwikis/thinktank/index.php/European_Commission_Machine_Translation

Elliott, D., S. Frank and E. Hasler. 2015. 'Multi-Language Image Description With Neural Sequence Models'. *CoRR*, abs/1510.04709.

Elliott, D., S. Frank, L. Barrault, F. Bougares and L. Specia. 2017. 'Findings of the Second Shared Task on Multimodal Machine Translation and Multilingual Image Description'. *Proceedings of the Conference on Machine Translation (WMT), Volume 2: Shared Task Papers*, 215–33.

European Commission. 2017. https://ec.europa.eu/info/resources-partners/machine-translation-public-administrations-mtec_en

Farajian, M. A. M. Turchi, M. Negri and M. Federico. 2017. 'Multi-Domain Neural Machine Translation through Unsupervised Adaptation'. *Proceedings of the Conference on Machine Translation (WMT), Volume 1: Research Papers*, 127–37.

Firth, J. R. 1957. 'A synopsis of linguistic theory 1930–1955'. In *Studies in Linguistic Analysis*. Oxford: Philological Society, 1–32.

Forcada, M. 2017. 'Making Sense of Neural Translation'. *Translation Spaces* 6(2): 291–309.

Forcada, M. L., M. Ginestí-Rosell, J. Nordfalk, J. O'Regan, S. Ortiz-Rojas, J. A. Pérez-Ortiz, F. Sánchez-Martínez, G. Ramírez-Sánchez and F. M. Tyers. 2011. 'Apertium: A Free/Opensource Platform for Rule-Based Machine Translation'. *Machine Translation* 24(1): 1–18.

Frey, C. B. and M. A. Osborne. 2017. 'The Future of Employment: How Susceptible are Jobs to Computerisation'. *Technological Forecasting and Social Change* 114: 254–80.

Gardner, D. and M. Davies. 2007. 'Pointing Out Frequent Phrasal Verbs: A Corpus-Based Analysis'. *TESOL Quarterly* 41: 339–59.

Goltz, N. 2017. 'Linked Democracy 3.0—Global machine translated legislation and compliance in the age of artificial intelligence'. *SSRN Electronic Journal*. https://researchcommons.waikato.ac.nz/handle/10289/11197

Harnad, S. 1990. 'The Symbol Grounding Problem'. *Physica D: Nonlinear Phenomena* 42(1), 335–46.

Hearne, M. and A. Way. 2011. 'Statistical Machine Translation: A Guide for Linguists and Translators'. *Language and Linguistics Compass* 5(5): 205–26.

Henderson, J. B. 2010. 'Artificial Neural Networks'. In A. Clark, C. Fox and S. Lappin (eds.) *Handbook of Computational Linguistics and Natural Language Processing*. Chicester: John Wiley & Sons, 397d–5a.

Hutchins, W. J. 1986. *Machine Translation: Past, Present, Future*. Chichester: Ellis Horwood.

Hutchins, W. J. (ed.) 2000. *Early Years in Machine Translation. Memoirs and Biographies of Pioneers*. Amsterdam/Philadelphia: John Benjamins Publishing.

Hutchins, W. J. 2004. 'Two Precursors of Machine Translation: Artsrouni and Trojanskij'. *International Journal of Translation* 16 (1): 11–31.

Hutchins, W. J. 2006. *The First Public Demonstration of Machine Translation: The Georgetown-IBM System, 7th January 1954*. Updated version of paper originally presented at the AMTA Conference, September 2004. www.hutchinsweb.me.uk/GU-IBM-2005.pdf

Hutchins, W. J. and H. L. Somers. 1992. *An Introduction to Machine Translation*. London: Academic Press.

Internetlivestats. 2018. www.internetlivestats.com/internet-users/#trend

Jakobson, R. 1959. 'On Linguistic Aspects of Translation'. In R. Brower (ed.) *On Translation*. Cambridge, MA: The Harvard University Press, 232–9.

Johnson, M., M. Schuster, Q. V. Le, M. Krikun, Y. Wu, Z. Chen, N. Thorat. 2016. 'Google's Multilingual Neural Machine Translation System: Enabling Zero-Shot Translation'. *Transactions of the Association for Computational Linguistics* 5: 339–51.

Joscelyne, A. 1998. 'AltaVista Translates in Real Time'. *Language International* 10(1): 6–7.

Karamanis, N., S. Luz and G. Doherty. 2011. 'Translation Practice in the Workplace: Contextual Analysis and Implications for Machine Translation'. *Machine Translation* 25(1): 35–52.

Kenny, D. 2011. 'Electronic Tools and Resources for Translators'. In K. Malmkjær and K. Windle (eds.) *The Oxford Handbook of Translation Studies*. Oxford: Oxford University Press, 455–72.

Kenny, D. 2012a. 'The Ethics of Machine Translation'. In S. Ferner (ed.) *Proceedings of the NZSTI Annual Conference 2011*, 121–31.

Kenny, D. 2012b. 'Linguistic Approaches to Translation'. In C. A. Chapelle (general editor) *The Encyclopedia of Applied Linguistics*. Hoboken, NJ: Wiley-Blackwell, 3439–46.

Kenny, D. and S. Doherty. 2014. 'Statistical Machine Translation in the Translation Curriculum: Overcoming Obstacles and Empowering Translators'. *The Interpreter and Translator Trainer* 8(2): 276–94.

Koehn, P. 2010a. *Statistical Machine Translation*. Cambridge: Cambridge University Press.

Koehn, P. 2010b. 'Enabling Monolingual Translators: Post-Editing vs. Options'. In *NAACL HLT 2010 Proceedings*. Los Angeles, CA: ACL, 537–45.

Koehn, P. 2016. 'The State of Neural Machine Translation (NMT)'. *Omniscien Technologies Blog*. 30 November 2016. https://omniscien.com/category/blog/ last accessed 30 January 2018.

Koehn, P. 2017. 'Neural Machine Translation'. Draft chapter for the book *Statistical Machine Translation*. https://arxiv.org/pdf/1709.07809.pdf

Koehn, P. and R. Knowles. 2017. 'Six Challenges for Neural Machine Translation'. *First Workshop on Neural Machine Translation*. https://arxiv.org/pdf/1706.03872.pdf

Kuhn, T. 2014. 'A Survey and Classification of Controlled Natural Languages'. *Computational Linguistics* 40(1): 121–70.

Langlais, P., S. Gandrabur, T. Leplus and G. Lapalme. 2005. 'The Long-Term Forecast for Weather Bulletin Translation'. *Machine Translation* 19(1): 83–112.

Lommel, A. 2017. 'How Augmented Translation Affects the Language Services Industry'. *Common Sense Advisory Blog*. 05 July 2017. www.commonsenseadvisory.com/default.aspx?Contenttype=ArticleDetAD&tabID=63&Aid=39818&moduleId=390

Malmkjær, K. 2011. 'Meaning and Translation'. In K. Malmkjær and K. Windle (eds.) *The Oxford Handbook of Translation Studies*. Oxford: Oxford University Press, 108–22.

Manning, C. D. and H. Schütze. 1999. *Foundations of Statistical Natural Language Processing*. Cambridge, MA: The MIT Press.

Melby, A. 1995. *The Possibility of Language*. Amsterdam/Philadelphia: John Benjamins Publishing.

Microsoft. 2018. https://blogs.msdn.microsoft.com/translation/2016/11/15/microsoft-translator-launching-neural-network-based-translations-for-all-its-speech-languages/

Mitchell, C. 2010. 'Translation and Materiality. The Paradox of Visible Translation'. *Translating Media* 30(1): 23–9.

Moorkens, J. 2017. 'Under Pressure: Translation in Times of Austerity'. *Perspectives* 25(3): 464–77.

Moorkens, J. and S. O'Brien. 2017. 'Assessing User Interface Needs of Post-Editors of Machine Translation'. In D. Kenny (ed.) *Human Issues in Translation Technology*. London and New York: Routledge, 109–30.

Nagao, M. 1984. 'A Framework of a Mechanical Translation Between Japanese and English by Analogy Principle'. In A. Elithorn and R. Banerji (eds.) *Artificial and Human Intelligence*. Amsterdam: Elsevier Science Publishers, 173–80.

O'Hagan, M. (ed.) 2011. *Translation as a Social Activity. Community Translation 2.0. Special Issue of Linguistica Antverpiensia* 10/2011.

Poibeau, T. 2017. *Machine Translation*. Cambridge, MA: The MIT Press.

Pontin, J. 2018. 'Greedy, Brittle, Opaque, and Shallow: The Downsides to Deep Learning'. *Wired*. 02 February 2018. www.wired.com/story/greedy-brittle-opaque-and-shallow-the-downsides-to-deep-learning/

Raley, R. 2003. 'Machine Translation and Global English'. *The Yale Journal of Criticism* 16(2): 291–313.

Reynolds, M. 2017. 'Google Uses Neural Networks to Translate Without Transcribing'. *New Scientist*. www.newscientist.com/article/2126738-google-uses-neural-networks-to-translate-without-transcribing/ last accessed 04 April 2017.

Sereda, S. P. 1982. 'Practical Experience of Machine Translation'. In V. Lawson (ed.) *Conference Proceedings: Practical Experience of Machine Translation*. Amsterdam/New York/Oxford: North-Holland Publishing Company, 119–27.

Somers, H. 1993. 'Current Research in Machine Translation'. *Machine Translation* 7: 231–46.
Somers, H. 1999. 'Review Article: Example-Based Machine Translation'. *Machine Translation* 14(2): 113–57.
Turovsky, B. 2016. 'Ten years of Google Translate'. https://blog.google/products/translate/ten-years-of-google-translate/
Way, A. 2009. 'A Critique of Statistical Machine Translation'. *Linguistica Antverpiensia* 8: 17–41.
Weaver, W. 1949. 'Translation'. www.mt-archive.info/Weaver-1949.pdf
Wiggins, D. 2017. 'Riding the Machine Translation Hype Cycle—From SMT to NMT to Deep NMT'. *Omniscien Blog*. https://omniscien.com/riding-machine-translation-hype-cycle/ last accessed 01 December 2017.
Wittgenstein, L. 1968. *Philosophical Investigations*. 3rd edition. Oxford: Basil Blackwell. Translated by G. E. M. Anscombe.

27
Literary translation

Leena Laiho

27.1 Introduction

'Literary translation' as a notion is challenging to define (see Hermans 2007; Wittman 2013: 438). In this chapter, it is understood as a translation of a 'literary work of art'. The concept of 'work' as a vantage point is seen as constructive although the notion is currently often replaced with 'literary texts'. As a notion, it covers texts 'that are held to exhibit literary features' (Boase-Beier, Fawcett and Wilson 2014: 1). As a piece of art, a literary work per se can be looked at from many perspectives: from a metaphysical point of view through to production for the literary market. When translated, a literary work becomes an 'original'. In the translation context, the notions of author, text and literary work receive additional significances. New questions arise: who are the authors of the translated work, what kind of a work is the translation, what is the relationship between text and work, etc. Any answer reflects metaphysical commitments and, ultimately, the notion of identity: under which conditions two pieces of writing can be regarded as one and the same work of literature, and when not (see Laiho [2007] 2009). Does a literary work persist in another language from the original and, if not, is it another work, or no work at all, just a version? Indisputably, only in the philosophy of art can explicit ontological assertions be expected; otherwise, even implicit references are rare, especially in the recent cultural climate in which Western thinking is questioned. However, the aspect of the original-identity relation is useful even for regarding postmodern views on literary works and translations, which tend to see both as 'textual tissues'. The original, therefore, appears in another light, as described by Susan Bassnett (1998: 27), who in reference to Roland Barthes writes: 'Isn't it obvious that all texts are a tissue of quotations, for how can anything be truly "original" unless it has been created by someone who has never encountered anyone else's work?' From that point of view, the identity discussion looks non-essential. However, should it not be seen as illuminating the phenomenon of literary translation, in much the same manner as any other consideration that draws its conceptual tools from other academic disciplines (see Boase-Beier, Fawcett and Wilson 2014), as a heuristic tool?

Heuristics, moreover, explain the selection of approaches considered here as emerging trends in the research of literary translation. The approaches presented in this chapter show the diversity of the field and contribute to understanding the open concept 'translation', as described by Maria Tymoczko (2005: 1085): 'the definition of translation is intertwined with aspects of almost all research in the field of translation studies'. The selection aims to reflect possible theoretical frames originating in other disciplines (natural science, philosophy, etc.) and delivering specific knowledge about the phenomenon otherwise non-accessible, expressed by Tymoczko (2005: 1090) as follows: 'Framing translation in a variety of ways is therefore productive because it responds to the nature of translation as an open category and a cluster category'. Seen against the background of Tymoczko's statement, and Wittgenstein's idea of *family resemblance* also referred to by Tymoczko (2005: 1085; 2003), the approaches presented here need not be understood as opposing each other; on the contrary, they, ontology included, can be seen to be in a complementary relationship.

27.2 Critical issues and topics

In literary translation research, key notions (even if no longer conceived as binaries but approached rather in terms of differences and similarities) are 'author'/'translator', 'original'/ 'translation', 'work'/'reader' or 'text'/'meaning'. These are the relationships which seem to be crucial when addressing different theoretical approaches. Let us first explore two actors important in literary translation: the translator and author. Clearly, paying attention to the author and translator cannot be avoided, whatever the focus. However, the same is true about the original and translation, as stated by Bassnett and Trivedi (1999: 2): 'One problem that anyone working in the field of translation studies has to confront is the relationship between the text termed the "original", or the source, and the translation of that original'. Further concepts such as creativity, voice(s), hybridity, third space and self-translation characterize the scholarly discussion on translation in general and recent theorizing on literary translation in particular. When examined closely, these concepts appear to be worthy of consideration in light of the basic notional constellation of original–translation and/or author–translator, although not everybody agrees with this assumption, such as Lawrence Venuti and others who wish to abandon the division (see Flynn 2013: 13). Instead of binaries, notions such as hybridity, third space and voice(s) are currently conceptual tools for approaching the phenomenon of literary translation, indicating future directions as well.

27.2.1 Translator–author

Let us take another abstraction level and look at authorship and, as its notional counterpart, 'translatorship', the latter with a slightly different accent to that employed by Toury (1995: 53), who primarily refers to socially definable professional abilities and suitability as determined by norms. Although it was not until the late seventeenth and eighteenth centuries (Bracha 2008: 193) that literary works began to be seen as the intellectual property of the individuals regarded as creators, the Romantic convention of 'authorship' has powerfully defined the Western literary scene (Venuti 1995). In scholarly approaches to literary translation, notions of originality, creativity, faithfulness and equivalence all allude to authorship discussions. Even when 'authorship' is still present in translation discourse, the conventional way of thinking about literature in all its aspects was successfully challenged by Roland Barthes' 'death of the author' (Kuhiwczak 2003: 116), the emergence of deconstruction with Jacques Derrida's notion of *différance* and also post-structuralism. The dethroning of 'meaning' as something inter-subjectively identifiable and, thus, transferable as the core of a literary work (see Arrojo 2010: 248) crystallizes the new way of thinking that causes a

Leena Laiho

reassessment of the status of author and original. Stephen Davis Ross (1981: 8) describes why a new attitude was welcome: 'In what ways . . . must a translation be similar to its original? . . . The most natural answer is that a translation ought to have the same *meaning* as the original. Unfortunately, neither meaning nor similarity is a clear notion'.

A literary work to be translated today is not necessarily primarily an aesthetic object to be presented as such in another culture and language. It has been given further significances and functions – it can be used as a medium for cultural exchange with cultural impact, and political and ideological purposes can be central in translating. (On 'committed approaches', see Brownlie 2003, 2010; Lefevere 1992). This means that the emphasis is placed on translation as decision making for certain aims, differing from translation as decision making per definition, as advocated by Jiří Levý [1967] (2000), for whom the translation process resembles a game, necessitating consecutive decisions and moves. Venuti (2000: 468) stresses the tendentiousness of decisions: 'Translation never communicates in an untroubled fashion because the translator negotiates the linguistic and cultural difference of the foreign text'. There is the Other to be encountered in translation, and this encounter is best served by a foreignizing translation with neither fluency nor illusion of an original as the aim, unlike domestication (see Venuti 1995). Therefore, to think of translation in terms of aesthetics is thinking un-contextually, according to Bassnett and Trivedi (1999: 6): 'Translations are always embedded in cultural and political systems, and in history. For too long translation was seen as purely an aesthetic act, and ideological problems were disregarded'. It is clear that as a result of the 'cultural' turn, the key notions addressed here appear differently.

27.2.2 Translator–creation–translation

As long as the superior status of an original based on the author's authority has been taken as given when it comes to translation, the translator's action can be ranked as secondary, especially with respect to creation (see Bassnett 2011, etc.). The secondary character of the translator's role in describing translation, according to Piotr Kuhiwczak (2003), appears in the use of binary divisions: speaking in terms of source-oriented vs. target-oriented translations, etc., refers to 'the anxiety that a translated text, always [has] its *other* against which it may be compared' (2003: 116), and such anxiety even gives reason to speak of 'parasitic activity'. However, any categorical answer to the question of whether a literary work of art after being translated into another language should be regarded as the creation of the original author alone would be too simplistic. We know that a literary translation is a new literary entity that did not exist before the translator's activity. Due to the initial creative act behind the original work of literature (idea, plot, structure, style, etc.) being ascribed to the author of the artefact, the translator's creative effort in producing this new literary entity is complex: what if there is no copy of the original left, just a translation – does the literary work exist? This complex relationship has been discussed in recent scholarly literature although not necessarily from this point of view. The parallel existence of two literary entities – original and translation – will be discussed later when considering metaphysical approaches as a trend in current research.

There are translation scholars who, by definition, regard the creative contribution of a translator as central (O'Sullivan 2013) and who raise the idea of taking a translator to be the co-author of a translated work (see Alvstad 2014: 276). Besides scholars, the issue of co-authorship has been addressed by literary translators themselves (Zeller 2000; Kahn 2011; etc.). Following Venuti (2008), such inclusivity would erase the translator from the misery of invisibility. A less radical solution would be to present the translator as such, visibly on the book cover. Although the literary practices described represent issues that could be seen as trivial, the overall message is not trivial – it is a stand on the issue of authorship and translatorship, with the aspect of creation as the core. The linkage between these practices and paratextual means and elements is addressed by Cecilia Alvstad (2014), who argues for a 'translation pact' to make the reader receive a translation as the original work, a view which at least seems to conflict with the demand for visibility and the aspect of translators' creativeness. Alvstad's argumentation will be returned to later when introducing current research.

Does a translator create, or can a translator even be regarded as an author, and what is an author? Dictionary entries are the point of departure for Christiane Nord (2011: 21–9) in considering the notion of 'author': she gives the definition of an 'author' as 'a person who originates or gives existence to anything'; 'authorship', in its legal respect regarding an 'author' as a creator, is linked to the *responsibility* 'for something that is created'. Nord makes a compromise between this view of creation and postmodern thinking, which is sceptical of anything truly being a new creation, and therefore of the very notion of authorship (see Bassnett 1998, etc.). She proposes that a translator must have 'some kind of text' as an 'offer of information' (1998: 21). As a functionalist, Nord emphasizes the purpose (or *skopos*) of translation and the task of a translator: after having processed the initial text, a translator has to make the new readers an offer of information – that is, a translation – to which the audience has access. Thought-provokingly, Nord places the focus on the role of target text readers, their culture and not so much on the contents of the original. Consequently, focus is not on the notions of equivalence or fidelity. On the contrary, it is stressed that there can be various translations of the same original work – into the same language and even by the same translator – for different purposes. Although Nord is primarily known as a scholar of non-literary translation, her contribution illuminates many recent views on the relationship between the original and translation. The idea expressed by Walter Benjamin [1923] (2012: 76) that translation continues the life of an original can also be seen to be present for Nord (2011: 25) – for her, the fact that works are translated is enriching: 'the translator widens the scope of a text, giving it a larger and more diversified audience'. From the receivers' point of view, Nord also sees in literary translation a qualitative growth: the literary repertoire of the target-culture profits from 'new models and patterns'. If for Benjamin an original's after-life is to be understood more in terms of a literary work's identity, for Nord, cultural-pragmatic aspects are foregrounded. But what is common for both views is that they do not see any loss in translation. Benjamin's thinking of the afterlife of a work as being significantly determined by language challenges the translator to re-think the discrepancy between meaning and the way of expressing the meaning.

The question of creation and originality is addressed by Piotr Kuhiwczak (2003) from another perspective: he focuses on literary translation as an activity, asking whether it can be compared with creative writing, as some think. He would not draw parallels between translating and creative writing, although he sees the issue of originality in writing as complex and much 'original writing' as 'based on crude imitation, if not plagiarism, such as by "popular literature" using "worn-out formulas"'(2003: 115–16). Although creative writing is included in literary translation, the translator, for Kuhiwczak (ibid.), is not only a writer – he or she is a literary critic as well. Literary translation has 'characteristic features of both creative writing and literary criticism', and about the latter activity he mentions Ezra Pound as having reportedly said that 'there was no more thorough form of literary criticism than translation' (ibid.). Because of the 'critical faculty' a translator is supposed to have, translating might occasionally be even 'more challenging than writing' (ibid.). Do we actually have similarities with André Lefevere's (1992) view of translation as the rewriting of an original text here, although the aspect of manipulation is missing? A further feature of both approaches could also be that Lefevere draws parallels between translation and criticism: 'The same basic process of rewriting is at work' in both (Lefevere 1992: 9).

Hu (2004), arguing from a non-Western perspective (an emerging trend in Translation Studies; Bassnett 2014: 146; Tymoczko 2003; etc.), criticizes the lack of focus on the subjectivity and creativity of translators in (Western) Translation Studies. He believes that scholarly discussion has been too long marked by thinking in binaries: emphasis has been placed either on a source text-centred or target text-centred approach. Hu (2004:115) proposes considering the active, creative role of the translator in a translation process by introducing the notion of 'translator-centredness' to do justice to 'translators' creativity and authority in translation processes involving literature'. Although Hu discusses translation as selection and decision making with respect to all forms of translation, his examples represent literary translation, where translational creativeness and subjectivity are most apparent. The discussion of different views on the 'translator' reveals that the role of the 'translator' has many aspects in Translation Studies; however, within the context of the philosophy of art, it becomes even more complex, as here the question of whether literary works of art are created or come into existence in some other way is likewise far from simple. (On 'ontology' and 'creation', see Davies 2006: 81–108; Rohrbaugh 2005: 241–53; Davies 2007: 17–30).

If the notion of 'translator' appears different from different perspectives, the same is true for 'translation' and 'original'. Hybridity is one of the keywords in recent discussion about translation, as mentioned earlier. Post-colonial theory in particular has made us aware of the interwoven and mixed character of cultural entities as a part of the debate on phenomena such as 'plurilingualism and linguistic creolization', 'transculturalism and transtextualization' or 'diasporic cultural expression', as Sherry Simon (2011: 49) writes. Simon is not in favour of regarding translation by definition as a hybrid in terms of culture or language. The reason is that, unlike actual hybrid translations, not all translations show observable traces of a confrontation and tensions between separate cultural, political and linguistic existences. (On 'hybrid text', see Schäffner and Adab 2001). In its incoherence, a text and a translation can appear as a space between, as a third space, using the terms of Homi Bhabha and, ideally, the translation can expose the political conditions and suppressive power relations from which this hybridity originates (Simon 2011). Similarly to Tymoczko, Simon (2011: 52–3) advocates 'an enlarged idea of translation' including translation practices that engender and express interference, such as 'self-translation', 'bilingual writing' and 'unfinished translation'.

27.3 Current contributions and research

By introducing current investigations into literary translation, specific studies and writings are used here to provide an insight into approaches and possibilities, and conceptual and applied means. Some examples are introduced in more detail than others, decided by their heuristic value or by their complexity suggesting a more thorough presentation. The first approach explores the issue through phenomenology, as a 'readerly experience' (Scott 2012: xi). The second concentrates on reading, the focus now being on readers constructing meaning as 'interpretive communities' – using Stanley Fish's notion (1980; see Baer 2014: 336). The framework is sociological. The third addresses the relationship between the author and translator as a fictional representation, using corpus research. The study is an example of interdisciplinary research. The fourth, similarly, represents the interdisciplinary approach using a model originally from science, in order to describe the holistic scene of translation. The fifth poses the question of identity as a metaphysical issue, and the sixth answers it in the context of literary studies and translation sociology.

27.3.1 Translation as reading

Translation as reading is considered here based on Clive Scott's *Translating the Perception of Text: Literary Translation and Phenomenology* (2012), which focuses on poetry translation but provides an insight into translation in terms of phenomenology. From this perspective, the relationship between original and translation appears different (see also Cook 1986). The reader experience is crucial: a source text is nothing or just a linguistic entity without a reader perceiving the written text. According to Scott (2012: xi), translation can be understood as a 'mode of readerly response to text'. What kind of a response does he refer to? It is to be defined in terms of the 'psycho-physiological responses of reading', as in the description of the translator's task: *'translating not an interpreted text* but *the phenomenology of reading'* (ibid.). Scott, basing his arguments on Maurice Merleau-Ponty's philosophy, distances himself – as he says – from hermeneutic-minded phenomenologists such as Heidegger or Gadamer who emphasize the significance of understanding the meaning of text, and thus the role of interpretation in all reading. For Scott, approaching a text is not an attempt to trace the 'authorial or textual intention-to-mean'; the textual encounter he is focused on is the 'readerly availability-of-sense' of texts (2012: 3).

Literary as a term is defined through its effect on the reader and not in terms of any cultural or institutional status of texts; it represents something that cannot be sealed forever and must be 're-defined' or 're-invented' continually. Scott (2012; 15) writes: 'It is a readerly perception, that a text is able to bring a reader to'. For Scott, literary translation is a 'translation *into* literary', which is ideally directed at polyglot readers who know the source language and text and are able to approach the translation as a translation – see Friedrich Schleiermacher's notion of foreignization [1813](1963) – unlike monoglot readers, who take interlingual translation as an 'informational service'. A literary translation, according to Scott (2012: 15), means 'a perceived excess of the signifier over the signified'. Signifiers are translated into other signifiers – against the background of meaning as something non-fixable, as a 'project of the signifier' that by definition can never be finished – an idea that alludes to Derrida and the deconstructionist understanding of meaning.

In this context, the relationship between original and translation appears quite different from approaching translation as interlingual, as 'translation proper' in terms of Roman Jakobson ([1959] 1992, cited by Scott 2011: 215). Scott (ibid.) regards the narrowed conception of language that the 'translation proper' has promoted as problematic; the paralinguistic – 'vocal input such as pausing, loudness, tone, intonation' – are excluded, like 'the involvement of language with other senses'. Equivalence and fidelity are not issues for translation for polyglots. A translator for Scott (2011: 214) should write out of the 'centre' of language; a translation is recontextualization. Scott (2011: 20) asks that one is ready to 'accept that the translation of phenomenology of reading' means developing 'a new kind of translation', a 'multilingual and multi-sensory translation'.

From the perspective of ethics, Scott's view militates against any traditional notion of 'translation ethics firmly rooted in Platonism', which would suggest that 'translators can and should recover the *true* meaning of the text' (Van Wyke 2013: 550). Finding its culmination in 'fidelity' as 'the basis for understanding the ethical duty of translators', traditional ethics, according to Ben Van Wyke (2013: 549), has not succeeded in defining 'fidelity' unequivocally, nor the object to which faithfulness should be shown. Therefore, a translator acting in accordance with phenomenological translation philosophy is perhaps guided by faithfulness towards himself or herself in three roles: as a perceiver; as a promotor of the language of the original text; and finally as a translator into *literary* 'mode'. Designed for a specific framework of reference, this type of ethics is hardly generally applicable. Could it be seen to represent a strictly contextualized form of ethics, allowing a variety of translations and '*good* translations'? In addition, the translator working within a phenomenological context hardly remains invisible; thus, he or she could contribute to making the whole scene of translation more visible, as desired by Van Wyke (2010: 114).

27.3.2 Translation and readerliness

Reading is also the key notion for Brian James Baer (2014), who follows the 'post-positivist take on reading, predicated on the death of the traditional author', which he believes introduced new approaches to textual meaning. The notion of readerliness, based both on Roland Barthes' readerly texts as interpretively open and Mikhail Bakhtin's heteroglossic texts, refers to readers of literary translations as co-creators constructing the meaning of a work. Consequently, authority, traditionally the 'unitary' supremacy of the author, is challenged by readers, who are many. The readerliness of translations, Baer continues (2014: 334), differs from non-translated writings: in addition to the intended foreignness in translations, the translations always 'carry traces of their foreign origins' through paratexts and signs on the 'textual surface' and other interventions. Therefore, a translated text might be 'associated with a kind of doubling, an inherent multi-voicedness or heteroglossia' (ibid.). How translations (of world literature) are read in different 'interpretive communities', especially in controlled circumstances (Soviet Russia, and so on), and which meanings and significances the readers give to works, are questions that research on the readerliness of translated literature tries to answer (see 2014: 336–42).

The framework of approaching literary translation in Baer's essay is clearly the sociology of translation. Translations are regarded in the context of the target-culture, indeed as a part of it, as pointed out by Baer (2014: 336), quoting Gideon Toury's (1995: 29) view of translations as 'facts of the target culture'. The relationship between original and translation seems, with this approach, like a continuum – an aspect that has not been considered by Baer in addressing the interpretive communities as an object of study.

27.3.3 The author–translator relationship as fictional representation

Thought experiments in philosophy are a useful tool for investigating the nature of things. Could fiction be used for the same thing? Parallels have been drawn between literary fiction and thought experiment – both 'advance our understanding of the worlds and ourselves' (Elgin 2014: 240). Thus, like a thought experiment, fiction can be thought to illustrate translation. This idea is employed analytically by Judy Wakabayashi (2011) in her corpus study on fiction. Wakabayashi (2011: 88) explores 'the range and nature of imaginary relationships between authors and translators of works of fiction in the light of postmodern questioning'. She distinguishes several types of representations of author–translator relationships to be discussed. According to Wakabayashi (2011: 101), her corpus-study of fictional depictions makes no claim to describe the real situation; however, the approach might be fruitful for further considerations on the issue, offering as it does new insights. Ideally, although fiction is fiction, it 'can provide models for alternative realities'.

Wakabayashi's study represents current research in various aspects. First, her approach is theoretically well embedded. Second, a study using corpus research methods is timely and relevant to the field of Translation Studies in terms of methodology. Third, it approaches phenomena in Translation Studies in an interdisciplinary manner by exploring scholarly notions in the context of another discourse, that of fiction. The author–translator relationship is a convoluted field to explore, and the point of view of the author is important with respect to the translator and the question of creation or creativity. In addition, in this study, the researcher is involved in thought experiments in two ways. Fictional depictions as such can be regarded as thought experiments, most obviously when the idea of a fictional original, and thus 'pseudo-translation' (Toury 1995: 35), are explicitly elements of a fictional text; this is the case in Barbara Wilson's story 'Mi Novelista' (1998) in which a pseudo-translation is followed by two pseudo-originals, the first one written by the pseudo-translator herself, the other by a 'plagiarizer' (see Wakabayashi 2011: 93–4). The example of a fictional original resembles a thought experiment introduced by Gregory Currie (1991: 328 ff.) in the context of the philosophy of art. In his thought experiment, there are two identical literary works of art, neither of them a copy of another; curiously, the works are written by two different authors 'word for word the same'. Whether these two texts are one and the same work or two different works is the question Currie asks in order to demonstrate differences in philosophical approaches to answering it, as will be presented in Section 27.3.5. This aside into the philosophy of art shows how thought experiments can be useful for considering theoretical aspects; it also indicates how disciplines outside Translation Studies are concerned with notions such as author, original and the Other.

27.3.4 Translator-centredness model

Central to Hu (2004) introducing the concept of 'translation-centredness' is a more adequate depiction of the reality of translation that would do justice to the creative and subjective aspects of the translator's work. Hu (2004: 107–8) believes that although there are approaches in Translation Studies that pay attention to the translator's role in the translation process, hardly any of these discuss the issue of 'translator' systematically and theoretically; even the post-colonialists, who argue for the visibility and 'subjective involvement' of the translator, tend to focus on other aspects of translation, such as ideology and gender, instead of the translator. Linguistics-based or hermeneutics-based approaches fail to recognize the active role of the translator in decision making.

In the proposal by Hu (2004: 114), translators' behaviour is the perspective for investigating translation. It is therefore easy to see that 'adaptation and selection are translation phenomena, and translators adapt and select in translating'. With this focus, translation can be regarded as the 'eco-environment of translating', referring to the 'worlds of the source and target text and language' and including the varying factors and aspects of translation holistically, from linguistic to social aspects, from authors to readers. In reference to the 'Darwinian principle of *Natural Selection*', Hu (ibid.) describes translating in terms of adaptation, which he sees as the best fit for the 'specific translational eco-environment' of selection, including the decision making that leads to the 'final target text'. Hu (2004: 115) visualizes the model by means of a figure showing the translator-centredness in translation and 'the angles from which the adaptive and selective transfer can be carried out' – there are items such as 'language', 'communication', 'culture' and 'society', the latter including 'esthetical' or 'philosophical' aspects.

Hu (2003: 284–5) exemplifies his model by looking at sonnet translation. When a sonnet by Shakespeare is to be translated, the selection of a translator already has the features of natural selection: the fittest translator in terms of poetry translation in the particular eco-environment of literary translation is selected as the first stage. This also can be seen as the adaptation of a translator to the source text, fitting the special environment. In the next stage, from *a* translator comes *the* translator, which involves an adaption to the particular constraints of the project. Here begins the dominance of the translator 'making decisions and thus selecting the form of the final target text'. In that a selectee becomes a selector, Hu refers to the 'dual identity' of translators. Ecologically inspired, the concept, according to Hu, is about 'a translator's individual survival and career' (ibid.). It is supposed to give the translator's role more significance and support translators' creativity.

It is hard to disagree with Hu when he claims that understanding translating in this manner would highlight the centrality of the translator as a decision maker (see Levý [1967] 2000). A further advantage is the holistic view taken of the issue of translation. As a properly structured framework, it allows the description of different relationships between translational factors and aspects. Being ecologically motivated, it enables the multiple interdependencies between the various aspects to become visible, interdependencies which in translation theories are often only loosely contextualized. Further, the model is general enough to be extended to include specific objects of study or focused on particular aspects. Being translator-centred, it reflects recent research interests in the framework of literary translation, such as phenomenological approaches, the various author–translator discussions or numerous studies on the status of translators. Accepting the relevance of Hu's model presupposes a positive stance towards the trend outside the natural sciences of describing phenomena in ecological terms (eco-cinema, eco-linguistics or eco-aesthetics). Either way, the model can be useful for understanding literary translation as a multi-perspective object of study.

How, then, does the model stand with regard to the ontological issue of the relationship between original and translation? Is the question of whether the translation is the same work as the original or another work possible or relevant in the framework of eco-translation? Let us imagine that we have a world of target text and language, aesthetically and philosophically influenced by a view which advocates the idea of a literary work of art as translatable in the sense of a work retaining its identity when translated. What kind of philosophy of art is then needed? Whatever the approach to the ontology of literary works of art, it cannot be based on the 'identity of language and syntactic identity within the language', as proposed by Nelson Goodman (1976: 209). Goodman's proposal would make translatability impossible. If a philosophical view is to define the identity of a literary work through the work's 'core meaning' and authorial intentions (see Section 27.3.5), as suggested by Arto Haapala (1989), this sameness could be reached through a 'correct' interpretation by a translator working in the hermeneutical tradition. These issues are discussed in the next section.

27.3.5 Translatability as an issue in the philosophy of art

The most natural framework for investigating the question of whether a literary work can be translated is that of the philosophy of art. Let us first examine an approach which takes the meaning of a literary work as an essential criterion in defining the work's identity. There are ontological views, according to which, put simply, a *good* translation is able to preserve all the central meanings of the original. The notion of 'core-work' (Haapala 1989; see Laiho [2007] 2009) accurately describes the issue of the central content which must be present in every acceptable translation of the work in order to justify it being called the same work. Although fascinating as an idea, and as such corresponding to the obvious common sense view on literary translation (Hewson 2011: 1–2; etc.), it raises the question of defining 'meaning'. A strict definition might be problematic. Then again, do cultural entities such as literary works need to be exactly describable semantically? Accepting the idea that works have a 'meaning' that reflects authorial intentions and that this meaning through interpretation is at least partly inter-subjectively traceable is not unproblematic either, as far as the identity of a literary work is concerned. Translation hermeneutics or semiotics to some extent entail the assumption of works being entities with meanings as their 'cores' and, consequently, interpretable or approachable.

Whether two works are identical is not decided by a 'meaning' being identical, to use the terms of Goodman and Elgin (1988). The identity is based on more formal qualities: being the same work requires that two textual entities are identically written, as mentioned earlier. Literary works, for Goodman (1976: 210), are 'characters' like the word 'chat', although typically larger entities (unless we have a work consisting of one word). For two characters to be the same, they must be identical in the same language (Goodman and Elgin 1988: 59). They must be identical in every textual detail, even in punctuation, and they are thus identical works, even when written by two different authors and in a different genre, because identifying works is not based on interpretation. The paradox is addressed by Currie (1991: 328 ff.; see Davies 2007: 26 ff.), introducing a kind of parallel to Jorge Louis Borges' *Pierre Menard, autor del Quijote* [Pierre Menard, Author of the Quixote'] (1944; see Laiho [2007] 2009): a manuscript is unexpectedly found, 'word for word the same' as Jane Austen's *Northanger Abbey*, already published, without any semantic or syntactic differences, and with the same title. The only difference is the genre: Austen wrote a burlesque to satirize the Gothic novel which is the genre of the other *Northanger Abbey* manuscript. The thought experiment is used by Currie to illuminate the absurdity of identifying literary works with texts, as Goodman and Elgin do – for them, a translation of a work can never be the same as the original. '[A] translation of a work', as Goodman (1976: 209) writes, 'is not instance of that work'.

What is the principal difference between the two philosophical approaches? Haapala's approach postulating a core-work sees translation as possible, Goodman's does not. Should we ask what kind of entities these literary works are metaphysically taken to be? They are different. Allowing a work to be translated without the work losing its identity represents an ontological view of literary works as Aristotelian types that do not exist beyond their tokens [*types* represent ontologically 'a general sort of thing' and *tokens* their 'particular, concrete instances', see Wetzel 2014] but are present in them, which explains the idea of a core-work (Haapala 1989: 189). The notion of literary works as language-specific characters originates from the sort of nominalism that denies the existence of abstract entities such as types as manifest in the definition of works (Goodman 1976: 210; see Wolterstorff 1995: 312). It appears that a type-token model for the ontology of literary works of art does not impede the translatability of literary works. On the other hand, only certain kinds of types and tokens are in favour of works being translated and still preserving their identity. Let us examine another way to define a type and token. The ontological hypothesis of Currie (1989; see Laiho 2013: 128) defines literary works of art (like all kinds of works of art) as action types. According to his Action Type Hypothesis, the types need to be enacted so that a work can be said to exist. How does this happen? A literary work will be enacted when an author x arrives at a certain word sequence – the structure S of a work – via a specific heuristic path Z. For two works to be identical as action types they must share a structure S and a heuristic path H, which is understood as a very broad notion referring to 'all the circumstances' which brought the author to arrive at the structure. These are the two constitutive elements of the works, the third being the invariable defining the relation 'x discovers y by means of z' – that is, **D**. Interestingly, the author is not a constitutive element; thus, authorship can vary, just as the time of enacting [τ] is irrelevant to identity. A literary work as an action type can be expressed in the form [x, S, H, **D**, τ]; the only accessible textual entity is solely an *instance of the* *structure* of a work and not of the literary work itself. Consequently, a work is only indirectly approachable, which is one aspect in Currie's theory that can be criticized as counterintuitive.

Why then use the Action Type Hypothesis for considering literary translation? There are several reasons why this model is fruitful for exemplifying the complexity of literary translation and its relationship to an original in light of recent theoretical considerations on the topic. As pointed out earlier, the criterion of 'being the same' as used by Currie is based on structure and heuristics. Reconstructing the same heuristics, one of the two identity conditions, may not be an insurmountable problem: a translator who is working hermeneutically might be seen as able to reconstruct the path of the authorial arrival at structure (like a literary critic; Currie 1989: 68–9). The structure, by contrast, is a problem. How can a translation have the same structure, defined as a word-sequence, as the original? This is clearly impossible: a translation cannot be the same work as the original. Currie's view on performing a work, as exemplified by a musical work of art, could be used to describe translation: performing is seen as representing the event type 'playing of sound structure S' and as different from composing a work. Translation, accordingly, could be regarded as the event type of performing or presenting a structure. Translating the specific word structure S presupposes, naturally, that the translator has identified the work behind the structure, the heuristics as intentions, etc., like a literary critic. After identifying the work, the translator has to decide on the manner of presentation – whether to use a feminist approach, to translate hermeneutically, to foreignize or domesticate, etc. – in order to produce literary products as specific presentations.

27.3.6 Translation as if an original: the translation pact

Cecilia Alvstad (2014) presents a view on literary translation that, at first glance, seems to conflict with the poststructuralist line of thought according to which, as an extreme, a literary translation should be seen as an independent literary text and not as the same work as the original. The 'translation pact', which Alvstad (2014: 271) elaborated on the basis of Philippe Lejeune (1975, 2000), is the key notion for understanding original and translation as the same work. Sameness is addressed here not from the point of view of ontology but from that of literary studies and translation. The sameness achieved through the pact works as a kind of make-believe that invites one to accept the deal, which seems to work inasmuch as 'readers, including critics, literary scholars and other professional readers, often talk and write about translations as if they were originals composed solely by the author' (Alvstad 2014: 270).

How does this happen? According to Alvstad, the agents collectively involved in a wider context in producing translations, such as authors, publishers and co-editors, all contribute to the 'rhetorical construction' that makes the reader re-construct for translated works only an 'implied author' but no additional 'implied translator'. More concretely, there are paratextual elements and practices indicating that a work is a translation. Conventions such as showing the translator's name inside the book or giving the translated title with the name of the original author on the book cover create the frame for reading. As a consequence, the reader reads translated works in a similar way to the manner he or she would read an original. Regardless of the fact that there are two agents 'accredited as the creators of the text' – that is, the author and translator – the illusion of an original written by the author arises for the readers, in correlation with the practice of unambiguously foregrounding the author in terms of paratextual means. The illusion is not necessarily destroyed even if the translator is present in the text of the translation itself, through footnotes, for instance; quite the contrary, as this might even be seen as strengthening the pact. The explanation (Alvstad 2014: 282) is to be found in the narratological nature of the pact: 'there can only be one structuring principle in a work'; readers do not therefore tend to need to 'reconstruct an implied translator', as proposed in the literature. One might ask whether the pact is designed to sustain the translator's invisibility – departing from the recent trend in Translation Studies – and to serve other agents, especially publishers, but not the translator. The invisibility advanced through the pact is rejected by Alvstad, for whom the pact can be regarded as highlighting the significance of a capable translator's work – as shown, for instance, in footnotes explaining translation choices – and consequently increasing trust in the translator. However, keeping in mind that Alvstad's (2014: 271) aim is to elaborate a theoretical framework for understanding 'why professional readers often write about translations as if they were originals', we can think the pact as a description. As described by Alvstad, this pact is at work if accepted by readers; if the invitation to make-believe is not felt to be convincing, because the translator's presence is seen as 'distorting', then the pact is 'challenged or even broken'.

27.4 Future directions

The research presented in Section 27.3 gives an idea of the variety of aspects to be found in approaching literary translation. It is to be expected that these ways of approaching literary translation will characterize future research as well. Translation Studies, being highly multidisciplinary, will make use of the concepts and methods of other research areas, as an expression of conceptual openness. Future objects of study include self-translation, voice(s) and ethics of translation, all linked with 'work identity'. Methodologically, corpus studies in literary translation (e.g. Baker 2000) is an emerging trend producing research knowledge and new types of data otherwise not available.

27.5 Summary

This chapter aims to show how conceptual tools contribute to the understanding of literary translation as a complex phenomenon consisting of the fields of translation and art. They share relevant questions, reflected in scholarly discussions in Translation Studies and the philosophy of art. Due to the different scopes of the two fields, their emphases diverge. Translation Studies focus on analysing different translation approaches to explain and define literary translation and philosophical concepts appearing as implicit factors in the background; the philosophy of art is concerned with defining a literary work of art in terms of ontology and identity, and the question of translatability is hardly addressed. Both theoretical approaches thus offer insights into the domain of the other. While a philosopher, for example, tends to see translation rather as a relative uniform activity, a translation scholar most likely looks at translatability as a challenge from the point of view of the possibility of transferring certain features and not as a metaphysical issue.

Both approaches can profit by viewing central concepts from the perspective of the other: a philosopher can use translation knowledge to explicate translatability more analytically, while a literary translator can profit from the fact that philosophy represents a more abstract level of approach. Undoubtedly, the benefit of the interdisciplinary approach is more obvious in the context of theory than on the level of practice. The question is whether a literary translator actually gains any advantage from knowing that notions such as 'author', 'translator', 'original' or 'translation' are described in Translation Studies in such varied ways, or that these notions are indirectly linked to the question of the identity of a literary work of art. If we accept that interplay between theory and practice is crucial for every academic field, we can see the importance of conceptual tools here. The decisions a literary translator makes are theoretically properly embedded and, consequently, can be described more analytically. The view taken in this chapter is best described by Jean Boase-Beier (2006: 147): 'for translators, as for any practitioners concerned with theory, the theory is another possible tool, a way of broadening the mind, an added perspective'.

Related topics

Current trends in philosophy and translation; translation theory and philosophy; equivalence; ethics; meaning.

Further reading

Baker, M. (2000) 'Towards a Methodology for Investigating the Style of a Literary Translator', *Target* 12(2): 241–66. (The paper delineates a methodical framework for exploring literary translators' individual styles, using a corpus of English texts translated from different languages.)

Connor, P. (2014) 'Reading Literature in Translation', in S. Bermann and C. Porter (eds) *A Companion to Translation Studies*. West Sussex: John Wiley & Sons, 425–37. (The chapter addresses the analysis of literary translation with two distinct orientations: translation as a process or product hardly conjoined although 'not mutually exclusive'.)

Holman, M. and Boase-Beier, J. (1998) 'Writing, Rewriting and Translation: Through Constraint to Creativity', in J. Boase-Beier and M. Holman (eds) *The Practices of Literary Translation: Constraints and Creativity*. Manchester: St. Jerome, 1–17. (The article is focused on the nature of creativity in original writing and literary translation, both of which activities are subject to different kinds of constraints; however, the author and translator both create.)

Howell, R. (2002). 'Ontology and the Nature of the Literary Work', *The Journal of Aesthetics and Art Criticism* 60(1): 67–79. (The paper gives an overview of ontological approaches to a literary work. Because of the variety of the works of literature, the same ontological mode cannot cover all the possible variants.)

References

Alvstad, C. (2014) 'The Translation Pact', *Language and Literature* 23(3): 270–84.

Arrojo, R. (2010) 'Philosophy and Translation', in Y. Gambier and L. van Doorslaer (eds) *Handbook of Translation Studies*, vol. 1. Amsterdam and Philadelphia: John Benjamins, 247–51.

Baer, B. J. (2014) 'Translated Literature and the Role of the Reader', in S. Bermann and C. Porter (eds) *A Companion to Translation Studies*. Chichester: John Wiley & Sons, 333–45.

Baker, M. (2000) 'Towards a Methodology for Investigating the Style of a Literary Translation', *Target* 12(2), 241–66.

Bassnett, S. (1998) 'When is a Translation not a Translation?', in S. Bassnett and A. Lefevere (eds) *Constructing Cultures: Essays on Literary Translation*. Clevedon: Multilingual Matters, 25–40.

Bassnett, S. (2011) 'The Translator as Writer', in C. Buffagini, B. Garzelli and S. Zanotti (eds) *The Translator as Author: Perspectives on Literary Translation*. Münster: LIT Verlag, 91–102.

Bassnett, S. (2014) *Translation Studies* [4th edition]. London and New York: Routledge.

Bassnett, S. and H. Trivedi (1999) 'Introduction: Of Colonies, Cannibals and Vernaculars', in S. Bassnett and H. Trivedi (eds) *Post-colonial Translation: Theory and Practice*. London and New York: Routledge, 1–18.

Benjamin, W. [1923] (2012) 'The Translator's Task', tr. by S. Rendall, in L. Venuti (ed) *The Translation Studies Reader* [3rd Edition]. London and New York: Routledge, 75–83.

Boase-Beier, J. (2006) *Stylistic Approaches to Translation*. Manchester: St. Jerome.

Boase-Beier, J., A. Fawcett and P. Wilson (2014) 'Introduction', in J. Boase-Beier, A. Fawcett and P. Wilson (eds) *Literary Translation: Redrawing the Boundaries*. Basingstoke: Palgrave Macmillan, 1–10.

Bracha, O. (2008) 'The Ideology of Authorship Revisited: Authors, Markets, and Liberal Values in Early American Copyright', *The Yale Law Journal* 118(2): 186–271.
Brownlie, S. (2003) 'Distinguishing Some Approaches to Translation Research', *The Translator* 9(1): 39–64.
Brownlie, S. (2010) 'Committed Approaches and Activism', in Y. Gambier and L. van Doorslaer (eds) *Handbook of Translation Studies*, vol. 1. Amsterdam and Philadelphia: John Benjamins, 45–8.
Cook, D. (1986) 'Translation as a Reading', *British Journal of Aesthetics* 26(2): 143–9.
Currie, G. (1989) *An Ontology of Art*. London: Macmillan.
Currie, G. (1991) 'Work and Text', *Mind* 100(3): 325–40.
Davies, D. (2007) *Aesthetics and Literature*. London and New York: Continuum.
Davies, S. (2006) *The Philosophy of Art*. Oxford: Blackwell Publishing.
Elgin, C. (2014) 'Fiction as Thought Experiment', *Perspectives on Science* 22(2): 221–41.
Flynn, P. (2013) 'Author and Translator', in Y. Gambier and L. van Doorslaer (eds) *Handbook of Translation Studies*, vol. 4. Amsterdam and Philadelphia: John Benjamins, 12–19.
Goodman, N. (1976) *Languages of Art: An Approach to a Theory of Symbols* [2nd edition]. Indianapolis and Cambridge: Hackett Publishing Company, Inc.
Goodman, N. and C. Z. Elgin (1988) *Reconceptions in Philosophy and Other Arts and Sciences*. Indianapolis and Cambridge: Hackett Publishing Company, Inc.
Haapala, A. (1989) *What is a Work of Literature?* Helsinki: The Philosophical Society of Helsinki.
Hermans, T. (2007) 'Literary Translation', in P. Kuhiwczak and K. Littau (eds) *A Companion to Translation Studies*. Clevedon, Buffalo, Toronto: Multilingual Matters, 77–91.
Hewson, L. (2011) *An Approach to Translation Criticism: Emma and Madam Bovary in Translation*. Amsterdam: Benjamins.
Hu, G. (2003) 'Translation as Adaptation and Selection', *Perspectives: Studies in Translatology* 11(4): 283–91.
Hu, G. (2004) 'Translator-Centeredness', *Perspectives: Studies in Translatology* 12(2): 106–17.
Kahn, M. (2011) 'How to Deal with Dialects in Translation?', in C. Buffagini, B. Garzelli and S. Zanotti (eds), 103–16.
Kuhiwczak, P. (2003) 'The Troubled Identity of Literary Translation', in G. Anderman and M. Rogers (eds) *Translation Today: Trends and Perspectives*. Clevedon: Multilingual Matters Ltd., 112–24.
Laiho, L. [2007] (2009) 'A Literary Work—Translation and Original: A Conceptual Analysis Within the Philosophy of Art and Translation Studies', in Y. Gambier and L. van Doorslaer (eds) *The Metalanguage of Translation*. Amsterdam: Benjamins, 105–22.
Laiho, L. (2013) 'Original and Translation', in Y. Gambier and L. van Doorslaer (eds) *Handbook of Translation Studies*, vol. 4. Amsterdam and Philadelphia: John Benjamins, 123–9.
Lefevere, A. (1992) *Translation, Rewriting and the Manipulation of Literary Fame*. London and New York: Routledge.
Levý, J. [1967] (2000) 'Translation as a Decision Process', in L. Venuti (ed), 148–59.
Nord, C. (2011) 'Making the Source Text Grow: A Plea Against the Idea of loss in Translation', in C. Buffagini, B. Garzelli and S. Zanotti (eds), 21–9.
O'Sullivan, C. (2013) 'Creativity', in Y. Gambier and L. van Doorslaer (eds) *Handbook of Translation Studies*, vol. 4. Amsterdam and Philadelphia: John Benjamins, 42–6.
Rohrbaugh, G. (2005) 'Ontology of Art', in B. Gaut and D. McIver Lopes (eds) *The Routledge Companion to Aesthetics* [2nd edition]. London and New York: Routledge, 241–53.
Ross, S. D. (1981) 'Translation and Similarity', in M. G. Rose (ed) *Translation Spectrum: Essays in Theory and Practice*, Albany: State University of New York Press, 8–22.
Schleiermacher, F. [1813] (2012) 'On the Different Methods of Translating', tr. by S. Bernofsky, in L. Venuti (ed) *The Translation Studies Reader* [3rd edition]. London and New York: Routledge, 43–63.
Schäffner, C. and B. Adab (2001) 'The Idea of the Hybrid Text in Translation Revisited', *Across Languages and Cultures* 2(2): 167–80.
Scott, C. (2011) 'The Translation of Reading: A Phenomenological Approach', *Translation Studies* 4(2): 213–29.

Scott, C. (2012) *Translating the Perception of Text: Literary Translation and Phenomenology*. Oxford: Legenda.
Simon, S. (2011) 'Hybridity and Translation' in Y. Gambier and L. van Doorslaer (eds) *The Handbook of Translation Studies*, vol. 2. Amsterdam and Philadelphia: John Benjamins, 49–53.
Toury, G. (1995) *Descriptive Translation Studies and Beyond*. Amsterdam and Philadelphia: John Benjamins.
Tymoczko, M. (2003) 'Enlarging Western Translation Theory: Integrating non Western Thought About Translation' [pdf] Available at www.soas.ac.uk/literatures/satranslations/tymoczko [accessed 20 June 2016].
Tymoczko, M. (2005) 'Trajectories of Research in Translation Studies', *Meta* 50(4): 1082–97.
Van Wyke, B. (2010) 'Ethics and Translation', in Y. Gambier and L. van Doorslaer (eds) *Handbook of Translation Studies*, vol. 1. Amsterdam and Philadelphia: John Benjamins, 111–15.
Van Wyke, B. (2013) 'Translation and Ethics', in C. Millán and F. Bartrina (eds) *The Routledge Handbook of Translation Studies*. London and New York: Routledge, 548–60.
Venuti, L. (1995) 'Translation, Authorship, Copyright', *The Translator* 1(1): 1–24.
Venuti, L. (2000) (ed) *The Translation Studies Reader* [1st edition]. London and New York: Routledge.
Venuti, L. (2008) *The Translator's Invisibility: A History of Translation* [2nd edition]. London and New York: Routledge.
Wakabayashi, J. (2011) 'Fictional Representations of Author-Translator Relationships', *Translation Studies* 4(1): 87–102.
Wetzel, L. (2014) 'Types and Tokens', *The Stanford Encyclopedia of Philosophy* (Spring 2014 Edition), Edward N. Zalta (ed.), available at https://plato.stanford.edu/archives/spr2014/entries/types-tokens/ [accessed June 2017].
Wilson, B. (1998) 'Mi Novelista', in *The Death of a Much-Travelled Woman and Other Adventures with Cassandra Reilly*. Chicago: Third Side Press, 195–215.
Wittman, E. O. (2013) 'Literary Narrative Prose and Translation Studies', in C. Millán and F. Bartrina (eds) *The Routledge Handbook of Translation Studies*. London and New York: Routledge, 438–50.
Wolterstorff, N. (1995) 'Ontology of Artworks', in D. Cooper (ed) *A Companion to Aesthetics*. Oxford: Blackwell, 310–14.
Zeller, B. (2000) 'On Translation and Authorship', *Meta* 45(1): 134–9.

28
Mysticism, esotericism and translation

Philip Wilson

Introduction

If, within the context of this *Handbook*, the relationship between mysticism, esotericism and translation is designated an 'emerging trend', it is in the sense of a new level of enquiry, not of a new conjunction, for the relationship is very old. In view of the increasing amount of academic research into mysticism and esotericism from historians, philosophers and theologians (see Magee 2016) it is appropriate to investigate the links between the phenomena for three reasons. First, many mystical and esoteric texts are studied in translation. Second, it is possible to use new philosophical tools to reconceptualise the connections that have been made in the past. Third, translation is still described in terms that point to the world of the spirit; a recent survey of literary translation by Chantal Wright (2016), for example, describes it as a 'spiritual endeavour' (2016: 7), a 'meditative practice' with a 'spiritual dimension' (2016: 18), a 'metaphysical enterprise' that 'gives us an insight into the nature of language and thought' (2016: 19). In this chapter, I shall investigate the options available to researchers in these areas.

It is important to be clear about what is meant by 'mysticism' and 'esotericism'.[1] Western mysticism originated in Ancient Greek mystery religion. At Eleusis, adherents were initiated into *ta mysteria* [the mysteries], which would lead to *gnosis* [knowledge], a 'direct perception of the ultimate truth of what is' (Magee 2016: xvi). Mysticism is thus an epistemic project to reveal the underlying metaphysics of the universe, and it is this claim to absolute and ineffable knowledge that distinguishes mystics (James [1902] 1985: 380). Mysticism flourishes within religious frameworks such as Christianity (Nelstrop, Magill and Onishi 2009) or Zen (Reps 1957), but also within secular contexts: Iris Murdoch argues for a 'natural way of mysticism' (1992: 301), whilst Andrew Weeks views the Middle High German courtly romance *Tristan* by Gottfried von Strassburg as mystical in its 'anarchic apotheosis of love' (1993: 60) and notes how the themes of mysticism have been 'widely current in the everyday culture of twentieth-century life' (1993: 234). Even if *gnosis* is by definition incommunicable (Scholem 1964: 3–4), mystics paradoxically claim to find ways of expressing what cannot be expressed. The Counter-Reformation Spanish poet John of the Cross (1991), for example, employs erotic imagery in order to show the nature of mystical union with God.

Esotericism[2] consists of those intellectual trends ignored by the Enlightenment, mainstream religion and the academy – for example, alchemy, astrology and magic (Hanegraaff 2013: 13). In contrast to mysticism, esotericism can be evaluated because it leads to communicable knowledge (Scholem 1964: 3–4): an astrologer may or may not successfully predict the future. If mysticism is *gnosis*, esotericism is *technē* [practice, technique], although not just any practice because esoteric practices are held to be those that are founded on *gnosis*, typically on the mystical teaching that all things are one, so that mysticism gives rise to esotericism and not the other way round (Magee 2016: xxx).

The boundary between mysticism and esotericism is fluid, so that a figure like Jakob Boehme is seen by some as mystic and by others as esoteric. Mystical and esoteric phenomena are often conflated as 'mystical' by authors, although contemporary researchers stress that two different traditions are at stake. Thus Kabbalah [Hebrew: reception], a Jewish tradition of great importance in the history of translation, is frequently described as mystical, and does have mystical aspects (see later), but can be seen as esoteric because of its reliance on traditional wisdom rather than on individual experiences of God (Dan 2006: 4). Walter Benjamin's enormously influential 1923 essay 'The Translator's Task' ([1923] 2012), which draws on the Kabbalah, can analogously be viewed as esoteric because it is about *technē* – that is, the practice of translation – but relies on *gnosis* – that is, a mystical view of language – in order to make points about the translator and his or her work.

Mysticism and esotericism together constitute a 'hidden intellectual history of the West' (Magee 2016: xv). Contemporary researchers begin their enquiry into this history as they find it manifested in texts. With respect to mysticism, for example, we cannot possibly access directly the ineffable experiences of, say, Julian of Norwich, but we can access her writings (Katz 1992: 4). Esotericism, whilst a matter of practices, can also be approached through the texts written by practitioners, such as the works of Emanuel Swedenborg.

Many canonical philosophers have addressed mystical and/or esoteric questions, including Benjamin, Collingwood, Derrida, Heidegger, Kierkegaard, Murdoch, Parmenides, Plato, Plotinus, Spinoza, Schopenhauer, Weil and Wittgenstein. In Plato's *Symposium*, for example, Socrates describes the ultimate destiny of the soul in terms of initiation into absolute beauty; philosophers must leave behind earthly things, even philosophy itself, in order to ascend to an ineffable and transcendent reality that is not of this world (*Symposium* (1994) 211b). There is a parallel with the Greek mystery religions, in which initiates rise to a new level of awareness. Philosophy, mysticism and esotericism are not distinct. For Martin Heidegger, for example, philosophy degenerates into sterile rationalism without mysticism, whereas mysticism without philosophy is irrational, as John Caputo argues (1978: 7). The philosophers Immanuel Kant and Georg Friedrich Wilhelm Hegel read Swedenborg and Boehme, respectively, facts that are not denied but usually never mentioned by scholars (Magee 2016: xiv). George Steiner describes how '[n]umerous elements of Gnostic speculation, often with reference to Hebrew, are evident in the great tradition of European linguistic philosophy' ([1975] 1998: 64). In addition, contemporary work in analytic and in feminist philosophy attempts to understand what is going on in mystical texts (see Nelstrop, Magill and Onishi 2009). Philosophy can therefore supply tools when we turn to examine the links between mysticism, esotericism and translation.

What are we to make, for example, of the assertion of Alexander Pope in 1715, that when he translated Homer he was conscious of the need to 'keep alive that spirit and fire which makes [Homer's] chief character' ([1715] 2007: 195)? Pope's image demands effort on the part of the reader. He draws on the Biblical descent of the Holy Spirit as tongues of fire upon the apostles at Pentecost (Acts 2: 4), which reversed the curse of Babel (see later). We might therefore ask if the image is mystical. Enquiry can make clearer what is at stake in such a pronouncement, and can illuminate the nature of translation, mysticism and esotericism, as well as suggesting approaches to the translation of mystical and esoteric texts and the theorisation of translation.

Enquiry may even lead to the conclusion that the long associations between translation and hidden traditions should be brought to an end. David Bellos, in a sustained attack on Benjamin's 'The Translator's Task', not only dismisses that essay but claims that a great deal of writing in contemporary translation studies consists of 'mystical nonsense', and that scholars ought instead to strive for 'philosophically, linguistically and historically informed thinking' (2010: 206). Nonsense of any kind ought to be avoided in scholarship, of course. Two questions face researchers. First, whether the study of mysticism and esotericism is a way of discovering important truths about the world and ourselves, and thus potentially about translation, or whether it is incompatible with scholarly objectivity (Magee 2016: xxxii). Second, whether the nature of mystical and esoteric writing raises particular difficulties for translation and how (if at all) these can be overcome (see Wilson forthcoming). That major philosophers have paid attention to mysticism and esotericism is one reason to take the enquiry seriously, even if we end up agreeing with Bellos. As Theo Hermans says of 'The Translator's Task':

> Of course, we can dismiss Benjamin's musings as 'mystical vagaries', as André Lefevere did at a time when only he and George Steiner had read Benjamin, but this nonchalance sits uneasily with the fact that the essay, however out of this world it may seem, nevertheless grew out of the Western tradition and is now one of the most celebrated and most quoted texts in modern translation studies.
>
> (2013: 82)

Historical perspectives

Translators of sacred texts have long been viewed as working under the inspiration of God. Philo Judaeus (1997), for example, discusses in c. 20 BCE the third-century BCE translation project known as the Septuagint, when 70 translators are said to have rendered the Hebrew scriptures into Hellenistic Greek. Each isolated translator was alleged to have written exactly the same target text. Philo remarks that the translators worked 'as if possessed ... as though dictated to by an invisible prompter', and describes them 'not as translators but as prophets and priests of the mysteries' (1997: 14). Such recreation of the target text is mystical, defying scientific explanation at least in the eyes of Philo, whose choice of vocabulary links the translation to the mystery religions.

The tendency to see translators as inspired also enters secular writing. Few translators in the modern world hope for the sort of divine intervention that produces the Septuagint (Hermans 2007: 9), but mystical and esoteric imagery is frequently encountered in classic statements on translation, as in Pope earlier. David Damrosch writes of the 'utopian view' of translation as a 'mystical mirroring process that would somehow bring the original work, entire, into the translation' (2012: 419). The esoteric poet Novalis, for example, claims that there are three types of translation: the grammatical, the transformative and the mythic. Of these three, mythic translations are the noblest, for they 'reveal the pure and perfect character of the individual work of art', and give us not the actual work of art, but its ideal ([1798] 1997: 68). Modern translators and translation theorists continue to use such imagery when describing translation. Antoine Berman, for example, sees translation as involving labour on the letter, by which he understands an activity 'more originary than the restitution of meaning' – that is, a restoration of the 'particular signifying process of works' and a complementary transformation of the translating language ([1985] 2012: 252–3). Wright comments that his description 'conjures up both a mystical and an unsettling event' (2016: 37). It may be that there is a mystical aspect to creative translation activity.

Jean Boase-Beier argues that it is still not known how translation works, even though all people who know more than one language can and do translate (1998: 33). It is therefore not surprising that translation is often described metaphorically because we naturally look for metaphors in order to describe what puzzles us and can best be understood indirectly (St. André 2010: 2). Mysticism and esotericism are fields from which translators and translation theorists have drawn metaphors. Benjamin describes translation as follows:

> Just as fragments of a vessel, in order to be fitted together, must correspond to each other, so translation, instead of making itself resemble the sense of the original, must fashion its own language, carefully and in detail, a counterpart to the original's mode of meaning, in order to make both of them recognisable as fragments of a vessel, as fragments of a greater language.
>
> ([1923] 2012: 81)

Benjamin uses here imagery from the Lurianic Kabbalah, where '*tikkun*' [redemption] is seen as a process of repair (Dan 2006: 75–80). He undermines the view of equivalence as invariant transfer that has dominated Western views of translation (Venuti 2012: 502) by comparing translation to the process of putting fragments back together. For Benjamin, translation is about non-equivalence. The Kabbalah sees texts as objects of transformation; a text is holy precisely *because* it can be transformed (Scholem 1996: 12). Kabbalistic imagery is therefore a particularly appropriate way to thinking about translation. Iain McGilchrist argues that:

> we need metaphor or *mythos* in order to understand the world. Such myths or metaphors are not dispensable luxuries, or 'optional extras', still less the means of obfuscation: they are fundamental and essential to the process. We are not given the option not to choose one, and the myth we choose is important: in the absence of anything better, we revert to the metaphor or myth of the machine.
>
> (2010: 441)

The non-mechanistic nature of Kabbalistic imagery explains both its prominence in writings about translation and the popularity of Benjamin's essay, because many translators stress that what they do is not an exercise in calculus but a recreation (Weinberger and Paz 1987: 34).[3]

One metaphor that has been prevalent in writing on translation, both in translation studies and in philosophy, is that of the Tower of Babel (Genesis 11: 1–9), in which God is shown scattering human beings and confusing their languages as a punishment for trying to build a tower to heaven. Authors who have used Babel when discussing translation include Barnstone (1993), Benjamin [1923] (2012), Berman [1985] (2012), Derrida (1985), Lapidot (2012), Ricoeur [2004] (2006), Scott (2012), Shelley ([1840] 2002) and Steiner [1975] (1998).[4] Jacques Derrida, for example, argues that in Babel God 'at the same time imposes and forbids translation' (1985: 170), thus making translation both a necessary and an impossible task, much like the mystical quest for union with God. As with that quest, we have a paradox, yet this paradox has made positive contributions to translation studies and philosophy, and sets the terms for twenty-first-century debates – for example, the current discussions on untranslatability (Cassin [2004] 2014). Recent interpretations of Babel are more positive. Clive Scott, developing a phenomenological view of translation, argues that Babel shows 'God's pushing humanity back on its proper course – the development of fruitful alterity' (2012: 8); Elad Lapidot sees the story as being about empowerment (2012: 99), and uses this reading to theorise the reason for translating philosophical texts in the first place: philosophy is 'looking for meaning in words' (2012: 104).

In the aptly named *After Babel* ([1975] 1998), Steiner traces a history of translation and draws on a variety of esoteric writings, including the Kabbalah:

> More justly amazed than modern linguistics at the whole business of man's [*sic*] estrangement from the speech of his fellow man, the tradition of language mysticism and philosophic grammar reaches out to intuitions, to deeps of enquiry, which are, I think, often lacking from current debate.
>
> ([1975] 1998: 61)

Hidden traditions illuminate aspects of translation that otherwise might be missed, a strategy still used by contemporary translation theorists. Willis Barnstone, for example, writes: 'A translation is a friendship between poets. There is a mystical union between them based on love and art' (1993: 166). Barnstone, as I interpret his words, is not suggesting that something supernatural is going on when a poem is translated, as in the account of the translation of the Septuagint described earlier, but offers a perception of the translation process. To translate a poem is an exercise in imagination. He uses mystical imagery in order to change the way that his readers see translation, which he describes as: 'the first acknowledgement of a string of original Buddhist rebirths' (1993: 166); a 'movement from darkness into light and back to darkness (1993: 268); a 'zoo and a heavenly Zion' (1993: 271). Such images are an indirect way of supporting Steiner's view of translation as 'not a science, but an exact art' ([1975] 1998: 311). They force readers to look at translation in a non-mechanistic way by appealing to what Paolo Fabbri, in a discussion of Kabbalah and translation, calls the 'passions and interests that cut deep through conceptual paradigms' (2009: 195). Such imagery allows writers to put forward a holistic approach, as in Robert Pirsig's esoteric novel *Zen and the Art of Motorcycle Maintenance*, where the narrator comes to realise the need to see technology as 'a fusion of nature and the human spirit into a new kind of creation that transcends both' (1999: 291). Not to see a motorcycle as more than the sum of its parts is to fail in maintaining one. The way we look at things is crucial, and mystical and esoteric writers challenge our viewpoints.

Critical issues and topics

Steiner turns to mystical and esoteric writings because they illustrate two important but apparently contradictory tendencies in how we view language: the universalist and the particularist ([1975] 1998: 77) (see Chapter 14, this volume, for a full presentation of Steiner's position). We long to discern universal patterns in language, but we constantly become aware of the differences between languages. Writing in linguistics, Roman Jakobson asserts that languages differ in what they must convey, not in what they may convey ([1959] 2012: 129). (Any language can translate any text, but it will be constrained by grammatical features such as gender.) Writing in philosophy, John Searle asserts that local cultural factors make activities such as translation difficult, whilst the shared background we have as human beings makes them possible (2011: 122). (It is difficult for me to translate an Old High German poem,

465

given its different culture, but if I remember that the people depicted in the text feel pain, as I do, I have a way in.) Writing in translation studies, Bellos argues that translation can take place because we are all different and yet all the same (2011: 338). These three examples show how an ancient debate continues to flourish.

By examining what modern philosophy makes of *gnosis*, we can advance this debate. According to perennialist theorists of mysticism, such as William James ([1902] 1985: 379 ff.), the mystic encounters something totally other, some ultimate reality, and then expresses this experience indirectly in the language of his or her tradition. Translation has similarly been seen as an attempt to reach *gnosis*, to restore the language of Eden, when, according to the Kabbalah, words and objects 'dovetailed perfectly' (Steiner [1975] 1998: 61). Such a longing for perfect equivalence can be traced to 'the exemplary essentialism of the Platonic tradition' (Arrojo 2010: 248). Plato's influence on Western mysticism and esotericism is vast (Nelstrop, Magill and Onishi 2009: 23), and the Platonic desire to return to a language preceding Babel, to what German philosophers have termed an *Ursprache* [original language], has marked a great deal of mystical and esoteric writing, as well as writings about language and translation. In Plato's *Cratylus*, Socrates defends the view that 'everything has a right name of its own, which comes by nature... a name is not whatever people call a thing by agreement... there is a kind of inherent correctness in names' (*Cratylus* (1926) 338a). Translation would then be a simple process of finding equivalents. There would be a mystical level of meaning lurking behind the languages we have after Babel – that is, the 'pure language' referred to by Benjamin ([1923] 2012: 81). The Kabbalah thus envisages a time when translation will be unnecessary (Steiner [1975] 1998: 498). (There is a parallel debate in contemporary philosophy of mind and language about the language of thought and its relation to natural language – see later.)

The human longing for a perfect language can be seen in how some languages – such as Arabic, Hebrew and Sanskrit – have been viewed as mystical – that is, transcendentally sacred (Katz 1992: 16). For Muslim scholars, for example, the Arabic Qur'an is untranslatable because it is a 'linguistic miracle', of which the meaning cannot be fully captured by human beings (Abdul-Raof 2005: 162). There have also been esoteric attempts to create languages with a logically perfect match between word and object, based on the view that 'from an engineering perspective, language *is* a kind of disaster' (Okrent 2009: 11). However, in a post-Wittgensteinian climate, it is difficult to investigate any language other than the ones we have (*PI* 336). Attempts at creating a perfect language have foundered: languages succeed *because* of irregularities, not in spite of them (Okrent 2009: 17). Ludwig Wittgenstein, engineer turned philosopher, uses in his later work the metaphor of an irregular and chaotic ancient city to describe language (*PI* 18), and stresses that nothing about language is hidden (*PI* 126) (see Chapter 4, this volume). If Benjamin's 'pure language' ([1923] 2012: 81) is seen as a perfect level of meaning to which translators can aspire, then the disquiet expressed by Bellos (2010: 206) is reasonable (see Chapter 5, this volume, for an argument that Benjamin's notion of pure language is *not* to be understood just in linguistic terms).

By looking at recent work in analytic philosophy, we can question the perennialist view of *gnosis*, and find a different way forward. Steven Katz argues that pure – that is, unmediated – experiences do not exist (1978: 26). Experiences are 'inescapably formed by prior linguistic influences, such that the lived experience conforms to a pre-existent pattern that has been learned, then intended, and then actualised in the experiential reality of the mystic' (1992: 5). Katz's contextualist approach turns attention to the language found in mystical texts, so that the nature of that language becomes central to enquiry, which is appropriate in the context of translation studies. Mystical and esoteric writings are often performative rather than descriptive. In Zen Buddhism, for example, instruction is often given by the *kōan*, a paradoxical anecdote on which a student meditates, such as the story of one hand clapping (Reps 1957: 34–5). Katz asserts:

> In posing the *kōan* the master is *not* attempting to pass information of a doctrinal or dogmatic sort to his student – although what is taught by the master and what is learned by the student does carry such content in an extended or a translated sense.... Here language performs an essential mystical task, but it is not a *descriptive* task.
>
> (1992: 6)

The student is enlightened upon realising that any answer to the problem of the sound of one hand clapping will be dismissed. The sacred sound *Om* in Hinduism similarly neither says nor tells something but does something (1992: 10).

Wittgenstein's later work can be applied to *gnosis*. In contrast to his early work (see later), he makes no attempt in the 1951 *Philosophical Investigations* to define or even to address mysticism. He introduces a number of tools, however, which can be used in such an investigation (see Chapter 4, this volume). The language-game, for example, is a way of describing human activities such as telling a joke, solving a mathematical puzzle or reporting an event (*PI* 23). As Peter Tyler argues, if we apply Wittgensteinian tools, we have a new way of looking at mystical (and, by implication, esoteric) texts:

> We are no longer concerned with finding ghostly... 'entities' or categories that lie 'behind' mystical discourse... Mystical discourse possesses meaning qua mystical discourse; its language-games are embedded in a practice or 'way of life' that enables reference to occur.
>
> (2011: 52)

From this point of view, for example, Benjamin ([1923] 2012) is using language performatively in order to raise questions about the task of the translator by forcing his readers to form new pictures of what goes on when people translate. Whether the reader accepts his language-games is, of course, another matter, but the way he writes may be closer to Zen than to any supposed science of translation.

Current contributions and research

I describe three examples of how research in translation studies enters into dialogue with philosophy in order to address mystical and esoteric phenomena.

- *Using analytic philosophy to theorise mystical accounts of translation*

Hermans (2007) investigates Joseph Smith's English version of the 1830 *Book of Mormon*. The way in which the translation is described in Mormon tradition can be seen as mystical, and resembles the translation of the Septuagint described earlier:

> Smith dictated his translation virtually without hesitation, guided as he was by 'the gift and power of God', as indeed the title page of the *Book of Mormon* has it, and also by Urim and Thummim, the two 'seer' or 'interpreter' stones which enabled him to read, understand and render into fluent English the otherwise incomprehensible signs on the gold plates.
>
> (2007: 3)

Hermans turns to the analytic philosopher J.L. Austin's theory of performative speech acts, in a process of triangulation that is exemplary for investigating mysticism, esotericism and translation (2007: 5). Austin argues that words can have a performative as well as a descriptive aspect because some speech acts are exercitive – that is, they bring something about. Thus, if somebody names a ship in the right circumstances, then that ship has been named: 'It is a decision that something is to be so, as distinct from a judgement that it is so' (Austin 1962: 154).[5] Austin's insight allows Hermans to theorise translations such the *Book of Mormon* as equivalent to a source text 'only if the felicity conditions for its success are fulfilled' (2007: 5): the *Book of Mormon* will be typically accepted as an authentic translation within the Mormon Church and not outside it. Translation is not a mystical act per se: it becomes a mystical act only in circumstances that allow it to be described as such.

- *Building translation theory from hidden traditions*

Lawrence Venuti (2012) conceptualises an approach to translation using the tradition of hermeneutics. Hermeneutics is a discipline that grew out of the interpretation of sacred texts and that has strong links with the Kabbalah's notion that meaning is not stable (Ogren 2016: 101). By looking to hidden traditions, we can find ways forward. Venuti rejects what he calls the instrumental model of translation, which treats translation as 'the reproduction or transfer of an invariant which the source text contains or causes, typically described as its form, its meaning or its effect' (2012: 485); instead he advocates the hermeneutic model, which 'treats translation as an interpretation of the source text whose form, meaning and effect are seen as variable, subject to inevitable transformation during the translating process' (ibid.). Venuti gives Cicero, Quintilian, Jerome and Nida as examples of the instrumental model; Schleiermacher, Goethe, Hölderlin and Berman as examples of the hermeneutic (ibid.). The hermeneutic model is preferred because it offers 'a more sophisticated account of translation that is not only comprehensive but ethical' (ibid.). (See also Chapter 24, this volume, for an account of translating Levinas in dialogue with Levinas's own work and with Jewish hermeneutic traditions.)

- *Applying what philosophers have said about hidden traditions to translation*

Wittgenstein investigates the esoteric practice of magic in a response to James Frazer's 1890 anthropological study *The Golden Bough*. Frazer describes various rituals of so-called primitive peoples as being in error, and Wittgenstein argues that he has failed to see that a different form of life is in question:

> What a narrow spiritual life on Frazer's part! As a result: how impossible it was for him to conceive of a life different from that of the England of his time!
> ('Remarks on Frazer's *Golden Bough*': 125)

There is a failure of imagination because Frazer projects his own form of life onto the people he studies, so that Bosnian Turks, for example, are condemned for making a mistake when they perform an adoption ritual that mimics the act of giving birth. As Wittgenstein comments: 'it is surely insane to believe that an error is present and that [an adopting mother] believes that she has given birth to the child' (ibid.). I use Wittgenstein's remarks in my own work as a translation theorist in order to show that 'any translator must be aware of his or her own form of life and avoid seeing the other as merely a version of himself or herself' (Wilson 2016: 33). It is all too easy for the translator to judge things only from his or her own point of view, but close examination of a phenomenon forces reconsideration.

Wittgenstein's reflections also give us reason to take mysticism and esotericism seriously. Commenting on magical practices, he writes that 'it will never be plausible to say that mankind does all that out of sheer stupidity' ('Remarks' p. 119), because an 'entire mythology is stored within our language' ('Remarks' p. 133). As Steiner notes: 'There is, above all, a clear sense, persistent... in Wittgenstein, of the numinous as well as problematic nature of man's [sic] life in language' ([1975] 1998: 64). What begins as an enquiry into magic ends by revealing truths about how we speak and write. As Wouter J. Hanegraaff concludes about magic: 'Beware of the power of words!' (2016: 404).

Recommendations for practice

The first recommendation is addressed to translators; the second to those who theorise translation, whether in translation studies or in philosophy.

- *Translating mystical and esoteric texts*

Like all texts, mystical and esoteric works rely on translation for their 'continuing life' (Benjamin [1923] 2012: 76). Nobody can command the languages necessary for any comprehensive investigation into these areas, and thus whole areas of research are closed down to scholars because of the lack of reliable translations (Hanegraaff 2013: 172). The production of reliable translations – whatever the term 'reliable' might mean – is therefore a priority, and insights into *gnosis* and *technē* will be useful to any translator, if we assume that to theorise is to put a translator in a better position to translate (Boase-Beier 2010). Mystical and esoteric texts represent a 'subversive and transgressive kind of writing' (Cupitt 1998: 3). The translator who pays attention to such transgressiveness will be less likely to see his or her task as involving competent use of a dictionary and nothing more. Peter Tyler, for example, notes how the translation from Greek to Latin of the mystical writings of Pseudo-Dionysius by John Scotus Eriugena, carried out about 862, is successful because it is both intelligible and yet retains 'something of the wildness and rough edge of the original' (2011: 67). Eriugena employs tactics such as the coinage of Latin words (e.g. *superdeus* [over-god]) in order to maintain the mystical performative discourse of Pseudo-Dionysius. Over one thousand years later, translators of mystical texts similarly need to be aware of how such texts function, so that they can adopt suitable strategies in order to represent them to the reader. One recent example of a radical translation of a mystical writer is by Edwin Kelly (2014), who presents in contemporary English parts of Julian of Norwich's Middle English *Revelations of Divine Love*. Kelly uses typography to show the struggles that Julian had to record her visions of Christ. The target text contains excised words, forward slashes, Roman numerals, non-standard use of upper and lower cases, and obsolete letters. Kelly thus attempts to maintain the style of the source text and the evident difficulty that Julian had to record her experiences (2014: 7). The translator of a mystical text must re-imagine the struggle that an author had to express what he or she considered to be inexpressible (see Wilson forthcoming), in line with Wittgenstein's advice that grammar tells us what kind of object anything is, so that we can see theology as grammar (*PI* 373). By implication, mysticism is also grammar.

Philip Wilson

- *Looking to non-Western traditions*

Investigating mysticism, esotericism and translation can encourage translation scholars and translators working within Western paradigms to look outside to other traditions (see Introduction). Many cultures have produced texts that have been classified as mystical and esoteric, and Steiner notes that every civilisation has 'its version of Babel, its mythology of the primal scattering of languages' ([1975] 1998: 59). A recent work in translation studies that investigates a non-Western mystical tradition is Douglas Robinson's *The Dao of Translation* (2016), which turns to Daoism. Robinson's purpose is to set up 'an East–West dialogue' between Chinese thinkers such as Laozi, author of the *Daodejing* [Classic of the Way and Virtue] and Western thinkers such as Pierre Bourdieu (2016: viii). The Dao [Way] is frequently described as mystical because it has traditionally been seen as unknowable (2016: 10), but Robinson follows the philosophical translation of the *Daodejing* by Ames and Hall (2003), which translates Dao not as 'way' but as 'making one's way' or 'making life significant'. The Dao is thus seen as *technē* rather than *gnosis*, allowing Robinson to conclude:

> 'D(a)oing translation' could thus be paraphrased 'waying translation' or 'making one's way to/through translation': not just translating but feeling-becoming-thinking translating as a socioecological emerging, shaped and guided by collective habits.
>
> (2016: 192)

Translation theory and practice are linked, and Robinson's approach to a mystical phenomenon becomes a means of reconceptualising translation and pushing our understanding of it in new directions. The book is another indication that the intellectual issues that cluster round mysticism and esotericism are still relevant (see Robinson 2016: 7).

Future directions

As well as continuing to work on areas that have been central to enquiry, such as the Kabbalah, scholars can expand their philosophical investigations to include fields such as alchemy, astrology, magic or panpsychism (which is now a research topic in the philosophy of mind; see Putnam 1988: 120–5).

Writings in the continental tradition, such as Benjamin, can be brought into dialogue with those in the analytic tradition, such as Katz (see Introduction for thoughts on how such a dialogue might be constructed).

Feminist readings of mysticism are significant because the writings of female mystics offer descriptions of 'the female struggle for self-awareness' that escape perennialist classification (Nelstrop, Magill and Onishi 2009: 18). Links can be made with feminist views of translation (see Chapters 16 and 20, this volume).

Dialogue with philosophy of mind also shows new ways of proceeding because mysticism and esotericism may indicate important truths about the (translating) mind. Peter Carruthers (2006), for example, gives a general account of how natural language can be theorised as translation out of the language of thought (mentalese), and neuroscientists are now examining mysticism and esotericism. Arzy and Idel (2015), for example, offer a neurocognitive approach that applies techniques from neuroscience to the ecstatic Kabbalah. They conclude that neuroscience can both shed light on mysticism[6] and learn from it: 'The ecstatic Kabbalah mystics may ... be considered pioneering investigators of the human self, consciousness, and mind' (2015: 4). (For cognitive approaches to translation see Chapter 25, this volume.) We can extend the use of 'translation' in order to describe *gnosis* itself, following Gershom Scholem, in his description of Moses receiving the commandments from God:

> To hear the *aleph* [first letter of the Hebrew alphabet] is to hear next to nothing; it is the preparation for all audible language, but in itself conveys no determinate, specific meaning.... In order to become a foundation of religious authority, it had to be translated into human language, and that is what Moses did.
>
> (1996: 30)

Mysticism and esotericism show that there are two stages in translation, each of which involves a translation: first, something is translated out of the mind into natural language; second, an utterance in one natural language can be translated into other natural languages. Both stages demand investigation using tools from cognitive science. The specific notion of translating the ineffable into natural language, even if only indirectly, raises important notions of translatability (Cassin [2004] 2014). As Bellos argues, translation itself may be problematic for those who believe in the ineffable (2011: 155) (see Wilson forthcoming).

Concluding remarks

Gabriel Marcel distinguishes between a 'problem' and a 'mystery' (1970: 127). A problem is something that is ultimately capable of solution, even if not yet (such as a mathematical puzzle that requires more computing power than currently available); a mystery is something that is in principle unsolvable (such as a religious belief), in which we can only participate. Many apparent mysteries have turned out to be problems. Gravity, for example, was once seen as a force far beyond our comprehension. Even if gravity still eludes total explanation, it is now considered to be a problem. *Gnosis*, in contrast, is still usually viewed as a mystery, which is unsurprising in view of its roots in Greek mystery religion. For the early Wittgenstein of the *Tractatus Logico-Philosophicus*, for example, mysticism is an attitude to the 'problems of life', which remain untouched even if all scientific questions have been answered (*TL-P* 6.52); the mystical is thus 'not *how* the world is, but *that* it is' (*TL-P* 6.44). But can we fence off *gnosis* in this way?

Philo describes the Septuagint's translators as 'prophets and priests of the mysteries' (1997: 14) as if they were adepts of initiation cults. Recent work in psychology, however, suggests that inspiration has more to do with the nature of the brain. Mihaly Csikszentmihalyi (1996) describes the process he calls 'flow', which in the context of translation is defined by Robinson as the ideal and subliminal state 'in which translating is fastest, most reliable, and most enjoyable' (2003: 213). Flow sounds like divine inspiration. Hildegrund Bühler reports how many translators describe entering a mystical space beyond language (1996). However, flow is explicable, not mysterious, and both Csikszentmihalyi (1996) and Robinson (2003) offer strategies for cultivating it. We have a problem, not a mystery. And the same may be true of other so-called mystical phenomena. As Karl Marx argues: 'All mysteries which lead theory to mysticism find their rational solution in human practice and in the comprehension of practice' ([1888] 1970: 122). This takes us back to Bellos's contention that research in translation studies needs to eschew 'mystical nonsense' (2010: 206). I conclude with three possible responses to the challenge.

First, mysticism and esotericism can indeed be dismissed as nonsense, together with their interface with translation. Perhaps the very idea of *gnosis* is seen as incoherent, or perhaps it is thought that such matters are best passed over in silence, following a remark by Wittgenstein (*TL-P* 7). The approach of the researcher who takes this option will be methodologically hostile.

Second, researchers may continue to investigate and even to use the language of mysticism and esotericism when addressing translation, even if they do not commit themselves to the forms of life associated with the language. After all, as McGilchrist argues, metaphors are how we come to understand the world (2010: 42). What matters is to progress in such understanding. Philosophy shows translation theorists that rigorous enquiry can inform our thinking on hidden traditions and that 'mystical' and 'esoteric' are not just terms of reproach to throw at any opinion we regard as 'vague and vast and sentimental' (James [1902] 1985: 379). Scholarly distinctions can be made when phenomena are investigated. Robinson, for example, in his study of Daoism and translation mentioned earlier, discusses the 'Daoist radicalism' of the 'abductive' approach to translation of Ritva Hartama-Heinonen, according to which signs translate themselves without the translator having to make any effort, such as looking words up, editing or even (presumably) learning languages (2016: 12 ff.). Robinson argues that such a 'utopian' attitude (compare the earlier remark by Damrosch) would make it very hard for any translator to make a living (2016: 34), and rejects her position. Yet he goes on to find more fruitful ways of engaging with the Dao (see earlier). The approach of the researcher who takes this second option will be methodologically agnostic, just as an expert on Plato need not be a card-carrying Platonist (Magee 2016: xxiii). Such a researcher can throw away the ladder of *gnosis* after investigating texts, to adapt an expression from Wittgenstein (*TL-P* 6.54), and yet still discover truths about being human in a world that needs translation. Hanegraaff argues that methodological agnosticism is the proper response for *all* scholarship on these matters (2013: 11–12).

Third, there is nothing to stop any researcher viewing translation as a 'spiritual endeavour' (Wright 2016: 7), a 'meditative practice' with 'a spiritual dimension' (Wright 2016: 18) or a 'metaphysical enterprise' (Wright 2016: 19) that offers an insight into language, to use terms cited at the beginning of this chapter. The approach of the researcher who takes this option will be methodologically committed.

Which of the three options is taken will depend upon belief – that is, upon the metaphysical framework that the researcher brings to issues of *gnosis* and *technē*. Belief, like metaphor, is something that we cannot do without. As Graham Ward argues, it is endemic to the human condition and goes all the way down to the dispositional (2014: 188). We see this in how people categorise writers as mystical and/or esoteric. For *A*, John of the Cross is a great poet but nothing more; for *B*, he is a mystical writer who manages to offer a proxy that suggests what it might be like to become one with God. For *C*, the Kabbalah represents an interesting hermeneutical tradition and nothing more; for *D*, it offers a methodology for communicating truths about ultimate realities. These four opinions are explained by the foundational beliefs – that is, the metaphysical frameworks of *A*, *B*, *C* and *D*. We all inevitably bring a metaphysical framework to any investigation. The metaphysical framework is what Wittgenstein calls the 'decisive movement in the conjuring trick ... the very one that seemed to us quite innocent' (*PI* 308).

Metaphysical frameworks are either dualist or monist, depending on whether one sees a reality behind this world or not.[7] In a post-Wittgensteinian world, the dualist will have problems justifying his or her position when it comes to language and the world we live in, but mystical and esoteric phenomena will be easy to explain because they purport to latch on to a transcendent realm of meaning. The monist has a more justifiable philosophical position, but will find mystical and esoteric phenomena difficult to explain, even if they do tell us a lot about ourselves – if only that we long for a Platonic view of the world and of language to be the case. Dualists will tend to be either methodologically agnostic or methodologically committed in their approach to mysticism and esotericism. Monists will tend to be either methodologically agnostic or methodologically hostile. The role played by belief in the enquiry is a further indication that this emerging area of research is important, no matter which methodological option is taken.[8]

Related topics

Wittgenstein; Benjamin; Derrida; equivalence; feminism; meaning; Shelley's Plato; Levinas: his philosophy and its translation; cognitive approaches to translation; literary translation.

Notes

1 The context of this chapter is mostly Western, but the distinctions can be applied to non-Western traditions (see Magee 2016: xxxi).
2 Alternative terms for esoteric traditions include 'occult', 'hermetic' and 'gnostic'. The final term also refers to theological traditions chiefly within Christianity.
3 Benjamin's essay is of tremendous importance when considering the subject matter of this chapter and demands more analysis than space allows (see Chapter 5, this volume).
4 *Babel* is also the title of a scholarly translation journal, whilst the translating Babel fish first appears in the comic science fiction of Douglas Adams.
5 There are similarities with the approach of Katz (1978, 1992).
6 The ecstatic Kabbalah is usually seen as mystical rather than esoteric.
7 What constitutes 'real' is a vigorous debate in contemporary philosophy of science and of mind and again demands more analysis than space allows.
8 Thanks to the following for their advice and support: Jean Boase-Beier, Sam Earle, Tom Greaves, Gareth Jones, Silvia Panizza, Shyam Ranganathan, Davide Rizza and Richard Woods.

Further reading

Benjamin, W. [1923] (2012) 'The Translator's Task', tr. by S. Rendall, in L. Venuti (ed.) *The Translation Studies Reader* [Third edition], London and New York: Routledge, 75–83. (The most influential esoteric statement on translation, drawing on imagery from the Kabbalah.)
Hermans, T. (2007) *The Conference of the Tongues*, Manchester: St. Jerome. (An example of triangulation of phenomenon, philosophy and translation theory: see the investigations of the Septuagint and the *Book of Mormon* (chapter 1), and of the Catholic doctrine of transubstantiation (chapter 4).)
Magee, G.A. (ed.) (2016) *The Cambridge Handbook of Western Mysticism and Esotericism*, Cambridge: Cambridge University Press. (A survey of current research. Magee's Introduction is particularly illuminating.)
Steiner, G. [1975] (1998) *After Babel* [Third edition], Oxford: Oxford University Press. (Important for its historical overview of the links between translation and alternative traditions and for Steiner's argument that such traditions have a lot to tell us about language, and therefore about translation.)

References

Abdul-Raof, H. (2005) 'Cultural Aspects in Qur'an Translation', in L. Long (ed.) *Translation and Religion: Holy Untranslatable?* Clevedon: Multilingual Matters, 162–72.
Ames, R.T. and D.L. Hall (2003) (trs) *Daodejing: 'Making Life Significant'; A Philosophical Translation*, New York: Ballantine.
Arrojo, R. (2010) 'Philosophy and Translation', in Y. Gambier and L. van Doorslaer (eds) *Handbook of Translation Studies*, Amsterdam: John Benjamins, 246–51.

Arzy, S. and M. Idel (2015) *Kabbalah: A Neurocognitive Approach to Mystical Experiences*, New Haven and London: Yale University Press.
Austin, J.L. (1962) *How to Do Things with Words*, Oxford: Clarendon.
Barnstone, W. (1993) *The Poetics of Translation*, New Haven and London: Yale University Press.
Bellos, D. (2010) 'Halting Walter', *Cambridge Literary Review* 3: 194–206.
Bellos, D. (2011) *Is That a Fish in Your Ear?* London: Particular Books.
Benjamin, W. [1923] (2012) 'The Translator's Task', tr. by S. Rendall, in L. Venuti (ed) *The Translation Studies Reader* [Third edition], London and New York: Routledge, 75–83.
Berman, A. [1985] (2012) 'Translation and the Trials of the Foreign', tr. by L. Venuti, in L. Venuti (ed) *The Translation Studies Reader* [Third edition], London and New York: Routledge, 240–53.
Boase-Beier, J. (1998) 'Can You Train Literary Translators?', in P. Bush and K. Malmkjær (eds) *Rimbaud's Rainbow*, Amsterdam: John Benjamins, 33–41.
Boase-Beier, J. (2010) 'Who Needs Theory?', in A. Fawcett, K.L. Guadarrama García and R. Hyde Parker (eds) *Translation: Theory and Practice in Dialogue*, London: Continuum, 25–38.
Bühler, H. (1996) 'Zur Deverbalisierung im Übersetzungsprozeß', in A. Lauer, H. Gerzymisch-Arbogast and E. Steiner (eds) *Übersetzungswissenschaft im Umbruch*, Tübingen: Narr, 259–69.
Caputo, J. (1978) *The Mystical Element in Heidegger's Thought*, Athens: Ohio University Press.
Carruthers, P. (2006) *The Architecture of the Mind*, Oxford: Clarendon Press.
Cassin, B. [2004] (2014) (ed.) *Dictionary of Untranslatables*, tr. by S. Rendall, C. Hubert, J. Mehlman, N. Stein and Michael Syrotinski, ed. by E. Apter, J. Lezra and M. Wood, Princeton: Princeton University Press.
Csikszentmihalyi, M. (1996) *Creativity*, London: HarperCollins.
Cupitt, D. (1998) *Mysticism after Modernity*, Oxford: Blackwell.
Damrosch, D. (2012) 'Translation and World Literature', in L. Venuti (ed.) *The Translation Studies Reader* [Third edition], London and New York: Routledge, 411–28.
Dan, J. (2006) *Kabbalah: A Very Short Introduction*, Oxford: Oxford University Press.
Derrida, J. (1985) 'Des Tours de Babel', tr. by J.F. Graham, in J.F. Graham (ed.) *Difference in Translation*, New York: Cornell University Press, 165–207.
Fabbri, P. (2009) 'The Untranslatability of Faith', tr. by C. O'Sullivan, in M. Baker (ed.) *Translation Studies*, Volume 1, London and New York: Routledge, 184–97.
Hanegraaff, W. (2013) *Western Esotericism: A Guide for the Perplexed*, London: Bloomsbury.
Hanegraaff, W. (2016) 'Magic', in G.A. Magee (ed.) *The Cambridge Handbook of Western Mysticism and Esotericism*, Cambridge: Cambridge University Press, 393–404.
Hermans, T. (2007) *The Conference of the Tongues*, Manchester: St. Jerome.
Hermans, T. (2013) 'What Is (not) Translation?', in C. Millán and F. Bartrina (eds) *The Routledge Handbook of Translation Studies*, London and New York: Routledge, 75–87.
Jakobson, R. [1959] (2012) 'On Linguistic Aspects of Translation', in L. Venuti (ed.) *The Translation Studies Reader* [Third edition], London and New York: Routledge, 126–31.
James, W. [1902] (1985) *The Varieties of Religious Experience*, London: Penguin.
John of the Cross. (1991) *Collected Works*, tr. by K. Kavanagh and O. Rodriguez, Washington: ICS.
Katz, S.T. (1978) 'Language, Epistemology and Mysticism', in S. Katz (ed.) *Mysticism and Philosophical Analysis*, London: Sheldon Press, 27–74.
Katz, S.T. (1992) 'Mystical Speech and Mystical Meaning', in S. Katz (ed.) *Mysticism and Language*, Oxford: Oxford University Press, 3–41.
Kelly, E. (tr.) (2014) *And After This I Saw: Selections from the Work of Julian of Norwich*, Norwich: Gatehouse Press.
Lapidot, E. (2012) 'What is the Reason for Translating Philosophy? I. Undoing Babel', in L. Foran (ed.) *Translation and Philosophy*, Oxford: Peter Lang, 91–105.
Magee, G.A. (ed.) (2016) *The Cambridge Handbook of Western Mysticism and Esotericism*, Cambridge: Cambridge University Press.
Marcel, G. (1970) *Being and Having* [no translator credited], London: Fontana.

Marx, K. [1888] (1970) 'Theses on Feuerbach' [no translator credited], in K. Marx and F. Engels (eds) *The German Ideology*, London: Lawrence and Wishart, 121–3.
McGilchrist, I. (2010) *The Master and His Emissary*, New Haven and London: Yale University Press.
Murdoch, I. (1992) *Metaphysics as a Guide to Morals*, London: Penguin.
Nelstrop, L., K. Magill and B. Onishi (2009) *Christian Mysticism*, Farnham: Ashgate.
Novalis [Friedrich von Hardenberg] [1798] (1997) 'Grammatical, Transformative, and Mythic Translations', tr. by D. Robinson, in D. Robinson (ed.) *Western Translation Theory from Herodotus to Nietzsche*, Manchester: St. Jerome, 213.
Ogren, B. (2016) 'Kabbalah', in G.A. Magee (ed.) *The Cambridge Handbook of Western Mysticism and Esotericism*, Cambridge: Cambridge University Press, 95–106.
Okrent, A. (2009) *In the Land of Invented Languages*, New York: Spiegel and Grau.
Philo Judaeus [c. 20 BCE] (1997) 'The Creation of the Septuagint', tr. by F.H. Coulson, in D. Robinson (ed.) *Western Translation Theory from Herodotus to Nietzsche*, Manchester: St. Jerome, 12–14.
Pirsig, R. (1999) *Zen and the Art of Motorcycle Maintenance*, London: Vintage.
Plato [c. 380 BCE] (1926) *Cratylus*, tr. by H.N. Fowler, in *Plato* Volume 4, London: Heinemann, 6–191.
Plato [c. 380 BCE] (1994) *Symposium*, tr. by R. Waterfield, Oxford: Oxford University Press.
Pope, A. [1715] (2007) 'The Chief Characteristic of Translation', in D. Robinson, *Western Translation Theory*, Manchester: St. Jerome, 193–5.
Putnam, H. (1988) *Representation and Reality*, Cambridge, MA: MIT Press.
Reps, P. (ed.) (1957) *Zen Flesh, Zen Bones*, London: Arkana.
Ricoeur, P. [2004] (2006) *On Translation*, tr. by E. Brennan, London: Routledge.
Robinson, D. (2003) *Becoming a Translator*, London and New York: Routledge.
Robinson, D. (2016) *The Dao of Translation*, London and New York: Routledge.
St. André, J. (2010) *Thinking through Translation with Metaphors*, Manchester: St. Jerome.
Scholem, G. (1964) *Jewish Mysticism in the Middle Ages*, New York: Judaica.
Scholem, G. (1996) *On the Kabbalah and its Symbolism*, tr. by R. Manheim, New York: Schocken.
Scott, C. (2012) *Translating the Perception of Text*, London: Legenda.
Searle, J. (2011) 'Wittgenstein and the Background', *American Philosophical Quarterly* 48(2): 119–28.
Shelley, P. [1840] (2002) 'A Defence of Poetry', in D.H. Reiman and N. Fraistat (eds) *Shelley's Poetry and Prose: Authoritative Texts, Criticism* [Second edition], New York: Norton, 478–508.
Steiner, G. [1975] (1998) *After Babel* [Third edition], Oxford: Oxford University Press.
Tyler, P. (2011) *The Return to the Mystical*, London: Continuum.
Venuti, L. (2012) 'Genealogies of Translation Theory: Jerome', in L. Venuti (ed.) *The Translation Studies Reader* [Third edition], London and New York: Routledge, 483–502.
Ward, G. (2014) *Unbelievable*, London and New York: I.B. Tauris.
Weeks, A. (1993) *German Mysticism*, New York: State University of New York Press.
Weinberger, E. and O. Paz (1987) *19 Ways of Looking at Wang Wei*, London: Asphodel.
Wilson, P. (2016) *Translation after Wittgenstein*, London and New York: Routledge.
Wilson, P. (forthcoming) 'Translation and Mysticism: Demanding the Impossible', in M. Akashi, W. Józwikowska, D. Large and E. Rose (eds) *Untranslatablity: Interdisciplinary Perspectives*, London: Routledge.
Wittgenstein, L. [1921] (1990) *Tractatus Logico-Philosophicus*, tr. by C.K. Ogden, London and New York: Routledge.
Wittgenstein, L. [1967] (1993) 'Remarks on Frazer's Golden Bough', tr. by J. Beversluis, in *Philosophical Occasions*, Indianapolis and Cambridge: Hackett, 118–55.
Wittgenstein, L. [1953] (2009) *Philosophical Investigations*, tr. by G.E.M. Anscombe, P.M.S. Hacker and J. Schulte, Chichester: Wiley-Blackwell.
Wright, C. (2016) *Literary Translation*, London: Routledge.

29
Toward a philosophy of translation

Salah Basalamah

Introduction

This chapter examines the different attempts at articulating a philosophy of translation as reflected in the discipline of Translation Studies (TS) and related disciplines. Following a definition of what a philosophy of translation strives to be, a review of past works on the topic will lay out the background of current research in this field. The chapter will next engage with some critical views on relevant contributions, and then outline some objectives and tasks of a future philosophy of translation.

Historical perspectives

Early in its development, TS apparently abandoned the tempting quest for a general theory (Holmes 2004). Approaches to translation have since evolved without any unifying model being explicitly proposed. Jean-René Ladmiral suggested speaking only of theorems (1978) – that is, fragments of theories that are to be applied in a casuistic manner. Over fifty years ago, the 'linguistic turn' was initiated; the 'cultural turn' occurred some twenty years later and, most recently, some have called the reliance on sociological theories in TS the 'sociological turn' (Pym 2010; Wolf and Fukari 2007; Snell-Hornby 2006; Inghilleri 2005; Tyulenev 2014). However, this account is subject to challenge – take, for instance, Rainier Grutman's assertion (2009) that nothing really new has been devised since Even-Zohar and Toury in the 1970s and 1980s.

But TS has certainly evolved, and during this evolution, translation as an object of study has increasingly moved from being viewed as a linguistic transfer 'process' to being seen as a final 'product', sometimes to be compared to its source text, sometimes to other (re)translations. However, the study of translation as a process has not been abandoned, and in more recent TS scholarship such study typically occurs within sociological investigations that seek to uncover how the social production of translations unfolds (Simeoni 1998; Hermans 1999; Casanova 2007; Heilbron 1999; Gouanvic 2005; Buzelin 2005; Sapiro 2008; Tyulenev 2012). The process can also be found in cognitive science (Gutt 1991), in neurophysiology (Kurz 1994), or in more recent studies on the neuroscience of translation (Tymoczko 2012), which investigate the representation of translational activities in the brain.

Critical issues and topics

Notwithstanding these debates around the process and the product of translation, as well as the shift from an earlier focus on the text to the more recent emphasis on the agent (Chesterman 2009), a properly philosophical approach to translation has been rather scarce in TS. A probable reason may be that other than linguists, comparative literature scholars, and other neighboring disciplinary affiliates, scholars who were trained in philosophy did not integrate the field into their scholarship or choose to investigate its potential. Perhaps the wider horizons of philosophical investigations have proven to be more appealing or more open than TS to a larger diversity of objects of study.

Another reason for this reservation may be a paradox affecting the nature of translation: on the one hand, translation epitomizes a casuistic activity that can hardly submit itself to generalizations – hence the theorems of Ladmiral (1978) and the absence of a general theory (Holmes 2004). At the same time, translation constitutes one of the specific disciplines of the humanities and therefore is subject to some degree of generalization due to the need to conform to the conventions of academic research (Passeron & Revel 2005; Lacour and Campos 2005).

'Thinking by case', according to Jean-Claude Passeron and Jacques Revel, is a possible effect of an 'underground epistemological revolution' (Passeron and Revel 2005: 15) that may have disconnected the humanities from their positivist approach in favour of a more flexible one, like that of constructivism. If the singularity of a translation can symbolize the status of a case-study and the peculiarity of its reflexive process in the humanities, then consequently translation has the potential to become an epistemological exemplar and play a role in the shaping of an entire epistemic culture (Knorr Cetina 1999).

In order to explore that potential and the extent to which translation can expand its semantic field, the task of defining TS's object of study needs to be undertaken from a philosophical perspective. In other words, if the concept of translation is to be understood beyond its traditional (Western) sense of meaning transfer, then the philosophical task of definition would entail a broader perspective, situating translation in a wider ontological framework or perceiving it from a bird's-eye vantage point. However, although this task of definition usually takes place within philosophy, TS should bear the responsibility for this inquiry in order to 'lift the most pertinent aspects of the philosophical debate into our own discipline and add the philosophy of translation to Holmes' map . . . ' so much so that Kirsten Malmkjær 'would like to see it as a branch of Translation Studies in its own right' (2010: 202).

As another indication of the breadth of the concept and its ability to overcome its own semantic limitations, translation has been widely used in different fields as a metaphor (Guldin 2015). In that capacity, it can be used to portray processes as diverse as genetic decoding (molecular biology), dream interpretation (psychoanalysis), transfer and exchange of knowledge (medical research), as well as the change of internet protocol addresses (networking), TV or radio retransmission (broadcasting), and property transfer (law), among many other still unexplored fields. However, despite the significant conceptual expansion that the figurative use of translation is offering, it – at least as demonstrated by Rainer Guldin (2015) – has not yet revealed its philosophical functions or scope.

Additionally, it can be noted that translation is also used metaphorically in daily speech as in, for example, 'this idea must be translated into concrete action'. According to Kobus Marais (2014), however, these translational metaphors have only played a marginal role in translation theory. His observation may be challenged by the ubiquity of the 'metaphors we live by' (Lakoff and Johnson 1980) and by keeping in mind how daily language is pervaded by them, as is even the very process by which we think (Fauconnier and Turner 2002, 2008). This thought should trigger our philosophical curiosity and lead us to reflect on the reasons that will be explored later in this chapter.

Current contributions and research

This overview does not indicate where an actual 'philosophy of translation' could be found. The reason is that neither the earlier mapping of TS (Holmes 2004) nor the latest (van Doorslaer 2007) account for a subcategory of this denomination. Therefore, within the discipline, the topic 'philosophy of translation' exists only in fragments – that is, articles and parts thereof (e.g. Ladmiral 1988, 1989, 1992, 1997, 2010; Tymoczko 2007; Weissbrod 2009; Malmkjær 2010; Blumczynski 2016). For example, in *Sourcier ou cibliste. Les profondeurs de la traduction* [Source or Target-oriented. The Depths of Translation], Ladmiral (2014) philosophizes the practice of translation rather than reflecting philosophically on the concept of translation and its potential ability to reshape the whole discipline. As a result, no matter how philosophical his approach may appear, he does not relate translation to wider conceptual, disciplinary, or primary matters of intellectual life that must transcend the immanent and narrow preoccupations of language transfer and its prescriptions. Philosophizing the activity of translating thus does not necessarily imply the advent of a philosophy of translation.

But there is an exception to this state of affairs. The only book in translation that has announced itself as a 'philosophy of translation' – although not in its title – is Marais (2014). Considering the singular status of Marais' work and its potential impact (which will be explored later in this chapter), the question that should be answered is whether there should be any space allocated to a philosophy of translation *inside* the discipline.

While the philosophy of translation does not seem to occupy much territory within TS, it has for much longer played a greater role in philosophy. When philosophy needed to tackle the complexities of language and interpretation, it often adopted translation as a particular object of study of its own (Heidegger 1996; Derrida 1985; Ricoeur 1996; Jervolino 2006; Benjamin 1989; Sallis 2002; Gadamer 2004; Quine 2013; Davidson 1984; see Chapters 3, 6, 7, 8 and 9, this volume). Whether in the revelation of paradoxes of language, or as a heuristic conceptual tool to better understand other interpretive processes in language and culture, translation has served as an inexhaustible cognitive device that puts common beliefs in perspective, and explains what superficial perceptions would not permit us to apprehend. But one should not confuse the mere appeal to translation in philosophy of language, hermeneutics or analytical philosophy (as illustrated by the previously cited authors) with a hypothetical philosophy of translation. More promising is the fact that the very role of translation moves in the former group from being a supporting (pedagogical) subject of reflection to a core object of study, although a philosophy of translation cannot content itself with taking place within the boundaries of only one or a few disciplines but would necessarily venture to expand its field of investigation to all.

One would expect philosophy, more than other disciplines, to model intellectual flexibility by revealing its verbal-centric propensity and to have a certain measure of transdisciplinary porosity in order to explore many fields of knowledge and even some uncharted territories of the translational concept. However, it has so far been primarily deepening the arcana of language, together with some of its specific features and uses (e.g. metaphors). On the other hand, not only have philosophers naturally tended to view matters through their particular philosophical *Weltanschauung* (Heidegger, Gadamer, Derrida, Ricoeur), they have also been seldom interested in thoughts specific to non-philosophical disciplines, unless these contributed to their own arguments. The question then turns back to TS: what stance should it take with regard to the philosophical dimensions offered by the translational concept?

As a possible response, it could be argued that TS is still a growing discipline that has not reached its limits or its latest stages of maturation. Therefore, it is to be expected that it would initially go through some deep crises – which it may already be starting to undergo – before it reaches the degree of maturity required to move to a new paradigm (Kuhn 1996). Some signs of unrest may already be detected with the most recent studies trying to stir the more established categories that TS has been working with and building upon for the last few decades (Basalamah 2016).

A case in point is Michael Cronin's *Eco-Translation* (2017), whose titular concept 'covers all forms of translation thinking and practice that knowingly engage with the challenges of human-induced environmental change' (2017: 2). Although not explicitly introducing itself as a philosophical investigation, Cronin's book is nevertheless a daring and creative effort to explore a new research territory that TS has never delved into. It should be kept in mind that one 'task of the philosopher is . . . to express in coherent meaningful terms what is usually only implicit in the way we live . . . . [or to describe] this effort that draws the boundary line between practice and theory, between understanding life and living it' (Macmurray 1936: 2–3). Viewed through this lens, *Eco-Translation* could be considered a philosophical undertaking in its own right. In urging humanity to embrace post-anthropocentrism, the notion of eco-translation develops an overarching scope that does amount to a philosophy of life more generally, but does not address directly enough the conceptual stakes of a philosophy of translation.

Another example may be the most recent work of Piotr Blumczynski (2016), which is more directly philosophical. Drawing on the reflections of Stefano Arduini and Nergaard (2011) in their inaugural issue of the online journal *Translation*, Blumczynski's book 'attempts to demonstrate the epistemological potential of translation . . . [and] aspires to a truly transdisciplinary endeavor in that it draws from and makes connections to various disciplines' (Blumczynski 2016: Introduction § 4). This book is a conceptual study of translation which attempts to 'claim new territories for translation' (Introduction § 9) by 'applying a translational interpretant . . . to insights originally formulated in other areas' (Introduction § 5). Blumczynski shows the flexibility of the translation concept and how translation can be found in many fields of knowledge, provided one is capable of seeing the potential of its applicability beyond initial disciplinary boundaries. However, it should be noted that while this conceptual investigation is presented as a journey through four disciplines of the humanities only, chapter 5, which focuses on anthropology and ethnography, inexplicably ventures into the social sciences. Additionally, philosophy (chapter 2) is only a part of the entire demonstration, not the study's overarching focus. As such, philosophy cannot be the lens through which the study considers its subject and at the same time one of the areas where translation occurs under different guises – in this case hermeneutics, understanding, and interpretation. Finally, Blumczynski's work does not even constitute the inception of a philosophy of translation in TS but is simply a 'translational methodology' (Blumczynski Ch. 1 § 7) aimed at 'chasing translation through several different fields' (Blumczynski Introduction § 11) and spotting it virtually everywhere. In other words, like Guldin (2015), who has tracked the metaphor of translation as used in other disciplines, even beyond the humanities, Blumczynski's book is yet another strong indication that conceptual research is a legitimate form, although less represented, of investigation in TS and that the concept of translation is, if not ubiquitous, at least increasingly 'enlarging' (Tymoczko 2007).

Despite the previously discussed works, and as alluded to earlier, Marais' (2014) attempt to formulate a full-fledged philosophy of translation seems to be the most promising to date. Not only is its content clearly philosophical in that it proposes an overarching view of TS's object of study, of the way it is situated in its system, and of how TS extends its disciplinary territory beyond traditional boundaries; his book is also an explicit 'effort to propose a philosophy of translation ... from the perspective of complexity' (p. 10). Interestingly, as suggested in the last words of the quote, this philosophy is seen from an allegedly even further vantage point – that of complexity. However, complexity is not a philosophy in its own right but, rather, is usually considered a 'theory' or a 'science' (Gershenson et al. 2007). It has been brought into being in order to study complex systems as part of 'General System Theory' (von Bartalanffy 1968), in which concepts and principles are deemed to be applicable to all domains of knowledge. In fact, several works on complexity consider their subject to be a part of the philosophy of science (Gershenson et al. 2007; Santos 2012; Rescher 1998), and a useful conceptual tool to account for the complexity of natural phenomena. So much so that Edgar Morin, a philosopher, argues that 'all most advanced sciences arrive to [sic] fundamental philosophical problems ... they thought they have eliminated' (Morin 2007: 24). This means that the abstract nature of complexity issues pertaining to the philosophy of science entails a philosophical reflection that distinguishes between 'generalized complexity', which applies to all fields, and 'restricted complexity', which applies only to the sciences (2007: 27). However philosophical this endeavor may be, it does not in itself amount to a philosophy of its own. Morin, confirming this point, observes that '[s]till today there is the illusion that complexity is a philosophical problem and not a scientific one' (2007: 24).

Notwithstanding the field which complexity is applied to, Marais' work (2014) moves beyond that of Maria Tymoczko (2007). Marais contends that Tymoczko conceptualizes translation only as an object of study – that is, a cluster concept (Marais 2014: 88) – while one rather needs to conceptualize the entire field of study – that is, 'the lens through which you look at reality' (2014: 89). For Marais, 'TS becomes the field of study that studies all reality from the perspective of inter-systemic relationships' (2014: 97). He advocates for 'a widening and philosophical strengthening of the foundations of TS in which a future field devoted to inter-systemic relationships could develop'. He calls this emerging field 'inter-systemic studies' (2014: 105). No matter how bold these proposals may be, Marais has not explained how his translation concept as 'one particular instance of the category of inter-systemic semiotic phenomena' (2014: 96) actually applies to all of reality. His pioneering work also leaves further questions unanswered, for example: how can one advocate for an all-systemic perspective, which cannot be but reductionist by definition, while at the same time calling for complexity – that is, literally a non-reductionist approach (2014: 98–9)? Where does Marais' philosophy of translation stand in Holmes' map of TS? Does his philosophy help with designing an 'ontology' (2014: 97) or an 'epistemology' (2014: 102)?

Overall, the philosophy of translation that has been developed so far – especially in its most recent versions – clearly indicates the direction that TS research is taking. In fact, all these works show that TS research is increasingly self-conscious regarding its own development and, like metatheory and translation, is becoming self-reflective. However, the question consistently remains whether this type of conceptual research amounts to a philosophy, and whether it is moving TS research forward to the degree that the concept of translation is effectively becoming 'ubiquitous', not only in the humanities, but also beyond.

Future directions

A philosophy of translation should incorporate not only the various perspectives on translation as an object of study but also its uses – metaphorical and beyond – and a broad vision of

TS's potential in terms of what it could contribute to human knowledge as a whole. In fact, rather than merely being a figurative representation of something else, translation has the potential to be seen as a philosophical paradigm in itself (Ricoeur 1996, 2007), which could be studied and applied outside the bounds of language, culture (Bachmann-Medick 2009), and even metaphor (Guldin 2015). Even if hermeneutics (Heidegger, Gadamer, Steiner, Berman) and the anthropological–postcolonial concept of 'cultural translation' serve as starting points for this broader philosophical investigation (Basalamah 2013), it should at the same time be clear that any philosophy of translation needs to be conceptualized within a reorganized structure of TS, which may require the creation of a new sub-discipline. The main objective of the new sub-discipline would be to delineate the epistemological underpinnings of TS and their extent – within and outwith the discipline. Initially, some more generic definitions of translation need to be provided in order that they may be tested against empirical studies undertaken in various subfields of TS and, at a later stage, in other disciplines of the Humanities and Social Sciences that have not yet been investigated in relation to TS, such as communication, political science, and education.

Additionally, in order for a proper philosophy of translation to get off the ground, there are at least four sets of questions that it must be able to address. The first deals with the multiplicity of notions and field affiliations behind the single term 'translation'. Like all other preliminary philosophical investigations, TS would seek a typology of the multiple definitions of the concept of translation in the Humanities and well beyond. The second set of questions concerns the reasons for the spread of occurrences of the concept of translation in many disciplines, albeit sometimes in metaphorical forms. As a matter of fact, the concept of translation, while it may be found in numerous domains of knowledge, is not 'ubiquitous' (Blumczynski 2016), as criteria of 'translationness' must exist that would distinguish it from processes comparable but not identical to it. But even in the many instances in which the concept of translation encountered is deemed compliant with the criteria of 'translationness', it still raises the question of why it exists outside its traditional semantic field as 'translation proper' (Jakobson 1959/2000: 114) and, more importantly, whether TS should be concerned by these 'external' instances. The third set of questions deals with the relationships between fields of knowledge, conceptual understandings, cooperation, and development. Here, it is proposed that researchers reflect on the ability of translation to act as a metaconcept that facilitates knowledge-expanding inter-disciplinary interactions. This set of questions leads to the fourth and last, which raises the issue of the role of translation in the formation of global knowledge or *Collective Intelligence* (Levy 1994). If translation is about regulated transfer-transformation processes within the boundaries of the relevant disciplines, then at the metatheoretical level it would make sense to reflect on how overall knowledge moves, transforms, and grows, both on the local and global scales. As such, all four sets of questions constitute a sort of preamble to the formation of a philosophy of translation conceived of as a sub-discipline of TS.

From object of study to archetype

Once this philosophy of translation has been suitably conceptualized and positioned within the boundaries of TS and its more immediate surroundings, scholars might undertake an investigation of the ability of a philosophy of translation to contribute to deepening the understanding of the translation concept as a heuristic tool in the wider framework of the three knowledge cultures (Kagan 2009) – and not in the Humanities only. In order to pursue such an investigation, the concept of translation cannot be defined as a mere object of study exclusive to TS but rather must be viewed as an archetypical concept that pervades many fields of knowledge, even if that concept – whatever shape or content it may take – cannot but constitute the legitimate and natural center of the discipline. As such, the concept of translation would gain a more fundamental status and might aspire to become a founding structure of various specific phenomena that appear in many disciplines.

For instance, drawing on the sociology of actor network theory (ANT), translation could be the defining feature of an assemblage (Latour 2005) of a variety of political movements that would not coalesce without an effort at finding a form of equilibrium among them, or a 'chain of equivalence' as Chantal Mouffe would put it (2005: 53). This would be even better captured by the concept of translation, which moves these groups from a state of fragmented powerless political constellation to a reorganized, although still diverse, and reoriented plurality that becomes empowered to direct itself toward a consensual course, and to confront a common political adversary in an agonistic relationship. Translating political movements into a coalition of dissenting forces against a single adversary would entail the transformation of some secondary differences, as well as some primary similarities, into a new political aggregation of powers that would have the ability to confront its shared challenge.

Boaventura de Sousa Santos (2006, 2016) illustrates this phenomenon by describing the dynamics of the grassroots networks of social movements which gather at the World Social Forum (WSF). Santos critiques the Western political-theory principle of modernity, which states that social change must originate from a constructed unity of action by a 'privileged agent of change . . . to represent the totality from which the coherence and meaning derive[s]' (2006: 131). He refutes this type of general theory, offering in its place 'a negative universalism' that he calls 'the work of translation' (132). Against the traditional verticality involved in organizing plurality, translation, according to Santos, allows for counter-hegemonic horizontal discourses. The horizontal orientation of these discourses emphasizes the diversity of movements. It also promotes equality, mutual respect and recognition, as well as the crucial process of dialogue and debate that entails the exchange and reciprocal integration of meanings from a multiplicity of cultural and ideological horizons. Besides the general goal of uniting this plurality into a counter-hegemonic agency, translation seeks to accomplish a more specific objective, which is to base the articulations of practices and knowledges on what unites [these movements] rather than on what divides them. Such a task entails a wide exercise in translation to expand reciprocal intelligibility without destroying the identity of the partners in translation (Santos 2006: 133).

The complex medium which this translational process relies on entails the creation of 'in every discourse or knowledge, *a contact zone* that may render it porous and hence permeable to other NGOs, practices, strategies, discourses and knowledges' (ibid. emphasis in original). Drawing on the concept elaborated by Mary-Louise Pratt (2008), Santos observes that the unification of the global social movement network involves working through the intricacies of a 'contact zone', defined by Pratt as a 'social spac[e] where disparate cultures meet, clash, and grapple with each other, often in highly asymmetrical relations of domination and subordination' (2008: 7). Although Pratt considers this contact zone a privileged locus for power relations 'such as colonialism and slavery, or their aftermaths as they are lived out across the globe today' (ibid.), it is clear that if Santos ultimately uses it in order to exert resistance against the domination of the global neoliberal hegemony within the global social movement network, he must view it as a pacified space where '[t]hrough translation work, diversity is celebrated, not as a factor of fragmentation and isolationism, but rather as a condition of sharing and solidarity' (ibid.). Hence, translation takes place in the very workings of the multiple-meaning negotiations that must happen when each frame of reference presents itself to the other in order for it to be understood, learned, and integrated by the others in the process of expanding the area of their commonalities.

In this case, the objects of translation are two-fold: both knowledge and practice. Like the two sides of a coin, the knowledges and practices of the social movements and non-governmental organizations (NGOs) are the kernels of meanings that make up the substance of translational transactions. As an example of knowledges, Santos compares the concept of human rights, which represents the Western idea of human dignity, to alternative ideas from non-Western cultural horizons that are similar but nonetheless different in some respects. In order for the movements and organizations gathering at the WSF to identify shared concerns, such as human dignity, they need to experience the translation process whereby they would have to expound their respective understandings and conceptual constructions and search for the coincidences, intersections, and common grounds. At the same time, in order that their respective identities do not get dissipated, they must not neglect to identify where over-lappings cannot occur. Hence Santos has 'been proposing a translation of concerns for human dignity between the Western concept of human rights, the Islamic concept of *umma* (community) and the Hindu concept of *dharma* (cosmic harmony involving human and all other beings)' (Santos 2006: 134). By practices, Santos means 'knowledge practices' for understanding the methods other local movements and organizations use to resolve issues they encounter and overcome hurdles embedded in different cultures and locales, and for relating these to their own methods and issues. In the words of Santos, '[w]hen dealing with practices ... the work of translation focuses specifically on mutual intelligibility among forms of organization, objectives, styles of action and types of struggle' (2006: 138).

This example shows that, conceived of as an underpinning configuration that gives shape and a shortcut mental access to an abstract and complex sociopolitical phenomenon, translation cannot be restricted simply to a convenient metaphor that parallels the traditional interlinguistic transfer process – as could typically be the case with a transmission or reproduction activity, for instance. It is, rather, the representation of a connective, transformative, and creative mechanism that could take place in many other fields of knowledge, and reality at large.

It appears that the concept of translation is widely present in many areas of life and in the three cultures of knowledge – the Humanities, the Social Sciences, and Natural Sciences – and their practices. But, most interestingly, the concept of translation, when defined at a higher level of abstraction, demonstrates the capability of conceptually unifying the disparate instances into an 'archetype'. In fact, in order to be considered as such, these instances need to have – albeit not all sufficient and necessary but common – characteristics. Four may be recognized at this stage. The concept of translation as an archetype needs to be capable of 1) connection, articulation and negotiation to reassemble *disparities*, 2) transfer in order to move – whether ideational or physical objects – through *space*, 3) transformation so that the latter objects can move through *time*, and 4) functionality and regulation, as this form of meta-translation is *regulated* and *purposeful*, albeit not always consciously.

Moreover, following Carl Gustav Jung's definition of archetypes as 'the hidden foundations of the conscious mind' (1970 § 53), the notion of translation rises to that higher level of abstraction and generalization, suggesting that the archetype of translation is one of those 'templates for organizing the universal themes that recur over and over again in human experience' (Meadow 1992: 188). This means that 'translation as an archetype' is *the template of all phenomena* and processes featured by the dialectical relationships of 1) *connectedness, articulation and negotiation,* 2) *transfer and/or* 3) *transformation.*

It should also be conducted *in a purposeful and regulated manner*, with or without a subjective intent.

This overview is a clear indication that such an abstract notion of translation requires a rather overarching function to recognize and describe all concrete or metaphorical occurrences of translation at the levels of semiotics (signs), statements (elaborate verbal signs), theories (complex concepts), and worldviews (collective frames of reference). However, one could wonder about the usefulness of such a rather highly abstract concept and its cross-secting scope. For the purposes of this chapter, suffice it to say that the concept of translation as archetype could serve as a heuristic tool 1) within disciplines in order to bridge sub-disciplines, 2) between disciplines so that cooperation could take place to respond to particular issues requiring more than one expert perspective, and 3) across disciplines, even across disciplinary cultures. In fact, what is proposed here is not a simple concept but a freshly coined *conceptual template* that may serve to offer a space for a philosophy of translation, and propose for TS an intra-, inter- and trans-disciplinary research programme that could, *retrospectively*, identify and explain instances of functional articulations, transfers, and transformations, as well as, *prospectively*, suggest heuristic methods to illustrate new instances of connections, transfers, and transformations – that is, translations.

As an example of translation within a discipline, in the field of education the transformation of the learner and the instructor during the learning/teaching interaction, as well as the process of the learner becoming an educator, would be deemed *translational*. It could be argued that both instances of transformation/articulation conform, on the one hand, to the criteria of what differentiates a translation occurrence from a simple change and, on the other hand, to a dialectics of ontologies and epistemologies in that any form of knowledge learning is conducive to an ontological transformation. If in this case *Education is Translation* according to Cook-Sather (2006), then TS needs to take stock of this development occurring not only outside its disciplinary jurisdiction but also outside its epistemic culture, such as in education, which is situated in the social sciences.

The horizon of transdisciplinarity

However, beyond the notion of archetypical translation – the transcending metaconcept of translation as exemplified through the educational conceptualization mentioned earlier – one could ask: what larger purpose would it serve? If translation, as it is conceived of at a higher level of abstraction, allows us to consider the connection, transfer and/or transformation of any types of objects and subjects, it follows that the very knowledge that a metaconcept reflects about is a prominent one to contemplate in the context of the relationships of its multiple sources and cultures – that is, disciplines. A functional and useful philosophy of translation would embrace the epistemological task of thinking about the relationships, communication, and integration processes of academic disciplines among themselves. It would consider how this task could lead to a greater ability to address concrete real-world problems.

In Margaret Somerville and David Rapport's co-edited book on transdisciplinarity (2000), which has become a standard reference in the field, it is remarkable to find that the concepts of translation, language, and communication have been used regularly by several of its contributors to convey their respective understanding of their objects of study. For instance, in a reflexive synthesis on the book's contributions, Julie Thompson Klein, a leading scholar on the topic of transdisciplinarity, evokes some of the metaphors that have shaped the reflections on the central topic of the book., For example, '[c]alling to mind the cautionary tale of the tower of Babel, [Roderick] Macdonald stressed that all communication requires translation across disciplinary languages. His example of a team-taught seminar on law, language, and ethics exemplified the necessity of translation in creating a shared meta-discourse on a common objective' (Thompson Klein 2000: 11). In turn, Gavan McDonell emphasized that '[t]here is always the necessity to engage in interdisciplinary translation, and it is almost inevitable that there will be attempts to establish the dominance of a particular language game' (McDonell 2000: 29). These examples and others, despite their more direct reference to translation, show that beyond the primary metaphorical uses of the term, there is a paradigmatic dimension to the concept which articulates one of the central issues of the notion of transdisciplinarity: its definition. If being transdisciplinary is to implement a form of translation, then the test is to see whether the defining features of transdisciplinarity correspond to those of translation.

For instance, Roderick Macdonald (2000) insists that 'transdisciplinarity is not the bridging of existing disciplines; it is their transcendence by a new epistemology' (2000: 69). He views it as 'a label for an epistemology that renounces existing intellectual disciplines. It necessarily claims for itself transcendent explanatory power.... By definition, transdisciplinarity is primarily about epistemic constructs' (2000: 70). As such, this understanding of transdisciplinarity would mean that there is a metadisciplinary level where boundaries are subsumed into an undifferentiated epistemology that is concerned only with how knowledge is constructed rather than how it addresses actual real-world issues. On the opposite side of this conception is the position of Desmond Manderson (2000) who contends that,

> the nature of transdisciplinary study does not seek to find a 'higher level' of knowledge that is in some sense unified or superior... The aim of bringing together diverse disciplines in a transdisciplinary project is not to *transcend* that knowledge base but rather to *transform* it... The concept of dialogue between different languages captures what I see as important in transdisciplinary scholarship... We live in Babel. But as this dialogue develops, we each learn new concepts and images through a growing appreciation of the richness and difference of the language of the other. These new words and approaches are then able to be incorporated into our own languages. A dialogue between disciplines does not transcend them any more than a dialogue between languages renders each language obsolete. But such a dialogue is a crucial learning experience through which we learn, and change, and grow.
>
> (Manderson 2000: 92, emphases in the original)

Manderson not only emphasizes his rejection of Macdonald's definition of transdisciplinarity (a horizontal and dialogical convergence of different but equal disciplines that learn from each other rather than a transcendence to disciplinarity that deals with epistemic constructs only); he also reaches a very 'translational' conclusion about the type of relationship that should exist between disciplines. He envisions neither their transcendence to a higher level of knowledge nor their submission to the hegemony of one discipline over others, but rather their mutual transformation. As a matter of fact, one of translation's lessons when it is conceived of as a conversation, as in hermeneutics (Gadamer 2004) or in education (Cook-Sather 2006), is the mutual reshaping of every party engaged in the translational process. Even in linguistic translation, one of the learning experiences translators undergo consists of discovering their own transfiguration in the course of their translational effort, no matter how limited it may be.

Going back to the *raison d'être* for the metaconcept of archetypical translation: it is to contribute beyond the traditional boundaries of TS in at least two ways. On the one hand, with the awareness that 'boundaries between disciplines are changing: by increasing specialization through internal differentiation within the disciplines, and by the integration of disciplines' (Hirsh Hadorn et al. 2008: 28), an archetypical translation conception would venture into a stream of research that enables the connection, exchange, and mutual transformation of disciplines. On the other hand, with the growing need for these types of transversal programmes of research, the archetypical translation framework would involve a transdisciplinary approach via its integrating of scientific disciplines, of problem fields, and of actors in the life-world (2008: 33).

Whatever the fate of such a proposal may be, the fact of the matter is that we still work in a disciplinary research context, and transdisciplinarity cannot for the time being be dismissive of disciplines. Hence, as long as we acknowledge this state of affairs, a philosophy of translation with a transdisciplinary objective would devote itself to, and find its *telos* in, the promotion of a multi-directional learning process. That process must utilize concepts and methods from various disciplines so that each discipline is empowered to conceptualize reality from perspectives other than its own. As a result, each discipline will expand its tools for understanding complex realities by adding at least one dimension of conceptualization to the confines of its traditional boundaries.

By way of conclusion, like Margaret Somerville (2000), who considers transdisciplinarity a 'self-reflexive' exercise 'to examine the limits of the concepts and methods of each discipline, and to seek new theories, concepts, and methods' (2000: 95), I propose that a philosophy of translation could be a synoptic disciplinary space in which the creation of an archetypical metaconcept of translation might encourage self-reflexivity not only within TS, but also in the transdisciplinary dialogue that most advanced forms of research attempt to engage in.

Related topics

Current trends in philosophy and translation; translation theory and philosophy; culture.

Further reading

Large, D. (2014). 'On the Work of Philosopher-Translators', in J. Boase-Beier, A. Fawcett and P. Wilson (eds.) *Literary Translation: Redrawing the Boundaries*, Basingstoke: Palgrave Macmillan, pp. 182–203. (Large begins his survey of philosopher-translators by discussing the translation of philosophy and the philosophy of translation.)

Scott, C. (forthcoming) *The Work of Literary Translation*, Cambridge: Cambridge University Press. (An attempt to write a philosophy of translation by a scholar influenced by phenomenology.)

References

Arduini, S. and Nergaard, S. (2011). 'Translation: A New Paradigm', *Translation Journal*, inaugural issue, 8–17.

Bachmann-Medick, D. (2009). 'Introduction: The Translational Turn', *Translation Studies. The Translational Turn*, 2(1), 2–16.

Basalamah, S. (2013). 'De la Cultural Translation à la Philosophie de la Traduction', *Doletiana*, vol. 4. Available at: www.raco.cat/index.php/Doletiana/article/view/276137 Accessed on January 30, 2018.

Basalamah, S. (2016). 'Mapping the Gulfs of Translation Studies'. *QScience Connect*, 16(1). Available at: www.qscience.com/toc/connect/2016/1 Accessed on January 30, 2018.

Benjamin, A. (1989). *Translation and the Nature of Philosophy. A New Theory of Words*. London: Routledge.

Blumczynski, P. (2016). *Ubiquitous Translation*. London: Routledge.
Buzelin, H. (2005). 'Unexpected Allies. How Latour's Network Theory Could Complement Bourdieusian Analyses in Translation Studies', *The Translator*, 11(2), 193–218.
Casanova, P. (2007). *The World Republic of Letters* trans. M. B. DeBevoise. Cambridge: Harvard University Press.
Chesterman, A. (2009). 'The Name and Nature of Translator Studies', *Hermes – Journal of Language and Communication Studies*, 42, 13–22.
Cook-Sather, A. (2006). *Education is Translation. A Metaphor for Change in Learning and Teaching*. Philadelphia: University of Pennsylvania Press.
Cronin, M. (2017). *Eco-Translation. Translation and Ecology in the Age of the Anthropocene*. London: Routledge.
Davidson, D. (1984). *Inquiries into Truth and Interpretation*. Oxford: Oxford University Press.
Derrida, J. (1985). 'Des Tours de Babel' trans. J. Graham, in J. Graham (ed.) *Difference and Translation*. Ithaca and London: Cornell University Press.
Fauconnier, G. and Turner, M. (2002). *The Way We Think: Conceptual Blending and the Mind's Hidden Complexities*. New York: Basic Books.
Fauconnier, G., Turner, M. (2008). 'Rethinking Metaphor', in R. Gibbs (ed.) *Cambridge Handbook of Metaphor and Thought*. New York: Cambridge University Press.
Gadamer, H. G. (2004). *Truth and Method*. London: Continuum International Publisher.
Gershenson, C, Aerts, D., and Edmonds, B. (2007). *Worldviews, Science and Us. Philosophy and Complexity*. Singapore: World Scientific Publishing & Co.
Gouanvic, J.-M. (2005). 'A Bourdieusian Theory of Translation, or the Coincidence of Practical Instances: Field, "habitus", Capital and Illusion', *The Translator*, 11(2), 147–66.
Grutman, R. (2009). 'Le virage social dans les études sur la traduction. Une rupture sur fond de continuité', *Texte, Revue de Critique et de Théorie Littéraire*, 45/46, 135–52.
Guldin, R. (2015). *Translation as Metaphor*. London: Routledge.
Gutt, E.-A. (1991). *Translation and Relevance: Cognition and Context*. Oxford: Basil Blackwell.
Heidegger, M. (1996). *Hölderlin Hymn 'The Ister'* trans. W. McNeill and J. Davis. Minneapolis: Indiana University Press.
Heilbron, J. (1999). 'Toward a Sociology of Translation. Book Translations as a Cultural World-System', *European Journal Social Theory*, 2(4), 429–44.
Hermans, T. (1999). *Translation in Systems: Descriptive and System-oriented Approaches Explained*. Manchester: St. Jerome.
Hirsh Hadorn, G., Hoffmann-Riem, H., Biber-Klemm, S., Grossenbacher-Mansuy, W., Joye, D., Pohl, C., Wiesmann, U., and Zemp, E. (eds.) (2008). *Handbook of Transdisciplinary Research*. Springer Science + Business Media BV.
Holmes, J. (2004). 'The Name and Nature of Translation Studies', in L. Venuti (ed.) *The Translation Studies Reader*. 2nd ed. London: Routledge, 172–85.
Inghilleri, M. (ed.) (2005). *Bourdieu and the Sociology of Translation and Interpreting*, special issue of *The Translator*, 11(2).
Jakobson, R. (1959/2000). 'On Linguistic Aspects of Translation', in L. Venuti (ed.) *The Reader of Translation Studies*. London: Routledge, 113–18.
Jervolino, F. (2006). 'Pour une philosophie de la traduction: À l'école de Ricoeur', *Revue de Métaphysique et de Morale*, 50(2), 229–38.
Jung, C. (1970). *Collected Works of C. G. Jung*, Vol. 10. 2nd ed. Princeton: Princeton University Press, 29–49.
Kagan, J. (2009). *The Three Cultures. Natural Sciences, Social Sciences and the Humanities in the 21st Century*. Oxford: Oxford University Press.
Knorr Cetina, K. (1999). *Epistemic Cultures. How the Sciences Make Knowledge*. Cambridge and London: Harvard University Press.
Kuhn, T. (1996). *The Structure of Scientific Revolutions*, 3rd ed. Chicago: University of Chicago Press.

Kurz, I. (1994). 'A Look into the "Black Box" – EEG Probability Mapping During Mental Simultaneous Interpreting', in M. Snell-Hornby et al. (eds.) *Translation Studies. An Interdiscipline*. Amsterdam: John Benjamins, 199–207.
Lacour, P. and Campos, L. (2005). *Thinking by Cases, or: How to Put Social Sciences the Right Way Up*. Available at: www.espacestemps.net/articles/thinking-by-cases-or-how-to-put-social-sciences-back-the-right-way-up/ Accessed on January 30, 2018.
Ladmiral, J.-R. (1978). *Traduire: théorèmes pour la traduction*. Paris: Gallimard.
Ladmiral, J.-R. (1988). 'Les Enjeux Métaphysiques de la Traduction. À Propos d'une Critique de Walter Benjamin', *Le cahier*, 6, 39–44.
Ladmiral, J.-R. (1989). 'Pour une philosophie de la traduction', *Revue de métaphysique et de morale*, 94(1), 5–22.
Ladmiral, J.-R. (1992). 'La Traduction: Philosophie d'une Pratique', in C. Pagnoulle (ed.) *Les Gens du Passage*. Liège: Université de Liège, 120–36.
Ladmiral, J.-R. (1997). 'Les 4 âges de la traductologie. Réflexions sur une diachronie de la théorie de la traduction'. *L'histoire et les Théories de la Traduction*. Actes. ASTTI Berne et STI Genève, 11–42.
Ladmiral, J.-R. (2010). 'Philosophie et Traduction', *Nottingham French Studies*, 49(2), 6–16.
Ladmiral, J.-R. (2014). *Sourcier ou Cibliste. Les Profondeurs de la Traduction*. Paris: Les Belles Lettres.
Lakoff, G. and Johnson, M. (1980). *Metaphors We Live By*. Chicago: University of Chicago Press.
Latour, B. (2005). *Reassembling the Social. An Introduction to the Actor–Network Theory*. Oxford, Oxford University Press.
Levy, P. (1994). *L'intelligence Collective: Pour une Anthropologie du Cyberespace*. Paris: La Découverte.
Macdonald, R. (2000). 'Transdisciplinarity and Trust', in M. Somerville and D. Rapport (eds.) *Transdisciplinarity: reCreating Integrated Knowledge*. London: EOLSS Publishers, 61–76.
Macmurray, J. (1936). *Interpreting the Universe*. New York: Humanity Books, 1996.
Malmkjær, K. (2010). 'The Nature, Place and Role of a Philosophy of Translation in Translation Studies', in A. Fawcett, K.L. Guadarrama Garcia and R. Hyde Parker (eds.) *Translation: Theory and Practice in Dialogue*. London: Continuum International Publishing, 201–18.
Manderson, D. (2000). 'Some Considerations about Transdisciplinarity', in M. Somerville and D. Rapport (eds.) *Transdisciplinarity: reCreating Integrated Knowledge*. London: EOLSS Publishers, 86–93.
Marais, K. (2014). *Translation Theory and Development Studies. A Complexity Theory Approach*. London: Routledge.
McDonell, G. (2000). 'Disciplines as Cultures: Towards Reflection and Understanding', in M. Somerville and D. Rapport (eds.) *Transdisciplinarity: reCreating Integrated Knowledge*. London: EOLSS Publishers, 25–37.
Meadow, M. J. (1992). 'Archetypes and Patriarchy: Jung and Eliade', *Journal of Religion and Health*, 31(3), 187–95.
Morin, E. (2007). 'Restricted Complexity, General Complexity', in Gershson et al. (eds.) *Worldviews Science and Us Philosophy and Complexity*, Singapore: World Scientific Publishing Co, 5–29.
Mouffe, C. (2005). *On the Political*. London: Routledge.
Pratt, M. L. (2008). *Imperial Eyes. Travel Writing and Transculturation*. 2nd ed. London: Routledge.
Passeron, J.-C. and Revel, J. (eds.) (2005). *Penser par cas*. Paris: Éditions des Hautes Études en Sciences Sociales.
Pym, A. (2010). *Exploring Theories of Translation*. London: Routledge.
Quine, W. (2013). *Word and Object*. Boston: MIT Press.
Rescher, N. (1998). *Complexity: A Philosophical Overview*. New Brunswick: Transaction Publishers.
Ricoeur, P. (1996). 'Reflections on a New Ethos for Europe', in P. Kearney (ed.) *Paul Ricoeur: The Hermeneutics of Action*. London: Sage Publications.
Ricoeur, P. (2007). *Reflections on the Just*, trans. D. Pellauer. Chicago: University of Chicago Press.

Sallis, J. (2002). *On Translation. Studies in Continental Thought*. Minneapolis: Indiana University Press.
Santos, De Sousa B. (2006). *The Rise of the Global Left. The World Social Forum and Beyond*. London: Zed Books.
Santos, De Sousa B. (2016) *Epistemologies of the South. Justice against Epistemicide*. London: Routledge.
Santos, G. (2012). 'Philosophy and Complexity', *Foundations of Science*, 18(4), 681–6.
Sapiro, G. (2008). 'Translation and the Field of Publishing: A Commentary on Pierre Bourdieu's "A Conservative Revolution in Publishing"', *Translation Studies*, 1(2), 154–66.
Simeoni, D. (1998). 'The Pivotal Status of the Translator's Habitus', *Target*, 10(1), 1–39.
Snell-Hornby, M. (2006). *The Turns of Translation Studies*. Amsterdam: John Benjamins Publishing.
Somerville, M. (2000). 'Trandisciplinarity: Structuring Creative Tensions', in M. Somerville and D. Rapport (eds.) *Transdisciplinarity: reCreating Integrated Knowledge*. London: EOLSS Publishers, 94–107.
Thompson Klein, J. (2000). 'Voices of Royaumont', in M. Somerville and D. Rapport (eds.) *Transdisciplinarity: reCreating Integrated Knowledge*. London: EOLSS Publishers, 3–13.
Tymoczko, M. (2007). *Enlarging Translation, Empowering Translators*. Manchester: St. Jerome.
Tymoczko, M. (2012). 'The Neuroscience of Translation', *Target*, 24(1), 83–102.
Tyulenev, S. (2012). *Applying Luhmann to Translation Studies: Translation in Society*, London: Routledge.
Tyulenev, S. (2014). *Translation and Society: An Introduction*. London: Routledge.
van Doorslaer, L. (2007). 'Risking Conceptual Maps: Mapping as a Keywords-Related Tool Underlying The Online Translation Studies Bibliography', *Target*, 19(2), 217–33.
von Bartalanffy, L. (1968). *General System Theory: Foundations, Development, Applications*. New York: George Braziller.
Weissbrod, R. (2009). 'Philosophy of Translation Meets Translation Studies', *Target*, 21(1), 58–73.
Wolf, M. and Fukari, A. (2007). *Constructing a Sociology of Translation*. Amsterdam: John Benjamins Publishing.

Index

activism 185–6, 245–6, 251, 404
actor–network theory (ANT) 159–60, 162, 482
aesthetics 448, 454
affect 401–3
After Babel: Aspects of Language and Translation 34–5, 57, 142, 225, 238, 257
agency 179, 248, 250, 422, 477, 482; feminism 329; feminism 260; Nietzsche 34, 44, 46
alētheia 52–3, 55, 57
analytic philosophy 3, 105, 157, 190, 231–2, 311–12, 316, 466, 467–8
anthropology 210–11, 217, 479, 481
aphorisms, Nietzsche 41–3
archetypes 481–4
Arendt, H. 329–30, 339
Aristotle 227–8, 238
Arrojo, R. 233–4, 245, 259 *see also* Nietzsche, F.
art, philosophy of 446, 450, 453, 454–6
artificial intelligence 428–9, 436–8
aspect-seeing 63, 66, 73
associations, professional 247, 249
Atherton, M. 327–8, 332
audiences 337 *see also* readers
Austin, J.L. 183, 468; context and pragmatics 197, 197–8, 200; Derrida 144; equivalence 233; Levinas 396; linguistics 276; meaning 299; philosophical translation 312, 314
authorship (authors) 347–8, 446–7; critical issues and topics 447–50; originality 456–7; Schleiermacher 17, 22, 26–9; translatability 454–6; translation and readerliness 452; translation as reading 451–2; translator-centredness (model) 453–4; translators relationship 452–3

Babel (tower of) 349, 351, 462, 464–6, 470, 485; Derrida 141, 151; Gadamer and Ricoeur 98
Badiou, A. 157–9, 165, 168
Barthes, R. 296–7, 347–8, 446–7, 452
being 52, 54
Being and Time 52, 59–60
Benjamin, W. 76–8, 151–3, 449, 462–4, 466–7; consequences 85–6; critical issues and topics 80–3; equivalence 225–7, 235; future directions 86–7; historical perspectives 78–80; meaning 295–6, 300–1; research 83–5
Bennington, G. 375–7, 380–1, 386–8
Berman, A. 25, 96, 100, 245–6, 463
bias 260–1, 263
Blumczynski, P. 478–9
Böhme, J 229–30
Book of Mormon 467–8
boundaries 44, 82, 215, 235, 478–81, 485–6
Braun, E. 228–31, 233–5
Bryant, L. 162–5, 168
Butler, J. 333, 337–9

Callon, M. 159–60
canonization 330, 337
Carnap, R. 108, 113–17, 232, 316
Cassin, B. 165–8
Catford, J.C. 293–5
Celan, P. 81, 85–6, 401
Celenza, C.S. 345
censorship 220, 261, 264–6, 352
character (language) 225, 229, 231–4, 238
charity 122, 126–31, 138, 248
Chaucer, G. 308, 316
Chesterman, A. 246–8, 301
Chomsky, N. 81, 109–10, 114, 231, 239, 272, 283–4
Cicero 228–30, 289, 308–9, 312–14
clauses 272–4
cognitive approaches 411–12; emotion 417–18; expertise 415–17; machine-translation 418–21; meaning 412–15; organization 421–4
colonialism 219, 301, 310, 482
colonization 34, 40–1, 185, 260
commitment 188, 348; context and pragmatics 191; culture 209; Davidson 124, 138; ethics 246; feminism 324, 326, 329, 331, 336; Gadamer and Ricoeur 99; literary translation 446; Quine 105, 115–16
communication 17, 19–20, 22, 214; intercultural 215–16, 218–19

Index

complexity 480; feminism 325, 330; Heidegger 49; literary translation 450, 456; Wittgenstein 65, 73–4
conceptual schemes 122, 133–4
consistency 362, 368–70
content 105, 108, 115
context 17, 23, 29, 195–7; critical issues and topics 199–201; current contributions and research 201–4; historical perspectives 197–9; practice recommendations 205–6
continental philosophy 3, 157, 161, 184, 185, 188, 190, 311, 393, 470
controversies, scholastic 63–6
cooperation 481, 484
correspondence, formal 293–5
creation 448–50
Crisp, R. 243–4, 247–50, 252
Cronin, M. 246, 429, 479
cultural translation 217, 296, 337–8, 481
cultural turns 215, 218–19, 250, 448, 476
culture 173–6, 179–88, 209, 477–8, 481–4; current contributions and research 218–19; definition 210–13; ethics 245–6, 251; exchange 307, 309–12, 448–50; functioning 215–18; future directions 220–1; Gadamer and Ricoeur 92–3, 96, 98–101; Levinas 393; literary translation 452–3; practice recommendations 220; research methods 219–20; translation 213–15
current trends 157–9; end of translation 168–9; flat ontology 162–5; new sophistics 165–8; sociology 159–62

Dasein 59, 79, 338, 365, 398
data-driven MT 435–7
Davidson, D. 106, 107, 109, 115, 117–18, 122–3; charity, interpretation and indeterminacy 126–31; further views 131–4; historical perspectives 123–6; Tarski's truth 135–8
deconstructionism (deconstruction): current trends 157; Derrida 144, 146, 386; ethics 245; literary translation 447, 451; Nietzsche 38, 41
Defence of Poetry, A 349–50
deinon 54–6
deontology 248–51
Derrida, J. 141–3, 316, 347, 375–7, 464; Benjamin 151–3; critical issues and topics 382–5; current contributions and research 386–8; eliminativism 144–7; equivalence 226, 232, 234, 236–9; feminism 338, 340; future directions 388–9; historical perspectives 377–81; Levinas 393, 397–400, 402–5; literary translation 447, 451; meaning 295–7, 296–7; Nietzsche 36, 41, 44; practice recommendations 388; readability and iterability 148–51; relevant translation 153–4; signifier and signified 147–8; transcendental signified 143–4

Derrida Seminars Translations Project (DSTP) 376–7, 381, 386–7
determinacy and indeterminacy 105, 106–9, 111–15
development 476, 480–1, 484
dialectics 20–1
difference 19–22, 24, 30–1, 447–8, 453, 455
discourses 236–8, 271–4, 277, 279–83
domestication 58, 159, 187, 448
dominance 245, 259, 454, 485

education 186, 481, 484–5
eikos logos 347–8
eliminativism 144–7
elision 264–6
Emad, P. 55, 60–1, 316–18
emotion 417–18
epistemology 188–9
equity 186
equivalence 224–6, 238–9, 482; contemporary thought 236–8; Isocrates to Humboldt 228–31; language and Saussure 226–8; meaning 293–5, 299–300; relativism 234–6; universalism 231–4
erasure 326, 327–8, 330, 340
Ereignis 60, 316–17
Ergun. E. 330–1
escape routes 330, 333, 336
esotericism 461–3, 471–3; critical issues and topics 465–7; current contributions and research 467–9; historical perspectives 463–5; practice recommendations 469–70
ethics 185–8, 243–4; future directions 251–2; Gadamer and Ricoeur 98–100, 102; key figures 244–6; Levinas 391, 405; Nietzsche 34, 43; questions in translation theory and practice 246–51; Schleiermacher 18–19
Eurocentrism 173–6, 179
evangelism 34
Even-Zohar, I. 190, 218, 245, 300, 476
evidence 104–5, 109–13, 115–16
evolution, cultural 106, 216
exclusion 327, 329, 340
existentialism 236, 311, 395
experiences, women's 324, 330, 333
expertise 415–17
explanations 109

facts 349
failure 196, 204
fairness 186
faithfulness 391–4, 398, 405
feminism 256–9, 266–7, 297–8, 324; critical issues and topics 329–37; current contributions and research 337–9; future directions 339–40; historical perspectives 326–8; invisibility and naming 262–4; sexuality, censorship, and

491

Index

elision 264–6; translation 259–60; translation studies (TS) 260–2
fidelity 243, 245, 404 *see also* faithfulness
Flotow, L. von 257, 259, 261, 329, 334, 336; ethics 245; meaning 297–8
forms of life 71–4, 182, 468–9 *see also* language-games
Frazer, J 468–9
Frege, G. 312, 314; context and pragmatics 197; Davidson 123; equivalence 228, 231; linguistics 275; Quine 105

Gadamer, H.G.: historical perspectives 90–1; issues and topics 91–6
gender 34, 41, 244, 245, 256–9, 266–7; invisibility and naming 262–4; sexuality, censorship, and elision 264–6; translation 259–60; translation studies (TS) 260–2; of words 383
genres 202, 271–3, 277; analysis 279–80
Gentzler, E. 244
Gestell 59
globalisation (antiglobalisation) 187, 215, 239, 246, 375–6, 389
gnosis 461–2, 466–7, 469–71
Golden Bough, The 468–9
grammar 272–3, 277, 280, 282–4
Grice, P. 198

Habermas, J. 91, 234
Hamann, J.G. 79, 81, 229–30
Hegel, G.W.F. 358–9, 364–71
Heidegger, M. 311, 316–18; hermeneutics 49–51; translation and words 51–6; translation practices 56–61
Heraclitus 226, 228
Herder, J.G. 17, 19, 229–30
Hermans, T. 245, 290, 463, 467–8
hermeneutics 468, 478–9, 481, 485; equivalence 234–6; ethics 451; feminism 453–6; Heidegger 49–51; Schleiermacher 22–5
Hickey, L. 299
history 76, 78–83, 86; Gadamer 90–1; Ricoeur 96–7
Hölderlin, F. 35, 54–8, 82, 318
holism 131–2
Humboldt, W. von 310, 361; Benjamin 79; equivalence 228–31, 233–4; Nietzsche 35, 40; Schleiermacher 18

ideas 349–50
identity 260, 457
images (imagery) 348, 351
indeterminacy 104, 106–14, 126–31, 176–80, 183–4, 293
individuals 210–13, 215
instability, of meaning 296–7
institutions 324, 327, 330–2
interactions 481, 484
international phonetic alphabet (IPA) 271
interpretation 34, 36, 41–6, 122–3, 134–8, 477–9
interpretation, radical 126–31, 135
intimacy 199, 238–9, 380
Introduction to Metaphysics 53–4, 57, 59
intuitions 105–6
invisibility 43, 245, 262–4, 296, 448, 457
Isocrates 228–31
iterability 148–51

Jakobson, R. 98, 175, 177, 465; Benjamin 77; culture 214; Derrida 143; equivalence 224; ethics 245; literary translation 451; meaning 290–1, 301; MT 429
Jews 403–6
Jowett, B. 347, 351–2, 354–5
justice 176, 185–8, 191; Derrida 154, 389; ethics 243, 246, 250–1; feminism 329, 337; Levinas 397–8, 406

kōan 466–7
Kant, I. 311, 314–17, 358–64, 366–71
Katz, S. 466–7, 470
kernels 291–3
knowledge 461–2, 465, 477–5; Schleiermacher 20, 22–3, 26, 29–31; women's 324, 329, 334–5, 337–8
Kourany, J. 327, 340
Krell, D.F. 317–18
Kripke, S.A. 123–4, 137, 197

labour, human 428
language 17–18, 30–1, 173–6, 477–8, 481, 484–5; Benjamin 76–7, 79–86; Davidson 123–6, 131; Derrida 141–3, 151–4; dialectics 20–1; eliminativism 144–7; enrichment 309; ethics 18–19; Gadamer 91–6; Heidegger 41–3, 49, 51, 55–8, 60; hermeneutics 22–5; methods of translation 25–30; Nietzsche 34–7, 39–46; Plato 21–2; as presentation 226–8; readability and iterability 148–51; Ricoeur 96–101; signifier and signified 147–8; transcendental signified 143–4
language-games 63, 66, 68–71, 73–4, 182, 467
language pairs 249, 283
language, pure 295–6
languages, 177–85, 187–9 *see also* mother tongue
Latour, B. 160–3, 168
Lefevere, A. 190, 218–20, 244, 289–90, 449–50, 463
Leibniz, G.W. 313, 359–60; equivalence 229, 231; feminism 332; Gadamer and Ricoeur 99; Schleiermacher 17
Levinas, E. 391–3; faithfulness 393–4; hermeneutic 'reduction' 400–1; infinite translation 403–6;

multilingualism 397–400; 'otherwise of being' 395–7; respecting style 394–5; silence 401–3
Levine, S. 298
linguistic turns 157, 161, 476
linguistics 271; critical issues and topics 284; discourse and conversational analysis 281–3; genre analysis 279–80; historical perspectives 283–4; phonemics, phonetics and phonology 271–2; pragmatics 275–7; psycholinguistics 278–9; semantics 275–6; sociolinguistics 277–8; text 280–1; words, clauses and sentences 272–4
literary translation 446–7; critical issues and topics 447–50; current contributions and research 450–7; future directions 457
Liu, L 332, 335–7, 340
logical positivism 116, 181, 311
Logie, J. 347–8, 355
logocentrism 141–2, 152; Benjamin 152; eliminativism 144–7; signifier and signified 147–9; transcendental signified 143–4
logos 226–30, 235–6, 238
love 346, 353–4
Lucretius 307–9, 313

machine translation (MT) 348, 350, 428–9; Benjamin 77; cognitive approaches 411–12, 418–24; critical issues 437–9; current trends 154; equivalence 239; feminism 333; historical perspectives 429–34; methods 434–7; Nietzsche 35 *see also* data-driven MT
Malabou, C. 324, 328–9, 339
manifestation principle 122, 123–6, 129, 131–4
Marais, K. 477–80
marginalisation 337
markets 248, 251
Marxism 38, 76, 78–9, 236
matrices 225, 229–30, 236
meaning 174, 176, 178–81, 183, 189, 300–1; Benjamin 295–6; Catford 293–5; charity, interpretation and indeterminacy 126–31; cognitive approaches 412–15; Davidson 122–3, 131–4; equivalence 225–9, 231–9; Gadamer and Ricoeur 90, 92–6, 99; Hickey 299; historical perspectives 123–6; instability 296–7; Jakobson 290–1; Levine 298; literary translation 447–52, 454–5; MT 437–8; Nida and Taber 291–3; Quine 104–13, 115–19, 293; reduction to 142–3; Ricoeur 295; sense of sense 289–90; Toury 299–300; truth 135–8; von Flotow 297–8 *see also* context
mediation 159–62, 168
metaphors 477–81, 483–5
migration 246, 250, 252, 332
mind, philosophy of 470–1
models 411–16, 418, 420–4
monism, anomalous 122, 132–3

morphology 272
mother tongue: current rends 158; Davidson 127; Derrida 384; ethics 244, 250; feminism 258; Gadamer and Ricoeur 94, 100–1; Levinas 397; linguistics 278; Schleiermacher 24
multilingualism 397–400
mysticism 461–3, 471–3; critical issues and topics 465–7; current contributions and research 467–9; future directions 470–1; historical perspectives 463–5; practice recommendations 469–70

naming 262–4
narrators 346–7
'negative sentence' 401–3
Nelson, S. 352–3
networks 482
networks, neural 429, 437
neural MT 434–8
neuroscience 239, 421, 470, 476
Nida, E.A. 187, 468; cognitive approaches 413; context and pragmatics 198–9; equivalence 224; ethics 245; linguistics 283–4; meaning 291–3; Nietzsche 37
Nietzsche, F. 34–8, 239; aphorisms 38–41; language, subject and interpretation 41–3; post-Nietzschean approaches 43–6
Novalis 38–9, 79, 165, 463
Nye, A. 228–9, 231

objects 481–4
observation 122, 129
O'Neill, E. 327–8, 330
ontology: flat 162–5; new sophistics 165–8; sociology 159–62
opacity (MT) 438
Ordinary Language philosophy 232–3
organizations 411, 417, 421–4
originality 34–8, 41–6, 446–7; author–translator relationship 452–3; creation 448–50; reading 451–2; translatability 454–6; translator–author 447–8; translator-centredness (model) 453–4
originality (original) 456–7
otherness 25
'otherwise of being' 395–7

panpsychism 470–1
Parmenides 58, 165, 166–7, 226, 228, 313
Partee, M.H. 227–8
personality 277
phenomenology 236, 450–1; Gadamer and Ricoeur 91, 93, 96–7; Levinas 391–3, 396–7, 402, 405–6
philosophers, feminist: critical issues and topics 329–37; current contributions and research 337–9; future directions 339–40; historical perspectives 326–8

Index

Philosophical Investigations 64, 112, 137, 180–1, 198, 232, 313, 467
philosophical translation: critical issues and topics 477–8; current contributions and research 478–80; development 307, 309–11, 313, 315; future directions 480–1; historical perspectives 476; object to archetype 481–4; transdisciplinarity 484–6
philosophy 173–6, 190–1, 476–81, 484, 486; Benjamin 76–80, 84–7; epistemology 188–9; Quine 176–80; Rawls 185–8; Wittgenstein 180–5 *see also* analytic philosophy, continental philosophy
phonemics 271–2
phonetics 271–2
phonology 271–2, 282
Plato 21–2, 226–8, 231–2, 345–7; critical issues and topics 347–54; future directions 354–5
poetry 314–16, 401 *see also* Shelley, P. B.
politics 432–3, 439, 448, 450, 481–3; Gadamer and Ricoeur 90, 93, 96, 98–9, 101
polysystems (theories) 218
postcolonialism 185, 481; culture 217–19; ethics 245; feminism 330, 338; Heidegger 41; literary translation 450, 453; meaning 301
poststructuralism 34, 236, 238, 297
power 257–9, 262, 264, 450
practices, translation 56–61
pragmatics 195–7, 275–7; critical issues and topics 199–201; current contributions and research 201–4; historical perspectives 197–9; practice recommendations 205–6
presentation, surveyable 66, 74
probability, numerical 433, 435–6
programs 411–12, 416, 418–20, 422–4
psycholinguistics 271–2, 278–9, 282
Pym, A. 217, 226, 246, 250, 377

Quine, W.V. 104–5, 176–81, 183–5, 189, 234–6, 293; determinacy and indeterminacy 106–9; evidence and explanation 109–13; fitting versus following rules 113–16; intuitions about meaning 105–6; meaning 116–19

racism 186
Rawls, J. 176, 185–8
re-expression 105
readability 148–51
readerliness 452
readers 328–30, 449–53, 456–7; Schleiermacher 17, 21–2, 25, 27–30
reading 451–2
recapture 104–6, 111–12, 118
reciprocity 186, 188, 334, 395
recognition 328, 330, 340
reduction, hermeneutic 400–1

reflexivity 477, 484, 486
relationships 248–9, 446–51, 454, 456; author–translator 452–3; human and MT 438–9
relativism 166, 225, 227–30, 233–9
relevance theory 284
religion 461–7, 471
representation 226–8
research 83–5, 476–81, 484, 486; MT 430–1, 433–5, 438–9
responsibility: ethical 245, 251; moral 97; MT 439; social 246, 248; translators 46, 296, 298, 334, 381, 449
rhythm (linguistic melody) 40, 84, 348–9, 399–401
Ricoeur, P. 90, 225–6, 234–8, 295; historical perspectives 96–7; issues and topics 98–102
Robinson, D. 38, 40, 290, 352, 470–2
rule-based MT 434–5
rules 108, 110, 113–16
Russell, B. 65, 180, 198, 231–2, 290

Sanaakkut Piusiviningita Unikkausinnguangat (Sanaaq) 256–7, 263–6
Sapir, E. 234–6
Sapir–Whorf hypothesis 230, 234, 291
Saussure, F. de 98, 144, 175, 226–8, 283
Schleiermacher, F.D.E. 17–18, 30–1; dialectics 20–1; ethics 18–19; hermeneutics 22–5; methods of translation 25–30; Plato 21–2
scholarship, historical overview 34–8
Scholem, G. 76, 78–81, 84, 404, 461, 471
Searle, J. 183, 233–4, 276, 465; Derrida 144–8, 377; Levinas 397
self-reflection 85, 180, 480
self-reflexivity 165
self-translation 329, 447, 450, 457
semantics 195–203, 275–6
sentences 272–4; negative 401–3
sexuality 249, 252, 256, 261–2, 264–6, 340
Shelley, P.B. 345–7; critical issues and topics 347–54; future directions 354–5
signified 147–53
signifier 141–2, 143, 145–50, 152–3
signifying 400–1
silence 401–3
similarity 448
Simon, S. 259, 261, 329, 334, 338; ethics 245; literary translation 450
skopos (theory) 216
Smith, J. 467
Soames, S. 231–2
social interaction *see* triangulation
social movements 482–3
societies 209–16, 219
Society for the Study of Women 326
sociolinguistics 271–2, 277–8, 282
sociological turns 250, 476
sociology 159–62, 210–11, 213

sophistics, new 165–8
Sophocles 35, 53–6
sources 392–3, 405–6
de Sousa Santos, B. 329, 336, 482–3
speakers 272–3, 275–7, 279–82
speech act theory 183–4, 233–4, 276, 280
Spivak, G. 245, 316, 338–9; Derrida 375, 377–8, 381, 386–8
statistics 433, 435, 437–8
Steiner, G. 462–5, 469–70; Benjamin 85; Derrida 142–3; equivalence 225–6, 228–35, 237–9; ethics 245; feminism 257, 261; Heidegger 57; Nietzsche 34–6, 38
structures 411, 413–14, 420–4
style 394–5
subject, the 41–3
surface structure 291–3
symbols (symbolism) 437
Symposium 346–8, 351–4

Taber, C.R. 291–3, 413
talk 122, 132
Tarski, A. 108, 122, 133–8
Task of the Translator, The 35, 77–82, 84, 86, 296
technē 462, 469–70, 472
technologies 246, 248–50
technology 428–9, 432–4, 439
tension 394–5
terminology 359–60, 362, 365
texts 271–4, 277, 279–81, 283–4, 382–3, 446–7; author–translator relationship 452–3; creation 448–50; interpretation 307–8, 310–13, 315–18; mystical and esoteric 469–70; originality 456–7; reading 451–2; translatability 454–6; translator–author 447–8; translator-centredness (model) 453–4; without meaning 144–7
texts, philosophical: future directions 317–18; historical perspectives 307–12; how? 315–17; who? 314–15; why? 312–14
texts, sacred 463, 468 *see also* religion
theory of justice 185–7
thought (thinking) 50–8, 60–1, 122–9, 132–3
thrownness 97
tikkun 81, 83–5, 464
tone 394–6, 399–401, 406
Toury, G. 476; ethics 245; linguistics 283; literary translation 447, 452; meaning 290, 295, 299–300; Wittgenstein 74
Tractatus Logico-Philosophicus 63–4, 180, 471
traditions, philosophical 307–9, 313
traditions, hidden 465, 468–69
traditions 34–8
training 435–6
transcendental signified 142–8
transdisciplinarity 484–6
transformation 34, 41, 44, 46
translatability 454–6

translation 80, 82–3, 142–3; concept of 477–84; end of 168–9; Gadamer 91, 93–6; new sophistics 165–8; ontology 162–5; practices 39, 327, 331, 450; relevant 153–4; Ricoeur 98–102; role of 34, 38–9; sociology of 159–62; subversive 298 *see also* literary translation
translation methods 25–30, 411–12, 414, 417, 419, 424
translation, radical 104, 107–8, 110, 180, 293, 469
translation, theory 173–6, 190–1; epistemology 188–9; Quine 176–80; Rawls 185–8; Wittgenstein 180–5
translationness 481
translator-centredness (model) 453–4
translators 34–41, 43–6, 314–15, 447–50, 456–7; art, philosophy of 454–6; authorship (authors) 447–8; creation 448–50; Gadamer 93–4, 95–6; historical 307–12; reading 451–2; relationships 452–3; Ricoeur 99–101; training 411, 414, 416–18, 420, 422
trends, current *see* current trends
triangulation 122, 124–6, 129
trust 245, 248, 251
truth 52–3, 159, 166–8; Davidson 122, 125, 129, 133–8

uncanny 54–5
understanding 479, 481, 483–6; Gadamer 90–6; Heidegger 50–4, 56–60; Ricoeur 96–102; Schleiermacher 17, 19, 22–3, 25–9
universalism 225, 227–8, 230–4, 236–9

Venuti, L. 187, 312–13, 317–18, 468; Derrida 375; ethics 243, 245; Heidegger 58; linguistics 283; literary translation 447–8; meaning 291, 296–7, 301
Vico 229–30, 310
violence 235, 312; Derrida 383n12; feminism 261, 266, 328; Gadamer and Ricoeur 101; Heidegger 54–5, 57; Nietzsche 39
visibility 34, 43, 46

wealth 186
Western, Educated, Industrial, Rich and Democratic (WEIRD) 244
Whorf, B.L. 234–6 *see also* Sapir–Whorf hypothesis
Wittgenstein, L. 175–6, 179–85, 189, 232; application 66; aspect-seeing 73; evaluation 73–4; forms of life 71–3; language-games 68–71; scholastic controversies 63–6; using 66–8
Wolff, C. 314
women 315, 324, 330, 333 *see also* experiences, women's; feminism
words 49–56, 58–61, 272–4; grounding of 51–6

yoga 205

Printed in the United States
by Baker & Taylor Publisher Services